"There are few peace activists who have the dedication of Brian Willson, as there are few activists who inspire me more. I hope Brian's story can inspire a new generation of activists to fight with all they have for peace, justice, our planet, and humanity."

—**Cindy Sheehan,** The Peace Mom

"In a world filled with violence, oppression, the madness of war, and the destruction of the environment, many are searching for hope—and those individuals who give us hope.

This is where Brian Willson comes in. Like many of us, he bought into the lies of war and violence. But something happened along his journey, and Vietnam was only the beginning. He discovered the truth and he followed it, no matter the cost. I encourage you to read this book about a great peace-maker and a great lover of mother earth. You will be filled with hope."

—**Roy Bourgeois**, June 7, 2010, founder, SOA Watch

"Brian Willson is one of a few modern men for all seasons. His memoir is an introduction to a way of living that could save a planet perilously drifting toward extinction. He takes the philosophy nonviolence or 'do no harm' and applies it to the violence we are doing to the planet and one another. (Personal note: perhaps we are a species that should be extinguished. At least 99 percent of us.) Caution! Read at the risk of being inspired."

—**Charlie Liteky**, Congressional Medal of Honor recipient, Viet Nam

"The 1960s to the 1980s . . . for progressive activists in the United State there perhaps was never a period quite like it—Vietnam to Nicaragua to El Salvador, one long protest against the barbarity of American imperialism. S. Brian Willson was there, here and everywhere, devoting his life, sacrificing his legs to a munitions train. A marvelous 'journey,' he calls it, for the boy who was 'convinced that the United States could do no wrong,' a loyal anticommunist, who served in Vietnam, then traveled the length of Latin America to oppose U.S. foreign policy and support the numerous victims of that policy. Sadly, that policy continues, but Willson's memoir can well serve as a guide and inspiration to a new generation of progressive activists. We've learned a lot."

—**William Blum**, author, *Killing Hope*

D0089291

"This stunning and comprehensive memoir is three overlapping books in one. First, there is a detailed narrative of major events in Brian Willson's life. He grew up as an all-American boy in upstate New York and hoped to become an FBI agent. When drafted for service in Vietnam he volunteered for the Air Force. Witnessing the indiscriminate bombing of Vietnam villages changed his outlook forever, and led to his water-only fast against the Contra War in Nicaragua and the loss of his legs on the tracks at Concord Naval Station.

Next, there is Brian's research-in-depth in societies victimized by U.S. imperialism. Along with scouring relevant histories, he went to Vietnam, Nicaragua, El Salvador, Colombia, occupied Palestine, Ecuador, Brazil, Iraq, Cuba, and most hopefully, Chiapas, and talked at length with ordinary people. Everywhere he found two things: on the one hand, desperate poverty caused by multinational corporations headquartered in the United States and the effects of brutal American military intervention; on the other hand, remnants of an ancient way of life characterized by mutual aid and self-reliance in small communities, and connection with the natural world.

Finally, Brian Willson takes us with him on his spiritual journey. He asks us to recognize that Americans face an unprecedented choice between an ongoing, shameful narcissism in which we ravage the world and endanger humankind for the sake of material things, and a life grounded in horizontal rather than vertical relationships that is slower, smaller, more dignified, and in the end more satisfying."

—**Staughton Lynd**, historian

"S. Brian Willson is an American hero who gives me inspiration and hope. In this book, he takes us on an amazing journey through his life as an all-American young man. He was an excellent student, an all-league athlete, a Conservative Baptist, a Republican and a strong believer in the American way of life. In 1969 he had an epiphany in Vietnam that changed his life forever. He has had many incredible experiences along the way, including being run over by a U.S. Navy train, where he lost both of his legs while protesting U.S. foreign policy in Central America. Brian now stands for peace, justice and fairness for all people of the earth. I love his mantra: 'We are not worth more, they are not worth less.' This book should be required reading for all high school and college students in America."

—**Cynthia McKinney**, former Green Party presidential candidate

"This Brian Willson is no throwaway American. This was a soldier in wartime, this was a protester after war taught him its lessons, and finally, this was a sacrificer in carrying protest to the nth degree. I was busted with him but I never gave the ultimate as he gave. This book is about a patriot, the kind of patriot you don't find anymore, the kind of patriot who loves and believes in his country so much he surrendered his legs in telling his country it's wrong. Read this book."

—**Edward Asner**, actor

"Brian Willson has lived one of the more interesting and inspiring lives of any peace activist in recent American history. His story deserves to be read and absorbed by people of all persuasions: militarists as well as antimilitarists."

—**Peter Dale Scott**, author, *The War Conspiracy: JFK, 9/11, and the Deep Politics of War*, poet

"Brian Willson's life story teaches us to 'walk the talk,' guided by one of the finest prophets of our time. Brian teaches us that we can't control the U.S. government. It is every bit as reckless as the train which ran over him. Brian asks people to stop fuelling 'the train.' If we can't control our own government, can we at least stop actively helping it? For many years, he traveled all over the world to campaign against weapons and war, but his conscientious objection to voracious resource consumption spurred him to design a new life style. With impeccable logic, Brian challenges us stay closer to home so that we can avoid consuming more than our fair share of energy. By living simply and working hard for justice, he aims to attain right livelihood. By studying his writing and following his lead, we bolster our chances to build a better world."

—**Kathy Kelly**, Voices for Creative Nonviolence

"I write as a witness to S. Brian Willson.

It was the privilege of the Office of the Americas to be part of the Nuremberg Actions at the Concord Naval Weapons Station in California. And this is the site where Brian and his fellow veterans gathered on the tracks to stop a munitions shipment to Nicaragua. The munitions train did not stop, in fact it speeded up as it approached the protesters. It was here at Concord that Brian lost both of his legs and received a brutally fractured skull.

And after Brian's rapid recovery, it was our privilege, during the peak of Reagan's homicidal war on the Nicaraguan people, to travel over much of Nicaragua with this wounded hero. We flew at tree-top level in a worn out helicopter to see the devastation.

Brian Willson represents millions of young women and men whose lives have been severely damaged by unnecessary, illegal and immoral imperial wars conducted by our nation. He urges us to a new way of life. This book must be required reading for every high school and college student. Their lives depend on it."

—**Blase Bonpane**, PhD, director, Office of the Americas

"Brian Willson and I went to Nicaragua in 1988 to witness the Sopoa Peace Summit between the Contras and the Sandinistas. The love and respect shown him by the people there was heartfelt and heart-warming (he had knelt in front of a train in the well-publicized protest of the shipment of weapons to be used against the citizens of Nicaragua by the Contras, who were trained and equipped by the U.S. and who wanted to destabilize the Sandinista government). In hospitals full of children and farmers who had lost limbs because of land mines planted by the Contras, we was obviously and immediately one of them. He'd done it for them and they loved him for it.

Brian Willson's courage, compassion, and commitment to fighting for freedom, justice, and human rights are an inspiration to the rest of us and a lesson in how to handle Adjustments in our Plans."

—**Kris Kristofferson,** actor, singer, songwriter

"Brian Willson's courage, integrity, and dedication to peace and justice and to a sustainable society have been an inspiration to all of those who seek to change the course on which we are lurching towards destruction. His memoir should be read and pondered, and its lessons should be taken to heart by those who hope to create a more decent world."

—**Noam Chomsky,** linguist, historian

"Brian Willson's memoir boils with alchemy that has turned pain and caring into moral insistence and political resistance. After seeing what war really does, he lives every day with the wounds of military madness and the imperatives of struggling for social sanity. This book takes us away from the false comforts of clichés and cardboard images, replacing them with a genuine account of injustice writ large and insistence on humane values. With this superb narrative of his own life, Willson invites us to think more clearly and feel more deeply."

—**Norman Solomon,** author, *War Made Easy: How Presidents and Pundits Keep Spinning Us to Death*

"Brian Willson is a hero in our midst. Descended from early settlers, like most small-town boys, he was born and bred to serve his country, to do his patriotic duty, and to not ask questions about the worthiness of his government. His military service in Vietnam shattered all illusions about the war itself and the government he was serving. Remaining duty bound, principled, and determined, he has spent the past four decades as a nonviolent activist against U.S. military interventions, and since 1988, has walked on 'third world legs.' We are fortunate to have this book, this testament to the transformative power of consciousness."

—**Roxanne Dunbar-Ortiz**, historian, writer, activist

"No one has gone deeper into the heart of American militarism and moral despair than Brian Willson, paying an immeasurable cost, only to come out intact on the other side. His brilliant extended reflection not only gives us light but also hope: this is what it means to be an upright human being in a world of violence and lies. He can't be stopped! Thank God Willson has written his story: we Americans need it desperately."

—**Mark Rudd**, author, *Underground: My Life With SDS and the Weathermen*

"Brian Willson is a modern-day prophet in the classical sense."

—**Jack Ryan**, ex–career FBI agent turned peace activist

"There is much for us all to learn from Brian Willson's life story. Brian's life touches upon all the important events and changes of the Vietnam/Woodstock generation. From all-American Boy to Vietnam veteran to martyr to the cause of antiwar to content green citizen. In the blink of an eye he was transformed into a symbol of the generation's struggle to build a brand new world. His book takes us through the events that led him to that moment on the train tracks in Concord through the personal transformation that took place in him as a result of that experience. Well written and historically important."

—**Country Joe McDonald**, musician and activist

"Brian Willson's life journey is a remarkable story of courage, commitment, and the unconquerable human spirit. It should be required reading for anyone concerned about the past, present, and future of this country. As Americans, we need to understand the connections between our materialism and militarism and the suffering of others and the plight of the planet. Willson convincingly establishes those connections in an unforgettable memoir."

—**Richard Falk**, professor emeritus of international law,
Princeton University

"Brian Willson's *Blood on the Tracks* is not like anything I've ever read before. Born on July fourth, Brian could not have been a more patriotic boy growing up, but his memoir shows how the humanity within each of us can bring down the barriers that separate us from our fellow human beings. This book is not just a personal journey; it is also historical, geographical, political. It takes us through lands ravaged by U.S. imperialism, through broken lives, lost dreams, and stolen hope, but it also describes inspiring alternatives, struggles for self-determination and sustainability. Change is possible, but it must first begin within ourselves. I recommend this book to you, and to everyone you know."

—**Camilo Mejia**, author, *Road from Ar Ramadi: The Private Rebellion of Staff Sergeant Camilo Mejia*, refused a second tour to Iraq based on conscience for which he was jailed in a military prison for nearly a year

"From the Bible reading of his youth, I'll bet author Brian Willson was familiar with the graphic mandate in Deuteronomy (and Jeremiah and Paul): 'Rip
the foreskins from your heart.' Vietnam did precisely that for Willson as he
watched, close up and personal, the slaughter of innocents. For example,
performing a bomb-damage assessment one day, the author suddenly discovered a young mother lying at his feet clutching three small children with
'blackened blood drying on their shrapnel-riddled bodies.' All four were dead.
Napalm had melted most of the mother's face but her open eyes seemed to
be staring intently into his. He felt 'a lightning bolt through my entire being
... She is my family,' he concluded, 'We are all one.'

Add courage and community to circumcised heart, and you get Willson
deciding eighteen years later to try to stop trains delivering munitions to ships
leaving California for Nicaragua. The aim: heading off the killing of other
'family' members by Contra terrorists illegally armed by the Reagan administration. After exhausting political avenues, Brian and two companions gave
the Naval base notice they would be sitting in the train tracks on Sept. 1, 1987,
in an attempt to block the delivery of arms. The train, though, was ordered
not to stop. Rather it accelerated to three times its permitted speed. Willson
lost both legs—and, almost, his life. The brutal incident was captured on film
and audiotape, and the book includes many revealing photos.

At an ecumenical worship service earlier that morning, Willson noted
that the munitions carried by train to port are 'going to kill people, people
like you and me ... we must put our bodies in front of [the trains] to say,
stronger than ever, that this will not continue in our name. The killing must
stop and I have to do everything in my power to stop it.' He then spoke
directly to 'people [folks like so many of us today] who ask what they can do
to support us. What they can do is come to the tracks and stand with us to
stop the trains ... only we can do it.'

Willson's work provides an opportunity for those who lack direct experience with the slaughter of innocents in Vietnam and Nicaragua—sorry, I
mean Iraq, Afghanistan, and Pakistan—to get a feel for what is actually being
done today in our name, and a challenge to find ways to stop it. Do you think
enough of us can handle the truth? As Cesar Chavez pointed out again and
again, there are always 'enough of us' and what's needed is **action.** I'm convinced that, once Willson's perceptive book is allowed to sink in, still more of
us will find our way onto the tracks."

—**Ray McGovern**, Ecumenical Church of the Saviour,
Washington, D.C., former CIA analyst

"S. Brian Willson's story is one of the most compelling and fascinating I have ever known. Indelibly marked by his wartime experiences in Vietnam, Brian subsequently educated himself about U.S. history and politics and became a determined peace and justice activist. In 1987, while participating in a well publicized blocking action with other veterans, Brian was struck and nearly killed by a Navy munitions train carrying weapons destined for Central America. Although he lost his legs in the assault, Brian has never stopped walking his talk. I met with him at those same tracks about six weeks later. His is an important message, and I highly recommend this book."

—**Martin Sheen**, actor

"*Blood on the Tracks* is a powerful story of Brian's conversion from a right-wing Republican born on the fourth of July to a world citizen willing to risk his life for the belief that we are all one human family and need to act on that belief. Brian believes that we all have a responsibility to live our lives in such a way that we do not kill or cause harm to other people or allow our government to kill other people in our names and with our tax dollars. Brian's story is an inspiration and powerful example for all of us who want to live in a world where peace and justice and living in harmony with the earth prevail rather than wars, poverty, horrendous injustice and environmental destruction.

Must reading for everyone who cares!"

—**David Hartsough**, director, PEACEWORKERS; cofounder, Nonviolent Peaceforce

"A remarkable and exceptional book! Brian Willson is an American hero, citizen of the world, and passionate man of peace. His extraordinary life is an inspiration to us all!"

—**Ron Kovic**, Vietnam veteran, author, *Born on the Fourth of July*.

Blood on the Tracks

The Life and Times of S. Brian Willson

A Psychohistorical Memoir

S. Brian Willson

Blood on the Tracks: The Life and Times of S. Brian Willson
S. Brian Willson
© 2011 PM Press

ISBN: 978-1-60486-421-2
Library of Congress Control Number: 2010916475

Cover: John Yates / www.stealworks.com
Interior design by briandesign

10 9 8 7 6 5 4 3 2 1

PM Press
PO Box 23912
Oakland, CA 94623
www.pmpress.org

Printed in the USA on recycled paper, by the Employee Owners of Thomson-Shore in Dexter, Michigan.
www.thomsonshore.com

Contents

Special Author's Acknowledgment

Over the years I've been writing this memoir, I wondered whether it would actually happen. I had writer's block that wouldn't quit. Some parts of my journey are burdened with shame and denial, others with disbelief, and I feared becoming vulnerable as I dredged up details I did not want to remember or discuss. Plus the writing process itself can be very challenging. But the therapeutic benefits of telling my story spurred me on.

Memoirs are, of course, based on memories, and memory can be tricky. Details are apparently recorded in one part of the brain, the hippocampus, while emotions and visceral feelings such as fear are in another part, the amygdala. Studies of the brain and nervous system reveal how traumatic experiences are processed and recorded within the dynamic interconnections among various portions of the brain. This memoir is not intended to be reporting the truth about events, but only how I remember and understand them. I have written hundreds—even thousands—of pages of various accounts of my life's journey, essays, anecdotes, and various analyses that accompanied my waking up process, but I had not been able to assemble them into a flowing, concise narrative. In 1992 I did publish (with the wonderful assistance of historian Staughton Lynd) a short book titled *On Third World Legs* (Charles H. Kerr) but its distribution was very limited, and much was necessarily left out.

As I was reading some personal correspondence in early 2004 while anguishing over the latest U.S. barbarism in Iraq and Afghanistan, I came upon an old letter from Gloria Emerson. A *New York Times* correspondent in Viet Nam from 1970 to 1972, Gloria published *Winners and Losers* in 1976—for me the most meaningful and passionate book written about the Viet Nam War. In her letter, she shared something quite touching: "I have a photograph of you, always before me, with the sign, 'Veterans Fast For Life.' Your courage is contagious." Though it felt good reading her words, it was a stretch to believe them, and besides, I don't feel particularly courageous. So I wondered if her comments were genuine.

Nevertheless, I contacted Gloria to belatedly thank her for the solidarity message, and to chat about how to complete a readable memoir. Surprisingly, she said that she had been waiting many years for my memoir, long overdue, and that the world needed to hear my story. She thought of me often, she said, and was very happy I had contacted her, saying she could see the anguish in my face from the photo, a "burden" which she knew intimately from her own experiences. Such validation!

As we talked on the phone and exchanged letters (e-mail for her was an "abomination"), it became clear that Gloria was as genuine in personal communication as she was in reporting the pain and suffering of the people in the Viet Nam War, on both sides, civilians and military alike. Gloria was still haunted by what she saw in Viet Nam and what she learned about the nature of the United States as a society. She confessed matter-of-factly that she would try a lobotomy to erase her memories if she thought it would work. I know that feeling.

But Gloria hadn't only been exposed to Viet Nam and Cambodia. She had also covered the Nigerian Civil War in 1968, and the one in Northern Ireland in 1969. Later she reported on apartheid in South Africa, the civil war in El Salvador, and occupation of the Palestinians in the Gaza. The latter led to her 1991 book, *Gaza: A Year in the Intifada*. She had a deep empathy for underdogs and was keenly sensitive to structural injustices wherever she saw them. She obviously sensed in me a kindred spirit: like her, I was infuriated about the behavior of the United States, while carrying deeply within the visceral knowledge of its egregious consequences on others. Thus she said, "Please, Brian, complete your memoirs. Get up each morning and pretend you are writing 'Dear Gloria notes' about a particular phase of your life, or an anecdote, or story, then share them with me. I believe that soon the pieces will begin to fall together."

In May 2004, out of the blue, Gloria asked if I would like to have a number of books from her Viet Nam library. I was stunned by her offer and, after a brief hesitation, I accepted with great appreciation. Before long, three large, very heavy boxes arrived. In mid-June, Gloria sent me a letter with a 1986 photo showing a number of books by Viet Nam authors displayed on the steps of the U.S. Capitol in solidarity with the Veterans Fast for Life. Her book, of course, was among them. She also sent the U.S. Army "Code of Conduct" card from her personal file that had been issued to U.S. troops during Viet Nam enumerating their expected conduct, including in the eventuality of capture. The code begins with the words, "I am an American fighting man. I serve in the forces which guard my country and our way of life." The concluding words: "I will trust in my God and in the United States of America." The card was sent, she said, "for a laugh."

Though I knew she took great pride in writing by hand or on a manual typewriter rather than on a computer, I did not know that she had recently been diagnosed with Parkinson's Disease, which would make typing or handwriting increasingly difficult. Thus I was rocked by grief when I learned that Gloria took her own life in her Manhattan apartment on August 4, 2004 (after months of careful preparation). Little did I know that the gifts of the books, the photo, the Code of Conduct card, had been part of Gloria's plan to distribute her personal possessions before moving on to the next world.

In her final letter to me, written just after Ronald Reagan's death in June 2004, she commiserated, "It has been awful to swallow the canonization of Reagan when he was so despicable, his presidency so terrible. The blather about him has been non-stop." Gloria knew of course that I had been caught up in Reagan's war on domestic dissent, disguised as a war on terror. She was indeed a kindred spirit.

Though I never successfully wrote more than a half dozen "Dear Gloria notes," and they never came together as a memoir, my interactions with Gloria Emerson became the motivational force I needed to complete my memoir. It was finally with the astute assistance of professional editor Jo Ellen Green Kaiser that I was able to craft a readable memoir. Whether this story is highly regarded or not will be determined by the readers. At least I can rest with the knowledge that I have completed what I set out to do many years ago.

I'm honored to dedicate this book to Gloria Emerson, a unique woman who felt deep anguish and possessed great passion, who believed in me for many years, and who finally got her wish—that my memoir be written.

S. Brian Willson
February 2011

AUTHOR'S CONVENTIONS

Throughout this book you will notice certain conventions that differ from publishing industry standards. These are not a result of editorial sloppiness but rather author's preference.

U.S. American—Although *American* is commonly used to refer to a person or other entity originating in the United States of America, I feel that it is presumptive and arrogant to do so, considering that the USA is but one country of many on the American continents.

American Way Of Life—This phrase is capitalized throughout the book to emphasize the destructive nature of a way of life that demands a disproportionate amount of the world's resources. As an acronym, it signifies being AWOL ("absent without leave" in military jargon) from our humanity and the natural systems of the planet that sustains us.

Viet Nam—Except where included in a reference citation, I have chosen to write the name of this country as two words (as it is done there, rather than its Westernized one-word form) in honor of Vietnamese culture.

Viet Cong or VC—In most cases, except when quoting others, I have tried to avoid using Viet Cong, translated as "Vietnamese Communists," as it was considered a derogatory nickname by the South Vietnamese puppets who coined it. Instead, I refer to Vietnamese who fought against the U.S. as members of the National Liberation Front (NLF).

Note: The names of U.S. military officers I encountered have been changed to protect their identities.

INTRODUCTION

by Daniel Ellsberg

The people sitting on the tracks at the Concord Naval Weapons Station on September 1, 1987, were expecting to be arrested. Either that or they would succeed in arresting the train, slowing the delivery of munitions to maim and kill people in Central America.

Having been in that position myself—on the tracks at the Rocky Flats Nuclear Weapons Production Facility in Colorado, nine years earlier—I can hear the skeptical reaction such actions evoke: "But you won't really stop the transport; the train will always get through."

To which the answer of those on the tracks is: "Not without arrests. Not invisibly, anymore; not smoothly, on time, without effort or reflection from within the bureaucratic system; not without public question, comment, controversy, challenge. Not, anymore, with the presumed consent of all American citizens."

As my son Robert put it, as we drove handcuffed in a police van past the tracks at Rocky Flats where we had just been arrested: "There should have been people sitting on the tracks at Auschwitz."

An overstated analogy? Not for Rocky Flats, where the plutonium triggers for all U.S. thermonuclear weapons were produced: each one of those thousands of warheads, a portable Auschwitz. But not for Concord Naval Weapons Station, either. As described in a manifesto by Brian Willson, July 4, 1987, "Concord, possessing both conventional and nuclear munitions ['bombs, white phosphorus rockets, missiles, grenades, ammunition'], shipping arms to military operations in Central America, the Pacific theater, the Philippines and South Korea, and the Middle East, including the Persian Gulf, is the largest munitions storage shipping depot on the West Coast."

The manifesto continued, "The vision for the Nuremberg Actions includes the daily upholding the law of nations and our own Constitution by placing ourselves—our bodies—in front of the trains and trucks carrying munitions of death from their bunkers to the piers for placement on ships, some destined for Central America where we can predict a specified number of human beings who will be killed and maimed once transported past our vulnerable bodies."

Why "Nuremberg Actions"? The statement asserted rightly that "the use and manner of use of our munitions in Central America is illegal under international and Constitutional law" and that the Nuremberg Principles obliged citizens to oppose aggressive war and to uphold international law by disobeying "commands furthering the illegal conduct and to refrain from participating any further" in it.

Willson wrote, on July 4, "Violence is our business to stop—non-violently. None of this is possible as long as we are unable or unwilling to pay the price or endure the risks of living and working for justice and peace." On September 1, Willson and other citizens were saying, in effect: "We withdraw our consent to this death-dealing transport. To carry it on, you will have to move us off the tracks by arresting us . . . or else, you will have to do it over our bodies."

Faced with these alternatives, the authorities at the base made unannounced choices: not to make arrests that day; and not to obey regulations requiring the train to stop if there was *anything* in front of it on the tracks. They gave secret orders to the train crew *not* to stop if there were human bodies ahead. Those orders the crew obeyed. They may or may not have been ordered to speed up, to three times their regulated speed at the base; in any case, that is what they did.

• • •

That day S. Brian Willson proved that the risk he was willing to run and the price he was willing to pay to live and work for justice and peace was as great as the price the State was willing to inflict on those who challenged its illegitimate actions and authority. There was no real limit on the latter price: as Brian—and I—had witnessed in Vietnam in ways that changed our lives, and as I had recognized earlier in reading secret nuclear war plans.

Such unbounded violence can be contained and transcended only by the unlimited civil courage that Brian exhibited that day, and by large-scale resistance, as he had put it on July 4, "that stems from an affirmation of life—equally—for all people of the earth."

"All people." "Equally." Those thoughts were spelled out two months later, on the morning of the train assault, in his notes for that occasion (supplied to me by Brian). They raise themes of profound import if they were to be taken seriously and acted on: as it turned out that they were, by Brian and his companions on the tracks.

"The authorities will be notified of the resistance action on the tracks so that they will have the choice of suspending movement of munitions, removing our bodies, or running over us. One truth seems clear: Once the train carrying the munitions moves past our human blockade, if it does, other human beings in other parts of the world will be killed and maimed. **We are not**

worth more. They are not worth less. [emphasis added] Let us commit to ourselves and the world that we will claim our dignity, self-respect and honor by resisting with our lives and dollars, no matter what it takes, any further policies designed to kill others in our name, in each of our names ultimately."

"*We are not worth more. They are not worth less.*" Meaning, if it means anything at all: "It is worth giving our lives to save theirs. It is worth risking our lives to reduce the risk to theirs."

Who really thinks that way, or acts that way? Well, often, members of a family; or a combat team, about each other (not about "the enemy" or *their* families); perhaps, to some extent, a community, a nation; "us." But how many feel that way about the lives of strangers, "others," "them"? Not very many, yet. Not Brian himself, much earlier in his life, before a path of experiences that awakened him to the moral reality of a familyhood that encompasses all humanity, indeed all life on earth.

The open eyes of a dead woman in Vietnam, killed, with her infant, by American bombs, the missing limbs of amputees in Nicaragua maimed by American mines, brought him, by a kind of terrible grace, to a greatly expanded sense of the "we" with rights and needs like his and our own, with just demands on our consideration, concern, compassion, and if necessary self-sacrifice.

This is the story of one man's evolution from being a normal, ordinary, patriotic American—capable of acquiescing, even participating in a war of horrendous destruction against people in Indochina ("enemies," along with their families and other "collateral damage")—to becoming a human who risked and sacrificed his legs to try to stop our carnage in Central America: one who ever since has devoted his life to warning fellow humans about the harm they are inflicting and the dangers they are posing to all others and to most forms of life on the planet.

In the era of nuclear threats and of manmade, consumption-driven climate change, nothing less than that same change in consciousness and in compassionate action—exemplified in Brian Willson's life and present lifestyle—on a mass basis can save this species from decimating itself and extinguishing most others in the relatively short run.

Is that at all possible? For humanity, as it is, in time?

The inspiration that this particular life-story presents is that it answers "yes" to that challenge. If one person (and of course, there have been many others, though not often so dramatically) can change their own awareness and their lives this way, then others of us can. It can't be ruled out, it can't be proven to be impossible, that *enough* humans can change themselves and history to stop the train that is heading now . . . to hell on earth.

That might seem a dishearteningly cautious way to put our prospects. In truth, the odds are not good. There is no guarantee that the train will stop, no matter how many bodies are on the tracks. But the stakes could not be higher, and it is inspiration enough for many of us to keep in sight, as this story helps us do in unsurpassed fashion, that despite all obstacles we do have a chance.

No reader, I believe, will finish this book without a sense of awe at the human spirit that is revealed in it and of gratitude for the map that Brian Willson has provided, in his life and this account of it, of the way out.

Foreword

I t is the week of March 13, 2008. I sit for hours at my computer, watching video footage of young Iraq and Afghanistan veterans talking, slowly and carefully, about what it feels like to fight a war. These are the Winter Soldier Iraq/Afghanistan Hearings, based on similar hearings conducted thirty-seven years earlier by Vietnam Veterans Against the War.

> On April 18, 2006, I had my first confirmed kill. This man was inno-cent. I don't know his name. He was walking back to his house and I shot him in front of his friend and his father. The first round didn't kill him. He started screaming and looked right into my eyes. I looked at my friend and I said, "Well, I can't let that happen," so I shot him again. It took seven people to carry his body away. We were all con-gratulated when we made our first kill. I was congratulated on mine.
>
> I just want to say that I'm sorry for the hate and destruction that I've inflicted on innocent people. . . . I'm sorry for the things that I did. I am no longer the monster I once was. [Jon Turner, 3rd Battalion, 8th Marines, www.ivaw.org.]

As I look at the faces of these soldiers and hear their stories, I cry nearly uncontrollably, my chest heaving, as I did during my first flashback in 1981. Politicians say that every war is different and necessary, but those of us who have fought in wars know all wars are the same.

> Later, we were going house to house in a village. Two guys were pointed out to us as troublemakers. We tossed the hut. There was nothing there. We took the guys anyway. Their mother was kissing my feet, crying. I don't speak Arabic, but I speak human. She was saying, "Why are you taking my sons, my boys? They haven't done anything." I was powerless to help her. . . . We never went on a raid where we got the right house, much less the right person. Not once! [Hart Viges, 82nd Airborne, www.ivaw.org.]

I would probably not let myself cry so much if my partner, Becky, was home. Ironically, she is in Viet Nam on a humanitarian project that addresses some of the damage we caused in that war forty years ago. If she heard me, she would want to soothe me, but I don't need or want to be soothed. Though the words of these soldiers shake me, their testimony indicates the power of transformation. It reveals the presence of soul, that indispensable characteristic of the human condition that is so often submerged under the pressure to conform and obey authority.

> I joined the military after September 11, 2001, out of a desire to protect our country. I believed the President and members of his cabinet when they claimed that Saddam Hussein posed a serious threat to the United States, and then was shocked to learn that Congress, the American public, and the international community had to one degree or another been deceived or frightened into supporting the March 2003 invasion of Iraq. [Thomas J. Buonomo, 2nd Lieutenant, U.S. Army, www.ivaw.org.]

I was once a young man, very much like the young men and women who have gone to Iraq. I grew up believing in the red, white, and blue. I believed that the United States had a sacred mission to spread democracy around the world. Viet Nam was my generation's war. I did not volunteer, but when I was drafted, I answered the call. It was in Viet Nam that my journey toward a different kind of knowledge began.

I did not become a full-fledged activist after I returned from Viet Nam. Instead, I resumed law school. I believed, like most people, that Viet Nam had just been a terrible mistake. Like many vets, my brain could not process the horrors I had seen there, and so for many years I had no visceral recollection of the worst of the atrocities I witnessed. I believed, as so many people now believe, that if we just had better politicians, or better laws, we would never have to fight a war like Viet Nam again.

I spent a decade after Viet Nam struggling against a prison system that locked up impoverished Black men for long years while it gave shorter sentences to White men. I spent years lobbying Congress for prison reforms, only to see that our legal system almost always worked in favor of those protected by privilege even at the expense of human rights. Finally one day, when I was working in one of those prisons, I experienced a flashback that revealed the true horror of the war I had been a participant in. Everything clicked into place.

Viet Nam was not a mistake any more than the Iraq War is a mistake. There neither was nor is anything different about these wars. They are part of a pattern of brutality written into our country's DNA. Since the first European settlers raped, pillaged, and massacred the local Indian populations in order to claim the land for themselves, we in the United States have felt it our manifest destiny as exceptional people to gain ever more material goods, even at the expense of anyone and everyone else, and the earth. We continue to treat others as inferiors.

I was dismayed at the way we were treating the Iraqis that we were there to liberate. Though our rhetoric spoke of freedom and liberation, our actions spoke only of self-preservation. [Ronn Cantu, Sergeant, U.S. Army, www. ivaw.org.]

For over four hundred years, the United States has expanded, first filling this continent, and then taking its empire overseas to the Philippines, Cuba, Haiti, Korea, Viet Nam, Nicaragua, Iraq, ad nauseum. As I tried to understand why I had gone to war in Viet Nam, I began to journey around the world, witnessing the impact of both overt and covert U.S. intervention in nations such as Nicaragua, El Salvador, Cuba, Brazil, Argentina, Palestine, Iraq, Korea, and elsewhere.

After spending significant time in Nicaragua, I realized that a whole different way of life was possible than the one into which I had been born. We didn't have to spend all of our time getting more and more. Life was actually fuller and richer when lived simpler and slower. The *campesinos* (farmers) in Nicaragua were poor—unfairly poor—but their goal in life was not to become rich. Though there were always exceptions, for most campesinos, community and extended family were more important than individual wealth. Preserving their dignity was more important to them than living a long life.

I believed, during these years, that if I could explain how the United States was forcing its way of life on people who didn't want it, if I could prove the harm that U.S. bombs and economic policies were doing to people who didn't want our "help," that I could convince the people of the United States to change government policy. I used all my legal training in this project: on these trips, I took detailed notes, wrote reports for a variety of non-governmental agencies, and checked my facts.

After each trip, I brought that information home, marched in protests, lobbied Congress, and spoke out at churches and universities. When those approaches didn't work, I helped organize the Veterans Fast for Life on the steps of the Capitol. Nothing, however, seemed to stop the behemoth of U.S. intervention as it sought continued prosperity through domination. Finally, we decided to go directly to the source of Nicaraguan suffering—the Concord Naval Weapons Station that shipped U.S. arms to the Contras of Nicaragua by way of El Salvador.

On September 1, 1987, at a well-planned and -publicized nonviolent action conducted on railroad tracks crossing public land between two sections of the naval base, I was run over by a munitions train. In one instant, I experienced, in my own body, the brute force of U.S. power that so many poverty-stricken villagers feel every day around the world. I survived, but my legs were taken from me. Since then, I've been walking on Third World Legs.

My body healed long ago, but that does not mean my healing has ended. My journey continues. I realize now that the U.S. engine of prosperity cannot be stopped until we change our very way of life. Each one of us must choose between an American Way Of Life that values selfish material prosperity and a way of life that values our collective humanity.

We don't have much time to choose wisely. Today, our national addiction to material comfort is so grotesque that, though we comprise only 4.6 percent of the world's population, we consume anywhere from 25 percent to nearly half of the world's resources. Our sky is filled with pollutants, our seas with plastics, our lands covered with pools of toxic waste. In our desperate desire for more, we are now waging war on our own home, the earth itself. The drive to consume, consume, consume is literally consuming our hospitable planet.

I no longer travel the world. I don't want to use the fuel or pollute the skies. But my journey continues. This book is my witness to the wars we have fought against others, and that we are now inflicting upon ourselves. There is no escaping the consequences:

> See, you can't wash your hands when they're covered in blood. The wounds carry on. This is what war does to your soul, to your humanity, to your family. [Iraq veteran Hart Viges, *The Independent* UK, September 24, 2005.]

All of us are covered in the blood of war through our complicity with the American Way Of Life. The deep understanding we must find is that this blood is our own, not just that of others. This book chronicles my journey toward that understanding. I walk with the millions of people around the world who are on similar journeys.

PART I

All-American

CHAPTER 1

July 4, 1941

B ooks have beginnings and endings, but I don't think of my life that way. The journey is what is important, not the destination. I may have an idea or an experience today that changes everything I thought or did the day before. As Gandhi said, life is an experiment with truth, every day.

I was born on July 4, 1941, in Geneva, New York, in the heart of the beautiful Finger Lakes region of Central New York State. I still have a drawing I made when I was very small of a Fourth of July parade. In the drawing, a boy holding a U.S. American flag leads the parade, followed by a fire truck. I suspect I am the one carrying the flag. Typically, as a young child, I had assumed that all the floats, marching bands, and fireworks were for me. After all, it was my birthday. Of course, I found out as I grew up that my personal story was only a tiny part of a much bigger story.

This book about my life is also about that bigger story, the story of U.S. America, the America that stretches from the North Pole to the tip of Patagonia, and the even larger story of our way of living in this world, on this earth. I've learned that, in life, everything is connected. My experiences growing up in small towns in upstate New York connect me to the history of the United States of America, to the Indigenous people who were here before me, and to the people I met in Viet Nam, Nicaragua, Cuba, Mexico, and elsewhere. However, it took me a while to sort out all those connections. In fact, I am still learning about them.

Arrowheads

My family lived in three different homes in my first nine-and-a-half years, but none were more than a mile and a half from Geneva General Hospital, where I was born. My mother often commented on how much I liked to be outdoors all day long as a toddler, even in the heavy snows of winter. Since my earliest years were during World War II, we shared a large lot with many neighbors who worked their victory gardens. My father had been too young to serve in World War I and too old for World War II, though he did serve as a neighborhood air raid warden, looking for visible lights from homes during the many blackout alerts. Geneva was close enough to the East Coast that fear of German bombings was high.

As I got a little older I would occasionally accompany my father on Saturdays when he went door-to-door selling—or trying to sell—the famous Fuller Brush line of products. On Sundays, my mother made sure my older brother and I got into our best clothes for Sunday services at the nearby First Baptist Church, where my father was a deacon and my mother sang in the church choir. As one of the regular attendees in children's Sunday School, I was recognized as the polite boy who always opened doors for seniors and who sometimes played clarinet at church events. My Sunday School teacher later described me as "very cooperative, no problem whatsoever . . . just an ideal little boy."[1] Our family was as all-American as you can get. My parents, who had both grown up in small towns in western New York State, were staunch Republicans who believed in the value of hard work. My father was ardently against the New Deal and labor unions, and held the kind of racist views that then seemed mainstream. Both my older brother, Dwight, named after famous evangelist Dwight L. Moody, and I played ball, rode bikes, and generally lived the kind of small-town lives depicted in Norman Rockwell paintings. One of my fondest childhood memories is playing with my tough steel construction toys—bulldozer, boom crane, road grader, earth-hauler, power shovel, and dump truck—creating a small road system in our yard. If I got lucky, I might find a flint stone arrowhead right in my own backyard. Later, when I got old enough to ride my brother's hand-me-down balloon-tired bike, I would cycle a mile to the fascinating Seneca Burial Mound (not far from the hospital where I was born), which was a treasure trove of arrowheads.

Before long, I had a box of arrowheads. I would feel each one with my fingers, noting its texture, shape, weight, size, and sharpness while enjoying the subtle color variations of dark-grey, blue, and black. Some had a glassy appearance. I often wondered what life had been like for the ancient peoples who had once lived and prospered on the very ground on which I played.

At the time I knew little about the Seneca Nation, or the powerful Six-Nation Iroquois Confederacy of which they were a part—just that they existed. Like my family, friends, and community, I assumed they were inferior to Europeans. In second grade, I drew a crude picture of a large cowboy firing a rifle at close range directly at a much smaller "Indian" boy whose arrow is just leaving his bow. The bullet's trajectory is shown just as it is about to enter the young "Indian's" head.

I was already on a journey I didn't even know about, one that would take me back to New York State as an adult to speak to the remaining Indigenous Seneca and around the world to speak to the Indigenous peoples of Chiapas, Nicaragua, Palestine, and Viet Nam. But that would come much later.

Four Corners

In December 1950, during Christmas vacation, my parents took me out of fourth grade and moved our family 150 miles further west, to the tiny farming community of Ashville, New York. I had grown fond of my Geneva elementary school and my neighborhood friends, so leaving brought me great sadness. I was learning to play the tonette and my dairy farm scene had been selected the best painting in art class.

One consolation of the move was that I would see my brother Dwight more often. Nine and a half years my senior, he was a sophomore at Fredonia State Teachers College, located in the county where we now lived. My parents had made the move to a run-down, 110-year-old house in an effort to lift our family out of serious financial straits. Our new home was set on two-thirds of an acre, and the vegetable and fruit gardens we planted became an important part of our family's home life and sustenance.

Instead of selling Fuller Brushes, my father took a job selling insurance door to door, but success remained elusive and my parents struggled to make ends meet. There was little money for new clothes for a rapidly growing schoolboy, but fortunately, each year, a rich uncle generously purchased a full set of clothes for me—larger sized shirts, pants, coats, underwear and shoes. (Many years later, after this same uncle left a small fortune to my mother, I discovered that he had made his millions as a stockholder in IBM, which had become the wealthiest corporation in the world after its business alliance with Nazi Germany to automate the Holocaust, tracking Jews and Gypsies from points of apprehension to concentration camps to extermination.)[2]

Ashville was a village of 350 people located about twenty miles south of the town of Westfield (population 3,000), where my mother had been born in 1907. Her father had been hired as a "Christian bookkeeper" for Dr. Charles Welch, president of Welch's Grape Juice. Dr. Welch was a teetotaler who developed his juice as a nonalcoholic alternative to wine for use in Methodist communion. Ashville was also twenty-five miles southwest of Shumla, a hamlet of fifty people, where my father had been born.

The village, typical of its day, possessed most necessary services to which residents could walk: general stores, feed mills, a diner, churches, library, grange hall, barber shops, blacksmith, fire hall, post office, grade school, and a garage. The volunteer fire department had one of the town's first TV sets and invited villagers to watch boxing and wrestling every Friday night. The farthest I ever traveled was our Sunday trips to the First Baptist Church in nearby Jamestown and occasional trips with my dad three miles to the next town's movie house to see the latest Randolph Scott westerns. Regular attendance at church was required, and my perfect Sunday School attendance earned me five straight summers of church camp on a pristine lake in western New York State.

Most of my activities, from walking to school, fishing and playing sports, going to the local Methodist Youth Fellowship, Boy Scout meetings, and weekly supervised youth recreation, happened within two-thirds of a mile of my home.

I suppose that some of my current ideas about the importance of small, local, sustainable living come from my experiences growing up around those four corners, even as, in hindsight, I realize it was a parochial, stereotypical 1950s McCarthyite town, filled with racism, sexism, and an unspoken classism.

Like Apple Pie

My life revolved around the outdoors. I spent warm days fishing at or swimming in Goose Creek, which meandered through our village. My friends and I rode our bikes around town, played pickup ball, and traded baseball cards. In the winter, I was the town's most ardent sidewalk shoveler. In summer I regularly mowed lawns, earning plenty of money which I added to the numerous tips I received for shoveling snow during our heavy winters. At night, kids came to my house to play basketball almost any time, since I had rigged up in our backyard the only outdoor lit court in town.

I bought so many baseball trading cards the general store ordered an extra box each week, just for me. Nevertheless, up until eighth grade, I was a terrible athlete. Being the last kid selected for teams was emotionally painful, and the feelings of rejection and exclusion could be intense. No one wanted "Brian the Brain."

In seventh grade, while my brother was serving in the U.S. Army in Germany, I was learning more about New York State history and that of the Seneca "Indians" and the Iroquois Confederacy of which they were a part. Our textbook, *Exploring New York State*, explained that the "Empire State" motto originated in 1783 when George Washington suggested that the territory, now clear of "Indians," become the "seat of empire" of "vast power and wealth." Our text described how Washington had ordered his army to "crush" the Indigenous people because of their threat to frontier settlements, from which the "primitive" inhabitants "never recovered." "All their villages were destroyed, their fruit orchards, their growing crops, their stores of food," "their power was gone forever." Just as well. They possessed "no machinery of any kind," "almost the entire area was covered with thick forests" unlike today when "more than half the land of New York is cleared for ploughing and pasture," and "like more civilized peoples, the Five Nations never thought of conserving their natural resources."[3] So now I knew more about the history of those arrowheads, or so I was led to believe.

My life changed dramatically halfway through eighth grade. In some miraculous way, my hands, eyes, and feet finally became coordinated. Suddenly, I was a good athlete. I could dribble and shoot the basketball, hit and field the softball, and smoothly perform gymnastics. Instead of the last kid picked for teams in gym class, I quickly became the first. Then I became the captain and could pick a team myself. I finally felt accepted by the other boys.

By the time I had finished eighth grade in June 1955, the fact that I, a boy, was valedictorian was not so embarrassing because I was now a respected athlete, rather than just "Brian the Brain." In those days, and in that district, eighth grade was the big graduation because so many kids in the rural area, especially boys, either did not go to high school, or knew they would never finish. I nervously gave the valedictory address on "Sportsmanship" at commencement. My mother saved that speech. Ironically, my address was somewhat prophetic. One of my conclusions was that being a "good sportsman" requires "not giving up easily when handicapped."

By age fourteen, I rode the school bus for the first time to Chautauqua Central High School ten miles away. I loved high school. I was a member of the National Honor Society and twice elected to Student Council. I was the first baseman on our summer Babe Ruth League baseball championship team. In my senior year, our Chautauqua "Indians" basketball team went to the semifinals but lost in the first round. I was selected to be on the league's all-conference second basketball team, and was the first baseman on our high school sectional championship baseball team, the latter honor a first ever for our school.

Going from being one of the least popular kids to one of the most popular helped me to feel empathy for others. I still remember a large Indigenous boy in high school who had a leg withered by polio without the expensive brace. He loved to play intramural sports but some kids didn't want him to play because he couldn't run well. As one of the two intramural team captains, I applied a principle that everyone on the team would play at least half of each game. I didn't want him to feel rejected.

A poster of St. Louis Cardinal's Stan "The Man" Musial, my boyhood "hero," hung over my bed. In the summer after my junior year, I turned down an opportunity to study in France as an American Field Service (AFS) foreign exchange student in order to play semipro baseball. Scouts watching those games often sat behind my father in the bleachers. Upon graduation, St. Louis expressed an interest in offering me a chance to play in the low minors if I chose not to attend college where playing amateur sports was prohibited at the time if signing any professional contract. I chose college where for three years I played basketball and baseball.

Lucky

While I flourished outdoors, life inside my home was difficult. My father was a very hard man to live with. He was a teetotaling fundamentalist, anticommunist, antiunion, racist and virulently anti-Semitic. By 1960 he feared, along with many others, the post–World War II threat of a Communist takeover and, with Kennedy's presidential candidacy, a Vatican-directed Catholic takeover as well.

Those fears led him to passively support organizations such as Robert Welch's John Birch Society (JBS), George Lincoln Rockwell's American Nazi Party (ANP), Willis Carto's Liberty Lobby (LL), and the New York Catskill Branch of the Ku Klux Klan. He also was a regular subscriber to billionaire H.L. Hunt's right-wing *Life Line* newsletter. These were all extremist organizations that embraced a politics of hate. This was not just run-of-the-mill racism. These groups were possessed by a venomous, perhaps criminal psychosis, and advocated violence against communists, Jews, Catholics, and Blacks, as well as Eastern European and Italian immigrants. Today we would call them terrorist organizations.

When Rockwell, the leader of the American Nazi Party, was assassinated in 1967 in Arlington, Virginia, by one of his jealous lieutenants, the ANP dissolved into three groups, leaving my father confused as to who was the legitimate American Nazi figurehead. This diverted my dad's attention to Carto and his *Liberty Letter*, which later became *The Spotlight*. Among other things, Carto repeated Rockwell's belief that the Jews concocted the Holocaust and, instead of having been incinerated, they died as happy rich people in New York City. This hatred is a strange and dangerous phenomenon, and I struggled to understand why my father embraced it.

My parents were intelligent people, though they possessed small-town, conservative, patriotic values. They were raised with the typical Eurocentric racism against people of "color." They both were early graduates of the Dunkirk, New York Business Institute, where my mother was class president in 1928 and gave the welcoming address at commencement. My father was a math whiz. They were solidly middle class from 1931–1944 because my dad had a steady, well-paying job in the office of a successful flour mill, essentially providing bread as a food staple. Thus, they were comfortable during the Depression. But at the age of forty, in 1944, my father lost his job when a larger milling company purchased the mill. Never again did he find stable employment that adequately paid the bills.

Fear of failure wields intense emotional power. One way that people seek relief from such anxiety in an individualistic, acquisitive society is by becoming addicted to consumption, only to discover that more is never enough. Other escapes are racism, classism, fundamentalism, and sexism. My father was not a big consumer, perhaps because he was born into an agricultural town that valued saving over consumption. Instead, he became xenophobic, projecting his fear of failure onto alien others, who he believed prevented him from succeeding. The organizations he joined used his anxiety to convince him to support repressive authority systems—religious, political, social, economic—that identified "enemies" while creating mechanisms to control and eliminate them.

These repressive organizations don't actually solve anyone's problems. Instead, they play insidious tricks to satisfy the deep psychological need for security without addressing people's real problems—either the generations of fear-based racism, or the structural injustices that preserve class divisions.[4] Ironically, permanent security is found only in community and through collective efforts. But in a market-driven, get-what-you-can culture, we are taught to be individualistic and narcissistic, and to reject collectivity and community. In his own way, I think my father was reaching for community when he joined groups like the American Nazi Party, but it was a false community formed through rejection rather than acceptance, hatred rather than love. Until we address the root of our anxiety, the shadow within, and learn to embrace mutual respect for each other and the earth, there will be no healing, just more fear, hatred, and war.

It has been a challenge for me to understand the politics and psychology of my immediate family. I have been embarrassed at times, worried at others, that I might become hateful like them. Yet my parents were doing what many adults do—finding fault with others rather than seeking healing within themselves and honestly addressing the structural injustices of the larger political-economic system. Materialism and the need for chronic denial about its deleterious consequences make resorting to addictions an "easy" out. But, of course, it is a Faustian bargain, as we sell our souls for a dollar just to "keep up with the Joneses" or to maintain someone else's image of ourselves.

Though I later came to understand that I fundamentally disagreed with my parents' views, especially those of my father, his politics were not my main problem when I was growing up. While his racial, ethnic, and religious prejudices did seem extreme to me, I agreed with my father's anticommunism, which was typical for the era. I would regularly join him and my mother in listening to Fulton Lewis Jr.'s radio show, in which Lewis would often reveal which U.S. government employees had recently been exposed as members of the Communist Party. It was the McCarthy era, and we were all worried the Communists were going to take over the country.

My mother was a warm, nurturing parent. My father, however, was emotionally cold and tyrannical. As a teenager, if I slept in even a few minutes past seven in the morning, my father would be pinching the skin on the right side of my neck, gruffly yelling, "Get up, get up!" He had grown up on a farm where he had to wake up early most mornings to milk cows and do other farm chores prior to walking four miles to school. I think he resented the comparative luxury of my sleeping in until seven.

Our relationship only got worse as I got older. By the seventh or eighth grade, it was uncomfortable for him to carry on *any* conversation with me other than giving orders, or making critical comments about my behavior or school performance. I dreaded working in the garden with him, as he would often express displeasure about some chore I'd performed that had not met his standards.

Having been abruptly moved from friends and familiar environs halfway through fourth grade, I had a lot of pent-up anger. I'm ashamed to say that all that anger came out soon after we moved to Ashville in the extremely cold, snowy winter of 1950–1951. When we moved, my paternal grandmother had given me her dog Lucky, a part water spaniel, I think as a way of helping me adjust to my new home. I had always loved playing with Lucky when we visited my grandmother, and I was grateful to have her.

Yet, not long after acquiring Lucky, in the confines of my bedroom, I spent about two days physically torturing her into absolute submission. It was my own monster manifesting itself, my desire to make sure this innocent creature was literally more of an underdog than I was. I kept this dark secret to myself for over forty years, until it came out during a therapy session with an astute psychiatrist. I am still bothered by the memory. My torture was so severe it left Lucky with a permanent slight limp in her left-rear leg.

Following this despicable act of sadism, I started feeling sick from my actions. Something in me changed, and I was able to see myself and Lucky in a new way. This episode with Lucky helped to teach me how much anger I had inside and how anger can enable a decent person to do indecent things.

Lucky also taught me a lot about forgiveness. Even though I had tortured her, Lucky was my best friend until her death four years later. She accompanied me on many outings—to the playground, the swimming hole, to my favorite fishing spot on Goose Creek, and overnight on Boy Scout campouts. As a water spaniel, she especially loved swimming in the creek while I was trying to fish. She is the only dog I ever saw get a running start and jump off a creek bank into a deep pool of water, then dog-paddle back to the creek edge. Shaking herself, she would repeat the jump several times, especially on hot days. It didn't make for good fishing, but I loved watching her jump in the water.

What really astonished me was that Lucky, after only a few months, somehow figured out on her own how to time her two-thirds-mile walk from our house to my elementary school so as to greet me when I exited the school each day at 3:15 p.m. I vividly remember walking home with Lucky each afternoon in spring of 1954 to find my mother ironing clothes as she listened to radio broadcasts of the famous Army-McCarthy Hearings. These explosive hearings, covered even in my school's *Weekly Reader*, were adjudicating a dispute between the Army, which claimed that McCarthy was seeking preferential treatment for a friend of his in the Army, and McCarthy, who was accusing the Army of employing Communists in its defense plants. There was a moment when Army Secretary Joseph Welch asked the obstreperous McCarthy, "Have you no sense of decency, sir, at long last? Have you left no sense of decency?" It caught McCarthy by surprise and some believe it was the beginning of the end of his popularity, much to the disappointment of people like my parents. In December 1954, the Senate condemned McCarthy for conduct unbecoming a U.S. Senator. He died of alcoholism in the Bethesda Naval Hospital in 1957 at age forty-eight. My teetotaling parents were shocked.

When I was in eighth grade, Lucky contracted throat cancer and died soon after being diagnosed. It was my first experience with death. I grieved as I buried her remains in our backyard in a little private ceremony. I laid a large stone over her gravesite, then erected a wooden cross that could always be seen from our kitchen window. Lucky had taught me the awesome lesson of the power of forgiveness.

Lucky's lessons, however, took time to sink in. As a teenager, I still had not yet figured out what to do with all that anger inside of me. That anger came roaring back one Saturday morning when I was fourteen. By that time I was physically bigger than my dad, both taller and heavier. That morning, when my father pinched my neck in his usual way, I lurched straight up, grabbed the shirt around his neck with both hands, and whirled the two of us through the air. My father ended up on his back, smashed against a cast iron radiator not far from my bed. I kicked his head with my bare foot against the radiator. As he yelled in pain, I screamed at him, "Don't you ever lay your hands on me again, you son-of-a-bitch!"

The entire matter had been so sudden, so quick that I think each of us was in shock. We never talked about it as a family, though I'm sure both my parents turned to Jesus to help them through the experience. I know that my father never did touch me again, but our relationship deteriorated even more. For me, it became another reason to be afraid of my anger and what it could do. I went into denial, just like my parents.

CHAPTER 2

At Bat

I don't want to leave the impression that my father never supported me. Though he was cold and emotionally distant much of the time, he showed his loyalty during my high school years by attending every varsity baseball and basketball game I played. As I was a starter on the baseball team all four years, and on the varsity basketball team for two and a half years, this was quite a commitment on his part. It was also unusual, especially for baseball games that were played in the afternoon hours. Many fathers had day jobs away from their farms, but because my dad was a door-to-door salesman, he chose to take time off to travel to both home games and away games, some as many as forty miles distant, to see his son play baseball. And he was not one of those fathers who harangued his son during the games, a big relief for me.

While I was a senior in high school I read FBI Director J. Edgar Hoover's *Masters of Deceit* (1958), a book describing the nature and tactics of the American Communist Party. The book appealed to me because it offered concrete clues for "spotting" Communist front activities; I dreamed that I, too, like our family's radio commentator hero, Fulton Lewis Jr., could be uncovering the names of known Communists. The book inspired me to think about becoming an FBI agent.

My brother was a bit aghast at the rabidity and simplicity of my anticommunist views. He had apparently been exposed to professors in college who taught U.S. and western history from a critical perspective. He had studied at Columbia University following his discharge from the Army in 1956, before getting a job teaching U.S. American history at nearby Jamestown High School. Nonetheless, he tolerated his little brother, and we shared a passion for the St. Louis Cardinal baseball team, an interest we share to this day, though our enjoyment is somewhat diluted by big money domination of the sport.

Ashville was located near Chautauqua Lake, home of the famous Chautauqua Institution that still offers annual summer lectures and intensive educational programs. My high school was located directly across the street from the main entrance. I often attended sermons and lectures given by some of the nation's most eloquent, primarily conservative preachers and political leaders, and musical events with celebrity performers. Some famous people in the United States have spoken at Chautauqua, including feminist Susan B. Anthony, inventors Alexander Graham Bell and Thomas Edison, Henry Ford, Helen Keller, and nine presidents, including Teddy Roosevelt, Franklin Roosevelt, and Bill Clinton. Philosopher William James visited in 1899 and remarked how its small-town values informed nationwide programs.

During the two years I spent at nearby Jamestown (New York) Community College (JCC) while living at home, my career ambitions changed from wanting to become a professional baseball player to becoming an all-American spy. The new president, John F. Kennedy, had stressed his passionate commitment to stopping Communism in its tracks, declaring that "our frontiers today are on every continent."[5] I decided I would go to bat for the real home team, my country. After graduating from JCC, I attended George Washington University (GWU) in Washington, D.C., expecting to be working in the FBI's junior agent program. I had already endured the required FBI interviews and fully expecting to be accepted.

A "Free" Cuba

At GWU I studied mathematics and Russian during the 1961–1962 academic year, assuming my acceptance in the FBI. My ambition was to work as a counterintelligence agent to assist in foiling any plans the Russian Communists had for undermining the "noble" U.S. American government and its "free" society. I was particularly concerned about the Cubans.

During my senior year in high school, Fidel Castro had marched into Havana as part of what we were told was a Communist revolution. As a sophomore in community college, I ardently followed the attempts by anti-Castro Cubans to retake their island from "Castro's Communists" by invasion at the Bay of Pigs. I was depressed when the CIA-led invasion was crushed in April 1961. I believed President Kennedy when, within a week of the defeat, he told a meeting of newspaper publishers that "our way of life is under attack."[6]

Later I learned that at the end of April, only a few days after Kennedy launched the ill-fated Bay of Pigs invasion, he had approved a one-hundred-man increase in U.S. advisers to Viet Nam. In early May he dispatched four hundred Green Berets to begin illegal, secret counterinsurgency actions in Viet Nam, especially in the north, and in Laos.[7] Little did I know then how much that secret decision and others to follow would affect me and most men in my generation.

During my year at GWU, I lived in Mrs. Christian's twenty-five-man boarding house near Dupont Circle. Much to my delight, a number of the boarders were Cuban professionals who had fled their island after Castro's revolutionary triumph. We spent many family-style dinners discussions around the twenty-foot-long rectangular dining table. During these conversations, I learned that these bankers, ranchers, lawyers, and doctors had fled their homeland due to what they termed the "ruthless" policies of Fidel Castro and his band of unruly revolutionaries. Their beloved leader, Fulgencio Batista, was forced to flee in January 1959 and took millions of pesos with him from the Cuban treasury to the safety of the Dominican Republic, run by fellow dictator Rafael Trujillo. In the summer of 1959, Trujillo and Batista had actively plotted to quickly overthrow the new Cuban revolutionary government, but to no avail.

I thought it terrible that, from among the nearly 1,200 prisoners among the CIA-financed and -trained Cuban Brigade 2506 taken captive in April 1961 by Castro's forces at the Bay of Pigs, there were family members who had owned and now lost more than nine hundred thousand acres of land—nearly ten thousand houses, seventy factories, and five mines, three banks and ten sugar mills, twelve cabarets and gambling establishments.[8] I had great sympathy for a doctor in the house who had fled the Dominican Republic after U.S. ally General Rafael Trujillo was assassinated on May 30, 1961, only six weeks after the ill-fated Bay of Pigs invasion. This doctor claimed to have been a close personal friend of Trujillo's, which added some intrigue to our living room discussions.

The Cuban expatriates were confident that President Kennedy planned another invasion later in 1962 to topple Castro, and that they would in fact soon be returning to Cuba. When I and other residents of the rooming house asked them how they could be so confident, they just smiled and said their insider contacts were reliable. Historical documents proved them correct.

Historians have now revealed that on November 30, 1961, President Kennedy created The Cuban Project, also known as "Operation Mongoose," to launch aggressive CIA covert operations against Cuba and assassination plans against Castro. It became the largest CIA operation ever, with six hundred case officers, three thousand resident Cuban agents, and more than a hundred ships and smaller craft working out of Miami under fifty-five front companies.[9] The Pentagon had been instructed to prepare contingency plans for a military invasion of Cuba in the fall of 1962, using as many as a hundred thousand troops. The Cuban missile crisis put an end to that plan.

In February–March 1962, the Joint Chiefs of Staff prepared and approved a formal, spectacular plan to create a pretext for a new invasion of Cuba. The plan, codenamed "Operation Northwoods," contemplated concocting an explosion of a U.S. naval ship in Guantánamo Bay, faking casualties, then blaming it on Castro. Innocent people were to be shot on U.S. streets, boats carrying refugees fleeing Cuba were to be sunk in the high seas, a series of violent attacks were to be carried out in Washington, D.C., Miami, and elsewhere, and planes would be hijacked—all to mobilize the people of the United States against Cuba.[10] Fortunately, "Operation Northwoods" was never formally approved!

My first roommate at the boarding house was a young Guatemalan man named Angelo, who was in Washington to study English. He sometimes practiced his language lessons with me, but he enjoyed drinking and partying more than studying. From a wealthy family, Angelo claimed his father was a ministerial official in the Guatemalan government headed by dictator Miguel Ydígoras Fuentes. Learning that his son was not doing so well in Washington, Angelo's father ordered him to catch a Greyhound bus to a school in Iowa where he was less likely to be distracted from serious English language study.

Neither of us knew at the time that many of the anti-Castro Cubans confined in prison after capture by Castro's forces had been trained by the CIA in Guatemala. I later learned that, in June 1960, Ydígoras had provided the CIA with a location for a training camp in a remote corner of southwestern Guatemala, one hundred miles west of Guatemala City on a large wealthy coffee plantation. In return, Ydígoras was to receive a lot of cash (which apparently was never paid) and an increase in the Guatemalan sugar quota in the U.S. market.

At the time, I knew nothing of the earlier, successful CIA-directed coup against democratically elected Jacobo Arbenz in Guatemala in June 1954. If I had known, I certainly would have asked Angelo about it. Many years later, I met one of the four CIA officers, Phil C. Roettinger, who had worked directly for CIA Director Allen Dulles in planning and carrying out the June 1954 coup. Some estimate that 250,000 Guatemalan Mayas died between 1954 and 1996 as a consequence of this coup, and over 300,000 families experienced detention and torture. Guatemala has never recovered from the severe destabilization from that coup.

During the same month that President Eisenhower was planning the illegal overthrow of Guatemala, he launched other illegal, covert warfare and paramilitary operations in South Viet Nam more than a month *before* the Geneva Agreements formally ended the eight-year French-Indochina War.[11] So, as I was completing seventh grade in tiny Ashville, New York, our president was making secret decisions that would impact my life fifteen years later, when as an Air Force officer I would witness the murders of Vietnamese people in farming villages nine thousand miles away from my own home.

Born Again

The boarding house had a strange mix of men. In addition to the Cubans, several "born-again" Christians regularly added Bible talk to the conversations. My family had been Baptist, and I had been baptized at age twelve, as was the custom in my church. In high school, however, I felt distant from the church, and told my minister I didn't believe I had made a thoughtful choice about being a Christian. To his credit, he gracefully accepted my recanting of Baptism. At the boarding house, one of the "born-again" Christians convinced me that I should reconsider my earlier renouncement of my Baptism, and attend his Nazarene church where I might be encouraged to have a "salvation" experience.

I was feeling a bit out of sync in Washington. I was a small-town boy not used to the big city. In Ashville, I knew most everyone and their parents and grandparents. I knew where people lived and how they lived. I missed the outdoors and connections to nature I enjoyed back home.

With all these connections severed, it made sense that I sought the one connection that could always be there for me, the connection to God. And so, at one of the Nazarene services, I did walk forward to the altar during an emotion-laden moment and uttered the magic words of salvation: "I ask forgiveness of my sins, Oh Lord. I now accept Jesus Christ as my personal Lord and Savior."

I immediately felt relief as many of the other worshippers held me and repeated over and over, "Bless you, son, now you have entered the Kingdom of Heaven, you have been saved." For a number of months after that experience, I became a "street preacher," spending my weekends on Dupont Circle where there were plenty of impoverished drunkards, both men and women, as well as many worn prostitutes. I would "preach" to them, in small groups or one on one, about their need, and the benefits, of "giving their lives over to the Lord."

For reasons I never understood, I received a form rejection letter in the spring of 1962 from J. Edgar Hoover stating that I was *not* accepted for the FBI junior agent program. I was greatly disappointed, almost depressed. I had assumed I was the perfect patriotic young man the FBI was looking for. I decided to leave Washington at the end of the school year and pursue a career in the Baptist ministry instead of the FBI.

To an American patriot, a career as a conservative Christian minister or a career as an FBI agent are not so different from one another. Both aim to preserve the American Way Of Life under God. As a "born-again" Christian, I'd be able to serve my God-endowed country equally well as a preacher of the Gospel. In 1962 I transferred to small (four-hundred-student), conservative Eastern Baptist College, just west of Philadelphia, Pennsylvania, where for two years I studied Greek, religion, anthropology, and sociology, and how to "live right" before the Lord.

CHAPTER 3

Seeking a Calling

The years from 1962 to 1965 were a time of change and painful growth for me. I was in my early twenties and living far from my family. For the first time in my life, I began to question what I had been taught.

Since my parents were not able to help me financially, I felt a certain freedom from worrying about meeting their career expectations for me. I worked numerous jobs to pay my way through college and I never had difficulty finding work, whether gardening or mowing lawns, cashiering at restaurants, sweeping floors, selling dictionaries door-to-door, setting pins at the bowling alley, or driving trucks. One of my best jobs was working as a Teamster, delivering fresh milk to hotels and restaurants one summer, and Coca-Cola to country stores and bars the next.

Religion permeated daily life at Eastern Baptist College. Every class began with a prayer. My first year there, as a junior, I played varsity basketball and baseball—and we prayed before every game. I enjoyed that immersion in religion at first. But by my second, senior year, in 1964, I began reading and questioning more.

One book I remember vividly—not assigned classroom reading—was *Silent Spring* by Rachel Carson. I was struck from the very first page where Carson dedicates her book to Albert Schweitzer, quoting him, "Man has lost the capacity to foresee and to forestall. He will end by destroying the earth." Wow! Chapter 1, "A Fable for Tomorrow," starts with the words, "There was once a town in the heart of America where all life seemed to live in harmony with its surroundings," which immediately reminded me of Ashville. Within two pages, Carson asks, "What has already silenced the voices of spring in countless towns in America? This book is an attempt to explain." I wondered whether spring was silenced in *my* little town. For the first time I was being exposed to the notion that our highly industrial, pesticide-based way of life might be poisoning plants and animals, and ourselves. In those days chemicals were bringing us "miracles," and to question motives of corporations was unheard of in my circle.

Though Carson's book is associated with more progressive political thought, my fundamental political views were not changed. My first semester at Eastern I read Barry Goldwater's book, *The Conscience of a Conservative*

(1960), which further motivated me to consider patriotism from a conserva-tive political perspective in my career plans. In 1964, as a senior, I supported Goldwater for president. I was especially supportive of his foreign policy, pleased that he was advocating bombing various targets in North Viet Nam and using atomic bombs to defoliate its forests.[12]

In April of 1964, during one of our required college chapel services, a speaker talked about U.S. foreign policy and the growing problem of Communist advances in Southeast Asia, especially in Viet Nam, where U.S. advisers and military equipment were attempting to fortify the "democratic free forces" there. There had been recent disturbing reports of four U.S. advis-ers having been killed in fighting in the Mekong Delta, and of U.S. planes having been shot down. During the discussion following the presentation, I remember rising to make a comment. I said something to the effect of, "The United States is obligated to bomb the godless Communists into oblivion, once and for all." I could not have known then that five years later I would be an eyewitness to the immediate after effects of barbaric bombings and their horrific annihilation of human beings.

Though within a few years I would grow to oppose Goldwater's poli-cies, history reveals that, as the war candidate, he had said what he actually believed, and therefore possessed a fair amount of integrity as U.S. politicians go. President Johnson, on the other hand, used his fraudulent peace platform to trounce Goldwater in the 1964 presidential election.

Even as he ran for his first full term on a peace platform (after assuming the presidency upon the death of JFK), Johnson was already secretly escalat-ing the war that President Kennedy had, in effect, begun. In February 1964, nine months *before* the election, President Johnson initiated covert military operations against North Viet Nam, hoping to provoke a reaction that, in turn, would politically "allow" overt and escalated U.S. aggression.[13] He also authorized secret bombings of the Ho Chi Minh Trail *inside* the sovereign country of Laos.[14] That same spring, Walt Rostow, one of Johnson's key aides, drafted a resolution authorizing aggressive war against the North.[15] Despite this covert war planning, as late as October 21, 1964, candidate Johnson said, "We are not about to send American boys nine or ten thousand miles from home to do what Asian boys ought to be doing themselves."[16]

The truth is that the U.S. American people had no real choice in the 1964 elections—both candidates wanted to go to war against the Vietnamese people. One was truthful about it, the other a sneaky, lying scoundrel. Sound familiar?

U.S. presidents have a long history of lying about their covert plans for going to war. During World War I, President Woodrow Wilson's sympathies

clearly lay with the British. Nevertheless, he proclaimed U.S. neutrality, rec-
ognizing that a majority of U.S. Americans wanted no part of war in Europe.
In 1916, he sought reelection successfully on the popular slogan, "He Kept
Us Out of War."[17] But soon after his second inauguration, Wilson asked
Congress for a declaration of war, promising this would make the world "safe
for democracy" and be a war "to end all wars." In 1940, President Franklin D.
Roosevelt promised a platform of peace and neutrality that later proved to be
a lie.[18] The fact is that U.S. presidents have always been ready to go to war to
preserve the American Way Of Life.

Leaving the Ministry

As my conservative political convictions continued to grow, my rigid religious convictions were weakening. Without intending to leave my calling, I
began to question many of the tenets of my faith. I remember one of my
main concerns at the time was about petitionary prayer. Baptists, like many
other denominations, often ask God's help for very specific outcomes, which
seemed questionable to me. Perhaps because I was relatively self-reliant as
a child, making my own money and taking care of some of my own needs, I
didn't understand why we would ask God to provide us with what we desired.
Didn't asking God for an expected outcome imply that we were above God?

As the year went on, I also began to doubt the Virgin birth, the Trinity,
and the authenticity of religious salvation experiences. As I began to grasp
the power of metaphors, I took the Bible less literally and instead developed
an appreciation of the Scriptures as a literary work. My questions were troubling to enough of my dorm fellows that I was added to their list of people to
be prayed for at weekly devotional meetings.

I was not too happy about being prayed over. The other students seemed
to be very rigid about interpretation of the Bible, and too judgmental about
those who might be questioning it. It made me feel uncomfortable—and
the experience, though minor, served as an early warning sign about fundamentalist beliefs in general. I had not rejected Baptism or Christianity at that
point. Actually, I thought my theological questions would make me a better
Baptist. But I came to realize that going to seminary would mean I would
have to conform my beliefs to those of others with whom I increasingly disagreed. And my questioning was being provoked and supported by my reading
of a specifically religious book, English Bishop John T. Robinson's, *Honest to
God*. Robinson, taking ideas from Dietrich Bonhoeffer and Paul Tillich, was
shaking up the religious world at the time by stating unequivocally that God
is not "out there," that God as a separate being simply does not exist, but in
fact is the ground of our very being.[19]

My mini-revolt against Baptist beliefs came to a head near the end of the year, while I was standing in a preregistration line for enrollment at the seminary connected to the college. I was talking with another student about whether, once we became preachers, it would be most important to "save" someone first or to address their socioeconomic conditions. My position was, you address their socioeconomic conditions first. That seemed obvious. The person I was talking with emphatically said, "No, you have to bring them to Jesus first."

I was so disheartened by that conversation that I left the preregistration line and decided I'd rather not attend seminary if it meant regularly engaging in that kind of conversation. I made a quick decision to apply to law school instead to explore a growing interest in criminal law.

Volunteer Prisoner

I was accepted at the Washington College of Law of the American University, Washington, D.C., and began classes in September 1964. After enduring the gruesome requirements of the first year of law school, I began to feel bored, needing some hands-on reality. By the fall of 1965, after beginning my second year, I arranged an internship to live in and work at the District of Columbia Jail with the enthusiastic support of Professor Howard Gill of the Correctional Administration program at American University.

Back then, almost everyone, including many conservatives, was interested in the possibilities of prisoner rehabilitation. It was only after I actually began spending time in the jail that my conservative veneer began to crack.

The D.C. jail held nearly 1,400 prisoners, over 95 percent of whom were African Americans, cramped in space designed for *half* that number. As part of my internship, I slept in an old jail cell and regularly ate with the prisoners or guards, at my choosing. Of course, I was free to come and go—and most days I drove back and forth to classes in my 1956 Chevy. In exchange for "room, board, and laundry," I worked for the jail's classification office, interviewing incoming prisoners from court to gather basic information.

During my "residence" at the jail I witnessed attempted suicides by two prisoners using a bedsheet wrapped around the frame of an upper bunk. On another occasion, I briefly assisted jail officers in preparing incoming prisoners for their showers. As I was helping a half-frozen, inebriated, elderly Black man undress and remove his high boots, his frozen foot dropped off right in my hands. His leg, it turned out, was gangrenous, and the foot tissue must already have been dead.

Imagine: here I was, a college law student, holding this man's foot in my hands. I was shocked and horrified! The man was so out of it that he didn't seem to even notice his foot had left his body. Later, I visited him in the jail infirmary until he was transferred to a public rehabilitation facility. As his only crime was public intoxication, I am sure the prosecutor must have dropped the charge. I felt so bad about that old man who now only had one leg.

These experiences opened my eyes to a whole different world. I was well aware of the danger some of these men posed to society. Nonetheless, I knew a little of what being an underdog felt like, and I began to feel empathy for these men. As I witnessed the harsh and dehumanizing realities of prison life, many of the naïve and parochial values of my rural, White, working-class background began to be seriously challenged.

I was the only White man to attend Black Muslim meetings in the jail. I also began reading *The Autobiography of Malcolm X*. I had grown up surrounded by discussions about race, but only from my father's warped, racist perspective. Though I had always disagreed with my father's racist views, I hadn't really been exposed to any alternative thinking about the subject. Race was avoided in my college and law school, and I had been surrounded by people identified as "White" (including the anti-Castro Cubans). Now I was exposed to a new framework for thinking about politics and race in the United States, one that drew deeply on psychology and class analysis. Malcolm X and other Black Muslim thinkers exposed the U.S. American promise of "equal justice under the law" as a lie. I had never heard such talk before—and I found myself feeling very afraid that they might be right.

Dickey's Story

I also got a very different view of U.S. society from my boss at the jail, Mr. Orange C. Dickey, its director of classification. Dickey, already in his mid-forties, seemed a shy man of few words, but over time he revealed more and more of his interesting life story. Originally from a small town in central Pennsylvania, he made enough money to attend Penn State by apparently being a successful bounty hunter tracking down wanted fugitives. He soon became an enlistee in the U.S. Army Criminal Investigation Division (CID) and was assigned in 1943–1944 to Italy investigating theft of U.S. food and supplies increasingly found in the black market.

Dickey soon was investigating Mafia chieftains, some of whom had been recruited to *cooperate* with Allied military forces to facilitate the invasion and occupation of Sicily in July 1943 and to aid in the overthrow of Mussolini and collapse of mainland Italy. This cooperative relationship between the Mafia and the Office of Strategic Services (OSS) and Office of Naval Intelligence (ONI) is one of a number of guarded secrets about World War II.[20]

Dickey eventually learned that Vito Genovese (the former overseer of Lucky Luciano's gambling and narcotics network in New York until he was forced to flee indictments in 1937) and the Sicilian Mafia figure Don Calogero Vizzini were ringleaders in the massive black market and drug operation in Italy. Though Genovese had supported Mussolini in the late 1930s, he switched sides in 1943. He became the official civilian interpreter for Colonel Charles Poletti, head of the Allied Military Government in southern Italy and Sicily, and the unofficial liaison between the U.S. military and the mob, while restarting the black market right under their noses. In fact, Genovese used his role in the military to commandeer Allied military trucks and bribe Allied military drivers to smuggle stolen foods and supplies to their markets. Dickey documented this intimate relationship between prominent U.S. military and civilian personnel in the Allied Military Government, the Mob, and the black market operations.

Singlehandedly, Sergeant Dickey apprehended Genovese in August 1944. After nine months of delaying tactics in Italian courts, Dickey handcuffed himself to Genovese in May 1945 for the sail from Naples to Brooklyn for trial. However, once Dickey got back to Washington, the War Department (as it was still appropriately named) to which Dickey had submitted his report, decided that its "hot" revelations should be kept secret with no action taken.

Meanwhile, the prime witnesses against Genovese were murdered or disappeared and he was released. Genovese resumed direction of Luciano's drug operations in New York while Luciano was still in Great Meadows Prison in upstate New York. In 1946, New York Governor Thomas Dewey commuted Luciano's sentence based on confidential reports that the latter had apparently provided helpful information concerning potential sabotage on the docks of New York, and had also aided the Allied war effort by furnishing contacts in Sicily and Italy. Never having been a U.S. citizen, Luciano was quickly deported to Naples, Italy, where he resumed the black market and drug operations earlier operated by the now-absent Genovese. His February 1946 sendoff from New York Harbor to Italy was attended by Frank Costello and Meyer Lansky, among other mobsters.

Dickey, of course, had been terribly disappointed, depressed, and outraged by the futility of his yeoman efforts to apprehend Genovese in Italy and bring him to justice in the United States. But worse, Dickey now faced the wrath of both the underworld who sought revenge for his capture of Genovese, and Dickey's own government who wanted his knowledge of U.S. complicity in black market and drug operations to remain a secret. Living quietly in a small Maryland town in the late 1940s, he nonetheless received death threats and feared his house would be firebombed. He moved a number of times in an attempt to live a safe, quiet life, ending up at the jail. Working long hours there offered him security at his workplace.

The one thing that troubled Dickey more than anything else was the proven complicit connection during World War II between civilian, military, and intelligence officials of the U.S. government and known mobsters, all rationalized under the cover of protecting "national security." He would say over and again, in his quiet unassuming manner, that this reality suggested to him that our government had no integrity, that they could not be trusted to tell the truth or uphold the law. He was distressed that the government also had covered up widespread narcotic trafficking to protect its covert assets.

Little did I realize, as I sat listening to Dickey, how my own experiences and studies would verify his concerns about government complicity in the systematic commission of crimes around the world. At the time, I still couldn't believe that my own government would do anything really wrong.

In fact, even as I listened to Dickey's stories about the Mafia's links to the U.S. government, and the Black Muslims' description of racism and economic injustice in our system, I was teaching high school students in a local Methodist Sunday school how terrible Communism was and how wonderful we were in taking responsibility for implementing God's justice on earth.[21] I did not yet grasp just how distorted and dangerous this position was. During one class, less than two months before entering the Air Force, I brought in a news article from the *Washington Star* that reported a formal position adopted by a prestigious world church group condemning the U.S. bombings of Viet Nam.[22] We decided to respond in writing by declaring that as Christians we believed that such bombings, though regrettable, were necessary to preserve democracy, once and for all, from a world threatened by Godless Communism.

In November 1965, shortly after taking up residence at the jail, I read a news story about a young Quaker who immolated himself on November 2, 1965, near the Potomac River entrance to the Pentagon, within view of Defense Secretary McNamara's office window, as a protest against the U.S. bombing in Viet Nam. I did not think much of it at that moment, except to note that the country was full of kooks. It was two or three weeks later while reading in my cell that I reread the news account of the immolation. I noted the man's name: Norman Morrison.

My God! I must have gasped in the isolation of my cell. Norman Morrison! Norman Morrison was a model young man who had graduated from Chautauqua Central School seven years before me. He was the first Eagle Scout I had known, the polite boy who had dated our neighbor's daughter. Though I was only eleven years old when he graduated from high school, he was one of the boys in the area that I looked up to. What had gotten into him, I wondered? Had he gone off the deep end? The article reported that at age of thirty-one he had been the executive secretary of the Stony Run Friends Meeting in Baltimore, Maryland, with a wife and three children. His one-year-old daughter, Emily, was with him when he went to the Pentagon on that fateful afternoon of November 2, though luckily she was not harmed. Three and a half years later, on a late spring day in 1969 in Can Tho City, South Viet Nam, I would finally begin to understand Norman's mysterious action.

CHAPTER 4

Enlisted

I was surprised and distressed to receive my draft notice in March 1966. It wasn't that I didn't want to fight. Unlike many armchair warriors who did whatever they could to avoid serving, I actually tried to enlist in 1964 but was rejected for a foot condition. Since then, I had assumed I was exempt from the draft with a II-S student deferment.

I learned, however, that since I came from an agricultural county where there were many absolute farming deferments, my school deferment was only preferential. I would have to enter the military even though I was still enrolled in a combined university program, earning a master's in correctional administration and a law degree. The one small consolation was that the Selective Service Board agreed to delay my induction until the end of spring semester, granting me time to enlist in a more personally favorable military program.

Many years later I discovered that another twenty-five-year-old graduate, like me a student from a rural area, had received a II-S school deferment in 1966, but was allowed to continue his deferment five times. His name was Dick Cheney.

Up until this time, I had remained a total and passionate believer in U.S. involvement in Viet Nam. However, I was not a gung-ho, combat-seeking young man. So I chose to enlist in the Air Force officer program. I had found out that the Air Force had its own corrections system, so I thought that my emerging academic background in criminal law and corrections/criminology could be put to good use there. The Air Force recruiter in Jamestown, New York, agreed, virtually assuring me a corrections career field, though it technically required volunteering for the Air Force security police. I was accepted in May 1966 for the Officer Training School (OTS) class to begin in September 1966 at Lackland Air Force Base (AFB), San Antonio, Texas. Little did I know what was in store for me!

After ten-and-a-half weeks at Lackland, I was commissioned a second lieutenant in the U.S. Air Force with 113 other young men, all but three of whom were White. Now having spending money for the first time, I purchased a marina blue Corvette Sting Ray fastback before I left Texas to prove that I was now a successful, cool man. I drove the Corvette east, first to visit my parents in western New York State, then on to Washington, D.C., to report for my first duty. While I was in training, President Johnson's secretary of defense (an Orwellian job description if there ever was one), Robert McNamara, told the president that in Viet Nam "we're going to just snow the place under with bombs, and I'm doing it purposely to make them cry."[23] McNamara knew what carpet-bombing would do to a country. As a young Army Air Force officer toward the end of World War II, he worked alongside General Curtis LeMay in the 1945 planning and coordinating of a thousand preatomic firebombings of sixty-seven Japanese cities. The war in Viet Nam was just heating up.

New Talk

I was initially assigned to the headquarters of the Air Force Systems Command (AFSC) in Washington, D.C., as an installation security police and law enforcement staff officer developing command-wide security regulations for military installations. AFSC primarily had responsibility for designing new weapons systems and it possessed research and development facilities at a number of bases throughout the United States that included nuclear weapons systems which required elaborate security measures.

I spent most of 1967 writing security regulations, evaluating security requirements, and learning practical operational aspects of security and law enforcement functions. In early 1967, I was sent to Northwestern University near Chicago to study at their well-known Traffic Institute. This was to prepare me for future work relating to traffic law enforcement and security operations on military bases.

This was a white-collar-type assignment. But the military isolates its members from the civilian community and replaces civilian laws with a strict system of obedience. Military training employs a set of rewards and punishments to break down selfhood and to induce organizational loyalty. The aim is to create well-trained automatons locked into a hierarchical authority system. Perhaps because I grew up resisting my father, I have had a difficult time obeying authority blindly; even so, I am shocked at the extent to which I did obey orders, especially later.

By early 1968, I was growing restive and bored. One night, looking, frankly, for a girlfriend, I wandered into Washington's All Souls Unitarian Church. A singles' club there sponsored a series of Tuesday evening talks. It was just coincidence that the speaker that Tuesday night was eighty-one-year-old U.S. Senator Ernest Gruening, Democrat from Alaska, and that he was speaking soon after the famous Tet Offensive had shaken U.S. confidence in its ability to "win" the war.

Gruening had been one of only two senators (the other was Democrat Wayne Morse of Oregon) who had voted *against* the Gulf of Tonkin Resolution on August 7, 1964, only seventeen days before the scheduled Democratic presidential convention in Atlantic City, the resolution granted open-ended authority to the president to "take all necessary measures" in waging military action against the people of Viet Nam, and by extension Cambodia and Laos. The vote in the House was an astonishing 416–0; in the Senate, 88–2, with only Gruening and Morse voting *no*. In his presentation Gruening detailed the substantial fabrication of facts that comprised the Tonkin Gulf incident. I felt uncomfortable and was unsure if I should even be there.

I stayed, though, and later came back for more Tuesday night talks. The tall woman who had introduced Gruening turned out to be the president of the singles' club that hosted the Tuesday night talks. She was a young lawyer working with the Civil Rights Division of the U.S. Department of Justice under the direction of then–Attorney General Ramsey Clark. Her name was Julie. She would become my wife before the end of the year, shortly before I was shipped to Viet Nam.

Julie's job at the Department of Justice was to protect voting rights in Alabama. Early in our relationship, she told me that FBI agents in Alabama were actually a hindrance to her work. She had learned to maneuver around them to gather her evidence, since they were clearly not cooperating with enforcement of the 1965 Voting Rights Act. I was jolted by this revelation and dismayed. Apparently my hero, J. Edgar Hoover, believed that civil rights workers were the real problem in the United States, rather than the Jim Crow laws they were designed to combat.

Here I was, a small-town boy who had wanted to be an FBI agent fighting against Godless Communists, now wondering if Hoover should step down. I wasn't calling myself a Christian anymore, in the Baptist sense of the word. As I look back, I can see that these changes came in stages. Often, people will say, "I woke up one day and found God," or "I woke up one day and found Marx," but that's not how my changes have happened. Rather, my life has been a journey, and at each stage I have taken little steps that gradually shifted the direction of my path. Radical change is possible, but for me it has generally happened gradually.

If I had had any of the careers I had wanted from the start—if I had become a baseball player, an FBI agent, or a minister, or a lawyer—my journey would likely have been very different. The security of a career would probably have made me comfortable and kept me inside the box. Instead, I have been freer to unfold in an organic way. Even when I was at my most conservative, I went to Chautauqua lectures, Black Muslim meetings, and lectures at a Unitarian church. I was surprisingly open to hearing new ideas. And that openness allowed me to take the little steps that eventually led to radical change, though not without initial resistance.

In 1968, along with going to my daily Air Force job and listening to Ernest Gruening claim the Gulf of Tonkin was a fraud, I resumed academic studies in Law and Corrections at the very institution, American University, I had left when drafted in 1966. Though I wasn't able to finish law school before going to Viet Nam, I was able to obtain my master's degree in criminology/ corrections in the summer of 1968.

As part of my master's degree project I gathered personal data through interviews with Washington, D.C., prisoners serving time at its maximum security prison in Lorton, Virginia, twenty miles south of Washington. I was interviewing there on April 5, 1968, the day after Martin Luther King Jr. had been assassinated in Memphis. As the news was ricocheting around the world, riots of rage erupted in as many as 125 cities, including Washington. Fearing a riot, the guards asked me to quickly leave the prison. As I drove north on Interstate 95 to return to Washington I noted plumes of smoke rising from several locations in the city. The guards were right. In fact, the rioting was so intense in Washington that I couldn't get to my southeast apartment for a week. Until things quieted down, I stayed at a private officers' club near the Dupont Circle neighborhood where I had lived in 1961–1962 while studying at George Washington University. Dupont Circle was now full of military troops with tanks and half-tracks, rather than the drunks and prostitutes I had remembered in my preaching days there in 1961–1962.

Not long after I got back to my apartment, more than a week after King's murder, I received a telephone call from my father. He wanted to tell me how fortunate the nation was now that King was dead. I felt so sick I didn't speak to my father for nearly a year. I remember crying after that call, wondering how it was that my father could possess such hatred, such fear of people he knew virtually nothing about. We had become very different, even more than I had known.

King had called for a Poor People's Campaign to begin in May. He envisioned building a huge shantytown on the Washington Mall to house as many as a half million poor. It was to be a massive undertaking of indefinite duration intended to force the government to stop all funding for the Viet Nam War and redirect it toward abolishing poverty and restructuring U.S. society. The government was terrified of a popular uprising and had convened briefings for Washington-based military police and security personnel such as myself; we were to assist local police with the aim of thwarting the effort. I was dreading any such orders. Use of the military in this way was technically against the law since the 1878 Posse Comitatus Act prohibited use of military in civilian law enforcement functions. I didn't want any part in an illegal maneuver. Besides, I thought King's plan was a good idea.

As it turned out, I was never called up. Once King was assassinated, the Poor People's Campaign fizzled. My solidarity visits to the Mall in late May and early June during an extra rainy spring revealed a disappointingly small number of residents in plywood, canvas and plastic shacks—probably fewer than two thousand—camping in ankle-deep mud. It wasn't going to be a serious problem for the government after all. Subsequent reports revealed that the Poor People's Campaign had in fact been infiltrated by a number of Military Intelligence officers.[24] Now, many years later, I have come to believe that this plan to organize thousands in a quasi-city on the mall was likely the final straw of King's historic, dynamic leadership that led to his murder.

Preparing for Combat

In the fall of 1968, I received orders for Air Force combat security police ranger-type training. I was ordered to leave Washington, D.C., for a U.S. Army base in Kentucky, where I would be prepared for missions called "Operation Safeside," an experimental ranger unit. Being in the Air Force, I couldn't understand why I had been chosen for this Army ranger–type assignment and, frankly, I wasn't happy about leaving my cushy job in D.C. to fight a war I no longer felt so enthusiastic about. A few of the other officers would gladly have swapped their desk jobs for this chance to actually fight the war. I was not one of them.

My new squadron was actually headquartered at a Tactical Air Command (TAC) Air Base in central Louisiana where I was to report first, before trekking off to dreary Fort Campbell, Kentucky. When I arrived in Louisiana, I privately shared with my new commander that I had not volunteered for this unusual Air Force assignment and found its ranger aspects inconsistent with my basic nature. He was understandably irritated, and immediately informed me that he knew of another officer who had wanted this plum assignment, and it was a pity he got stuck with me. I asked about a switch and he responded that it was too late.

So off I went, with more than 550 other airmen, to begin training as members of the 823rd Combat Security Police Squadron commanded by Lt. Col. Kalman. Why were airmen being sent to an Army training and staging base to learn ranger tactics? The long story was that some officers in the Air Force had been Army Rangers in World War II, and they wanted to expand the Air Force's role within the U.S. military by creating a counterinsurgency-style security unit. The short story was that the Air Force brass no longer trusted the Army to protect its air bases after the devastating 1968 Tet Offensive.

Viet Nam, like Iraq, was not supposed to be a long war. In fact, by December 31, 1967, the United States was confident we were going to win. The U.S. Embassy in Saigon sent out invitations to its New Year's Eve party saying "Come see the light at the end of the tunnel."[25] General Westmoreland was so cocky that he taunted the enemy Viet Cong: "I hope they try something because we are looking for a fight."[26] On January 22, 1968, outgoing Secretary of Defense Robert McNamara declared to the U.S. Senate that there were no regular North Vietnamese army units operating in the Mekong Delta.

Part of my journey has been seeing and hearing history repeat itself: thirty-six years after Westmoreland's outrageous and traitorous taunt, President Bush the Younger jeered at the Iraqi opposition to his illegal invasion, saying that the U.S. military could easily handle the Iraqis and, like Westmoreland, said, "Bring them on!" Forty years after Robert McNamara declared premature victory in Viet Nam, George W. Bush stood on the USS *Abraham Lincoln* with flags flying and declared victory in Iraq on May 1, 2003. Both Westmoreland and Bush believed that nothing could possibly stand in the way of the United States. They underestimated the anger and tenacity of a people who are wrongly attacked.

In January 1968, U.S. military personnel at Binh Thuy Navy base were feeling so comfortable that they erected a large banner at the entrance of their base, "Wishing Our Vietnamese Friends A Happy Year & A Successful TET" (Tet being the Vietnamese Lunar New Year) with corresponding Vietnamese translation. The Vietnamese did have a successful Tet. On the night of January 30, 1968, somewhere between sixty-seven thousand and eighty-four thousand forces of the armed branch of the National Liberation Front (NLF)/People's Liberation Armed Forces (PLAF)—which we derogatorily termed the Viet Cong—and the North Vietnamese Army (NVA) launched a series of coordinated attacks along a seven-hundred-mile, nonlinear front throughout the country.[27] The surprise Tet Offensive lasted for several weeks and targeted South Vietnamese cities and military installations stretching from the southern Ca Mau Peninsula and Mekong Delta to northern sections near the DMZ. There were at least twenty-four major battles, and U.S. dead approached four thousand in February and March alone. The myth of U.S. invincibility had been shattered.

During the Tet Offensive, each of the ten primary U.S. and Vietnamese air bases were hit with a recorded 1,030 rounds. Twenty-four U.S. and Vietnamese fixed-wing aircraft had been destroyed, 236 seriously damaged.

Hundreds of Army and Marine helicopters and small aircraft were destroyed. Tan Son Nhut and Binh Thuy air bases each received a minimum of eighteen different attacks in February and early March 1968. By the end of the war the U.S. had lost over 3,300 fixed-wing aircraft, and suffered the total destruction, loss, or severe damage to more than 10,640 helicopters.[28]

The United States responded to the Tet Offensive by unleashing all the conventional firepower it had, largely directed at the rural civilian population. The CIA escalated its Phoenix program, arresting, torturing, and assassinating thousands of civilians to "neutralize" the NLF infrastructure. The Air Force intensified aerial strikes, including B-52 saturation bombings, bombs containing napalm, and lower altitude strafing. Meanwhile, scared, angry, and often racist ground troops conducted search-and-destroy "attrition" missions, often systematically exterminating villages. This was the context in which the My Lai massacre occurred on March 16, 1968, though news of My Lai was to be covered up until Sy Hersh revealed it more than eighteen months later in November 1969 (many other such massacres went unreported in the Western press). My USAF mission was a small part of this stepped-up response to Tet.

Given the devastating damage that had been experienced by the Air Force during the 1968 Tet offensive, the Pentagon concluded that neither the Army nor the Marines were capable of adequately securing Air Force bases. Bombing was escalated after Tet, making security for fighter/bomber and other aircraft even more important. Thus, the Air Force felt compelled to create its own special combat security forces, and intended to prepare these units for worldwide assignment, in hot or cold climates, to be able to quickly secure new air bases established in hostile environments. We were told Guatemala was on the list. I didn't have a clue what was happening there and wished I had quizzed my earlier Guatemalan roommate.

My specific assignment in the "Operation Safeside" mission was to head up one of the dozen newly trained combat security sections (similar to an Army platoon) comprised of five six-man fire teams and two three-man mortar units assigned to secure specific Air Force bases threatened by guerrilla ground and mortar attacks. We supposedly possessed greater mobility than regular Air Force security police, with heavier firepower, advanced detection equipment, and intense training modeled directly on the Army's Ranger course at Fort Benning, Georgia. The 550-plus-man 823rd Combat Security Police Squadron (CSPS) was part of the 82nd CSP Training Wing headquartered at Fort Campbell, Kentucky.

As an officer of the 823rd, I received extra security training in strategic-, combat-, counter-, and technical-intelligence principles. This took up as much as a third of my time at Fort Campbell, an orientation distinctly different from regular security police training.

Kill! Kill! Kill!

I had been developing doubts about the war and about the morality of the U.S. government. But I was still a small-town boy who had been taught to obey the authorities and fulfill my obligations. I never would have dreamed of becoming a conscientious objector, or defying orders, as some of the draft dodgers were doing in those years. I went to Fort Campbell in Kentucky, prepared to do my best.

During the national presidential campaign that concluded with Richard Nixon's election five weeks before the start of our training, frustration with the war had led to suggestions for using nuclear weapons in Viet Nam. That was very disconcerting to me and had made me ever more anxious at the start of this combat training.

During our twelve-week training period, I had an experience that revealed a very different Brian. About a month into our training we had our bayonet exercises. We were told to affix the bayonet to our M-16s, then repeatedly plunge it into a dummy one hundred times while screaming *Kill! Kill! Kill!* as loudly as possible. Of course, most combat-oriented military units are routinely subjected to this basic drill. But I had not signed up for a combat-oriented military assignment.

I couldn't do it. I affixed the bayonet, but when it came time to plunge it into the dummy's body, I stopped cold. In my head I wanted to comply—I really wanted to follow orders. But my body stubbornly refused to cooperate with my brain's directives. My arms seemed to have a powerful voice of their own. I could not plunge the bayonet into even an inanimate dummy.

Much later, I came to understand that the human body has its own wisdom, one older than the thinking mind.[29] At the time, though, I had no idea what was happening. My hesitation understandably angered the training sergeant, provoking him to shout the order again and again. I tried again, struggling to overcome my bodily resistance. Exasperated, the sergeant started yelling right into my ear and pushed up against me. My legs buckled and I dropped to my knees. Humiliated, I became angry, and decided that whatever happened, I would not follow orders to plunge the bayonet.

All of a sudden, Brian Willson, all-American boy, had an attitude problem. Faced with war protesters at home and a resurgent guerrilla war in Viet Nam, the military wasn't thrilled about dealing with yet another problem case in its ranks. I asked to see the squadron commander, but he was not interested in hearing my concerns. Instead, he carried on with the same kind of yelling I had heard from the sergeant, but was even more abusive. Face red, he told me I was looking at twenty years in Leavenworth prison. He got ever louder, his body exploding with rage, until one of his arm gestures struck me and I stumbled, unbalanced, to the floor.

I am a pretty big guy and was an all-around athlete. It's not easy to knock me down. What strikes me now, looking back, is how anxious and scared I was, how cowed by authority. I was already off-balance, both mentally and physically, when these men were shouting at me. I was getting a taste of how war impacts ordinary people, turning otherwise regular guys into brutes. Though the commander seemed taken aback for a moment by his out-of-control behavior, his anger quickly resumed. He called me a coward and accused me of being "an ally of the VC." Our operations officer, a more professional, straight-laced, career security police officer, a major, was also present in the room. He read to me from a copy of the UCMJ (Uniform Code of Military Justice), informing me that I was facing five years in military jail for failure to obey orders. Well, I thought, five years is a lot better than twenty. And, I wondered, if my commander thought I was an ally of the "VC," why on earth would he want me in his squadron? As the major later said, I was getting a "royal chewing out."

Shortly thereafter, the commander, outraged with my "poor attitude," considering me disloyal for my "self-admitted failure to accept the responsibilities" as an officer, and fearing a deleterious effect on the morale of other members of the squadron, placed me on something called the Officer Control Roster for 180 days.[30] He ordered me to see the squadron chaplain, a Southern Baptist it turns out, who shamed me over and over for about twenty minutes without hearing a word I had to say. He concluded that I was disturbed, requesting an immediate assessment by an Air Force psychiatrist. The psychiatrist, a very kind man, met with me for several hours and concluded that I was of sound mind, recommending a reassignment that would not conflict with my ethical concerns. But Colonel Kalman said that since I was of sound mind I would have to comply with the orders as they were—a classic "Catch 22"! I was depressed.

Not long after, while I was still at Fort Campbell, the commander of the 82nd Combat Security Police Wing, a full colonel and my commander's boss, ordered me to his office. He said the action taken by the 823rd commander was "inappropriate" and removed me from the Control Roster. He shared with me his desire for "preventing any . . . unnecessary unfavorable publicity to the U.S. Air Force," and informed me that headquarters leaders at Tactical Air Command (TAC) would send the Judge Advocate to Fort Campbell if necessary because they "do not want a situation to develop which would embarrass General Momyer," the head of TAC and the former commander of the Seventh Air Force in Viet Nam. He reiterated that his job was "to maintain the standards of discipline." The 82nd wing commander was very polite and respectful to me, and surprisingly suggested that I consider an administrative separation from the Air Force for "unfitness."

This was another step in the journey, another decision for me to make. I wasn't ready, however, to understand fully what my body was trying to tell me. Despite my growing doubts about the war, I wasn't ready to abandon all that I had believed so fiercely as a child and young adult. And I wanted to protect my manhood and ego; I didn't want to seem weak. So I told the colonel that I was very fit—physically, psychologically, and politically—to accept an order to Viet Nam but in a different, noncombat-type assignment more suitable to my temperament. He repeated that the Air Force had no plans to reassign me and that the choice was up to me: possibly receive an administrative discharge for unfitness, be court-martialed if I refused to deploy when ordered, or comply and get on the plane when it departed.

I chose to comply. At the time, I rationalized my decision by telling myself that I was not asking to avoid Viet Nam, but to receive a more traditional assignment. I now know that disobedience would have been the more noble, honest decision. My body was telling me I did not want to hurt another person. My political opinions had changed, and I had qualms about the war. Yet, I did not possess sufficient courage to disobey a direct order to deploy.

Ironically, though I never completed the bayonet training, my official Air Force records state that I "successfully completed" the twelve weeks, 708 hours of combat security police training school. Whether I had successfully completed the combat security training or not was of no concern to them. What was important to them was that my body voluntarily walked onto that plane leaving for Viet Nam. General Momyer would not be embarrassed.

CHAPTER 5

Us and Them

My Safeside unit shipped out to Viet Nam on March 7, 1969. On the books, my unit was permanently located at a TAC base in central Louisiana, and only assigned Temporary Duty (TDY) to Viet Nam. Congress, politically nervous about a continuing war that was to have been short in duration, had mandated a maximum limit of permanent troops in Viet Nam, a limit Johnson, and then Nixon, had already exceeded. Temporary Duty allowed the Pentagon to move troops to Viet Nam for 179 days without being considered permanent. The plan for us was to be in Viet Nam for 179 days, return to the United States for one month, and then rotate back to Viet Nam. U.S. official military force levels peaked in South Viet Nam in April 1969, with 543,400 troops. It is not clear how many other thousands of troops were present TDY, or how many were covert operators not on any books whatsoever.

We landed first at Cam Ranh Bay in south central Viet Nam's II Corps along the South China Sea, about 190 miles northeast of Saigon. We then flew a short twenty-minute hop to Phan Rang Air Base, the headquarters for the in-country Safeside operations. Our 823rd commander, Lt. Col. Kalman, ordered my particular unit to the small Binh Thuy Air Base in Phong Dinh Province in the Mekong Delta. Someone in the room mentioned that Binh Thuy was nicknamed "mortar alley," due to it being the most attacked 7th USAF base up to that time.

Since the beginning of the hot war in 1965, Binh Thuy had indeed been the most attacked air base in Viet Nam. Mortars had exploded *inside* its perimeter a total of forty-five times—far more than any other base at the time. Most recently, in the seven and a half weeks from January through the start of Tet 1969, Binh Thuy had been hit three times with a total of 129 mortars, killing two and wounding five. It had also been penetrated once in late January with a small "VC" sapper squad. One plane and a helicopter on missions from Binh Thuy in January also had been shot down, with three aircrew presumed dead.

Binh Thuy was the only 7th USAF air base in IV Corps. It was ninety miles southwest of Saigon on the south side of the Bassac River, the southernmost tributary of the Mekong four-river Delta system. Cambodia was sixty miles to the northwest. Can Tho City, the fourth-largest city in South Viet

Nam, was seven miles southeast along the river, and site of a CIA Provincial Interrogation Center (PIC). My unit's job was to augment the 632nd Security Police Squadron that had valiantly defended Binh Thuy during Tet 1968 from at least eighteen attacks. Only Tan Son Nhut had been attacked as often. New intelligence suggested stepped-up attacks after Tet 1969. Apparently 7th Air Force determined that the 632nd needed reinforcement.

Our plane touched down at Binh Thuy just before midnight on March 8, 1969, only two weeks after the beginning of the new Tet assault on February 23. Within these two weeks, the U.S. had already suffered well over three thousand casualties, and on this night the "VC" had attacked fifty military targets, including Binh Thuy. The timing of our arrival was very eerie. I remember seeing flashes and hearing loud explosions, and the pilot screaming at us to hurry so he could become airborne again. We were quickly taken to a nearby bunker where we hunkered down until it was determined safe to move, then taken to our sleeping quarters, which were fortified with steel and sandbags. Though mild compared to the experiences of others, those first few minutes were enough to make the war real to me, even though none of the incoming mortars actually landed inside the base perimeter.

A fellow officer in the 823rd told me he believed our commander's friend who had eagerly volunteered to be in the 823rd, was the operations officer, a captain, at Binh Thuy. He was right. I was already unhappy with the assignment; now I would be working every day with a man who had wanted my job. I couldn't believe it. My commander had told me on several occasions that he would do whatever was necessary to keep me from making captain. Was it just a coincidence that he paired me with someone who already had contempt for me, a set up likely to create bad blood? Had he assigned me to Binh Thuy to make sure his ally would watch me like a hawk and prevent me from promotion? I don't doubt it. Though I tried to treat him with soldierly respect, the operations officer and I had an acrimonious relationship from the moment of my arrival to the date of my departure.

Melvin Laird, Nixon's secretary of defense, was in country at the time of our arrival, setting up the details of Nixon's plans for "Vietnamization." Nixon suggested in a major speech that the problem with Viet Nam was that the war had been "Americanized"—instead of supporting the Viet Nam people, we were fighting their war for them. Nixon's plan was to "turn the war back over to the locals."

The very idea that the Vietnamese had not already been deeply engaged in the war is an example of the deep racism of our national psyche. Hundreds of thousands of ARVN troops had been trained and armed by the United States, with many killed or maimed in what was essentially our desire to beat back the threat of "Communism." U.S. troops were in Viet Nam because of our own deluded political imperatives. Our presence had created, then escalated the war, resulting in the murders of thousands of villagers. Now we were going to pull out, and blame the wreckage on the local population.

Laird was calling for increased use of bombings by both South Vietnamese and U.S. pilots in the expanding areas called "free-fire zones." He promised increased armaments to South Vietnamese ground forces, and offered greater numbers of planes for its air force. Intensification of the Phoenix "neutralization" program was underway. Rumors had it that U.S. Marines had invaded Laos on the same day we arrived at Binh Thuy as part of "Operation Dewey Canyon I." Ten days later, Nixon's "secret" carpet bombings in Cambodia started. These bombings were glibly, sadistically called the "Menu" bombings—they used code names, believe it or not, of "Operation Breakfast," then "Dinner," "Snacks," and "Dessert." They did not end until August 1973! Nixon was not the only president to secretly bomb Cambodia. President Johnson had actually initiated bombings over Cambodia as early as October 1965 in support of numerous illegal secret ground operations by CIA and Special Forces.[31]

It was a tense moment and an intense time. I learned that on the day of our arrival, the nearby Can Tho Army Military Police commander had been fragged, and though he escaped serious injury, there were thirteen total casualties, including two killed. That made me even more nervous. After all, I was an officer, too, and I knew I would have to be in contact with the Can Tho MPs if my men were involved in barroom brawls. Officers were not very popular in Viet Nam. I wondered what I was getting into.

After our arrival to supplement the 632nd security police, I was designated by its squadron commander, a major, to be in charge of the night security forces. Thus, I coordinated the positioning of not only my own men, but the security personnel from the regular 632nd security police, as well as a unit of South Vietnamese, around the perimeter of the base. Because of the history of attacks on Binh Thuy, and uncertainty as to when mortar attacks or NLF sapper probes could happen, I was in a constant state of hypervigilance. Almost from the start, I got the sense that the war was mad and out of control, with bombing campaigns for no clear reason, and accomplishing no clear purpose except killing.

During my tenure at Binh Thuy from early March until early August, the base was actually hit inside its perimeter with mortars only three times, with no casualties—much to my relief, though there were at least ten other warnings of incoming mortars or recoilless rifle attacks where the explosions occurred *outside* the perimeter. One attack virtually demolished the mess hall and shrapnel from another mortar round destroyed the air conditioning in my housing unit—a trailer. Being on high alert every night naturally became nerve-wracking, but we were in a much more enviable position than those being sent out on patrols in the jungles.

Nearby Can Tho airfield, and sectors of its city, were also hit on a number of occasions, including the Ben Xe Moi whorehouse district where, of course, there were generally a number of airmen and other military personnel present.

During July there were five sapper probes of our perimeter, but only one that might have penetrated. It was inconclusive because there was no damage, though reportedly two persons were spotted running on base and two unexploded grenades were found in the petroleum storage area. A similar penetration had been suspected on an earlier occasion, but also with no conclusive evidence. Also in July, two planes and two helicopters from Binh Thuy, each on separate missions, were shot down, with at least seven crew members presumed dead. And three patrol boats from the nearby Binh Thuy Navy base had been destroyed with all crew believed dead.

On two occasions airplanes returned to Binh Thuy with their pilots mortally wounded, once in late March or early April, another in late May. In the first case, I was on the flightline and witnessed the landing. I saw the pilot in the front seat of a T-28 slumped over with a bullet hole in his left temple, a stream of blood cascading down his cheek. A Vietnamese copilot in the rear seat had brought the plane down safely.

For nearly a month, from early June to the beginning of July, my unit was temporarily dispatched from Binh Thuy to Phan Rang Air Base, 250 miles to our northeast in II Corps, to help build new bunkers and fortify perimeter security as it was being increasingly attacked by rockets. In the three weeks prior to our arrival at Phan Rang, it had been attacked on six occasions, with nearly a hundred rockets causing five casualties.

The day we arrived, three 107 mm rockets exploded a little after four in the afternoon, killing two and wounding eight. I was walking with an Aussie officer when he apparently heard the air ripple preceding a rocket and threw me down to avoid shrapnel. The explosion was huge—rockets have much more explosive power than the mortars I experienced at Binh Thuy—and debris landed all around us. When it was all clear and the Aussie officer and I had gotten up and resumed walking, he pointed out what looked like the remains of one of the two men killed that day. What a way to start our new bunker-building assignment at Phan Rang. I was shaken up for several days, especially since the rocket attacks continued, though mercifully with only one more airman wounded while I was there.

I was lucky to have a confident, experienced NCO—a professional soldier—working with me, especially at Phan Rang. My section was ordered to fill thousands of sandbags and construct a number of bunkers, but we were not provided any of the materials or equipment. My NCO said, "Don't worry, lieutenant, I'll take care of it." I wouldn't have had a clue how to proceed, but he knew just what to do. He discovered where to get the bags, confiscated an "idle" military dump truck, found and paid a local Vietnamese sand-pit operator to fill several truckloads, then brought those loads of sand to base for our bunker construction projects. We paid out of our own pockets for the labor of the Vietnamese power shovel operator and for the sand. Between negotiating for materials, filling the sandbags and building the bunkers, all the while participating in regular perimeter security and being on the lookout for incoming rocket attacks, the weeks I spent at Phan Rang seemed endless. It was a relief when I finally got back to Binh Thuy in early July, a day before my birthday.

Many of us believed there was an active drug trade going through Binh Thuy. It was rumored that Nguyen Cao Ky, South Viet Nam's vice president, who visited the base often, was involved in this drug trade. On one occasion I escorted Ky from his plane to the local Vietnamese commander Colonel Anh's quarters, where the two men liked to play tennis on a nearby lighted court. Alfred W. McCoy later revealed that Binh Thuy acted as a transshipment point from Vientiane, Laos through Phnom Penh, Cambodia, then down the Bassac River Tributary of the mighty Mekong to Binh Thuy Air and Navy Bases on their way to Saigon.[32] It shouldn't have been a surprise that one illegal activity would beget another.

Us

I tried not to pay too much attention to any of the rumors swirling around the base. My focus was on my men and night security. Many of the men were understandably determined to pass as much of the war as they could by drinking or spending time with girlfriends or prostitutes off base. Almost every evening, I would travel the few miles to the Ben Xe Moi district on the west side of Can Tho City to make sure all my men were back to the base in plenty of time for their nighttime sentry duties. My policy was that everyone had to be on base two hours before their 2030 (8:30 p.m.) duty was to begin.

Ben Xe Moi was typical of the scenes that emerged around concentrations of GIs. Young Vietnamese women, desperate for survival cash, sold their bodies to U.S. military personnel. On one occasion I had to corral two of my men from one of the regular Ben Xe Moi "dens" after the time at which they were to have returned for night duty. When I barged in, they slapped the prostitutes in apparent frustration, knowing their time was up. I was sickened by their display of power over these young women.

Though we freely dispensed condoms to the troops, they were not necessarily used. One of my men contracted gonorrhea six times, once causing him to miss security duty. The military doctor counseled me, as his commander, to insist that condoms be used, with threat of disciplinary action. This was the only time I threatened one of my troops with serious disciplinary action.

A number of men received "Dear John" letters from their wives or girlfriends back home. Such rejection letters were devastating, and I would spend time in the barracks comforting these soldiers. Though I was only a few years older than them, I served as a father figure in these situations.

I thought that being there for my men was part of my job, but apparently there was a fine line between counseling the men and being their buddy. Military protocol insisted on a strict separation of officers from enlisted personnel. Officers ate separately, had markedly better sleeping quarters, and our own officers' club, sometimes featuring officers-only entertainment. Beyond giving orders or supervising duties and operations, contact with enlisted men was considered "fraternization" and was prohibited. At least that was my experience at Binh Thuy. We had been taught that we were fighting for equality and liberty, but those values were not exactly modeled in the military.

I had difficulty with military hierarchy and tended to ignore the protocol. Other officers noticed. On one occasion, for example, the 632nd operations officer, my nemesis, saw me using the enlisted men's urinal (not a difficult piece of investigative work, since only a chest-high barrier separated the urinal from the internal road adjacent to it). He told me that urinating in an enlisted men's facility was a violation of the UCMJ, amounting to fraternization and conduct unbecoming an officer. How ridiculous, I thought.

Frankly, I considered other conduct a lot more unbecoming. For example, some of the men, including officers on the base, referred to the Vietnamese as "gooks," whether they were on "our side" or the other. Some of the worst comments about the Vietnamese were made by the U.S. pilots who came to Binh Thuy for brief periods to carry out bombings, recon, or psyops missions. Listening to them during the few times I spent at the officers' club, I quickly learned that the U.S. was conducting daily bombings of Vietnamese villages. The pilots would laugh while discussing the operations that were leading to destruction of "easy," undefended tiny Delta village targets, ostensibly full of "Viet Cong."

One evening while watching pornographic movies on the patio of the officers' club, pilots were eating steaks and drinking beer with their Vietnamese whores when the siren went off warning of potential incoming.

I, of course, joined everyone else in scrambling into the club's bunker. There were distant explosions but apparently none of them hit inside our base. The clicking sound of the nearby movie projector could be heard from inside the bunker as the film continued. When the all clear sounded, couples resumed their seats to continue watching the flick, or went into the nearby "fucking hooches" as if nothing had happened. The scene was so surreal I felt like I was watching a Fellini movie.

I began to question the bombings of the villages. From my reading and early observations, it seemed most of the inhabitants were civilians. I had spent my first weeks in Viet Nam studying every intelligence report I could find, striving to discern the locations of various local villages, wondering whether they possessed particular political affiliations. An irregular newspaper, the *Binh Thuy Times*, and the daily military paper, *Stars and Stripes*, reported on various operations that were "bloodying the enemy's nose." From my perspective as an officer in charge of combat security at the base, the bombings seemed not only inhumane and illegal, but actually threatened the security of our base by increasing the outrage of the Vietnamese. Outraged people tend to organize against those who are hurting them. I also couldn't understand why we were bombing these people when doing so was clearly against the U.S. Rules of Engagement which incorporated the Nuremberg Principles that strictly prohibit targeting civilians or their infrastructure, for example their villages and homes.[33]

Them

During my first month in Viet Nam I continued to receive confirmation that the United States was bombing inhabited villages. I was part of security discussions in the Central Security Control (CSC) bunker where maps of supposed NLF sightings were marked. "Intelligence" reports discussed during those meetings indicated an increasing number of villages were "enemy-friendly" and were therefore now identified by U.S. and Vietnamese officials as being within "free-fire zones."

If a village or specified population area was *suspected* of paying taxes to the NLF (as they were required to do by units of the South Vietnamese forces), or *suspected* of having been visited by an NLF unit during nighttime maneuverings, or *suspected* of being the source of food for an NLF unit, or if a muzzle flash was *believed* to be spotted by U.S. observers, the villages in those areas *automatically* became "legitimate" targets for bombing. I was told that leaflets printed in Vietnamese were being dropped from planes into these villages in advance, to notify the residents that they were living in a newly designated "free-fire zone," urging them to move to a safer place. The fact that the

Vietnamese often did not leave their villages after the dropping of the leaflets was perplexing to the U.S. military, and it greatly contributed to the notion that the Vietnamese did not value life as much as we supposedly did.

I did meet one disaffected C-47 psyops pilot who was about to be sent back to the United States for his refusal to fly more missions. "John" told me the psyops leaflet program was a joke. He said the leaflet translations were poor and often landed in areas far outside the targeted villages. Besides, there were no particularly safe places to move to. He knew, he said, that the intelligence that selected the target villages was often "made up" and he had begun to simply fly his missions without dropping the paper. He was the only person I met during my tenure in Viet Nam who shared my antiwar position, and we hung out together at Binh Thuy for the few days before he returned to the States. I do not know what happened to him.

Gradually, I came to understand why so many Vietnamese chose to face death and remain in their villages after being informed that their village was a "free-fire zone." Like other Indigenous people around the world, including those from the United States, the Vietnamese were deeply attached to their ancient lands. Buddhist, Taoist, and Confucian religious traditions all stress the importance of living close to ancestral burial locations. Additionally, the U.S. military would not allow residents to take their farm animals with them when they left their villages, not recognizing that these sacred creatures were key to the villagers' economic well-being and considered to be part of their family.

I became increasingly irate to think that even though we claimed to cherish life, we regularly bombed these ordinary village people literally to pieces. I was beginning to think we had it exactly backward. Our motto had become "We must destroy a village to save it," an Orwellian phrase that, in itself, should have alerted us all to the criminally misguided nature of what we were doing in Viet Nam.

I became aware that our misunderstanding and fear of the Vietnamese people extended to individuals as well as to local villages. On one occasion early in my tour, at a perimeter security location near dusk, the 632nd operations officer met me on the road that paralleled the western edge of the base. He pointed out to me two or three barely visible Vietnamese apparently fishing in one of the waterways, probably five to six hundred meters out from our perimeter. In fact, I wasn't sure that I could positively see them.

To me, men fishing was a familiar sight and I had paid little attention to it. In fact, it reminded me of my own carefree days fishing along Goose Creek as a boy. This officer, however, said he needed to remind me that the entire area around the base had been declared a "free-fire zone," and that it was important that my unit enforce it by killing these fishermen. I told him that the Vietnamese had been fishing in these waterways for generations, and that I was not going to shoot at them unless they were shooting at us. He said they could be scoping out specific targets at our base in preparation for night mortar attacks or sapper probes. Though this was theoretically possible, I replied that I was not going to fire at them or order my men to do so.

Intelligence reports did indicate that the NLF had in the past sent mortars into Binh Thuy from small boats in the adjacent Tra Noc Canal. But the wide canal also made them easy targets of AC-47 Spooky gunships. In fact, I had already called in Spookies on several occasions after spotting personnel in the canal with a starlight scope. But the waterways that crisscrossed the vast region around Binh Thuy were narrow and numerous, and served as one of the main food sources for the many people living in the villages surrounding our base.

The captain gave me a direct order to shoot at the Vietnamese fishers. I asked him if he was really giving me an order. He took his M-16 and thrust it at my chest, ordering me to grab it and ready myself for aiming and shooting at these people. I refused to put my hands on his M-16. The fact that I never carried my M-16 in Viet Nam angered him. He then yanked his gun back and positioned himself to fire at the Vietnamese. I ordered him not to fire, as in my judgment it would needlessly alienate the Vietnamese, which could, in turn, endanger our base by inciting subsequent attacks. We briefly scuffled. Furious, he jumped into his Jeep and hurriedly drove off, telling me I would pay for this.

In military terms, this scuffle demonstrated a management failure. The Air Force had dispatched a combat security police unit, with someone like me as the officer-in-charge, to supplement an existing security police squadron that had its own chain of command and history of securing the base before our arrival. Real differences of opinion concerning security were bound to come up, especially between two officers who did not get along. In this situation, as an officer responsible for combat security, I truly believed that in shooting these fishers, I would increase the risk of attacks on our base. The operations officer, I suppose, believed these fishers posed a real threat. He was right.

It didn't help that the operations officer truly despised me. Yet it was also true that I increasingly believed what we were doing in Viet Nam was wrong. Knowing we were killing civilians every day certainly did affect my own decisionmaking process.

In my own mind, I was still a good boy, trying hard to do my job protecting the base and my men. Within a month, however, I began to get a reputation as a gook-loving kook. My critical views were understandably irritating other NCOs and officers, who began to confront me, declaring that I was "as good as a VC." This is what my own commander had accused me of back at Fort Campbell.

Curiously, after these confrontations, Colonel Anh, the Vietnamese tactical wing commander at Binh Thuy, sought me out for conversation. I hardly knew the man. He commended me for my studious efforts to learn situation and intelligence reports. One of the few positives in my evaluation reports from Binh Thuy was that I kept my superiors "well informed with accurate situation reports which greatly aided higher headquarters in the evaluation of security conditions in the Binh Thuy area." Colonel Anh wanted to ask me a favor. I listened.

Mai Ly

Colonel Anh was under tremendous political pressure from the newly funded "Vietnamization" policy to dramatically increase bombings by South Vietnamese pilots over a wide region in the Delta. Admiral Zumwalt, commander of naval forces in Viet Nam, had personally welcomed a new light attack squadron of OV-10s and helicopters at Binh Thuy to protect the increased boat patrols of Delta waterways. Secretary of the Navy John Chafee had made a visit as well. The first of the new Cessna A-37B fighter-bombers being turned over to the South Vietnamese Air Force had arrived at Binh Thuy in early April, replacing most of the Douglas A-1 Skyraiders and North American T-28s. A fresh cadre of newly trained South Vietnamese A-37B pilots had just arrived from the United States.

In early April, the hamlet of My Thuan in the District of Binh Minh in southeastern Vinh Long Province just across the Bassac River was overrun by the NLF, causing many casualties. Then, on April 10–11, there was another night of mortar and rocket attacks throughout Viet Nam. Though Binh Thuy escaped attacks that night, the nearby sacred Dinh Thanh Temple on our side of the river had been attacked with four casualties. Even more significant from a military and political perspective, the large city of Vinh Long, a Provincial capital fifteen to twenty miles northeast of Binh Thuy, was hit with a hundred mortars, causing well over a hundred casualties. Furious, Colonel Anh chose to respond with vengeance to ensure a massive increase in "VC" body counts.

Anh asked me to accompany a Vietnamese lieutenant (nicknamed "Bao") to visit freshly bombed "targets." I was a bit startled at this request. The purpose of our visit, as Anh described it, was to perform a quick estimate of the pilots' success at hitting their specified targets. The military sometimes took aerial photographs of bombed targets, but ground recon teams (Personnel Damage Assessments/PDAs) or the fearsome death-squad CIA-trained Vietnamese Province Reconnaissance Units (PRUs) were better suited to conduct these assessments.

Apparently there were no ground recon units available in April. The majority of the ARVN's 9th Delta Division was tied up in "Operation Rice Farmer," assisting the U.S. 9th Infantry Division's eight thousand troops in provinces immediately west, north and east of Vinh Long, especially in Kien Hoa where the brutal "Operation Speedy Express" was being conducted. Thousands of other troops in IV Corps were operating immediately south of the Saigon area. By the end of 1968, the PRUs, primarily CIA assassination units, were under orders to identify and "neutralize" (disappear, torture, murder) three thousand suspected members of the "VC Infrastructure" every *month* as part of the Phoenix program.[34] Too much else was going on to send ground troops our way. Vinh Long had apparently, at least temporarily, slipped through the cracks.

Anh was particularly interested in having a U.S. American officer perform the documentation because a recently captured NLF suspect tortured at the CIA's Can Tho Province Interrogation Center had confessed that the South Vietnamese pilot corps had been infiltrated. Anh suspected that among the wave of recently arrived, freshly trained South Vietnamese pilots, there might be some who would intentionally miss their designated targets, or worse, defect to Cambodia.[35]

There was another possible explanation for my being asked to perform this unusual, extra-duty assignment. Conducting damage assessments was very unpopular. When PRUs were not available, this duty was sometimes assigned to unpopular officers, especially as punishment for known fraternizers. A Viet Nam scholar, Douglas Valentine, reported this phenomena in his elaborate chronicling of the Phoenix program.[36] In fact, my Company Grade Officer Effectiveness Report rated me poor in leadership and judgment, primarily because I "was extremely well liked by [my] men . . . due, in part, to a very marked tendency to over-identify with them."

The first target Bao and I visited was just northwest of Highway 4 in southern Vinh Long Province, north of the Bassac River, four or five miles as the crow flies from Binh Thuy, and perhaps eight or nine miles south of Sa Dec. With Bao in the passenger seat of my Jeep, I drove to Can Tho and then took the ferry north across the Bassac River to Highway 4. Within a couple miles we turned onto a side track and soon we saw plumes of smoke behind some high grass. The bombing reportedly had occurred within an hour or so prior to our arrival.

We got out of the Jeep. As I walked cautiously through the high grass toward the smoke, I heard low moans, then increasingly loud roars. I looked to my right, and saw a water buffalo, a third of its skull gone and a three-foot gash in its belly. I couldn't believe it was still alive. I felt sick to my stomach.

Soon, even more pitiful sights came into view. Out of the corner of my eye, perhaps eighty feet toward center-left, I saw one young girl trying to get up on her feet, using a stick as a makeshift cane, but she quickly fell down. A few other people were moving ever so slightly as they cried and moaned on the ground. Most of the human victims I saw were women and children, the vast majority lying motionless. Most, I am sure, were dead. Napalm had blackened their bodies, making many of them nearly unrecognizable.

My first thought was that I was witnessing an egregious, horrendous mistake. The "target" was no more than a small fishing and rice farming community. The "village" was smaller than a baseball playing field. The Mekong Delta region is completely flat, and the modest houses in its hamlets are built on small mounds among rice paddies. As with most settlements, this one was undefended—we saw no antiaircraft guns, no visible small arms, no defenders of any kind. The pilots who bombed this small hamlet flew low-flying planes, probably A-37Bs, and were able to get close to the ground without fear of being shot down, thus increasing the accuracy of their strafing and bombing. They certainly would have been able to see the inhabitants, mostly women with children taking care of various farming and domestic chores. They had the option to abort their mission based on their own observations from the air. They could have been back, safe and sound in Binh Thuy, in less than fifteen minutes. Instead, they had come back with a big thumbs-up, mission accomplished.

Colonel Anh need not have worried about any of his pilots missing their targets. The buildings were virtually flattened by explosions or destroyed by fire. I didn't see one person standing. Most were ripped apart from bomb shrapnel and machine gun wounds, many blackened by napalm beyond recognition; the majority were obviously children.

I began sobbing and gagging. I couldn't fathom what I was seeing, smelling, thinking. I took a few faltering steps to my left, only to find my way blocked by the body of a young woman lying at my feet. She had been clutching three small, partially blackened children when she apparently collapsed. I bent down for a closer look and stared, aghast, at the woman's open eyes. The children were motionless, blackened blood drying on their bullet and shrapnel-riddled bodies. Napalm had melted much of the woman's face, including her eyelids, but as I focused on her face, it seemed that her eyes were staring at me.

She was not alive. But at the moment her eyes met mine, it felt like a lightning bolt jolted through my entire being. Over the years I have thought of her so often I have given her the name "Mai Ly." (I simply rearranged the letters of My Lai, location of the infamous March 1968 massacre of Vietnamese villagers by U.S. forces.)

I was startled when Bao, who was several feet to my right, asked why I was crying. I remember struggling to answer. The words that came out astonished me. "She is my family," I said, or something to that effect. I don't know where those words came from. I wasn't thinking rationally. But I felt, in my body, that she and I were one.

Bao just smirked, and said something about how satisfied he was with the bombing success in killing communists. I did not reply. I had nothing to say. From that moment on, nothing would ever be the same for me.

I was experiencing such a shock that it did not occur to me to seek medical help for those who still might be alive in the village. We just walked away from the moaning of those still alive. They did not count as human beings. Though I was crying inside, I did nothing. In our return drive to Binh Thuy, we passed directly by the Army's 29th Evacuation Hospital next to Binh Thuy and I did not even think of stopping to report the critical need for medical attention in that village. Bao, who knew how to describe the village's location, said nothing. I soon learned that few people survive the suffocation and burns that result from napalm bombing.

I now knew, viscerally, the evil nature of the war. But more than that, I knew that these bombings had deliberately targeted inhabited, undefended villages, and therefore murdered countless civilians. And those murders had been planned and carried out as part of a policy created by the U.S. government, with the complicity of their Vietnamese puppets. The policy was genocide. Those Vietnamese people who chose with their words and deeds not to openly support the U.S. presence and the Thieu government were considered totally expendable. I had no choice—God help me!—but to admit that my own country was engaged in an effort that was criminal and immoral beyond comprehension.

During that same week in mid-April, Bao and I went to four other bombing "targets" in south central Vinh Long Province, and they too were inhabited hamlets or Vietnamese settlements, similarly destroyed. Though that week remains a blur, I estimated that we documented somewhere between seven and nine hundred murders of Vietnamese peasants, all due to low-flying fighter-bombers who could see exactly who and what they were bombing. There was clearly no further need to document the pilots' "successes." All had hit their targets—collections of unarmed fellow Vietnamese farmers and families clustered in easy view from low flying bombers. Colonel Anh was pleased. He was not even interested in any formal report.

I could not talk about this experience for twelve years, and the thought of it still creates tremors in my body. I often find myself crying at the thought of it, and at times feel a rage that nearly chokes me.

After Viet Nam, I knew that my own government, the government for which I had hoped to work, was not only criminal but psychotic. Buried deeper inside me, however, was an even more radical epiphany, the truth Mai Ly offered me through her open eyes. *She is my family.* It would take me many years to understand the real meaning of this experience—that we are all one—a lesson that continues to deepen and expand as I grow older.

MAP 1
Viet Nam's Mekong Delta Relating to Brian's Duties

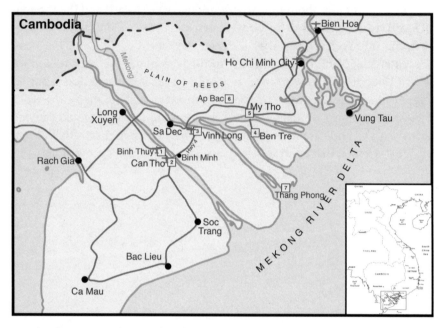

Area in Viet Nam's Mekong Delta relevant to my duties as commander of a USAF 823rd combat security police unit dispatched in 1969 to tiny Binh Thuy Air Base supplementing its regular security. By then, Binh Thuy had been attacked forty-five times, most for any of the ten 7th Air Force bases. And, from January–August 1969, it received at least sixteen mortar attacks, of which six hit inside its perimeter, causing seven casualties, had six aircraft shot down with ten crew killed and six suspected sapper penetrations. In 1969, the area was sprayed with five dozen Operation Ranch Hand herbicide missions, including five paralleling Binh Thuy's perimeter. Knowledge of locations of friendly units and intelligence of roaming NLF units tended to lower my anxiety.

1. Binh Thuy Air Base, along the Bassac River, the lowest of four Mekong tributaries, where I served March–August 1969. HQ for 74th Tactical Wing of South Vietnamese Air Force fighter squadron of A-37Bs as well as CIA planes. Binh Thuy River Patrol Boats were next door.
2. Nearby city of Can Tho (pop. 1 million), fourth-largest city in South Viet Nam, location of Can Tho Army airfield, 10th PSYOPs Battalion, and Phong Dinh Provincial CIA Interrogation Center.
3. Vinh Long (pop. 100,000), capital Vinh Long Province, was attacked with a hundred mortars on April 10–11, 1969, causing 120 casualties, which provoked launching of incessant bombings of villages in the province, all in "free-fire zones." Home to 2nd Brigade, 9th Infantry Division.
4. Ben Tre (pop. 140,000), capital Kien Hoa Province. Bombings in February 1968 destroyed 85 percent of the city. USAF Major Chester L. Brown circled above the

city directing air and artillery fire, proclaiming, "It became necessary to destroy the town in order to save it."

5. My Tho (pop. 200,000), capital Dinh Tuong Province, near the home of U.S. 9th Infantry Division and 7th ARVN Infantry Division.

6. Battle of Ap Bac, west of My Tho, where, on January 2, 1963, 230 NLF troops defeated three thousand ARVN soldiers.

7. Thang Phong, tiny hamlet in Kien Hoa Province on South China Sea where, on February 25, 1969, Lt. Bob Kerrey's Navy SEAL team murdered twenty-four villagers, including women and children. Kien Hoa was being marauded by U.S. 9th Infantry's Division's "Operation Speedy Express" and escalation of Phoenix assassination program, both part of Nixon's "Vietnamization." Kerrey later became a U.S. Senator from Nebraska, presidential candidate, and president of the New School in New York. Kerry described the murders as "an atrocity." "Speedy Express" murdered an average of sixty-one Vietnamese peasants every day for 180 days.

Note 1: Provinces of Dinh Tuong (My Tho), Kien Hoa (Ben Tre) and Vinh Long were sources of the first major peasant revolts in November 1940 against the French and Japanese. Viet Nam became a virtual colony of Japan, no more palatable to its people than French or U.S. occupation. This region remained the most revolutionary area in all Vietnam.

Note 2: The triangle formed by Can Tho, Vinh Long, and Sa Dec contained dozens of villages and hamlets in "free fire zones" mercilessly bombed in spring 1969. While assessing the "success" of bombings in five of these undefended, inhabited fishing hamlets, I witnessed the results: hundreds murdered, mostly women and children, producing a personal epiphany possessing "irreversible knowledge" of the war's criminality.

PART II

Pax Americana

CHAPTER 6

In Country: Viet Nam

After a couple of months in Viet Nam, I continued to wake up, asking more questions. Just how many villages were we regularly bombing? How many civilians were we killing?

By fate, part of my job was to document bombing casualties in Vinh Long Province. If those numbers were multiplied across the country, I knew the total number of dead and wounded must be enormous. In fact, a consensus has emerged that, from the official invasion of Da Nang on March 8, 1965, through the cease-fire on January 27, 1973, a period of nearly ninety-five months, over six million Southeast Asians were killed (or, as I would now say, murdered).[37]

Over 2,100 people were being killed each day, 88 every hour.

I was only seeing a fragment of that killing: I began seeing the war in a new way. Before going to Viet Nam, I had listened to Senator Gruening at the Unitarian church describe the Gulf of Tonkin attack as a fraud, but I had been skeptical—after all, I had been brought up listening to Joe McCarthy on the radio, telling us that the "reds" were going to ruin our way of life and it was our duty to fight them. Now I was fighting the "reds" and finding out that most of them were simply rural villagers, farmers, and fishers.

On my trips in April to visit the "targets" of our bombings, what I found were the blackened, mangled and maimed bodies of women and children, innocents who had been destroyed by U.S. napalm. As I looked at their bodies, I suddenly remembered the time when I had tortured my dog, Lucky. The land of my birth, the land of "liberty," was in the grip of the very same monster I had once discovered resided within me. Our arrogant way of life, the American Way Of Life, was itself AWOL from the world of universal humanity.

Free-Fire Zones

The war did not stop to allow me time to assimilate the tragic deaths of young women, children, and old men. As the night security force commander, I had work to do, assuring security posts were alert and perimeter posts were briefed on the latest intelligence. Despite my increasing concerns about the war, I took my job very seriously. I wanted to make sure my men and I left Viet Nam alive, and my adrenaline was working.

As part of intelligence gathering, I was tasked with riding every morning with my nemesis, the 632nd operations officer, in a small observation helicopter called a "loach," to make notes of any significant movements of personnel on the ground in the areas of Phong Dinh and Vinh Long Provinces around Binh Thuy. Sightings of any "VC" would have been unlikely since they operated mostly at night. On one flight, the pilot noted a difficulty stabilizing our loach, apparently a problem with the rear rotor blade due to ground fire or mechanical malfunction. The pilot descended quickly and we experienced a hard landing, not quite a crash, in a rice paddy somewhere in southern Vinh Long Province. I fell from the open door of the helicopter into the paddy, luckily walking away with only bruises and sprains. There was a small ARVN (Army of the Republic of Vietnam) detachment nearby which provided us security while we repaired the rotor blade sufficiently to fly at low altitude back to Binh Thuy. Later we discovered there was a functional design problem with these particular Hughes helicopters' rear rotor blades such that they proved to only have one-sixth of their programmed life expectancy. I stopped participating in these missions after this, not just because I feared a more serious crash, but also because I felt they were a needless exercise that did not add any intelligence of value.

I was more comfortable reading regularly prepared intelligence reports, maps and the local news, both the irregular *Binh Thuy Times* and the daily Saigon version of the military newspaper, *Stars and Stripes*. From a base and personal safety perspective, I wanted to keep track of the various ground and bombing campaigns, and particularly the changing intelligence about where and when NLF units might target Binh Thuy with mortars or sapper attacks. But the mounting casualty statistics caused me to be increasingly troubled as I came to realize my job was defense in the service of offense: in essence, I was protecting pilots and planes so that they could continue what I considered to be mass murder.

Starting in 1965, the United States and the South Vietnamese had used aerial bombardment in rural areas as the central feature of their counterinsurgency strategy.[38] Hamlets were numbered on maps, identified only by their grid coordinates. The local Vietnamese, of course, had names for these little villages, but those names were irrelevant as far as the military was concerned. All our bombers cared about were the coordinates—and often, they did not even worry if their bombs fell outside of those areas. In fact, testimony at the Bertrand Russell International War Crimes Tribunals in Sweden and Denmark in 1967 revealed destruction by bombings of 307 Catholic churches and 116 Buddhist pagodas. And, U.S. intelligence personnel admitted that hospitals were routinely targeted, "the bigger the better." Classified USAF bombing manuals defined hospitals, schools and churches as "psycho-social targets designed to destroy civilia order and morale."[39]

In 1969, these bombings were stepped up. "Vietnamization" had begun; the United States was seeking to "secure" the country so it could pull out and let the South Vietnamese take over. The number of South Vietnamese fighter-bomber sorties (one round-trip mission per plane) jumped from 2,100 in April to 2,700 in May, nearly a 30 percent increase, and to 3,000 in July.[40] Most sorties were carried out by Cessna A-37Bs, especially effective in low-altitude daylight operations where there was no presence of antiaircraft defenses. Undefended, inhabited villages were perfect targets for these pilots—in effect, one turkey shoot after another.

Pilots knew they were targeting civilian villages, but that no longer mattered. By 1969, the vast majority of land in the Delta was designated as lying within "free-fire zones." These were areas in which the U.S. and South Vietnamese military forces were authorized to shoot or bomb any person, animal, or object, no questions asked—in effect, genocide zones. All buildings destroyed by bombs in such zones were considered "VC structures," a policy that originated as early as October 1961, despite the fact that almost all of them were peasant homes and farm buildings.[41] The aim appeared to be solely to increase body counts.[42] Certainly, no one seemed worried if planes missed their targets or killed civilians. In densely populated Phong Dinh and Vinh Long Provinces, alone, a combined one million people lived in over 120 identified villages, and each village contained a number of hamlets.

Though the 7th Air Force claimed to coordinate most aerial operations, there were so many planes and so many pilots—and so much machismo among many of the pilots—that it was not unheard-of for pilots to operate on their own whim over vast territory. For example, Major Richard Secord, later to have a starring role in the covert Iran-Contra affair, worked out of the CIA base at Udorn, Thailand, and other airstrips such as Nakhorn Phanom from 1966–1968 coordinating CIA's and USAF's 7th Air Force systematic secret bombings resulting in the murder of thousands of peasants in northern Laos.[43] According to author Roger Warner, Secord enjoyed spending his free time dropping bombs. In an interview, Secord told Warner that on slow days he simply "buzzed across the Mekong on bombing and strafing runs, if he thought his CIA bosses wouldn't find out, and they didn't . . . Getting airborne was a welcome relief from working in an office. If Secord had to break the rules to fly, it didn't trouble him much. He had come to see that in the Laos war a lot of the rules didn't make sense."[44]

On my own base, it was never clear how much Colonel Anh was coordinating with 7th Air Force his A-37 bombing missions in Vinh Long and Phong

Dinh Provinces. I wondered whether many of those aerial campaigns were of Colonel Anh's own making. I often visited the CSC bunker on the base, where we had maps stuck with pins. On one map, each pin allegedly represented an enemy target; on another the supposed location of NLF sightings. Any Vietnamese settlement suspected of collaborating with the "Viet Cong," no matter how minimal the evidence, was included in the "free-fire zone" and received a pin indicating imminent destruction.

It became clear to me that the object of the U.S. and South Vietnamese bombings was to kill with abandon anyone still living in the countryside. To paraphrase U.S. Air Force Major Chester L. Brown's infamous remark during the Tet offensive, it appeared we were destroying the countryside in order to save it.[45]

Body Counts

I was so distressed about this situation that I flew to Tan Son Nhut Air Base in Saigon on April 19, 1969, to meet with my immediate superior, Captain Joel, and the chief of the 823rd Combat Security Police Squadron intelligence section, Captain Paul. I wanted to share my shocking experiences of witnessing the immediate aftermath of a series of bombings from low-flying fighter bombers where hundreds of vulnerable villagers in Vinh Long Province were intentionally murdered. I wanted to know what my superiors knew about this.

We examined the many maps of the ten primary in-country air bases mounted on a long wall with pins and annotations identifying up-to-date intelligence sightings of supposed "VC" units. Comparing the map information with the records, such as they were, of the most recent bombings identified in 7th Air Force and other reports, we suspected that some of these were the same bombing runs I had witnessed. At the first "target," I had estimated 120–130 bodies, mainly women, children, and elderly, all civilians. The after-action report from 7th Air Force listed a hundred "VC" dead at what seemed to be the same location. If that was the same "target," it was a lie.

Captain Paul's reports that bombings had destroyed "VC" units in the general areas of the villages I had examined, but with the same "VC" units mysteriously reappearing elsewhere a few days later, was the clincher. Paul said to me, "You confirmed my suspicions that we weren't killing VC." Thus, the approximately seven to nine hundred bodies I had counted in the five bombed villages in Vinh Long Province were in fact civilian deaths (murders), not "VC."

The Vietnamese census listed the population density in Vinh Long Province as 810 persons per square mile. Generally, each village was made up of much smaller hamlets, often five to ten per village. But hamlets were further broken down into clusters of families living in "settlements." Average family size was 6.3. Thus, there were several thousand settlements recognizable from the air, most of them in officially designated free-fire zones, all of them considered "enemy targets."

This kind of intelligence gathering drove me crazy. My home county in western New York State, Chautauqua, had a population of 135,000 in an area roughly one-third larger than Vinh Long Province, with a density of 130 persons per square mile. Chautauqua had dozens of small towns throughout its area outside its two small cities, Dunkirk and Jamestown. I tried to imagine what it would be like living in my small village, knowing it was in a target zone, but not knowing *when* we would be bombed.

I tried to imagine that my town, or nearby towns, were being bombed not because of anything we had done, but simply because they were towns in "free-fire zones," essentially genocidal regions. It was hard to even imagine: with the exception of the bombing of Tulsa's prosperous African American neighborhood in 1921 by the National Guard in one of this country's largely unknown racist riots where perhaps several hundred were killed and more than a thousand Black homes, businesses, and churches were destroyed, I am not aware of any other U.S. Americans being subjected to bombings in their villages and cities.[46]

I also tried to imagine what it would be like to know that my grandparents, aunts or uncles were being killed—and considered enemy dead—just because they had grown up and made a living in a town that some foreign government now considered a "free-fire zone." What did it mean that people were being slaughtered—by U.S. firepower from low-flying airplanes—just for living in their ancestral homes?

The U.S. military's official reports were listing the mass murders of civilians as military deaths of enemy combatants. Viet Nam, it turned out, was a war of body counts. Who the bodies were did not matter. Just as earlier in U.S. history, it was said that the "only good Indian was a dead Indian," now official U.S. reports were essentially saying, the "only good Vietnamese is a dead Vietnamese." Human beings were reduced to "VC dead"; villages reduced to grid coordinates. We had lost our humanity.

Hue

I unexpectedly learned a bit more about how this bombing campaign felt to the Vietnamese people one day in late April or early May when I naively decided to take a little jaunt north of Can Tho City. I crossed the Bassac River Ferry, meandered up Highway 4 only a couple of miles in traffic with ARVN trucks, then briefly turned onto a narrow elevated side path. I was in the Binh Minh district of southeast Vinh Long, not far from where the bombings had taken place in April, but closer to Highway 4.

I didn't go very far before I saw dark smoke billowing into the sky. That likely meant bombs or artillery or both. Holy shit!, I thought, at any moment a bomb could be dropped on me. I quickly turned around to race back to Highway 4.

Just then, I saw out of the corner of my eye an old man running down the road away from the smoke. He was whimpering. When he noticed me, he quickly ran into tall grass, perhaps 150 or 200 feet away. I think of this man so often I have given him a name, "Hue." Like "Mai Ly," he is deeply etched into my consciousness.

As I sped the short distance to get back onto Highway 4, my hands and feet were trembling so much I had to stop to gain my composure. A water buffalo stood nearby—alive and healthy—but in my mind, I saw the wounded water buffalo I had seen a few weeks earlier in the bombed village. Yet here, the landscape seemed undisturbed. In fact, as I looked around, I saw an old woman calmly walking down the road, carrying a yoke across her shoulder, bags full of produce hanging on either end.

One moment, one place, was so full of death—Mai Ly with children in her arms, the old man running from his burning village; another was so serene, a water buffalo grazing on the grass, an old woman going about her day. Death and destruction had become so banal, so ubiquitous, it was now simply part of daily life for these villagers.

I placed my head on the steering wheel of my Jeep and closed my eyes. I think I was crying. When I opened my eyes I was in the same eerie place, both psychically and physically. The water buffalo was still standing there, and the old woman was still slowly walking toward the highway. Smoke was heavy in the air behind me. I opened my Swiss Army knife and jabbed the point of the blade into the palm of my hand in an attempt to wake myself from this nightmare. Fuck! I was awake. Hue and Mai Ly—these people's pain was not a bad dream but a horrific reality.

As Good as a "VC"

The reality, I realized, was that I was nearly nine thousand miles from my home agricultural village in New York, tasked with providing security for fighter-bomber, reconnaissance and observation planes waging a genocidal campaign against simple and humble farming people who had likely never traveled more than a dozen miles from their homes. That we glibly labeled Vietnamese as "communists" to justify killing them because they wanted their independence revealed the extent of our madness, extraordinary arrogance, and utter ignorance.

Our side had thousands of fixed-wing aircraft and helicopters conducting countless reconnaissance, logistics, and combat support and bombing missions, dozens of offshore Navy ships bombarding the mainland, and numerous armed patrol boats in the three thousand miles of navigable waterways in the Delta. We were using hundreds of thousands of small arms, automatic weapons, and pieces of artillery. And we were on the soil and waterways and in the airspace of another sovereign country, just as the French had been before us. It was preposterous to actually believe that this land of farmers and fishers who wanted to be free of colonization had been a threat to France, or posed a threat to the United States. Not only was this war delusional, it was diabolical!

I couldn't keep silent about what I was witnessing, especially since I still believed in the American Way Of Life. I still believed that if only my fellow officers really understood what was happening, they would stop it. After all, the U.S. Rules of Engagement clearly prohibited killing civilians or destroying their infrastructure.

So one day, when I was in the CSC bunker with other officers reviewing maps and reports, I questioned what we were doing. Why, I asked were the pin markers on our maps, markers meant to identify enemy targets, clearly on the coordinates of inhabited civilian hamlets? Why were we bombing civilians? These were Nuremberg crimes and they were the result of official policy, day-in and day-out.

I didn't get a good answer. Instead, the other officers and noncoms would argue with me, defending the bombing runs. A visiting major, about six feet five in height, whom I had never seen before, was so angry he physically forced me out of the bunker.

Who was the real enemy of our country? Was it them or was it us (including me)?

CHAPTER 7

Letters Home

Less than three weeks after I landed in Viet Nam, I wrote to my two U.S. senators, Jacob Javits (R-NY) and Charles Goodell (R-NY), and to President Nixon's secretary of defense, Melvin Laird, asking if they really knew what was happening on the ground. Interestingly, Republican Goodell, a Korean combat veteran, became a leading dove—he was the first senator to introduce legislation (in fall of 1969) requiring withdrawal of U.S. troops by the end of 1970.

I became increasingly enraged at the conduct of the war. My awareness of atrocities was expanding since, as a security officer, I spent time studying military and CIA reports, conversing with U.S. Army soldiers in Can Tho, making personal on-site assessments of bombed villages, and talking with pilots at Binh Thuy.

From gathering this data, I very quickly learned that the falsified casualty reports and casual killings of civilians were not just aberrations at our air base. They were happening across the country. Now, more than forty years later, I know that the war was even more vicious and cruel than what I saw in country. Worse, much of what happened in Viet Nam has been repeated over and again, now in Iraq, Afghanistan, and Pakistan.

Viet Nam and Iraq

The torture that has occurred at Guantánamo Bay, Bagram, and Abu Ghraib is nothing new. In 1970, a U.S. construction consortium, "The Vietnam Builders," constructed isolation cells at the draconian Vietnamese prison on Con Son Island. These were the infamous "Tiger Cages" where so-called hardcore "VCI" suspects were regularly tortured and beaten while bolted nude to the floor, handcuffed to a bar, or put in leg irons, begging for food, while lime was thrown on them. This was under direction of the U.S. government–funded "Corrections and Detention Division of the Public Safety Directorate."[47] As at Guantánamo, most of the prisoners were not even the people we sought; at Con Son Island, many of the prisoners were not "VCI," but in fact the Buddhist students so hated and systematically repressed by the Diem and subsequent regimes.[48]

"The Vietnam Builders," which had built warships for the U.S. during World War II, was the largest-ever construction consortium, going by the name RMK-BRJ, which stood for Raymond International, Morrison-Knudsen, Brown and Root, and J.A. Jones Construction. In addition to building prisons, the consortium received at least two billion dollars in lucrative no-bid contracts to turn South Viet Nam into a virtual military territory, employing over 8,500 U.S. Americans and 51,000 Vietnamese, constructing six naval bases, twenty airfields, a number of hospitals and storage depots, and twenty base camps housing 450,000 military personnel.[49] In Iraq, the no-bid contracts went to the same people, the firm now called KBR, Inc. In 1998, Brown and Root, a subsidiary of Halliburton based in Houston, merged with the M.W. Kellogg Co. of Dresser Industries, thus KBR.

The use of mercenary forces was also an important part of the U.S. war machine in Viet Nam. South Korean mercenary forces alone (fifty thousand at any one time drawn from three large divisions and brigades), paid 100 percent by the U.S, were in II Corps coastal provinces from Qui Nhon south to Phan Rang from September 1965 until March 1973. They committed a series of My Lai–scale massacres with the aggregate numbers of known murders committed running into the thousands. Quakers documented at least twelve separate massacres of a hundred or more civilians carried out by Korean mercenaries, and dozens of other massacres of twenty or more unarmed civilians plus countless individual murders, robberies, rapes, tortures, and destruction of land and personal property.[50]

During several conversations in Can Tho *mamasan* restaurants with soldiers from the Army's 9th Infantry Division, I heard gloating accounts of how they were "kicking ass" in Kien Hoa Province, fifty miles to the northeast. They were part of "Operation Speedy Express" which was softening up villages with bombing and artillery barrages before cleaning up with ground sweeps. At the time I had no idea how systematic the killings were, though intelligence reports claimed Kien Hoa was being successfully "cleared." But I did know from the bombing patterns in adjacent Vinh Long Province that there was an insane obsession with killing as many Vietnamese as possible to prove that "Vietnamization" was working. It was all show for the U.S. American politicians and the American body politics. Reducing U.S. casualties at the expense of Vietnamese had the effect of calming the antiwar movement.

Terror, atrocity, massacre and genocide are what the Viet Nam War was all about. Time-Life Books published a series on Viet Nam in which the authors described the war as "a continuum of terror," "a strategy of terror," and "a contagion of slaughter." Nor can the blame for those atrocities be laid at the feet of individual soldiers. As Christian Appy concluded in his moving chronicle, *Working-Class War: American Combat Soldiers and Vietnam*,

"American military policy did not . . . make atrocities by individual soldiers inevitable, but it certainly made it inevitable that American forces *as a whole* would kill many civilians" (201). As I later came to understand, the atrocities we committed in Viet Nam were not the work of out-of-control soldiers, nor were they a one-time aberration. They were a continuation of the particular belief in manifest destiny that has shaped this country's values since our forbearers brutally terrorized and murdered the Indigenous people living in North America four hundred years ago.

The massacre at My Lai is well known. Yet there were many others. Less than two weeks before my arrival at Binh Thuy, on February 25, a U.S. Navy SEAL team herded together twenty-four peasants in Thang Phong village in Kien Hoa Province some fifty miles to the east of Binh Thuy and shot them all. The leader of that seven-man SEAL team was Lt. Bob Kerrey, who was later to become a U.S. senator from Nebraska, a Democratic U.S. presidential candidate, and the president of the New School in New York. In 2001, when confronted by journalists about his role in the massacre, he confessed that it felt like an atrocity had been committed that night.[51]

The commander of the feared 9th Infantry Division at the time was Major General Julian Ewell, who enjoyed the nicknames "Bloody" and "Butcher of the Delta." Some of the Division's aircraft sported painted slogans like "Our business is killing, and business is good." According to Daniel Ellsberg, Ewell "so completely freed his helicopter gunners from restraints against firing on sampans in canals lined on both sides with housing that the Division reported body-count ratios of 'friendly' to 'enemy' dead unmatched in the history of the war, or perhaps in any war."[52] Ewell was famous for yelling at his troops, "get a hundred a day, every day."[53] When the six-month Speedy Express campaign centered in Kien Hoa was completed on May 31, 1969, the 9th Division claimed its members had killed nearly eleven thousand "enemy" while capturing fewer than 750 weapons. If that figure is accurate, then members of that division had killed an average of sixty-two Vietnamese per day during their six-month operation. The overwhelming majority of them were undoubtedly poor peasants.

The U.S. military had other ways of enforcing its Pax Americana beside mass murder. Agent Orange did the job nearly as well as napalm. Years after leaving the military, I learned that between January 1969 and August 1969, the months just before and during my time at Binh Thuy, at least sixty-three Operation Ranch Hand missions had been flown in Vinh Long and Phong Dinh Provinces, spraying herbicides on the surrounding countryside. Over forty of the missions were within a ten-mile radius of Binh Thuy, and five of those directly paralleled our base perimeter. These herbicides included the major defoliants Agent Orange (with Dioxin), Agent White (with Tordon, containing picloramic acid), and Agent Blue (an arsenic-laden desiccant intended to destroy food crops, especially rice, by dehydration).

Between December 14, 1965, and June 27, 1970, the U.S. reportedly sprayed a total of 137,579 gallons of Agents Orange, White, and Blue just in the area of Can Tho and its surroundings.[54] This chemical warfare destroyed 60 percent of Viet Nam's mangrove forest, nearly 10 percent of its food crops, and exposed a large percentage of the population (and most U.S. soldiers) to some of the most toxic chemicals known. In particular, dioxin, the most toxic by-product of Agent Orange, is considered one of the most potent cancer-causing substances ever studied, one thousand times more toxic than strychnine, one hundred thousand times more poisonous than cyanide.[55] The mutagenic effects on offspring continue to this day, affecting 12 percent of the Vietnamese population, and are estimated to last for ten generations.

The Vietnamese View

When I defended Vietnamese civilians, other officers frequently responded that the Vietnamese really were not like us—that they did not cherish life as we did. I was sure that this could not be the case.

People sometimes ask me how I became the kind of activist who would sit down on railroad tracks to block a munitions train. As I reflect back, I remember these painful moments that comprise my journey, directed, if at all, by a sense of curiosity and openness. The other officers chose to remain on base and speculate about the Vietnamese. They seemed, for the most part, content not to question our typically racist views, shrouded in the belief of American exceptionalism. I decided I wanted to learn more about the Vietnamese, both for purposes of base security—and for my own sanity.

I sometimes ventured into settlements in and around Can Tho City where Colonel Anh, the Vietnamese Binh Thuy base commander, seemed known and liked. Anh had given me the names of a couple of people who worked at a local orphanage who spoke conversational English and could offer me some cultural, maybe even strategic information. I was never certain that these conversations offered any helpful information for intelligence purposes, but I certainly learned more about Vietnamese cultural life. I began to understand just how much their ancestral land meant to the Vietnamese people. Like other Indigenous people I would meet later in my life, the Vietnamese fishers and rice farmers could not imagine life away from their food sources and rice paddies, their farm animals, their fishing waterways, and the ancestral burial grounds near their settlements. That they remained didn't mean they accepted what was happening to them.

By this time I was making it obvious in my conversations that I disagreed with U.S. bombings of villages. I generally couched my criticisms of the war under international law, explaining that people who have been the victims of criminal invasions and occupations have the right to defend themselves in various efforts to repel the aggressors. This, I thought, might open some space in our conversations, though in hindsight it could have endangered my life.

The couple of Vietnamese I talked with seemed careful about how they described the presence of the U.S. military forces, or even the ARVN, walking a fine line in order to survive. It should be noted that the ARVN, the South Vietnamese army, was corrupt and often brutal—hardly an organization most villagers would willingly support.[56] I began to sense under their politeness, most Vietnamese people were at least sympathetic to the NLF, and definitely angry at our destructive presence there.[57]

The Vietnamese needed to be cautious in expressing their opinions. The CIA-directed Phoenix program, and particularly its Civil Operations and Rural Development Support (CORDS) "pacification" effort under U.S. military control, had been intense after Tet 1968.[58] Feared Province Reconnaissance Units (PRUs), in essence assassination squads, were tasked with identifying, interrogating, and assassinating any member of Vietnamese society who was perceived to be a member of what they called the "Viet Cong Infrastructure" ("VCI"), its officers and decision-makers.

The French had operated more than eighty prisons. At Can Tho itself was a five-hundred-bed prison that often held two thousand prisoners. Diem had put thousands of political prisoners into dozens of detention camps. President Thieu had locked up thousands of political prisoners in forty-two provincial jails and four large national prisons. According to *Time* magazine, in December 1972, Thieu was holding eighty thousand political prisoners.[59]

Major torture was occurring at the CIA Province Interrogation Center in Can Tho.[60] There were reports of smaller torture centers near Binh Thuy Air Base, and at the Can Tho Army airfield as well, but I never knew if that was true. I did learn later that CORDS had in fact disappeared or murdered *thousands* of men and women in the villages who had been perceived as leaders within the political wing of the National Liberation Front, what we called the "VCI," and there were plenty of reasons for even ordinary villagers to fear being added to the list, and then disappeared.

In 1971, Phoenix director and future CIA chief William Colby said thousands had disappeared or died in Thieu's prisons, and 28,000 supposed members of the "VCI" had been captured under Phoenix, with 20,000 killed.[61] The Thieu regime actually boasted that Phoenix had killed 40,994 suspected enemy civilians from August 1968 through the middle of 1971 and that 84,000 had been "neutralized."[62] Despite this effort to rid South Viet Nam of its "civilian enemies," a 1970 CIA report indicated that 30,000 people inside the Thieu government were regular cooperators with the "NLF/VCI,"" and that the number may have been as high as 50,000.[63]

Doing My Homework

As questions about the war continued to arise for me, I began spending more time in our little base library. It was there that I found three books that greatly aided my education about the history of Viet Nam, and the way the French, and then the United States, sabotaged the Vietnamese people's deep aspirations for independence.

The first, *The United States in Vietnam*, written by Cornell University professors George McTurnan Kahin and John W. Lewis, provided a tremendous historical overview of Viet Nam, and details of the French and U.S. wars of aggression.[64] The other two were written by French journalist Bernard Fall, an expert on the Viet Minh/Viet Cong, *Hell in a Very Small Place: The Siege of Dien Bien Phu* and *Street Without Joy*.[65] Fall was killed by a booby trap explosion somewhere northwest of Hue on his sixth trip to Viet Nam in February 1967 while accompanying U.S. Marines on a mission.

From these books I learned that the United States, starting under President Truman, had been militarily and financially aiding France since the 1940 in its efforts to militarily defeat the Vietnamese independence movement and recover their former colony. The use of atomic weapons was even considered by the U.S. in its attempt to rescue the French from their defeat at Dien Bien Phu in May 1954. Fortunately, the French government refused the offer, saying, "But it will kill our men too!"

The United States never intended to honor the 1954 Geneva Agreement that had temporarily divided the country until mandated unifying elections were held in 1956. Our government intelligence indicated that Hồ Chí Minh would be elected president, and that was unacceptable. The CIA was planning sabotage as early as spring of 1954. In June, a Catholic Vietnamese, Ngo Dinh Diem, who at the time had been living in a Maryknoll Seminary in the U.S., was brought in to be our puppet leader in primarily Buddhist Viet Nam. To create a core constituency for Diem, the CIA had brought nine hundred thousand Catholic Vietnamese from the north to the south to support his presidency, and many of the young men from this group became Diem's ARVN forces.

I was embarrassed that I knew nothing of this history. In my ignorance, I had joined the U.S. military and been complicit in murdering countless

Vietnamese who simply wanted to be independent from colonial forces. I began feeling ashamed, though I tried to push the feeling aside so as not to be disabled by an increasing sense of personal invalidity. How could I have achieved bachelor's and master's degrees, and been halfway through law school, and not known anything about this history?

Ode to Norman Morrison

Reading these books brought me into contact with the base librarian, a beautiful young Vietnamese woman who was a library science graduate of nearby Can Tho University, a university destroyed during Tet 1968. I remember her name as Anh Ly, though some Anglicized her name as "Annie."

I was impressed by An Ly's relatively good English, and by her passionate interest in books. The library was full of music tapes, and most airmen came there to listen and tape music to take home with them. What interested me was that she had collected a small selection of very recent books (some mentioned above) that contained extremely honest and critical accounts of Vietnamese history and the tragic policies of U.S. and French imperialism. It didn't appear that anyone else had checked out these books. Could I have been the first GI who was reading these books? I don't know.

One day, when I was checking out a book, she asked me if I would like to come to her family's house in Can Tho City for a Sunday dinner. I was startled. After hesitating, I agreed. She drew me a map directing me through Can Tho city streets to her family's house. What happened during that dinner turned out to be another one of those unpredictable life-changing moments.

I was nervous, of course, about going to her house. I trusted Anh Ly, but she could have been creating a trap to kidnap or kill a U.S. military officer. I also wondered if going to a civilian's house would be sanctioned by my military superiors—or even if this was a set-up by some on the base to accuse me of being a traitor. As I drove to Anh Ly's house, I nervously kept checking my rear view mirror to see if I was being followed. I was relieved when I finally parked my Jeep in her pleasant but modest neighborhood.

Anh Ly introduced me to her family. We had a wonderful Vietnamese meal, but what was incredible was the topic of much of the conversation. As they tested out the extent of my feelings about the U.S. and its war against their country, knowing of my outspoken opposition to it, they began to share their own sentiments. This was a very political family. One of her uncles was languishing in one of President Thieu's prisons for his political opposition while serving in the South Vietnamese legislature. It was the first time in my life I was involved in a passionate and informative conversation about the nature of revolution, of people struggling for autonomy from outside invaders.

After the meal, Anh Ly and one of her brothers wanted to sing some music accompanied by their Vietnamese instruments. After a few songs in Vietnamese, they said they wanted to sing a special song, and they ended by translating it into English. It was called "Ode to Norman Morrison," about a U.S. American whose sacrifice meant a great deal to the Vietnamese.

When I heard the name, Norman Morrison, I began to tremble. Norman was the young Quaker man who had immolated himself in view of Secretary of Defense Robert McNamara's window in the Pentagon parking lot on November 2, 1965, in protest of the U.S. war, especially the incessant bombings. This was the man I had scoffed at when I had read about his death. I had never given Morrison another thought.

The family then nervously but proudly showed me the postage stamp that had been issued by the North Vietnamese government with Norman's face looking down from the clouds upon U.S. antiwar demonstrators below. Possession of that stamp was prohibited in the South, so this family kept it well hidden, which explained their nervousness when they showed it to me. I was overcome with emotion and awe.

I began weeping. This Vietnamese family, of course, knew nothing of my connection with Norman. I tried to explain what was happening to me in the moment and my memories of him. I finally understood Norman's deep anguish about the war. Like him, I was feeling, in the deepest recesses of my soul, the anguish and frustration of trying to express outrage at the atrocities being arrogantly inflicted on innocent people in a distant nation. At that moment, Norman became my hero.

Norman was not the only U.S. American to immolate himself in anguished response to the barbaric war waged against the Vietnamese. There were at least eight others from March 1965 to May 1970, ranging from sixteen to eighty-two years of age, including three women. Five of the immolations occurred in California.[66] In addition, there were at least seventy-six Vietnamese, mostly Buddhists, who likewise sacrificed themselves to end the repressive Vietnamese government policies and the massive killings by the U.S. military.[67]

CHAPTER 8

Conduct Unbecoming

My time in Viet Nam came to an abrupt end.

On August 2, 1969, I was confronted by two shocking developments within hours of each other. In the morning, a couple hours after completing my night shift, as I was walking to my quarters for a nap, I was abruptly greeted by an Army captain representing himself as a lawyer from nearby Can Tho Army Airfield. The short conversation occurred while we were standing not far from the CSC building. He first read me what I believe were Article 31 rights, then showed me three or four pages of typed charges against me, all alleging violations of the Uniform Code of Military Justice (UCMJ).

I didn't know who signed the papers. It was such a surprise I didn't even think to ask for a copy. I was nearing the date when I would be rotated back to the States anyway. I wondered why, if they were going to bring charges, they would do so now? At the time, however, I wasn't thinking clearly. My stomach was tied into knots and my mouth felt dry as I looked at the typed charges: fraternization with enlisted men, conduct unbecoming an officer, theft of government property, disaffection, sedition. It seemed surreal.

Later that same day, while I was still processing in my mind these charges, I was handed a telegram a little after 1600 hours (4 p.m.) by a personal courier from my squadron chain-of-command contact at Tan Son Nhut in Saigon. The telegram ordered me to get on the "first available aircraft for processing to return to CONUS" (Continental United States).

Officer's Privilege

I suppose I should not have been surprised by the charges, but I was. Despite my views on the war, I had tried my best to do a good job in Viet Nam. In fact, one reason I had turned so strongly against the war was because, from the moment I landed, I had been focused on base security, and seriously read numerous military and intelligence reports that came to Binh Thuy about conditions and activities in the Delta. My first impressions of Viet Nam were from reading reports filled with reports and images of bombed villages and dead Vietnamese.

I genuinely believed that the intentional bombing of noncombatant villagers, in addition to being in violation of both international and U.S. constitutional law, was harmful to base security—and in the long view, I was right about that. Official Air Force records disclose that its ten primary air bases collectively were hit on average once every nine and a half days over the four-plus years prior to my arrival in March 1969. As the bombings of villages dramatically accelerated under "Vietnamization" in the spring of 1969, the air bases were attacked more than twice as often, on average once every 4.6 days for nearly four years until the ceasefire in January 1973.[68]

Had superior officers engaged me in dialogue, it might have helped our unit more effectively carry out its mission, such as it was. But it also would have threatened the hierarchical model upon which the military is based. I had already figured out from observing the way officers treated enlisted men that the military itself was not just a tool to win a war, but a mechanism for enforcing a way of life. What I was just starting to understand was that, in order for the military to be able to hear and understand the criticism we were making, their whole culture would need to undergo a radical transformation.

The military tradition of separating enlisted men from officers on base was enforced even in war zones such as at Binh Thuy. As an officer, I was privileged. For living quarters I had an average-sized, air-conditioned trailer all to myself, while my men lived in barracks. While the men were expected to keep their barracks spic and span, I had at my disposal a *mamasan* who regularly cleaned my living space and made my bed in return for very little compensation. Officers had both an outdoor patio where they could watch porno movies, as well as a special air-conditioned lounge in the officers' club, while enlisted men had to go off-base for those kinds of amusements. Enlisted men were not allowed into officer's living quarters, and officers generally went into the enlisted men's quarters only to issue orders or for formal briefings.

I quickly ran afoul of this prohibition against fraternization. In order to supervise my men, I had to spend time with them. It seemed smart to go to their barracks and talk to them when they got a "Dear John" letter in the afternoon, because I had to count on them later that evening. The military did not work that way, however.

This same officer was also a stickler when it came to military dress code. Early on, he threatened to issue an Article 15 (administrative punishment) to one of my men for not wearing his military cap or helmet when walking from his barracks to the chow hall. I personally thought we had a lot more important things to worry about than whether the men were wearing their caps. In many ways, I was very naïve about the military culture of which I had become a part.

I can now see, looking back over my life, that I have always had a tendency to fight against authority. I prefer taking my own path, not being told what to do by others. At the time, however, it seemed to me just common sense that my men would be more likely to listen to me if I created a truly respectful work environment. I found that when I treated my men as fellow human beings instead of as military inferiors, they were more likely to be at their duty stations, awake and alert. It was that line of thinking that led me to dispense with all saluting in my unit. That angered some of the other officers, who said I was a bad example.

Despite closeness with my men, I never talked to them about politics or the war. I felt that my duty as an officer was to make sure my men fulfilled their assigned mission without getting killed or injured. Ironically, it was my concern for my men that led to many of the charges against me.

A Tale of Two Jeeps

My interactions with the 632nd operations officer came to a head one night in the middle of May. Just after midnight, I was in the latrine when I heard the first of many explosions: it was a mortar and recoilless rifle attack. I ran to my Jeep—only to find it missing.

When the base came under attack, I normally rushed out to the perimeter road to support my men at their various positions. I regularly carried extra water, C-rations, and sometimes candy bars in the Jeep. But now, with no Jeep, and no time to waste, I ran as fast as I was able to the perimeter.

I spent much of the rest of that night on foot, walking along the perimeter road, visiting my men in their positions. Finally, in the wee hours of the morning, I saw a slow-driving Jeep, lights out, coming toward my position. Lo and behold, this was my Jeep, driven by the 632nd operations officer. Furious, I grabbed his camouflage shirt, ordered him out of my Jeep, and told him in no uncertain terms that he had seriously impeded the functioning of my unit's mission and my ability to carry out my unit responsibilities. Furthermore, I told him I was going to write him up for a serious incident report and submit it to 7th Air Force in Saigon for severe disciplinary action.

I did write up that report, cataloguing this officer's major interference with and violations of Air Force command procedures in a combat situation. If I had submitted it as a formal complaint, it would have led to an investigation and doubtless interrupted this officer's expected automatic promotion. He pleaded with me to not send it. I offered him a deal. If he would withdraw the Article 15 that he had filed against my troop for not wearing a hat, stay away from my men's barracks, and promise never to use my Jeep again, I would not send the report. I did tell him I planned to keep a copy in case there was cause to submit the report at a later date.

He never bothered me or my men again in any overt way, though the acrimony between us continued. I also suspect he had something to do with the charges brought against me in August, given that he was a good friend of Lt. Col. Kalman, the 823rd commander, though I will never be able to prove it.

I could only guess at the origin of most of the charges against me. "Fraternization" and "conduct unbecoming" had already been verbally threatened against me by many of the officers who did not like my friendly and respectful manner of relating to enlisted men. The charges of sedition, though false, could have been made by anyone, since virtually all the officers and noncoms on the base had heard me voice my disagreement with the military campaign in Viet Nam every day for months.

It took me a while, though, to figure out the charge of "theft of government property." It turned out to be a problem involving one of my jeeps. My unit possessed three jeeps, but usually only my NCO and I had need for them, which left one generally unused. The 632nd was short jeeps. On one occasion First Sergeant Myron of the 632nd had asked if he could borrow our extra Jeep to go into Can Tho. I shouldn't have agreed, since I suspected this career NCO had an alcohol problem, but I did. The next day I learned that the first sergeant had collided with a South Vietnamese troop truck on the busy highway between Binh Thuy and Can Tho. The investigating MPs deemed him drunk at the scene before towing the severely damaged Jeep to their compound in Can Tho. He had been taken to the 29th Army Evacuation Hospital between Can Tho and Binh Thuy with a broken leg and numerous other injuries.

The commander of the 632nd assured me that sooner or later my Jeep would be repaired or replaced. A few weeks later a Jeep was returned to me. I was very appreciative. Out of curiosity, but not really caring, I asked whether it was an entirely different Jeep or the same Jeep with new parts and body pieces? I was told it was the original Jeep completely repaired. As it turned out, however, the Jeep had been replaced: the serial number on the "repaired" Jeep was different from the one identified on my equipment manifest list. Thus the basis for the charge of "theft of government property" was based on the fact that the original Jeep's serial number was still on my manifest list but was unaccounted for. Joseph Heller of *Catch-22* fame could not have found better material.

A Failure of Leadership

The absurdity of the theft charge strongly suggested to me that at least two officers had worked together striving to get me court-martialed. I already knew of the wrath of my own 823rd commander who had promised I would never make captain, and that of his friend, the 632nd operations officer at Binh Thuy. The nature and timing of the charges were too coincidental.

My 823rd operations officer, Major Maynard, also from our squadron headquarters at Phan Rang, visited me for inspections and oversight on two occasions. On the evening of the major's first visit, he accompanied me for several hours as I made my rounds among my men. On that particular evening, a sighting by one of the Vietnamese sentries suggested one or two men might have penetrated our Petroleum On Line (POL) area. This, indeed, was serious, as there were countless gallons of fuel stored there that, if ignited, could destroy a whole section of the base.

With the major in my Jeep, I quickly drove toward the POL area and called to tell my NCO and the fire teams at perimeter locations to be extra watchful for any sappers. A Vietnamese sergeant was already present with other security personnel as I popped several illumination flares from those strapped to my uniform. I also called for a Spooky gunship that provided extra illumination.

I looked around and noticed Major Maynard kneeling near the far side of my Jeep's front wheel-well, no doubt to protect himself from any imminent explosion. I moved toward him and asked that he please get off the ground because I might have to quickly move the vehicle depending on how the situation unfolded. I didn't want to run over him, or have to even think about it, in this tense moment. He moved slightly, but remained crouched on the ground next to the Jeep. We never found anyone in the area, and it did not blow up. We were both relieved.

Later, in the wee hours of the morning, the major wanted to critique my performance and that of my men. To this day I cannot remember what his beef was. I do remember him saying that my unit's military bearing was ragged—which I'm sure it was, technically, though my men got their jobs done, and done well.

What he ordered me to do as a kind of punishment for my unit's supposed defects was, however, ridiculous. I was to give my men hour-long marching drills on the flightline every morning for one week after they had completed their nine-hour nightly stint. He left the next morning and I, of course, never complied with that order. No one ever said anything more about it, though what other officers might have reported to my squadron's headquarters at Phan Rang was not shared with me.

In a subsequent written evaluation, the major concluded that I displayed poor leadership skills. He wrote in his report that I "encountered certain difficulties in working with others"; my antiwar views "expressed on a number of occasions tended to create friction"; that my judgment was negatively affected by my "tendency to overidentify" with the enlisted men, though he noted that I "was extremely well liked" by them; that I exhibited poor performance "under stress"; and that I "in no way displayed a particular out-standing affinity for the control and use of resources." He did say that the sincerity of my views "cannot be doubted for a moment," and that I possessed "courage" of my "convictions." He even acknowledged that "in another career field, given a challenge compatible with [my] personal feelings, [I] could perform outstandingly," which had been, of course, my consistent argument while in combat security police ranger training at Fort Campbell.

By early August it was certainly true that I did have an "attitude problem" about the war and my role in it. For several months I had felt strongly that what our country was doing in Viet Nam was terribly wrong, and I believed it was my duty as a citizen to talk about it.

When you sense a different truth, when you awaken, you face a choice, and if you choose to follow that truth, a new journey unfolds. And once you are on the journey, the choices become clearer on the new journey. But these choices are sometimes difficult, making it tempting to revert to former, more comfortable, familiar habits.

My first leap came with a realization that plunging the bayonet into another is in effect plunging the bayonet into oneself. I saw that as the great lesson for humanity. Some would call it the principle of karma—what goes around comes around. Everything is interconnected in an undivided whole as modern physics is teaching us.

Nonetheless, when I left Viet Nam I was distressed by the major's criticisms of me in April, and terrified, in August, that I would be court-martialed and sent to military prison. Bravery is much easier to come by in hindsight.

CHAPTER 9

Sent Home

As soon as I received the telegram ordering me back to the United States, I began to pack and say good-bye to my men and my NCO. Within thirty-six hours I was on a flight to Phan Rang, then back to Saigon where I spent another day or two in the busy Tan Son Nhut terminal building waiting for an available seat on a returning plane.

After 151 days in Viet Nam, I arrived in the United States around August 5, 1969. My final destination was England Air Force Base near Alexandria in central Louisiana, the actual home of the 823rd. My wife, whom I was able to call from Saigon, greeted me there.

I honestly had no idea what would happen next. When someone suddenly announces there are fifty-some charges against you, you get nervous. However, no one at the personnel office where I went to report claimed to know anything about me, and surprisingly no one knew anything about any charges or orders.

I was puzzled, but decided to take a thirty-day vacation leave and traveled with my wife to New England. We were at a B & B in Woodstock, Vermont, on August 16 when I read in the morning newspaper about an extraordinary cultural gathering of five hundred thousand people a hundred miles away, ironically in Woodstock, New York. I was ecstatic to learn of it. At our breakfast table that morning was a couple from Connecticut still grieving the recent death in Viet Nam of their only son. When I shared that I had just returned, the mother reached for my hands and, as I clasped hers, we both broke into tears. After breakfast our conversation latched onto a hope that perhaps the Woodstock event was the beginning of a cultural revolution that would make war impossible.

Suddenly I felt tremendous relief! The nightmare that began the day I reported for Air Force ranger training at Fort Campbell, Kentucky, exactly eight months earlier on December 16, 1968, was over. Eight months of daily chronic dry mouth and anxiety dissipated in seconds with the thought that revolution was in the air. I felt at that moment that Viet Nam was behind me. Little did I know that many years later a flashback would force emotional processing of these experiences and that healing would necessitate dredging up the memories I began to blank out at this point in my life.

Woodstock—Vermont and New York—gave birth to the real Brian, still unfolding.

Flower Power

I picked up some of the hippie vibe, however, during my New England vacation. When I reported back to England Air Force Base in September, I came in my pre-owned VW Beetle, having earlier sold my fancy Corvette Sting Ray. I had decorated the Beetle with a bunch of flower decals as a way of making a kind of antiwar statement. I drove this flower-power car right up to the base—and was promptly stopped by security police at the gate who told me that the decals on the car violated some Air Force regulation prohibiting inappropriate political propaganda.

After a few conversations, I was able to convince the base chief of security police that I couldn't take the decals off. He and I both knew that I needed a car, since I was being housed off base, and a flower-power Bug would not be easy to sell or trade in Louisiana. We reached a compromise: the security police would simply not recognize my vehicle when I entered the base. What that meant in practice was that they would not salute the blue officer's sticker on my bumper, as they were required to do for officers entering the base. What a deal! I hadn't been saluted virtually the whole time in Viet Nam and didn't want to start now.

At the personnel office, I received new orders assigning me to serve as the executive support officer for the chief of the supply squadron on the base. I thought it best not to ask about any pending charges, and, to my surprise and relief, no one ever mentioned them again, though they continued to weigh on my mind until my final discharge in 1972.

Later, after I was discharged, I sent for my records and there was no mention of any charges in my files, nor any mention of me being put on the Officer Control Roster—even though I have a copy of the Control Roster notification in my own files. All I can imagine is that the 82nd wing commander at Fort Campbell headquarters, or his superiors at Tactical Air Command (TAC) headquarters in Langley, Virginia, smelled trouble with the charges against me and quickly stopped the whole court-martial process and shredded the papers, including the Officer Control Roster action.

The last thing the military wanted, in the fall of 1969, was to go through a court-martial of an officer. Courts-martial are public affairs, and nothing could be worse for the military at that moment than to hand the media a story about an officer who was adamantly against the war. They had enough on their hands.

During the first week of September 1969, U.S. Army Lt. William Calley was charged with the massacre of hundreds of civilians at My Lai, more than ten weeks before the details were publicly revealed by investigative reporter Seymour Hersh.[69] On September 23, the heated trial of the Chicago Eight began. On September 25, U.S. Senator Charles Goodell (R-NY), my own senator, surprised everyone when he filed legislation requiring the withdrawal of U.S. troops from Viet Nam by 1970. There was a vigorous national campaign organizing demonstrations throughout the United States for the upcoming mid-October War Moratorium, which was followed by a massive antiwar protest in Washington on November 15.

Within the military itself, the first recorded mass mutiny among troops in Viet Nam had occurred in late August[70] though there had already been sixty-eight smaller mutinies in 1968 as subsequently reported by the Army.[71] All these events pointed toward a new *zeitgeist*; the change I felt in myself was taking place against the backdrop of a much larger cultural shift.

Troublemaker

The tension at England AFB was palpable. Antiwar protests were heating up around the country, including small demonstrations in various locations in Louisiana. Officers on base were on the lookout for any sign of subversion among the troops. The atmosphere was such that the smallest thing—such as the flower decals on my car—would make the officers nervous.

Without planning on it, I already had been identified as a troublemaker. During that fourth year of my Air Force active duty commitment, I was called into the office of the base wing commander on five separate occasions. Ironically, only one of those had anything directly to do with my antiwar beliefs.

As in Viet Nam, at England AFB I tried hard to keep my own personal views about the war separate from my Air Force duties. My job as the executive support officer for the chief of supply largely involved addressing personnel issues related to housing, family, personal debt, alcohol and drug abuse, health problems, career counseling, criminal behavior, and so forth. I worked hard to do my job well.

What I couldn't do, however, was deny my own humanity, or that of those around me. I was troubled when I witnessed acts of discrimination and elitism. I guess I was still the kid in high school who, as team captain, had made the rule that all the boys, including the Indian boy with polio, should be able to play on the intramural team. What I discovered was that the military at home, like the military in Viet Nam, had a different set of rules.

The first time I was ordered to the wing commander's office, it took me several minutes to grasp why I was there. My wife, Julie, a lawyer working at the local legal aid office, was teaching a college-level sociology class on the base. In one of her classes, she mentioned that racism existed in the U.S. military. When asked what evidence she had, she said her husband, who worked on the base, had provided examples of discrimination. Apparently, someone in the class reported this to an officer who in turn told the wing commander.

Being called to the wing commander's office is not something any officer takes lightly—it's like being a middle manager at a large corporation being called in to see the CEO, except in the military you don't get fired if you've done something wrong; you get court-martialed. My fears were real: on at least two of the occasions when called to the wing commander's office, I remember the presence of an Air Force JAG lawyer. For someone who was still a good boy at heart and who really wasn't aiming to cause trouble, these visits made me anxious.

The wing commander quickly got to the point. He claimed that I had shared confidential information about critical base matters in an inappropriate manner with off-base personnel. Even though I wondered how serious this might be, it didn't seem to be in the court-martial category. I replied that we both knew racism was rampant on base, as well as off, and that if the commander wanted to pursue a charge of "conduct unbecoming an officer" he could address my attorney wife. He didn't.

It is worth noting that only eighteen months before my conversation with the wing commander about racism in the military, President Johnson's Kerner Commission (also known as the "Riot" Commission) had concluded that the United States was "moving toward two societies, one Black, one White, separate and unequal." It blamed the 1960s "riots" of rage on "White racism," i.e., the hatred of African Americans by Whites. When national commissions were acknowledging the presence of institutional racism, it was foolish for the wing commander to pretend it didn't exist, particularly in Louisiana. This was, after all, the state in which Homer A. Plessy brought his suit against Louisiana's 1890 "separate car law" that required separate railway cars for Blacks and Whites—a law the Supreme Court upheld in *Plessy v. Ferguson*, essentially legalizing Jim Crow for the next fifty-eight years.

Race Privilege

My second visit to the wing commander was also related to race relations on base. As the supply squadron executive support officer, I had started an investigation of off-base housing discrimination allegations that were brought to my attention by Black members of our squadron. At the time, former defense secretary McNamara's executive decree was still in force forbidding housing discrimination within a five-mile radius of any military installation. England AFB had barracks for single enlisted men, and fairly nice individual housing for upper-rank married officers. Everyone else had to live off base, as was my case, though it was also my preference.

Several Black enlisted members with families described for me their deplorable living conditions and the unavailability to them of decent, affordable housing in the area. I investigated and discovered, for example, two families living in unheated and uninsulated shacks less than five miles from base, each with an outhouse, but both sharing only one cold-water spigot at the edge of the dirt road in front of their shacks. There was no indoor plumbing whatsoever.

The base housing office, whose job it was to investigate these kinds of complaints, had a reputation of being unresponsive to Black housing concerns. I decided to do some initial probing and selected one of the Black airmen to do a phone survey with me. We each separately made appointments by telephone to look at the same advertised rental units on the same day, then compared notes. The Black airman was turned down at all but one of the units. I was accepted at all of the same units, except for one, but that was because it had been rented just before I got to the place.

The airmen were right: there was blatant housing discrimination off base. This was not a surprise. But I didn't feel that I would be the best advocate given my reputation on base. I had heard that there was a Catholic chaplain on base who was very empathetic to enlisted men's concerns, especially minority ones, and I decided to talk with him. If he was sympathetic, and prepared to be an advocate, I would turn the facts over to him. The chaplain seemed very sympathetic and open to pursuing the case, so I gave him the information from our housing survey.

I was therefore quite surprised to be ordered to the wing commander's office once again, this time charged with violating the base chain of command to the detriment of the Air Force. At first I once again didn't know what I had done. But soon it became clear that the chaplain had reported our discussion on housing discrimination, and the perception of a do-nothing housing office, to the wing commander. Boy, did I feel betrayed. I was told that the housing office, which was known for its pattern of ignoring McNamara's no-discrimination decree, would take care of the matter! I was not surprised when the matter got buried at the housing office. Morale among Black airmen in our squadron continued to deteriorate.

Exercising My Rights

A third charge was again race-based. During the 1969 Christmas season, the largest department store in Alexandria was picketed by local Blacks who demanded fair employment opportunities. The store's clientele was heavily

Black, but had no Black sales employees. Some of the clients in my wife's local legal aid office were part of the picket. One rainy December Saturday, my wife and I chose to take umbrellas and sandwiches to the picketers. We delivered them to the folks at the picket line in front of the store and remained with them for perhaps an hour or two.

The very next Monday, I was again ordered into the wing commander's office. I remember a JAG lawyer being present. The wing commander asked whether I had advocated civil disobedience at any time since I had been in Louisiana. I said that although I believed civil disobedience was sometimes necessary to effect social change, I had not had any reason to participate in such action up to that point.

I had actually participated in a couple of antiwar rallies on weekends, but they had all been legal and had not used civil disobedience as a tactic. Eventually, I figured out he had called me in about the workers' picket. I told him that while I had attended the picket, I had not used civil disobedience since I only walked in circles in front of the store. Surely, the First Amendment allowed me to do that. I suggested he might want to discuss this matter with my lawyer wife. Again, the matter was dropped.

By this time, I had begun to suspect that these visits to the wing commander might not have much to do with the so-called charges against me, but with the antiwar expressions with which I was involved off base, and my reputation of questioning the war that preceded my being assigned there. At one meeting, I recall he smiled at me and asked if he had to worry that I might plant a bomb on the base. I could tell that he wasn't serious, but simply threw the question out to make a point. I, in turn, smiled as I shook my head.

I am sure this wing commander must have thought I was a spoiled fruitcake. He had started his career as a pilot during World War II and had been shot down in France in December 1943 after flying a "successful" bombing mission over Germany. He was a prisoner of war in the German Stalag Luft 1 Prison Camp until liberation in May 1945. His subsequent career had mostly been in unconventional aerial warfare and he had been vice-commander of a special clandestine aerial operations unit in Southeast Asia before coming to England AFB. Obviously, he had invested many years of his life in the culture of war and couldn't relate to anyone who questioned that culture. In the language of the '60s, he just "didn't get it."

Working for Peace

I kept my sanity during this year thanks in part to the community I found at the tiny Alexandria, Louisiana, Unitarian Fellowship. I had first met my wife in 1968 at a Unitarian lecture in Washington, D.C., and we both joined the

Fellowship. I thrived in this new atmosphere, among people openly committed to justice and the search for deeper meaning in life. This small group of people, who met Sundays without any minister or paid staff, provided me with a real home for my new heart and political perspective. At this stage of my life, it was important for me to be gathering with people who were politically aware, who supported critical thinking, and who supported one another in questioning authority. I became very involved, and soon began helping with the recruitment of interesting speakers for our Fellowship's Sunday services.

Virtually everyone in this small group of twenty to twenty-five people was either vigorously against the war or open to criticism about it. Most also had been working for racial harmony and integration during their adult lives. During the year I was a Fellowship member, our little group helped initiate the Rapides Parish Inter-Racial Coalition in concert with a number of other local Black and White leaders and concerned citizens. Our building became the regular meeting place for a series of discussions focusing on school desegregation, often generating intense debate. The first major court-ordered desegregation plan had just been legally imposed in the parish.

We also lived out the reality of racial integration in a way that sometimes shocked the locals in surrounding central Louisiana towns. Even in 1969, Blacks and Whites in Louisiana did not usually spend time together outside of work. We picnicked together, shared other social times, and rode to and from meetings together. These seemingly simple activities were interesting enough to get us regular coverage in the local newspaper, *The Alexandria Daily Town Talk*.

While I was never really worried about myself, there were members of the Fellowship who were threatened for participating in this coalition. During evening meetings at our small Fellowship building we posted people outside to stand guard in case of trouble. When we drove people home from the meetings, we traveled in small caravans. My experiences with the U.U. Fellowship and the Inter-Racial Coalition helped me stand firm for equal rights for my fellow airmen when I came back to base on weekdays.

One initiative I helped spearhead during that year involved the remote, sprawling, Angola Penitentiary complex. Angola was created on the site of three old cotton plantations that had been worked by slaves from Angola, Africa. In an irony not lost on Black people, three-quarters of today's five thousand inmates on this former plantation site are Black.

I had heard about Angola during my coursework on corrections systems: *Collier's Weekly* had headlined Angola "America's Worst Prison" in 1952, after thirty-one prisoners slit their Achilles tendons to protest conditions.[72] What I hadn't realized was that a large number of families were unable to visit their loved ones locked up in Angola. This was because of the location of the prison itself. Nicknamed "The Farm," Angola was situated on a bend of the east bank of the Mississippi River, just below the Mississippi state line. The site was very difficult to reach: from Baton Rouge, you had to drive seventy-five miles up Highway 66. From Alexandria, it was seventy miles to the southeast, plus required crossing the Mississippi River by ferry. No public transportation reached the site, and many of the families of inmates did not have cars or could not afford the ferry fees.

It has been reported that 85 percent of the prisoners sentenced to Angola are lifers and will never leave.[73] Thus many poor Angola prisoners were virtually exiled from their families—often never able to see or touch them again. After learning this, our Fellowship chartered a bus to take relatives on weekend visits to Angola. Many years later, Sister Helen Prejean would make Angola Penitentiary and its death row famous with her book, *Dead Man Walking*, which became a Hollywood movie by the same name.

The Fellowship also helped me give voice to my antiwar feelings. Like many vets, I had repressed the most horrendous episodes of my Viet Nam experience: I would not remember seeing Mai Ly's face for many more years. Each entanglement with base bureaucracy, however, reminded me of the stupidity of the war we were fighting, and the carnage we were creating. With support from the Fellowship, I was able to present a series of five classes on Sunday afternoons on the history of French, then U.S. aggression in Viet Nam.

I based this lecture series on the books I had read at Binh Thuy base library and since returning home—most importantly Kahin's and Lewis's *The United States in Vietnam*.[74] My theme was that the French and U.S. wars in Viet Nam—both part of the long history of Western colonialism—had egregiously contravened the wishes of the majority of the Vietnamese people. As such, they were acts of naked aggression prohibited by the Nuremberg Principles and international law. I was happy to learn later that a plainclothes representative from the Air Force Office of Special Investigations (OSI) sat in on some or all of the five classes and reported on them to the England AFB wing commander.

More than twenty years later, I inadvertently learned that an uncle of mine had been interviewed in 1969 by the FBI in the government's apparent efforts to learn more of my background, though the family never wanted to talk about it, and didn't. The repeated office visits to the wing commander were surely only one way the Air Force tried to keep an eye on me.

History Lessons

When I was called into the wing commander's office a fourth time, it was in regard to the Fellowship lecture series. Very concerned that I was telling lies about U.S. policy and the war, he admonished me that my behavior was unbecoming an officer. I was furious and conveyed to him that it was my First Amendment right to express my views out of uniform and off duty. I demanded that he meet with my wife and perhaps an ACLU attorney. He backed off.

The fifth and final time I saw the wing commander, I was with my own commander, Major Deng, chief of the supply squadron. A native Chinese man born in Formosa (Taiwan), he had been a pilot in Viet Nam and was now stuck in Louisiana as a squadron commander with his Chinese wife and two adorable children. I know that he was irritated with me because of my increasingly contemptuous attitude about the military, but he always treated me with respect.

We were visiting the wing commander because of what I thought to be a truly ridiculous situation relating to the annual inspector general (IG) review of the base's compliance with Tactical Air Command regulations about everything from the appearance of lawns and buildings to flightline procedures. Commander Deng, a career officer, was about to receive poor marks from the inspector general because the supply squadron had flunked a building inspection. The squadron failed its inspection, apparently, because there were girlie pictures on the walls of the enlisted men's barracks. The wing commander had gotten involved because his base would get a recorded infraction due to any subordinate unit's black mark.

I was the fall guy in this situation. I had not directly ordered removal of the pictures. Back then, few women served with enlisted men, so there were no sex discrimination issues to worry about in the barracks, and I felt perhaps the pictures helped the men's morale. I had told the major that I would not give a direct order to the men to take down the pictures, though I would brief them of the inspector's wishes, and post his order on the barrack's bulletin board. After I did this, the majority took down the pictures, but a few did not.

Well, as you can imagine, the inspector was very upset when the next day he discovered a few pictures still on the wall. My boss and I were brought into the wing commander's office for a scolding. Though I was not given the floor during the formal IG briefing, I did make my case during a break—I told the wing commander I thought the directive was unfair to the enlisted men since the plush officer housing on the base was not equally inspected. I will never forget the wing commander's response to me. He said that the right of officers to not have their personal living quarters inspected was a matter of RHIP—Rank Has Its Privileges. Case closed!

Here was a fine example of elitism in action. Hierarchy and class, married to White privilege, were the hallmarks of military society. Yet we were at war theoretically to protect equal justice for all and democracy. Increasingly, I understood these words of equality to be a social myth covering over the secret that we live in a society committed to exploitation enabling immense profits for a small number of people. We had not been fighting for freedom in Viet Nam, or equality, but for the continuation of U.S.-based material prosperity that would benefit only a few at the expense of many.

The war came home to me and the heart of our society in a more profound way on May 4, 1970. I was driving my car to the base gym to play basketball when I heard on the radio that the Ohio National Guard had shot a group of students at Kent State University who had been demonstrating against Nixon's April 29 invasion of Cambodia. Four students were murdered and nine others wounded. Shocked and grief-stricken, I pulled off the road. I couldn't drive. I couldn't fucking believe it.

Free at Last!

Finally, August 1970 arrived. I had been counting the days until I could leave the military, X-ing off the squares on my calendar, worried that something unexpected might interfere with my getting out. According to my papers, my final day was to be September 13, but the Air Force was gracious enough to grant me a fourteen-day early out so I could return to law school. And so, I was honorably separated from active duty on August 30, 1970, as a captain.

It wasn't until the fall of 1972, however, that I was finally clear of any military jurisdiction. I had signed up for a six-year commitment, four years active and two years in the inactive reserves. When I received my final honorable discharge, I breathed a sigh of relief. I was finally free after six years of being employed by an institution involved in chronic lies, systematic brutality, infuriating hierarchy, and the most pathological version of patriotism imaginable.

Despite the threats and admonishments directed against me during my time in the military, I was never convicted of any military crime and never subjected to a court-martial. Despite having had official charges read against me in August 1969, no record of such charges can be found in my official Air Force records. There is no record of the Air Force offering me legal counsel; there is no record of lawyers reading my rights. There is no record of being placed on the Officer Control Roster. There is nothing! These omissions only make me believe even more strongly that the office visits I was ordered to make to the wing commander in Louisiana were designed mainly to keep me quiet. They wanted to get rid of me as quickly and quietly as possible.

Much of what I learned during my military service in Viet Nam, and then in Louisiana, I realized only later. What I discovered at the time, for the first time in my life, was that I was a reasonably intelligent, thinking individual. I was becoming aware of social justice but I knew virtually nothing about history. It is a mystery to me why it took going to war and walking into the belly of the beast to realize the power of history.

Growing up in "America" conditions us to believe in our exceptionalism. We are insulated psychologically and intellectually from the rest of the world, just as the oceans on our east and west have insulated our country geographically. In the United States, going along with the mythology of the "American Way Of Life" has, at least until recently, generally guaranteed a comfortable material life.

There's a reason for our comfort, however, that becomes visible when we are able to look beyond the illusions of the myth. As early as 1948, George Kennan, head of the State Department's Policy Planning Committee, authored the following, brutally honest internal document:

> We have about 50 percent of the world's wealth, but only 6.3 percent of its population. . . . Our real task . . . is to devise a pattern of relationships which will permit us to maintain this position of disparity without positive detriment to our national security. . . . We should cease to talk about . . . unreal objectives such as human rights, the raising of the living standards, and democratization . . . [W]e are going to have to deal in straight power concepts.[75]

Being in Viet Nam had revealed to me the reality of this "position of disparity." I was staggered at the amount of destruction my country was unleashing with its expensive, sophisticated technology, in a country with an ancient history and comparatively simple way of life. Disparities between rich and poor have only continued to grow. Today, the United States comprises only 4.6 percent of the world's population while it continues to consume grotesquely disproportionate percentages of the globe's resources. In 2006, a study by the United Nations University found that the richest 10 percent accounted for 85 percent of the world's total wealth.[76] One recent report concluded that the average rates at which people in the "First World" consume resources like oil and metals and produce wastes such as greenhouse emissions is thirty-two times higher than in the "Third World."[77]

No matter how you cut it, the disparities in wealth and income are obscene, a morally untenable reality that is totally unsustainable. Even when I was still in Viet Nam, I wondered what this inequality would mean for our world. Others, apparently, had the same question. Though I wasn't aware of it at the time, the comprehensive study, *The Limits to Growth*, conducted at MIT from 1970 to 1972, reported that the growing human footprint on our earth— dependent upon the oil-based technologies we were so proud of—was exceeding the carrying capacity of the planet and, within our lifetimes, would begin to have a significant negative impact on both human societies and the earth itself.

As it turned out, 1968 was the peak year for quality of life in the United States.[78] Ever since, pollution, depletion of natural resources, and growing inequality between rich and poor have led to a deterioration of quality of life for ordinary people in the United States.

The earth has available only 1.8 global hectares per person of biocapacity (ecological footprint) to satisfy living needs for housing, clothing, food, transportation, etc. The average person in low-income countries uses 0.8 hectare, in middle-income countries, 1.9 hectares, or slightly above what is possible, and high-income persons, 6.4 hectares, or already three-and-a-half times what the earth can provide. But in the United States today, the average is 9.6 hectares per person, which is twelve times that of the consumption of an average person in low-income countries.[79]

Noam Chomsky has described how we are able to pull this off, echoing historian William Appleman Williams's earlier analysis in his astute study, *The Tragedy of American Diplomacy*.[80] Chomsky describes our material prosperity as being the result of honoring "The Fifth Freedom," the freedom to rob, pillage, and murder others to feed our insatiable consumptive lifestyle.[81] We did not invade Viet Nam to help the Vietnamese. We invaded to eliminate a dangerous example of an independence movement that, if successful, could pose a serious threat to the U.S. and corporations' nearly unlimited, "free" access to the rich resources of the rest of the world.

We invaded Viet Nam on the claim that the Vietnamese (and the rest of the world) were threatened by an unyielding Soviet Union that would impose its communist vision upon the rest of us. What I was to discover was that the American Way Of Life was at least as unyielding and imperial.

Years later, President George H.W. Bush said, at the 1992 Rio de Janeiro summit, "The American Way Of Life is not negotiable." Presidents before and since have agreed. In a report sent by the U.S. National Security Council to President Harry Truman in 1950, report author Paul Nitze asserted the unique right and responsibility of the United States to impose its "order among nations" so that "our free society can flourish." The report warned that not holding to this standard would have a "drastic effect on our belief in ourselves *and our way of life*" [emphasis added].[82] How ironic that it has been the United States, rather than the Soviet Union, that has succeeded in imposing its will globally and monolithically in order to ensure the fulfillment of the *American* Way Of Life.

I did not know any of this back in the 1960s. U.S. history was taught to me as a narrative of democracy and freedom, not as a story of exploitation dating back to our genocide of the "Indians." Like so many others, when I got to Viet Nam I lacked any critical frame of reference with which to assess the veracity or propriety of contemporary rhetoric and policies. In *Nineteen Eighty-Four* (1949) George Orwell prophesied how democratic governments could easily become totalitarian by using language to destroy the past, i.e., eradicating memory in order to rewrite history and therefore control the present and future such that "war is peace."[83] Gore Vidal has called us the "United States of Amnesia."[84] As I've studied the U.S. role in Viet Nam and elsewhere, I've come to understand that our country is AWOL from the rest of the world—Absent Without Official Leave from Planet Earth. We pursue our American Way Of Life without understanding that this way of life destroys other people, destroys the ecosystem and will soon destroy ourselves.

Being addicted to the American Way Of Life requires chronic denial of its dependency upon massive exploitation and waste. After my experience in Viet Nam, however, I could no longer remain in denial. Once I woke up to the catastrophic consequences of my ignorance, little could put me back to sleep.

PART III

The Criminal Injustice System

CHAPTER 10

No, Justice

One week after leaving the Air Force, I was back in Washington, D.C., attending law school. Like many vets, I wanted to put Viet Nam out of my mind. I was so overwhelmed with anger every time I thought about the war that it seemed easier not to think about it at all.

Putting aside the war seemed possible, back then. Like many people who suffer from post-traumatic stress disorder, I actually had forgotten the most traumatic incidents that had happened to me. I remembered the anxiety and fear when I heard the incoming mortar warnings, and I remembered very clearly my reports about the bombings—I remembered the research I had done. But I didn't retain any memory of Mai Ly's eyes or seeing the bloody, gashed water buffalo or the villagers' strewn bodies. I didn't remember the look on the face of the old man who ran from the bombing of the village across the Bassac River north of Can Tho.

In D.C., my wife Julie found a terrific job as assistant general counsel for the U.S. Bureau of Prisons and we bought a house in the quaint Georgetown section of Washington. I planned to settle down and resume the life I had left before the war.

I was surprised at how much life had changed while I was in the Air Force. When I had last been a full-time law student at American University in 1966, male students had been required to wear a coat and tie to class. On my return just four years later, men and women both were wearing beads, sandals and jeans to class. A lot of the guys had beards and long hair. In the military, I had been the "long-haired guy," but in civilian life, with my near-crew cut and simple clothes, I looked pretty conservative.

Those last two years in law school were a difficult time for me. In many ways, it was important for me to return to my "career" and to civilian life. I wanted the normalcy I had lost in Viet Nam. At the same time, ideologically, I had gotten a lot more radical in my thinking. I was passionately antiwar, and had begun to question many aspects of American society. I had one leg in the past and one leg in the future.

Not Ready for Revolution

A few of the other law students were also Viet Nam veterans. Like me, they didn't want to discuss the war in any detail, but we spent time together between classes, even though they were generally some three or four years younger than me. We shared a passion for change, and we talked a lot about the need for revolution. One guy was going to meetings of the Weather Underground and I accompanied him one evening.

The Weather Underground people were very vibrant and passionately antiwar, but their reliance on violence as a tool for change turned me off. Still, they possessed a tremendous commitment to end human suffering at the hands of patriarchal structures that few others could match. I tried the Communist Party, too, but when I went to their meeting, it was so rigid and fundamentalist I felt like I was back in a Baptist church. My wife and I went to the Unitarian church in Washington, D.C., where I found wonderful people who opposed the war, but they didn't have the intensity I craved. I was having difficulty finding a group I was comfortable with that shared my rage and passion.

Looking back, I regret not having been active with Vietnam Veterans Against the War (VVAW). I still had a difficult time thinking of myself as a vet because I was not a grunt, and I thought only grunts were legitimate vets. I hadn't experienced their hell. I also was trying my best to put Viet Nam behind me.

That said, one of the most vivid memories I have of those years was six days in April 1971, when over a thousand Viet Nam vets gathered on the Washington Mall to protest the war. This action was a follow-up to the January 31 to February 2 Winter Soldier Investigation (WSI) hearings in Detroit, Michigan, convened and coordinated by the VVAW. At the hearings, 117 veterans testified about their war crimes, with the hope that their testimony would educate U.S. citizens about the horrors of war in general, and the crimes committed during this war in particular.[85] Even as the veterans publicly confessed their war crimes—for healing as much as anything—they were learning that VVAW had been monitored by the FBI since their formation in 1967.[86]

The April action in Washington, D.C., was called "Dewey Canyon III," a "limited incursion into the country of Congress," after "Dewey Canyon I," the code name for the U.S.-directed invasion of Laos that took place from January 22 to March 18, 1969 despite congressional prohibitions. The day I arrived in Viet Nam, March 8, 1969, was reportedly the day the U.S. Marines joined the South Vietnamese in the Laos military operation.

The second invasion of Laos from January 29 to April 6, 1971, named "Dewey Canyon II," also saw the U.S. 9th Marines supporting South Vietnamese troops. In that battle, the South Vietnamese lost half their forces while the U.S. suffered more than 1,400 casualties, lost 108 helicopters with another 600 damaged, and had seven fixed-wing aircraft shot down.[87] The "Dewey Canyon III" protests focused on the illegality of the U.S. actions in Laos, Cambodia, and Viet Nam itself.

When the "Dewey Canyon III" antiwar action started, I walked over to the Washington Mall from my nearby Public Defender Service office to check it out. I ended up spending my lunch hour hanging out there. After a day or two of that, I brought my fatigues to my job (I was working while in law school), and changed clothes after work to spend the night with the veterans—there was a court battle around whether they were allowed to sleep on the Mall at night and I wanted to support them and be part of the whole thing. I wasn't an organizer, I wasn't active with any VVAW group, and I didn't want to tell anyone I had been an officer or what my role had been in Viet Nam. But for the very first time, my feelings and views were being validated by others who understood what war was really about.

It was during "Dewey Canyon III" that John Kerry gave his famous speech, "How do you ask a man to be the last man to die for a mistake?" to the Senate Foreign Relations Committee. I stood near the door of the packed hearing room at the Capitol to listen. Tears ran down my cheeks as Kerry testified.

Perhaps the most moving moment for me, though, came on the last day of that protest, Friday, April 23, 1971. I watched as, one by one, nearly a thousand vets stepped up to a microphone near the chickenwire fence the police had hastily erected on the west side of the U.S. Capitol building. Veterans made brief statements and then threw their war medals over the fence toward the steps of Congress. Kerry was among them. I remember one vet saying, "These medals are drenched in the blood of the innocent." The war was still on, and here were hundreds of vets, each saying, in his own way, "Fuck this war." Again, I was moved to tears. I felt so validated.

The following Monday freshman congressman Ron Dellums (D-CA) conducted four days of "Ad Hoc Hearings on Command Responsibility on War Crimes in Vietnam" at which twenty-four Viet Nam veterans testified, including five West Point officers and a civilian witness to the secret, systematic U.S. bombings that annihilated ancient inhabited cultures in Laos.[88]

The intensity of the antiwar protests continued through that spring. After the Dellums hearings, large May Day demonstrations blocked streets and intersections in Washington, D.C. More than thirteen thousand persons were arrested, one of the largest number in U.S. history for a protest event. Protesters overwhelmed the five-thousand D.C. police force, leading the Justice Department to justify using U.S. Army and National Guard troops under a new made-up doctrine called "qualified martial law."[89]

I was not personally involved in these activities, but I was intimately aware of them because my wife Julie, as assistant legal counsel for the Federal Bureau of Prisons, was dispatched to be the overseeing warden at an emergency overflow detention center in Virginia. Julie's two youngest sisters had come to Washington to be part of the protests and had stayed at our house. They described how, on Sunday, May 2, as they peacefully gathered with thousands of other protesters along the Potomac River, the police maliciously attacked them in phalanx formations, beating them. During the next day, Monday, a workday, each was arrested while blocking intersections and taken to separate detention facilities. One sister was sent to RFK Stadium in Washington, and the other was transported to the facility in Virginia, where my wife got to witness her own sister being brought through intake in handcuffs.

Several days later, Julie was chastised by her siblings for being complicit in the war machine. Complicity, I thought. Yes, how easy it is to be complicit to "maintain order" while national policies commit mass murder and mayhem on an hourly basis, causing egregious disorder and destruction elsewhere. I knew that Vietnamese were being murdered every day. The statistic I learned later: more than eighty-six Southeast Asians were being murdered every hour of every day that the war dragged on.[90] Yet, I myself had not participated in the May Day protests. I had not yet walked very far on my journey.

Many years later, in the 1980s, I became acquainted with antiwar veterans who had been active in VVAW during those tumultuous times. One of those was David Cline. Dave had a *psychic* experience similar to the one I had in Viet Nam. After Dave was shot and injured by an NLF soldier, he killed that soldier. Then he realized they were the same. David Zeiger, producer and director of the documentary film *Sir! No Sir!*, about GI resistance during the Viet Nam War, captures what Dave Cline felt in words that ring true for me as well:

> Then it hit him that there was no real difference between the two of them. Finally, the epiphany: It was the NLF soldier who was fighting for a just cause, while Dave and his comrades were fighting for a lie. In typical Dave Cline fashion he concluded in 1970, "I had to kill a revolutionary to become a revolutionary."[91]

Dave Cline served several terms as national president of Veterans For Peace. He was able to come back to the United States and become active right away, organizing soldiers against the war. For me, though, it took longer. Dave's working-class childhood apparently had led him to distrust authority early on, whereas the American way had really looked good to me right through college.

I had always been proud of being a good ol' all-American boy, and it took me many years to reconcile who I had become with who I had planned on being.

I remember one particular day when I was a kid and my brother Dwight and I were hitting balls on a baseball field. One of us would hit, and the other shag down the fly balls. After a couple of hours, as the sun was setting, a wonderful feeling came over me. It was just a perfect day, a magical moment, and I got goosebumps just thinking about how perfect it all was. I turned to my brother and said, "Isn't it fantastic that we live in America?" At that moment, the American Way Of Life embodied all that was good and right and true. My brother looked at me with surprise at my sentimentality.

Who wants to give up that myth? It's like a drug. After Viet Nam shocked me awake, it would take more than a decade of personal experiences dealing with the U.S. injustice system—a type of "rehab"—before I could accept the truth and put the myth aside.

Public Defender

Meanwhile, I struggled with my law school classes. The problem wasn't the work itself; I just wasn't very motivated, especially with the excitement of antiwar protests happening all around me. I did not want to quit, however. It was important to me to be done with military life and prepare for a new civilian life and career.

I turned to the professor who had inspired me to combine penal and criminal law in a joint master-law degree program. He had helped me get my internship at the Washington, D.C., jail. He again suggested I do hands-on work while finishing law school. Fortunately I was able to acquire a job as a full-time caseworker with the D.C. Public Defender Service. That work entailed interviewing criminal defendants in order to develop personalized alternatives to prison, called treatment plans, which the pubic defender would present to the judge at sentencing.

Many of the clients were heroin addicts, some of them Viet Nam vets. I would meet with each of them, and attempt to visit their places of residence if they were free pending trial. If they were in jail, unable to post bond, I visited them there. I would then prepare a written report outlining what I believed was an appropriate plan to help that person live his life while reducing his chance of future encounters with the criminal system. I would suggest methadone clinics, schooling, health care, and other interventions. I enjoyed this work, which was very different from dealing directly with the court system and its bureaucracy.

So for the years 1970 to 1972, I went to law school part-time on the GI Bill while seeking to put theory into practice by getting the criminal justice system to personally address the lives of the mostly poor and Black people revolving through its doors. Before I completed my final semester of law school, long-time friends from Chautauqua County, New York, visited me in Washington to ask if I would be the Democratic candidate for sheriff in the fall elections, using my military background, my law degree, and my background in corrections. At first the idea sounded like a joke, but after a couple of weeks I began to think perhaps it would be a worthwhile experience. My candidacy was short-lived, however, because I was still registered as a Republican, and the old guard of the Democratic Party refused to endorse me.[92]

I resigned from my Public Defender Service job after graduating from law school in May 1972 in order to prepare full-time for the bar exam. I was pleasantly surprised to learn in December that I had successfully passed the exam. Life looked good—until I heard, less than a week later, that Nixon had ordered intensive "Christmas bombings" over the densely populated areas between Hanoi and Haiphong. It had been hard for Julie and I to accept that Nixon had won the presidential election, and now our worst fears about him were coming true. I couldn't enjoy the holidays knowing the United States was bombing Vietnamese villagers during that time.

I was formally admitted to the District of Columbia Bar on January 26, 1973. A day later, the Paris Peace Accords were signed by the U.S. and North Viet Nam, implementing an immediate cease-fire and, in effect, preparing for an end to the Viet Nam War. I was thrilled! But I was soon shocked and depressed to learn that President Nixon reneged on a provision to provide more than $4 billion in reconstruction aid to Viet Nam, using millionaire Ross Perot's campaign to link the issue of MIAs that existed in all wars, with POWs in this particular war. In other words, the claim was that the North Vietnamese were intentionally withholding a certain number of U.S. prisoners following the signing of the Accords. Thus, no reconstruction aid to Viet Nam would be provided. Furthermore, if some prisoners had not yet been released, withholding the promised aid was likely to ensure they would not be released until the aid was released. Nobody in U.S. circles was at all concerned about the two to three hundred thousand Vietnamese missing in action. And today the privately designed black and while POW flags fly on buildings around the country reminding the public that the Vietnamese remain our enemy.

I began my law career by taking a couple of indigent federal criminal cases in Washington. Working as a kind of independent contractor for the government, I was to be paid by submitting vouchers to the federal court for my work preparing a defense, both research and court time. I'm afraid my career as a lawyer was very short-lived, however.

The very first time I went to court on behalf of a client, I was stunned to realize that I was unable or unwilling to conform to the protocols of courtroom respect. I had a hard time rising when the judge came in. It was the same feeling I had had when I was asked to plunge the bayonet into the dummy. I knew I was supposed to stand up for the judge when the bailiff issued the order to rise; I understood that I would have to rise for the judge regularly in order to pursue my criminal law career; but I just couldn't bring my legs to unfold and rise.

We had killed perhaps six million people, most of them civilians, in Viet Nam, Laos, and Cambodia, but none of the policymakers who planned and directed that systematic mass killing were being held to account. Our country's political leaders had committed the supreme international crime by viciously attacking without provocation the people of Southeast Asia, violating every international law by which the United States had agreed to abide, but no one was willing to prosecute these crimes.

A month after the 1971 May Day demonstrations I was able to read portions of the explosive *Pentagon Papers* as published in the *New York Times*. The *Pentagon Papers* was an extraordinary, forty-seven-volume secret history of U.S. involvement in Viet Nam from the end of World War II to spring of 1968. At the same time, I was mesmerized by a filibuster being conducted by a freshman U.S. senator from Alaska, Mike Gravel, who sought to block renewal of military conscription by reading from the floor of the Senate the complete version of the *Pentagon Papers*, subsequently published in October by Beacon Press. Thus I, along with other U.S. citizens, learned that all the claims of war critics were true after all, including the willful deception of the U.S. people. Commissioned in June 1967 by Johnson's secretary of defense, Robert McNamara, it took thirty-six analysts eighteen months to compile the nearly three thousand pages of narrative and four thousand pages of documents.

The *Pentagon Papers* revealed that U.S. politicians and policymakers cared little about the fate of the Vietnamese people; the objective had become one of simply avoiding humiliation and defeat. They also showed that we did not inadvertently slip into a war, but that it had been produced deliberately against the wishes of the Vietnamese people. Former U.S. Marine, Rand Corporation, and Defense Department official Daniel Ellsberg, one of the papers' authors who, with Tony Russo, originally leaked the *Pentagon Papers*, describes this devious history in his essay, "The Quagmire Myth and the Stalemate Machine."[93] It should be required reading for all U.S. citizens, along with the *Pentagon Papers* themselves.

Nor did the U.S. government confine its illegal acts to other countries. At home, the government suppressed any kind of critical dialogue in our society by illegally instituting monitoring measures. I had already watched military troops put down protesters, including my sisters-in-law. Later that year I would learn, with the rest of the country, about the Nixon Watergate scandal. It revealed the existence of an insidious network of domestic surveillance far beyond Nixon's July 1970 Huston Plan, an episode "of lawlessness and impropriety at the highest levels of government."[94] J. Edgar Hoover himself had warned Nixon that these actions were clearly illegal even as he was willing to participate.[95]

Eventually, I learned of the FBI's COINTELPRO programs, which had conducted more than two thousand illegal actions against U.S. citizens from 1956 to 1971; the CIA's Operation Chaos, which kept tabs on three hundred thousand U.S. citizens; the National Security Agency's thirty-year Operation SHAMROCK, which kept a massive watch list of people while analyzing 150,000 overseas telegraphic and telephone communications *per month*, and a long-standing joint FBI-military program, which conducted domestic intelligence first initiated by President Franklin Roosevelt in 1936 with broad investigative scope using the "fundamental tool" of paid informants exacting "an adverse impact on the rights of individuals."[96]

In Viet Nam, the CIA used the term "neutralize" as a polite way to describe the murder, incarceration, and torture of Vietnamese peasants. Here at home, Hoover's FBI was using the same term in reference to Martin Luther King Jr. Hoover talked about using "avenues aimed at neutralizing King as an effective Negro leader."[97] Would we stop at nothing to preserve the status quo? And now Nixon was dishonoring the legal Paris Peace Accords.

Meanwhile, I was working in a federal criminal court in Washington, D.C., supposedly upholding the law by ensuring due process for people considered serious criminal threats to our society. In actuality, these people were the same impoverished drug addicts I had met in the public defender's office. Given the crimes being committed by our country's leaders at home and abroad, the whole idea that we were dispensing justice and preserving order in the courtroom seemed farcical, and I just couldn't rise and pay my respects to that.

Building Prisons

Fortunately, I had an alternative job waiting. Again, Howard Gill, my old professor, invited me to work as a penal consultant with him in Cincinnati, Ohio, assisting an architect in planning a new regional criminal justice complex. Within two weeks, I left the idea of law practice—forever as it turned out— and became a consultant in the development of a new prison complex in southwestern Ohio.

I chose as part of my research to live for nearly three months in the then-hundred-year-old Cincinnati Workhouse to interview as many of its current prisoners as possible. When it became clear that the study was going to take at least a year, with more work likely to follow, my wife Julie gave up her job and came out to join me in Ohio. We sold our house in Georgetown and bought a new one in the university neighborhood of Cincinnati.

My work required identifying the demographic character of the existing jail population in an effort to determine how many defendants coming through the Cincinnati criminal court system really required incarceration. How many were really violent or exhibited a pattern of reckless behavior endangering the public? In essence, I was establishing a rationale for estimating the size of a prisoner population and the number of cells or dormitory rooms needed to house them. I also identified the kind of treatment staff and programs that would be important to operate a humane complex and the number of office and other spaces needed in the overall design. In general I researched anything that would help the architect develop the new complex as a progressive treatment institution.

The architect had begun with a general preconception that the complex would have approximately seven hundred beds, about the number of confinees in the two local facilities at the time the study was initiated. After developing a profile of both the convicted criminals and the pretrial defendants who had not made bail, however, I concluded that the complex only needed 300–350 beds. Many of the criminals imprisoned were there for petty, nonviolent crimes like writing bad checks, possession of small amounts of marijuana, and other victimless crimes like prostitution, and so forth. And the vast majority of pretrial defendants were there because they could not afford the excessively high bail amounts.

It did not make sense to me that the state (with money from taxpayers) would spend $40,000 per bed in construction costs, plus $5,000–10,000 per year to incarcerate each of these seven hundred prisoners, when it could spend half that amount on incarcerating violent prisoners and use the rest to create constructive rehabilitation programs. At that time there were plenty of studies revealing that locking people up generally embittered them even more. The emphasis on prison as the *primary* policy not only avoided addressing the personal and social problems leading to illegal behavior, but also completely ignored the causative *structural* problems of economic and social injustice. Incarceration, throughout its history, has tended to worsen people's behavior. Focusing social resources on appropriate education, drug rehabilitation, and job training in general enables people to become more independent and "law-abiding."

Professor Gill seemed a bit surprised at my analysis, which essentially amounted to a critique of the U.S. prison system. I sensed we were drifting apart, a feeling brought home to me one day when the subject of the Viet Nam War came up. I never brought up the topic. One day, however, Professor Gill mentioned how concerned he was that the United States had not done what was necessary to "win" the war. I was shocked. I had simply assumed that anyone who was smart and aware of the world would be against the war. Yet here he was, an adamant supporter.

These conversations with Professor Gill about the war led me to ask deeper questions than I had asked before. I had always looked up to Professor Gill as a mentor. Now I had to ask myself: Who is wise and who is not? What parts of life can people see and what parts can they not see? I had begun, intellectually, to slip out of an old comfortable place to one that was increasingly uncomfortable. What were my blind spots? How many more assumptions were there of which I was still unaware?

These kinds of questions also started seeping into my prison work. I began, in fact, to question the whole idea of prisons. How can one trust a criminal selection process in a society that chooses to lock up mostly poor people while chronic injustices permeate the entire community—in fact, the entire nation? And worse, while the most violent offenders in the prison system might have killed someone, millions were murdered by men who had involved us in the Viet Nam War—men who possessed tremendous political and economic power and operated with virtual impunity as they enforced policies for profit that systematically destroyed lives and nations while degrading our vital natural environment. How can we pretend to have a rational and just criminal system when our government itself seems neither rational nor just?

Focusing on prisons and prosecution seemed like a distraction from these bigger issues. I wondered why citizens at large, including myself, continued to legitimize with our votes, tax dollars, and silence such a fundamentally unjust system? Was it that the middle class didn't care? What kind of chronic denial conveniently allowed us to pretend some people deserved misery, while others deserved prosperity? Did we not understand that an injury to one is ultimately an injury to all? Martin Luther King Jr. had warned us that an injustice anywhere is a threat to justice everywhere. It seemed to me that materialism had become our drug, preventing us from perceiving that inattention to the health of the whole would sooner or later make *all* of us sick?

These issues were troubling me as I prepared to make a presentation at the first press conference convened for the Cincinnati prison project. One of my roles was to offer a technical justification for spending public money on the portion of the project that dealt with incarceration. I couldn't bring myself to justify the architect's notion of a 700-bed complex. My research had told me something different. Instead, I briefed the press that it would be a waste to build a 700-person jail when the community only needed a 300–350 person jail and that the money saved would be better spent on proven rehabilitation programs to enable prisoners to become "law-abiding" citizens.

Well, telling the truth publicly got me fired. I was pretty naïve to think I would keep my job after making such a public rebuke of my employer's project. As it turned out, the architect recommended one 400-bed facility, a figure closer to my earlier recommendation, but the project was never approved by the politicians.

My penal philosophy and research approach, however, had attracted the attention of some political people I had met in Ohio and I was offered an interview for assistant state corrections commissioner. My career, I fantasized, was about to take off. If I had been appointed to that position it would have provided me a high-paying, professional corrections job, and enabled my wife, who was then working for a legal aid office in Cincinnati, to settle down as a lawyer in Ohio.

However, I had become far too critical of the criminal injustice system to become a reformist prison administrator, and I was beginning to realize that I was no good at "going along to get along." I would not be able to live with myself for very long doing work that required me to take public positions that were at serious variance with my beliefs. I could not comfortably take a political position, because I wouldn't be free to address the racial and class issues that required priority attention. So, after much thought, I declined further consideration for such an appointment.

In retrospect, I see this particular phase in my journey really began when I decided not to attend Baptist seminary. I decided then that it was better to choose a course that would validate my own ideas rather than try to mold them to fit in with the fundamentalist theology of my religion. I was just beginning to understand that every aspect of our society—including our political and judicial system—had its own fixed doctrines and systemic prejudices. They all shared a fundamental belief in what I would later come to call the American Way Of Life. I would eventually come to understand that we each have a choice: to live in the system or to challenge it; to embrace the American Way Of Life, or to question it and begin crafting a radically different way. At this point in my life, however, I could not yet imagine a different path.

CHAPTER 11

A Caged Society

I was at a loss as to what to do for many months after being fired from the penal consulting position. My wife Julie was enjoying her work at the Cincinnati legal aid office, but what was my work to be?

In the spring of 1974 I learned that the Unitarian Universalist Service Committee (UUSC) in Boston was launching a national justice program. When I inquired about the position, the executive director asked me if I would be interested in co-directing the program. What a break! Again, Julie sacrificed the career she'd begun in Cincinnati and she and I moved to Boston.

Once in Boston, I was able to convince the UUSC that this national justice program would be more politically effective if it provoked a national debate about the historic idea of incarceration as the *primary* policy of "law and order." I suggested creating a National Moratorium on Prison Construction. The board of directors agreed. I also suggested that the office should be located in Washington, D.C., and again, the executive director and board agreed. So, after only a couple of months in Boston, Julie and I picked up and moved to Washington. There I was again, in the nation's capitol, the belly of the beast.

I spent the fall setting up the national office for the Moratorium. Another organization with a long history of reformist involvement in the criminal injustice system, the National Council on Crime and Delinquency, then under the leadership of Milton Rector, asked if they could directly support us since they already had adopted a position supporting a national prison moratorium. That association worked out beautifully and they provided us office space not far from Capitol Hill.

Our goal was to educate the U.S. public about the history of the criminal justice system, its truly discriminatory pattern, and the research showing that its effectiveness at protecting society was largely illusory. Part of this work was to educate Congress and to influence state and local political jurisdictions across the country about the dangers of *increased* dependence upon the use of incarceration.

We faced an uphill battle. In the previous several years, a number of revelations had indicated that a deep criminality existed at the top of the U.S. political system. The *Pentagon Papers* had exposed that the U.S. government had committed international crimes, conspiring to start and then continue the war against Viet Nam. The Nixon government's engagement in illegal domestic operations designed to silence popular dissent had also started to leak out. Yet on June 17, 1971, only four days after publication of the *Pentagon Papers*, Nixon named drug abuse "public enemy number one in the United States" and Congress seemed ready to agree. Apparently, Nixon's massive state crimes against the Constitution, against international law, against the small countries of Southeast Asia, and against the U.S. American people were not considered serious threats to our society. Drugs were.

This new war on drugs served many purposes. One, it scapegoated poor, mostly Black drug users as the U.S. enemy number one, turning public attention away from the much more significant criminals who were running the country. Second, it pumped massive amounts of cash into rural areas, as prison construction brought good jobs. Not least of all, the rhetoric of the "war on drugs" bolstered the rhetoric of the "war on Communism." As a nation, we love wars. Maybe we are addicted to the feelings we derive from *thinking* we are in control over others, as we deny our own insecurity emanating from efforts to adapt to a self-centered, *unnatural* market-driven society.

One thing was certain: the new war on drugs would push states to send more people to prison. My job was to push back.

In the Belly of the Beast

My new national position entailed extensive travel, speaking, and writing, including preparation of testimony to be presented before various state legislatures and the U.S. Congress. I loved doing the research. I also felt highly engaged speaking about prisons in the context of the criminal injustice system, and the larger context of a society that had yet to deal with its systemic pattern of class and race discriminations. It was work I could be passionate about.

Increasingly, however, I found that I spent more and more of my time in D.C., rather than organizing in the states. Being at the center of so-called power in this country was seductive. I became, essentially, a lobbyist. After awhile, competent and sympathetic staff members on the Hill began asking me to write and analyze legislation on prison and criminal justice issues to aid their efforts at influencing their political bosses.

That opened my eyes. I realized that few of the congressional staff—let alone the congresspeople they served—had the time or energy to read through the often-arcane details of the legislation they voted upon. Why should I expect any of these people to know the kinds of details about prison administration and reform that it had taken me years to learn? Congress can't possibly know what they need to know to pass the legislation that constantly comes before them. Yet they do, every day.

The way the majority of congresspeople get their jobs done is by relying upon lobbyists to "educate" them and to draft the laws for them. This system is mutually beneficial. Money from corporations and other special monied interests funds election and reelection campaigns. In return, legislators invite lobbyists from these groups to write legislation, with the result that most laws in this country are created for the benefit of those groups. The only ones who lose out are the people the laws are supposed to serve.

In the nearly four years I spent as the coordinator for the National Moratorium on Prison Construction, I was one of only three or four persons in D.C. consistently lobbying for at least a temporary suspension to prison expansion and construction. I regularly competed for senators' and representatives' attention against tens of lobbyists from the prison construction industry, as well as all the other lobbyists representing countless interests walking in and out of the offices every day.

Draft legislation is a maze, because the more complicated it gets, the easier it becomes for changes to be hidden from lawmakers, and therefore the public. Prisons would sometimes appear in plans submitted to Congress, then upon careful scrutiny they would disappear in subsequent plans, but then reappear somewhere else. It was literally a full-time job to keep tabs on what prisons the prison construction lobbyists wanted where in order to match prisoner projections that were always changing from one month to the next. But one thing was constant: there was always intense political pressure to build more and more prisons, a momentum that would not stop.

One prison, for example, was hidden in an appropriations bill funding the 1980 Winter Olympics in Lake Placid, New York. The prison construction industry, with full complicity of Congress and the U.S. Olympic Committee, inserted language in an appropriations bill funding construction of the International Olympic athlete dormitories ensuring that these dormitories would be converted to a federal prison immediately upon conclusion of the games. The Olympics, ostensibly an international symbol of peace and harmony, had morphed into a way of funding prisons to incarcerate urban Black people in a remote area hundreds of miles from their lawyers and families! It was a deceitful plan, hatched in *secrecy*, to fund the de facto exile of Blacks. We fought that for two years—and lost.

This is an example of prison Keynsianism—a government economic strategy using discretionary and discriminatory policies to provide a "product" of urban Blacks (and other minority offenders, mostly males) to be shipped long distances to be caged in White rural communities in order to provide the latter with an expanded job and tax base. For example, in far northern California, depressed, rural, mostly White Del Norte County was rescued economically when the state constructed the draconian Pelican Bay Prison near the Oregon border to house primarily minority males from Los Angeles, 750 miles away. It is now the area's largest employer.

In that intense lobbying atmosphere, I felt like I was at war again. Every day, I would strive to outthink and outmaneuver the opposition. I became increasingly aggressive, plotting how I would beat the other guys' plans. I didn't like that feeling. I had been so relieved to leave the military and its aggressive posture, and now I was once again "securing the perimeter," trying to scope out my enemy's defenses. While the cause I was fighting for this time was just, I did not want to live my life as if every task was a battle. I felt there must be a better way to achieve justice.

Lock 'em Up

It also became clear that attacking prison construction head-on was not going to work. The more effectively my office did our advocacy work, the more aggressive the opposition became in their efforts to add prisons.

When we began our prison moratorium work in 1974 there were approximately 415,000 *total* prisoners in the United States, including juveniles, incarcerated in over 5,200 jails and prisons at the local, state, and federal levels. From 1925 through 1974 the *average* per capita detention rate (PCDR) for state and federal prisoners combined had been a rather stable 107 prisoners per 100,000 residents. In 1974, however, the PCDR jumped to 195, and then just kept going, rocketing to 770 in 2005, a rate that tops all other nations. That's a fourfold increase![98] To put these numbers into more concrete terms, between 1974 and 2004, more than two new jails or prisons were added to our national cage inventory every *week*. Today, the United States has more than 8,500 penal institutions, housing somewhere between 2,200,000 and 2,300,000 prisoners on an average day.

Who were these new prisoners? It's instructive to note that between 1972, when the Bureau of Prisons, at Nixon's request, unveiled its first master plan for new prison construction, and 1977, the Bureau opened twenty-one new penal facilities capable of housing nearly six thousand additional prisoners. In that same period of time the number of *non-White* federal prisoners increased by approximately the *same* number—six thousand. In effect, the initial prison expansion was reserved exclusively for non-White prisoners.

When prisons are built, they must be filled, and it's easiest to fill them with those living in poor, minority communities. Prison-building virtually guarantees Jim Crow racism through a kind of classic double-cross. Prison construction provides jobs to mostly rural, mostly White, lower-middle-class, relatively uneducated workers, while impoverished urban communities of color are egregiously ripped apart through the forced removal of its members.

In the 1970s, at the very same time the United States was paying to add thousands of cages that would be filled mostly by Black men, its politicians simultaneously proposed a moratorium on new public housing. While prisons were adding an average of fifty thousand beds each year, we were only building eight thousand affordable housing units.[99]

Thus, our society made a cruel choice. It essentially imposed a moratorium on public housing, ostensibly to cut costs, while choosing to dramatically escalate funding to construct prisons for the same impoverished class that would have benefitted from housing. Cages instead of houses were built for poor, urban Blacks while jobs were created for poor, rural Whites. The disparity in incarceration rates between African and White Americans is dramatic in the extreme.

Shockingly, 12.8 percent of Black men in their late twenties are incarcerated and on any given day, 30 percent of Black men in their twenties are under "correctional supervision."[100] At this rate, one-third of all Black males will go to prison during their lifetimes.[101]

It is instructive to compare these numbers to those of South Africa under apartheid. In 1993, in South Africa, the incarceration rate for Black males was 851 per hundred thousand. Only ten years later, in 2004, the U.S. incarceration rate for Black males was 4,834 per thousand, or 5.7 times higher!

Perhaps as startling is the fact that, according to the Department of Justice, as of December 31, 2006, on an average day there are nearly 7.4 million U.S. Americans on probation, in jail or prison, or on parole, i.e., under local, state or federal government "correctional" supervision—3.1 percent of U.S. adult residents.[102] As reported in the *Baltimore Sun* on February 29, 2008, one of every one hundred adults now is incarcerated.

Though Jim Crow *formally* ended thanks to court decisions and a long civil rights struggle in the 1950s and '60s, its poison resumed in the '70s under the domestic wars on crime and drugs administered by the criminal injustice system. In the 1960s, the U.S. political-economic system had been threatened with real people power. Terms such as a "crisis of democracy" and "an excess of democracy" were used by elite institutions like the Trilateral Commission, as they fearfully witnessed historically passive and marginalized people such as women, youth, and minorities aggressively asserting their voices into the collective, political arena.

The domestic "wars" on crime and drugs have been the system's response to this near breakout of democracy. Aimed particularly at low income and minority youth, the wars on crime and drugs have reversed many of the gains of the 1960s, reinstating an unequal Jim Crow system, ensuring that these communities remain deprived of dignity and justice.

An Ideology of Prosperity

A war raged, throughout the 1970s, on those unlucky enough to be poor, young, Black or Native American. In addition to the declared wars on crime and drugs, these years witnessed the cruel termination of free public higher education, a move that could only have been designed to prevent the education of the working class. Governor Ronald Reagan terminated free tuition in the University of California system in 1970, and President Gerald Ford threatened in 1975 to withhold federal aid from New York City unless it eliminated its free tuition at City University, which resulted in its termination in 1976, after 129 years of not charging tuition. Thus ended the last vestiges of free public higher education in the United States.[103]

The 1970s witnessed escalating attacks on labor as well, culminating in the 1980 election of Ronald Reagan to the presidency.[104] Running on a platform of "trickle-down economics," Reagan instituted huge tax cuts for the rich while imposing draconian slashes in domestic social safety net programs. The net result was an economy that reversed the gains of the New Deal and led to dramatic increases in disparity between rich and poor.

All these rollbacks stand as examples of a pronounced chipping away at the commonwealth by the oligarchy. Ronald Reagan stated forthrightly his belief that society's main job was to ensure that the wealthy prosper, and from that all else will follow. Denying the working class access to education also denies them entry into the upper classes in a society in which success is biased toward test scores and academic degrees.

Prison construction also serves the oligarchy. Philosopher and criminologist Jeffrey Reiman, in *The Rich Get Richer and the Poor Get Prison*, argues that the "failure of the criminal justice system [to reduce crime] yields such benefits to those in positions of power that it amounts to a success."[105] Reiman presents one of the best analyses of the criminal injustice system.[106] It is not the poor who breed crime, but poverty, which is why locking up poor people is such a failure. However, by suggesting that the problem is particular people (mostly young Black men) rather than their economic condition (poverty), and by suggesting that the solution is the lockup rather than socioeconomic programs, the criminal justice system perpetuates a powerful message. It is a message—part of a larger ideology, really—that legitimates disparities of wealth and privilege while diverting public attention away from the powerful and onto the powerless. This ideology also, conveniently, provides for a profitable crime-control industrial complex, a means to silence dissidents, and allows the rich a means to escape criminal prosecution (they don't, after all, fit our profile of a "criminal").

In 1972, historian William Appleman Williams, an extraordinarily astute observer of U.S. culture, came out with a new edition of his powerful book, *The Tragedy of American Diplomacy*, which really explained what I was seeing in my work in the criminal justice system. In his book, Williams ties together U.S. foreign and domestic policy, arguing that in both arenas the United States has pursued prosperity through expansion by any means necessary. I had seen this ideology at work in Viet Nam, and I was seeing it again in the prison-industrial complex. Cheap labor meant prosperity for the rich, so the poor had to be kept in line through the criminal injustice system, and had to be kept poor via trickle-down economics. Prison-building meant prosperity, so the U.S. had to keep building prisons, even if it meant creating more criminals to fill them.

When money and profit are the motivators, there is no end to the resources the already rich will use to achieve their ends. If the goal of the United States was really to achieve a just society, with "liberty and justice for all," then oligarchy would give way to democratic principles and we would see the emergence of real people power. Because the true goal of the United States is prosperity, however, our government will do virtually anything necessary, domestically and globally, for its continued expansion, even if that means supporting racism, classism and violence. As a nation, so far, we have decided to design a caged society committed to preserving powerful plutocracy rather than creating a free egalitarian community committed to justice and mutual respect. Materialism is our religion, masked by the false ideologies of "democracy" and "Christian charity."

After studying and experiencing the real workings of the criminal justice system, suddenly my job didn't seem quite so wonderful. As I walked past the monumental stone buildings that lined the Mall in Washington on my way to work, I started to feel as if I was in imperial Rome. Of course, these fortresses of stone in this "capital of liberty" were constructed by slaves. I looked at the tourists lining the steps of the Capitol building and I thought: "Wow, this is all mythology. It's a bastion of hypocrisy." I realized that those buildings, and the political structures they represent, are all part of a lie. The representatives in those buildings were not representing the people. Rather they were conduits for capitalism, working to preserve the insatiably consumptive American Way Of Life. My growing critique of U.S. society was validated by my discovery of Thorstein Veblen's *The Theory of the Leisure Class*.[107] Veblen, an original thinker born in rural Wisconsin in 1857, coined the term "conspicuous consumption"[108] in describing the misuse of wealth and waste of resources that characterizes so much of the American Way Of Life.

All during my time in Viet Nam, I had believed that if people only knew the truth, they would stop the war. I had written to my congressmen and my senators, hoping the truth would change their minds and their votes. When I got out of the military and started my career as a law-trained prison reformer, I had the same hope: if only people knew the truth about the prison system, if only they understood how racism and classism are toxic to human culture, if only they could learn how their dollars would go further if they went to rehabilitation or new affordable housing rather than prison construction, surely people would stop building prisons. What I discovered was that no one really cared much about the truth. What they cared about was money and power.

I had tried to change the system from within and discovered that the system as it is structured and valued is the problem. Furthermore, habitual cooperation with it on the part of the vast majority of the population legitimizes it, no matter how consistently destructive the results. I regretfully submitted my resignation and left Washington.

CHAPTER 12

Back to the Land

W hile I was working at the National Moratorium on Prison Construction, I started reading widely, not just about the criminal justice system but about the larger socioeconomic context, and even further, the evolution of the human condition. I knew in my bones that something was terribly wrong with the politics, economics, religion, propaganda, and values of a society that could rationalize systematic terrorism against the people and nation of Viet Nam. Learning about the prison-industrial complex confirmed my belief that Viet Nam was not an aberration.

The next step in my self-education was to look inward. This was my society and I had been conditioned by it. Now I wanted to know why it was that I had so *easily* been part of it.

I went looking for critiques of U.S. history, of capitalism, of "democracy," and so forth, as well as for visions of radical alternatives. I read a lot of conventional political commentary, as well as Marxist analysis. Not being a scholar in any discipline, and feeling very dumbed-down after Viet Nam, I was looking for essays a layperson could understand.

Many of my peers were drawn to Marxism. I totally appreciated the Marxist critique of capitalist society, describing the manner in which the productive economic structure separates people (owners and managers) from people (the workers), thus creating and depending upon class divisions, while alienating all people from their true nature as well as from Mother Nature. Capitalism is unable to universalize justice since it knows no limits to exploitation and expansion, no matter the costs to the health of the people or the earth. Reading Marx enabled me to see that imperialism is built into the very fabric of a capitalist society.

It wasn't as easy for me to buy into long-term Marxist solutions, however. I felt uneasy when the just ends sought (classless communism) were distinctly different in nature and quality from the transitional means proposed ("dictatorship of the proletariat"/state socialism) to liberate society from the problem (the "dictatorship of the bourgeoisie"/oligarchy). The transitional means themselves *could* lead to more human suffering through totalitarian rule.

In 1975, I stumbled across the work of anarchist thinkers. There was no set ideology, but they seemed to agree on some fundamental principles—

rejection of and noncooperation with top-down authority and hierarchy, cooperation and mutual aid with peers, voluntary associations, decentralization, networks in federations, and a rejection of the idea that the end justifies the means.

There are lots of differences among people who call themselves anarchists, with distinctions reflected in various names such as anarcho-syndicalism, anarcho-communism, mutualism, Buddhist anarchism, Christian anarchism, etc. As I learned about different anarchist movements, I saw that they often argue their differences among themselves as they stave off criticism from just about everybody else. I admit I get frustrated by this kind of infighting. Nonetheless, the ideas put forward by anarchist thinkers offered me glimpses of a different vision. I was not interested in being a particular kind of anarchist, but in studying key ideas that to me promised a sustainable direction if our species was to evolve. By 1974, I felt our whole society was functioning like a bunch of lemmings running at breakneck speed over a cliff. I was not happy to continue living in a world where Western-dominated, egotistical, delusional materialism was steering us toward omnicide.

A New Consciousness

Anarchists understood that we needed to develop a new kind of consciousness, one that was cooperative rather than authoritarian, based on interconnection rather than Cartesian dualism, ecological rather than mechanical. My military experiences with rigid authority structures, especially the class division created by the strict prohibition of fraternization, felt like a toxic poison in my body. I did not think those tyrannical methods were natural to the human condition—certainly not mine—and I wanted desperately to discover another way to live.

Of course, changing collective consciousness is a tremendous challenge, partly because our current consciousness, which was developed out of the thinking of René Descartes, so strongly favors separateness, neutrality, detachment, linear images, and a mind divorced from body and nature. Indeed, David Bohm, one of the originators of quantum physics, notes that the Cartesian way of thinking has pervaded our notions of order for twenty generations. Bohm makes the startling diagnosis that thought structures themselves continue to defend the unexamined assumptions of Cartesian thinking despite the cumulative evidence revealing their fallacy. Thus, Bohm, suggests, "thought is the problem"—if we can't change our thoughts, we won't be able to change how we interact with the world.[109]

These ideas finally gave me insight into how I was able to travel thousands of miles across the world to participate in bombing innocent civilians.

I had grown up as a Cartesian thinker. I thought about the world in terms of us and them, difference rather than similarity. When I could not thrust my bayonet into the military dummy, I simply had no thought structure for understanding what my body was telling me. In fact, my brain was telling me to ignore my body—that brain was superior to body. Ironically, it was my traumatic experiences in Viet Nam that led to the liberation of my thoughts and enabled me to begin seeing different patterns, new directions.

Others in the twentieth century have been making that same kind of shift in consciousness. Relativity theory and quantum physics have demonstrated the absolute interconnectedness of everything at every moment, everywhere.[110] These new mathematical and scientific theories undermine Cartesianism, which would have us split our feelings from our thoughts. Thinkers in many disciplines are now beginning to understand that we must recover the lost dimension of feelings and learn to listen, once again, to the body's viscera, the deeper source of human and natural connection. Anthropologist Ashley Montagu and political scientist Floyd Matson call this process *minding*—the marriage of thought with feeling.[111]

Anarchists generally, though not always, have understood this interconnectedness. Too often, anarchism is portrayed as a "do what you want" political theory. That's libertarianism. Anarchists do believe that as evolutionary beings we are naturally autonomous—but they also believe we are, as part of our fundamental nature, wired into social networks. While libertarians advocate a world of one against all, anarchists understand that as socially wired beings we choose innately, individually, and autonomously, to work together for the common good. Though some anarchists believe in violence as a way of throwing off oppressive power structures, the vast majority reject it as a method, despite popular reputation to the contrary. Most anarchists trust that, in general, people will make wiser decisions when they are free to do so within the web of their local community relationships, where familiarity serves as an organic accountability mechanism.

This research into anthropology and sociology, politics and biology— our fundamental nature—led me to the writings of a drop-out Russian prince, Peter Kropotkin. After leaving the Czar's officer corps, Kropotkin became a biologist—and arguably the world's first ecologist.

In *Mutual Aid: A Factor of Evolution* (1902), one of the world's greatest treatises on ecology, Kropotkin concluded that

> Society is based in . . . the conscience—be it only at the stage of an instinct—of human solidarity. It is the unconscious recognition of the force that is borrowed by each man from the practice of mutual aid; of

the close dependency of every one's happiness upon the happiness of all; and of the sense of justice, or equity, which brings the individual to consider the rights of every other individual as equal to his own.[112]

In the practice of mutual aid, which we can retrace to the earliest beginnings of evolution, we thus find the positive and undoubted origin of our ethical conceptions; and we can affirm that in the ethical progress of man, mutual support—not mutual struggle—has had the leading part.[113]

Kropotkin was acutely aware of the web of interrelationships that make up life. We are not just an individual living among other individuals. Each of us is a member of a village, just as we are a member of a family. Even as an adult within a family, one has the freedom to act as one likes—but the social mores of the family limit us. You know, for example, that there are certain things you cannot say or you will be shunned by your family. Whether you say them or not is your choice, one you need to think about carefully. For example, even though my politics alienated me from my parents, I still worked hard to maintain a connection with them.

Gandhi once remarked, "There is enough for everyone's need, but not enough for everyone's greed." This is the concept of mutual aid. Anarchists understand that mindless consumerism quickly translates into exploitation, injustice, and inequality beyond the view of our acquisitions. The solution is to live within the natural limits of our society and our planet. I can't use more energy than I create. I can't eat more food than my neighbors and I can grow. The aim is to create a "steady-state economy" where inputs and outputs are balanced.

For the first time in my post–Viet Nam exploration, I discovered political philosophies I could get excited about. But what would I do with them? Would they remain theoretical as I continued living, business as usual, as I had been taught and knew so well, along with everyone else?

The Meaning of Local

It's one thing to read about a philosophy or way of life, and another to see it lived. I had grown up embracing the American Way Of Life, with its emphasis on consuming more and more to become materially prosperous, in perpetual competition with others.

Many commentators have noticed that the United States has become more materialistic in the past hundred years, particularly under the spell of mass media and mass marketing techniques advocated by such P.R. giants as Edward Bernays. However, as I read more deeply into U.S. history, I realized that the American Way Of Life originates to the very official founding of our country, and even earlier. Some have argued that in "America," the settling colonists were drawn from more lower-middle-class elements such that our cultural tradition grew out of a petty (lower) bourgeois psychology.[114] One study of emigrants in the 1770s from England and Scotland revealed half were indentured servants or convicts.[115] But the drive to bourgeois prosperity was in fact incorporated into our 1776 Declaration of Independence with the phrase, "life, liberty, and the pursuit of happiness," words the Founders effectively intended to allow for serious pursuit of material prosperity by and for people like them—other White men of means. It was no coincidence that the Declaration was written the same year as Scottish economist Adam Smith published *An Inquiry into the Nature and Causes of the Wealth of Nations*. Both works actively defended the emerging capitalist economics of a class-based bourgeoisie ushered in by the industrial revolution, i.e., a materialistic philosophy.[116] Out of these origins grew the concept of "American Exceptionalism," dependent upon a global market to satisfy the "American Dream" of endless prosperity.[117] In our very constitutional founding the U.S. government joined with business elites to promote oligarchic profit—creating a national bank in 1790, imposing protective tariffs to aid fledgling industries, assuring immigration to provide cheap labor, and creating a publicly funded national debt to enrich a creditor class, etc.[118] James Madison, a major architect of the Constitution, advocated an "imperial republicanism"[119] with a central government secure over all subdivisions. He declared it important to "extend the sphere" so as to "make it less probable that a majority of the whole will have a common motive to invade the rights of other citizens,"[120] while assuring "one great, respectable, and flourishing empire."[121] These policies intrinsically fostered class divisions.

As a young man, I wanted a career so that I, too, could realize material prosperity. One of the first things I did when I started making money as a commissioned officer was to buy a 1965 Corvette Sting Ray with the largest engine made (427-cubic-inch) with a hump on its hood to house the huge carburetor. When I left for Viet Nam, I believed it was just a brief side trip on my journey to the "good life"—a life of material possessions and personal comfort.

In Viet Nam, my research and my minimal personal exposure to the Vietnamese way of life helped me understand the unique strength of their village system.[122] The word "village," as used by the U.S. military to describe small population centers in Viet Nam, I found to be inaccurate. We think of a village as a small but densely populated area of several hundred or thousand people, tied together by a main street and local government center. The Vietnamese did not live that way. Instead, they lived in clusters of strongly united and related families. These familial settlements of maybe several dozen people in turn were loosely joined into hamlets. The hamlets, each composed of maybe a dozen family settlements with a total population in the low hundreds, were then loosely joined into villages. When the U.S. government spoke of villages, in Vietnamese terms, that meant a number of hamlets over a several square mile area. The bombing targets I had witnessed in April 1969 were in effect not "villages," but settlements of families.

In Viet Nam, people generally did not move very far from the community in which they were born. Unlike most U.S. Americans I knew, Vietnamese people's lives were rich in local relationships.[123] One reason the war went so badly for the United States in Viet Nam is that the Thieu government, guided by the United States, tried to incorporate those villages into a national politics. The people simply didn't want to be incorporated into a larger, remote entity. When the Diem regime and then the Thieu regime tried to enforce nationalism by dragooning locals into de facto concentration camps far from their ancestral homes, it only angered the populace and strengthened the NLF."[124]

Viet Nam showed me that people power can exist separate from state power. When I returned from Viet Nam, however, it hardly seemed possible to imagine my own country as a series of decentralized villages. The modern state, with its corporatism, mass production, and mass consumerism, really have triumphed here. U.S. Americans are famously mobile. Very few people in the United States now live in the communities where their parents and grandparents lived. Many don't even know the people living right next door to them. We spend more time indoors with our televisions and electronic gadgets than outdoors with our neighbors. We are, sadly, more likely to compete with those neighbors than try to get to know them as fellow human beings. As a general rule, the American Way Of Life is often the antithesis of the strong, local community.

Appropriate Technology

When my wife and I moved back to Washington in 1974, we chose to live in the Adams-Morgan neighborhood. In 1971, when I was a law student, we had lived in Georgetown, which was (and continues to be) a center of elite, bourgeoisie political power in D.C. Adams-Morgan, in contrast, traditionally had been a poor, lower working-class, mainly Black neighborhood, close geographically to the center of the city but politically and spiritually miles away. When we moved there, it was experiencing the first wave of gentrification, and later became a mostly White, middle-class area. Back in 1974, however, Adams-Morgan was still very racially mixed. As I walked through the neighborhood each day en route to my office at the Moratorium, I would be reminded by the people around me of the importance of remaining involved in some way in the civil rights struggle.

On my walking route, I noticed a man who had a welding shop in his garage. His face seemed familiar, and one day as I walked by, it clicked: he looked like a man I remembered from photos—one of Goldwater's speech-writers during the 1964 presidential campaign I had nominally worked on at college. But this guy had a full beard with bib overalls, so it was hard to tell, and I was hesitant to approach a stranger. One day I finally found the courage to walk up the driveway. After introducing myself, I asked, "Are you Karl Hess, the Goldwater speechwriter?" The man just laughed. Turned out he was Karl Hess, but he had come a long way since his Goldwater days. He had undergone his own radical journey in those ten years, and identified himself as an anarchist.

In addition to welding frames for solar panels and fish tanks for inner-city homes, Hess earned income from refinishing antique furniture pieces and selling them at a local flea market. Hess did all his work using relatively simple tools, because of his feelings about capitalist manufacturing. He wanted to use only tools that could be made from local resources or from low-capital manufacturing: what British economist E.F. Schumacher, the author of *Small Is Beautiful*, called "appropriate technology."[125]

Karl Hess held appropriate technology meetings every Tuesday night in his shop. I started attending, and the most interesting guests kept showing up. I met Schumacher himself there, and Mildred Loomis, the grandmother of the countercultural movement, as well as homesteaders Helen and Scott Nearing and many others in the anarchist and decentralist world. Hess introduced me to provocative books about autonomy and decentralization, including his own, *Dear America*.[126]

Spending time with Karl Hess was nourishing to my spirit. I loved the idea of using practical tools and living within one's limits. I knew that the kind of military tools we had used in Viet Nam—from the M-16 I refused to carry to B-52s to napalm to Agent Orange—were wrong for people and for the planet. Their creation seemed the product of insane minds, funded by an apathetic, complicit population living in a kind of corporate totalitarianism.

Karl Hess—and the people I met at his workshop—made me realize that I could live my life differently. I didn't have to be so complicit. I didn't have to play the Washington game.

Wally and Juanita Nelson
In many ways, living in Washington helped me along my journey because so many of the people who became important influences in my life traveled through D.C. In addition to the weekly speakers I was exposed to at Hess's

welding shop were other people different than I had known, critical thinkers with many exciting ideas: people like Alger Hiss, the former State Department official accused of being sympathetic to the Communists, whose case Nixon had used to rise to power, and Ben Bagdikian, long-time media critic who wrote a seminal work on media concentration in the U.S.[127]

One week I traveled to Connecticut for an activist's training coordinated by the War Resisters League. There I met Wally Nelson, who, with his wife Juanita, became an important part of my journey. Wally and Juanita called themselves community self-reliance decentralists. They took the idea of living within limits literally, "living simply so that others might simply live."

Wally and Juanita Nelson lived in Deerfield, Massachusetts, on a homestead owned by Quakers. They had built their simple house themselves, and dug a well, but chose to live without plumbing and electricity. They fed themselves and made what small amount of money they needed by tending a large organic garden. They generally didn't use a car, though they drove a few miles a week in their old pickup to deliver their vegetables to local restaurants and farmer's markets. When they traveled further sometimes, to do workshops, speak to groups or visit friends, they took the bus.

The Nelsons lived this way purposely because they believed the world's problems could be traced to the oil economy and the exploitive American Way Of Life that most people mindlessly followed. They believed each person had a responsibility to consume only what he or she produced in cooperation with their neighbors in a local economy. They understood that without "walking your talk" you couldn't create an antidote to the American Way Of Life.

Wally was the child of a Black Baptist minister from Arkansas, but by the time World War II rolled around he was an adherent of nonviolent revolution without allegiance to any religion or government. He chose to be a war resister in World War II, even refusing work in the alternative service camps because he did not recognize the state. As a result, he was imprisoned for three-and-a-half years during the war. Juanita had been a reporter for an Ohio newspaper and interviewed him in prison for a feature story. They became partners after his release.

Two years later, Wally was one of sixteen courageous men who participated in the very first interracial "freedom bus ride," called the "Journey of Reconciliation," through the upper South in April 1947. The ride was co-sponsored by the biracial Congress of Racial Equality (CORE) and the Fellowship of Reconciliation (FOR), and it intended to test the 1946 Supreme Court decision, *Irene Morgan v. Commonwealth of Virginia*, outlawing segregation on interstate travel. Its members soon learned that the people in the South paid no attention to the Court's decision. The riders were assaulted by a group of Whites in Chapel Hill, North Carolina, on April 13, and three of the participants served thirty-day sentences on segregated North Carolina chain gangs for sitting together at the front of the bus.

I later met six others who participated in the 1947 "Journey of Reconciliation"—Worth Randle, Ernest Bromley, Jim Peck, Igal Roodenko, Joe Felmet, and George Houser—each of whom inspired my journey in some way. These people led me to meet or read about such figures as Chicago Seven defendant and anarchist Dave Dellinger and his wife Elizabeth; social ecologist and anarchist Murray Bookchin; popular historian Howard Zinn; linguist and critic of U.S. imperialism Noam Chomsky; and historians and lawyers for the poor Staughton and Alice Lynd. Ernest Bromley and his wife Marion were among the first tax refusers I ever met.

Wally and Juanita became tax resisters in the late 1940s. They didn't believe in hierarchy or bureaucracy. They knew they could live a good life of dignity with others without relying upon external authority structures or external inputs from afar. Most people who have grown up in the American Way Of Life would look at everything Wally and Juanita gave up as a great sacrifice. But they never thought of it that way. Life gave them joy. They admired the ideas of Henry David Thoreau, especially those expressed in his 1849 essay "Civil Disobedience". Thoreau's pronouncements resonated with them, such as "All men recognize the right of revolution; that is, the right to refuse allegiance to, and resist, the government, when its tyranny or its inefficiency are great and unendurable." Students who study Thoreau in school are rarely taught that he was a tax resister. He once declared, "I simply wish to refuse allegiance to the state, to withdraw and stand aloof from it effectually." Like Thoreau, Wally and Juanita embraced this kind of thinking. They wanted to stay grounded as human beings.

Knowing people like Wally and Juanita, and other role models, has enriched my own journey. The American Way Of Life teaches us that we have to be individuals and do everything on our own and for ourselves. But the Vietnamese villagers and the people I met at Karl Hess's shop showed me that there is another way of living, a life created through relationships. Life *is* the network of our relationships! Once I realized I was not on my own, that there were others who shared the same principles, I was able to start considering a different way of life.

Dairy Farm

Throughout the 1970s, I had focused on the prison system as a way of addressing the problems I saw in U.S. society. But eventually I came to realize that addressing the criminal injustice system without looking at the whole society doesn't work. There's no way to understand the criminal injustice system without looking at the political system, the economic system, the racist, sexist, and classist nature of our entire culture, and the history of structural injustices that date from our country's origins.

Inspired by the people I met at Hess's welding shop, and people like Wally and Juanita, I began to feel a need to get away from the rat race of Washington. I wanted to become a producer, rather than a consumer.

I think Wally and Juanita's lifestyle in particular appealed to me because I grew up in an area where most kids lived on a farm. I suppose I had a certain nostalgia for farming, but what I most wanted was to engage in real, manual labor after seven years of being in my head, writing essays, doing analyses, traveling and speaking, and sitting at a desk. And, to be honest, after working four years as a lobbyist, I was fed up. I didn't want to talk to anyone. I just wanted to talk to animals, trees, and plants, and to get my hands in the soil.

Julie and I seriously started looking to purchase a farm in 1976. We decided the best place to farm would be near where I grew up in western New York State. A high school classmate was a successful dairy farmer in the area. He was willing to teach me the ropes, but we needed to get a farm near his. I started visiting him on weekends, commuting from D.C. by airplane while still working at the Moratorium. In the end, this partnership didn't work out because our politics were very different. He was into big agriculture and big yields while I was interested in working on a much smaller scale. Also, he expressed anger that the United States had not "finished the job" in Viet Nam, and that shocked me. I learned from him, but I knew I didn't want to farm with him.

Nevertheless, during that year, Julie and I took some very big steps toward leaving the city and moving permanently to the country. Julie actively began looking to join a small law firm in or near Jamestown where she could practice. When she found one, she took an apartment there temporarily. I continued to commute every weekend from Washington as we looked for farms throughout Chautauqua County.

Finally, in early 1977, we found an old dairy farm in the township of Charlotte, between Sinclairville and Cherry Creek. We called our farm "Charlotte Highlands." The farm was only twenty-five miles from my parent's house and only two miles from where my paternal grandfather's depression-era farm had been. It was about twelve miles from where my father was born. When I submitted my resignation to the Moratorium, I packed up and moved to our farm, to what I believed and hoped would finally be my permanent home.

My parents were shocked—for one, that I had left law practice completely, and now, that I planned to be a farmer. They couldn't imagine me milking cows and spreading manure. For them, that was a step backward. They had done everything as parents to help me escape rural America, and here I was going back to the life they'd fled. They were starting to realize that I was definitely on a different path, choosing a way of life much different from their own.

That said, they actually liked coming out to see me at the farm. They hadn't really been able to understand what I did at the Moratorium, and what they understood of that work they hadn't liked. At least farming was something they could understand.

I started to build a network of relationships in Sinclairville and the surrounding area that were as rich in their own way as the relationships and networks I enjoyed in Washington. Julie and I were both active in the Jamestown Unitarian Church. The elected Charlotte Town Council members asked me to be the town tax assessor and building inspector. My wife was hired as the town attorney, supplementing her regular law business. A dairy farmer named Roger was my closest neighbor. He lived four miles to the east in Cherry Creek, where he served as a town supervisor. Roger graciously agreed to mentor me the first year I was farming. He was a real right-winger, but he was also interested in small, organic farming. We got along because he was not afraid to debate our political differences. We enjoyed friendly conversations in the barn around farming, politics, tax resistance, and everything else.

Schumacher's *Small Is Beautiful* and the fascinating works of economist Leopold Kohr gave me a refreshing frame of reference with which to critique what seemed the out-of-control industrial revolution and its worship of high technology and large size.[128] Schumacher stressed "intermediate technology" of small, practical tools,[129] while Kohr emphasized "appropriate size"—small nations and small administrative/political units, what today we would call bioregions.[130]

Reading Schumacher and Kohr gave me more confidence about walking a simpler talk, about being conscious of my consumption. I was particularly swayed by Schumacher's essay, "Buddhist Economics," in which he shared Gandhi's assertion that fear dissipates when we are liberated from *attachment* to wealth.[131] Schumacher explained:

> From the point of view of Buddhist economics . . . production from *local* resources for local needs is the most rational way of economic life, while dependence on imports from afar and the consequent need to produce for export to unknown and distant peoples is highly uneconomic and justifiable only in exceptional cases and on a small scale.[132]

"The marvel of the Buddhist way of life," he wrote, "is the utter rationality of its pattern—amazingly *small* means leading to extraordinarily satisfactory results."[133]

I had been looking for a way to be more involved in the civil rights movement, to heal the inequalities I had seen around me in Adams-Morgan, in the military, and particularly in the prison system. Schumacher was telling me that if I wanted to change the system, I must start with myself. He believed that only when each of us is able to live within our own footprint will we be able to create social and economic justice.

As I began farming I realized how, in every moment, there was an opportunity to practice awareness of the task at hand. I consciously treated my cows very kindly, even hugging them each before milking. I only had a total of thirty Jersey dairy cows, and never milked more than thirteen at any one time. They grazed on pastures kept without pesticides or herbicides, producing near-organic milk. I already had a large organic garden. I strived to practice what I believed.

In the long-term, economically, I don't know if I would have been able to sustain myself on that farm. I was about thirty years too early for the "organic movement"—few consumers in the 1970s wanted to pay a premium for organic food. My goal, at the time, however, was not to make money but to refute hypocrisy and simply to live the life I believed. That is difficult to do in a capitalist society, especially if one has debt, which ironically tends to feed capitalism's need for ever more consumption and spending, and, yes, ever more debt.

Coincidentally, the year I actually started farming, 1978, was the year that humankind claimed the *entire* sustainable yield of the planet. That is, we had exhausted the planet's ability to produce more than we can consume. This means that, since 1978, whenever one person consumes more than their average share, another person goes hungry.[134]

By 1979, I was becoming what some people would call radical, but as far as I was concerned I was simply embracing ideas and principles that made eminently good sense on my personal journey. In order to reduce my dependency on and support of the oil economy, I decided to trade in my 1952 John Deere tractor for draft horses. I had an Amish friend and a non-Amish draft-horse farmer who were happy to teach me the art of draft-horse farming, and I was an eager student. I put a $300 deposit down on a $1,200 buggy from one of the three local Amish buggy factories to replace my car.

Another notion that was simmering in my mind at the time was tax refusal. After my conversations with people like Wally and Juanita Nelson, Ernest and Marion Bromley, and Karl Hess, I couldn't help but feel that paying taxes made me complicit in killing other people through our national policies of war-making.

Saying Goodbye

Finally I felt I had found my spiritual home, but, as often happens, that gain required a loss elsewhere. The last tie to my old life was my wife. Julie had faithfully moved with me to Louisiana, back to D.C., on to Cincinnati, to Boston, then back to D.C., but in each case she was moving with a man who was searching to find some kind of a job in regular society. Now, she was living with a man who wanted to get away from the American Way Of Life, become a tax refuser, and pursue an older, slower, earth-connected life. Though I think she agreed with me in many ways, and intellectually wanted to support me, it became clear over time that this new way of life just wasn't for her. Our differences had begun to manifest in constant bickering and frequent explosive arguments.

Julie and I finally separated in 1980, and in a few months began divorce proceedings. We had bought the farm with money from her salary and a loan from her parents, and I knew I couldn't afford to pay the mortgage with what I would make as a farmer, at least initially. And so, sadly, I was forced to leave this land and begin searching, again, for a place to call home. I went to the Amish buggy maker to cancel my order, sadly forfeiting my $300 deposit.

I had felt so at home on the farm, so grounded, that I had begun to tell people that I would never leave, that I would die there. I grieved for years over the loss of that land. It was the closest I'd ever come to living the life I wanted. As fate would have it, I would never farm again. I wouldn't have the money to buy another farm until much later, when the government compensated me for intentionally running me over with their munitions train. Ironically, the very act that brought me the money made farming the way I had imagined it physically impossible. It is difficult to farm as an ambulatory double-below-the-knee amputee with prostheses. I can do a lot, but for farming I would not have the leg muscles and balance necessary to do a lot of the lifting and pulling work that labor-intensive farming requires. I have learned from these experiences that life cannot be taken for granted, that it is a content-rich journey, and that I need to go with the flow as it unfolds in each moment.

For awhile, I was angry with Julie for not enthusiastically wanting to be a part of the journey I was on, but I've come to realize that you can't force people to change. Julie was very angry with me for instigating our split-up. She thought I was crazy for wanting to begin active tax resistance. Of course, her reluctance was understandable and I could sense our estrangement. If change happens, it generally takes time and progresses at its own pace. People have to discover on their own their capacity to identify and solve the issues that are inherently part of being a human being. Each of us has to find the route to our own deeper, more authentic self.

It took me a long time to realize that to live as I wanted, to be true to myself, I would have to live from my heart. I knew I wanted to change my life when I left Viet Nam, but it took me at least six years and a lot of role models to even begin considering a different way of life. And even then, my journey wasn't finished. I knew what I wanted, but when I left the farm, I tried to go back to the kind of work I had been doing at the Moratorium. I hadn't figured out that I would only be at home with myself when all the aspects of my life supported a different, more radical way of living.

CHAPTER 13

Flashback

On January 2, 1980, I sadly watched from afar as my wife drove away from the farm and out of my life. I was out in the field on my 1952 John Deere tractor, spreading manure. It seemed fitting, somehow. The life I had lived up until that point was like compost—I was no longer who I had been, but all of my experiences were important ingredients for who I was becoming.

I realized I was too depressed to stay on the farm by myself until it sold. I found a young man who wanted to rent the farm and was willing to manage my Jersey cows along with his own. Meanwhile, I moved to my brother's house in nearby Jamestown, New York. I got a temporary job with the 1980 Decennial Census while trying to figure out what to do next. I fantasized about baseball umpire school, becoming a printer, or running a natural food business, and actually applied to Amtrak to be a train engineer. I wanted to duplicate the experience I had on the farm, in terms of being in close contact with what Marxists would call the means of production. However, I was not yet ready to live like my role models, Wally and Juanita Nelson, who existed virtually outside the system.

That spring I did something I had been putting off for a while, mainly because I hadn't been able to talk about Viet Nam much up until that time. I was sensing a readiness to begin sharing some of the more uplifting moments of my wartime experience. So, one day, with no notice, I knocked on the front door of Norman Morrison's mother's house in Chautauqua, New York. Hazel Morrison, very elderly at the time, opened the door and, after I explained my purpose, graciously invited me to come in and have a seat in her small living room. Clumsily, I began telling her of the incredible dinner in Can Tho City in late May 1969 where Norman had been so totally present. I remember having a difficult time because the emotional and historical content was so heavy. I could not help crying as I described for her the reverence these Vietnamese had for Norman. Hazel at one point said, "Norman would be very proud of you." After hearing my story, she pointed to an envelope that was conspicuously sticking out of a small basket sitting on a dresser to my left. It was an old airmail letter that had been typed. The letter contained a very heartfelt condolence message from a Vietnamese government official on behalf of President Hồ Chí Minh expressing the tremendous inspiration that Norman's sacrifice held for all their people. I began crying once again, just feeling the power of Norman's act and realizing how it had affected so many in Viet Nam.

After that meeting with Mrs. Morrison, I considered again the possibility of seeking an academic teaching position. By the 1970s it seemed I was already too radical to be even a college teacher. Nevertheless, during this period I applied to more than sixty colleges and universities that had announced job openings in the field of criminology. My application clearly stated that my approach to teaching criminology/penology was to present the subject in a more complete historical, political, social, class, and racial context. Despite holding an advanced degree in the field plus considerable work experience, I received only three responses, and in only one of those was I considered among the top three candidates.

At the one university where I was in the final three, a member of the selection committee confided that my holistic approach was exactly what was needed, but she thought other committee members found it too radical. For students to understand that the system was based on a generations-old history of structural class divisions and racial injustice was not going to serve them well in getting jobs in the system. I suspect that was the primary reason for receiving such a feeble response rate, and zero offers.

I felt stuck in an awkward transitional phase between one way of life and another, and didn't know how to proceed. Then, serendipitously, I got a call from Jack Backman, Senate Chair of the Massachusetts Joint Legislative Committee on Human Services. I had met Senator Backman several years earlier at a prison conference. He tracked me down and asked if I would like to become his legislative assistant in Boston working on prison, mental health and veterans' issues. I gladly accepted his offer, solving my problem for the moment.

I began working for Backman in June of 1980. He was actually quite radical for a politician and gave me the freedom to draft legislation on any issue I thought important. I liked the work—loved working with Backman—but was back in the corrupt system I had been trying to reject.

Facing Brutality

I worked in Backman's office for a little over a year. One of my priorities was to address complaints from prisoners and their families about prison conditions and brutality. One of the first things I did was to assemble letters the senator had received from prisoners, and records of phone calls from families of prisoners, to establish some kind of pattern. I soon discovered that prison conditions far outstripped any notion of brutality most of us could imagine. I already knew that prisoners were subject to occasional beatings or denial of necessities. What I didn't know and subsequently learned, however, was that along with physical assaults and arbitrary discipline, prison guards were subjecting prisoners to destruction of property, including blankets and reading glasses; medical negligence, including withholding insulin from diabetics; arbitrary and illegal denial of prisoners' access to courts, attorneys, and legal materials; intimidating behavior including ripping prisoners' clothes from their body; and, most brutal, unnecessary and assaultive rectal searches.

I believed that the frequency and manner in which rectal searches were conducted constituted torture, especially at Walpole State Prison. The complaints about rectal searches from the maximum-security sections of the prison were chronic, and daily. Every time a prisoner would leave his cell to see a lawyer, go to the law library, see a visitor (his wife and child sitting behind a solid window), or see a doctor (if he was lucky enough), he was subject to a rectal search upon leaving the cell, and another one upon returning to the cell.

Once subjected to a search, any resistance, such as slight body tensing or verbal grumbling, often meant being thrown to the floor by the guards who then forcibly spread the buttocks while restraining the prisoner's body flat on his stomach. Articulate prisoners who were known to file legal briefs were subjected to some of the worst treatment. It was not unheard of for a guard to handcuff a supposed recalcitrant prisoner to the bars with feet dangling above the floor, mace him, rip his clothes off, spread his buttocks forcibly apart, and film his anus while another guard "searched" it—essentially, an act of sodomy.

Rectal searches were not the worst guards would do. Prisoners often had boiling coffee or scalding water poured on them, and many had permanent scars from burns. Sometimes they would be repeatedly clubbed. These acts of violence were an outlet for sadistic expression by the guards; physical assault was a way they exerted total control over the prison setting.

It would have been easy for me to just blame individual guards, but my experience in Viet Nam suggested something more sinister. In Viet Nam, I saw first-hand the powerful force that social expectations exert over individual values and morality. I listened to pilots brag about their "kills" and then saw little children who had been machine-gunned and napalmed to death by those same low-flying pilots who could easily see their victims. Veterans of all wars talk about the same phenomenon: normal procedures ignored, human beings treated like animals, a kill-first-and-question-later mentality that arises out of the inhuman chaos and catastrophe of war.

After World War II, moral philosopher and political theorist Hannah Arendt, a Jew, watched the trial of Adolf Eichmann, the architect of the Nazi gas chamber policy, and was surprised to learn that he was "neither perverted nor sadistic." Instead, she wrote, Eichmann and many others just like him "were, and still are, terrifyingly normal." In his defense, Eichmann and many other Nazis argued they were simply law-abiding men implementing the policies of their government—policies that included exterminating millions of people.[135] Arendt named the ability of ordinary people to commit extraordinary evil as a result of social pressure or within a certain social setting, "the banality of evil."

The "banality of evil" was not unique to the Nazis. Just three months after the start of Eichmann's trial, a social psychologist at Yale University conducted a series of experiments to better understand the nature of obedience to authority. The results were shocking. Stanley Milgram carefully screened subjects to be Participants representing typical U.S. Americans. Briefed on the importance of following orders, they were instructed to press a lever inflicting what they believed were gradually escalating series of shocks at fifteen-volt increments every time the nearby Learner/actor made a mistake in a word-matching task. The Experimenter/authority figure calmly insisted that the experiment must continue, even when the Learners began screaming in pain. A startling 65 percent of the Participants administered the most dangerous level of electricity—a level that might have killed someone actually receiving the shocks. Additional experiments were conducted over the years at other universities in the United States, and in at least nine other countries in Europe, Africa, and Asia and all revealed similar high rates of compliance to authority. A 2008 study designed to replicate the Milgram obedience experiments while avoiding several of its most controversial aspects, found similar results.[136]

In his paper, Milgram announced the study's most fundamental lesson:

> Ordinary people, simply doing their jobs, and without any particular hostility on their part, can become agents in a terrible destructive process . . . The most common adjustment of thought in the obedient subject is for him to see himself as not responsible for his own actions. . . . He sees himself not as a person acting in a morally accountable way but as the agent of external authority. "doing one's duty" that was heard time and again in the defense statements of those accused at Nuremberg. . . . In complex society it is psychologically easy to ignore responsibility when one is only an intermediate link in a chain of evil action but is far from the final consequences. . . . Thus there is a *fragmentation* of the total human act; no one man (or woman) decides to carry out the evil act and is confronted with its consequences [emphasis added].[137]

Milgram reminded us that a critical examination of our own history reveals a "democracy" of installed authority no less tyrannical, thriving on an obedient population of insatiable consumers dependent upon the terrorization of others, citing destruction of the original Indigenous inhabitants, dependence upon slavery of millions, internment of Japanese Americans, and the use of napalm against Vietnamese civilians.[138]

In the same vein, a 1971 experiment designed to study the effects of overt authority on humans was conducted by psychologist Philip Zimbardo, coincidentally a New York City high school classmate of Milgram. Called the Stanford Prison Experiment, a volunteer group of twenty-four college students was selected, based on their history of being well-adjusted young adults, to play the role of prisoner or guard in a simulated prison setting at Stanford University in California. Originally designed to last fourteen days, Zimbardo had to end the experiment after six days because the "guards" became so physically abusive and sadistic, and the "prisoners" so depressed and emotionally disturbed, that he feared permanent harm was being done to the participants' psyches. Zimbardo himself was shocked at how quickly "ordinary" persons became perpetrators of evil. He concluded that almost anyone in the right "situational" circumstance can be induced to abandon deeply held moral principles and cooperate in violence and oppression, demonstrating an easy transformation from the good Dr. Jekyll to the evil Mr. Hyde.[139]

As I reflected on the situation at Walpole Prison, I realized I was not all that different from the guards. They had signed up to do a job guarding prisoners, and had become sadists. I had signed up to serve my country and had become part of a war machine that was killing Vietnamese people. Retired Army Lt. Col. Dave Grossman, a professor of military science, has argued that humans have a deep, innate resistance to killing that requires the military to develop special training techniques to overcome.[140] I had been unable to thrust my bayonet into a dummy during training. But if I had been an army grunt instead of an Air Force officer, and a few years younger, I wondered, would I have killed on command?

The military was very unhappy when I refused to use my bayonet, because the military is well-aware that men can only be made to kill by coercion. The tyranny needed to make an army work is fierce, as it knows it cannot allow dialogue about its mission and must quickly patch any cracks in the blind obedience system. As Milgram reported, "the defection of a single individual, as long as it can be contained, is of little consequence. He will be replaced by the next man in line. The only danger to military functioning resides in the possibility that a lone defector will stimulate others."[141] My commanders placed me on the Officer Control Roster, meted out royal scoldings behind the doors of their offices, threatened me with court-martial charges, shamed me over and over, and accused me of being a coward and traitor who was creating morale problems that interfered with our mission. They tried hard to get me to obey, and when I wasn't as obedient as they wished, they kicked me out of Viet Nam a month earlier than scheduled.

Zimbardo suggests a flip side to the social pathology of obedience to authority. Citing *situational* historic acts of heroism by a number of people including Rosa Parks who refused to sit in the "colored" section of the bus, McCarthy-era truth-telling journalists George Seldes and I.F. Stone, Army Sergeant Joe Darby who exposed the Abu Ghraib tortures, the first responders to the World Trade Center collapse on 9/11, Army Warrant Officer Hugh Thompson's intervention in the My Lai massacre along with his two door gunners, Glen Andreotta and Larry Colburn, and the repeated *historic* actions over a lifetime as exhibited by people such as Mohandas Gandhi, Zimbardo suggests the capacity of humans for the "banality of goodness" or the "banality of heroism" as well. But it does require certain situational factors and conscious preparation to constrain the systemic forces that tend to shape us into automatons capable of monstrous acts.

One of the first steps in creating a cultural breeding ground for good rather than evil, in my opinion, is to address the severe problems caused by a class-based society such as we have in the United States which insists upon preserving a capitalist economic system. Such a system inherently creates and depends upon class divisions that in turn produce insecurities, anxieties and various defense mechanisms, including violence against others. People need to feel emotionally secure—comfortable with themselves.

The guards at Walpole had gone through a deindividualization process similar to the one I had been exposed to in the military. In addition, class and race bias caused them to think of themselves as different—and better—than the prisoners. No one stood up to suggest otherwise. Together, these factors enabled the guards to act and feel without thinking. The dehumanization of powerless prisoners makes prisons inherently destructive to guards and prisoners alike.[142]

Facing Mai Ly

I reorganized my schedule so that I could go to Walpole every other week to begin interviewing a long list of prisoners to gather facts and statements about their claims against the prison and some of its guards. I would start my interview days early in the morning and, depending on the housing unit or cellblock, I interviewed prisoners on the cellblock tier itself, walking from cell to cell. If necessary, I would do this until late afternoon to maximize interview time without being interrupted by guards moving prisoners in and out of a visiting room.

By early June 1981, the prison report was mostly written and I had only a day's worth of interviews to conduct before completing it. So I returned to

Walpole for one final day of interviews. I spent the entire day on one tier of Cellblock 10, one of the worst places in the prison to be, whether as a prisoner or a guard. On this particular block I remember the prison walls were solid rather than barred, and the prison doors only had little openings about head high for communication or the delivery of meals.

It must have been sometime around 5 p.m. I was talking to the last prisoner at the far end of the block when my attention was distracted by a commotion at the other end, near the entrance of the cellblock on the same tier. I looked down the walkway and saw that two guards had pulled a prisoner out of a cell onto the walkway floor. One guard kicked the prisoner while the other guard hit him with a billy club, the prisoner screaming, the guards shouting.

That's when I flashed.

I had no warning. I had never experienced anything like it in my life. All of a sudden, I felt as if I was in a village in Viet Nam. I looked down and saw a woman lying at my feet, her eyes wide open, staring up at me.

If you have never had a flashback, you can't understand what it feels like. It's very, very different from having a bad memory pop into your mind. When I looked around me, I could only see this woman's eyes, dead children, the gored water buffalo lying on the ground. I smelled the burned corpses and buildings of that village. I literally could not see, hear, or smell the real world of the very noisy prison around me. My brain had replaced the sensory information of the world I was in with the sensory information it had stored from this traumatic event twelve years earlier.

A voice inside of me said, "You have to get out of this place. You have to get to a safe place." So I tried to get off that cellblock, but I couldn't walk straight. I staggered, grabbing the sides of the walkway, stumbling over bodies of Vietnamese villagers. Even as I exited the prison, I was reliving being in the village. I later found out that flashbacks can be as short as a few minutes or, in bad cases, as long as a few days. Mine lasted an hour or two, with after-affects for months. I somehow got off the cellblock and through the many locked doors I had to pass to get out of the prison. The whole time, I felt like I was in Viet Nam. I have no idea what the guards thought, but I got myself out of there and into my car, where I sat for probably an hour and a half, moaning, crying, and drooling.

That afternoon, I became a Viet Nam veteran.

Up until that moment, I'd been a very functional person. I had completed law school and become a lawyer, social worker, penal consultant, tax assessor, lobbyist, farmer. Yet that whole time, even though I had developed what some would call radical politics, I never claimed my identity as a vet. Partly, I felt guilty about having gone to Viet Nam and participated in a war that was unjust. Partly, I felt that only "grunts" who had faced death every day in the jungles of Viet Nam had the right to claim vet status. But to be honest, the main reason I didn't identify as a vet was that I just didn't want to think about my experiences there. I could not face the deeper emotional stress of what I had seen and heard and felt in Viet Nam.

The flashback opened me up. In one epiphanic and traumatic moment, Mai Ly's eyes connected with mine, and I realized that she was my family. She was me. I was she. I felt that I had died and been reborn.

Most of us follow a path set out for us by others. We hardly think about it, or if we do, we think only within the formula we are given. As a young man, at one time I thought my choice was to become a Baptist minister or a lawyer. It never occurred to me that what mattered most was the journey itself, and that I could not predict where I would go or what I would discover about myself and about the world.

Once you understand you are on a journey, then you realize that all the elements of life we usually concern ourselves with—how much money we make, where we live, what we do—are not that significant. You discover that there is something else, something beyond yourself, a whole other resource you can draw upon. I don't have a name for it. It's the Tao, the Life Force, the Great Spirit, the Spirit of Life, or God, if you will. It's way beyond you, yet you are part of it and it's inside of you. The box we are usually bound up in blocks this life force. The flashback shattered what was left of the box I was in and provided me access to this larger vision, the one that was first born when I stared into Mai Ly's eyes in April 1969.

My vision of Mai Ly was traumatic, but also very beautiful. As I looked into her eyes, I was immersed in a feeling of empathy and cooperation, a feeling that I was one with everyone else in the world. And I realized, you mustn't hurt other people because in the end you are also hurting yourself. When you plunge the bayonet into another person, you are plunging it into your own body.

Some would describe this principle as karma, or simply, "What goes around comes around." You experience what you do to others; when you hurt others, you hurt yourself. You can't defy that basic principle because if you do, you will pay. You may not pay right away, but you will pay. The currency is psychic pain, loss. Many veterans pay every day for the violence they inflicted on others, especially innocent civilians, as well as the violence that was inflicted on themselves and their comrades. Our world is paying now for the hurt we have done to the planet and all her inhabitants.

PART IV

The United States in America

CHAPTER 14

Without Leave

After the flashback, I could not continue to work. I started therapy, and within a few weeks took an extended leave of absence—one from which I would not return. I went back home to Jamestown to put my farm on the market and help attend to my mother, who had severe Parkinson's Disease, but mainly to recover and examine the new journey I was now on.

Before taking my leave of absence, I was able to complete my report on Walpole with the help of a Massachusetts prison support group, and submitted it to Jack Backman. The written report, *Walpole State Prison, Massachusetts: An Exercise in Torture*, was released to the public on June 9, 1981. No media covered it, the conservative governor and his public safety secretary did not want to see it, the corrections commissioner made no comment, and the legislature took no action. It was totally ignored.

Jack sent the report to Amnesty International in London, where it got but a brief mention in their annual report in 1982: they divulged that Massachusetts Governor King had responded to their inquiry with the assurance that "any allegation of wrongdoing, in any state correctional facility, is immediately investigated by the Commissioner of Corrections." That was the end of it.

A similar thing had happened in Cincinnati. There, I essentially had been told that it was economically better for the system to build a large prison without regard to how a thoughtful, just process would make society safer and healthier. Few Cincinnatians really understood what was going on, or could spend the time to study the prison plans.

Prosperity based on ignorance had also been the calling card of prison construction when I worked at the National Prison Moratorium. Lobbyists made the rules and Congress went along with them because more prisons brought in more money—and besides, neither congresspeople nor the public they represented had the time or energy to follow the complex and arcane path of prison legislation.

In my post–Viet Nam life I was discovering that you can work as hard as you can to reveal what is going on in the system; you can turn up hard, factual information; but more often than not, nothing will come of it because the system itself doesn't care. People are so busy pursuing their material lives that—even if they suspect or know that policies are "unpleasant"— they cannot stop what they're doing. So they just continue with business as usual.

I believe human beings do care, that empathy is an inherent archetypal characteristic. I also know from experience that denial is a powerful defense when we are faced with difficult truths. If I tell someone sitting in my living room a story about a prisoner who was tortured, offering facts and a detailed description of that torture, then the person listening to my story often will wince or look away—they will physically be unable to sit still while listening to that kind of story. The same thing occurs when vets bear witness.

Economic and political structures are not people, yet they are comprised of people—bureaucrats—who strive to keep their jobs. It's important to understand that the people who make decisions and materially benefit from economic systems are generally far removed from the effects of their decisions. Within the enclosed cocoon of their work world, bureaucrats experience the people impacted by the system as nothing, more or less, than statistics. Quite removed from the effects of their actions, from the feelings of the people affected, bureaucrats essentially repress knowledge of someone being tortured, someone being imprisoned. The system insidiously requires this kind of denial in order to maintain itself.

Making Connections

My flashback connected my work on prisons to what I had witnessed in Viet Nam. I realized that connection was not arbitrary. What I had witnessed at Walpole State Prison was the torture of prisoners. What I had witnessed in Viet Nam was the terrorizing and murdering of innocent civilians. Both groups were powerless. As I recovered from my flashback, I realized that the brutality I had witnessed in Viet Nam and in the prison system were both part and parcel of the American Way Of Life. Our country was founded on brutality, and our economic system continues to be sustained by brutality.

During the months I spent in Jamestown, I read voraciously, steeping myself in U.S. history. What I discovered continued to dismay me. I found a chronic *pattern* of malicious behavior directed by a Eurocentric government against any people who got in the way of our "progress." The cultural ethos that originated in the dispossession of Native Americans remains our "defining and enabling experience" as a nation.[143] When the Europeans first came to these shores, they eliminated the land's original inhabitants through a brutal process we would now call genocide or ethnic cleansing. This was our institutional holocaust. We took best of what native culture had to offer—the land itself, their agriculture, their medical knowledge, and their democratic political system—even as we raided their villages, destroyed their crops, and killed their people.

Why did the British "settlers" who arrived here attack native cultures rather than seeking business or trade, as the French and Russian traders did? They attacked because many were not "pilgrims" but rather *employees*, sponsored and directed to establish colonies on behalf of private, for-profit enterprises funded by English venture capitalists. Two early companies, the London (or South Virginia) Company, and Plymouth (or North Virginia) Company from England successfully acquired rights to possess this land from the Crown. Like contemporary Western oil companies that extract coal, oil, and diamonds in central Africa, the mandate for these colonial businesses was to extract resources for immense profits, without regard to the well-being of the native population.[144] In fact, many Europeans considered these "new" lands to be empty.

The Powhatan War (1607–1646) in what is now Virginia; the Pequot War (1636–1638), in what is now Connecticut; King Philip's War (1675–1676), in what is now central and western Massachusetts; Pontiac's Rebellion (1763–1766) in the Ohio Valley and Michigan areas; the Seminole Wars in Florida (1817–1858); and dozens of others of wars and hundreds of massacres throughout the 1800s accomplished the Europeans' goal of clearing the land for their own profit. Continental conquest was more or less finalized in December 1890 when the 7th Cavalry took revenge for its earlier 1876 humiliating defeat under Custer at Little Big Horn by massacring three hundred Sioux women and children at Wounded Knee in South Dakota. (Sixty years after the Wounded Knee massacre, the 7th Cavalry committed one of the first known massacres during the Korean War when it killed hundreds of defenseless civilians at No Gun Ri in July 1950.)

Some of our most revered "Founding Fathers" spoke quite clearly about their imperialist agenda. Benjamin Franklin, in 1751, argued that "surplus land"—that is, land once owned by the Indigenous people—was necessary to generate wealth.[145] Thomas Jefferson set out to create what he called an "empire of liberty," which in practice would mean "prosperity" for the White man and enslavement for everyone else.[146] Jefferson pursued this imperial vision by purchasing the Louisiana Territory through the exercise of extra-constitutional powers, authorizing the Lewis and Clark intelligence expedition,[147] and advocating preventive war in 1807: "If the English do not give us the satisfaction we demand, *we will take* Canada, which wants to enter the Union; and when, together with Canada, we shall have the Floridas, we shall no longer have any difficulties with our neighbors; and it is the *only way of preventing them*" [emphasis added].[148]

James Madison continued Jefferson's policies by declaring, in 1811, our country's right to control Florida and other Spanish possessions in all of the Western Hemisphere.[149] This imperial manifesto was finally given a name in 1823, when President James Monroe declared what became known as the Monroe Doctrine, that the United States had a right and obligation to fulfill its destiny by claiming the entire continent, North and South, in effect from "sea to shining sea." This was later popularized as "Manifest Destiny." The acquisition of this land mass was completed by President Polk, who concocted a war with Mexico in 1846 to gain additional slave territory we now call Texas, New Mexico, and California, as well as parts of Arizona, Nevada, Utah, Colorado, and Wyoming, adding nearly 1.2 million square miles to the country.

Claiming a wide swath of North America was not enough for U.S. imperial ambitions, however. As early as 1849, Senator Benton from Missouri urged America to initiate trade and "rich commerce" with Eastern Asia to "realize the grand idea of Columbus . . . carrying wealth and dominion with it."[150] We invaded Korea, a country with no army, in June 1871 with a twenty-five-boat Navy war fleet and one thousand sailors and Marines to force the "hermit kingdom" into opening new trade routes. We landed U.S. Marines in 1893 in Hawaii to conquer that island, annexing it in 1898. In 1898 with our newly built, superior Navy, several thousand troops stationed in Manila and thousands more in Cuba, we fought the Spanish-American War. When Teddy Roosevelt and his Rough Riders charged San Juan Hill on July 1, 1898, it was alongside Cuban soldiers who thought we were there to help liberate the island from Spain. However, it turned out that the war was largely a fight with Spain over colonial properties, enabling the U.S. to gain control over Cuba, the Philippines, Puerto Rico, and Guam.

The next year began the lingering "Philippine-American War," fought against an active guerrilla movement seeking Filipino sovereignty. Nearly 4,500 U.S. soldiers died in the campaign, but massacres of Filipinos were enormous with estimates of dead ranging from 250,000 to 1,000,000.[151]

We turned our attention from Asia back to Central America when we intervened in Colombia in 1903 to take control of its northern province, Panama, in preparation for building an Isthmian Canal. The period of the so-called Banana Wars[152] in Central America and the Caribbean from 1898 under President McKinley to Franklin Roosevelt's "Good Neighbor Policy" in 1934, saw at least eleven countries invaded by the U.S. Marines on at least thirty-four occasions, several occupied for extended periods, all with the aim of assuring U.S. corporate monopolies in the banana, sugar, and tobacco trade.[153] By 1930 the U.S. had sent gunboats more than six thousand times into Latin American ports as part of its assertion of power in Latin America.[154]

First the continental North American land mass, then Asia, then our neighbors to the South: we would stop at nothing to establish an empire that would provide a small number of U.S. citizens with a large percentage of the West's wealth. We were not a benevolent trading partner to the rest of the world but a bully, committing torture and genocide, invading other lands to gain resources for our own prosperity.[155]

I learned from studying U.S. history that the torture we carried out in Viet Nam was nothing new. In the early 1900s, when the U.S. attacked the Filipinos, who were fighting for their independence from Spain (and their subsequent U.S. occupiers), our Marines boasted of the success of their "water cures" (cf. water boarding) to extract information from the "treacherous gugus," many of whom died in the process.[156] President Teddy Roosevelt glibly claimed that the water cure was an old Filipino method of mild torture,[157] even while declaring that the defeat of the Filipino independence fighters was a "triumph of civilization over the black chaos of savagery and barbarism."[158] Almost a hundred years later, in 1996, it was revealed that the Pentagon's infamous School of the Americas (now the Western Hemisphere Institute for Security and Cooperation) at Fort Benning, Georgia, had been using manuals to teach practices such as execution, coercion, false imprisonment, and torture to Latin American military and security personnel.[159] It turns out that these manuals were based on lessons learned over decades of field operations, pulled together by U.S. Army counterinsurgency operatives in 1965 in a program known as Project X. These were used in the Phoenix program in Viet Nam, in Iran, and many Latin American countries,[160] and also incorporated techniques from another manual, *Psychological Operations in Guerrilla Warfare*, distributed to the Contras in Nicaragua.[161]

I remembered my early childhood drawing, in which I drew a cowboy pointing a gun at an Indian. Was this U.S. American character to me? Had the whitewashed history I had been learning at school conditioned me to assume I had the right to prove my superiority by exerting power over others? Was that why I had so easily agreed to participate in a war against Asians who clearly did not represent a threat to me or my fellow citizens?

Viet Nam had clearly not been an aberration, a "special circumstance" or a one-time failure. But I had to read back into the history of my country to understand that. What became clear to me was that if we do not know our own history, we have no frame of reference, no context, with which to judge current events.

Tax Refuser

One of the reasons my wife Julie and I separated was my serious consideration of becoming a tax refuser. After spending a summer reading through the real history of the United States, my mind was made up. I could not support a system that would bomb people around the world and imprison people here at home simply to maintain what increasingly seemed an addictive, materialistic way of life.

My wife thought I was being irrational. I understood her point of view, as it was also hard for me to take this next step. I was raised to obey authority. When I was commissioned an officer and later became a lawyer, I had taken an oath to uphold the laws of the land. As a young man, I never imagined I would have to defy my own government. Now, I was committing myself to be absent without leave—AWOL—from my own government by refusing to pay taxes.

As I struggled with that decision, I remembered, back on the farm, thinking to myself, "How can I tread more lightly on the earth when I'm contributing to killing people through paying taxes?" Sometimes, when no one else was around, I would weep over my complicity in the crimes of our government. At other times I was so angry I would scream. After leaving the farm and going to work for Jack Backman, taxes had once again been withdrawn from my paycheck. I had chronic ulcer-like stomach pain during much of that year from the stress of participating in a system I no longer accepted.

Over the course of my journey, I have learned to listen to my body. In Jamestown, after reading a more authentic history of the United States, I was finally determined to follow my gut, and began the challenge of becoming a tax refuser.

There is a difference between being a tax resister and a tax refuser. I don't resist the idea of paying taxes: I believe in supporting my local community. What I refuse to do is pay money to a government that will then use that money to wage wars. People have asked me, "Why don't you at least pay Social Security taxes?" Well, I would, except Congress constantly borrows against those funds to pay for wars. In fact, in 2007 and 2008, President Bush paid for the Iraq war substantially by borrowing against the Social Security Trust Fund.

Because I am a tax refuser, I had to be very scrupulous with the IRS. I worked with a certified public accountant beginning in 1983 to prepare accurate tax returns showing what the government's tax code claimed I owed, then I attached a letter to my returns indicating that I was refusing to pay based on the Nuremberg Obligation. When the IRS started sending me threatening form letters, I quickly sold my house to avoid tax liens. In 1985 I wrote once again to the IRS to explain my position. Here is an excerpt of that letter:

> Our country has signed the Nuremberg charter and principles which delineate the scope of individual responsibility in the face of illegal activities by a government. As I read the Nuremberg principles, com-

plicity in the commission of crimes against peace, a war crime, or a crime against humanity is a crime under international law. As such, it is also part of the supreme law of the United States under the Constitution. Nuremberg also requires responsibility of individual citizens to abide by international law even when ordered contrary by his/her government. Article VI of our Constitution makes this individual responsibility supreme law over orders by the government.

As the United States is engaged in wars and aggression against citizens of other nations, and is conspiring to do so as well, and uses the threat of first strike weapons as a plan to wage aggressive war, such behavior is clearly in violation of a number of treaties, the Nuremberg principles, and the United States Constitution. As such, I cannot in good conscience pay these taxes. Furthermore, by so doing, I am upholding the Constitution of my own country.

Many people still don't understand why I became a tax refuser, and it may seem bizarre to some, but it is *not* complicated. Ask yourself this question: "What would I do if someone came to my door and asked for 20 percent of my income to pay for this country to invade Iraq or Iran or whoever the current enemy might be?" Many people, my parents included, would readily give that money. Many of us, however, would only do so reluctantly. If we wouldn't give money to the government directly to pay for an unjust war, why would we give that money to the IRS when it will be used to pay for that same war?

To become a tax refuser, I had to accept that—like a soldier going AWOL from the army—I would probably be put in prison. My lawyers told me to expect that outcome sooner or later. But when I finally resolved this issue for myself, I felt really clean and free. I finally felt that I had begun to extricate myself from direct complicity in murder by actions of the U.S. government.

I do not have some peculiar desire to spend time in prison or to subject myself to needless deprivation. I believe that in a healthy human community, the ultimate legal and moral authority resides within the heart and mind of each autonomous citizen—in his or her conscience. When this government commits a *pattern* of behavior that consistently violates its own laws, then the government has relinquished its authority to act on behalf of its citizenry. I must act according to my conscience.

Henry David Thoreau had it right when, in the wake of the U.S.-concocted war against Mexico to acquire more slave property, he wrote in his essay "Civil Disobedience," "If a thousand men were not to pay their tax bills this year, that would not be a violent and bloody measure, as it would be to pay them, and enable the state to commit violence and shed innocent blood."

By linking the beating I witnessed at Walpole Prison to Viet Nam and the other acts of U.S. imperialism, my flashback had confirmed for me what the American Way Of Life really means. It was no longer going to be acceptable to support a system that bombed poor people in order to maintain our "nonnegotiable" way of life.

Last Days in the System

While I was recovering from my flashback, I stayed in touch with friends and colleagues. In early 1982 two new acquaintances were looking for a third partner in a natural dairy food business in Greenfield, Massachusetts. They bought only local milk, then manufactured all-natural kefir, eggnog, cottage cheese, and rennetless cheese, and then sold these products to health food stores in New England and down the East Coast as far as Washington, D.C.

After we agreed that I would join the partnership, it was decided that I would focus on marketing our products. Working in Greenfield meant that I would be in contact with Wally and Juanita Nelson, whose extensive gardens and small subsistence organic farm was located in neighboring Deerfield. In fact, I rented a room in the Traprock Peace Center that was literally a stone's throw from the Nelson's homestead. I thought that the natural food business would be a good match for my emerging anarchist and decentralist ideas about eating locally and treating the earth well. Since the fledgling business was not yet making profits, I would have sufficient deductions from a small paycheck so as to not have to pay taxes.

I also was attracted to the idea of a worker-owned business. My partners were interested in the Mondragón Cooperative Corporation, the world's largest worker cooperative, created in the early 1980s in a town of that name in the Basque region of northwest Spain. Mondragón now boasts over 120 employee-owned cooperatives with forty thousand worker-owners, and they are twice as profitable as other Spanish firms.[162]

The Mondragón cooperative was inspired by the Spanish anarchist movement, which flourished from the 1870s into the mid-1930s. I have heard some call it a decentralized, caring form of capitalism. Unlike the Marxist movements of the time, Spanish anarchism placed a strong emphasis on simple lifestyles—a total remaking of the person along community libertarian values with contempt for vertical authority structures and hierarchy, including a rejection of patriarchy. The Spanish anarchists placed a high value on spontaneity, local sufficiency, autonomy, and initiatives arising from small affinity groups. They did not want to be led by leaders but by liberated individuals residing in each community.[163]

Mondragón grew out of the history of a people—the Basques—who seemed to understand the natural workability of a small, cooperative environment. The Basques are believed to be the oldest surviving indigenous ethnic group in Europe. Like many other Indigenous peoples who have managed to maintain their cultures, the Basques believe in the value of local sufficiency and autonomy similar to today's Zapatista Indigenous in Chiapas, Mexico. Though the Spanish anarchists fell in 1936 when Franco forcibly won control of Spain, Mondragón marked its revival and later spurred the creation of worker-owned businesses around the world.

I dreamed our natural food business would become part of that kind of steady-state local economy. I saw us as being a logical lynchpin between farmer-owned dairies and worker-owned health food stores. But the reality turned out to be much different. I discovered that many dairy managers in health food stores expected bribes to get a few inches of shelf space for our product. My hardworking partners wanted to expand with more worker-owners, but our business was not yet generating sufficient cash. The organic movement did not really come into its own until the 1990s, and few consumers back in the 1980s understood that organic foods were healthier for bodies and for the planet than the cheaper, mass-produced, antibiotic-infused dairy products on supermarket shelves.

In an attempt to relieve the cash-flow crisis, my two partners decided a cost-cutting measure would be necessary to survive financially. We would replace our more expensive honey sweetener in our anchor product—seven flavors of kefir—with cheaper high-fructose corn syrup, that savvy health food customers would not buy if they knew it was an ingredient. The situation was further ethically compromised because the kefir would continue to be sold in our existing cartons that listed honey as the sweetener ingredient. As marketing director, I was alarmed. I had only been with the company a month or two and contemplated resigning, sharing publicly my reasons. Fortunately my partners restored honey as our sweetener. This disagreement was a warning to me, however, that it was going to be extremely difficult to create a sustainable worker-based business within a ruthless capitalist economy.

CHAPTER 15

Becoming a Vet

W hile I worked hard to sell our dairy products, I also began helping local veterans set up a small volunteer storefront counseling center. I realized I had to start dealing with my own issues as a veteran, and to do so I needed to talk with other vets. I found that many other vets were coping with the same problems, plus additional ones, especially illnesses and birth defects apparently caused by exposure to Agent Orange.

I had only been in the dairy business eight months when I learned that a group of Green Berets had landed in a military helicopter on the athletic field of a nearby high school, then moved quickly to the gymnasium where they conducted a hand-to-hand combat demonstration before a full school assembly. Angry, I shared this news with a Viet Nam veteran friend. Within a few days, we organized a press conference in front of the local military recruiter's office in Greenfield to announce formation of a new veterans speakers group (at least he and I, for starters) to seek equal time in classrooms to present an alternative, experiential perspective on the military. Soon the Veterans Education Project (VEP) was launched, a project that continues to this day.

I became increasingly active as a volunteer with the vets center—so active that by early 1984, after only two years as a partner in the dairy, I left the business to serve as the director of the newly established, state-funded Western Massachusetts Agent Orange Information Project office. A few months later, the local chapter of Vietnam Veterans of America (VVA) received money from the state to set up a fully staffed storefront for Viet Nam veterans and asked me to serve as its executive director. When I worked for Jack Backman, I had helped prepare legislation authorizing the creation of state-funded veterans' outreach centers—now I was directing one of them.

My work with veterans at the store-front center was the last position I held that was really part of the U.S. economic system. I asked to be paid as an independent contractor so that none of my income was withheld, and I refused, during these years, to pay taxes, though I filed honest and accurate returns. I had already sold my house, and now I converted my car to a long-term lease. I did not want any ownership of property that could be garnished by the IRS. Yet, my work with veterans necessarily kept me very engaged within the system.

John Kerry

In fact, I quickly became involved again in the kind of political work I had rejected when I left Washington. First, I was appointed to the Agent Orange subcommittee of the newly formed statewide Viet Nam Veteran's Advisory Committee under the joint auspices of Lieutenant Governor John Kerry and state Commissioner of Veterans Services John Halachis. Governor Dukakis also appointed me as a member of his statewide homeless veterans task force.

For that work, and my work at the vet center, I was awarded a special commendation by Governor Dukakis for "Humanitarian Service above and beyond normal expectations to your fellow Vietnam Veterans" in fall of 1985.

When John Kerry ran in 1984 for the U.S. Senate seat being vacated by the ailing Paul Tsongas, I volunteered for the campaign, along with several other antiwar Viet Nam veterans to solicit publicity and votes. The media nicknamed us "Kerry's Commandos," but we called ourselves the "Doghunters."[164] During this campaign, Kerry was accused by retired general George Smith Patton (a Viet Nam veteran known for his brutality)[165] of "near-treasonous activity" for returning his war medals at the 1971 Dewey Canyon III antiwar protest in Washington.[166] Kerry responded that he had not thrown his own medals, but those of a World War II veteran at the latter's request. Kerry invited reporters to view his medals and ribbons on display at his Boston apartment.[167] This revelation came as a shocking, hurtful betrayal—a deceit perpetuated for thirteen years. Though I tried to ignore it at the time, it troubled me deeply.

As Kerry's lead in the race continued to vanish, his ultimate victory was largely attributed to the "galvanizing energy" produced by the Doghunters, several of whom, myself included, became members of Kerry's first veterans advisory committee.[168] In Kerry's first term he quickly conducted a gutsy investigation of Reagan's covert efforts to fund the cash-starved, illegal Contra terrorists in Nicaragua through proceeds from drug trafficking under the cloak of national security. Kerry's 1,166-page report issued in December 1988 concluded that "senior U.S. policy makers were not immune to the idea that drug money was a perfect solution to the Contras' funding problems."[169] Despite this, only four months earlier, on August 10, Kerry chose to join a majority of his Democratic colleagues to give millions of dollars to the Contra terrorist forces in a close Senate vote (49–47), refusing to join the few principled Democrats who rightfully rejected any further money for the grotesque murder rampages in Nicaragua.[170] Though I was no longer an active member of Kerry's advisory group, I wrote a personal letter strongly urging Kerry to vote against any aid to the terrorists. I never received a reply. Though the Contras had officially agreed to stop fighting, the effect of granting additional monies predictably led to more acts of terrorism and the killing and maiming of hundreds of additional Nicaraguans. My subsequent trips to that country corroborated this.

I've noticed that at times my idealism wins out over my historical understandings. I had hoped that in John Kerry, the man who had spoken so passionately before Congress to end the war, the country would find a politician who finally would advocate for true democracy rather than the mantra of prosperity. I was wrong, of course. By the time Kerry ran for president in 2004, presenting himself as a war hero, he had voted in favor of the Iraq War. Similar to his vote during his first term when he supported illegal Contra aid, in his 2002 campaign for a fourth term, he again refused to vote with a minority of his courageous Democratic colleagues who opposed an illegal intervention against Iraq. This was a dramatic betrayal of the beautiful conclusion to his speech before the Senate Foreign Relations Committee more than three decades earlier: "[O]ur determination [is] to undertake one last mission— to search out and destroy the last vestige of this barbaric war . . . so . . . thirty years from now . . . we will be able to say 'Vietnam' and not mean . . . a filthy obscene memory, but mean instead the place where America finally turned and where soldiers like us helped it in the turning."

Each of us chooses his or her own journey. John Kerry chose a path that took him back to the American Way Of Life, a repudiation of the turning of America he once advocated, Meanwhile, I was walking a very different path, trying to get away from my country and its obsession with prosperity at any cost.

Vet Center

Most of my time at the vet center was spent not on politics but on people. The work was intense. Over a period of two years our office received nearly three thousand walk-ins, many who came in day after day looking for help and comfort. Our staff focused on several hundred serious cases. For some we filed formal claims with the VA. I assisted in negotiating surrender of three Viet Nam veterans who torched a Buddhist peace pagoda on New Year's Eve in a rural area of western Massachusetts. One of those veterans later was convicted of murder and is serving a life sentence in prison. The designated veteran chaplain for our local group, who had served in Thailand during Viet Nam, was convicted of numerous counts of sexual abuse of boys and is also serving a life prison term.

As director of the center I served as the crisis intervention counselor. I was often called into emergency situations in homes, bars, and on the street when a veteran in the midst of a crisis threatened harm to himself or others.

On eight or nine occasions I carefully (though with a rush of adrenaline) disarmed vets and confiscated their knives or guns, sometimes loaded, depositing them in a locked safe.

On one occasion I was called to calm a vet who had discharged a shotgun into the living room ceiling of his apartment as a mother and her children cowered in the corner. I was able to very slowly approach the man and gently coax him to lay his weapon on the floor. He collapsed into my arms. I held him for some time until he was calm enough to be transported to the VA hospital.

My leased car became an emergency vehicle transporting veterans to emergency rooms, detox centers, or the VA hospital twenty miles away. I regularly washed bloodstains off the upholstery. I sought out "bush vets" living in the woods who were brought to my attention by concerned neighbors who directed me to their sites. I advocated for a local vet abused by local police, leading to him receiving both an apology and a financial settlement.

During my tenure in Greenfield, a number of Viet Nam veterans in the region committed suicide, while others died of de facto suicide from alcoholism, drug overdoses, or suspicious single-car accidents. One familiar veteran, a Viet Nam "tunnel rat," asked one day to meet in my private back office. Sitting on the floor, Alan spent several minutes intensely pantomiming with his hands various sculpting motions. Then, looking at me with tears, he cried, "I want to resurrect the women and kids I blew away in one of the tunnels. I murdered them. It was for a lie. I need them to be alive so I can now live once again." I held Alan as we cried together. A year later he collapsed on a downtown sidewalk and died not far from our office. He had drowned his grief in alcoholism.

I was reminded how much our society chooses dishonesty about Viet Nam hoping its pain will go away. Wanting to learn more about the lives of the eleven men whose names were listed on Greenfield's "Vietnam" plaque in front of its police station, I was shocked to discover that only seven had died in Viet Nam. Three never served Viet Nam, dying in the late 1950s. A fourth died in an accident in Germany. When I brought this to the attention of local veteran leaders and political officials, no one could explain it, no one wanted to revisit the process that had been used to create the plaque, and no one wanted to correct it. I wondered how many other veteran memorials around the country reflect this kind of fraud on the truth?

Wesley Blixt, a reporter with the Springfield, Massachusetts, *Morning Union*, wrote a feature story reporting that the vet center was "a log book of crisis, despair and occasional threats," and that during my work there the center had "attracted regional attention, serving as a lifeline for some Viet

Nam vets, and as a focus of commitment for others." Next to serving in war, the experiences at the vet center were some of the most intense of my life.

United States Abroad

One reason I had begun working with vets was that I had become aware that many were experiencing what is now being diagnosed as post-traumatic stress disorder (PTSD). These symptoms were aggravated by Reagan's October 25, 1983, invasion of the tiny island of Grenada. Ostensibly the invasion was over the Cubans building a five-thousand-foot runway. Grenada possessed almost no military, but was a major world supplier of spices such as cinnamon, ginger, and nutmeg. This lawless venture served as a major news distraction from the deadly bombing just two days earlier in Beirut, Lebanon, that took the lives of 241 U.S. military personnel, mostly Marines. For vets, both of these military episodes brought flashbacks and bad memories of their time on the battlefield.

The context in which these events occurred proves instructive. Despite Jimmy Carter's claim to be the human rights president, the United States under his watch had supported a number of repressive regimes, from Somoza in Nicaragua, to Mobutu in Zaire, Suharto in Indonesia, and the Shah in Iran, among many others. Meanwhile, the years 1979–1980 were marked by people's revolutions for justice and independence around the world. Iranians deposed the U.S.-installed Shah, a ruthless dictator who had ruled them for twenty-six years; the Sandinistas threw out the U.S.-installed Somoza regime in Nicaragua, after forty-five years of tyranny; the Salvadoran revolution erupted in late 1979 to rid El Salvador of feudal-like conditions that enabled great profits for a few families affiliated with U.S. corporations; the South Koreans revolted in Kwangju in early 1980 against their repressive, U.S.-sanctioned rulers; and Russian troops moved into Afghanistan after Carter sent supplies to rebels seeking to overthrow a Soviet-friendly revolutionary government there. The United States was losing its puppets in at least three important geographic regions, even as our human rights president supported continued repression.

Unwilling to lose its imperial grip, the United States went on the offensive, first under Carter and then in an accelerated mode under President Reagan. With the memory of Viet Nam still too strong to enable a U.S. military return to Asia, the Reagan administration focused its energies on Central America, using Nicaragua, El Salvador, and Guatemala as examples to demonstrate U.S. imperial hegemony in a region that historically had been exploited in order to enhance the American Way Of Life. Reagan linked the Sandinistas, the new Nicaraguan government, to Communism, and began covertly supplying arms to a counterrevolutionary force called the Contras, which the U.S. created. He began granting large amounts of money to the repressive El Salvadoran government to put down its Indigenous rebellion, and later to the draconian Ríos Montt dictatorship in Guatemala.

The creation and use of anticommunist paramilitary forces was not new. Eisenhower used them in 1954 in the overthrow of Guatemala. Kennedy used them in 1961 in the attempted overthrow of Cuba, and then later to overthrow enemy governments in Laos and Viet Nam. Ford used them in 1974–1976 to overthrow a popular political organization in Angola after that country gained its independence from Portugal. Carter used them in Afghanistan in 1979, and they became the Taliban, who we are fighting today, the second generation of the Mujaheddin.

U.S. intervention in Central America and elsewhere did not surprise me after my reading of alternative histories of the United States.[171] Still, I was shocked when I read about the extent of U.S. support for the Contras in the November 8, 1982, issue of *Newsweek*. In that nine-page report, "A Secret War For Nicaragua," journalists detailed the measures by which Reagan was attempting to throw out the Sandinista government in Nicaragua. Virtually everyone who was following the news knew that the Contras were created, armed, and funded by the United States. The *extent* of U.S. involvement in training Contra troops in the United States, as well as in Honduras, and the number of U.S. military and intelligence personnel who were being employed to help them, were not so well known. The United States was also welcoming assistance from U.S. mercenaries, many of them Viet Nam veterans, to augment Contra training in Honduras, to provide combat support in Nicaragua's war zones, and to assist Salvadoran troops fighting the guerrillas there.

This coordinated military campaign was designed to destroy the very fabric of village life, like the United States had done in Viet Nam. Starting in 1982, Contra offensives destroyed roads and bridges, campesino farming cooperatives, pharmacies, schools, homes and entire village infrastructures, telephone and electrical transmission lines, and vehicles carrying goods to markets, terrorized teachers and other local leaders, sometimes beheading them. They were destroying the country to "save" it. On April 29, 1985, *Newsweek* published a series of gruesome photos of Contras executing Nicaraguan peasants in a field. Under U.S. supervision, Contras and/or CIA-paid operatives, the latter euphemistically called "unilaterally controlled Latino assets" (UCLAs), attacked the Nicaraguan port at Corinto and blew up its oil storage tanks; they mined harbors to blow up ships, and they used U.S.-supplied planes to bomb northern areas, on one occasion destroying the Managua Airport Terminal.

I felt like we were reliving Viet Nam all over again. Even the rhetoric was the same. Thomas Pickering, the U.S. ambassador to El Salvador, compared the Sandinistas to an "infected piece of meat that attracts insects," just as previous U.S. troops had called Southeast Asians "rodents."[172] Reagan called Nicaragua a "totalitarian dungeon." His CIA chief, William Casey, in early 1983, ordered his associates to dramatically increase economic warfare against the Nicaraguans: "Let's make them sweat, let's make the bastards sweat."[173]

Even as the Sandinistas were cast as less-than-human, Reagan called the terrorist Contras the "moral equivalent to the Founding Fathers,"[174] "our brothers" and "freedom fighters." [175] It was as if I was seeing the U.S.-Indian wars all over again. Instead of the European settlers fighting the "savage" Sioux, we were told the brave Contras were fighting the "malignant" Sandinistas who were spreading "cancer" under their demonic dictator, President Daniel Ortega. President George H.W. Bush later denounced Ortega as a "little man," "an unwanted animal at a garden party."[176]

I had to speak out. In 1985, I started speaking at public forums as a private citizen, making clear my opposition to Reagan's policies of brazen terrorism. A lot of us politicized vets had, by then, decoded our politicians' language, so when the Sandinistas, for example, were called "Marxist-Leninists" or Communists, we knew those words meant "poor people who are organizing for independence and therefore must be eliminated." I knew from Stanley Milgram's experiments that we, the American public, were like Pavlovian dogs, trained to obey. When politicians or media pundits say "Marxist-Leninist," the people say, "Go get them." My fellow citizens were not going to stop this carnage. Just as I had stood up for prison reform, I felt I had to stand up to support the sovereignty of the Sandinista government.

From Protest to Action

Just as I had kept my views on Viet Nam from my enlisted men when at Binh Thuy Air Base, I worked hard to keep my opinions about Reagan's policies in Central America out of my work life at the vet center.

Some of the vets were angered that I disagreed with our president. On September 1, 1984, two U.S. mercenaries based in a CIA camp in Honduras, both Viet Nam veterans, were shot down and killed in their Hughes 500 MD helicopter as they were strafing the inhabited town of Santa Clara in northern Nicaragua.[177] Interestingly, a local veteran complained that my vocal opposition to the Contras was not appreciated since, he said, his wife's relative, a guy named Powell from Memphis, was one of the two aircrew killed in the crash. Of course I maintained my right to freedom of expression on my own time away from the outreach center.

Colonel Oliver North of Reagan's NSC staff, in fine Orwellian fashion, called the mercenary operatives "nonofficial assistants."[178] At the same time news reports indicated that a unit of Fort Campbell's 101st Airborne Division was flying combat missions inside Nicaragua and had already suffered seventeen casualties in 1983 alone.[179] Other reports hinted that a number of covert U.S. military operatives were busy in several Central American countries. In increasing numbers, family members of U.S. KIAs in the region were beginning to doubt the veracity of the Army's explanation of the manner and place of death of their loved ones, as claims of "bodywashing" (concocted stories for KIAs) were circulating.[180] And in 1996, a special ceremony was held at Arlington National Cemetery for twenty-one U.S. soldiers killed "for the noblest, the most unselfish reasons" in the secret war in El Salvador. More than five thousand actually served in that dirty war.[181]

Through 1985, the anti-Sandinista rhetoric increased. In February 1985, at a news conference, Reagan said that he did not intend to "remove" the Sandinistas they would "say uncle" and agree to institute what the administration would regard as genuinely democratic changes.[182] On May 1, 1985, the president imposed economic sanctions against Nicaragua by declaring a national emergency due to that country's policies and actions constituting "an unusual and extraordinary threat to the national security and foreign policy of the United States."[183] By early June, an overt invasion of Nicaragua was becoming openly discussed (clearly a covert operation was already underway).[184] An intelligence official said, "an invasion of Nicaragua would [be so easy it would] be like falling off a log."[185] In August, Reagan officials took a clear step toward overt war when they said U.S. "differences with Nicaragua cannot be resolved as long as the Sandinistas remain in power."[186]

In preparing for war, it was clear that the United States was determined to create another Viet Nam, another senseless war against impoverished peasants that we could not win. Contrary to the rhetoric, the Contras were not freedom fighters who would gain the people's loyalty by bringing them democracy and American-style prosperity. Its bloody tactics, as designed by U.S. strategists, in fact were having the opposite effect. In September 1985, a former high-ranking Contra political official quit in disgust over the atrocities being committed by the Contras. Edgar Chamorro, the former communications director for the FDN Contra Directorate, declared in an affidavit:

> [It] was standard FDN practice to kill prisoners and suspected Sandinista collaborators. . . . We were told that the only way to defeat the Sandinistas was to use the tactics the Agency attributed to "Communist" insurgencies elsewhere: kill, kidnap, rob and torture . . . tactics reflected in an

operational manual prepared for our forces by a CIA agent who used the name "John Kirkpatrick" . . . The manual was entitled "Psychological Operations in Guerrilla Warfare." In fact, the practices advocated in the manual were employed by FDN troops. Many civilians were killed in cold blood. Many others were tortured, mutilated, raped, robbed or otherwise abused. . . . The atrocities I had heard about were not isolated incidents, but reflected a consistent pattern of behavior by our troops. There were unit commanders who openly bragged about their murders, mutilations, etc. . . . I frequently heard offhand remarks like, "Oh, I cut his throat." . . . When I questioned them about the propriety or wisdom of doing those things they told me it was the only way to win this war, that the best way to win the loyalty of the civilian population was to intimidate it and make it fearful of us.[187]

Chamorro also said that brigades would "arrive at an undefended village, assemble all the residents in the town square and then proceed to kill—in full view of the others—all persons suspected of working" for the Sandinista government, or the Sandinista Party.[188]

The truth of what was happening was out there, but many U.S. Americans were just not seeing it, perhaps not wanting to believe it. They did not necessarily support Reagan's policies, but they were not engaged enough to prevent him from carrying out his covert, "low-intensity" war. Based on my experience on the ground in Viet Nam, I knew that Reagan's covert war might seem to be "low-intensity" to comfortable, insulated U.S. American citizens, but that it would be extraordinarily intense and destructive for those living day after day in the violent *terror* zones.

Protesting seemed inadequate. I knew campesinos were being slaughtered. I decided that I needed to go to Nicaragua to see for myself what the Sandinista revolution was about and to separate the rhetoric from the reality. I also believed—and hoped—that the Sandinistas were true to their word, and could provide an example of a serious commitment to a socially just society. I was sick of the American Way Of Life, and felt I had to break free, once and for all, and find a different way to live.

In November 1985, I resigned from my work at the Greenfield vet center. On January 4, 1986, I was on a plane headed for Nicaragua.

CHAPTER 16

Dignity Trumps Longevity

I landed in Managua on January 4. I had signed up to take Spanish classes at a school in Estelí, a city of seventy thousand located in a mountainous region ninety miles north of Managua. A bus picked up the twenty or so of us who were going to study there, drove us to Estelí, and dropped us off with our host families.

My artist friend Dinny and I traveled together from Vermont. Dinny spoke some Spanish already. She and I actually stayed alternately with two families of campesinos, expanding our language learning opportunities. One household was headed by Asunción, whose son, Ramón, had been killed fighting Somoza in 1979, and whose son-in-law, Justo, had been killed in 1983 by the Contras while serving as a first lieutenant in the Sandinista army. Another son, Enrique, was also in the Sandinista army fighting the Contras.

The other family was headed by Alejandra, whose son Oscar also had been killed fighting Somoza. Alejandra had three other sons serving in the Nicaraguan army; one had been wounded and was recovering in a military hospital. Each family had a photo of their dead son hanging conspicuously on their living room wall.

These families lived in small, simple houses with part-tile, part-dirt floors. They had electricity to power a couple of light bulbs and a TV. They cooked in a semi-outdoor kitchen so the smoke could go right outside; they didn't have any indoor plumbing, so they used an outhouse. The houses' walls were pockmarked with machine gun bullets from the 1978–1979 Esteliano insurrection against Somoza's National Guard. They were lively houses, with grandchildren running around and a bunch of chickens in the backyard along with a pig or two.

While I was on the plane to Nicaragua I had read a 1985 Oxfam America booklet, *Nicaragua: The Threat of a Good Example?*[189] This booklet reminded me again of what historian William Appleman Williams taught was the "American" *weltanschauung*: achieving prosperity through expansion, with any impediment to that prosperity either assimilated or eliminated. I had not been in Estelí more than a couple of days before I began to encounter the realities of U.S. power. Each night I was kept awake by the sound of powerful explosions in the distance, with machine-gun fire tracers visible within three kilometers to the east of Estelí. I was not reading about Nicaragua anymore. I was there, hearing and seeing for myself how my country's money was being used to kill campesinos.

"Freedom Fighters"

On January 13, just over a week after I landed in Nicaragua, the U.S. National Security Council (NSC) launched an all-out campaign to convince Congress and the American people that the Sandinistas were a growing threat to all of Central America. Elliott Abrams, President Reagan's assistant secretary of state, began this new propaganda campaign with a nationally distributed op-ed piece in which he declared that there was "no question the Sandinista regime is repressive and undemocratic . . . subverting neighboring democratic countries."[190]

Abrams and the Reagan administration were asking Congress for an additional $100 million to fund "freedom fighters," that is, the Contras, to counter the "threat" the Sandinistas posed to neighboring "democratic" countries. In short, Reagan was asking for $100 million to fund terrorists, which meant many more civilians would be killed before this ugly "secret" war ended.

Abrams's op-ed was a part of a massive Orwellian campaign spearheaded by the White House in 1983 to manage "public perceptions," that is, to "manufacture consent."[191] Obsessed with eliminating the dangerous "virus" posed by Nicaragua's popular revolution, administration officials knew that the vast majority of Nicaraguans resisted the Contra "freedom fighters" and that the majority of U.S. Americans opposed Contra aid as well.[192]

The religious right was involved in this campaign as well. Pat Robertson, one of my parents' favorite TV evangelists, was quoted in *Time* magazine as saying, "The U.S. has a moral obligation to support 'freedom fighters' who battle 'satanic' Communism."[193] Robertson was adamant that the Contras be "saved" for Jesus and led religious services in their Honduran camps[194] as he publicly applauded their armed invasion of Nicaragua.[195]

Another of my parents' favorite TV evangelists, Jerry Falwell, set up his Liberty Federation in January 1986 to develop support for various U.S. foreign policy adventures, including Star Wars. This organization was instrumental in helping to increase funding for the Contras.[196]

Abrams's op-ed piece was followed four days later by a scathing condemnation of the Contras from former Contra director Edgar Chamorro: "During my four years as a Contra director, it was premeditated policy to terrorize civilian noncombatants to prevent them from cooperating with the [Sandinista] government. Hundreds of civilian murders, mutilations, tortures and rapes were committed in pursuit of this policy of which the Contra leaders and their C.I.A. supervisors were all aware."[197] Those who were paying attention understood that the Contras were terrorists undermining a popular elected government.

The Reagan administration set out to twist that truth around. Its Office of Public Diplomacy (OPD) aimed to negate news about the positive developments in Nicaragua's health care, literacy, and land reform programs, while discrediting Reagan's critics. To them, the public's opposition to Contra aid was simply an inconvenient fact that had to be reversed.

In OPD's first year of operations it sent materials to 239 editorial writers in 150 cities while arranging 1,500 speaking engagements.[198] The *Washington Post* described OPD's function as the selling of U.S. foreign policy. It seemed as if, in the eyes of the Reagan administration, the people of the United States were part of a foreign, enemy nation requiring a massive dose of propaganda delivered via covert CIA operations to subvert their ideas and change their minds.[199]

The OPD, of course, was not without historical precedent. In 1917, President Woodrow Wilson created the Committee on Public Information (CPI) headed by newspaperman George Creel, which carried out a relentless propaganda campaign to overcome public resistance to entering World War I. Using seventy-five thousand propaganda footsoldiers called "Four-Minute Men" throughout the country, a vast propaganda ministry asserted itself into every aspect of social life in virtually every community in the United States through lectures, entertainment, and news.[200] Among those who assisted was journalist and intellectual Walter Lippmann, who believed in the importance of the "manufacture of consent," and Edward Bernays, the father of modern public relations, who believed that democracy required the government to shape and guide public opinion to maintain order. This he called the "engineering of consent."[201] The power of the executive to assert its own will despite public opinion has since been a constant throughout much of modern U.S. history.

In case propaganda proved insufficient to move public sentiment toward favoring a Contra paramilitary victory, Reagan and his CIA director, William Casey, seriously considered a backup plan that would utilize U.S. troops in an illegal invasion. In that eventuality, a corresponding arrangement would be necessary to contain the anticipated substantial domestic opposition to it.

Casey, a former Office of Strategic Services (OSS) agent in Europe during World War II, had become a wealthy Wall Street tax lawyer before becoming Reagan's 1980 presidential campaign manager, and both men held great contempt for Jimmy Carter. Casey was known to be tough and cold, self-righteously proud that Western intelligence operations are ruthless and cutthroat.[202] As early as 1982, Reagan and Casey directed Oliver North in the NSC to draft contingency plans to suspend the Constitution under several scenarios, one of which was widespread internal dissent or opposition to a U.S. invasion abroad (i.e., in Nicaragua). Suspension of the Constitution, code-named REX-84, would mean turning government control over to the Federal Emergency Management Agency (FEMA), appointing military commanders to run state and local governments, and declaring martial law.[203] The plans also called for the detention of thousands of aliens and dissidents.[204]

What stunned so many, later, when these plans were exposed, was the Reagan administration's clear understanding that "prosperity" trumps "democracy." The power of the people was only a means to an economic end. When the people got in the way of the wealth machine, they were to be silenced. Reagan, Casey, and North were more than willing to implement the same policies "at home" that they were already using in Nicaragua.

The Real Enemy Is Us

I was not very surprised by Elliot Abrams's letter or the Reagan administration's new Contra campaign. After all, I had come to Nicaragua because I already understood that the administration was pursuing prosperity at the expense of democracy in Nicaragua. However, my experiences in Estelí effectively transferred my intellectual understanding into my viscera.

During my first weekend at Estelí, our language school class went to pick coffee in the mountains with a local coffee farming cooperative. While we were there we got word that Contras were attacking cooperatives on the east side of the mountain and that there had been several casualties. These attacks must have been related to the explosions and tracers I witnessed the previous nights. When we returned to Estelí on Sunday, I learned that the Contras had killed eleven people from three local farming cooperatives.

The next day, I was standing on the street behind my adopted family's backyard, which was about a block from the cemetery, when horse-drawn wagons came slowly by bearing the bodies of five women and a child, campesinos killed by the Contras. The simple caskets were open, and I could see the faces of the dead.

"My God," I said, "this is just like Viet Nam." I felt electricity up and down my body, just like I had during my flashback. I started crying, and Alejandra, one of the two women I came to call my Nicaraguan mothers, held and comforted me.

At that moment, Viet Nam and Nicaragua came together as the face of my country. I saw again Mai Ly's eyes. I saw Hue, the old man who had fled the U.S. bombing of his village. Like Mai Ly and Hue, the faces I saw in the caskets were supposed to be the faces of my enemies. I realized, at that moment, that the only real enemy was us. We U.S. Americans were, in effect, killing ourselves without even knowing it.

AWOL in Nicaragua

The American Way Of Life had killed Mai Ly, and the American Way Of Life was now killing campesinos in Nicaragua. And all of us citizens who paid taxes, who went about our day's business as usual, who voted for Tweedledee or Tweedledum, and who remained silent, were complicit.

The American Way Of Life keeps us chained to a frenetic rat race in which most of us spend all our time making a living, managing a household, paying taxes, buying all the things thought necessary to have a "good" life. We waste hours of our lives getting to and from work, getting to and from the mall, shuttling our kids to and from their activities. The price we pay is to give up interactive community and sustainable living for the desperate life of individualism in a materialist age.

Even worse, to maintain this way of life, we must constantly victimize the rest of the world. The countries that comprise the "First World" possess nearly a quarter of the world's population, yet consume somewhere around 85 percent of the world's resources. When the 75 percent of the people left with only 15 percent of the earth's resources fight back, the First World responds with violence. The system requires that they submit. The system requires their goods and their labor. Human beings are no longer considered part of the equation. Not only is this way of life grotesquely immoral and unjust; it is totally unsustainable.

In protest, I already had gone AWOL from U.S. society by becoming a tax refuser. Now, I realized, my life's work would be to educate others about the faces I saw—the faces of Mai Ly and Hue, the faces of the campesinos in Estelí. I had to make public how the American Way Of Life had caused citizens of the United States to leave behind their own humanity. Just as important, I had to find a better way of life for myself and others.

Though I had been moving in a different direction for several years, it took this day of seeing with my own eyes the deaths of these Nicaraguan innocents to make it crystal clear that we all exist together in a sacred interconnection. The mothers, children, fathers, and grandparents in Viet Nam, in Nicaragua—they are all my relatives, too. The knowledge that all life is sacred, including my own, was not just a fact perceived by my brain but something felt in my stomach and now seated deeply inside of me. I am not worth more than they are. They are not worth less than I am.

They Are Not Worth Less

In the little house in Estelí, Nicaragua, I could not stop sobbing over the dead I had seen. Another child and four men who had been killed in the attacks had been buried on Sunday before we returned from coffee picking. All eleven were murdered by U.S.-funded weapons with U.S.-trained and equipped terrorists in a U.S.-guided war. All night long, I talked in one-word-at-a-time, dictionary Spanish with my Nicaraguan family. They thought I was afraid. Rather, I was filled with sadness and rage. Finally, Alejandra found the words to comfort me. It took me a while to understand what she was saying since I knew virtually no Spanish, but her wise words speak to me still: dignity is everything, she said. Longevity is nothing.

Dinny aptly described Alejandra as luminous. Her words were not empty; she was a campesino revolutionary who had already lost a son to the revolution. This woman wasn't a Buddhist; she lived in the moment because she never knew when she would get the call that another son had been killed. She was willing to live that way, to consciously live each moment without worrying about the next one, in order to create a life that she felt was worth living.

For seventeen years I had allowed the dictates of my culture, the middle-class values of "reasonableness" and "credibility," to take precedence over the profound wisdom I had first become conscious of in the villages of Viet Nam's delta. I had learned about dignity when I looked into Mai Ly's eyes—and had then put that knowledge aside. The pull of the American Way Of Life is strong: it tells us that we can "have it all" as long as we are willing to deny our interconnectedness to everyone and everything else. We can "have it all"—but in the bargain we forfeit our dignity as human beings.

Since that moment in January 1986 when I saw those bodies on the wagons in Nicaragua, I have been committed to living and behaving as an equal human being in a global context. Living life this way in the United States is not easy. I have to question and redefine myself every day. How do my everyday activities—eating, keeping warm, moving from one place to another—impact those living elsewhere in the world? How do I spend my time? Am I sensitive about the well-being of others on this planet? I try to live my life as I imagine Mai Ly lived hers, as my Nicaraguan mother is living hers, with my mantra, I am not worth more than they are, and they are not worth less than I am.

I am often described as a peace activist, but I don't accept such labels. When I live my life with an awareness of the earth and of other people, I'm being human. We don't have a word for that. We have a word for driving a truck or making money on the stock market or believing in Karl Marx, but we don't have a word for being someone with their feet on the ground, striving to be connected to other people and to the planet.

It's easy to say these words, but it's not so easy to live them. Our conditioning is so deep, embedded over centuries and perhaps millennia, that once we grasp this new consciousness and embark on a new path of liberation, we can be assured that the remainder of our lives will be spent experimenting with these truths. We will make many mistakes, do "stupid" things, make discriminatory judgments, and probably harm other people, other species, and the planet in the process of this painful but joyous journey toward enlightenment. Nonetheless, it is our incredible opportunity and potential to do so.

Witness for Peace

After my "rebirth" in Nicaragua in early January 1986, I remained there for seven more weeks before returning to the United States. Based in Estelí, I occasionally would go to Managua on my own and meet up with other *internationalistas*. It was there I met Charlie Liteky at the Witness for Peace house.

At the time, Witness for Peace was a courageous faith-based group, primarily U.S. Americans, who for several years had been monitoring Contra attacks in the war zones and reporting on them publicly. They regularly received delegations from the United States to expose increasing numbers of citizens to the realities of the terror war. It was a tremendous service.

Charlie had been a Catholic chaplain in Viet Nam. He had been awarded the Congressional Medal of Honor for rescuing more than twenty wounded soldiers while under intense enemy fire. Though his epiphany and his own transformation to peace activist came many years after he left Viet Nam, by the time we met, Charlie agreed with me that our role in Viet Nam was immoral. His revulsion at what we were doing around the world deepened after he made visits to Central America in the early 1980s, where, among other groups, he met with Salvadoran Mothers of the Disappeared and later, Salvadoran refugees in San Francisco. Just as my work with prisoners had first led me to connect the Viet Nam experience with the American Way Of Life, Charlie's meeting with refugees fleeing repression and terror funded by the United States outraged him about the insulation of the U.S. society.

Charlie was in Nicaragua in 1986 because, like me, he sensed Nicaragua was another Viet Nam. We both believed that the United States was in a state of national moral emergency and we wanted to do something to stop this immoral war. When we met that first time in Managua, Charlie happened to mention that he had been deeply affected when learning of Norman Morrison's self-immolation in 1965 in protest of U.S. policy in Viet Nam. That was the first time I had heard any veteran mention his name, and I was duly impressed. We also talked about Bobby Sands and the nine other Irish hunger strikers who had died in Long Kesh Prison near Belfast in 1981, who were seeking recognition as *political* prisoners, not common criminals, for fighting against the seven-hundred-year British subjection of the Irish. Sands's funeral was attended by one hundred thousand people.

Charlie and I discussed the possibility of doing a similar direct action, fasting or even immolation in protest of the U.S. wars in Central America. We know this would seem crazy to most people living in U.S. America. But we were already living with a new consciousness. And what we saw happening around us every day in Nicaragua only reinforced our commitment to the revolution and our disgust and anger with our own government.

Reason for Anger

I think it may be difficult for many U.S. citizens to understand our level of anger, because of most people's ignorance of geopolitical reality. As I write this, I wonder how many U.S. citizens are sufficiently, personally impacted and outraged by the continued grotesque, illegal occupation of Iraq and Afghanistan to express resistance beyond petitioning a government that cares nothing of popular sentiments. With no universal conscription and no direct taxation for the occupation costs, only a small number of people are personally affected. Every day, as I write this chapter, the United States military is "targeting terrorists" in these countries, which means we are shelling villages and towns, usually killing civilians ("by mistake," it says), yet how many people read the small, quarter-column stories about these deaths buried in the "B" section of the newspaper or in the tiniest boxes online? How many U.S. citizens really understand that U.S. imperialism—our engine of prosperity—has a direct impact on the lives of millions around the world?

We don't know our own history, including our pattern of intervention in the tiny country of Nicaragua. We did not first become interested in Nicaragua in the 1980s. The tiny, impoverished country has been invaded at least a dozen times by U.S. forces since the 1850s, when a Tennessean named William Walker, seeking creation of new, profitable slave territory, imposed himself as president with the aid of a small band of mercenaries and quickly received formal U.S. recognition. Though Walker's adventure was short lived, over the years substantial U.S. extractive industries, businesses, and banking interests profited immensely from Nicaragua's cheap labor, abundant natural resources, and guaranteed markets. Any popular resistance or native restiveness threatened the stability of investors' profits.

In the late 1920s, Wall Street bankers Guaranty Trust and Brown Brothers invested in Nicaraguan mahogany and other timber.[205] A 1926 *New York Times* article reported that "extensive mahogany growths [were] owned by Americans on the east coast of Nicaragua" and the "payment of duties [export taxes] by American exporters of lumber" were in dispute. Export duties legally due to the Nicaraguan government were being confiscated to pay off loans owed to U.S. investors.[206] These and other economic factors helped cause a virtual civil war in Nicaragua, beginning in 1927, between the Conservatives, representing the minority elite, and the Liberals, representing the majority poor, whose small armed element was referred to by the U.S. as "bandits." Of course, the United States could not sit idly by while this "instability" threatened a significant source of prosperity for its elite class.

In January 1927, U.S. President Calvin Coolidge delivered a special address to Congress about instability in Nicaragua:

> I have the most conclusive evidence that arms and munitions in large quantities have been, on several occasions . . . shipped to the revolutionists in Nicaragua . . . [W]e have a very definite and special interest in the maintenance of order and good Government in Nicaragua . . . The United States cannot, therefore, fail to view with deep concern any serious threat to stability and constitutional government in Nicaragua tending toward anarchy and jeopardizing American interests, especially if such state of affairs is contributed to or brought about by outside influences or by any foreign power. . . . At the present time there are large investments in lumbering, mining, coffee growing, banana culture, shipping, and also in general mercantile and other collateral business. . . . There is no question that if the revolution continues, American investments and business interests in Nicaragua will be very seriously affected, if not destroyed.[207]

The northern regions of Nicaragua where I later personally witnessed the impact of Contra fighting had been the scene of intense fighting during the years 1927–1933, when more than five thousand troops conducted an early version of large-scale counterinsurgency operations. This was popularly called "Mr. Coolidge's Jungle War."[208] U.S. Marines occupied the country against campesino rebel resistance to stave off what President Coolidge and Assistant Secretary of State Robert E. Olds claimed in November 1926 were efforts by the Mexican government "to establish a Bolshevik authority in Nicaragua to drive a 'hostile wedge' between the U.S. and the Panama Canal."[209]

U.S. politicians feared Olds was itching for war with Mexico over its fertile Vera Cruz oil fields. But Olds insisted that Mexico was interfering in the affairs of Nicaragua and posing

> a direct challenge to the United States. . . . We must decide whether we shall tolerate the interference . . . in Central American affairs or insist upon

our dominant position. . . . Until now Central America has always understood that governments which we recognize and support stay in power, while those which we do not recognize and support fail. Nicaragua has become a test case. It is difficult to see how we can afford to be defeated.[210]

In January 1927, Coolidge's secretary of state, Frank B. Kellogg, repeated U.S. fears that Nicaragua's stability was threatened if it became a hostile Bolshevist regime in cahoots with revolutionary Mexico: "Formation of the All-American Anti-Imperialist League, under instructions from Moscow" was planned "to organize Latin America against the United States, one of the purposes . . . being to 'actively support Latin-American strikes against American concerns.'"[211] The dissident elements had formed a ragtag rebel army under the command of Augusto Sandino, whom the State Department accused of adopting "the stealthy and ruthless tactics which characterized the savages who fell upon American settlers in our country 150 years ago."[212] Moscow was thus used as early as the 1920s to justify U.S. intervention in the Western Hemisphere. And those who resisted were painted as illegitimate and criminal. As it would again in the 1980s, the U.S. was identifying Indigenous resistance to *our* illegal intervention as a crime—the totally unacceptable crime of self-defense.

Of the 13,000 Marines in the Corps in 1927, at least 1,500 were busy keeping calm in China and 1,100 were occupying Haiti, while another 3,000 sailed in warships. The majority of the balance, at least 5,000, were stationed in Nicaragua with a supportive unit of combat planes.[213] For six years, the Marines fought aggressively, though unsuccessfully, to subdue and eliminate the rebel army led by Sandino, which the U.S. described contemptuously as "bandits" (compare the similar terms "illegal combatants" in Afghanistan, "criminals" in Viet Nam, "savages" in the Americas).

Their tactics were similar to those used earlier against the various Indigenous nations resisting White European settlements—burning crops and killing horses and cattle, destroying food supplies, burning homes, and murdering large numbers of civilians. But with the added firepower made possible by the introduction of aerial bombardment, far greater destruction was exacted in Nicaragua in a shorter period of time. The Marines used fragmentation anti-personnel bombs, scattering shrapnel over wide areas, along with incendiary bombs, organized dive-bombing, machine-gun strafing of civilian population centers, and close air support of ground troop operations. They bragged about the "miracle of marine air" that produced "streets . . . strewn with the dead and dying."[214] Still, they could not defeat the cagey and committed campesino army.

The United States also manipulated elections to guarantee its continued control of Nicaragua's political process. During a demonstration in front of the U.S. Embassy during my first trip to Nicaragua in 1986, I met seventy-seven-year-old Bill Gandall who had been a young U.S. Marine fighting Sandino's forces in the late 1920s. He described the brutality that he and other Marines inflicted on the Nicaraguan people almost sixty years prior. He was quoted at the time in *The Washington Post*: "We never caught him [Sandino] because no matter how we tortured, we could never get people to inform."[215] He recounted his participation in the 1928 U.S. supervised elections, calling them "fraudulent," while describing the Marine's brutality: "I shot a guy at the polls . . . [and] after that, it was taking part in rapes, burning huts, cutting off genitals. I had nightmares for years. I didn't have much of a conscience while I was in the Marines. We were taught not to have a conscience."[216] I cringe at how history continues to repeat itself. As Barbara Tuchman so clearly articulates in *The March of Folly: From Troy to Vietnam*, the horrific patterns of war have played out around the globe for millennia.

Shaping a Response

A few days after the murders of the eleven campesinos, our language class visited the U.S. Embassy in Managua where we met with political "counselor" Garett Sweny. Reading from well-prepared notes, he informed us that peace in Nicaragua depended upon, among other things, the "fortunes of the Contras," which he numbered at more than twenty thousand. He stressed the positive importance of the U.S. economic embargo, including food shortages, implying that increasing people's suffering would sooner or later force the Nicaraguan people to "cry uncle," as Reagan had demanded a year earlier.[217]

The Republicans overwhelmingly supported increasing the "fortunes of the Contras," that is, sending the Contras more money for bullets and bombs, whereas the Democrats overwhelmingly supported starvation as the best path to regime change in Nicaragua. Hard imperialism or soft imperialism—take your pick!

During my time in Nicaragua I traveled around the countryside between Estelí and Managua observing as much as possible, meeting many Nicaraguan people and Sandinista leaders. In mid-February I visited a beautiful farm cooperative in the mountains not far from Estelí. There, the twenty members of the Leonel Rugama extended family told me that "during Somoza years we were like slaves to the protected landowners; since the Revolution it has been like paradise to work and own our land, and profit from hard work without a harsh boss who pays nothing."[218] Unfortunately, because of Contra terrorist activity, half of the family members had to take turns every night as defensive sentries to ward off threatened attacks.

It was while visiting this cooperative that we all heard the tragic news of a nearby Contra ambush of a truck carrying eighteen civilians, killing the Swiss driver, four women, and one child. This was just five weeks after the eleven Estelianos were murdered. Several other people had been kidnapped, murdered, and wounded during these weeks.

There was a Nicaraguan prison in Estelí for captured Contras and on one occasion a small group of us visited the prison staff and interviewed the prisoners. I remember several Contras described how they had been forcibly recruited, actually having been kidnapped from northern Nicaragua communities. Their CIA trainers in Honduras, they said, stressed the satanic behavior of the Sandinistas, saying, "they ate their babies."[219] Unfortunately, the tragic truth was that the Contra War was killing Sandinista babies.

Learning more about the Contra War, I offered to broadcast a speech on Radio Liberación in Estelí, asking the U.S.-funded Contras and their CIA advisers and mercenaries to lay down their arms. That speech was translated into Spanish and broadcast continuously for a week or two. This is what I would have called witnessing when I was a Baptist. Given the heavy propaganda of the times, however, I doubt my words influenced anyone to lay down their arms.

As the pressure built in the U.S. Congress for more Contra aid, or even an overt U.S. military invasion of Nicaragua, we heard that El Salvador was aiding Honduras in the U.S. paramilitary campaign to overthrow the Sandinista government. I nervously discussed this additional threat with my associates in Nicaragua. El Salvador had a large military air base at Ilopango just east of the capital city of San Salvador, and reports indicated Contra supplies were being flown in, and airplanes were departing from that base for missions over Nicaragua.[220]

I wondered how we might convince more U.S. Americans to come to Nicaragua to witness the war, stand with the people, and share their risks. In 1938, Gandhi had called for the formation of a people's nonviolent army of volunteers "equal to every occasion where the police and the military are required."[221] This "army" would be prepared to risk their lives as peacemakers, putting their bodies in the line of fire to prevent the killing of civilians.

In 1961, A.J. Muste, a long-time advocate of nonviolent resistance in the United States, along with activists from other countries, created an experimental peace brigade to be a nonviolent force to "revolutionize the concept of revolution itself by infusing into the methods of resisting injustice the qualities which insure the preservation of human life and dignity."[222] The Brigade's most important project established a training center for nonviolent action in Dar-Es Salaam, Tanzania, Africa.[223] In 1981, Peace Brigades International was founded based largely on this model. I was impressed with this idea, and began to think of doing something similar in Central America.

In 1983, I had attended the Vietnam Veterans of America founding convention in Washington, D.C., as a delegate of our local Greenfield VVA (Vietnam Veterans of America) chapter. My call at the convention for the creation of unarmed veteran observer teams in Central America was reported in *The Village Voice*, stirring controversy but no action. Now, in Nicaragua, the time seemed ripe to try this idea again. [224]

In February 1986, I first presented to a Nicaraguan solidarity official a written proposal to provide teams of veterans to live in war-ravaged communities working on construction projects. The Veterans Peace Action Teams would become a reality exactly one year later.

CHAPTER 17

Fasting for Life

Returning from the war zones of Nicaragua, I made a brief stop in Washington, D.C., for one more effort at lobbying. It seemed that it might be effective, given the questions in the media about the Contra War. I chose to focus my efforts on a particular congressman, Douglas Wayne Owens (D-UT), a fence sitter on Contra aid. A former Mormon missionary and member of the House Foreign Affairs Committee, he was admired for his honesty as a liberal congressman.

I personally presented Owens with voluminous evidence of Contra terrorism in Nicaragua—photos, survivors' written testimonies, audiotapes of interviews, and oral and written summaries of personal observations. After allowing me three or four minutes to summarize the evidence of U.S.-financed terrorism in Nicaragua, Owens looked at me and said: "Why should I believe someone who looks like you?" At the time I had long hair and a beard; my dress was neat but casual. Realizing that all the testimony in the world evidently didn't count, in Owens's eyes, if you didn't wear a suit, I came away from his office feeling utterly dejected.

Devastated by what I had experienced in Central America, and in Washington, D.C., I retreated to Chelsea, Vermont, to a cabin belonging to Dinny's parents, and secluded myself. I didn't want to see anybody. I didn't want to hear anyone say, "Hi, Brian, how are you?" I couldn't say that I was fine, and I didn't want to have to explain what I was feeling. I was intensely angry and elated at the same time: angry at U.S. policy and elated at how inspirational the Nicaraguan Revolution was.

For much of that spring and summer, I gave myself space to process what I had seen, heard, and felt. I worked as a roofer's helper to earn food and rent money. I allowed time for thinking, reflection, and meditative prayer. I knew that I had come far on my journey from the young man who hated the "reds" and believed the United States could do no wrong. I needed time to think about who I had become, and how to proceed on my new path.

Fearmongering at Home

Listening to and reading Reagan's pronouncements about Central America made me sick. On March 24, 1986, *Newsweek* reported that Reagan was proudly proclaiming, "I'm a Contra, too!" At that point I was hoping that Mr. Reagan would actually join the Contras on patrols and ambushes in Nicaragua and find out what it felt like to risk his own life while seeking to murder others.

It was not long after my return that Reagan made one of his most infamous fearmongering statements, insisting that defeat of his $100 million Contra aid package in Congress would mean "consolidation of a privileged sanctuary for terrorists and subversives just two days' driving time from Harlingen, Texas."[225] His claim was ridiculous, of course, but it did motivate me to later visit Harlingen to examine any preparations its residents were making to defend themselves against an invasion from Nicaragua, 1,200 miles to the south!

In late March, the administration's rhetoric became even more Orwellian when the State Department declared Nicaragua to be an aggressor state in Central America. Of course, the U.S. administration's aim was to negate Nicaragua's claim of self-defense under international law.[226] This is an old trick: an authority figure rhetorically identifies an enemy as being ready and able to invade our own country, threatening our "exceptional" way of life, in order to whip up popular support for war. Such claims may sound absurd later on, but we know from history how well they work: it is the big scary lies that evade critical thinking and public scrutiny. Hermann Goering, Hitler's second in command, explained it this way:

> Naturally the common people don't want war neither in Russia, nor in England, nor for that matter in Germany. That is understood. But, after all, it is the leaders of the country who determine the policy and it is always a simple matter to drag the people along, whether it is a democracy, or a fascist dictatorship, or a parliament, or a communist dictatorship. Voice or no voice, the people can always be brought to the bidding of the leaders. That is easy. All you have to do is tell them they are being attacked, and denounce the peacemakers for lack of patriotism and exposing the country to danger. It works the same in any country.

Twenty years earlier, in 1966, President Johnson had warned that if we didn't stop the reds in Viet Nam they would soon be attacking San Francisco.[227] In 1986, President Reagan expressed his enthusiasm for "rollback" of the evil Soviet empire and preventing what he called a Soviet beachhead in the Americas. Fifteen years later, in 2002, George W. Bush proclaimed that Saddam Hussein of Iraq was about to send weapons of mass destruction our way.

All of these were lies. However, Reagan's lies about the Sandinista revolution were so extreme that he was having difficulty winning the popular support he needed to overthrow a sovereign government. Even members of the usually passive U.S. media were curious why Reagan was so eager to throw money at the Contras.[228]

Why do we continue to allow this chronic pattern of national lying? As a society whose primary religion is materialism, our culture tends to be dominated by individualism, material acquisition, and competition. Our obsessive pursuit of materialism has preempted the evolutionary social-biological compact that guided our species for millennia. I believe human beings come into the world with the archetypal characteristics of empathy, cooperation, and mutual respect. We are wired as social beings. Yet these fundamental characteristics have been buried under an avalanche of narcissistic, egocentric behavior fueled by modern materialist culture. This goes against our evolutionary nature.

Our desperate attempts to ensure our personal survival in the frenetic impersonal world of materialism leave little psychic/intellectual space or time for us to be creatively engaged citizens in a wonderfully diverse world. Emotional insecurity tends to breed obedient and compliant consumers and worker-robots. It is easier to believe the propaganda and lies of the corporate nation state—which we legitimize with our taxes, votes, silence, and daily participation—than to begin a process of critical thinking that might disrupt our comfortable lives. With little memory of our collective political and psychological histories, we have no frame of reference with which to thoughtfully analyze current events. It is easier to trust the "experts" and silently assent to a vertical system that protects our individual pursuits of "prosperity" (even as it grotesquely enriches the oligarchy at the expense of much of the remainder of the world) than to consider our responsibility for all the consequences of each of our daily choices. And so we give up our power as genuinely autonomous beings within community, denial being a chronic defense mechanism, enabling the status quo to continue with only minor interference here and there.

Duncan Murphy

My experience with Congressman Douglas Wayne Owens would be the last time I ever directly lobbied a member of Congress in a Washington office. I turned instead to veterans' organizations, figuring that Congress might perhaps listen to a group of veterans. I traveled several times on Amtrak from Vermont to Washington, D.C., sometimes handing out leaflets on the street describing Reagan's war of terror against the people of Nicaragua and El Salvador. Washington was a familiar place and I found many people there who were like-minded. One of them was Duncan Murphy.

Murphy had served as an ambulance driver in World War II and took part in the liberation of the Bergen-Belsen concentration camp. It was that experience that started his journey as an activist against war. At an antiwar meeting in Washington, I noticed a man who looked a lot like the Shiloh driver who used to deliver weekly baked goods to my childhood home in western New York State more than thirty years earlier. I asked, "Did you used to deliver baked goods to homes in Ashville, New York, in the 1950s?" Yes, he had. And that was Duncan Murphy! This serendipitous meeting revealed how vital our local connections can be.

Opposing Contra Aid

Charlie Liteky was temporarily living in D.C., and we began meeting quietly to plan an action to protest the U.S. government's support of the Contras. We knew the Contra aid bill would come up for a vote in June, so we pondered nonviolent direct actions that might help thwart that vote. Our first idea was to pour a red liquid, representing blood, down the ribs bracing the dome of the Capitol building on the night of the vote. We seriously considered this dramatic tactic, but after spending a month casing the huge structure we decided we couldn't pull it off. As it turned out, it was just as well, since the office in which we were discussing this plan was bugged and we learned in June that we would have been arrested once we began to climb the dome on the evening of the vote.

Instead, we decided to embark upon a water-only fast if the bill passed. We hoped it wouldn't pass, of course, and in mid-April we helped organize a new veterans organization, the short-lived National Federation of Veterans For Peace. Four dozen veterans arrived from around the country, and we held a press conference announcing our vehement opposition to Contra aid. Charlie was named the new organization's coordinator. After the press conference we published newsletters and all the other things typically done when trying to organize a movement.

I worked hard on the lobbying front, but my experience in the halls of Congress did not give me much hope. In general, those in power do not want to hear about the crimes being committed on behalf of a system designed to maintain power and wealth.

On the same day of our veterans' press conference, April 14, 1986, U.S. Secretary of State George Schultz presented a college lecture, "Moral Principles and Strategic Interests," in which he declared that "negotiations are a euphemism for capitulation if the shadow of power is not cast across the bargaining table."[229] In other words, the United States preferred to "negotiate" by bringing a gun to the bargaining table. That gun was the Contras.

If that wasn't enough, we soon learned from Witness for Peace that on that same day a band of Contras had ambushed and burned a civilian pickup carrying Nicaraguan construction workers on the road to Wiwilí about three miles north of Pantasma, murdering three and injuring two others. The very next day, in another part of the world, nearly fifty U.S. warplanes dropped 350 bombs and missiles on Libya to send an "antiterror" message to Colonel Khadafi, another of the evil leaders *du jour*. These events severely aggravated me and some of the other veterans, and we wondered how we could endure these ongoing acts of barbarism. I returned to Vermont to get a grip on my emotions and to reflect on my next steps.

While in Vermont, I read another Witness for Peace report of a two-hour attack by two hundred Contras on a war resettlement community near Pantasma, twenty-five miles north of Jinotega city. Twenty houses were burned, three residents were injured as they fled, and one nineteen-year-old boy was seized and led away with his hands tied behind his back. I was haunted by what had happened to that young man, and I wondered again how this madness might be stopped.

On June 25, 1986, I rode Amtrak to Washington to personally witness the big $100 million Contra aid vote. The level of debate was beyond disappointing. Both sides seemed to agree that the Sandinistas were a totalitarian regime supported by the Soviet Union that was oppressing its own people while seeking to spread Communism throughout the hemisphere. The only debate was whether the Sandinistas should be starved out through an economic embargo or forced out by the Contra terror war. I was not surprised when the Contras won by a vote of 221 to 209.

Congress refused to honestly (i.e., overtly) implement policies that opposed the popular democratic revolutions in Nicaragua and El Salvador. They refused to openly use U.S. military force. Burned by Viet Nam, politicians did not want to conduct another U.S. military venture that might go awry. Instead, they relied on the creation of puppet national security states and covert actions in Central America that used terror to preserve the oligarchic status quo, such as in El Salvador and Guatemala, and counterrevolutionary forces such as the Contras to overthrow the people's-oriented government in Nicaragua.

I noticed the men in the gallery section to my right were Contra leaders. One of them was Adolfo Calero, onetime Coca-Cola baron in Nicaragua under Somoza, now the principal political spokesman for the Contras. As I exited the gallery into the hallway, I walked right by Calero, who was laughing heartily with his Contra friends. Congress had just given him $100 million to fund thousands of terrorists. I felt sick to my stomach.

Two days after that vote, the World Court rendered its final decision on Nicaragua's suit against the United States. In an unprecedented decision, the court ordered the U.S. "immediately to cease and to refrain from training, arming, equipping, financing and supplying the *contra* forces or otherwise encouraging, supporting, and aiding military and paramilitary activities in and against Nicaragua." The court also ordered the United States to provide reparations to Nicaragua, later determined at more than $17 billion. In response, Reagan declared the United States was not subject to the court's jurisdiction, though this country had been an initial signatory to the treaty creating the court and was subject to its charter.[230]

Phil Roettinger

During this difficult period, I was uplifted to read a personal account in the July issue of *The Progressive* magazine by ex–U.S. Marine colonel Phil Roettinger, one of the forty veterans who had attended our April 1986 press conference in Washington, traveling from his home in Mexico. His article, "The Company, Then and Now," described his role as a CIA operative, working under director Allen Dulles, to overthrow Jacobo Arbenz Guzmán in 1954. A former general, Arbenz had been democratically elected in 1951 as a reformist president of Guatemala.

Under Arbenz and his predecessor, Juan José Arévalo, workers and campesinos were able to freely organize in alternative political parties and strong labor unions for the first time in Guatemalan history, develop peasant associations, create committees to decide the fair allotment of land grants, and build the first women's organizations. At the time, Arbenz was in the process of nationalizing unused United Fruit Company land and redistributing the land to the poor campesinos, paying as compensation the land value as reported on the company's own tax returns. In addition, United Fruit and other companies were also being required to pay fair wages, though they were allowed to remain in the country. The grip of the U.S. corporations and the country's traditional upper classes was being broken, and rigid social hierarchies were being weakened by the explosion of vibrant local culture.[231]

These radical moves, of course, ended the subsidy of slave-like labor the companies had enjoyed and curtailed the huge profits they had come to demand. From the U.S. point of view, Arbenz was threatening the prosperity of U.S. businesses (a.k.a. "U.S. interests"). His land reform policies had to be stopped.

Dulles, United Fruit's lawyer at the time, accused Arbenz of being a puppet of the Soviet Union and convinced President Eisenhower to order his overthrow in 1954, an event that led to the murder of as many as two hundred thousand people over the next forty years. Phil Roettinger was part of that covert action against Arbenz. In his article comparing U.S. actions against Arbenz to those against the Sandinistas, he wrote, "It is painful to look on as my Government repeats the mistakes in which it engaged me thirty-two years ago. I have grown up. I only wish my Government would do the same."

It was validating for me to read another veteran's account of a personal transformation. Roettinger described his sense of responsibility for the egregious damage inflicted on others when he was so ideologically brainwashed—a feeling I knew so well. Phil and I later became good friends. He became like a father figure to me, and we shared several trips studying U.S. interventions in Central America and the Middle East.

A New Path

Phil Roettinger, Duncan Murphy, Charles Liteky—these three men, and many others, were all on a similar journey and it was no coincidence that our paths crossed. I don't know if I would have continued on the path I did without the support and encouragement of Charlie, Duncan, Phil, and other veterans. They affirmed for me that I was not insane, but that something was, in fact, insane about our way of life. They gave me the courage to do what came next.

Up until this moment in the summer of 1986, I had never taken on the U.S. government in a direct way. I had protested the Viet Nam War within official channels, writing letters to Congress and complaining to my superiors. My work on prison reform was all done through Congress and state legislatures. My work on behalf of veterans often entailed filing paperwork with the VA. I had attended rallies and protest marches, but I had never said, "I will put my life on the line to stop what my government is doing."

Immediately after the Contra aid vote, I went to a pay phone near the Capitol building and called Charlie at his home on the Pacific coast, even though it was after 11 p.m. his time. Immediately we started planning for a water-only fast to begin approximately September 1.

Planning the Fast for Life

Planning any direct action takes thoughtful preparation. The key for us was to make absolutely clear to the public why we were fasting. Reagan's terror wars were illegal and demonic. We wanted to increase public awareness of the horror and help build popular resistance. Our plan was simple. We would sit on the Capitol steps, the front porch of Congress so to speak, and drink only water. We would be proxies for the people in Central America, who were invisible in the United States, people who were dying because of U.S. policies. We wanted to do more than talk. We wanted to feel their anguish, and we wanted others to feel their anguish through us.

When you feel something, you start getting in touch with your passion and compassion. Things start happening. You act differently. I know this from my own experience. All of my thinking and talking about politics didn't mean anything compared to looking into Mai Ly's eyes or seeing the dead campesinos in Estelí.

We veterans had been trained to go to war, and to take the lives of "the enemy." We had trusted the "causes" our government declared necessary for "national security." We obediently participated in an unjust war, having believed everything we had been told. Some of us, myself included, were still hurting from having been betrayed so callously. Now, dictated by conscience, we were going to risk our lives for peace, to save the lives of the "enemy." I explained it this way to the media in a press release issued September 1:

> I and three other veterans of war have decided to embark upon the most important mission of our lives—a fast for life. Once having put our bodies on the line elsewhere in the waging of war, for issues we did not fully or even minimally understand, we now choose to put our bodies on the line here in this country in the waging of peace for issues we possess a clearer understanding of. We do so with a great affirmation for life—all life, whether for Nicaraguans, North Americans, Soviet citizens, etc.

Charlie Liteky and I continued meeting in July, and were soon joined by Duncan Murphy. Duncan's friend George Mizo, a highly decorated Viet Nam veteran, also wanted to join our fast. George had been a platoon sergeant in Viet Nam and was seriously wounded himself when most of his unit was wiped out in an ambush. He survived and became an uncompromisingly antiwar activist. The four of us decided to fast in shifts, with Charlie and George beginning the fast, followed two weeks later by Duncan and me. The idea was that if two people were close to death, the public would know that two more people were to continue the action.

Before embarking on the mission, Charlie wanted to renounce his Congressional Medal of Honor in protest of U.S. policies in Central America. On July 29, 1986, at a solemn ceremony at the Vietnam Memorial, he placed on the ground at the Wall's apex an envelope containing the medal and a letter addressed to President Reagan. In the letter's conclusion, Charlie wrote, "I pray for your conversion, Mr. President. Come morning I hope you wake up and hear the cry of the poor riding on a southwest wind from Guatemala, Nicaragua, and El Salvador. They're crying, 'Stop killing us!'"

When President Johnson draped the medal around Charlie's neck eighteen years earlier on November 19, 1968, according to Charlie, the president had said, "Son, I'd rather have one of these babies than be president." Charlie is believed to be the only recipient of the Congressional Medal of Honor to ever renounce it, and it is now on display at the Smithsonian Institution's National Museum of American History on the Washington Mall.

On August 13, 1986, the Senate passed a slightly different version of the $100 million Contra aid package that would go to a conference committee. As a result of this Senate vote less than three weeks before we were to begin the fast, U.S. Senator James Sasser (D-TN) predicted that the Contras could now be trained as regular army units and be ready to launch an invasion and seize a remote area of Nicaragua by spring 1987, likely with support required from U.S. Marines.[232] Knowing this made my heart race as I prepared for our action, especially as I learned only a few days later that Reagan was preparing to send U.S. soldiers to train Contra commanders to overthrow the Sandinistas.[233]

Fasting for Life

We began the Veterans Fast for Life on September 1, 1986. Charlie and George started their water-only diet that day, and Duncan and I joined them on the steps of the Capitol. I started a quasi-fast in preparation, eating mostly bananas and wheatgrass juice.

At first, the public didn't seem to notice. The Capitol police, mostly vets, would come over and joke with us, but we didn't have many other visitors. But by the second week, a support group of thirty or so people emerged. They sat with us on the steps, made sure we had sufficient water, and passed out educational leaflets. In the evening, we slept at the house of the Christic Institute (also an organization under FBI surveillance), and there we had lively discussions with our support group about the fast. The Church of the Savior on Massachusetts Avenue provided office space, out of which we developed press strategies with the help of a media coordinator.

A physician monitored our health on a daily basis—keeping track of blood pressure, electrolyte levels, and presence of essential minerals such as potassium necessary for the heart. We instructed the doctor not to bring us out of a coma if that were to occur to any of us deep into the fast, but to keep us abreast of any health-threatening diagnoses. I wrote instructions for my burial in Nicaragua if it came to that. Taking care of these details freed me to focus on the purpose and experience of the fast.

I want to make clear that none of us wished to die. We wanted to live. We wanted to be part of a new United States, a nation of people willing to embark on a radically new course of humility and honest justice. We would not stop fasting until we saw a sufficient response. We hoped that our fast would result in conspicuous nonviolent resistance, with the people of the United States rising up to protest the policies that were murdering Nicaraguans and Salvadorans. At the very least, we were going to fast until we saw that people actually understood that a different way of life was necessary. We wanted to make clear that dignity trumps longevity. We would rather die than live a way of life we could not believe in.

Once we started reaching out to the media, interest perked up. Our first wave of support came from church groups, many of them advocates of liberation theology. Many came from the sanctuary movement, from churches that had protected refugees fleeing repression from U.S.-financed wars in El Salvador and Guatemala. Every evening at six, someone from our support group would conduct a service on the steps. By the fifth week hundreds of people were joining us during our daily four-hour sit, spilling out into the east Capitol parking lot. As our bodies shrank, the crowds grew.

One of the people who supported the fast was an experienced faster himself—Mitch Snyder. A member of the Washington, D.C.–based Community for Creative Nonviolence (CCNV), he had fasted at length on several occasions on behalf of the homeless. He was a contemporary inspiration for our fast.

Many people, of course, didn't support the fast on philosophical or strategic grounds, including those who were vigorously opposed to Reagan's policies. The extraordinary nonviolent activist Phil Berrigan, for example, thought the action too death-oriented, too violent. Charlie Clements, who at the time was directing an effort to elect new U.S. senators who would oppose Reagan's terrorist policies, thought we should work on changing the election system. Allies within the Unitarian Church also believed we should work to effect change within the system.

But we were past that. We believed that the system was the problem and therefore could not be the solution. Just as I had left my Republican upbringing for political liberalism in the late 1960s, now I was leaving liberalism behind. I was becoming what some termed a radical. But being called a radical didn't feel quite right. I was simply expressing a basic truth about protecting international law and people's human rights, following my own conscience. I was simply becoming more human.

Signs of Change

A few days before the fast was to begin, a number of people were already protesting on the Capitol steps. Peter Yarrow of Peter, Paul, and Mary joined our assembly to play music in solidarity. After about two weeks of sitting on the front steps of the U.S. Capitol building, we started seeing some interest from the oligarchs who sometimes worked inside the building. On September 15, Senators Tom Harkin (D-IA) and Charles Mathias (R-MD), in separate press releases, brought attention to our "plea for peace" while urging the Reagan administration to "heed the pleas of these veterans." On September 23, Rep. Robert J. Mrazek (D-NY) in a speech on the House floor lauded the fast, and paid a special tribute to Charlie Liteky's strength of character for revealing the same courage in confronting U.S. apathy that he had showed in saving lives in Viet Nam. On the twenty-fourth day of the fast, my U.S. senator from Vermont, Patrick Leahy, inserted into the *Congressional Record* a statement in support of the fast with a news article attached to it.[234]

Not wanting to depend very much on the U.S. oligarchic political process, we traveled to New York on the weekend of September 20 to personally meet in private with the Mexican ambassador to the United Nations. Mexico was a leader in the Central American Contadora peace process, through which several nations were attempting to negotiate a cessation of U.S. aid to the Contras. He was pleasantly surprised because he said the members of his group had been waiting for signs that the U.S. people were prepared to more vigorously oppose the lawless policy.

Senator John Kerry (D-MA) made a strong statement on the Senate floor on September 25 about the fasters, asking other senators "to take note of the depth of their commitment and the concern which they express regarding our policy." On the same day, Mary McGrory wrote a column in the *Washington Post*, "Starving for Peace." On September 29, my Republican congressman from Vermont, James Jeffords, spent forty-five minutes talking to me on the steps about his determined opposition to Contra aid. Senator John Kerry visited with us on the steps several times throughout the fast.

On October 7, the thirty-seventh day of the fast, thirteen U.S. senators and seventy-five members of the House of Representatives issued a joint public statement saying they were "moved" by our "courage and sincerity" while reiterating their strong opposition to Contra aid. John Kerry urged us to end our "hunger strike" before we died.[235] A number of senators and representatives had joined us on the steps on October 3 for a conversation, including Senators Kerry, Don Riegle of Michigan, Chris Dodd of Connecticut, and Daniel Patrick Moynihan of New York. Soon after, we were visited by experienced faster Dick Gregory, Martin Luther King III, and Bishop Walter Francis Sullivan from Roanoke, Virginia.

Just two days before, on the thirty-fifth day of the fast, a politically explosive event had occurred when a plane dropping illegal arms to the Contras in southern Nicaragua was shot down. One crew member succeeded in parachuting to safety—Eugene Hasenfus, an arms kicker who had formerly done the same job for the CIA in Laos during the Viet Nam War. The CIA and Reagan of course denied any connection to Hasenfus, but the downing of the aircraft and Hasenfus's confession exposed what would become known as the Iran-Contra scandal. Eventually, it would be revealed that the United States had engaged in a doubly illegal covert action—illegally trading arms to Iran for U.S. hostages in Lebanon while using the cash gained from Iran to provide weapons to the Contras in Nicaragua in violation of congressional prohibitions.

The Reagan administration and its allies went into high gear to try to distract the public. On the forty-first day of the fast, six days after the Hasenfus incident, Senator Warren Rudman (R-NH), a member of the Senate Intelligence Committee, made the shocking accusation that we fasting veterans were the equivalent to Middle Eastern terrorists.[236] Very soon thereafter, a Plowshares group in Chicago chose to jam the locks on military recruiters' offices with gum, and left leaflets saying the action was done in solidarity with our fast. In response, the Chicago office of the FBI issued a priority communiqué to all its offices to investigate both the Plowshares group and the Veterans Fast for Life as terrorist suspects! This was something we didn't learn about for another year, when it made us wonder: was there a connection between Rudman's statement, confidential Senate Intelligence Committee discussions, and the FBI's rush to investigate us as domestic terrorist suspects?

The accusation issued by government officials toward us seemed not only ridiculous, but also very ominous. It demonstrated how frightened our supposedly democratic government is of free speech and of real resistance to its policies, even nonviolent resistance. The FBI was actually quite serious about the threat we posed. One agent from Peoria, Illinois, named Jack Ryan wrote a letter to his supervisors saying that because we were "totally nonviolent" he was "not willing to conduct this lead or be involved in this case." He was fired. His case went all the way to the Supreme Court, which refused to overturn the U.S. 7th Circuit Court of Appeals decision affirming his dismissal for disobeying a lawful order of a paramilitary organization such as the FBI. Apparently, government workers aren't allowed to tell the truth.

On the same day Rudman made his preposterous statement accusing us of committing the equivalent of terrorist acts by fasting, the New York Times reported that U.S. officials admitted illegally assisting private agencies and organizations to arm the Contras, the consequences of which were, of course, a war of terror against countless peasants, murder and mayhem.[237] The tide was beginning to turn, we hoped, though it was hard to be happy about these media stories: the hypocrisy of Rudman accusing us of being terrorists when the U.S. was arming terrorists was sickening.

As the fast went on, my parents became depressed worrying about my health. Many people thought we were crazy. But this was a cause we believed in. All of us had known we might die when we went off to war. That didn't deter us and no one tried to stop us from going, or at least no one had tried to stop me. But now that we were on a water-only fast and it seemed we really might die, people were pleading with us to stop. We all understood the irony. Why should we be willing to risk death for something we didn't particularly believe in, but not for something we believed in deeply? Other vets got it. By the end of September more and more veterans seemed to be expressing solidarity with the fast.[238]

By the second week of October, it was clear that increasing numbers of vets were incensed at U.S. policies and beginning to feel empowered. Throughout the fast, other veterans joined us for a few days here and there. The Hasenfus affair provided another stimulus to the movement. On the thirty-ninth day of the fast a number of vets from around the country joined us near the Vietnam Memorial to return war medals in protest of Reagan's wars.[239] Some people said the fast helped inspire a resurgence of the vets' peace movement. I don't know about that, but I know we did motivate a lot of people to engage in direct action.

On the forty-fifth day of the fast, there were more reports confirming the U.S. use of the Ilopango Air Base in El Salvador as the center of CIA-supported aerial operations for supplying the Contras.[240] Despite the continued efforts of the Reagan administration to create an aggressive, overt war against Nicaragua, it seemed that the tide might be turning. We certainly hoped so, for our own sake. Mail poured into our office. More and more people came to sit with us. And, as we sat on the steps, we got a call that we were invited to appear on *The Phil Donahue Show*. Finally, we had broken through to a mass audience.

The same day we appeared on the Donahue show, our doctor told us George was only a few days from death. Over a two-day period of discussion with our support group, and after initial disagreement among the four of us, we decided that the fast had been sufficiently successful. Indeed, the fast had definitely increased the education of the public and escalated expressions of opposition to Reagan's policies. During the last two days of the fast, Nicaragua's foreign minister, Miguel D'Escoto Brockmann, visited us. At midnight on October 17—forty-seven days after we had begun—we held public communion and broke bread together on the steps of the Capitol.

By this time, there had been five hundred documented actions around the country in solidarity with the fast.[241] When the staggered fast ended, Charlie and George had gone forty-seven days with no food, I had gone thirty-six days, and Duncan thirty-three. George recovered quickly and each of us resumed our respective political activities.

WAR HEROES ELEVATE COMMITMENT TO PEACE IN CENTRAL AMERICA ...

These men are participating in the **VETERANS FAST-FOR-LIFE** and have agreed to break their fast only if they recognize a "...significant signal of protest..." from U.S. citizens condemning U.S. government policies in Central America.

❝ In 1945 I was among those who helped to liberate the concentration camps. At that time, I made a vow to prevent those atrocities from ever happening again. Forty years later I went to Nicaragua and heard of the same atrocities from the lips of contra victims. ❞

Duncan Murphy, 66, of Sulphur Springs, Arkansas. Former member of U.S. Army Ambulance Corps and World War II combat veteran. Began Fast-For-Life 9/15/86.

❝ Central America is taking me back to Vietnam which was an illegitimate and immoral war built upon a lie...and so is this one... I find it ironic that conscience called me to renounce the Medal of Honor for the same reason I received it...trying to save lives. ❞

Charles Liteky, 55, of San Francisco, California. Former U.S. Army Chaplain, Vietnam veteran, and recipient of the Congressional Medal of Honor which he renounced on July 29, 1986 to protest U.S. policies in Central America. Began Fast-For-Life 9/01/86.

❝ You don't win hearts and minds by killing them. We don't promote democracy and freedom in Central America, we support markets. I've done everything my country asked me to do... I was a good student...good athlete...went to college and went off to war...but my government just keeps lying, violating the Constitution and international law. ❞

S. Brian Willson, 45, of Chelsea, Vermont. Former U.S. Air Force Security Officer and Vietnam veteran. Attorney-at-Law. Began Fast-For-Life 9/15/86.

❝ Once I was willing to risk my life in war... why not sacrifice it for peace? What the United States government is doing in Nicaragua is **NOT** being done in my name. ❞

George Mizo, 40, of Trenton, New Jersey. U.S. Army combat veteran of the Vietnam War. Began Fast-For-Life 9/01/86.

Veterans Fast for Life poster from September 1986 found at an October civil disobedience action at a Chicago military recruiting office that led the FBI to initiate an investigation of the fasters as suspects under "domestic security/terrorism" guidelines.

THE *BOSTON GLOBE* SATURDAY, OCTO   11, 1986 17

METRO/REGION

October, 11, 1986

Living/Arts 20

Rudman likens fasting veterans to terrorists

By Eduardo Paz-Martinez
Globe Staff

Sen. Warren Rudman (R-N.H.), in a letter released yesterday, compared fasting veterans protesting US policy in Central America to Mideast terrorists holding Americans hostage in Lebanon.

Rudman's statement, made in response to a veterans group's request for his support of the fast that began on the steps of the Capitol Sept. 1, was quickly blasted by Boston-area veterans as "absurd" and "poppycock."

"The veterans speak for the majority of the American people in opposing a policy of creating death and hunger in Central America," said James Packer, a

'Rudman is full of poppycock. His statement tells me he is in tune with the present administration. Rudman wants to go back to the 1950s.'
                                                    — Ron Armstead, a veteran

member of the Boston chapter of Vietnam Veterans of America. "Sen. Rudman's analysis is absurd."

Rudman, a freshman senator seeking reelection, sent the letter dated Oct. 3 to a New Hampshire chapter of the Veterans For Peace organization, which is supporting the four fasting men.

"In my opinion, their actions are hardly different

than those of the terrorists who are holding our hostages in Beirut until we agree to release their comrades in Kuwait, who we in fact have no control over," Rudman wrote. "The debate over this difficult and contentious issue is not furthered by attempts to hold government hostage."

Packer, one of several hundred local veterans who were scheduled to join the fasting veterans in Washington this weekend, said the group no longer takes Rudman seriously.

"Perhaps we are beginning to have some kind of effect on the decision-makers," he added. "As for Rudman, his statement speaks for itself. It's not to be taken seriously."

John Barr, a 30-year Marine veteran who saw combat in Korea and Vietnam and a member of the New Hampshire veterans' group, said the senator's letter "enraged" state veterans.

RUDMAN, Page 19

Rudman likens veterans fasting in protest to Mideast terrorists

■ RUDMAN
Continued from Page 17

Rudman, in a statement released by his office yesterday, said he did not intend to "offend anyone."

"But I stand by my basic message of the letter that while we all cherish our basic democratic right to dissent. I cannot support the actions of a few individuals seeking to impose their will upon a government by threatening to take their own lives," the statement added.

Rudman's comments were in direct reference to the veterans' fast. The four, Congressional Medal of Honor winner Charles Lipsky of San Francisco, George Miso of Watertown, Brian Willson of Chelsea, Vt., and Duncan Murphy of Arkansas, have said they will not end their fast until the United States changes its military policy in Central America.

Packer said Rudman's frank comments are proof that their opposition is "now being discussed in the halls of Congress and in the back rooms of the State Depart-

ment."

His reaction was echoed by others.

"Rudman is full of poppycock," said Ron Armstead, another veteran. "His statement tells me he is in tune with the present administration. Rudman wants to go back to the 1950s."

Armstead said the senator's antagonistic characterization will only cement the veterans groups' resolve. "It's very clear that what is going on in Nicaragua very much parallels our involvement in Vietnam," Armstead added. "The plane being shot down is one more factor in the development of what is going to happen."

World War II veteran Harry Landfield, a member of the Smed-

ley D. Butler Brigade who also planned to travel to Washington aboard the bus convoy, said Rudman "is blaming the victim."

"Anytime you disagree with any aspect of foreign policy, you are a 'terrorist'," he said. "The people in the hunger strike are pacifists of the first order."

Landfield, too, said he was not surprised to find Rudman issuing such a statement. "He's seeking reelection, isn't he?" Landfield asked.

According to an aide, Rudman served as an Army combat platoon leader in the Korean War.

October 11, 1986, the forty-first day of our water-only fast, this *Boston Globe* article reported comments of Senator Warren Rudman (R-NH), member of the Senate Intelligence Committee, comparing the fasters to Mideast terrorists holding U.S. Americans hostage.

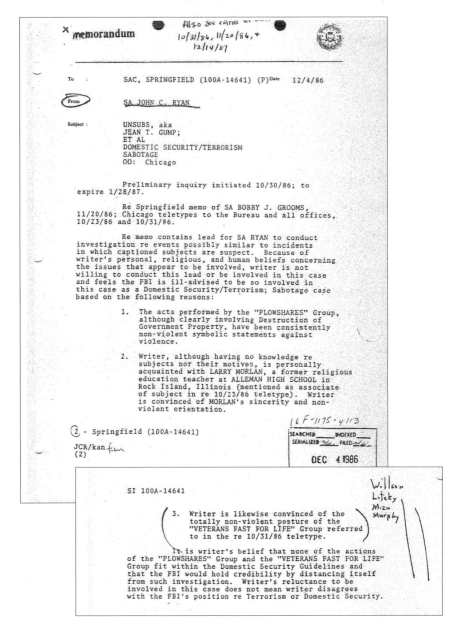

Also See entries
10/31/86, 11/20/86, +
12/14/87

memorandum

To : SAC, SPRINGFIELD (100A-14641) (P)^{Date} 12/4/86

From : SA JOHN C. RYAN

Subject : UNSUBS, aka
JEAN T. GUMP;
ET AL
DOMESTIC SECURITY/TERRORISM
SABOTAGE
OO: Chicago

Preliminary inquiry initiated 10/30/86; to
expire 1/28/87.

Re Springfield memo of SA BOBBY J. GROOMS,
11/20/86; Chicago teletypes to the Bureau and all offices,
10/23/86 and 10/31/86.

Re memo contains lead for SA RYAN to conduct
investigation re events possibly similar to incidents
in which captioned subjects are suspect. Because of
writer's personal, religious, and human beliefs concerning
the issues that appear to be involved, writer is not
willing to conduct this lead or be involved in this case
and feels the FBI is ill-advised to be so involved in
this case as a Domestic Security/Terrorism; Sabotage case
based on the following reasons:

1. The acts performed by the "PLOWSHARES" Group,
   although clearly involving Destruction of
   Government Property, have been consistently
   non-violent symbolic statements against
   violence.

2. Writer, although having no knowledge re
   subjects nor their motives, is personally
   acquainted with LARRY MORLAN, a former religious
   education teacher at ALLEMAN HIGH SCHOOL in
   Rock Island, Illinois (mentioned as associate
   of subject in re 10/23/86 teletype). Writer
   is convinced of MORLAN's sincerity and nonviolent orientation.

16 F-1175-4113

② - Springfield (100A-14641)

JCR/kan
(2)

SEARCHED_____ INDEXED_____
SERIALIZED_____ FILED_____

DEC 4 1986

SI 100A-14641

Willson
Litjeky
Mizo
Murphy

3. Writer is likewise convinced of the
   totally non-violent posture of the
   "VETERANS FAST FOR LIFE" Group referred
   to in the re 10/31/86 teletype.

It is writer's belief that none of the actions
of the "PLOWSHARES" Group and the "VETERANS FAST FOR LIFE"
Group fit within the Domestic Security Guidelines and
that the FBI would hold credibility by distancing itself
from such investigation. Writer's reluctance to be
involved in this case does not mean writer disagrees
with the FBI's position re Terrorism or Domestic Security.

FBI agent Jack Ryan's two-page letter from December 4, 1986, addressed to his
FBI superiors explaining his refusal to follow orders to investigate under "Domestic
Security/Terrorism Sabotage" guidelines, the Plowshares Group and the veterans of
the Veterans Fast for Life.

CHAPTER 18

In Country: Nicaragua

A fter the fast, I wasn't sure what to do with my life. I had mentally been prepared to die. Before the fast I had turned over my car to the bank, said contingent goodbyes to friends and family, and arranged for burial of my ashes in Nicaragua. Stopping the fast led to a feeling of liberation. I had my life back and was free to do anything.

I felt energized by the support we had received, especially from veterans. I had already proposed creating a group of veterans who would go to Nicaragua as unarmed witnesses, perhaps working on restoring facilities destroyed by the Contras. During the Fast for Life, I had plenty of time to reflect on this idea. I returned to the cabin in Vermont for a bit of secluded time.

Not Enough

As I recuperated in my cabin, I learned from Witness for Peace of another terrible Contra crime. A civilian transport truck with fifty-five passengers rolled over a Contra-placed antitank Claymore mine in the Pantasma valley on the road from Jinotega to Wiwilí, injuring at least thirty, of whom twelve died, and twelve others suffered amputated limbs. I felt sick to my stomach and wondered whether we had stopped the fast prematurely.

Then there was a report by John Greenwald in *Time* magazine that despite the fact that the Contra aid bill was not signed into law until October 17 (ironically, on the day we ended our fast), officials had likely released monies to Contra operations in *August*—after the Senate vote but before the aid was finally approved.[242]

When and under what conditions, I wondered, would a sufficient number of U.S. Americans step outside their comfort zone and mobilize to stop these crimes being committed in our names? Was our way of life so sacred that we were blind to its diabolical consequences? I didn't know what to do.

I heard about a rally at the General Electric plant (now owned by General Dynamics) in nearby Burlington, Vermont, to protest the manufacture of the Vulcan rapid-fire, multiple-barreled Gatling machine gun, which was used heavily in Korea and Viet Nam and was now being used in El Salvador. So on

October 25 I traveled to the rally, where I spoke about the incredible damage the Gatling gun inflicts on civilians.[243]

In an interesting but alarming irony, a federal investigation named me as a suspect in arms smuggling almost two years later. The feds claimed I was illegally smuggling Vulcan Gatling gun and antiaircraft parts into Guatemala under cover of the Veterans Peace Convoy. Brian Willson, a nonviolent protester, involved in gun smuggling! There was a Veterans Peace Convoy, and though I was an avid supporter I was not an organizer. The Convoy was actually transporting humanitarian aid on trucks and buses to Nicaragua in violation of Reagan's embargo. The federal investigation was a poorly disguised attempt to stop groups from supporting the Sandinistas and bringing in humanitarian aid to the campesinos. I was never personally interrogated so I thought nothing more about it.[244]

My next step soon became clear when the Nicaraguan government invited the fasters to celebrate the twenty-fifth anniversary of the founding of the FSLN (Frente Sandinista de Liberación Nacional, or Sandinista National Liberation Front) on November 8.[245] Charlie and his wife Judy remained in Washington to vigil, while Duncan, George, and I flew to Managua. We were greeted at the airport by Sergio Ramírez, the country's vice president. On November 8, we shared the podium with President Ortega and President Thomas Sankara of Burkina Faso addressing more than three hundred thousand people in Managua's large plaza. My speech criticizing U.S. policy was covered in the U.S. media.[246] That evening we were guests of President Ortega and First Lady Rosario Murillo for a performance of the Russian Bolshoi Ballet in the Rubén Darío Popular Theater.

Talking to Hasenfus

We were eager to meet with Eugene Hasenfus, as he was a direct link between the United States and the Contras. The Nicaragua government facilitated our meeting him, perhaps hoping it would bring more attention to the Iran-Contra connection in the United States. Whatever the reason, they arranged for us to travel with Hasenfus by helicopter, along with a Nicaraguan judicial team and an ABC-TV crew, to the remote October 5 crash site for an inspection.

At the crash site, debris was scattered over a wide area—twisted metal and parts of one of the plane's engines, numerous pieces of AK-47s, boots, portions of wooden ammunition boxes, water packets, etc. We initiated a conversation with Hasenfus there. He seemed quite willing to talk to English-speaking people who cared about his story.

We were allowed by the Sandinista authorities to meet with Hasenfus again on November 11 (Veterans Day in the U.S.) at Tipitapa Prison, located ten miles from Managua. At that meeting, he told us that he was paid $3,000 a month, and $750 for each overflight. He described his ten secret arms supply flights as originating from Ilopango, San Salvador, sometimes routed over northern Nicaragua from Honduras, other times routed south over the Pacific to Costa Rica before flying over southern Nicaragua.

He knew many details about the complex Iran-Contra funding scheme because he was in communication through his boss, Max Gomez, with Richard Secord and Oliver North, who controlled the Swiss bank account used to purchase the weapons. Hasenfus had lived since July 1986 in one of three safe houses established in fashionable neighborhoods in San Salvador to house the Contra resupply crew of nine pilots, seven mechanics, three kickers, and several other support personnel.[247]

Between July 17 and September 26, over sixty phone calls were made from the safe houses in San Salvador to various receivers, including Southern Air Transport in Miami (an airline conducting covert activities for the CIA), Secord's home in Virginia, Stanford Technology in Virginia (Secord's company), and Lt. Col. North's number at the NSC in Washington, D.C. The resupply team was nominally employed by Corporate Air Services of Quarryville, Pennsylvania, but the orders were believed to originate from Stanford Technology Trading Group International, Inc., Secord's private company.[248]

In trying to expose the crimes of my own country against the Nicaraguan people, I discovered that my government had been involved in a demonic deal to send arms to both Iran and the Contras. The deals were blatantly illegal, of course, but I already knew from my work in government how easy it was for Congress to look the other way. Indeed, many hearings were held when Iran-Contra became public, but no one was really punished. North never served jail time, and his conviction was overturned on appeal; he actually ran for the U.S. Senate in Virginia in 1994. Secord pleaded guilty for lying and was given two years of probation. He then became a corporate CEO. Earlier in his career he had been involved in the secret air war in Laos from 1966 to 1968, and had acknowledged that on slow days he simply "buzzed across the Mekong on bombing and strafing runs, if he thought his CIA bosses wouldn't find out, and they didn't."[249]

While Iran-Contra captured national attention, Hasenfus revealed to us that the arms were stored in a couple of warehouses at Ilopango. This dramatically exposed El Salvador's direct role in the Contra War, confirming numerous press reports. From other sources we learned that weapons from Secord's supply lines were sometimes mixed with privately donated weapons and weapons from Concord Naval Weapon Station, some of which were being stored in International Harvester's El Salvador warehouse.[250]

The intense Reagan-Bush war against impoverished, restive Salvadoran campesinos during 1980–1992 converted the Salvadoran society to a repressive national security state. The main Salvadoran military base at Ilopango in the eastern suburbs of San Salvador had become a huge military staging area, costing the government $500 million a year (more than $1.3 million a *day*) in CIA, State Department, and Pentagon funds. In return, we were training soldiers and financing the purchase of bombs, helicopters, fighter-bombers, and small arms to ensure that El Salvador's repressive government could destroy its own Indigenous revolution. Some of the arms Hasenfus was bringing to the Contras the day he was shot down actually were skimmed from supplies going for the Salvadoran government. It was an easy two-fer for the United States—sell enough light arms to El Salvador so that the excess can be supplied to the Contras under the table while keeping sloppy books to cover it up.

The supply line to the Contras could be traced directly back to the United States. I learned from a San Francisco Pledge of Resistance Freedom of Information request that the Concord Naval Weapons Station (CNWS) in California was shipping arms directly to El Salvador's Pacific coast port at Acajutla. Among the weapons shipped: several thousand white phosphorous rockets whose incendiary chemical fire fragments burn people's flesh to their bones,[251] over 2,700 general purpose 500- and 750-pound demolition and fragmentation bombs used to quickly destroy houses and whole villages; several million 7.62 millimeter linked cartridges for General Electric machine guns mounted on helicopter gunships that fire a hundred bullets a *second*; over 6,000 high-explosive rockets also used to quickly destroy houses and their inhabitants; and nearly 1,800 one meter fuse extenders to increase a bomb's impact and increase the likelihood of sending shrapnel into larger numbers of personnel.[252] I also possessed a written report from a missionary who witnessed bombing in Chalatenango, El Salvador, and was able to identify the markings on an unexploded bomb that revealed it had been shipped from CNWS.[253]

Hasenfus supplied the rest of the story. Most of the weapons shipped to El Salvador from CNWS were used directly against the Salvadoran people. However, some of those weapons, such as grenades and rockets, ended up in the hands of CIA operative Felix Rodriguez (aka Max Gomez).

Rodriguez was a Cuban-American veteran of the CIA's failed Bay of Pigs operation in 1961 who had an extensive history of working with the agency. At Ilopango, Rodriguez directed the twenty-five-person, five-plane Contra aerial supply operation coordinating flights and drops of arms. He answered directly to Oliver North and was assisted by another Cuban CIA veteran, Luis

Posada Carriles (aka Ramon Medina), a known terrorist responsible for the 1976 mid-air bombing of a Cubana airliner that killed all seventy-three passengers on board. Rodriguez was also in direct contact with Donald Gregg, Vice President George H.W. Bush's national security aide.

Some weapons provided by Secord's operation, known as "The Enterprise," were flown or trucked directly to Contra supply bases in Honduras such as Palmerola, El Aguacate, San Lorenzo, and Jamastran, which the General Accounting Office concluded had been illegally constructed or upgraded by U.S. engineers in 1984.[254] Weapons from private U.S. donors and Secord's international arms suppliers were flown directly from Ilopango to Contras deep within Nicaraguan territory, over either the Honduran or the Costa Rican borders.

Hasenfus was part of a four-man crew flying one of those missions when shot down on October 5, 1986. The plane was flying at an altitude of 2,300 feet about twenty miles north of the Costa Rican border when it was hit by a surface-to-air missile near San Carlos, Nicaragua. The C-123 air freighter was carrying thirteen thousand pounds of military supplies, including sixty AK-47s, fifty thousand rounds of ammunition, grenades and their launchers, jungle boots, and water packets originating from Brooklyn, New York.[255] Hasenfus survived because he was near the open door ready to kick out heavy boxes of military supplies attached to parachutes, and had on a parachute himself. The pilot and copilot, both of whom had served with Hasenfus in secret CIA operations in Laos in the 1960s and 1970s, were killed. The fourth crew member, a Nicaraguan, was also killed.

It was "Franklin," head of the Jorge Salazar Contra task force of 1,400 mercenary fighters stationed deep in central Zelaya Department, who was waiting for the guns and ammunition to fall from the sky that day. Despite not receiving the expected shipment, Franklin's band of terrorists had sufficient weapons eight days later to ambush a passenger bus traveling from Rancho Alegre to La Gateada, about thirty-five miles north of the ill-fated drop site. The group opened fire indiscriminately with rifles and machine guns, leaving two passengers dead and fifteen wounded; two others were kidnapped.[256]

As a trained lawyer I recognized that, thanks to Hasenfus, there now existed clear evidence to directly prove executive orders to murder and terrorize innocent human beings and legislative funding of those criminal activities. The U.S. Congress was funding the arms and approving policies of mass terror in at least two countries, Nicaragua and El Salvador. The crimes were directed by President Reagan and funded by U.S. taxpayers. I knew the victims and how they were being murdered or injured; I knew from Hasenfus that many of the weapons used in the attacks were coming from El Salvador;

and I knew from the Freedom of Information Act that many of the weapons in El Salvador were supplied by the Concord Naval Weapons Station.

U.S. in Honduras

While we were in Nicaragua, Reagan's war was heating up along the border with Honduras, and pretexts for a U.S. invasion were increasingly discussed. Honduran President Azcona and President Reagan accused the Sandinistas of physically invading Honduran territory.[257] News outlets reported that U.S. helicopters were ferrying troops to the border to do battle with Nicaraguan forces. I again felt sick to my stomach and took a day to center myself.

Viet Nam veterans acting independently as mercenaries had been working in El Salvador against the popular guerrillas and in Honduras supporting the Contras since late 1983 or early 1984.[258] Major C.A. McAnarney, logistics officer with the U.S. Military Group in El Salvador, facilitated eleven shipments of military supplies from the Civilian Military Alliance (CMA) mercenary group to the Salvadoran military from November 1983 to March 1984.[259] CMA was founded by Thomas "Tommy" Posey, a Viet Nam veteran, John Bircher, Klansman, and professional mercenary for whom the adrenaline of fighting Communism never ended. John Negroponte, U.S. ambassador to Honduras at the time, who was practically directing the Contra War against the Sandinistas,[260] facilitated an early 1984 meeting between Posey and officers in the Honduran military.[261] In a January 23, 1984, letter, Contra FDN commander Enrique Bermúdez responded to Posey's offer of military training and weapons: "We are willing to accept all the help that your organization is able to provide us so we can increase our fight against Communism and in favor of democracy."[262] In September, more than seven months later, two CMA helicopter pilots flying out of a CIA-Contra base in Honduras were shot down and killed in their attack helicopter in northern Nicaragua.[263] Despite this heightened exposure, Posey remained as determined as ever to kill more Sandinistas. He was pictured in *Newsweek* holding an automatic rifle as he stood next to a large banner depicting a hunting knife piercing a beret-adorned human skull with the inscription, "Kill 'Em All, Let God Sort 'Em Out."[264]

That some veterans actively supported the Contras had been dramatically exposed on September 1, 1984, when the CMA helicopter pilots were killed in Nicaragua.[265] This had been brought to my attention when I was director of the veterans outreach center. In 1986 the Contras consulted with the Pentagon, seeking ever more Viet Nam veteran mercenaries to help with their combat training in Honduras. At least one hundred veterans apparently arrived there in July 1986.[266] A similar number of veterans soon were participating in the nonviolent Veterans Peace Action Teams in Nicaragua and El Salvador, revealing the polarizing differences in perspective. Tommy Posey possessed particular disdain toward U.S. Americans sympathetic with the Sandinistas such as these veterans and proclaimed a desire "to draw a bead on one of them."[267] Subsequently, Posey exclaimed how "delighted" he was at the loss of my legs to a munitions train while protesting the shipment of arms to the Contras in September 1987.[268]

Exactly how dangerous the situation was for Nicaragua became clear to us on our last day there, December 7, 1986, when our small delegation had a personal meeting with Nicaragua's foreign minister, Maryknoll Father Miguel D'Escoto. During this meeting, D'Escoto took an important phone call from Honduran President Azcona warning that he (Azcona) was under intense pressure from the U.S. to dispatch pilots to bomb the small Nicaraguan towns of Murra in Nueva Segovia (pop. 5,000), and Wiwilí in Jinotega (pop. 2,900), fifteen miles apart from each other, a dozen miles from the Honduran border. D'Escoto immediately made calls to the Nicaraguan Army to watch for bombings while evacuating the residents. Though a warning was dispatched by military couriers, the bombings by U.S.-supplied Honduran jet fighters nonetheless murdered seven Nicaraguan soldiers and wounded twelve others, including four civilians, two of whom were children.[269]

A high-ranking Green Beret officer declared in a December 1986 *Los Angeles Weekly* article that a U.S. invasion of Nicaragua had been likely planned for April 1987, but was delayed by the Iran-Contra revelations that erupted after Hasenfus's plane was shot down. The frenzied U.S. rhetoric and troop movements in Honduras suggested, however, that an invasion was still imminent. We felt an urgent need to stop it.

Waging Peace

Eugene Hasenfus was not the only person of significance I met on this trip. I also met Holley Rauen, who was in Nicaragua with a U.S. health care delegation. We became quick friends, and eventually she became my partner.

When Holley and I returned to the United States, we immediately joined with the Bill Motto "Wage Peace" VFW Post 5888 in Santa Cruz, California to form a committee organizing veterans' peace teams.[270] In January of 1987, just three months after the Veterans Fast for Life ended, the Veterans Peace Action Teams (VPAT) became a reality. Headquartered in Santa Cruz, California, Holley and I became members of the first assembled and trained eleven-person team that traveled to Nicaragua in February 1987. *New York Times* had just reported that hundreds of U.S. paratroopers were simulating war games in Honduras near the border with Nicaragua.[271] We were under no illusions; we knew the assignment we chose for our veterans was a dangerous one.

Our first team arrived in Nicaragua on February 19. Its members were a broad mix of veterans. Gary Campbell was a Korean combat veteran serving as a Presbyterian liberation theology missionary in Nicaragua. John Schuchardt, an attorney and Plowshares activist, had been a Marine lieutenant who resigned his commission in protest of the Viet Nam War. He was accompanied by his wife Judith. Rick Schoos, a well driller and electrician, had been a helicopter mechanic in Viet Nam; Peter Eaves, a bicycle mechanic, had been a Marine at Guantánamo; John Poole, a chiropractor and baker, had been an Army grunt in Viet Nam; John Isherwood, a physician who had worked with the World Health Organization, was a World War II veteran of the British Army. Scott Rutherford, a former Navy officer now retired from federal government service, had helped organize our Veterans Fast for Life a few months earlier. Peter Nimkoff, an anthropologist and former U.S. magistrate in Florida, had been a Marine officer in the post-Korea period. Two other veterans, one of World War II and one of the Viet Nam era, chose to remove themselves from the mission after our training in the U.S. and our initial briefing in Nicaragua. Holley and I rounded out the team.

We immediately traveled into rural areas as assigned by the government. However, we soon convinced Sandinista officials to allow us direct access to more dangerous areas in the administrative departments of Jinotega and Matagalpa, which shared borders with Honduras, where some of the worst Contra atrocities had occurred.

For much of the first four weeks, we traveled by pickup truck to visit a different community each day with our backpacks and bedrolls. The first couple of days we saw overwhelming evidence that the Contras regularly attacked civilians and their community infrastructure, and unceasingly planted tank mines on roads, making travel by civilians treacherous. While traveling in Matagalpa Department, the small community of Tapasle was attacked not far from where we were and their new health clinic burned down by the Contras.[272]

On several occasions, we found spots where hundreds of wrappers of bandages and gauze pads were lying on the ground. These were likely locations where groups of Contras had regrouped to bandage their bleeding wounds after firefights with Sandinista troops. As I looked at the debris, I noticed that some of the first aid material wrappers were from U.S. companies and was reminded, even by this small example, that corporations were making money first inflicting, and then mending the wounds of war.

We spoke to many victims of Contra attacks, observing destroyed cooperative farms and homes, health clinics and schools, while noting that *all* bridges had been damaged or destroyed, and *all* power lines were down. One night we stayed at a community in the war-ravaged Pantasma Valley where Sandinista intelligence warned of an impending Contra attack. We were bedded down on the concrete floor of the school and could hear mortars and gunfire and see fiery explosions all night long as Sandinista soldiers lay in defensive positions around the village. I never slept a wink. Rather, I sat all night in ready alert on the edge of a concrete wall next to the school, while shallow-breathing to increase my listening ability, just as I had done in Viet Nam. I don't know what my response would have been if an attack had occurred.

At dawn, we sighed with relief along with the soldiers and residents. Then an exhausted mother staggered into the health clinic cradling her one-year-old baby, Roger, in blood-soaked clothing. She had walked with him for four hours, since the Contras threw a grenade into her house. Several of us watched as a local doctor removed grenade shrapnel from Roger's belly.

Dora

Writing about this mother reminds me of another young mother I met in northern Nicaragua named Dora. I asked Dora why she would risk her life to ride weekly on her cooperative farm's passenger truck to go to the market or health clinic in a nearby town. She couldn't understand my question. "Why would people want to hang out along the road to shoot us?" she asked.

As hard as I tried, I couldn't explain why people paid by the United States were ambushing trucks taking campesinos to health clinics or the market. How can one describe the utter demonic nature of Cold War politics, the paranoia behind them, and politicians' dependence on "plausible deniability" to cover up policies that, once known, would be totally unacceptable to the public?

Dora was right: what we were doing was not rational at a human level. It was rational only if you believed people were "viruses" that needed to be eliminated to enhance our own deluded sense of superiority—racial, political, cultural. But how can a twenty-two-year-old campesino living in the mountains grasp that? In fact, Dora was a victim of an ambush in which eighteen of the twenty-two passengers were murdered when a rocket-propelled grenade and hundreds of bullets overwhelmed the truck as it rounded a curve. There were 120 bullet holes in the truck alone. Her one-year-old was murdered, her four-year-old was shot through the face and shoulder, and she lost a six-month-old fetus, her left leg at the hip, and her left eye.

Most people can't really imagine the policies of terror. You have to experience them to fully understand them.

It's worth revisiting here a 1948 internal State Department document that best illustrates what the Cold War was a convenient cover *for*. The ability of the United States to crush popular movements erupting after World War II—simplistically called communists—required a rationale that the "evil" Soviet Union posed a global monolithic threat to our "freedom." (This policy of "containment" was later escalated by Ronald Reagan to a policy of "rollback.")

> We have about 50 percent of the world's wealth, but only 6.3 percent of its population . . . In this situation, we cannot fail to be the object of envy and resentment. Our real task . . . is to devise a pattern of relationships which will permit us to maintain this position of disparity without positive detriment to our national security. . . . We need not deceive ourselves that we can afford today the luxury of altruism and world-benefaction. . . . We should cease to talk about vague and—for the Far East—unreal objectives such as human rights, the raising of the living standards, and democratization. The day is not far off when we are going to have to deal in straight power concepts. The less we are then hampered by idealistic slogans, the better.[273]

Walk to Wiwilí

Frustrated by the continuation of the war, our group decided to embark on a more risky *satyagraha* action. We wanted to walk unarmed and undefended on a seventy-mile rural road through one of the most dangerous areas in all of Nicaragua—the remote but important, and heavily mined, trade road from Jinotega north through the Pantasma Valley to Wiwilí near the Honduran border. This was the same area that saw intense fighting between U.S. Marines and Augusto Sandino's forces fifty-five to sixty years before.

The devastating October 20, 1986, tank mine explosion of a passenger truck had occurred in the Pantasma Valley, but dozens of other vehicles had been destroyed on this road (and other roads) with dozens of civilian casualties, and the loss of many limbs. Wiwilí in northern Jinotega, and Murra fifteen miles further northwest in Nueva Segovia, had been the two villages bombed by the Honduran air force at U.S. direction in December. The destruction of Murra by Marine bombs in March 1928, fifty-seven years earlier, was still remembered by Nicaraguan campesinos.

Just four days before we were to start the walk, a *New York Times* headline reported that the "C.I.A. Gives Contras Detailed Profiles of Civil Targets" to be destroyed in a "spring offensive" (March 19, 1987). Spring was two days away! There was plenty of adrenaline flowing, I can assure you. Because of the danger involved, we needed official permission, since we planned to march toward Honduras close to dozens of Contra camps. Though the Nicaraguan government discouraged the walk, President Ortega finally okayed it. We wanted to walk directly into the heart of the war zone to bear witness to what our government was doing. We would continue to decide nightly where to bed down.

We briefed the U.S. Embassy in Managua of our plans on March 20. We met not only with U.S. Ambassador Harry Bergold and his information officer, Alfred A. Laun III, who not only informed us he had been a Phoenix operative in Viet Nam but warned us that if anything happened during our walk, "We [the U.S.] will hold the Sandinista Government responsible." We were reassured to receive advance notice that no investigation would be held if anything happened to us, as the "satanic" Sandinistas would be automatically blamed.

On Sunday afternoon, March 22, the day before the walk was to begin, we received a military briefing about watching for loose mounds of gravel on the road surface that might be concealing "antitank" mines and how to detonate them if necessary. We were to surround any suspected mine location with rocks. Later that evening, we received an intelligence briefing from the Sandinista military in Jinotega about locations of recent Contra sightings and attacks along the road, which of course made us very nervous. When we asked one of their officers, well-known Sandinista commander Omar Cabezas, what we might expect, he replied, "I think they are going to try to kill you."[274] We paused, looked at one another, and asked, "Do we really want to do this?" After a couple of hours of further discussion we all agreed to proceed. At the same time we were told that the U.S. was conducting its largest-ever war trainings in Honduras with fifty thousand troops.[275]

Our briefing disclosed that three days earlier there had been a serious Contra attack on the Monterey coffee cooperative eleven miles north of Jinotega. Two campesinos were murdered and six injured, and fifteen homes and all the coffee processing facilities and farm equipment were burned. Our route would take us through the destroyed cooperative, and we wondered where this band of Contras would be in a day or two. On that same day, March 19, the agricultural cooperative of El Cedro in rural Jinotega was attacked, resulting in the deaths of two people and total destruction of a house, the health clinic, and the food supply center.

On the day of our departure, Monday, March 23, a *Miami Herald* headline story, "Contras in Training for Major Offensive," suggested the threat of a broadened war for the Nicaraguans. And the 1987 March issue of the *Progressive* magazine reported that a former U.S. Marine intelligence officer was providing the Contras with a list of civilians in Nicaragua marked for assassination. Nicaragua was definitely a terror zone on many fronts, thanks to Reagan's "freedom fighters."

On the Road

We packed rice and beans and snacks. Each morning we would rise at dawn and get ready for the day's walk. Because I had numerous bone spurs on the bottom of my feet that made walking painful, especially on rough ground, I wrapped my feet with extra gauze bandages before slipping on my boots. It would take a few minutes to get our sleeping bags and bedrolls roped up, then prepare or locate a local breakfast. Some mornings we prepared enough rice and beans for several meals and ate them cold along the road.

Each day we wondered whether we would be confronted on the road by the Contras, or worse, ambushed from behind brush or trees along the road. We walked in two columns, one on each side of the road, each person about ten to fifteen feet behind or ahead of another. Looking forward or backward, each of us knew we should always see eleven others, including an unarmed Nicaraguan guide. Each of us was strategically paired with another walker and was responsible for always knowing where our partner was, especially when resuming our walk after a stop or break.

Our first day, we walked through the Monterey coffee cooperative, which had been destroyed only four days earlier. As we paused to observe the destroyed houses, farm houses, and equipment, knowing that a number of cooperative members had been murdered or injured, team member radical missionary Gary Campbell, who had witnessed the destruction of villages in Korea, said to me, "The books of God must ultimately be balanced." It struck me that there was a whole lot of balancing due after five hundred years of Eurocentric plunder, and that sooner or later we would have to pay a dear price for this.

There were many bridges on the road, and though each one had been damaged due to sabotage, they were still passable, with some having been substantially repaired. Again we found that all electric power lines had been destroyed over the entire distance from Jinotega to Wiwilí. The Nicaraguan government did not even attempt to keep the lines repaired because the prowling bands of Contras would easily destroy them again.

Perhaps it was just luck that we were not killed. During the first three days, we heard five firefights and mortars exploding ahead or behind us. The *Miami Herald* reported that the road we were on had "been the site of rebel ambushes and land mine explosions" (March 25, 1987). My partner Holley and I temporarily left the walk when President Ortega sent word asking me to speak at the national coffee harvest festival in San Ramón. This required reversing directions and driving south by Jeep with an armed escort over the road we had walked the day before. Soon after our departure, while driving over the Pantasma Mountain pass, we encountered a bloody ambush of an army kitchen truck that had occurred minutes earlier. Six people had been killed and nine others injured by U.S.-made M-79 grenades and small arms. Shells littered the road. We transported the injured driver to the hospital on our way to San Ramón.

Upon arrival at San Ramón, I shared the podium with President Ortega and Sam Nujoma, then president of SWAPO (Southwest Africa People's Organization), who three years later became the first president of liberated Namibia. My report on the ambush we encountered was covered by wire stories that appeared around the United States.[276]

On our drive back north to rejoin the walk as it approached Wiwilí, our route took us up, over, and down the treacherous, curvy Pantasma Mountain road and past the ambush site of the previous day. Eager to join our other comrades walking to Wiwilí, we kept driving after dark, turning out the Jeep lights to reduce our visibility and reduce our chances of becoming an ambush target. The driver carried an AK-47 under his seat and another Nicaraguan soldier rode shotgun with an AK-47 at the ready. Holley and I, anxious and fearful in the back seat, closed our eyes and held our breath as we slowly rounded each hairpin curve. Anticipating instant death, we wondered if we would hear the crack of the rifles or feel the bullets as they entered our bodies. We realized that this is what Nicaraguans experienced every day throughout the rural areas of the country.

We made it back just in time to join our group for a grand entrance into Wiwilí. As we entered the small city, we were greeted by several hundred campesinos, who walked the last couple of miles with us. We had a grand celebration with many of the town's residents at a makeshift stage. Since the town had no electricity, there was no refrigeration. Undaunted, the people had arranged for beer and soft drinks on ice to be flown in for the occasion. Those cold drinks sure hit the spot.

Sending a Message

All of us survived the walk unscathed. Although I personally was relieved to be alive, and felt deepened by the experience, what was most important was that our outreach effort had sent a powerful message of support to the Nicaraguan people and the Sandinista revolution, and equally to the Contras, who were worried that U.S. citizens, especially veterans, could so boldly obstruct their attempt to destroy the Nicaraguan Revolution.

Nicaraguan newspapers, radio, and television covered the walk every day. And the Contras warned us every day via their radio station that we were at risk if we chose to walk into areas ironically made dangerous only by them. The CIA had recently funded a powerful fifty-thousand-watt AM Contra radio station broadcasting from nearby El Salvador with regular programming and news.[277] On March 27, a news item in the *Miami Herald* reported that "Contra rebels warned 10 U.S. war veterans on a peace march in a northern war zone Thursday that the Sandinista government will be held responsible for 'whatever happens' to them." Though learning that was disquieting, it was not enough to stop our walk. Besides, the U.S. Embassy had already given us the same warning.

We also understood the walk amplified our message back home. Though press coverage in the United States was less than we would have liked, we discovered a number of news items in newspapers such as the *San Francisco Chronicle, San Francisco Examiner*, the *Boston Globe*, the Springfield, Massachusetts, *Morning Union*, the *Miami Herald*, the *Oakland Tribune*, and several wire stories that appeared in local papers around the country, including in my various hometown newspapers. A Dutch TV crew filmed our walk for European audiences. (The Dutch cameraman, Cornell LaGrouw, was killed two years later covering a firefight in El Salvador.)

I believed our style of active grassroots expression *might* be making a difference. Instead of talking the talk, I was walking the walk. I was validating my ideas with actions, experiencing life in Nicaragua as the campesinos do. What I discovered was that walking the walk was personally liberating and empowering for people I met. When we returned to the United States, I made public presentations and found many people receptive to the message. In 1985, a new version of an earlier, nearly defunct Veterans For Peace organization emerged and as we talked about our work in Nicaragua other vets seemed inspired to become active in their hometowns, and some considered participating in a Veterans Peace Action Team.

I had found this physical action to be profoundly meaningful, partly because it allowed me to directly associate with the victims of U.S. foreign policy as I placed myself directly in front of that policy. It was much more real than being a lobbyist in the system. I felt more on track.

Ben Linder

Before leaving Nicaragua in early April I revisited the Leonel Rugama Rugama cooperative near Estelí, where I had visited a year earlier. I wanted to see how they were faring and was alarmed to learn that the CIA was parachuting specially trained Contra commandos into Nicaragua's remote zones to commit sabotage.[278] On Sunday April 5, I arrived at the cooperative, eager to converse with my new friends. Sadly, I learned that two of the cooperative's adult male members had been kidnapped eight days earlier while they were butchering a cow. About thirty Contras were seen roaming the area. Later the men's tortured bodies were found. One had his head cut off, the other his testicles. One of the men left behind a wife and three children. With tears rolling down my cheeks I joined them in their solemn, prolonged wake. Photos of the two men were displayed next to their simple wooden caskets. This was a very sad note on which to be leaving Nicaragua.[279]

I scheduled one final visit before I left the country. On April 7, I traveled to Matagalpa hoping to meet a young, soft-spoken mechanical engineer from Portland, Oregon, named Ben Linder. Ben had moved to Nicaragua in 1983 after graduating from the University of Washington. A unicyclist, clown, and juggler, he was especially popular with the campesinos' children. In 1986 he moved to tiny El Cuá in the Department of Jinotega and assembled a team to construct a small hydroelectric plant in the neighboring village of San José de Bocay so that peasants could have a few light bulbs and refrigeration for medicines. Ben and I met at an ice cream shop in Matagalpa, and he shared with me how dangerous things had become for him and his Nicaraguan coworkers. In fact, I learned that the day before our VPAT members met at the U.S. Embassy to inform our ambassador of our intention to walk through the war zone, the agricultural cooperative of El Cedro, near the dam construction site, had been attacked by the Contras. Two residents had been murdered; one of them was a close friend of Ben's. During that attack, the health clinic, food supply center, and a home had been burned to the ground.

Sadly, Ben Linder himself became famous for being murdered by the Contras exactly three weeks after our visit, April 28, as he worked on the hydro project with his coworkers. David Linder, Ben's father, a retired hospital pathologist, traveled to Nicaragua and, after personally reviewing the autopsy and talking with the doctor who carried it out, concluded that "they blew his brains out at point-blank range as he lay wounded" after his legs had been seriously injured by grenade shrapnel.[280] Americas Watch, in a November 1987 report, concluded that Linder "appeared to have been summarily executed at the site of a hydroelectric project ... by the *contras* after an ambush."

Interestingly, the Contras initially admitted killing Linder, though they must have been chastised by their trainers and PR bosses in Washington, because they later changed their story and glibly blamed the murder on the nasty Sandinistas.[281] The major Contra field commander, Enrique Bermúdez, was eventually identified as the architect of the assassination. White House spokesman Marlin Fitzwater blamed Linder for his own death, saying that

U.S. citizens working in Nicaragua "put themselves in harm's way,"[282] while Vice President George Bush condemned Linder because "he was on the other side."[283]

Ex-Contra leader Fermín Cárdenas Olivas, also known as "Cain," told a reporter in an October 1989 interview that Bermúdez had directly ordered U.S. engineer Ben Linder's murder in April 1987 because he was a Sandinista, and his death would be a defeat for the Sandinistas by stopping the hydroelectric project being constructed in Nicaragua's remote northern mountains. Bermúdez reportedly offered a lucrative reward to the Contra who assassinated Linder at point-blank range. "Cain" himself was assassinated on December 1, 1989, shortly before he was to provide an affidavit for a wrongful death lawsuit brought by the Linder family against the Contra leadership, including Bermúdez.[284]

I heard about the assassinations of Ben and his coworkers shortly after joining an Easter Sunday veterans' march to Reagan's Western White House ranch in California's Santa Barbara Mountains. Three hundred vets, including Charlie Liteky and Duncan Murphy, went on that march and pounded crosses into the ground in front of Ronald Reagan's front gate, each cross bearing the name of a murdered Nicaraguan campesino.

Charlie and I decided to return to Nicaragua after Ben Linder's funeral to plan a people's walk on the remote road to the small hydroelectric plant where Ben had been murdered, to demonstrate that U.S. citizens were committed to completing the plant. The Contras took note and warned that foreigners were not safe in Nicaragua and that they should quickly exit the country.[285] Though the march was temporarily delayed, it did take place on May 16, with seventy participants. The Contras had indeed mined the road, but luckily the mines were spotted and removed without incident.[286] Ben Linder's dam was finally completed seven years later, becoming operational in May 1994.[287]

I was disgusted by comments made at a formal hearing on Linder's murder conducted in May by the House Foreign Affairs Subcommittee, when member Connie Mack (R-FL) admonished Linder's parents: "I can't understand how you can use the grief I know you feel to politicize this situation . . . I don't want to be tough on you, but I really feel that you have asked for it." Mrs. Linder responded, "That is the most cruel thing you could have said." Mack: "I don't consider it to be cruel, I consider it to be to the point." Elliott Abrams, assistant secretary of state, testified that Linder's death need not have occurred but for Nicaragua's "practice of permitting and even encouraging Americans . . . to travel in combat zones."[288]

Enraged, I envisioned additional teams of U.S. citizens traveling to Nicaragua to rebuild clinics and homes the Contras had destroyed.

Meanwhile, a second Veterans Peace Action Team headed to Nicaragua on May 29. They would rebuild the El Cedro health center near El Cuá destroyed by the Contras in a March 19 attack, not far from Linder's dam construction site, and it would be dedicated to Ben.

Green Empowerment, now in seven countries, grew from Linder's legacy and in Nicaragua works with the Association for Rural Development Workers–Ben Linder (ATDER-BL) building microhydro projects expanding electricity, drinking water, and watershed protection to thousands of villagers in the Cuá-Bocay region.

Their Legs Are Worth as Much as Mine

During this period, my life was filled with educational activism. I didn't have a job to earn money, though at times I worked as a day laborer, and sometimes people donated funds to help with traveling and speaking. My partner, Holley, was covering basic living expenses in her work as a midwife in Marin County, California, where we lived at the time with her thirteen-year-old son, Gabriel. I had substantially gone AWOL from the repressive, market-obsessed system I call the American Way Of Life.

I know that just hearing about the life I was living made some people angry. Here I was, a perfectly healthy person, choosing not to "earn my keep" even as I was criticizing the government that supposedly protected my exercise of free speech. I could almost hear my father making angry comments about me being a hypocrite, leeching off society, and so forth. Perhaps, what really drives this anger is fear—fear that I might be telling the truth; fear of questioning the status quo; fear of what people might find if they examined their own lives.

I couldn't avoid the grotesque realities of U.S. policy after my visits to Nicaragua. Over and over again, I had visited villages decimated by Contra attacks, bombed schools, clinics full of wounded, morgues full of dead, and freshly dug graves. During the first Veterans Peace Action Team mission, I visited over four hundred amputees in hospitals and homes who had lost limbs, mostly to U.S. land mines. As I spoke to the amputees, I expressed how sorry I was that they had to pay such a high price for defending their country from my country's terrorism, but I also wanted them to know that their example of courage inspired me. As I left one hospital, having seen nearly two hundred amputees in one day, I cried out, "Jesus Christ, their legs are worth just as much as my legs. My legs aren't worth any more than their legs!" Little did I know that this was a truth I was about to experience directly.

MAP 2
Northern Nicaragua impacted by Contras—VPAT Walk

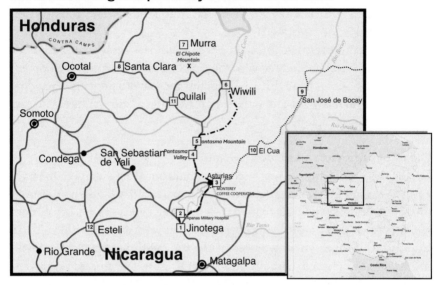

1. March 23, 1987, first Veterans Peace Action Team (VPAT) departs Jinotega City (pop. 50,000), one hundred miles northeast of Managua, beginning our seventy-five-mile walk to Wiwilí, considered the most dangerous region in Nicaragua due to the frequency of ambushes and mined roads.
2. VPAT visits many soldier amputees at Apanás Military Hospital.
3. March 24, 1987, VPAT visits Monterey coffee cooperative, northeast of Jinoega and south of Asturias, five days after a devastating Contra attack, killing two, injuring six, while destroying fifteen houses, coffee processing facilities, and farm equipment.
4. Pantasma Valley where a Contra-placed Claymore antitank mine blew up a civilian transport vehicle, October 19, 1986, killing twelve and wounding thirty-four, including twelve amputees.
5. March 27, we encounter Contra ambush on Pantasma Mountain, killing six and injuring nine. We ensure jeep takes injured driver to hospital.
6. Sunday, March 29, we arrive in Wiwilí (pop. 2,900), fourteen miles from Honduran border, after a seven-day walk through active Contra areas. *Every* bridge we walked on had been damaged by explosives, and *all* electric wires were down. Honduran pilots flying U.S. jets bombed the city on December 7, 1986, causing nineteen casualties.
7. Murra (pop. 5,000), thirteen miles from the Honduran border, also bombed, December 7, 1986. A few miles south is El Chipote Mountain, which for a time in 1927–1928 was headquarters for Augusto Sandino's rebel army fighting U.S. Marines in northern Nicaragua. It was the tenth time since 1853 the U.S. had invaded Nicaragua "to protect U.S. interests." The Marines dive-bombed the mountain city of Ocotal (pop. 30,000), July 27, 1927, using fragmentation bombs. The Marines reported "scores of men fell from the bombing and strafing" as

the "miracle of Marine air" created "streets . . . strewn with the dead and dying." Sandino reported massive destruction to crops and farm buildings, and murders of many animals and *campesinos*. Sandino's ragtag army, who the Marines called "bandits," never exceeded three thousand fighters. The twelve thousand U.S. Marines departed in January 1933, after a seven-year stalemate.

8. Santa Clara, six miles from the Honduran border, was attacked, September 1, 1984, by a Honduran-based CIA-helicopter piloted by two U.S. Viet Nam veteran mercenaries from Alabama-based Civilian Military Alliance (CMA). One woman and 3 children were killed before the helicopter was downed with both pilots killed. CMA sold T-shirts with imprint, "Kill 'Em All, Let God Sort 'Em Out."

9. San José de Bocay, where twenty-seven-year-old mechanical engineer Ben Linder and two Nicaraguan coworkers were murdered by Contras, April 28, 1987, while constructing a small hydroelectric plant.

10. El Cuá, near war-besieged El Cedro where second VPAT in May 1987 built a health clinic destroyed by Contras, dedicated to Ben Linder.

11. Quilalí (pop. 8,000), where Contras ambushed Dora, Erick, and twenty others in a transport truck, October 29, 1988, killing eighteen.

12. Estelí (pop. 100,000), a revolutionary city ninety miles north of Managua where I was first introduced to Nicaragua in January 1986.

PART V

She Is Me

CHAPTER 19

Blood on the Tracks

W hat did I have to do to stop the U.S. war against the Sandinistas? Though this now sounds egocentric, at the time I felt I had to answer this question.

For years I, along with thousands of others, had been *begging* Congress to stop the secret, illegal funding of the Contra terrorists, without much success. I had participated as a witness to this criminal war by cofounding and participating in veterans' peace team walks in the war zones. But those efforts and that of groups like Witness for Peace had not prevented increases in funding. On June 27, 1986, the World Court's order to the U.S. to stop all funding of these terror activities likewise had been summarily and blatantly ignored by both Congress and the president. Though our veterans' fast on September 1, 1986, had raised some awareness, Congress continued to send even more "humanitarian aid" and military funding to Contra bases in Nicaragua and Honduras. Now, with the revelation of the Iran-Contra affair, we knew that whether the aid approved by Congress was legal or illegal, humanitarian or military, a shadow government had been providing even larger sources of funding for the actual weapons the Contras used.

As I researched the Iran-Contra network, I discovered that Oliver North was not only getting money from Iranian weapon sales and a number of right-wing governments—including our stalwart ally Israel, which was providing many trainers and millions of dollars worth of weapons including surface-to-air missiles—but also from the oligarchs at home.[289] Wealthy businessmen like Joseph Coors of the Coors Brewing Company, Rich DeVos of Amway, Malcolm Forbes of *Forbes* magazine, Lew Lehrman of Rite-Aid,[290] Texas heiress Ellen Garwood of the Clayton Anderson fortune, and a slew of others, all willingly gave millions of dollars to the "freedom fighters."[291] Calling the Contras "God's Army," Pat Robertson and his Christian Broadcasting Network gave several million, while Jerry Falwell collected money through his Liberty Federation and funneled it to Oliver North for his secret war.[292]

Many of these preachers and groups had organized themselves into the Council for National Policy, whose mission was to coordinate fundraising for the Contras.[293] The council was a network of five hundred influential right-wing Christian activists. Members included U.S. senators and congresspeople; CEOs; TV evangelists; syndicated columnists; State Department and White House officials; retired and active-duty military officers, including covert operations veteran and retired General John Singlaub; and right-wing think tanks. These coordinated efforts raised millions of dollars from the U.S. American people for an illegal war abroad.

People like my own parents were giving money for "God's Army." My mother and father listened religiously to fundamentalist preachers like Pat Robertson, Tim LaHaye, Jerry Falwell, and read carefully the mail they received from conservative anticommunist organizations such as the World Anti-Communist League (WACL). They were giving money to the Contra cause even as I was fasting for peace!

A mix of rabid but naïve anticommunism, racist ideology, and fundamentalist Christian beliefs led people like my parents to support terrorist groups who in turn murdered innocent people in Central America who were largely impoverished due to my own country's historical polices of exploitation. The tragic absurdity of it all made me feel like I was watching a Fellini movie. But I couldn't leave the theater. This was real.

I realized that I had made a strategic error in trying to stop Contra funding. The money flowing to the Contras was not just coming from Congress. It was coming from an unhealthy society that was too wide, too deep, and too irrational to stop. Yet, just because I could not stop the flow of money for weapons didn't mean I was powerless. I could make a serious effort to stop the flow of the weapons themselves.

Vigils at Concord Naval Weapons Station

I returned to Northern California and began talking with other people who were interested in reviving a vigil at the Concord Naval Weapons Station (CNWS). The station had been a site for peace vigils since Viet Nam, in part because it was geographically located in the left-leaning Bay Area, but also because it was the largest Pentagon weapons depot on the West Coast, and because of the design of the base itself. Split into two separate parts, an inland area and a tidal area, a thin stretch of public right-of-way lay in between that included both sides of a public road.

Weapons were brought to CNWS from arms manufacturing plants around the country, and stored in the more than three hundred munitions bunkers in the inland area. Once they were ready for shipment, they were ferried either by truck on a road or by train on parallel tracks to the tidal port area. From there, they were put onto ships for transport. Because of the layout of the base, the trucks and trains regularly traveled across the public highway and its right-of-way to get from the inland area to the tidal area. In addition to storing vast amounts of conventional weapons, CNWS served as a major nuclear weapons depot housing more than three hundred nuclear bombs and warheads in the tidal area.[294]

Past vigils had taken place on that public road, plainly visible for hundreds of feet to the slow-moving drivers of the trucks and trains. Our vigil began there on June 10, 1987. We called ourselves Nuremberg Actions, honoring with the presence of our bodies the Principles of Nuremberg, which prescribe *disobedience* to illegal orders and encourages ordinary citizens to do whatever they deem reasonably necessary to *stop* government crimes. (The Nuremberg Principles emerged out of the Nuremberg trials conducted by the Allies to prosecute Germany's Nazi war criminals following World War II.) The first day of the vigil, several people blocked trucks transporting weapons on the road parallel to the tracks. Among them were Dave Hartsough, Dorothy Grenada, Russ Jorgenson, and Wendy Kaufmyn, and each was arrested.

We continued on with the vigil through the summer. People continued to get arrested, and we also were subjected to occasional violence. Some nearby residents were unhappy with our protests and on occasion drivers on the public highway would shout at us and throw bottles. In addition, the police, including the California Highway Patrol (CHP), who were called to CNWS to control vigilers and arrest blockers of munitions trucks, had become abusive. A legal observer at one of the early protests "witnessed a number of assaults on the demonstrators by the CHP . . . I saw painful ear holds. I saw them choking people and hitting them with batons and using dowels. One demonstrator was thrown onto a barbed wire fence." Another observer with the Pledge of Resistance reported, "It was clear the CHP was out of control . . . They were stopping people, pulling them out of cars."[295] We learned that, during the 1960s, some of the most violent harassment against antiwar protesters in California had occurred at CNWS.[296] However, none of us were seriously hurt, and the Marines on the base did not generally get in our way or participate in the arrests—they left it all up to the local police.

The act of vigiling at CNWS felt very concrete to me—we could actually see the weapons on some of the trucks and trains. We knew a percentage were going to El Salvador to kill the campesinos there, and some were going to Honduras to supply Contras at their sanctuary bases, or being loaded onto planes and dropped directly to the Contras in Nicaragua. Every bullet, every rocket, every bomb, every grenade, was intended to be expended against impoverished campesinos in El Salvador and Nicaragua. And by our actions, we were slowing them down, raising questions about their use. The link was direct and physical.

I was energized by the action, though a bit surprised that my companions thought nothing of blocking big trucks, knowing they were likely to go to jail. At the time, I felt like I was doing enough just being a support person.

Block the Train

After a couple of weeks of seeing so many trucks and trains pass slowly by our vigil, visibly loaded with rockets and bombs, I started "seeing" bodies inside the boxcars and on the flatbeds. The weapons just turned into bodies. I now think I was experiencing post-traumatic stress disorder, though I didn't realize it at the time. All I knew was that the rockets and bombs we saw on flatbed railcars looked, to me, like bodies of the dead.

These visions drove me to select a date on which I would begin to block trains and also begin another fast. As with the Veterans Fast for Life, I was again joined by two other veterans, Duncan Murphy from the 1986 fast and Reverend David Duncombe, a World War II and Korean War vet who was then serving as a university chaplain. Our plan was to fast for forty days while positioned every day on the tracks. We assumed we would be arrested, and made plans to fast in jail as well. We chose to begin on the first anniversary of our 1986 fast, September 1, 1987.

I decided that, since I was likely to face jail time for blocking trains, I would send another letter to the IRS clarifying my position on tax refusal based on the Nuremberg Principles. I wanted them to know that I owned no assets, but would be physically at CNWS for much of the fall or in jail in case they wanted to contact me again. Soon there was a message from the IRS tacked to our apartment door in San Rafael asking that I come to their office for a personal meeting. I complied, bringing two friends with me as witnesses, prepared to again make my case that, under Nuremberg, I was obligated to disobey the U.S. government's illegal order that I pay for its criminal wars. The agent refused to converse with me unless the witnesses remained outside our meeting room. I refused that request and he ordered us immediately out of the building.

I soon received correspondence telling me that IRS liens were being placed on any and all property I might own (I had none), that I would be subject to fines and other penalties, and possible prison time if they chose to go to federal court. I turned this matter over to my San Francisco attorney, asking him to sufficiently stall their proceedings to allow me to conduct the forty-day fast on the tracks beginning September 1. I did not hear from them again until 1989.

I now felt that I had fulfilled all my obligations and was free to devote myself to the protest on the tracks.

A Legal Vigil

Many people have told me I was stupid or crazy to think I could sit on the tracks and not get hit by a train.

All I can say is that I approached the project as a former military installation security officer. In my military training, I learned that facility commanders do not take chances when security is at stake, especially where explosives are involved. These trains were loaded with explosives. Further, Concord Naval Weapons Station had a 350-man Marine force securing the base. It was unthinkable that they would be unable to stop or arrest three peace protesters.

I personally had no desire to be killed, so in my lawyerly way, I did a lot of research on the topic. There had been a number of examples in U.S. history of people blocking trains, either in opposition to military policies where movement of nuclear weapons, military supplies or troops was being questioned, or during labor stoppages by railroad workers themselves.[297] Trains had always stopped, including at Concord.

Vigilers during the Viet Nam War sat on the tracks at CNWS and were arrested. Trains coming out of the inland part of the weapons base, by law, traveled at a speed limit of 5 mph and were required to stop if they saw *anything* on the tracks—a stalled car, a deer, a cow, an individual or group of people, or an undetermined object—and remove it before proceeding. The land was flat, and engineers had plenty of visibility and stopping distance as long as they traveled at the required 5 mph speed limit. The two spotters standing on the front cowcatcher platform on the very front of the slow moving locomotive were in constant radio contact with the engineer.

An event that happened several weeks before the beginning of our announced fast assured me that the trains routinely stopped as regulations require when any obstacle was on the tracks. From June until September, people were blocking munitions trucks *every day* on the road parallel to the tracks. I went to the base on many of those days to join the vigil in support of the blockers.

One Sunday in early July, a Korean War veteran, barely known to the Nuremberg Action folks, independently decided to get on the tracks to block the oncoming train. He hadn't planned that in advance—he just did it. He had not taken the nonviolent training that our group undertook to participate in civil obedience/disobedience actions. The locomotive was traveling at its normal speed, and the spotters standing on the cowcatcher radioed the engineer to stop the train. One spotter simply hopped off the cowcatcher and quickly grabbed the man's large hand-held cross and smashed it in two, then shoved the man off the tracks. He just as quickly jumped back on, and the train rolled down the tracks. That showed me that the crew made sure the tracks were clear of any obstacles before moving, as regulations strictly require and common sense dictates.

To make absolutely sure all officials and employees of the base would be aware of the nature of our vigil, I wrote a letter on August 21 to the commander of the naval base, Lonnie Cagle. In my letter, I explained that two other veterans and I planned to fast on the tracks for forty days beginning on September 1, 1987. I detailed the reasons for the fast, and asked for a meeting with him. I sent copies of the letter to the Contra Costa County sheriff, the Concord Police Department, the California Highway Patrol, and a number of elected officials, including Senators Alan Cranston and Pete Wilson of California, Representatives Barbara Boxer, George Miller, and Don Edwards of California, Senators John Kerry and Ted Kennedy of Massachusetts, and Patrick Leahy and Jim Jeffords of Vermont. It should be noted that the letter was not meant to ensure our safety since the train crew was required by regulation and law to stop whenever they observed any objects or people on the tracks. The letter was primarily for educational purposes.

The Naval Station certainly received my letter, as the commander cabled the information to his superiors in Washington on August 31, outlining our plan, and identifying me as "protest principal." Cagle wrote: "Fasters will not move for approaching rail traffic. Local sheriff and police offices aware of threat." Since the whole point of the train blockage was to protest the movement of armaments, I took every possible opportunity to publicize what we were planning to do and to explain our motives. On August 28, 1987, an article was published in the local *Contra Costa Times* titled, "Peace Group Sets Arms Blockade: Will Block Weapons Hauls at Concord Naval Station." That article reported "The weapons blockades will coincide with a 40-day fast beginning Tuesday."

With this sustained vigil, I believed I was taking another step in walking my talk. By sitting on the tracks, I would be putting my body directly between the weapons and the campesinos of Nicaragua. The three fasting veterans positioned on the tracks offered a valuable lesson: if the train crew could stop for the three of us, they could stop the train entirely, thus saving the lives of thousands of campesinos destined to be murdered by the weapons on that train. In the process, the train crew would be upholding international law, the Nuremberg Obligation, and the U.S. Constitution. We would be part of a process intended to prevent the killing of innocents, while forcing a reckoning with U.S. legal requirements to uphold international and domestic constitutional law.

Ten days before I started the forty-day fast on the tracks, Holley and I held a commitment ceremony, declaring to friends and family that we were partners.[298] We vowed we would be a family of resistance, "prepared for the risks . . . required, individually and collectively, to live and promote a radical transformation in our North American society . . . This path may require us to be separate from one another—due to work, travel, jail, injury or even physical death." It was a lovely celebration, with 150 people, music and food. Rita Clark, sister of Nicaragua's Foreign Minister Miguel D'Escoto, joined our ceremony. We were happy and focused on how our actions might make a real difference in the world. Being part of this movement was profoundly satisfying for both of us.

September 1, 1987

We began our vigil on September 1 a little after 10 a.m. with an ecumenical worship service on the tracks. Only a couple of news people showed up for the event, but forty or fifty people came to support us, including Holley and her son Gabriel who considered me his stepfather. A personal friend, Bob Spitzer, a psychiatrist who was an amateur videographer, was there to document our arrest on video. A professional photographer acquaintance, Andy Peri, was present to make certain we had a good photographic record of the expected arrests and the formal beginning of our action.

At the service, I shared my thoughts and feelings, speaking from my heart rather than from a prepared speech. This is a literal transcript of what I said:

> My hope is that today will begin a new era of sustained resistance, like the salt march in India and like the civil rights movement in the 1950s and 1960s where people, every day, realize that we, the people, are the ones that are going to make peace. Peacemaking is full-time. War-making is full-time. And so my hope is that we will establish or create a kind of action here that revives the imagery of the sustained resistance of the past such as in the salt march and the civil rights movement where people are committed every day to say, "As long as the trains move munitions on these tracks we will be here to stop the trains." Because each train that goes by here with munitions, that gets by us, is going to kill people, people like you and me.
>
> And the question that I have to ask on these tracks is: am I any more valuable than those people? And if I say "No," then I have to say, "You can't move these munitions without moving my body or destroying my body." So today, from the spirit of a year ago on the steps and then for five months in Central America and coming back, the Nuremburg Actions and today, I begin this fast for atonement for all the blood that we have on our hands and that I have on my hands.
>
> And I begin this fast to envision a kind of resistance, an empowering kind of spirit, that we hope to participate in with many people, saying, These munitions will not be exploded in our names and they will not be

moved any longer in our names, and we must put our bodies in front of them to say, stronger than ever, that this will not continue in our name. The killing must stop and I have to do everything in my power to stop it.

And I hope that when people ask us what they can do to support us: what they can do is they can come to the tracks and stand with us on the tracks to stop the trains. That's all we want. We want more people to join hands and say, "This will not continue. And only we the people can stop it." Thank you.[299]

At 11:40 a.m., Duncan Murphy, David Duncombe, and I took our position between the rails. Two others, Ellen Earth and Michael Kroll, held a large banner across the tracks immediately behind us, which stated in bold letters, "Nuremburg Actions: Complicity in the Commission of a Crime Against Peace, a War Crime, or a Crime Against Humanity, is a Crime Under International Law."

All morning, we had noticed a different mood on the base than there had been in the past. David Hartsough observed that at about 11:30 a.m. two truckloads of Marines armed with M-16s and wearing flak vests, drove within fifty feet of our vigil before driving away. This was highly unusual. At about 11:45 a.m. a carload of Marines again drove near the vigil. One of them shouted to Hartsough, "We hear there is going to be violence today." And there was a group of armed Marines who stood idly near our vigil, something that had not occurred since we started our presence on June 10.

Larry Reposa, CNWS fire chief, later admitted in a sworn statement to authorities that he had "a bad feeling about this situation" and had "requested an engine company to respond from the inland fire station and stand by."

As we sat on the tracks, we saw a train approach and stop. Nuremberg Actions organizers Bob Lassalle and Marilyn Coffee walked over to a CNWS official who was carrying a walkie-talkie and appeared to be in touch with the train. When Lassalle reminded this man that demonstrators were still on the tracks, the man turned away and refused to listen before replying, "I think you're crazy; I'm going to do my job." A subsequent investigation revealed that this man's boss, the chief civilian security officer at the base, had told him, despite the absence of sheriff's deputies, that the train should be authorized "to go ahead; we're going to have a confrontation sooner or later." As Lassalle was walking back toward the tracks, he tried to communicate the same message to a nearby truckload of Marines, when one of them remarked, "Well, there may be some violence out here today."

CHAPTER 20

"Here Comes the Train"

I have no memory of what happened on the tracks. Victims of severe trauma often lose any memory of the traumatic event. Doctors call this condition "retrograde amnesia." I can only reconstruct the events from eyewitness testimony and scientific evidence gathered at the scene.

The following is a transcript of an audiocassette recording by Bill Fisher, the one radio reporter who was present that day.[300]

VOICE: *Okay. Here comes the train.*

MALE VOICE: *We're not leaving the tracks, right?*

MALE VOICE: *We're not leaving.*

MALE VOICE: *It's planning, preparation, initiation, waging a war of aggression or a war in violation of international. . . .*

[INAUDIBLE DUE TO TRAIN WHISTLE]

[TRAIN WHISTLE IS HEARD FOR NINETEEN SECONDS BEFORE IMPACT]

[TRAIN WHISTLE CEASES]

MALE VOICE: *No.*

FEMALE VOICE: *Oh, my God! Oh, my God! Oh, my God! Stop the train! Stop the—Oh, my God!*

MALE VOICE: *Help.*

FEMALE VOICE: *Come help me!*

FEMALE VOICE: *Ambulance is here.*

MALE VOICE: *Look what you did, you're the murderers.*

GABRIEL: *You murderers! You killed my father! You killed my father!*

MALE VOICE: *Where's the fucking ambulance?*

MALE VOICE: *Get an ambulance.*

FEMALE VOICE: *My God!* [SIRENS]

[MULTIPLE VOICES—INDISCERNIBLE]

GABRIEL: *You killed my father! Killed my father! You did that, by God!*

MALE VOICE: *Stay right there.*

MALE VOICE: *We love you, Brian.*

HOLLEY: *I'm holding the bleeding.*

MALE VOICE: *You want me to hold that* [INDISCERNIBLE]

HOLLEY: *Yes. You have to press very hard so that no more blood comes out.*

MALE VOICE: *Relax. Real, real hard.*

HOLLEY: *Right here.*

[MULTIPLE VOICES—INDISCERNIBLE]

MAN OPERATING TAPE RECORDER: *The train—there's total confusion. There's a fire truck that came. There's still no ambulance. It's been five minutes since the train came barreling down the tracks, blowing its horn. The three men who were on the tracks had panic in their eyes and two of them jumped aside. One of them who was kneeling fell back under the train, had his foot rolled over and cut off. Was dragged and bumped and dragged again. His head split open. His other foot cut off. And finally bumped into the inside of the track where the train then pulled on and stopped 400, 500 feet down the road.*

The—I never saw the eyes of the guys in the caboose. There were two guys on the cowcatcher, sort of screaming and yahooing and "Here we come." The Marine guards who are around with their M-16s look panic-stricken. Now there are several veterans who are enraged and yelling and screaming at the soldiers who are starting to surround the crowd and keep people off the tracks. There is still no ambulance. There's been a County Sheriff and a firetruck and a military vehicle of some kind with an official person with a radio coming around calling for things.

Holley, Brian's wife, is holding his leg trying to keep it from bleeding. His skull is open, you can see his brain inside. It's probably a four or five inch gaping hole in his skull. He's stunned. Stunned—fuck! Grief, all around.

The man from the fire department is attempting to suture and bandage what he can but he—the military keeps telling people to step across the fucking yellow line. I can't believe it.

Why don't you guys do something constructive? Jesus Christ!

MALE VOICE: *The train was going full bore.*

FEMALE VOICE: *We heard the screaming. I—* [INAUDIBLE]

MALE VOICE: *Didn't touch the throttle. Didn't even touch the throttle.*

MALE VOICE: *Fucking unbelievable.*

MAN OPERATING TAPE RECORDER: *They've attached something to his nostril. I just picked up a huge chunk of bone. Duncan Murphy is leaning over Brian, trying to hold on to life.*

Brian's eyes are closed. I'm not sure at this point.

Gabriel, Brian's stepson, is still distraught and screaming. As you look around, some of the responses are changing from shock and grief to anger.

Here comes the ambulance. Five, six, seven minutes later.

This was not a surprise. This had been a well-publicized protest. Brian had sent letters to some fifteen or twenty people, the base commander amongst others, last week. Everyone knew full well that this was going to be a day where the train was going to be stopped and the train did not stop.

Looks like military nursing personnel have arrived. He's still blinking, still holding on. Brian is such a strong character.

FEMALE VOICE: *Let's get a small no-pressure dressing-bandage, a Kurlex.*

MALE VOICE: *I've got* [INAUDIBLE]. *I've got everything under control.*

MALE VOICE: *Okay.*

MALE VOICE: *John, is that the only way you can stop it, is with that?*

MALE VOICE: *—have a tourniquet.*

MALE VOICE: *Hold on, man.*

VOICE: *Let's make a hole.*

MALE VOICE: *Need anything, buddy?*

MALE VOICE: *No. Looking good. Looking good.*

FEMALE VOICE: *How you doing, guy?*

MALE VOICE: *Pretty good.*

FEMALE VOICE: *I'm Petty Officer McGee. I'm a Navy Corpsman, okay? Let us help you.*

MALE VOICE: *I couldn't tell you, myself.*

FEMALE VOICE: *Don't hold pressure. Just hold it there.*

FEMALE VOICE: *110 over 80 bp, Bob.*

HOLLEY: *You're doing good. Your blood pressure is good, honey. You're hanging in there.*

FEMALE VOICE: *You're doing great, guy. You're doing great.*

FEMALE VOICE: *How're you doing? You doing all right?*

FEMALE VOICE: *Yeah.*

MALE VOICE: *Okay. Keep your hands* [INAUDIBLE].

HOLLEY: *I love you, Brian.*

MALE VOICE: *We all love you, Brian.*

FEMALE VOICE: *Brian. Brian.*

MALE VOICE: *How many victims do you have?*

MALE VOICE: *What?*

MALE VOICE: *How many victims do you have?*

FEMALE VOICE: *Two that I—there's one minor victim down there.*

MALE VOICE: *Where's the other one?*

FEMALE VOICE: *Everybody's making a circle around you for healing, Brian.*

HOLLEY: *Honey, you've gotta be brave, okay?*

GABRIEL: *Why didn't you dodge it? I wanted you to dodge. Why didn't you dodge it? Dodge it. You should have dodged—My God, that's a piece of him! That's a piece of him!*

HOLLEY: *Tell him you love him, Gabe. Just tell him you love him.*

GABRIEL: *My God, that's a piece of Dad.*

MALE VOICE: *It's all right.*

HOLLEY: *Just tell him you love him.*

GABRIEL: *That's a piece of my Dad!*

HOLLEY: *Tell him you love him. Bring him up here.*

MALE VOICE: *It's all right.*

FEMALE VOICE: *Dan, tell him you love him.*

HOLLEY: *Hey, Gabe, listen, I'm going to go to the hospital with Brian and—*

VOICE: *I want to go with you.*

FEMALE VOICE: *I'll take you there.*

HOLLEY: *Okay, they'll take you and you meet us at the hospital, okay?*

FEMALE VOICE: *I'll take you there, Gabe. I promise you.*

FEMALE VOICE: *Okay? Okay? Okay?*

VOICE: *God.*

HOLLEY: *He's going to be okay, honey.*

GABRIEL: *No, it's not going to be all right, that's my Dad.*

HOLLEY: *Yeah, we know. You know? I know, honey, I saw the whole thing.*

FEMALE VOICE: *Right now we need to get out of the way so they can* [INAUDIBLE].

GABRIEL: *God, you have blood all over you!*

HOLLEY: *I was stopping the bleeding on his legs, honey.*

MAN OPERATING TAPE RECORDER: *They brought a stretcher now. They're placing Brian's torso, that's what it is. His legs are gone below the knees. His head is wide open. He's still hanging on. His blood pressure is pretty good. People have formed a semi-circle around him, holding hands, trying to help pump life.*

It's still a pretty confusing situation. Duncan Murphy is still hanging on, as is Holley. And the Corps is working to strap him to a piece of plywood now to lift him up into the ambulance.

Now there are police vehicles everywhere. Highway Patrol, Concord Police, County Sheriff; as well as all the military police. Lots of little radios calling someone somewhere.

The train is still stopped, ironically, down the track some 500 feet, meters, I don't know: some distance down the road with this little triangle of explosive or dangerous cargo highlighting the back of it.

The engineer is still standing on the cab looking back. The two guys on the cowcatcher, I don't know where they are. They are behind the fence and the sentries so we can't approach them. It's on military property and they're making it very clear that we don't cross the yellow line.

The young Marine guards whose responsibility that is, initially came out here trying to look serious but sort of with a chuckle. This was another day, another job. And all of a sudden it's a different day.

People are yelling. Some of the veterans are angry and yelling at the—I don't know—at the air, at the fates, at the gods.

This whole thing had been orchestrated and planned and the train didn't stop.

CHAPTER 21

What Really Happened

David Duncombe, who had been crouching on the tracks, was able to leap clear to the left. Duncan Murphy, also crouching, was able to leap straight up ten feet—a mighty feat for a sixty-six-year old man—and grab onto the hand railing above the locomotive's cowcatcher platform. I was *sitting* cross-legged, and was unable to jump off in time. I was the only one hit. Duncan suffered a gash on his shin bone when he jumped up to face the two spotters standing on the cowcatcher platform whose hands were holding the same railing that Duncan momentarily grabbed to stabilize himself before jumping off. Duncan and Holley were the first to reach me after the train's second and last boxcar had passed over my limp body.

I'm sure I would have died if Holley, a midwife by profession, hadn't been right there. Four other friends assisted a composed Holley in stopping my blood flow and kept my energy alive by talking to me while waiting for the arrival of the ambulance. One friend, David Hartsough, protected my exposed brain while Duncan bent over me, cradling my head. Also assisting was Steve Brooks, a former helicopter door gunner in Viet Nam and then-commander of the Bill Motto "Wage Peace" VFW Post 5888 in Santa Cruz, California. Former Green Beret medic Gerry Condon helped Holley stop the bleeding from the stumps where my legs had been.

Hartsough later told me how difficult it was to see my body being rolled and yanked from one side to the other under the locomotive, twisting and flopping around like a rag doll as it was moved fifteen to twenty feet further down the tracks. I was surprised to learn that I was conscious the whole time until anesthesia was administered about 3:30 p.m. at the John Muir Hospital trauma unit in preparation for extensive surgery. Before the ambulance finally arrived, my circle of healing friends later described my conversations with them. I was saying over and over that we must stop that train before more campesinos are murdered, while moaning about the pain I felt in my legs.

Holley had studied emergency medical care in preparation for our peace walk on mined roads in Nicaragua's war zones, so she knew how to use finger pressure as an alternative to a tourniquet for stopping blood flow and managed to stop my bleeding, stabilizing me right there on the tracks. An IV was always present in Holley's car trunk as part of her midwife medical kit, and she used it immediately to bring me fluids. Although the Concord Naval Weapons Station Fire Department did respond, taking my vital signs, the station's Navy ambulance crew arrived at the scene only to quickly leave again without providing medical assistance or transportation to a hospital since, as they declared to Holley, my body was technically not lying on Navy property. Many more precious minutes elapsed before the arrival of the county ambulance.

I Am Alive

When I awoke in the hospital a few days later, I assumed I was in a jail cell. I had been so sure I would be arrested that it didn't occur to me that I had been hit by the train. Numerous green plants adorned my room and Holley, sitting next to my bed, explained that I was in the hospital. I was shocked! I looked down and saw my body covered with bandages, splints and casts. My upper legs were in casts under the sheets. Since the bottoms of the casts were connected to pipes and extended to the foot of the bed where two feet were visible, I had no idea that my lower legs were gone. To the contrary, I felt sharp pain in what seemed to be my toes, heels, arches, and ankles. I would later learn that the feet were just rubber prostheses and I was experiencing severe phantom pain, pain mysteriously felt in parts of the body that had been severed. This pain was subsequently treated successfully with acupuncture despite hospital doctors' suggestion that I would likely be on morphine for many years to manage the pain.

Both of my legs had been mangled by the train, one amputated at the moment of collision, the other twisted backward and subsequently amputated during surgery at John Muir Hospital, both below the knee. My skull was also fractured—apparently part of my brain was visibly pulsating as it bled. On the right side of my forehead there was a hole in my skull the size of a lemon where a piece of my cranium had been completely dislodged and driven into my right frontal lobe. My left outer ear had also been nearly sliced off, but paramedics were able to save it from total severance until the surgeons sewed it back on several hours later. In all, I survived nineteen injuries, including less serious broken ribs, broken shoulder, broken wrist, a seriously damaged kidney, and battered mouth. It is a miracle I survived at all, let alone with the ability to continue walking.

Four days after going under the train when I became fully conscious, I was informed that as many as nine thousand demonstrators had assembled at the crime scene, outraged by what had happened. Joan Baez sang, and Jesse Jackson and Daniel Ellsberg spoke. All three of my fellow veteran fasters from the year before also spoke. One of them, of course, was Duncan Murphy, who barely escaped being run over, himself.

During that intense day, hundreds of people ripped up a lengthy section of tracks and stacked the railroad ties to build a kind of monument unequivocally saying, "You will not do that again!" Although within two weeks authorities had replaced the tracks and the munitions trains began rolling once again, they were confronted for many years with large numbers of people forming blockades.

My brother Dwight visited after I'd been in the hospital a week or so. I first saw him talking to a guard outside my hospital room door. As he approached my bed, he smiled to see I was sitting up and alert. As he gently hugged me, he jokingly asked if I was trying to be Superman, adding that this was not a good beginning to his recent retirement after twenty-nine years of teaching.

I was surprised to learn that the hospital was receiving more than two hundred phone calls an hour, requiring a phone bank of volunteers, and shocked that a few of those calls were obviously death threats against me. As a result, the hospital had posted twenty-four-hour security outside my door. Somehow, my action, and the government's criminal response, had hit a raw nerve with some people just as it had inspired others. It was strange to realize that some hated me enough to want me killed, while others saw me as a hero.

My spirits were greatly lifted by the thousands of letters that poured in from well-wishers delivered to my bedside in large postal bags. Among the letters was a note and package from the St. Louis Cardinals baseball team sending me "best wishes" and expressing appreciation "for being such a great Cardinal fan over the years." I was thrilled as I unwrapped a Cardinal batting helmet and a baseball autographed by all the Cardinal players. A bit later I received an autographed copy of Stan Musial's autobiography—my boyhood hero! I also received a note from the San Francisco Giants baseball team— "Good luck to you. . . . You are a very courageous man"—accompanied by a number of players' autographs on Giants letterhead. These gifts all brought big smiles.

"Don't Stop"

Everyone wanted to know what really happened. Luckily, we had the audio tape recording, the video footage, and many photos, as well as eyewitness accounts. All of these were eventually incorporated into a legal brief filed on my behalf, and also available for congressional testimony.

All the evidence confirms that the train initially came to a complete stop several hundred feet before the public highway crossing where our vigilers were positioned. It was a bright, sunny day, with visibility for at least 650 feet, and the two spotters standing on the front cowcatcher platform of the train were visible to those gathered around the tracks. We know the spotters saw us far in advance, because their superiors radioed to the county sheriff asking how long it would take for the sheriff's officers to reach the scene. Besides, it was the spotters' primary job to ensure that the tracks were clear and to communicate that via radio to the train engineer.

All this was standard operating procedure. What followed was not. Instead of waiting for the sheriff to come, the train started moving. In fact it accelerated to more than three times the 5 mph speed limit. The FBI examined the video footage taken by Spitzer and determined that the train was moving at 16 mph when it hit me.[301] Rob Morse's *San Francisco Examiner* column on September 6 described the coverup: "Here's what the Navy says: The train was going 5 mph. Willson probably jumped on the tracks. They didn't see him on the tracks. Here's what we see in videotape and photos: The train was galloping right along—at a speed TV technicians worked out to be 17 mph."

A photograph reveals a fresh burst of smoke pouring out of the train's stack at the time of impact, suggesting the train accelerated further after running over me. The subsequent official Navy report concluded that the crew had clear visibility for 650 feet, the crew never braked even after recognizing us on the tracks, and the train was accelerating to three times the speed limit at moment of collision.[302] The report recommended punishments for the base commander and crew for violating base safety and security protocols. The report also stated that I was fully prepared to be arrested, and that I was moving in the final seconds in an effort to avoid impact. The Federal Railroad Administration declared that this was *not* a railroad accident.

The train did not stop because the train crew had been instructed not to stop. Ed Hubbard, railroad supervisor at CNWS, in an official report said he "informed the train crew that the protesters had stated they were going to remain on the tracks and stop the train that day. [He] told the crew [that] if the protesters started climbing on the train [they should] continue until the train was inside the gates and the marines could take over." David Humiston, the engineer, reported to investigators "he was told by his supervisor, when going on duty that morning, *not to stop* outside the base area. This was to prevent anyone from boarding the locomotive or the cars it was pulling." The *only* place outside the base area was the precise small spot where our vigil was located on the right-of-way.

Ralph Dawson, one of the two spotters standing on the very front of the locomotive, similarly said he had been instructed *not to stop* if protesters started climbing on the train. According to the report, Dawson "felt the protester who had been hit [me] was beyond help, so he did not tell the engineer to stop, but allowed him to proceed through the gate and onto government property before stopping." An investigative reporter located official documents that were not made public to congressional investigators or the media. These documents also confirmed that the train crew had been ordered not to stop: "The engineer, conductor and supervisor of the Concord Naval Weapons Station train that ran over pacifist S. Brian Willson Sept. 1, 1987, told investigators they were under orders not to stop outside the base where demonstrators were expected to stand on the tracks."[303]

Just Following Orders

I came very close to being killed that day. I lost both my legs and have spent years recovering from the physical and psychological trauma of these injuries. I will never be able to realize my dream of farming my own land. Yet, I prefer not to dwell on these losses.

I believe that each of us chooses our path in life. The train crew chose to follow illegal orders, and for that I condemn them. But I also have empathy for them. They are living the way I used to live; they were brainwashed as I was into believing they were protecting the American Way Of Life by running us over. They later sued me for traumatic stress. I'm sure they do have post-traumatic stress syndrome, but I am not the cause. The cause of their stress, and mine, is a system that runs roughshod over individuals even while demanding our dumbed-down obedience to authority.

When the U.S. government offered a cash settlement for the egregious act several years later, it was a de facto acknowledgement that the Navy train crew and their superiors intended not to stop the train. By not stopping, the Navy's civilian crew was in fact simply following orders.

The actions of the train crew are an excellent case example of the Milgram experiment findings. Psychologist Robert Cialdini, an authority on influence and persuasion, has written a college text, *Influence: Science and Practice*, in which he cites Lieutenant Calley at My Lai and the train crew at CNWS as a demonstration of Milgram's critical finding: "the extreme willingness of adults to go to almost any lengths on the command of an authority."[304] We can speculate that, given a command not to stop, and faced with an immovable obstacle, the crew chose to obey authority rather than their own most basic feelings and moral ethics. They may even have sped up in order to get past us more quickly.

Whether the crew sped up on their own accord or on orders does not matter, in the end. When the Naval command gave the order to move the train forward, the message was that the government was willing to murder us in order to protect their cargo, cars full of weapons designed to kill other people, just like us, living in distant lands.

The U.S. government is so afraid of losing its grip on other countries and people, on the resources that enable our "prosperity," that it is willing to sacrifice its own people to the cause. The crew of the train were like grunts at the very end of a chain of command involved in a diabolical, criminal national policy. And we three were apparently seen as pests threatening to arouse others in the population from their slumber.

Like Mai Ly and the villagers in Viet Nam, like the eleven campesinos I saw being carried to their graves in Estelí, we were in the way of empire. We had to be eliminated.

Nuremberg Principles

Principles of International Law Recognized in the Charter of the Nuremberg Tribunal and in the Judgment of the Tribunal

As formulated by the International Law Commission, June–July 1950.

Principle I
Any person who commits an act which constitutes a crime under international law is responsible therefor and liable to punishment.

Principle II
The fact that internal law does not impose a penalty for an act which constitutes a crime under international law does not relieve the person who committed the act from responsibility under international law.

Principle III
The fact that a person who committed an act which constitutes a crime under international law acted as Head of State or responsible government official does not relieve him from responsibility under international law.

Principle IV
The fact that a person acted pursuant to order of his Government or of a superior does not relieve him from responsibility under international law, provided a moral choice was in fact possible to him.

Principle V
Any person charged with a crime under international law has the right to a fair trial on the facts and law.

Principle VI
The crimes hereinafter set out are punishable as crimes under international law:

a. Crimes against peace:
(i) Planning, preparation, initiation, or waging of a war of aggression or a war in violation of international treaties, agreements, or assurances;
(ii) Participation in a common plan or conspiracy for the accomplishment of any of the acts mentioned under (i).

b. War crimes:
Violations of the laws or customs of war which include, but are not limited to, murder, ill-treatment or deportation to slave-labor or for any other purpose of civilian population of or in occupied territory, murder or ill-treatment of prisoners of war or persons on the seas, killing of hostages, plunder of public or private property, wanton destruction of cities, towns, or villages, or devastation not justified by military necessity.

c. Crimes against humanity:
Murder, extermination, enslavement, deportation, and other inhuman acts done against any civilian population, or persecutions on political, racial, or religious grounds, when such acts are done or such persecutions are carried on in execution of or in connection with any crime against peace or any war crime.

Principle VII
Complicity in the commission of a crime against peace, a war crime, or a crime against humanity as set forth in Principle VI is a crime under international law.

(*Source:* United Nations General Assembly Resolution 95 (1). The Principles were formulated by the International Law Commission at the request of the General As-

---

Concord Naval Weapons Station (Calif.)

INTERFAITH SERVICE CONCORD
September 1, 1987 for

Interfaith Service
9-1-87

OPENING SONG

OPENING PRAYER

READING: Letter from 24-year old prior to mother's death

MOMENT FOR QUIET REFLECTION

SONG

READING: ISAIAH 58:5-12

MOMENT FOR QUIET REFLECTION

TIME FOR SHARING PRAYERS/CONCERNS

CLOSING PRAYER

CLOSING SONG

Copy of Nuremberg Principles we distributed at the Concord vigil site.

NUREMBERG ACTIONS
CONCORD
BEGINNING JUNE 10
NONVIOLENT RESISTANCE AT
CONCORD NAVAL WEAPONS STATION

Continue the large June 12-13 action – join a sustained, open-ended nonviolent action at Concord Naval Weapons Station, California.

The time has come to say No to the illegal and immoral crimes against humanity being waged against the people of Central America — Not just with our words but with our bodies and our lives.

After World War II the NUREMBERG trials spelled out the principle that individuals are responsible for obeying international law on human rights even if their governments do not.

THE VETERANS PEACE ACTION TEAMS are putting out the call to all citizens to uphold international law and decency, invoking the NUREMBERG CHARTER, to stop the illegal and immoral wars being waged against the people of Nicaragua, El Salvador and Guatemala.

A WORLD PEACE FORCE is emerging beginning with the sustained presence of individuals willing to put their bodies in the way of the trucks and trains that are transporting arms to ships at Port Chicago, bound for Central America.

We invite your participation in this ongoing, open-ended NUREMBERG ACTION beginning JUNE 10 at the Concord Naval Weapons Station. We ask all participants to commit to nonviolence in spirit and in deed with the personnel at the base, ourselves and the community of Concord.

This sustained action of nonviolent resistance is endorsed by the Pledge of Resistance and is being promoted in cooperation with local peace and justice organizations.

SCHEDULE
Wednesday, JUNE 10, 1987
8:00 AM: Sustained action on the tracks begins

Friday & Saturday, JUNE 12-13
Mass Nonviolent Action

Sunday, JUNE 14
8:00 PM: Evaluation of the first phase of ongoing action

STOP THE WAR IN ITS TRACKS!

No Arms to El Salvador!   No Aid to the Contras!
For Nonviolence Preparation and Information:
Pledge of Resistance: (415) 655-1177   Veterans Peace Action Team: (408) 426-7822

YES. I'd like to participate in the non-violent blockade of arms shipments at the Concord Naval Weapons Station by:

A ☐ Ongoing presence at the tracks.

B ☐ 1, 2 or 3 days at the tracks.

C ☐ 1 week per month at the tracks.

D ☐ Contribute $ _ _ _ _ for the project.

E ☐ Other support: (circle)
    office help, housing, food

Name: _____

Address: _____

City: _____ State: _____ Zip: _____

Phone: Day _____ Evening _____

Please detach and mail to:
Veterans Fast For Life / Veterans Peace Action Teams
P.O. Box 586, Santa Cruz, California 95061

Original poster announcing creation of the Nuremberg Actions Concord in efforts to halt shipments of lethal weapons destined for El Salvador and Nicaragua

COVENANT OF NONVIOLENCE

NUREMBERG ACTIONS - CONCORD

As a participant in the Nuremberg Actions at the Concord Naval Weapons Station, I commit to the following nonviolent discipline, and as part of these actions, I will reflect on these commitments:

1.   We will regard each individual as a human being and our attitude will be one of openness and respect toward all whom we encounter as we engage in our actions against U.S. intervention in Central America.

2.   We will use no violence, physical or verbal, toward any person. We will refrain from insulting remarks.

3.   We will not damage property.

4.   We will not run, use threatening motions, or jump suddenly on or off the tracks or roadways.

5.   As members of these nonviolent actions we will follow the directions of the designated coordinators. In the event of a serious disagreement one should remove oneself from the action.

6.   We will carry no weapons.

7.   While not denying feelings, we will harbor no hate. Should others express violence toward us, we will submit to that expression without returning the violence. We will also protect others from insults or attack.

8.   We will not bring or use any drugs or alcohol other than for medical purposes.

9.   We will show respect for the police

10. We will not evade the consequences of our actions.

11. We will be alert to the people around us and will be aware of when others need assistance. We will support each other in needs for peacekeeping

NONVIOLENCE TRAINING IS REQUIRED for all those who have not previously received it. All who wish to take part in these Nuremberg Actions are required to take a day-long introduction to the philosophy and methods of nonviolence. In addition, all participants are required to attend a special training and briefing for these actions at the Concord Naval Weapons Station.

6/16/87

NUREMBURG ACTIONS
MT. DIABLO PEACE CENTER
65 Eckley Lane
Walnut Creek, CA 94596
(415) 930-8505

Our Nuremberg Actions Covenant of Nonviolence.

VETERANS FAST FOR LIFE/
VETERANS PEACE ACTION TEAMS

June 2, 1987

Captain G.G. Mayes, Commander
Concord Naval Weapons Station (CNWS)
Concord, CA 94520

Dear Commander Mayes:

We are planning a nonviolent action beginning June 10th. We are writing you because we wish to maintain open contact with all law enforcement agencies and military personnel.

We are very concerned about the deepening U.S. militarization in and of Central America. Many of our group have experienced first-hand what our policy is doing to the people of these countries. The killing and maiming with our weapons is not only immoral, but illegal as well under international and domestic laws. A bi-partisan political process in our country has supported--for many years--a policy of destabilization, subversion, and terrorism in many countries in the world, including much of Central America. Some of us were once participants in carrying out some of these policies. No matter how much we pursue through political avenues the cessation of these policies of death, the policies not only continue, but they frequently escalate.

Under the Nuremberg Principles signed by the United States after World War II, individuals are obligated to do everything in their power that is reasonable to make known and stop violations of law by their superiors and government. The purpose, of course, was and is to prevent from ever happening again the horror of Nazi Germany which was sustained by the silence and complicity of the German citizenry. Today, the citizenry is WE The People of the United States. We are invoking the Nuremberg Principles at this time and are asking many people to join us. One of our Veterans Peace Action Teams is currently living and working in the northern war zones of Nicaragua and we expect some of them to join us when they return later this summer.

We are committed to stopping the weapons shipments from leaving the Concord Naval Weapons Station. We know that once they arrive at destination points they translate into death and maiming of many human beings. We ask you to join in this effort to stop further weapons shipments.

On Wednesday, June 10, 1987 at 8 AM a sustained, open-ended, nonviolent resistance campaign will begin at the facility for which you have been directed to oversee. The purpose: To stop weapons shipments. We welcome the opportunity to discuss in person why we feel so strongly about this matter and the plans for the on-going resistance. We propose to meet with you Monday, June 8th.

We look forward to hearing from you.

Sincerely,

cc: Major Warren
    Dan Tikalsky
    Ken DeLapp
    Rod Carpenter
    Cliff Kroeger   for Nuremberg Action Committee   Member, National Coordinating
    Harry Hart   Member, VPAT   Committee, VPAT
    Doug Sizamenes   Chris Ballin   S. Brian Willson

P.O. Box 586   •   Santa Cruz, California 95061   •   (408) 426-7822
                                              Home: San Rafael (415) 258-9740

My June 2, 1987, letter to Concord Naval Weapons Station (CNWS) base commander Mayes announcing our plans to commence a sustained nonviolent resistance at and along the railroad tracks on June 10.

```
TOD 156 2307Z JUN 87

  ORIG DIC

  INFO A/B/01/07/10
FTIUZYUW RUWMKNA2281 1562217-UUUU--RUWNSUU.
ZNR UUUUU
P R 052217Z JUN 87
FM WPNSTA CONCORD CA
TO COMNAVSEASYSCOM WASHINGTON DC
INFO CNO WASHINGTON DC
CINCPACFLT PEARL HARBOR HI
COMNAVBASE SAN FRANCISCO CA
CHINFO WASHINGTON DC
BT
UNCLAS
MSIG/UNIT SITREP/WPNSTA CONCORD/005/JUN//
FLAGWORD/UNITSITREP/-//
TIMELOC/042100Z/WPNSTA CONCORD CA//
GENTEXT/EFFORT TO BLOCK EXPLOSIVE RAIL AND TRUCK TRAFFIC/
BRIAN WILSON, COORDINATOR OF A PACIFIST ORGANIZATION KNOWN AS
QUOTE VETERANS FAST FOR LIFE AND VETERANS PEACE ACTION TEAMS UNQUOTE
INFORMED PUBLIC AFFAIRS OFFICER THIS COMMAND THAT ON 10 JUNE HIS
ORGANIZATION WILL BEGIN A PERPETUAL ATTEMPT TO BLOCK WEAPONS STATION
CONCORD EXPLOSIVE RAIL AND TRUCK MOVEMENT BETWEEN THE STATION'S
INLAND AND TIDAL AREAS BY PERMANENTLY STATIONING PERSONNEL ON RAIL
TRACK AND IN ROADWAY. HE FURTHER STATED THAT WHEN ONE PERSON IS
ARRESTED, ANOTHER WILL TAKE HIS OR HER PLACE FOR AS LONG AS THEY HAVE
PEOPLE REMAINING, WITH THOSE ARRESTED RETURNING TO THE SCENE AFTER
RELEASE FROM CUSTODY TO REPEAT ACTION. WILSON IS SAME PERSON WHO
FASTED IN WASHINGTON, DC, EARLIER THIS YEAR PROTESTING U.S. CENTRAL
AMERICAN POLICY WITH RESULTING HIGH VISIBILITY NATIONAL MEDIA
ATTENTION. MEMBERS OF GROUP HAVE BEEN SEEKING TO BUY OR RENT RE-
SIDENCE IN AREA TO HOUSE MARATHON PROTESTERS. WILSON SAYS THEY HOPE
TO KEEP EFFORT GOING FOR AT LEAST SEVERAL MONTHS. SINCE TRACK AND
ROADWAY INVOLVED EASILY ACCESSIBLE TO PUBLIC AND UNDER JURISDICTION
OF CIVIL AUTHORITIES, THIS SITUATION COULD REQUIRE PERMANENT POLICE
PRESENCE AND HAS SERIOUS SAFETY AND SECURITY IMPLICATIONS.
RMKS/AMPLFYING SITUATION REPORTS WILL BE FILED AS THIS INCIDENT
DEVELOPS//
BT
#2281
```

Official cable sent June 5 by CNWS commander to his superiors in Washington, D.C., in response to my June 2 letter to commander Mayes.

Retyped version for easier reading:

FROM: Commander, Concord Naval Weapons Station, CA

TO: Commander, Navy Sea Systems Command, Washington, DC

"Effort To Block Explosive Rail And Truck Traffic"

Brian Wilson (sic), coordinator of a pacifist organization known as 'Veterans Fast for Life and Veterans Peace Action Teams' informed public affairs officer this command that on June 10 his organization will begin a perpetual attempt to block weapons station Concord explosive rail and truck movement between the station's inland and tidal areas by permanently stationing personnel on rail, track and roadway. He further stated that when one person is arrested, another will take his or her place for as long as they have people remaining, with those arrested returning to the scene after release from custody to repeat action. Wilson (sic) is same person who fasted in Washington, DC, earlier this year protesting U.S. Central American policy with resulting high visibility national media attention. Members of group have been seeking to buy or rent residence in area to house marathon protesters. Wilson (sic) says they hope to keep effort going for at least several months. Since track and roadway involved easily accessible to public and under jurisdiction of civil authorities, this situation could require permanent police presence and has serious safety and security implications. Amplifying situation reports will be filed as this incident develops.

VETERANS FAST FOR LIFE/
VETERANS PEACE ACTION TEAMS

August 21, 1987

Captain Lonnie Cagle, Commander
Concord Naval Weapons Station (CNWS)
Concord, CA 94520

Dear Commander Cagle:
        This letter serves to introduce myself to you, announces an impending 40 day water only Fast as part of the Nuremberg Actions at CNWS, and requests a personal meeting with you.

        Last year I was one of 4 U.S. military veterans on a 47 day water only Fast on the steps of the U.S. Capitol in Wash., D.C., protesting our war policies in Central America. In 1966-1970, I was in the U.S. Air Force, serving as a security officer with intelligence functions in Vietnam in 1969. Since separation from the military I have worked in a number of capacities, including practice as an attorney and criminologist. I have also owned a dairy business and been director of a Vietnam Veterans Outreach Center for which I received a special commendation from Massachusetts Governor Michael Dukakis.

        A couple of years ago I became very suspicious of the U.S. policy in Central America. I resigned as director of the Outreach center and began a series of trips to see for myself. I have subsequently been to Nicaragua 4 times and to El Salvador and Honduras once each.

        I have walked and ridden 700 kilometers (430 miles) in the northern war zones of Nicaragua. I have talked with hundreds of Nicaraguan people: campesinos, government and church officials, military personnel and contras. I have talked with several hundred victims of the contra terrorists, most of them civilian casualties from anti-tank mines, ambushes, torture, grenade and mortar attacks. I also have talked with many widows and orphans. In El Salvador I talked with survivors of U.S. directed bombing missions. We are committing wholesale murder and maiming.

        CNWS is the largest munitions depot on the west coast, and was a major supplier of munitions during the Vietnam war. An April 1985 U.S. Dept. of Defense contract with the government of El Salvador has provided hard evidence of substantial shipments of munitions from CNWS to Central America. Additionally, in November 1986, I spent time with Eugene Hasenfus in Nicaragua discussing the flow of munitions into El Salvador, and their subsequent movement to bases in Honduras, some of which then travel to Nicaraguan-based contras from air drops on several flight patterns.

        Enclosed find copies of the April 4 and May 29, 1987, reports of Veterans Peace Action Teams observing and working in Nicaragua. The war is demonic. So-called Low Intensity Conflict is terrorist warfare of the most barbaric form. Our intervention into sovereignty violates a number of domestic and international laws.

        As part of a movement to uphold international and U.S. Constitutional law, and to stop the illegal and immoral U.S. war in Central America, I have been involved with many others in the Nuremberg Actions who have been present on a daily basis at CNWS since June 10, 1987. We plan a sustained presence that will include persons placing their bodies on the tracks and roadway, asking you and those moving the munitions to stop their movement.

P.O. Box 586   •   Santa Cruz, California 95061   •   (408) 426-7822
Home: San Rafael (415) 258-9149

My August 21 letter to new CNWS commander Cagle announcing our plans for a forty-day blocking action and fasting on the tracks commencing September 1.

In so doing, we will be upholding the law under the Nuremberg Principles agreed to by the United States, and Article VI of our Constitution which holds our treaties to be Supreme Law.

Commencing September 1, 1987, I plan to Fast on water only on the tracks for a period of 40 consecutive days. I will use this time in sacrificial reflection to atone for our complicity in death policies, and to envision resistance actions in response. Others will be joining, including one of the other members of the 1986 Veterans Fast For Life, Duncan Murphy. I want you to know in advance of this plan. If not incarcerated, deceased or otherwise disabled, I am committed, as the spirit moves me, to be physically on the tracks for part of each of the 40 days. This will be made clear to the public and the media. Other people are expected to be present either on or just off the tracks and roadway as part of the Nuremberg Actions. We believe, and shall affirm, our participation in civil disobedience, upholding domestic and international law with our bodies.

Because of the seriousness of these matters I ask that we have a personal meeting to discuss them. This action is not intended to harass you or any military or civilian personnel. As part of our philosophy of nonviolence, we are committed to treat every person with human respect. We must, however, do everything reasonable in our power to make known the crimes of our country and to stop them from continuing. We ask that you suspend movement of munitions, exercising your responsibility to uphold international law and the U.S. Constitution which considers treaties as part of itself. Under Nuremberg, every citizen, including military personnel, is duty bound to uphold the law, even when ordered otherwise by superiors. I would like to discuss with you your views and response to our concerns.

Some of us have decided to put our bodies on the line to save lives of other people who are worth no less than us. Our killing and our complicity in it must stop! I hope that you will respond so that we can set up a mutually convenient time to meet.

Sincerely,

S. Brian Willson

Enclosures
C:

R.C. Oliver, CHP	Michael Dukakis, Gov Mass.
R. Rainey, CC Sheriff	J. Kerry, US Sen Mass
G. Straka, Concord CP	E. Kennedy, US Sen Mass
K. DeLapp, Concord PD	P. Leahy, US Sen Vt
B. Boxer, US HR CA	J. Jeffords, US HR Vt
G. Miller, US HR CA	T. Harkin, US Sen Ia
A. Cranston, US Sen CA	D. Bonior, US HR Mi
P. Wilson, US Sen CA	D. Edwards, US HR CA
Variety of other pol. officials & media	

```
                        DISTRO:

ORIG: D1C  INFO: A/B/10/09/07    TOT: 311523Z AUG 87
PTTUZYUW RUWMHNA3397 2431445-UUUU--RUWNSUU.
ZNR UUUUU
P 311445Z AUG 87
FM WPNSTA CONCORD CA
TO COMNAVSEASYSCOM WASHINGTON DC
COMNAVBASE SAN FRANCISCO CA
INFO CNO WASHINGTON DC
CINCPACFLT PEARL HARBOR HI
CHINFO WASHINGTON DC
BT
UNCLAS
MSGID/UNIT SITREP/WPNSTA CONCORD CA/008/AUG//
REF/A/UNIT SITREP/WPNSTA CONCORD CA/052217Z JUN 87/005/NOTAL//
AMPN/PREVIOUS REPORT RELATED TO THIS INCIDENT//
GENTEXT/INCIDENT IDENTIFICATION AND DETAILS/COMMANDING OFFICER
RECEIVED LETTER FROM GROUP IDENTIFIED AS VETERANS-FAST FOR LIFE AND
VETERANS PEACE ACTION TEAMS ADVISING THAT PROTESTORS PLAN TO
FAST FOR 40 DAYS ON RAILROAD TRACK USED TO TRANSPORT MATERIAL
BETWEEN STATION INLAND AND TIDAL AREAS. LETTER AND NEWS ARTICLE QOUTING
PROTEST PRINCIPAL, MR. S. BRIAN WILLSON, STATES FAST TO BEGIN 1 SEPT
AND THAT FASTERS WILL NOT MOVE FOR APPROACHING RAIL TRAFFIC. LOCAL
SHERIFF AND POLICE OFFICES AWARE OF THREAT.
SHOULD POTENTIAL INTERRUPTION OF RAIL SERVICE OCCUR, THEY
WILL BE REQUESTED TO REMOVE PROTESTOR(S). COMMANDING OFFICER'S
ASSESSMENT: INTERRUPTION OF NORMAL STATION OPERATIONS NOT ANTICIPATED.
LOCAL MEDIA ATTENTION HAS OCCURRED. NATIONAL MEDIA ATTENTION POSSIBLE
SINCE FASTERS ACHIEVED NOTIRIETY DURING FAST ON CAPITOL STEPS IN
WASHINGTON DC LAST SEPTEMBER//
RMKS/AMPLFYING SITUATION REPORTS WILL BE FILED SHOULD INCIDENT
DEVELOP//
BT
#3397
```

Official cable sent August 31 by CNWS commander to his superiors in Washington, D.C., in response to my August 21 letter, where he clearly states "that fasters will not move for approaching traffic" with "national media attention possible" and that law enforcement "will be requested to remove protestor(s)"

Retyped version for easier reading:

FROM: Commander, Concord Naval Weapons Station, CA

TO: Commander, Navy Sea Systems Command, Washington, DC

"Previous Report Related To This Incident//Text: Incident Identification And Details"

Commanding Officer received letter from group identified as Veterans Fast for Life and Veterans Peace Action Teams advising that protestors (sic) plan to fast for 40 days on railroad track used to transport material between station inland and tidal areas. Letter and news article quoting protest principal, Mr. S. Brian Willson, states fast to begin 1 Sept and that fasters will not move for approaching rail traffic. Local sheriff and police offices aware of threat. Should potential interruption of rail service occur, they will be requested to remove protestor(s) (sic). Commanding officer's assessment: Interruption of normal station operations not anticipated. Local media attention has occurred. National media attention possible since fasters achieved notoriety during fast on capitol steps in Washington DC last September. Amplifying situation reports will be filed should incident develop.

Comment: The August 31 cable makes clear that Navy officials understood precisely the nature of our action—to fast on the railroad tracks for forty days and not to move for approaching rail traffic. Further, the cable informs Washington of the Navy's planned response—to remove us from the tracks.

COME TO THE CONCORD, CA. NAVAL WEAPONS STATION –
(Port Chicago Highway near Clyde, Ca.)
    Participate in the:

    * On-Going NUREMBERG ACTIONS, Uphold International Law
      With Your Body Or Your Presence On Or Near The Tracks;
    * 40 Day 1987 VETERANS/CITIZENS FAST FOR LIFE AND PEACE,
      Commencing September 1 on the Railroad Tracks

FOR MORE INFORMATION, Contact: Mt. Diablo Peace Center, Chuck Goodmacher; (415) 933-7851; or Veterans Peace Action Teams, Scott Rutherford, (408) 426-7822

Sherry Peters / The Hartford Courant

Veterans Duncan Murphy, left, and S. Brian Willson after 3 weeks
into the 1986 Veterans Fast For Life.

DUNCAN MURPHY and BRIAN WILLSON

And OTHERS

Will FAST ON WATER ONLY For 40 Days On The Railroad Tracks As Part Of The NUREMBERG ACTIONS.

This FAST Will Provide A Substantial Period Of
Time In Sacrificial Reflection, Within A Resis-
tance Atmosphere, To ATONE FOR OUR COLLECTIVE
COMPLICITY In Death Policies, And To ENVISION
RESISTANCE ACTIONS In Response To Those Poli-
cies.

Original poster announcing our plans to commence on September 1, 1987, a forty-day, water-only fast on the railroad tracks at CNWS while blocking munitions trains.

As a two-year-old in Geneva, New York, in the 1940s, I loved to play in the snow, no matter how deep or how cold. I didn't want to be penned up in that damned crib.

One of my second grade drawings—large White man shooting a small "Indian," Geneva, New York, 1948–1949.

My older brother Dwight and me, 1945.

"Lucky," my Water Spaniel best friend from fourth to eighth grade.

Eighth grade valedictorian photo, Ashville, New York, Union Free School, June 1955.

I stand second from left, Boy Scout Troop 41, Ashville, New York, July 1953.

I stand amidst the snow banks as a teenager in 1957 on Ashville Hill overlooking Chautauqua Lake (visible top right). My family moved to Ashville, located in the snowbelt south of Lake Erie, when I was nine. I enjoyed the long winters because of tobogganing, sledding, and snowshoeing and because I loved to shovel neighbors' walks and driveways to earn money.

My older brother Dwight, Mom, Dad, and me, Ashville, ca. 1957.

Pitching on a makeshift mound in front of our house in Ashville, ca. 1957.

I sit front left, Student Council, Chautauqua Central High School (New York), 1958–1959.

I stand fourth from left, co-captain, Chautauqua Central High School "Indians" varsity basketball team, 1958–1959. Bill Cornell, third from left, and I were selected to Southern Division's all-conference second team, New York Section VI.

I kneel front right, co-captain and first baseman, Chautauqua Central High School "Indians" baseball team, Class C, Section VI champions, 1959.

I rest my hand on a stack of more than sixty family bibles found in my parents' home after their deaths in 1989, many purchased from evangelist Jerry Falwell. [PHOTO: JIM WISE]

Ron Kovic and I flash peace signs at a Berkeley teach-in against the U.S. war in Iraq, 1990. We share the same birthday, July 4, Ron born in 1946 and I in 1941. [PHOTO: MARC FRANKLIN]

I stand in the back row, eighth from left, one of 115 graduates of U.S. Air Force Officer Training School (OTS), November 25, 1966, Lackland Air Force Base, San Antonio, Texas. Left: Blown-up headshot.

I sit on the Binh Thuy Air Base flightline, March 1969, holding a walkie-talkie and looking pensively at a pallet of body bags. I commanded a special Combat Security Police unit at Binh Thuy. Notice Operation Safeside star patch on my left shoulder. [PHOTO: DAMAGED POLAROID]

I lean on an armored personnel carrier (APC V-100), Binh Thuy, 1969.

I stand with my immediate superior, Captain Joel, Tan Son Nhut Air Base, Saigon, who wrote on the back of this photo from April 19, 1969, "Pacifist and Warrior."

I stand right, commander in front of a portion of my combat security unit after dispatch to Phan Rang Air Base, June 1969. [PHOTO: USAF]

My combat security unit fire teams engaged in training maneuvers along Phan Rang Air Base perimeter, June 1969. [PHOTO: USAF]

This is an enlarged view of a postage stamp issued by North Viet Nam depicting U.S. Quaker Norman Morrison's face overlooking antiwar demonstrators. The stamp was issued shortly after his immolation on November 2, 1965, in view of Secretary of War McNamara's office at the Pentagon. Morrison was the first Eagle Scout I knew. He graduated in 1952 from Chautauqua Central High School (New York), seven years ahead of me. There were at least eight other U.S. Americans who immolated themselves between March 1965 and May 1970 in anguish over the war. They ranged in age from sixteen to eighty-two. There were at least seventy-six Vietnamese who immolated themselves, most of them Buddhists.

Campaign photo during my ill-fated run for Sheriff of Chautauqua County, New York, 1972.

Copy of my official District of Columbia Bar membership ID, January 1973.

Top: I pose next to my Corvette Sting Ray after commissioning as a Second Lieutenant, 1966.
Bottom: Home from Viet Nam, I graduated to this flower-power Volkswagen Beetle.

Dewey Canyon III encampment of more than a thousand Viet Nam veterans on the Washington Mall near the Capitol building, April 18–23, 1971, organized by Vietnam Veterans Against the War (VVAW). Dewey Canyon III was a nonviolent "limited incursion into the country of Congress" to stop war funding, using a variety of tactics—guerrilla theater, conventional lobbying, even veterans attempting to turn themselves in as war criminals. On April 23, the veterans returned war medals over a hastily erected fence near the west steps of the Capitol—medals of dishonor drenched in the blood of the innocent. This action escalated FBI targeting of VVAW. Dewey Canyon I and Dewey Canyon II were the illegal, secret U.S.-orchestrated invasions of Laos, 1969 and 1971, respectively.

As coordinator of the National Moratorium on Prison Construction, I speak to a recently released prisoner from New York's Attica prison while attending a 1975 New England prison conference.

I stand second from left, War Resisters League class of trained organizers, 1978. [PHOTO: WALTER GOODMAN]

My mentors, Juanita and Wally Nelson, radical homesteaders, in front of their self-built home in Deerfield, Massachusetts, 1983. Wally served three and a half years in prison during World War II for refusal to participate in the war, even refusing alternative service in a civilian public service camp. Wally was on the first Freedom Ride in 1947 to test desegregation in the south. He and Juanita were founders of Peacemakers in 1948, seeking radical change through nonviolence and publishing the *Handbook on the Non-payment of War Taxes.* Wally and Juanita each did time in prison for tax refusal, even as they live on less than $5,000 a year. They are role models for disobedience to following orders, and teach that tyranny can only exist with compliance of the people.

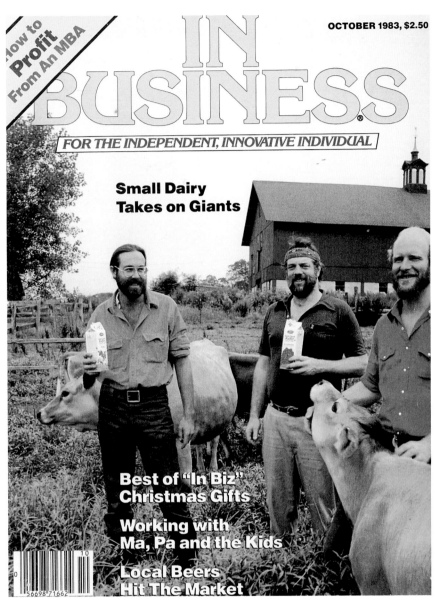

OCTOBER 1983, $2.50

How to Profit From An MBA

IN BUSINESS

FOR THE INDEPENDENT, INNOVATIVE INDIVIDUAL

Small Dairy Takes on Giants

Best of "In Biz" Christmas Gifts

Working with Ma, Pa and the Kids

Local Beers Hit The Market

I pose with my two business partners in New England Country Dairy for the cover photo of *In Business* magazine, October 1983. The feature article, "The Dairy that Dared," by James Ridgeway, told of our early success in being an independent dairy product distributor for small owner-operators. [PHOTO: WESLEY BLIXT]

I stand, center, in protest, Greenfield, Massachusetts Commons, October 23, 1983, after 241 U.S. Marines were blown up in Beirut, Lebanon. Also holding signs are Viet Nam veterans Joe Bangert, left, and Rob Stenson, right.

As director of the Vietnam Veterans Outreach Center, Greenfield, Massachusetts, I talk with another veteran in front of our office, 1985.

Facing page: I sit, front left, one of twelve Viet Nam veterans at Senator John Kerry's (D-MA) black-tie victory party, June 1985, where he thanked us for our role in his 1984 election victory. Kerry sits in middle. I was struck by Kerry stressing that his initials, "JFK," for John Forbes Kerry, would aid in his aspirations to the White House. The media nicknamed us "Kerry's Commandos" as we flew around the state in a campaign helicopter. Cameron Kerry concluded that our efforts pulled his brother's campaign out of a nose-dive by providing the much needed "galvanizing energy." [PHOTO: RICHARD SOBOL]

Left to right: George Mizo, Duncan Murphy, Charlie Liteky, and I begin an open-ended, water-only Veterans Fast For Life (VFFL), September 1, 1986, on the steps of the U.S. Capitol, to protest President Reagan's terrorist policies in Central America. [PHOTO: RICK REINHARD]

Left to right: Charlie Liteky, Roanoke Bishop Walter Sullivan, George Mizo, comedian Dick Gregory, Martin Luther King III, me, and Duncan Murphy, late September 1986. [PHOTO: RICK REINHARD]

October 3, 1986, thirty-third day of the fast, George Mizo explains the fast to Senators, L to R, John Kerry (D-MA), Donald Riegle (D-MI), Christopher Dodd (D-CT), and Daniel Patrick Moynihan (D-NY). I stand with baseball cap to the left of John Kerry. [PHOTO: RICK REINHARD]

Charlie Liteky speaks at a press conference in a U.S. Senate room on thirty-seventh day of the fast, October 7. Sitting, left to right, are George Mizo, Duncan Murphy (behind George), me, Congressmen David Bonior (D-MI), Leon Panetta (D-CA), and Senator Charles Mathias (R-MD). [PHOTO: RICK REINHARD]

Weary fasting veterans after forty days. Left to right: George Mizo, me, Duncan Murphy, and Charlie Liteky. The fast ended at the conclusion of the forty-seventh day after our TV appearance on *The Phil Donahue Show*, and our monitoring doctor notifying us of George's precarious health. By this time we'd already received word that five hundred solidarity actions with our fast were taking place around the country. [PHOTO: BILL BECKER]

I speak before three hundred thousand Nicaraguans in Managua's Plaza of the Revolution, November 8, 1986, on the twenty-fifth anniversary of the founding of the FSLN. Fellow fasters are Duncan Murphy, to my left, and George Mizo, to my right. The Nicaraguan government invited the fasters to the event. Charlie Liteky remained vigiling in Washington [PHOTO: TOM KOREN]. The Sandinistas are named for Augusto César Sandino, who led the Nicaraguan peasant resistance against U.S. Marine occupiers, 1926–1933.

Left to Right: Duncan Murphy, George Mizo, and I plead for an end to war and creation of military veterans, Managua press conference, U.S. Veterans day, November 11, 1986. [PHOTO: CHRIS VAIL]

November 11, 1986. I look on as George Mizo shakes hand of Eugene Hassenfus in southern Nicaragua near the crash site where a secret U.S. Contra supply plane was shot down when hit by a surface-to-air missile fired by a nineteen-year-old Sandinista soldier on October 5, 1986. Hassenfus, a Viet Nam veteran mercenary, parachuted to safety as he was about to kick military boots and AK-47s out the plane's door when it was hit. Three crew members, two of them Viet Nam veterans, were killed. A Nicaraguan Judicial Tribunal brought Hassenfus, now their prisoner, to view the crash site, and invited us to accompany them. [PHOTO: CHRIS VAIL]

I announce the formation of the eleven-member Veterans Peace Action Team (VPAT) at a press conference in a U.S. Senate Hearing Room, February 17, 1987, as I point to map of Nicaragua's war zones where we plan to document Contra terrorism. Left to right: VPAT members Rick Schoos, John Schuchardt, me, and John Poole. [PHOTO: PAUL BRUBAKER]

VPAT members hold a banner in front of U.S. Embassy, Managua, March 1987. Left to right: Scott Rutherford, U.S. Navy; Jim Bush, U.S. Army; Peter Nimkoff, U.S. Marines; John Poole, U.S. Army; John Isherwood, British Air Force; Rick Schoos, U.S. Army; Joe Ashley, U.S. Navy and Army; me, U.S. Air Force; John Schuchardt, U.S. Marines; and Peter Eaves, U.S. Marines. Not shown: Holley Rauen and Judith Williams.

I speak at a March 20, 1987, Managua press conference announcing VPAT's plan to walk unarmed seventy-five miles through dangerous Nicaraguan war zones. Rear, left to right: Holley Rauen, John Schuchardt, and Judith Williams. The day before, we briefed Alfred Laun III at the U.S. Embassy of our plans. He proudly shared with us his role as a Phoenix operative in the U.S. assassination program in Viet Nam. He declared that the Sandinistas would be held responsible for "whatever happened to us," apparently no investigation necessary. [PHOTO: CHRIS VAIL]

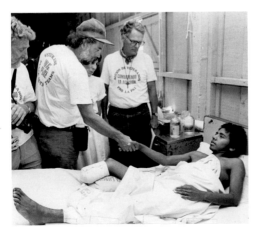

March 1987. I shake hands with a Nicaraguan soldier whose leg had been amputated after being injured in an explosion of a Contra-planted landmine. Left to right: VPAT members John Isherwood, Holley Rauen, and John Schuchardt. [PHOTO: CHRIS VAIL]

Walking on the second day from Jinotega to Wiwilí with our WAGE PEACE banner, March 24, 1987. Left to right: me, Holley Rauen, Judith Williams, and Scott Rutherford. [PHOTO: BRENTON KELLY]

Hole in the ground where an 81 mm mortar exploded minutes before our VPAT arrival in front of home where a mother and children were present (in background). Nearby Nicaraguan soldiers appear as VPAT members gather. Left to right: Peter Eaves, me, unidentified Nicaraguan, Joe Ashley, and John Schuchardt.

March 28, 1987. President Ortega listens as I report witnessing aftermath of a bloody ambush on Pantasma Mountain the day before that killed six and wounded nine.

I shake hands with President Ortega at the national coffee festival in San Ramón, March 28, 1987, as a smiling Dwight Nujoma, future president of Namibia, looks on. [PHOTO: CHRIS VAIL]

Local villages greet VPAT arriving in Wiwilí, March 29, 1987, after walking seventy-five miles in seven days. I am third from the left wearing VPAT t-shirt and a headband.
[PHOTO: CHRIS VAIL]

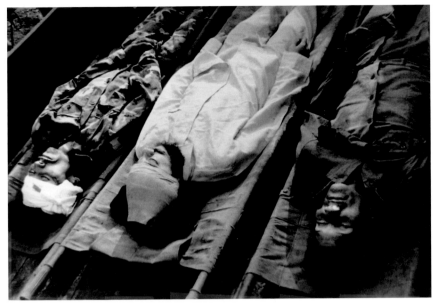

The body of Benjamin Linder, twenty-seven-year-old mechanical engineer from Portland, Oregon, lies in white between Nicaraguan Sergio Fernández (left) and Pablo Rosales, after the three were murdered by Contras, April 28, 1987, at the site of their hydroelectric project in San José de Bocay, Jinotega, Nicaragua. [PHOTO: GARY HICKS]

Mural of the festive clown, juggler, and unicyclist Ben Linder as he entertained Nicaraguan children when not working on small hydroelectric projects.

Happy faces at location of planned blocking action at Concord Naval Weapons Station, about 11 a.m., September 1, 1987. Left to right: photographer Andy Peri, Michael Kroll, unidentified, Duncan Murphy, me, Bob Lassalle, Marilyn Coffey, and David Duncombe. [PHOTO: ANDY PERI]

View of blockers at 139 feet available on September 1 to spotters standing on front of the locomotive in radio contact with the engineer. Despite the official Navy Report concluding we were observable for 650 feet, the crew did no braking whatsoever as it accelerated to over 16 mph in a 5 mph speed zone. [PHOTO TAKEN BY MY LAWYERS FROM FRONT OF SAME LOCOMOTIVE ON A SIMULATED RUN AUTHORIZED BY THE FEDERAL COURT IN PREPARATION FOR TRIAL]

Just before noon, September 1, U.S. Navy locomotive hauling two boxcars past the main gate (right) loaded with explosives near our blockade, with two spotters standing on the front platform. [PHOTO: RANDY BECKER]

About one second before I was struck. You can see the legs of the spotters on the locomotive's platform. Note my right hand pushing against the rail in an effort to lift myself up and off the tracks. [PHOTO: ANDY PERI]

Moment of impact. Note my right hand is now separated from contact with the rail, indicating my body has been struck and knocked backwards. [PHOTO: RANDY BECKER]

Black smoke surges out of the locomotive exhaust stack as the train crew accelerates to more than three times its legal speed limit after I have been struck. [PHOTO: RANDY BECKER]

My severed lower right leg lies next to tracks as my mangled legs lie on the rails in the direction of train travel, indicating my body has been turned completely around after impact. Witness David Hartsough described my body tossed around like a rag doll under the train. [PHOTO: ANDY PERI]

An anguished Holley looks helplessly at my body under the first boxcar of munitions. [PHOTO: ANDY PERI]

Holley rushes to my aid after second boxcar has passed and my crumpled body straddles the two rails. Left to right: Pierre Blais, Holley, Duncan Murphy (behind Holley with arm reaching downward), David Duncombe, Gerry Condon, and Gabriel Ortega (Holley's son). Duncan and David had been fellow blockers, narrowly escaping being run over. [PHOTO: ANDY PERI]

Holley immediately begins attending to my severely wounded body. My severed lower right leg can be seen to the left of the rail opposite my crumpled water jug. My St. Louis Cardinals baseball cap lies on the other side of the rail, lower right. The train continues down the tracks. [PHOTO: ANDY PERI]

Anguished faces. At left, Ellen Earth gasps as she moves away from the scene while a kneeling Gerry Condon (with back to camera) and Holley (visible over Gerry's right shoulder) earnestly seek to stop the flow of blood from my legs. Duncan closely cradles me as David Hartsough holds his left hand on my bleeding head. [PHOTO: JOHN SKERCE]

Closeup of my severely wounded body as friends seek to stop the bleeding around my head and legs. Steve Brooks (in green hat with hands on Duncan's back) joins Gerry, Holley, Duncan, and David. Steve, a door gunner in Viet Nam, was commander of the VFW Post 5888 in Santa Cruz. Note the yellow line running diagonally across tracks on the left demarcating the public right of way from Navy property (left of line). The Navy ambulance refused help, telling Holley my body wasn't lying on Navy property. [PHOTO: RANDY BECKER]

Gerry Condon comforts an exhausted Duncan Murphy who has my blood stains on his t-shirt and my bloodied pants at his feet (cut off by ambulance medics), as police casually stand around. To the credit of the Navy Fire Department, its crew did assist Holley with emergency first aid. [PHOTO: JOHN SKERCE]

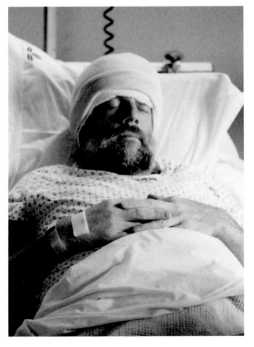

In John Muir Trauma Hospital, Walnut Creek, in early September with my wrapped head. While I was recovering in the hospital from September 1 to 29, blocking actions at CNWS escalated, as they continued to do for several years thereafter. [PHOTO: HOLLEY RAUEN]

Jesse Jackson and Joan Baez console Holley at CNWS on September 5, 1987, as thousands of demonstrators gather to protest the September 1 attempted murder. [PHOTO: T. ROCAMORA]

Holley speaks to the estimated five to nine thousand protestors gathered at CNWS on September 5, 1987. [PHOTO: RUFUS DIAMONT]

Tracks being ripped up on September 5, 1987. [PHOTO: HOLLEY RAUEN]

Increased numbers of demonstrators create a permanent encampment blocking every train for nearly two and a half years after I was run over.

A typical arrest of nonviolent train blockers at CNWS, late September 1987.
[PHOTO: CAROL KATONIK]

Actor Martin Sheen joins me on the tracks in October 1987 where he is arrested for blocking a train. Ex-CIA agent Phil Agee stands in the rear between Martin and me in front of the sign. [PHOTO: CAROL KATONIK]

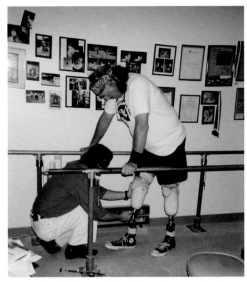

Police use unruly tactics in arrests of more than two thousand protestors during around-the-clock blocks of every munitions train for more than two years. Quaker David Hartsough, left, and UCC Minister David Wiley, right, had their arms broken.

Being fitted for prosthetic legs by premier San Francisco prosthetist, Wayne Koniuk, who has fitted me with seven sets of legs over the years. [PHOTO: BECKY LUENING]

I testify before U.S. House Armed Services Committee, November 18, 1987, Washington, D.C., investigating the Concord train assault. The committee censored all but four of my forty-seven pages of written testimony. My visibly indented skull shows a hole where a piece of my skull the size of a lemon was completely dislodged and thrust into my right frontal lobe, destroying it. My outer left ear had been sliced off but was sewn back on and restored to near its original state. Other injuries included a broken right shoulder, cracked ribs, broken right wrist, two broken elbows, damaged right kidney, extensive abrasions on arms and shoulders, and multiple cuts inside my mouth. [PHOTO: HOLLEY RAUEN]

Dancing next to wheelchair. This photograph was part of a 1989 USSR exhibition, *Positive Negatives: Portraits of Courageous Russian and American Public Figures.*
[PHOTO: JOCK MCDONALD]

January 1988, four months after nearly being killed, I sit between Dan Ellsberg, left, and actor Ed Asner during an eleven-day water-only fast on the U.S. Capitol steps protesting Congress's continued funding of the Contra terrorists in Nicaragua. [PHOTO: BILL LEDGER]

Ex-CIA officer Phil Roettinger, to my right, and singer-songwriter Kris Kristofferson join me at government peace talks with the Contras, March 21, 1988, in Sapoa, Nicaragua. Holley stands behind Kristofferson's left shoulder. Michael Kroll, who held the Nuremberg Banner behind me at Concord on September 1, 1987, stands directly behind me. Blase Bonpane of the Office of the Americas stands behind, and between Kristofferson and me. The Sapoa Accords, signed March 23 by the Contras and the Nicaraguan government, agreed to a ceasefire, amnesty, and designated safe zones for those demobilizing. [PHOTO: MARK BIRNBAUM]

I am joyfully dancing at a U.S. citizen's protest in front of the U.S. Embassy in Managua, March 1988.

I entertain Nicaragua war amputees with my stumps painted as puppets, "Moe" and "Joe," as Blase Bonpane, holding the microphone, translates the puppet show. Chavarría Rehabilitation Hospital, Managua, March 1988.

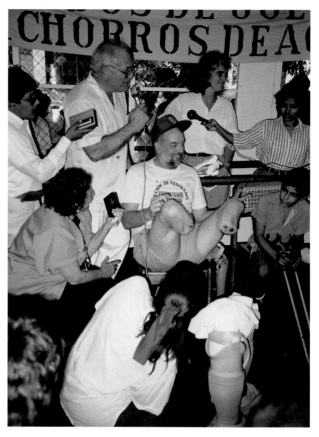

Holley and I stand with our U.S. delegation and Nicaraguan troops next to a military helicopter on banks of Rio Coco, March 1988. Honduras is visible behind the helicopter. [PHOTO: MARK BIRNBAUM]

I am in relaxed conversation between Nicaragua's foreign minister, left, and President Daniel Ortega, March 1988. [PHOTO: GARY CAMPBELL]

With Holley and Daniel Ortega. We clasp raised arms after Ortega presented me Nicaragua's highest award, the Augusto César Sandino Medal, seen pinned on my shirt. March 29, 1988. [PHOTO: INFORMATION OFFICE, PRESIDENT OF NICARAGUA]

Kris Kristofferson and I converse before boarding a Sandinista helicopter to visit campesinos in war-ravaged El Cua, October 1989. [PHOTO: MARK COPLAN]

I exit a helicopter after landing in the remote Jinotega village of El Cua, October 1989.
[PHOTO: MARK COPLAN]

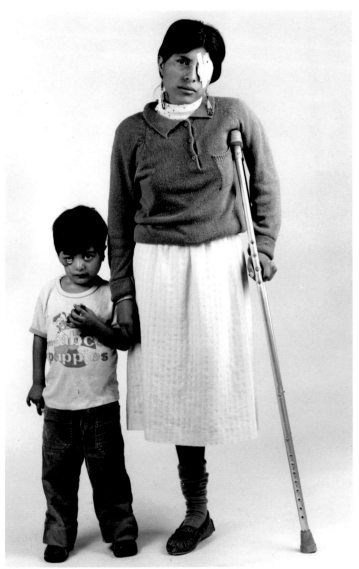

Dora and Erick, two of only four survivors from a Contra ambush of a Nicaraguan transport truck carrying twenty-two campesinos to a health clinic near Quilali not far from the Honduran border on October 29, 1988. The truck was hit by a rocket-propelled grenade and at least 120 bullets, several of which struck Dora, Erick, and her one-year-old son Marlon, whom she was holding in her arms. Dora lost one leg to multiple bullet wounds, lost her left eye to bullet shrapnel, and lost her six-month-old fetus to bullet wound-induced blood poisoning. Erick was shot through the face and tear duct, and through the right shoulder, resulting in a permanently withered arm. Marlon received bullet shrapnel in his skull and died two days later. This and dozens of other ambushes occurred despite the Contras' agreement at Sopoa in March to stop all combat operations. [PHOTO: MARVIN COLLINS]

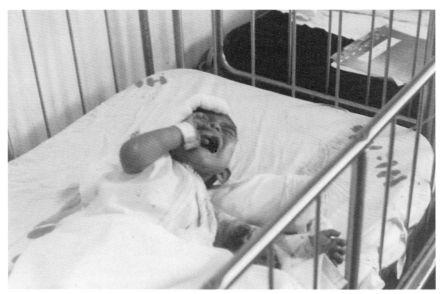

Marlon, Dora López's baby, one day before dying from
bullet shrapnel injuries to his head inflicted in October 1988
ambush. [PHOTO: HOLLEY RAUEN]

Upon return to the U.S. from my March 1988 trip to Nicaragua, I join with Jack Ryan,
recently fired from the FBI for refusing to investigate six of us as domestic terrorists,
at our first joint public appearance at Boston's historic Faneuil Hall, April 9, 1988.

In 1995 I ride a mule into a remote southern Nicaraguan rainforest to visit a new ecoforest community created by ex-Sandinista soldiers and Contras, accessible only by foot or pack animal. [PHOTO: JOANNE CALKINS]

Veteran's peace delegation to the Middle East visits ex-Nablus Palestinian Mayor Bassam Shaka at his home, September 15, 1991. Shaka's legs were blown up by an Israeli-planted car bomb explosion at his home in 1980. Kneeling: Bill Kelsey, left; one of Shaka's sons, right. Standing, left to right: Rick Droz, one of Shaka's sons, John Schuchardt, Mark Birnbaum, Ellen E. Barfield, Larry Egbert, me, and Phil Roettinger. [PHOTO: RICK DROZ]

I stand in Rafah, Gaza, on the border with Egypt, at the "Flat of Shouts," September 1991. Palestinians in the background call across the security fence to other family members permanently caught for years on the other side of Israeli-imposed no man's land. Palestinians do not have passports and are not able to travel across borders. [PHOTO: RICK DROZ]

I lean on my walking stick in the Amirya underground bomb shelter in a middle-class neighborhood of Baghdad struck by two U.S. "smart" missiles at 4:30 a.m., February 13, 1991. The missiles murdered hundreds of women and children who took shelter here while their husbands and older boys remained in their homes expecting to be bombed. The U.S. claimed that this shelter was one of Saddam Hussein's military command bunkers. [PHOTO: RICK DROZ]

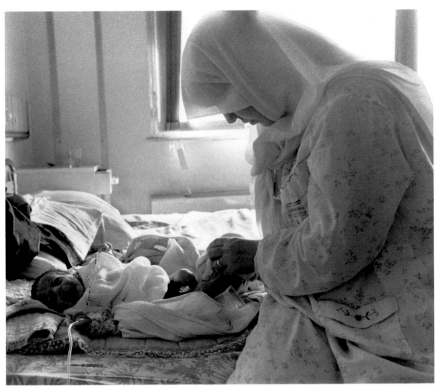

One of thousands of Iraqi children under two years of age suffering and dying as of October 1991 in epidemic proportions from malnourishment and gastroenteritis caused primarily by economic sanctions and bombed water and sewer facilities. [PHOTO: RICK DROZ]

I am attending a conference in Panama City with over a hundred other U.S. citizens, November 29–30, 1989, in efforts to deter an anticipated U.S. invasion. The U.S. invaded three weeks later, on December 20.

The destroyed, heavily populated El Chorillo neighborhood of Panama City, shortly after being bombed by the United States. Impoverished El Chorrillo bore the brunt of the estimated two to six thousand killed. U.S. forces were in country seeking to arrest one person, Manuel Noriega. [PHOTO: PANAMA HUMAN RIGHTS COMMISSION]

U.S. troops wearing the insignia of the 193rd Infantry Brigade, Airborne, control people in the streets of Panama City, December 1989. [PHOTO: PANAMA HUMAN RIGHTS COMMISSION]

Murdered Panamanian victims of the U.S. invasion in a temporary morgue, Panama City, December 1989. [PHOTO: PANAMA HUMAN RIGHTS COMMISSION]

Left to right: Daniel Ellsberg, me, and David Dellinger, with ex-CIA agent Phil Roettinger behind, carrying crosses of Salvadoran dead at a demonstration at the Pentagon protesting U.S. aid to the death squad–oriented El Salvadoran government, October 17, 1988. [PHOTO: RICK REINHARD]

Four weeks after the protest at the Pentagon, I am headed for meetings with the FMLN guerrillas in the mountains of Chalatenango, El Salvador, November 13, 1988. Veterans' delegation member Phil Roettinger (in blue baseball cap) stands on left; delegation member Dave Silk (in white shirt) stands on the other side of the mule.

Our veterans' delegation meets with the three FMLN* guerrilla commanders of the central region of El Salvador in a small town in the Department of Chalatenango, March 13–14, 1988. Front, left to right: David Lynn, Raul Valdez, and Dave Silk. Rear: Dimas Rodriguez, Douglas Santamaria, me, Phil Roettinger, and Milton Mendez.

*The FMLN is the Farabundo Martí National Liberation Front. Farabundo Martí (1893–1932) was a Salvadoran revolutionary activist killed in the government repression of the 1932 peasant revolution. A U.S. military attaché acknowledged in 1931 that masses of Salvadorans were starving as the country's forty or so controlling families owned everything, living as kings supported by U.S. investors. In 1932 restive peasants and trade unionists revolted under Martí's leadership but were readily crushed by General Martínez, the oligarchy's hero, with as many as thirty thousand murdered, including Martí. The U.S. quickly acknowledged Martínez as El Salvador's political leader. Not much changes.

Three of thousands of assassinated torture victims in El Salvador: José Luis Cornejo Calles, 27; Manuel de Jesús Santamaría, 25; and Javier Santamaría, 16. Cuscatlán, El Salvador, January 31, 1988. [PHOTO: NON-GOVERNMENTAL HUMAN RIGHTS COMMISSION]

December 2000. I am visiting one of the thousands of organic gardens in Havana created as part of Cuba's necessary response to the sudden lack of oil after the fall of the Soviet Union. Cuba was forced to directly address peak oil, and their response serves as an example for the rest of the world. [PHOTO: BECKY LUENING]

President Jean-Bertrand Aristide of Haiti meets our veterans' delegation at the Presidential Palace, Port-au-Prince, June 18, 1991, 133 days after his inauguration as the first democratically elected president of Haiti, and 105 days before the U.S.-sanctioned coup that ousted him. Left to right: Aristide, me, unidentified Haitian, my brother Dwight, Aristide's aide Jean Juste, and ex-FBI agent Jack Ryan. The Presidential Palace was destroyed in the earthquake of January 12, 2010, that killed three hundred thousand, leaving one million homeless in a nation of ten million. In 2004 Aristide was kidnapped in the middle of the night from the Presidential Palace in a second coup, flown out of Haiti on a U.S. plane, and exiled to South Africa. Note: Due to its vast resources, Haiti was once described as the "Pearl of the Antilles" (a.k.a., West Indies) at various times by France, Great Britain, Spain, and later the United States. The U.S. militarily intervened in Haiti's internal affairs at least nineteen times between 1857 and 1900, and U.S. Marines occupied the country from 1915 to 1934 and in 1919 bombed civilians in putting down a peasant rebellion.

In the Zapatista village of San José Del Río, Chiapas, Mexico, I am documenting daily movements of harassing Mexican military units in April 1996 as part of the international Civilian Peace Camps in San Cristóbal, Chiapas. [PHOTO: CATHERINE RYAN]

I visit the Kent State campus in 1995, on the twenty-fifth anniversary of the murder of four students and wounding of nine others, by the Ohio National Guard, May 4, 1970. I stand at the location where some of the students lay dying. [PHOTO: FREDD LEE]

Dave Cline and I hug in 1988, a few months after my recovery. Dave was a longtime Viet Nam veteran activist, serving as president of Veterans For Peace, 2002–2007.

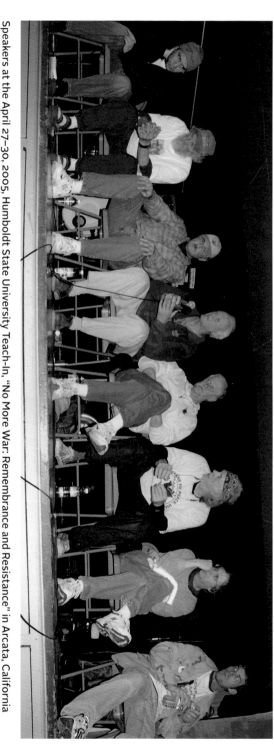

Speakers at the April 27–30, 2005, Humboldt State University Teach-In, "No More War: Remembrance and Resistance" in Arcata, California on the thirtieth anniversary of the end of the Viet Nam War, and the thirty-fifth anniversary of the lethal shootings at Kent State in Ohio and Jackson State in Mississippi, in May 1970. Left to right: Camilo Mejía, Iraq Veterans Against the War (IVAW); Charlie Liteky, recipient of Congressional Medal of Honor in Viet Nam; Joe Lewis, survivor of severe wounds at Kent State; Jack Ryan, ex-FBI agent turned peace activist; Jim Russell, survivor of wounds at Kent State; me; Mike Hastie, medic in Viet Nam, photographer activist; Tim Goodrich, IVAW. [PHOTO: DON MADDOX]

On site as the framing takes shape for my straw-bale house in Wendell, Massachusetts. I hired a crew of three to help build the house.

I begin placing straw bales in the walls of what became a solar-powered, straw-bale home, Wendell, Massachusetts, 1996.

My completed self-designed/built, active/passive solar, straw-bale home, Wendell, Massachusetts, 1998.

My 1984 Chevy S-10 pickup truck chassis converted to all electric adjacent to my arm-powered handcycle, both providing most of my local transportation.

Farallones-model composting toilet at our home in California, 2003. This model is taken from former California State Architect Sim Van der Ryn's book, *The Toilet Papers: Recycling Waste and Conserving Water* (1978, 1995). [PHOTO: BECKY LUENING]

July 2006. I am handcycling on U.S. Route 30 from Portland to Longview, Oregon, on a group cycle ride to Seattle for the national Veterans For Peace Convention.
[PHOTO: JIM RUSSELL]

Becky Luening, Pedro Kropotkin, and I stand in front of our homemade greenhouse behind raised vegetable beds that are part of our permaculture edible landscape. Pedro is named after one of my anarchist mentors, Russian Peter Kropotkin, using a Spanishized version of his first name. [PHOTO: JENNIFER BARKER]

CHAPTER 22

S. Brian Willson, "Terrorist"

Naturally, I wanted to understand why the military had ordered this particular train to keep going, when trains had stopped in the past. The short answer was provided by the Navy itself. In depositions, Navy employees claimed that they had to keep the train going to prevent it from being boarded. Of course, we had no intention of boarding the locomotive. We had plainly stated that our goal was to stop the train. We were nonviolent. But the U.S. military doesn't understand nonviolence. They can't comprehend it.

Since we protesters were willing to break the law to protest illegal U.S. policy, the government assumed we were violent. In fact, I later discovered the FBI had issued a warning that Duncan and I were "domestic terrorist suspects." The FBI had decided and undoubtedly communicated to the Navy and other government agencies that Duncan and I were terrorist suspects who, despite our history of nonviolent actions, were planning to hijack a train loaded with weapons that traveled on only three miles of restricted tracks. Faced with this terrorist fantasy, their decision was to plow through our group without regard to consequences, an action equivalent to attempted murder.

Code Name: Terrorist

I first learned that I had been labeled a terrorist from a newspaper article brought to my attention three weeks into my hospital stay. The story reported the firing of John C. "Jack" Ryan, an FBI agent based in Peoria, Illinois, who "lost his job for refusing to investigate peace activists" classified as domestic terrorists.[305]

I believe I was first targeted by these covert agencies in late September or early October 1986. The Veterans Fast for Life had begun, and an increasing number of news items about the fast appeared.[306] Hundreds of groups around the country were creating political actions in solidarity with our fast. We also were having some impact on Congress. My senator from Vermont, Patrick Leahy, stood before the U.S. Senate on September 24, 1986, and lauded the purpose and importance of our fast. On October 7, a statement signed by thirteen U.S. senators and seventy-five members of the House of Representatives supporting the goals of our fast was publicly presented to the media at a well-attended press conference that appeared on national TV.

By October 11, 1986, the backlash had already begun. Senate Intelligence Committee member Warren Rudman (R-NH) issued a press statement at which he compared we fasters to Middle Eastern "terrorists." Meanwhile, a covert investigation, perhaps by the secret Iran-Contra group, had likely already begun, although I can only speculate. The Veterans Fast for Life office was broken into on one occasion with computer records sabotaged, followed by a burglary at our temporary residence that was also arguably overseen by a government agency, as only lists containing names and addresses of fast supporters were taken.

On October 31, 1986, the FBI officially declared members of the Veterans Fast for Life "domestic terrorist suspects." That included, of course, Duncan and me. The October FBI memo from the Chicago office was sent to *all* FBI offices indicating that the Plowshares group and the Veterans Fast for Life group were both part of "an organized conspiracy to use force/violence to *coerce* the United States Government into *modifying its direction"* [emphasis added].[307]

Jack Ryan, a veteran of more than twenty-one years of documented exemplary FBI service, wrote a response on December 4, 1986, to his superiors, refusing to take part in the investigation. Ryan, who subsequently has become a close friend, concluded that the acts performed by the Plowshares group and Veterans Fast for Life were "totally non-violent," and that none of the actions under investigation "fit within the Domestic Security Guidelines." Interestingly, Ryan, whose sincerity was never questioned by the FBI, was fired for writing that memo—as it turned out, while I was recovering in the hospital. He appealed his firing all the way up to the Supreme Court, where he lost. According to federal court records, "never in the history of the FBI had an agent flatly refused to carry out an investigation" of an "unsolved federal offense." Ryan was the first, and hopefully not the last. The court ruled that "obedience is a high value" in a paramilitary organization such as the FBI.[308]

Jack has said repeatedly that the origin of the FBI investigation into the two groups that included Duncan and I as members, was suspicious for two reasons: (1) the national investigation officially was triggered by acts of local, *minor* vandalism—apparently the "terrorist act" of gumming locks at Chicago military recruiting offices; (2) the locally initiated October 31, 1986 national FBI communication *already possessed a code name*, extraordinarily unusual, suggesting a preconceived "terrorist" investigation already in the works.

COINTELPRO . . . Again

Since U.S. citizens are taught so little factual history, we often think that government policies are unique to our present generation. As it turns out, I just happened to get caught up in the paranoia and madness of the "global war on terror" that Ronald Reagan first promulgated twenty years before George W. Bush built his entire domestic and foreign policy on it.

From the moment Reagan took office in 1981, he began signing Executive Orders, National Security Decision Directives, and Intelligence Findings that essentially revived the secret, illegal, government domestic spying program, COINTELPRO, which was supposed to have been terminated ten years earlier. On December 4, 1981, it was reported that Reagan decided to "press covert action in Nicaragua and El Salvador."[309] On the same day, he signed Executive Order No. 12333 reauthorizing all the earlier criminal activities of COINTELPRO and more. The National Security Agency (NSA), the CIA, and the FBI were granted wide authority to conduct domestic surveillance and infiltration, and to *expose and destroy* efforts of individuals and groups *anywhere* perceived as terrorists, especially those opposed to Reagan's policies in El Salvador and Nicaragua.[310] Even more explicitly, on April 3, 1984, Reagan signed National Security Decision Directive 138, "Combating Terrorism," by authorizing both preemptive and retaliatory attacks on "terrorists."[311] On July 19, 1985, it was reported that the congressional budget included at least $15.2 million for covert domestic counterterrorism activities by the FBI and CIA.[312] The next day, July 20, 1985, Reagan signed National Security Decision Directive 179 by which he created a Task Force on Combating Terrorism chaired by Vice President George H.W. Bush, former head of the CIA, who, in turn, created a "Terrorist Incident Working Group" chaired by the NSC's Oliver North.[313]

On January 20, 1986, while I was in Nicaragua, Reagan ordered a National *Program* for Combating Terrorism to be covertly coordinated by North with special staff, under direction of Vice President Bush's Task Force [emphasis added].[314] This office secretly employed members of the Pentagon's covert Intelligence Support Activity (ISA) to conduct classified domestic operations in concert with FBI and Secret Service agents, analogous to Nixon's earlier criminal White House "Plumbers" unit.[315] By July the FBI was conducting a number of domestic counterintelligence/counterterrorism surveillance operations apparently approved by North's secret group.[316]

On July 5, 1987, just three weeks after we started our vigil at CNWS, the nearby *San Jose Mercury News* broke an alarming story revealing the existence of a Reagan-initiated contingency plan under authorship of the NSC's Oliver North to suspend the Constitution under several scenarios, one of which was the U.S. invasion of Nicaragua. In such case, the national government would be turned over to FEMA (Federal Emergency Management Agency), state and local governments would be turned over to military commanders, and martial law would be declared, with thousands rounded up and detained.[317]

The following week, during the Iran-Contra hearings in Congress, I was stunned when House member Jack Brooks (D-TX) asked Lt. Col. North of the NSC, "Were you not assigned, at one time, to work on plans for the continuity of government in the event of a major disaster?" Co-Chair Senator Daniel Inouye (D-HI) cut Brooks off, saying, "That question touches upon a highly sensitive and classified area, so may I request that you not touch on that, sir?" The very scary issue that the *San Jose Mercury News* had revealed a week earlier was not allowed to be discussed by the Iran-Contra Committee. I felt increasingly that we the people had no governmental oversight.

My fears were not unfounded. During the Reagan years, there were hundreds of suspicious harassment incidents and break-ins, presumably ordered by the government, at least two hundred of which involved entry into private homes or organization offices.[318] Over 1,600 groups were targeted,[319] and nearly seven thousand U.S. citizens were seriously investigated as "terrorists."[320] As the FBI expanded its investigations under the auspices of "international terrorism," efforts were directed "specifically against individuals who definitely display their contempt for the U.S. government by making speeches and propagandizing their cause."[321] The FBI claimed that much of this surveillance was conducted at the request of the CIA and the NSC,[322] agencies that would be involved in the indefinite detention of activists in the event of a U.S. invasion of Nicaragua.[323]

The FBI director at the time, William Sessions, admitted in a December 14, 1987, letter to Congressman Don Edwards (D-CA) that six people from two organizations, Silo Plowshares and Veterans Fast for Life, "were developed as suspects . . . under the domestic security/terrorism caption." Sessions explained that from the pattern of conduct,

> [I]t was reasonable to conclude a political motive, by two or more persons engaged in activities in violation of Federal law. . . . Such investigations are initiated when the facts or circumstances reasonably indicate that two or more persons are engaged in an enterprise for the purpose of furthering political or social goals, wholly or in part, through activities that involve force or violence and a violation of the criminal laws of the United States.[324]

Duncan and I, two of the four participants in the Veterans Fast for Life, were included among these suspects, but what "force or violence" Sessions believed we committed or planned to commit remains a mystery.

U.S. Government: Terrorist

All evidence about the train incident at the Concord Naval Weapons Station points to one fact: the train carrying explosive cargo was required by the base's own rules and regulations to stop for *any* obstacle or object on the tracks, whether the crew had advance notice or not. On September 1, 1987, an egregious crime was committed. The train did not stop because the engineer and two spotters were ordered *not* to stop. The crew chose to ignore our presence, violating the most basic of human and safety concerns, not to mention legal requirements.

The government defense argued that they believed Duncan, David, and I were planning to "board the train," i.e., to hijack it.[325] This was first brought to my attention during an official interrogation in the hospital. Government officials apparently imagined we might take over the train and somehow use the weapons it carried, so that national security required that the train not stop. To reiterate: the government and its agents, at several levels in its chain of command, participated in an attempted murder—just as numerous eyewitnesses had quickly concluded and as suggested by several journalists— deliberately running over us because they believed we were terrorists who planned to "hijack" the locomotive.[326]

I was flabbergasted by the investigator's question, "Did you plan to board the train?" But the question took on a much more serious meaning when, a couple of days later, I read the story in the newspaper about an FBI agent being fired for refusing to investigate the participants in the Veterans Fast for Life as "domestic terrorist suspects." Holy shit! *Me? A terrorist?* Suddenly an explanation for the drastic criminal action of the government began to take shape.

The government's rationale for accelerating the train directly at our Concord action "was a paranoia understandable only in the light of the counterterrorist files which the FBI had already accumulated on Willson [and Murphy]. . . . Crew members . . . were under orders to keep moving . . . the product of the administration's counterterrorism mind-set." This was the joint conclusion of Peter Dale Scott, Berkeley English professor at the time, a well-known political author and former Canadian diplomat, and Jonathan Marshall, a long-time progressive journalist who at the time was the *San Francisco Chronicle* economics editor.[327]

Even President Reagan's daughter, Patti Davis, was incredulous. In a letter written to me a few days after I was hit, she expressed her "dismay" at her father's

> aggressively anti-Sandinista rhetoric and to his absurd references to the Contras as "freedom fighters." . . . Nothing that I've felt during these years equals the sickness in my heart over what happened to you. . . . It symbolizes . . . everything that is wrong and unjust in this world, and in this

country. . . . I am sure you sat down with the confidence that you would walk away from that confrontation, and onto another . . . and another until your message was heard. But you will walk again; all of us who have prayed and shed tears for you will be your legs.

The crime committed at Concord Naval Weapons Station was so egregious that it triggered a congressional hearing. However, at that hearing, conducted in November 1987, only four witnesses were called. (None of the more than forty eyewitnesses were allowed to testify.) The existence of orders to not stop the train was *not* shared with Congress since certain key reports were never made public. And my forty-seven-page written testimony submitted for the record was redacted to only four pages. My representative at the time, Barbara Boxer, was furious because, among other things, she said, "The Navy not only softened its report, it won't release all of it." She explained the reason: "They don't want to give it to the public because they are afraid of a lawsuit."[328]

The only useful information to come out of the hearing was that the Navy investigator acknowledged that the authorities knew of me and my past activities prior to September 1, and they considered me a serious protester, and "the protest principal." Also, as early as June when we first started our vigil at the tracks, Concord City Police Officer Ken Delapp said he knew of my fast in Washington the year before and was nervous that groups of veterans might be coming to the tracks, bringing others with them.

Clearly, the Reagan administration did not want its covert surveillance techniques revealed, nor its readiness to kill its own citizens. Congress could have exerted more pressure, but chose not to. In fact, throughout the 1980s, Congress generally supported Reagan's war on terror.[329] My discoveries came only through the relentless efforts of independent journalists and, later, through my pursuit of justice in the courts.

Accused and Accuser

In one of the many bizarre ironies of this incident, I first went to court over the train assault as a defendant. The train crew sued me in February 1988, claiming I had caused them to suffer post-traumatic stress by being on the tracks and getting myself run over. The suit was so bizarre that a number of news magazines covered it, including the *New Yorker* (February 8, 1988), *People* (February 15), and *U.S. News and World Report* (May 23).

Tom Steel, a thirty-seven-year-old San Francisco lawyer and member of the National Lawyers Guild, represented me. Already an accomplished human rights attorney, his calm counsel guided me through what turned out to be an arduous three-year ordeal. To meet the suit of the train crew, Tom advised me to countersue. Because we could not convince the district attorney for Contra Costa County or California State or U.S. attorney generals to bring criminal charges against the train crew and their Navy superiors, we were forced into civil court. I sued the government under the Federal Tort Claims Act and, separately, sued the train crew under a federal civil rights act.

What followed was a long slog through the cesspool of the legal system—piles of paperwork, accusations filed back and forth through what seemed like hundreds of motions, and numerous pretrial depositions. With Tom Steel and my partner Holley, I endured forty cumulative hours of depositions over five separate days by John Penrose, the U.S. Attorney for San Francisco, working hand-in-hand with a number of attorneys from several private law firms representing the train crew and apparently paid for by the U.S. government. The train crew sat directly across the table from Holley and me. In Rob Morse's October 30, 1989, *San Francisco Examiner* column, he reported that seven law firms were part of an extraordinarily expensive effort by the government in "fighting Willson."

At the end of the first day of these depositions, Penrose stood up and gestured to the wall behind the spot where Holley and I had been sitting, pointing to a photo of President Reagan and Vice President Bush hanging directly above us. Penrose looked straight at Holley and me and said, "It was really tough—every time I'd look over to your side of the table, I'd see those two faces on the wall." Maybe he was trying to tell us he was a Democrat, or trying to establish some rapport. But Holley wasn't buying any of it. She immediately responded, "How do you think I felt looking across the table at the three men who tried to murder my partner?" He had nothing to say.

If I had felt contempt for the legal system before this case, I felt it more strongly after. Since I had opened a civil suit, my whole life was available for examination. The lawyers for the train crew and government used this opportunity to seek details of my political, professional, even personal, activities. They subpoenaed my two passports, seeking to know for each country, for every trip, who met me at the airport, who drove me, where was I going, what was my purpose, who hosted me, etc. They wanted names. I refused to provide names if I thought doing so would bring harm to people. And the truth is, often I couldn't remember the names of the people involved in hosting my trips.

My deposers were particularly focused on how I got to spend time with Eugene Hasenfus, the Contra arms kicker who parachuted to safety when his plane was shot down over Nicaragua. They kept asking, who was paying me, who was I working for? They assumed I was a spy for the Sandinistas because they couldn't imagine that someone would do what I was doing—spending weeks, months, years organizing opposition to my government's covert and overt war against Nicaragua—unless I was paid to do so. They couldn't conceive of someone working for an ideal without pay. According to the offhand discussions I overheard during breaks in the deposition proceedings, I was certain that the government wanted to prove I was a foreign agent for Nicaragua, in which case I could have been charged with violation of the Foreign Agents Registration Act which requires registration with the Department of Justice. If I had been convicted of violating the act, I could have been sent to prison for several years.

The case ended as oddly as it had begun. A trial date had been established and in preparation we conducted a mock trial that lasted several days. We hoped to develop the best strategy to prove that the government was negligent, since the government is liable for the negligent acts of its employees. The law makes it clear, however, that the government cannot be sued for the *criminal* behavior of its employees.

After deliberating for a few hours, the mock jury ruled there was no negligence because the facts indicated beyond a reasonable doubt (the criminal standard) that on September 1, 1987, the U.S. government had intended for the train crew to run me over. The train crew had only done their duty as ordered: not stopping, then accelerating the train when people were clearly visible on the tracks. Thus, the jury ruled there was criminal intent, but not negligence.

In short, we had such a strong case that if we went to court we would lose. All the government had to do, if we proved a crime had been committed, was to declare that the government can't be liable for criminal behavior of its employees. This is the law.

When it became clear that it would be nearly impossible to prove *mere negligence* rather than intention (criminality), we began to consider a settlement strategy. Tom and his firm had already spent hundreds of thousands of dollars on the case. He needed to be able to pay himself and the others who had helped him with the case. Settling with the government seemed to be the best way to accomplish that.

However, the idea of settling the lawsuit made me feel physically sick. I wanted a trial for all to see what really had happened. My consolation was that the settlement allowed Tom and his team to continue their work. Settling the case also proved I was right. The fact that the government could not prevail in showing I was negligent or criminal in my behavior has proven to many skeptics that it was, in fact, the government that was the criminal in this case.

Absent Without Leave

I finally left John Muir Hospital on September 29, 1987, exactly four weeks after arriving there in an ambulance. I had endured the amputation of both my legs and a major brain surgery. The latter entailed thoroughly cleaning my brain of grease and dirt, then extracting the piece of my skull that had lodged in my frontal lobe.

Upon leaving the hospital, I went directly to the tracks, escorted by nearly three dozen war veterans along with Holley and Gabriel. With difficulty, I disembarked from the automobile and slowly navigated with my walker toward the hundreds of protesters there to greet me, many of whom had been encamped at the site since September 1. It was an overwhelming moment. Steve Brooks, commander at the time of the renegade Santa Cruz VFW "Wage Peace" Post 5888, of which I was a member, conducted a ceremony in honor of the resistance actions.

No trains ran between noon on September 1 and September 12. From that point until sometime in January 1990, a period of nearly 875 *consecutive* days and nights, *every* train—and nearly every truck—that attempted to transport munitions to awaiting ships at nearby Sacramento River's loading dock, was blocked. Nuremberg Actions exploded with members. The coordinating committee hired staff and a nearby house served as headquarters. Dozens of volunteers took turns populating a permanent camp at the crime scene. Numerous solidarity events were organized to accompany the regular blocking actions. Various notables showed up, even to be arrested, such as actors Ed Asner and Martin Sheen. Former CIA operatives Phil Roettinger and Phil Agee came to speak. Former CIA administrative officer Jim Wilcott became part of the permanent vigil until his death due to cancer in 1994. Political clown Wavy Gravy performed at the site. Jefferson Airplane founder Paul Kantner and Joan Baez's sister, Mimi Fariña, appeared on several occasions. U.S. Navy officials came to realize it had been a terrible mistake to run that train.

From 1990 to April 2002, numbers dropped off, but people continued to be present twenty-four hours a day, seven days a week, to make selective blocks. The durability of Nuremberg Actions' commitment was mindboggling. For nearly 5,700 *consecutive* days, from September 1, 1987 to early April 2002, protesting citizens were present at the crime scene to remind CNWS authorities and base employees of the illegality of their continuing movement of weapons. Angry passing motorists sometimes threw dead animals at protesters, and on several occasions shots were fired into Greg Getty's nearby camper at night, on one occasion missing his sleeping body by only a few feet. Getty turned out to be the most insistent of all the protesters, being present every day through the years until April 2002, and from that point present every week until 2009. He was arrested and jailed numerous times.

All told, more than two thousand arrests were made, with some people serving as much as six months in jail. One of those was Reverend David Duncombe, who on September 1, 1987, jumped off the tracks just in time. Duncombe was arrested dozens of times and also served jail time. In the first few months after the assault in which the government took my legs, gruff arresting police broke the arms of at least two nonviolent protesters, Quaker David Hartsough, and Reverend David Wiley, who nonetheless continued their blocking with arms in casts.

After leaving the hospital, I remained in San Francisco while I learned how to walk on prostheses and adjusted to my new body. People marveled at the speed of my recovery and my ability to walk once again on artificial legs. My secret was that I was blessed with the devoted services of two very special health care practitioners. Wayne Koniuk, one of the finest prosthetists in the country, volunteered countless hours, carefully fitting my new legs and regularly fine-tuning the fit over and again, to ensure comfortable walking. We have remained a team all these years. Physical therapist Tom Koren volunteered dozens of hours at my home teaching me to walk on my stilt-like legs. When I returned to the hospital in late February 1988 for a second round of brain surgery, I surprised the staff by walking into the reception room. During this operation, the surgeon inspected the healing of the right brain lobe before installing a protective plate into my skull.

By March, the doctors were done. Physically, I was physically healed. My spirit, however, had a huge hole in it. Brad Kessler, in an October 1987 article for the *Nation*, wrote that "for those who saw the terror on the tracks . . . it was like a metaphor of what happens to those who dissent from administration policies: they get run over." I had literally been run over by my own government.[330]

While confined to my bed recuperating from injuries, I had a lot of time to think. Throughout my life, even as I had dissented from the war in Viet Nam, questioned the lock-up-and-throw-away-the-key mentality of our prison system, and protested U.S. funding of the Contra War, I never imagined that my own government would try to kill me. Call me a terrorist? Yes. Imprison me? Yes. But kill me? No.

After all, I was—and am—a W.A.S.P. People like me are usually protected from this kind of repression, unlike other unfortunate members of our society. Now, I felt the lash of authority on a cellular level. The American Way Of Life is inherently violent. Our prosperity is based on taking resources from others in order to feed our insatiable appetites. Our affluence is built on three genocides or their equivalent:

- the theft of this land by force, resulting in the murder of millions of Indigenous peoples;

- the theft of people's labor, resulting in the enslavement and death of millions of African Americans;
- the theft of the world's resources, leaving millions murdered and billions impoverished throughout the "Third World."

Historically, our country has enjoyed near total impunity in taking whatever it wants, while conveniently denying the grievous harm done to others. I had the audacity to question the pursuit of prosperity. But our empire cannot tolerate too many probing questions.

Yet, questions were all I had left. What do you do when you realize that the way of life in which you have been raised is not just a lie but is actively destroying the lives and livelihoods of millions of others, and even the future habitability of the planet itself? What do you do when you realize that your way of life can only be sustained through violence? As someone who had long opposed the institutionalized violence of my country, and finally become a victim of that violence, I felt I had no legitimate choice other than to cast off the American Way Of Life and instead study and practice nonviolence as a way of pursuing revolutionary change.[331]

As I recuperated in my hospital bed, I understood that what happened to me on September 1, 1987, was not an aberration, but a tragic continuation of a national pattern. Since the 1600s, our European ancestors used terror against those who refused to assent to our aggressive advances, and subsequently against those who dissented from official government policies. The train assault was the ruthless application of Reagan's "go anywhere, do anything" policy. It was a warning shot fired at dissent and free speech everywhere, with the possible added bonus of permanently silencing a couple of particularly irritating peace activists.[332]

I have become convinced that the American Way Of Life cannot become less violent, because violence is at the very core of its "prosperity." Violence enables U.S. citizens to gain a much larger share of the world's resources than anyone else. It is our belief in our "exceptionalism" that rationalizes it.

Most citizens of the United States are usually well insulated from any knowledge of the brutal tactics our government uses to protect the American Way Of Life. What happened to me, however, is a normal experience for millions of people around the world who have been victims of U.S. policy, especially when they organize against their oppressors.

In an instant, I had literally become one with all those others who had been maimed and murdered in the struggle for justice. I was no longer sharing only an intellectual and emotional affinity with the downtrodden. I had become one of the legless, one of the victims, of the American Way Of

Life. I had merged with Mai Ly, with Hue, with the mothers and children in caskets on their way to the cemetery in Estelí Nicaragua. I was one with the millions of campesinos around the world killed, maimed, terrorized, and impoverished by the policies of my country.

Now, I understood that the American Way Of Life cannot be fixed. From now on, I would declare myself Absent With Out Leave from that way of life. My quest would be for an alternate way of life that I could promote. I thought about the villagers in Viet Nam and the campesinos in Nicaragua, and it seemed to me that these peoples lived a simpler life in tune with the earth that was not inherently violent, destructive, or imperial.

Our national imperial project is necessary to feed our rapacious appetite. What if we could live without all those consumer goods? What would happen if we gave up our oil-based, market-driven economy? What would a simple, sustainable life, based only on what we had at hand, look like?

The train changed me forever. In effect, my legs have become Third World Legs. They are the indisputable evidence of the burden and gift of being engaged in the struggle for justice.

BRIAN'S PATH TO BEING LABELED A "TERRORIST" BY THE U.S. GOVERNENT (IT'S EASIER THAN IT LOOKS.)

CONTEXT: President Reagan issued a number of secret directives essentially reviving COINTELPRO, authorizing the CIA, FBI, and other intelligence agencies to conduct domestic surveillance of "terrorists," including preemptive raids, the latter described as "a license to kill." On January 20, 1986, when I was in Nicaragua, the National Security Council (NSC) initiated an effort to coordinate the combating of terrorism. Six months later, on July 18, the FBI initiated domestic counter-terrorism operations as part of this plan. Hundreds of break-ins occurred, over 1,600 groups were targeted, and nearly seven thousand U.S. citizens were seriously investigated as "terrorists." Those publicly condemning U.S. foreign policy were investigated by the FBI at the request of the CIA and NSC under auspices of battling "international terrorism."

1986

January-February: I travel to Nicaragua wanting to help prevent another Viet Nam. I broadcast translated radio messages directed to Reagan's Contras and their advisors.
September 1: Veterans Charlie Liteky, George Mizo, Duncan Murphy and I begin water-only, open-ended Veterans Fast for Life (VFFL) at the U.S. Capitol protesting Reagan's outlaw policies in Nicaragua and El Salvador.

October 5: On the thirty-fifth day of the fast, a U.S. mercenary plane dropping arms to the Nicaraguan Contras is shot down. Eugene Hasenfus, a Viet Nam veteran, parachutes to safety and confesses after capture.

October 11: On the forty-first day of the fast, U.S. Senator Rudman (R-NH) compares us fasters to "Mideast Terrorists," as reported in the *Boston Globe*.

In **October,** our VFFL office is broken into at night and its database of supporters taken. The home where we sleep is broken into during the day with information of our supporters taken. These burglaries are part of a pattern in which dozens of offices opposing Reagan's Central American policies are broken into with records stolen but valuables left intact.

October 17: We four veterans end our fast after forty-seven days. The *New York Times* reports our statement: "We have 500 documented solidarity activities." The *Times* describes the fasters' new strategy: "They hope to recruit hundreds of other veterans who will be willing to go with them to Central America, where they will try to intervene with Nicaraguan rebel offensives."

October 25: I speak at a protest at the GE plant in Burlington, Vermont, where the rapidfire Gatling gun is manufactured. The media reports my plans to send observer teams to war zones in Nicaragua.

October 30: Plowshares action gums locks at Chicago military recruiting offices in solidarity with our veterans' call for civil disobedience protesting Reagan's policies; two VFFL pamphlets are left at scene.

October 31: FBI sends national directive: "SUBJECT: Domestic Security/Terrorism Sabotage," ordering investigations of the Plowshares group and our Veterans Fast for Life, described as "an organized conspiracy to use force/violence to coerce the U.S. Government into modifying its direction."

November 5: VFFL fasters George, Duncan, and I travel to Nicaragua.

November 8: We fasters share podium with President Daniel Ortega at the FSLN's twenty-fifth anniversary before three hundred thousand people in the Managua Revolutionary Plaza. The *New York Times* reports that I am one of the main speakers; the *Philadelphia Enquirer* quotes me: "We smell, taste and feel another Vietnam."

November 8: We fasters are guests of President Ortega and First Lady Rosario Murillo at a performance of the Russian Bolshoi Ballet. Our presence is reportedly condemned by U.S. Secretary of State Shultz.

November 9: George, Duncan, and I accompany Nicaragua judicial team and prisoner Eugene Hasenfus to CIA plane's rural crash site.

November 11 (U.S. Veterans Day): We vets hold Managua press conference condemning U.S. policy, after which we conduct a three-hour prison visit with Hasenfus in which he describes ten covert aerial missions.

December 13: Duncan, Charlie, and I join with others to protest training of Contras at a Florida military base.

1987

February 19: I help organize an eleven-member Veterans Peace Action Team (VPAT) to travel to Nicaragua's war zones to learn firsthand from witnesses and survivors of Contra terrorism.

March 23–29: Our VPAT team walks seventy-five miles through war zones; Contras issue radio threats against us.

April 7: Just before returning to the U.S., I meet Ben Linder at a Matagalpa ice cream shop. Linder, an engineer from Portland, Oregon, is building small hydroelectric projects in war zones.

April 28: Linder and two Nicaraguan coworkers are murdered by Contras.

May 2: Faster Charlie Liteky and I travel to Nicaragua to organize citizens' walk to Linder's murder site.

June 10: I help launch Nuremberg Actions (NA) to protest munitions trains at Concord (California) Naval Weapons Station carrying weapons destined for El Salvador and Nicaragua. NA intends to uphold the Nuremberg Obligation by obstructing prohibited aggressive attacks by the U.S.

September 1: One year after beginning our 1986 fast, two other veterans and I begin a well-publicized forty-day water-only fast at a location on the tracks at Concord where previous blockades had always been handled routinely by removal and arrests. On this day the train accelerates to more than three times its 5 mph speed limit and runs over me, despite two "spotters" standing on the locomotive's front platform in radio contact with the engineer as per routine. Navy officials later admit planning a "confrontation" and ordering the train crew "not to stop outside the base area" to "prevent anyone from boarding the locomotive," supposedly fearing a hijack despite protesters' nonviolent demeanor and presence of a security force of 350 armed Marines. Navy ambulance medics refuse to offer assistance, saying my body is lying just off Navy property.

September 17: The Peoria, Illinois, *Journal Star* reports experienced FBI agent John Ryan was fired for refusing orders to investigate as "domestic terrorists" the nonviolent Plowshares group and the VFFL fasters for protesting U.S. policies that Ryan describes as "violent, illegal, and immoral." I read the article while in the hospital where I am under twenty-four-hour armed guard due to numerous death threats.

November 18: A congressional hearing about the train assault censors forty-three of my forty-seven-page testimony. The Navy testifies that it knew of me prior to September 1, identifying me as a serious protester who had notified the base commander of train blockade beginning September 1. The Navy concluded the train was speeding 12–16 mph; blockers were visible to train crew for 650 feet; and crew never braked for the blockers.

December 14: FBI Admits Terrorist Investigation: FBI director William Sessions admits that six people from two organizations—Silo Plowshares and Veterans Fast for Life—were considered suspects under the domestic security/terrorism caption. From the pattern of conduct, he says, "it was reasonable to conclude a political motive, by two or more persons engaged in activities in violation of Federal law . . . Such investigations are initiated when the facts or circumstances reasonably indicate that two or more persons are engaged in an enterprise for the purpose of furthering political or social goals, wholly or in part, through activities that involve force or violence and a violation of the criminal laws of the United States."

1988

August 19: Newspapers report that federal investigators identify me as a suspect in illegal smuggling of Vulcan Gatling gun and antiaircraft parts into Guatemala under cover of the Veterans Peace Convoy. The Convoy was transporting humanitarian aid to Nicaraguan campesinos on trucks and buses in publicized violation of Reagan's embargo. The investigation was a poorly disguised attempt to stop groups from supporting the Sandinista revolution. Though I was not accompanying the Convoy, I publicly supported it while it was in a standoff for two weeks with U.S. Customs at the Mexican border before the vehicles were released. Fortunately, nothing came of it.

LATVIJAS
MIERA AIZSTĀVĒŠANAS
KOMITEJA

ЛАТВИЙСКИЙ
КОМИТЕТ
ЗАЩИТЫ МИРА

RĪGĀ, GORKIJA IELĀ 11-a   TEL. 229859   РИГА, УЛ. ГОРЬКОГО, 11-a   ТЕЛ. 229859

98 - IO/II 1987

S.Brian Willson
249 Bahia Place
San Rafael
California 94901 USA

Dear Mr. Willson!

In the end of October Peace wave, coming over Latvia, activated thousands of peace movement activists. Many of them - in factories, in schools and elsewhere, expressed deep solidarity with you, dear Mr. Willson.

Your heroism, truly patriotism and conviction in the struggle for peace now is known practically to every body here in Latvia.

Here we send you signature lists collected in different parts of Latvia.

We wish you all the best!

Sincerely yours,

Biruta Shneidere

Vicepresident of Latvian Peace
Committee
Gorky Str. II a
Riga, 226010
U.S.S.R.

One of thousands of letters I received from the Soviet Union, this one informing me that my "conviction in the struggle for peace now is known practically to every body here in Latvia."

Sept. 6, 1987

Dear Brian,

For the past few years I have listened, with growing dismay, to my father's aggresively anti-Sandinista rhetoric and to his absurd references to the Contras as "freedom fighters". But nothing that I've felt during these years equals the sickness in my heart over what has happened to you. It symbolizes to me everything that is wrong and unjust in this world, and in this country.

I can only hope that this tragedy will not take from you the faith and committment that led you to those tracks in the first place. I am sure you sat down with the confidence that you would walk away from that confrontation, and onto another . . . and another until your message was heard. But you will walk again; all of us who have prayed and shed tears for you will be your legs.

Thank you for your courage,

Patti Davis

Patti Davis

President Reagan's daughter sends me a powerful message: "You will walk again . . . All of us who have prayed and shed tears for you will be your legs."

PART VI

Third World Legs

CHAPTER 23

Becoming a Hero

On Sunday, March 20, 1988, twenty-four days after my final surgery, my partner Holley and I returned to Nicaragua. This time we were accompanied by ten people, including singer-songwriter Kris Kristofferson and Blase Bonpane of the Los Angeles–based activist group, Office of the Americas.

It was a tense time to be traveling to Nicaragua as President Reagan had just declared that the Sandinistas had invaded Honduras, suggesting a major U.S. military response was considered.[333] In fact, on March 16 Reagan launched "Operation Golden Pheasant," sending more than three thousand U.S. paratroopers to Honduras. Meanwhile, Honduran pilots flying U.S. warplanes began bombing portions of northern Nicaragua.

However, there were also indications that the tide might be turning. Congress was finally beginning to understand that Oliver North, with Reagan's tacit blessing, had set up a secret government agency to aid the Contras. The same day Reagan launched his Honduran operations, a grand jury brought a twenty-three-count indictment against four key Reagan aides, including Oliver North, involved in the illegal Contra operation, We hoped our trip to Nicaragua honoring its sovereign government, would encourage the Sandinistas to continue their social reforms until the political climate changed in the United States.

Me, a Hero?

President Daniel Ortega greeted our delegation with a huge smile as we stepped off the plane in Managua. He gave me a big hug, and then accompanied me arm in arm from the tarmac into the terminal building. Hundreds of Sandinista children handed me flowers.

I was escorted to Daniel's Jeep and climbed into the passenger seat—Holley rode in the back with Foreign Minister Miguel D'Escoto and Kris Kristofferson. As Daniel drove away from the airport we soon encountered mobs of people lining the streets. Daniel drove slowly, our windows fully open, as people reached in and touched my arm, shouting, "Brian, Brian!" I realized that, through the act of literally putting my body between them and the locomotive of U.S. imperialism, I had become a hero in the eyes of the Nicaraguan people.

Kris, who as a successful singer-songwriter knew how it felt to be famous, tapped me on the shoulder from behind and asked, "How are you dealing with this?"

I really couldn't say at that moment: I was too overwhelmed. Looking back, I tend to see my journey in a larger context. I don't experience myself as heroic because I know I am not alone in knowing how delusional our idea of "American exceptionalism" really is. Many others came before me, protesting against the American Way Of Life, and I expect and trust others will come after me. That's part of the reason I wrote this book—to encourage you, the reader, to embark on your own journey of liberation.

Though the train sought to terminate my journey, it could not extinguish my spirit. That is true for each of us. No matter what happens, when we are true to what is deepest within us, our spirit seeks to reclaim our humanity from the patterns of conditioned obedience to the antihuman economic and political systems in which we live.

In my opinion, anyone who participates in constructive alternatives to our current system, or who dares to disobey the illegal and immoral orders that perpetuate systemic violence, is a hero-in-progress.

A Hopeful Trip

During that first evening in Managua, our entourage stopped to address the crowd from makeshift stages. My impromptu solidarity messages (translated by Alejandro Bendaña, secretary general to Nicaragua's foreign minister) drew cheers from the crowd.

The next day we drove in a convoy to Sapoa, eighty miles south of Managua on the border with Costa Rica to observe the first "peace" talks between the Contras and Sandinistas. Reagan's Contras were represented by Adolfo Calero, among others, and the Sandinista team was headed up by the President's brother, Sandinista Defense Minister Humberto Ortega. The road from Managua to Sapoa was lined with cheering campesinos who were hopeful that the U.S.-financed and directed terrorism would finally stop. The fact that the Nicaraguan government had agreed to these direct talks had baffled the Reagan administration. They didn't understand how desperate the campesinos were for peace.

From Sapoa, we toured more of the country, spending ten days in all. We visited tired but happy Sandinista combat troops on the banks of the Rio Coco at the border with Honduras. They had just successfully driven thousands of Contra terrorists back into their sanctuary camps in Honduras, causing more than a thousand casualties. We visited hundreds of injured in several hospitals, met with U.N. officials, and conducted a number of meetings with various Sandinista and opposition groups. During this time the "Ernesto Che Guevara Organization of Disabled Revolutionaries" (ORD), injured combatants of the war, recognized me with a special award. The next day, I was notified of another special recognition from the war wounded of the Farabundo Martí Front for National Liberation (FMLN) in neighboring El Salvador.

On March 29, in a nationally televised ceremony held at the national convention center, President Ortega, on behalf of the Nicaraguan people and the Sandinista government, awarded me the country's highest honor—the Order of Augusto César Sandino in the Maximum Grade, "Batalla de San Jacinto." The Battle of San Jacinto took place on September 14, 1856, when an early version of a campesino army defeated the first U.S. armed invasion of their country led by U.S. filibuster William Walker. The Medal of Sandino had only been awarded to a handful of people, including Nelson Mandela and Fidel Castro.

It was exhilarating to be visiting that country in the midst of a people's revolution. While people were exhausted by the war, they were also enthusiastically optimistic about the possibilities that lay ahead. The memory of Somoza was still fresh. "Under Somoza," one person told me, "we were like slaves. But under the revolution, we are free." These words really capture the spirit of the Sandinistas at that time.

In the United States, a number of people shared with me their concern that the Sandinistas were Communists. I got sick of hearing that line as a justification for terrorizing the population. There was a tiny Communist Party in Nicaragua with virtually no power. But even if there had been a large Communist Party, why the concern? In Nicaragua, when people were asked if they were Communists, they just laughed—it was an absurd question.

The Sandinistas were revolutionaries. They had spent years fighting a powerful U.S.-supported and financed repressive regime, and had triumphed. Their form of government was similar to that of European Social Democrats—a mix of socialism, private enterprise, and state-run cooperatives.

I had my own concerns about the Sandinista government, but they were far different from those of the Reagan administration. I had become friends with President Daniel Ortega, Sandinista Foreign Minister Miguel D'Escoto, and other government officials, and several times attended gatherings with the nine-member Sandinista *Comandantes*. I questioned the continued quasi-cult aura surrounding the Sandinista leadership, just as I was critical of the U.S. government's top-down structure.

However, I thought the changes they were making were exciting, and I understood that the experiment of creating a just society was still unfolding.

I believed the revolution would succeed if given a chance. And, whatever my own feelings about Nicaragua's style of governance, it really was none of my business. What the United States was doing in Nicaragua *was* my business.

Like the vast majority of people living in what we call the "Third World" (a term connoting inferiority that has both racist and classist overtones), Nicaraguans lead simple lifestyles. It is diabolical that a large, powerful country such as the United States expends such toxic energy to interfere with the Nicaraguan people and their culture. The people want basic dignity in their lives, with decent health care, a little land to grow their food, and basic education. Those of us who live in the largely White, middle-class "First World" take for granted a life free of severe hardship, where health care, food, and education are readily available.

Of course, on closer examination, we discover the myth of this image of ourselves, since vast swaths of U.S. Americans have not benefited from a system that egregiously violates human rights while failing to meet basic human needs, despite rhetoric to the contrary. And now the short-lived, post–World War II middle class itself is deteriorating. And what can I say about an education system that doesn't value critical thinking? In fact it teaches obedience.

My excitement about the Sandinista revolution, and simultaneous depression about my own country's continued criminal behavior, prompted me to consider moving to Nicaragua despite the fact that my Spanish was very poor. The Sandinistas even generously offered me a hotel building in Managua as a place to host visitors and have offices. Of course I appreciated the offer, but graciously turned it down. However, I did continue to explore the idea of acquiring a farm in the Estelí or Jinotega area where I could share with others my interest in sustainable, small-scale organic agriculture.

At Sapoa, Humberto Ortega shook my hand and said, "You bring us good fortune." I only wish that were true. It was difficult for me to witness the Contra spokespersons smiling arrogantly, knowing that President Reagan was their boss, and just pretending to talk peace while serious-faced Sandinistas were doing everything they could to end the terror war. After all, secret documents disclosed Reagan's intentions to "block" any treaty[334] and that it was literally scared of a "peace breakout."[335] And Reagan's successor, President George H.W. Bush, held such contempt for President Ortega, he referred to him as "Danny," and called him "an unwanted animal at a garden party."[336]

The accords agreed upon were reasonable, but given the recent history of peace talks in Nicaragua, I did not expect the Contras to demobilize as they had promised, as long as the U.S. continued to give them arms, daily intelligence on Nicaraguan troop locations, stipends, food, and more. Reagan was obsessed with overthrowing the Sandinista government.

As William Appleman Williams wrote in his book *The Tragedy of American Diplomacy*, the United States has long operated on the principle of advancing our prosperity for a few through endless expansion at any cost. When the U.S. hits an impediment, it must be assimilated or eliminated. The Sandinistas were striving for local democratic socialism and popular justice, a virus that had to be stopped before infecting other poor. Thus, for the U.S., a serious impediment to unfettered prosperity.

CHAPTER 24

Fighting Empire in El Salvador

N icaragua was not the only Central American country with which Reagan was obsessed. He felt just as paranoid about El Salvador.

The two countries were mirror images of each other. Nicaragua had a revolutionary government, which the United States wanted to overthrow, so it created a counterrevolutionary force, the Contras. El Salvador was run by U.S. puppets, one of whom was moderate President José Duarte, whose government knowingly supported the oligarchy of wealthy coffee-landowning families. This system was righteously challenged by a revolutionary movement of the people. In one country, we supported a puppet government against a people's revolution; in the other, we supported a puppet revolution against a people's government.

In both cases, the U.S. goal was to maintain these countries as modern versions of banana republics. To ensure the profits of U.S. corporations and thus help maintain U.S. prosperity, the United States needed to ensure access to the natural resources of these countries—sugar, coffee, bananas, gold, corn, livestock, textiles, forests—at a fraction of the cost it would take the U.S. to produce. Viruses spreading poor people's power had to be eradicated.

For our country to extract resources from another country requires a pliant and nondemocratic government—thus the U.S. desire to "cure" any people's movement toward democracy and universal fairness, so that it will not spread like a virus and "infect" other impoverished countries whose resources we covet. If these countries do not play along, we do not think twice about overthrowing them. That's how U.S. empire works. Our rhetoric is about freedom, but our actions are about repression and exploitation.

I first became aware of the situation in El Salvador after hearing the shocking news of Salvadoran Archbishop Oscar Romero's assassination on March 24, 1980, only a day after he had addressed members of the Salvadoran military and security forces with the following words: "In the name of God and in the name of this suffering people whose cries rise to heaven each day more loudly, I beg you, I beseech you, I order you in the name of God: *Stop the repression*" [emphasis added].[337] While his death was attributed to right-wing paramilitary squads, I sensed the hand of the United States. I had already learned that as early as 1961, fearing another Cuban-style people's revolution, the U.S. had dispatched military personnel to El Salvador, including Green Berets, to squelch a reformist coup. Though this was one of the earliest uses of secret warriors such as Green Berets, intervention of this kind became habitual, repressing restive poor populations virtually everywhere, including creation of death squads.[338]

Less than a week after Romero's murder, Salvadoran security forces fired on a crowd of mourners at Romero's funeral, killing thirty-nine and wounding two hundred. Two days later, on April 1, the U.S. sent $5.7 million in riot control equipment to El Salvador.[339] It was subsequently revealed that former Army Major Roberto d'Aubuisson, the prominent strong-arm leader of the country's right-wing oligarchy, had presided over a meeting of active-duty Salvadoran military personnel in a private "safe" home on March 22, where attendees drew straws for the "privilege" of murdering Romero.[340] This was confirmed in detail by the 1993 El Salvador Truth Commission.

D'Aubuisson had strong links to the United States. An early student at the U.S. Army's School of the Americas (SOA), he had attended the U.S. Public Safety Program at the International Police Academy in Washington, D.C., in the 1970s, where he had clearly made friends in high places.[341] The relationship between President Reagan and d'Aubuisson was such that former U.S. ambassador to El Salvador Robert White claimed that Reagan "chose to conceal the identity of Archbishop Romero's murderer" while entertaining d'Aubuisson as "an honored guest at our Embassy."[342] The Reagan administration also knowingly allowed d'Aubuisson to solicit funds from wealthy Salvadorans living in Miami: White testified before a congressional committee that six wealthy Salvadoran landowners living in Miami had held regular meetings to hatch plots to "organize, fund, and direct death squads through their agent, Major Roberto D'Aubuisson."[343]

My first public appearance after the train assault was on October 30, 1987, in Marin County, California, when I shared the podium with White, who explained the diabolical nexus between Salvadoran death squads and the highest levels of the U.S. government.

In both Nicaragua and in El Salvador, my government was using the "Communist threat" to wage a war against impoverished, restive campesinos in order to guarantee our access to their resources, and ensure defeat of threatening people's movements—Viet Nam all over again.

In Latin American societies, often the ordinary people ("serfs") working for the landowners ("lords") didn't have enough food to survive. That's why people revolted. During a 1988 trip to El Salvador one young rebel summarized his people's fight against the government and the feudal-like system it was preserving, quite precisely: "If you struggle, you may die, but with dignity," he told me. "If you don't struggle, you die of starvation. You have no alternative."

When the U.S. sends money and arms to fight *against* people's movements, we are supporting the impoverishment of others in order to maintain our own prosperity. In effect, our lifestyles are *subsidized* by the brutal exploitation of others, and destruction of the ecosystem itself. I wanted to experience the perspective of the people we were harming. I wanted to hear their stories. The lawyer in me wanted more evidence to grasp the issues.

To El Salvador

In 1986, when Duncan and I were in Nicaragua after the fast, we decided to go to a labor conference in El Salvador. We were aware the U.S. was playing an expansive role in protecting the repressive Salvadoran government while using Salvadoran military infrastructure for the Contra War.

It was only a short flight, and since we were traveling without visas we flew in late at night to increase our chances of getting through the airport's customs and immigration checkpoint. Our "intelligence" from Salvadorans in Managua

"U.S.-FINANCED TERROR"

What happened after Romero's March 1980 assassination is now well known. The United States financed a six-billion-dollar reign of terror for twelve years with rampant death squads and widespread torture using various Salvadoran security forces and paramilitaries taking their instructions from the CIA and U.S. military.[344] More funds were spent than on the CIA's murderous adventure in Afghanistan. Every U.S. diplomat, military officer, and intelligence operative working with El Salvador's political and military leaders knew most of those involved in organizing and carrying out death squad terror—precise information on murders, kidnappings, and death squad activities.[345] The resulting carnage—seventy-five thousand total murdered—ultimately couldn't be kept from the media. Even so, it is not well known that the U.S. had financed Special Forces activities and death squads since the early 1960s.

The first known large massacre of civilians carried out by U.S.-funded Salvadoran military forces took place on May 14–15, 1980, near the Chalatenango village of La Arda along the Rio Sumpul, one of the rivers that forms the border with Honduras. At least six hundred people were butchered, cut to pieces with machetes, while women were tortured and drowned. Pieces of bodies were found in the river for days afterwards. Church observers got the news out immediately, but the mainstream U.S. media decided it was not newsworthy.[346]

On November 27, 1980, seven political leaders of the opposition Revolutionary had tipped us that wives of security personnel working the late shift would typically come to the airport and wait to pick up their husbands, anxious to get home before midnight. And it was true: when we arrived, the immigration officials ignored the fact we did not have an advance visa, as their wives were impatiently standing next to them. Nonetheless, there was atmosphere of repression at the international airport, with armed police and military *everywhere*.

The labor conference was hosted by the harshly persecuted National United Workers of El Salvador (UNTS), and one of their activists met us, incognito, as we left customs. He whispered to us to not talk of anything political until we got to our hotel room in San Salvador, which he told us had been checked for bugs. The next morning we went to the university conference site and met Julio César Portillo from the UNTS Executive Committee. He had already survived several attempts on his life, including one by the feared Treasury Police and another by an army brigade. Later he showed us scars from bullet wounds incurred during these assassination attempts. This experience was typical for El Salvadoran activists, a fact we would be reminded of repeatedly during our discussions at the conference.

Democratic Front (FDR) attending a meeting in San Salvador were kidnapped, tortured, then murdered.[347] Five days later, four U.S. church women working in El Salvador were kidnapped after leaving the international airport, raped, then shot in the head at close range with hands tied behind their backs. They were discovered buried in shallow graves soon after the crime was committed. This gruesome event shocked El Salvador, the United States, and the world.

Despite this escalating reign of terror, however, Reagan only increased financial aid and the number of military advisers President Carter had sent to El Salvador.[348]

The series of massacres continued throughout 1981, culminating in one of the most gruesome slaughters of the entire war. During two weeks in December, three thousand members of the elite Salvadoran counterinsurgency Atlacatl Battalion, trained by U.S. Special Forces at both the U.S. Army's School of the Americas in Georgia and in El Salvador, went on a rampage in the northern Morazán Department. Residents in nine hamlets, including El Mozote, were machine-gunned, tortured, and burned at will, with as many as one thousand murdered. News of the massacre was delayed, but eventually reached the North American public on January 27, 1982, with front-page stories in the *Washington Post* and the *New York Times*. In a *Twilight Zone*–like performance true to his character, the very next day President Reagan certified that the Salvadoran government was making progress in abiding by international human rights standards.[349] But the reign of terror was just beginning.

We heard about systematic torture of labor and other activists being carried out at the draconian Mariona Prison in northern San Salvador, as well as in other locations, reportedly encouraged and supervised by Green Berets.[350] A detailed, graphic torture report was smuggled out of the prison and eventually revealed to U.S. Americans by the Marin California Interfaith Task Force (California).[351]

We were surprised to meet fifteen other U.S. veterans attending the labor conference and, together, we wrote and issued a statement offering our solidarity to the Salvadoran people while condemning U.S. policy that supported the repressive regime. After the conference ended, Duncan and I hurried to the airport and flew back to Managua. Back in Nicaragua, we experienced a dramatic difference in atmosphere. Despite the war being waged by the Contras, there was still a feeling of revolutionary excitement and relaxed freedom there.

Return to El Salvador

When I returned to El Salvador in 1988, the situation had deteriorated further. Villages suspected of being sympathetic to the FMLN were increasingly being bombed by the Salvadoran government, and I knew by then that the armaments were coming from the Concord Naval Weapon Station.

I had decided to travel again to El Salvador after consulting with Phil Roettinger, the ex-CIA agent I had met in April 1986 at our veterans press conference in Washington, D.C., organized in opposition to Contra aid. He had written an interesting op-ed piece that had appeared in March 1986 about his role in the overthrow of the democratically elected Arbenz government in Guatemala in June 1954.[352]

After his CIA role in Guatemala, Phil was assigned to Mexico City in 1960 to assist in various destabilization and propaganda campaigns intended to overthrow Fidel Castro in Cuba. It was during this time that he realized he was in the wrong job, because the campaign disillusioned him. He left the CIA and never again lived in the United States.

After our veterans' press conference in 1986, Phil and I began to collaborate as activists and witnesses against the criminal activities of the U.S. government. A retired Marine Corps colonel, Phil became active in Veterans For Peace. He always looked like he was still in the military. He maintained a rigid, erect six-foot-six posture, had a short-cropped brush cut, and always wore a hat with colonel leaves emblazoned on the bill. He stood out!

In November 1987, Phil became the president of a group of ex-CIA, National Security Council (NSC), and military security agents organized by long-time CIA veteran John Stockwell. Called ARDIS (Association for

Responsible Dissent), the group's announced intention was to campaign for an end to covert activities by the U.S. government. Other members included Phil Agee (ex-CIA, Uruguay, Ecuador, Mexico); David MacMichael (ex–National Intelligence Council estimates analyst, El Salvador-Nicaragua); Ralph McGehee (ex-CIA, Thailand, Viet Nam); Dan Ellsberg (ex–Rand Corporation, revealed *Pentagon Papers*); and Jack Ryan (ex-FBI agent).[353] For a short time I served as their vice president.

We turned our attention to El Salvador. More than a thousand people demonstrated at the Pentagon on October 17, 1988, to protest U.S. support for the El Salvador government. During the half-day long blockade of the building, Phil and I locked arms with Dave Dellinger, Daniel Ellsberg, Charlie Liteky, Korean activist Kiyul Chung, and many others. Police lifted employees over our bodies in lieu of making arrests.[354] That day Phil and I discussed the idea of organizing a veterans' trip to El Salvador. Shortly, we would see some of the newspaper coverage of the Washington action posted on office walls inside the U.S. Embassy in San Salvador.

On November 10, 1988, our delegation of five U.S. veterans, along with Frankie Herrera, our translator and all-around support person, flew into San Salvador. The next day we met with Reynaldo Blanco, president of the nongovernmental Human Rights Commission (CDH). Blanco's predecessor, Hebert Anaya, had been murdered nearly a year earlier, the second CDH president murdered in four years. On our way to his office, our driver made a series of detours and diversionary stops to ensure we were not being followed.

Blanco informed us that in 1988 alone, there had been 1,049 assassinations, 1,828 violent political deaths, 961 civilians captured, and 274 civilians disappeared in El Salvador. He showed us gruesome photographs of torture/murder victims and current lists of over 400 torture victims by name and date of capture. He told us the war would quickly end if the huge amount of U.S. aid was terminated.

When we asked Blanco how he could handle a job that was likely to lead to his death, or at a minimum put him in a constant fear of assassination, he calmly smiled and said, "This is my work for the people. Whatever happens, happens. I try to be careful. I think carefully about how and when to travel while moving my office from place to place. I try to always have others around me. Work for justice is dignified."

Meeting the FMLN

After intense meetings in San Salvador we hired a van and a driver and headed north into the heart of the Chalatenango "conflict zone," just a few miles from the Honduran border. There we planned to meet with revolutionary leaders from the Farabundo Martí National Liberation Front, or FMLN. We knew we would have to travel through about a dozen military checkpoints along the highway; if we were stopped, we could be turned back or even detained, because the El Salvadoran government did not want people traveling into areas where they might meet with the FMLN guerrillas, or witness the almost daily bombings and strafings of civilians by Salvadoran Air Force pilots flying U.S. fighter bombers and attack helicopters.

To increase our chances of passing through the checkpoints undetected, we left at one in the morning, and every time we approached a military checkpoint, our driver would creep very slowly with lights out, carefully easing the van over the sharp speed bumps to avoid making noise. As fortune had it, the soldiers manning the dozen checkpoints were all lying asleep in their ponchos along the roadside. We arrived in Chalatenango City about 4 a.m. Shortly after sunrise, we observed a Salvadoran helicopter gunship (a U.S.-supplied Huey) strafing a cluster of civilian houses less than a half mile from our location. After another three or four miles, we disembarked and began walking on offroad rocky mountain paths, less than seven miles from the Honduran border. Walking on these paths was difficult for me with prostheses, so I was relieved when we were met, as planned, by an FMLN scout who had brought a mule for me to ride. We vigilantly avoided Salvadoran Army patrols as well as any helicopter activity within sight and earshot of our slow-moving procession.

When we reached a certain point on the mountain trail, we saw a person on a knoll ahead of us waving an FMLN flag. We were now in what was considered "guerrilla territory" for that day. The next twenty-four hours were intense, as we accompanied FMLN guerrillas to observe the war from the ground. We visited the besieged communities of San Antonio Los Ranchos, Guarjila, and San José Las Flores, all within four-and-a half miles of each other. When we were in San José Los Flores, we were only three-and-a-half miles from the Honduran border.

Dimas Rodríguez, Douglas Santamaría, and Milton Mendez, the three leaders of the Joint Command for the Central Front of the FMLN—departments of Chalatenango, La Libertad, and San Salvador—were our hosts that day. Dimas welcomed us, "on behalf of the General Command which has been informed of your presence here at this war. Your presence is an honor to us." He described a recent A-37 bombing attack with white phosphorous and an attack the same day in Flores with saturation bombing dropping forty, five-hundred-pound bombs and twenty-four rockets as close as one-hundred meters from where we were talking. He reported that U.S. advisers carrying M-16s were frequently seen in the field next to 105 mm artillery.

Dimas concluded his remarks with these words:

> We will continue to struggle until we reach a change that is for true peace
> with justice. . . . We will defeat them in the long run because our people
> can no longer stand it. . . . You have already seen the level of poverty here.
> The lack of food, clothes, medicine. You can see and feel the reality. . . .
> People demand solutions to meet immediate problems. That's when the
> death squads and military show their true colors. It won't end until there
> is a real change in this regime. With our rifles, shovels, stones and sticks
> we will eventually defeat those planes, tanks and ships. . . . Our victory
> will be your victory.

After making this statement, Dimas presented me with a solidarity gift—a
green FMLN daypack that I still have in my possession. A number of other
guerrillas met with us during the night, including a number of young women
who contributed to the discussion. Dimas was killed one year later during the
nationwide FMLN offensive in November 1989. He was the highest-ranking
guerrilla killed in that campaign.

I was amazed by the way these guerrillas could take a night off in the
midst of the war to eat, talk, sing, and dance with us. The whole community
turned out for this party, which was held on the town's lone basketball court.
They could celebrate because they were acting in community, for their land
and their people.

U.S. Operatives

Upon leaving the guerrilla communities, our delegation retraced our steps
back toward Chalatenango City. Once there, we spotted the regional military headquarters. Our "intelligence" informed us it was in the back of this
building where the U.S. advisers in the region maintained an office. With
the six-foot-six Phil Roettinger leading the way, the five of us walked past a
Salvadoran security guard posted outside the military gate. Phil commanded
in Spanish, "at ease," and the soldier saluted us, probably thinking we were
either U.S. CIA operatives or military advisers in casual dress. We walked on
with confidence toward the back of the building.

At the rear of the building we saw a pallet loaded with rice from Agency
for International Development (AID) sitting next to a door. The door easily
opened the door and the five of us walked into a large room. We surprised
two U.S. military advisers, a captain from Puerto Rico and a sergeant from
the Midwest, who were discussing the most recent attacks by the FMLN
against Salvadoran army soldiers at El Paraíso, Ojos de Aguita, and San José
Las Flores (where we had just been). Surprisingly, they welcomed us with no

questions after we introduced ourselves as U.S. *veterans* assessing the situation in El Salvador. There was a huge map of El Salvador on the wall with pins designating locations of Salvadoran military garrisons, recent attacks by the FMLN, and plans for new movements against the guerrillas.

We had been talking with them for at least half an hour about the situation in the region when suddenly the sergeant jumped from his seat and called his boss in San Salvador, U.S. military attaché Colonel Wayne Wheeler. The sergeant asked Phil to get on the phone with Wheeler, who quickly asked us to leave and ordered the advisers to say nothing more to us. After we left the headquarters, we visited the Chalatenango gravesites of Maryknoll Sisters Ita Ford and Maura Clarke, two of the four U.S. missionaries who had been raped and murdered in December 1980 by Salvadoran National Guardsmen. Ford and Clarke, along with Ursuline Sister Dorothy Kazel and lay missioner Jean Donovan, had been invited by Salvadoran Archbishop Romero to assist internally displaced mothers and children before he himself was murdered in March 1980.

After witnessing the heart of the revolution, we returned to San Salvador on November 15, where we participated in a large rally for peace with thousands of Salvadorans.[355] Several Huey helicopter gunships hovered over this nonviolent rally the entire time, creating deafening noise and huge dust clouds intended to intimidate and terrify the participants. One of them hovered not more than twenty-five feet directly above our veterans' delegation, with the pilot, the door gunner, and a soldier with an M-16 looking directly down at us. Nobody panicked, however, and the rally sent a signal to both the Salvadoran and the U.S. government that the people were unwilling to accept continued repressive rule.

The day after the large peace rally, we visited the September 1988 massacre site at remote San Francisco in San Vicente Department east of San Salvador. On November 17, we met with Colonel René Emilio Ponce, chief of staff of the Salvadoran Armed Forces, who told us it was imperative that El Salvador "not go the way of neighboring Nicaragua," and that the Communist guerrillas must be defeated. Our meeting with Ponce took place almost exactly one year to the day before he orchestrated the massacre on November 16, 1989, of six Jesuit priests, their housekeeper, and her teenage daughter at the Central American University (UCA) during the FMLN offensive that ultimately forced the right-wing Arena government to the table with the guerrillas.

It was this massacre that provoked U.S. Maryknoll priest Roy Bourgeois, a decorated Viet Nam veteran, to expose the School of the Americas (SOA) at Fort Benning, Georgia, as a de facto school of assassins, since so many of its graduates had been identified as architects of massacres, as well as those officers carrying them out. Bourgeois also exposed that the SOA manuals trained its students in torture. In 1990, Bourgeois started a water-only fast with a dozen others at the gates of Fort Benning, launching an ongoing effort called SOA Watch. I joined in that fast for a week. Every year since then, SOA Watch has organized a large demonstration of as many as twenty-two thousand at Fort Benning to mark the anniversary of the November 16, 1989, massacre. Each year a number of people are arrested and imprisoned, some for as long as a year, for acts of civil disobedience—namely, crossing the property line onto the military base.

One of the priests murdered in the 1989 massacre was Father Ignacio Ellacuría, the university rector known for his courageous leadership in pursuit of justice for the poor. I remember reading parts of the 1982 convocation address he gave at Santa Clara University in California, in which he called the values of those living in the industrialized countries inhuman, because we insist on using the majority of the world's resources by force, thereby assuring that justice cannot be universalized for everyone. That principle stuck with me. Like Ben Linder and so many others, Ellacuría was assassinated for fostering the universalization of *justice*.

Finally we went to the U.S. Embassy for a face-to-face meeting with Colonel Wayne Wheeler, which Phil had arranged by phone from the Chalatenango military headquarters. Our meeting with him lasted nearly two hours. He furiously admonished us for going outside the city of San Salvador without an embassy-granted "safe conduct pass," though it is not likely the staff there would have issued us one. We honestly confessed that we knew of no regulation for a safe conduct pass in what we were told was a democratic country.

He said it was not safe for us in the countryside. We told him how we traveled to the war zone and that our extensive meetings with the guerrillas were very educational. We explained that it was safe for us because we wanted only to participate in dialogue and did so without carrying threatening weapons such as M-16s. Of course he was aghast to hear of our exploits.

A Viet Nam veteran himself, this was Wheeler's second tour in El Salvador. He described what he called the recent FMLN "terrorist attack" on the El Paraíso Garrison in September, where the guerrillas used homemade launchers to propel mortars inside the barracks. They had hit an ammunition dump, killing four and wounding forty. With strange logic, he criticized the FMLN for dragging off their own wounded and dead, "a dirty tactic like the 'VC' and North Vietnamese Army used in Viet Nam to conceal their casualty figures from us." He claimed there was no relationship between the death squads and the military.

While Wheeler mostly toed the U.S. line, we were surprised by some of what he said. For example, he admitted that there were 125 U.S. advisers currently in El Salvador even though the congressionally imposed limit was 55. We later learned that numbers were manipulated by altering job titles and by assigning U.S. military to temporary duty in the country, so that more advisers could be stationed there with little accountability.[356] Indeed, I later discovered that, during the twelve years of the U.S.-funded Salvadoran war against the guerrillas, five thousand U.S. advisers served secretly in El Salvador under Presidents Carter, Reagan and Bush, with twenty-one of them acknowledged as killed in action.[357]

Wheeler was not totally blind. He expressed fear that U.S. aid would be cut off if the recent San Francisco massacre (the site we had visited two days earlier) was not thoroughly investigated. He said "I will pack up my bags and leave, if this San Francisco massacre is not investigated thoroughly." He admitted to not seeing much light at the end of the tunnel, but said he thought the U.S. should remain one more year to evaluate the effectiveness of the next Salvadoran elections.

Before the meeting ended, Phil put a bee in Wheeler's bonnet. Phil looked straight at him and told him of his CIA participation in the 1954 overthrow of democratically elected President Arbenz in Guatemala. He then asked Wheeler: "Do you know that you are confusing communism with people's land reform and that one day you will have to live with what I think of every day, that I participated in a lie that led to the murder of thousands of innocent people?" Wheeler was stunned by Phil's question.

A year later, during the big FMLN offensive that began on the evening of November 11, 1989, Wheeler found himself barricaded inside his home with his family as guerrillas and government forces fought over Escalon Circle in the wealthy area of Avenida Escalon. The seizure of San Salvador in 1989 took Salvadoran military officers and their U.S. advisers by surprise. U.S. Army Major Eric Warren Buckland, a psychological operations specialist within the Salvadoran High Command, said the offensive "was like the fall of Saigon." The strength and scope of the siege was so overwhelming that for the first four days the Salvadoran High Command feared that the country might fall.[358]

I left El Salvador hopeful that their revolution would succeed.

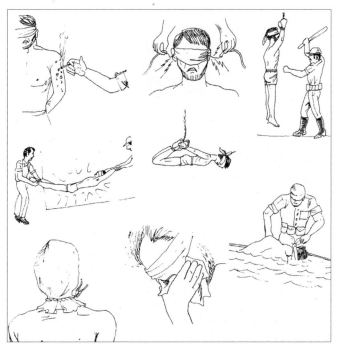

Drawings of some of the forty torture techniques smuggled out of the draconian Mariona Prison in San Salvador. Many of these were explicitly taught to Latin American soldiers at the U.S. Army's School of the Americas (SOA), now called the Western Hemisphere Institute for Security Cooperation (WHISC), and overseen by Green Berets in El Salvador [DRAWINGS: NON-GOVERNMENTAL HUMAN RIGHTS COMMISSION].

Note: Despite the U.S. reputation for being a society committed to justice, facts reveal otherwise. For example, the UN Convention Against Torture and other Cruel, Inhuman or Degrading Treatment or Punishment, adopted in 1984, established as international law that absolutely no torture or other degrading treatment is permissible under any circumstances. And though the U.S. formally signed the Convention in 1988, it has a history of using torture long before, and after—as revealed in Iraq and Guantánamo in the 2000s. During the U.S. conquest of the Philippines, 1899–1903, brutal U.S. military practices against Filipinos under the Teddy Roosevelt administration included the water cure (a version of water boarding). A May 31, 1902, *New York Times* story reported President Roosevelt boasting that bravery of U.S. soldiers enabled "the triumph of civilization over the black chaos of savagery and barbarism." The 1931 Wickersham Commission Report on Lawlessness in Law Enforcement under President Hoover, concluded that the "third degree," i.e., the willful infliction of pain and suffering on criminal suspects, was "widespread" throughout the entire criminal justice system to coerce detainees. These practices inflicted suffering through physical brutality, threats, sleep deprivation, exposure to extreme cold or heat— also known as "the sweat box" and blinding with powerful lights and other forms of sensory overload or deprivation. And, in early 1982, the *New York Times* reported that Green Berets oversaw torture of suspects and detainees in El Salvador. And it continues with impunity.

CHAPTER 25

Coca-Cola Colombia

A s an activist, I have learned how critical it is to understand the historical contexts that inform the kind of structural injustices I saw in El Salvador, Nicaragua, and elsewhere. Since I learned virtually no authentic history during my formative years, I have spent much of my life studying the role of the United States in creating and maintaining these structural injustices. One of the most telling cases in this history is the sad story of Colombia, a country I visited in the early 1990s to better understand what was happening to our Latin American neighbors.

A History of Oppression

Colombia signed its first treaty with the United States in 1846, authorizing the U.S. to build a railroad across the Isthmus in its northernmost state of Panama. At the time, Colombia stretched north into the Isthmus, and the treaty was designed to facilitate commerce across it. U.S. investments increased in Colombia in the 1890s, with many large corporations pouring billions into the area—for development of mining, railroads, sugar, electricity, agriculture, banks, etc.[359] Oil was discovered in Colombia in 1921 and brought even more investments.

By the early 1940s, Laurance Rockefeller, third generation of the wealthy Rockefeller family, owned 1.5 million acres of prime agricultural land on the Magdalena River valley in Colombia where he raised cattle, harvested mahogany, and built hotels, while his brother Nelson owned a large ranch in neighboring Venezuela. About the same time, Robert W. Johnson, founder of Johnson & Johnson drug company, was seeking legal control of the numerous botanical plants found in the Amazon Basin (including Colombia), used in the manufacture of market drugs, as he fiercely competed with German companies such as Bayer.[360]

President Eisenhower, concerned that the encroachment of so-called "communists" in Latin America would interfere with the "stability" needed by these corporations to realize profits, had ordered the coup of a democratically elected Guatemalan government in 1954. A year later, with U.S. assistance, the Colombian Army under General Alberto Ruiz Novoa, an officer who had headed the Colombian regiment under U.S. command in the Korean War, set up the first counterguerrilla training center in Latin America to confront this alleged communist menace. It was named the Lancero School.[361]

Ruiz Novoa's school soon proved woefully inadequate, however, so in 1958 Eisenhower ordered an antiguerrilla specialist team to Colombia to discuss with its new president, Alberto Camargo, methods for ridding the country of emerging "red republics" in the lower Magdalena River valley. These were new communities comprised of thousands of internal refugees who were fleeing the terrible Colombian civil war (*La Violencia*) that had started in 1948. These aggrieved and terrified peasants had moved onto unused rural lands, setting up their own local governments while creating a territory of experimental peasant republics challenging the legitimacy of the central government in Bogotá.[362]

This phenomenon of people withdrawing their allegiance to a central authority to create local self-reliant communities was not unique. It was similar, perhaps, to Maya peasants abandoning servitude to their city-state kings in 900 A.D., or to the brief decentralized liberation socialism of the Basque region in Spain in the mid-1930s. It could be seen as a prelude to the Zapatista decentralist revolution in southern Mexico in the 1990s. All these actions display an archetypal human characteristic of seeking autonomy within local self-reliant social groupings.

The Cuban Revolution of January 1959 provided the political impetus Eisenhower needed to overthrow these "red republics." He acquired open congressional support for his Overseas Internal Security Program (OISP) which sent counterinsurgency specialists to Colombia to formally advise security forces on eliminating the threat of the rebellious poor.[363] After President Kennedy announced the Alliance for Progress in Latin America in 1961, he chose Colombia to be a laboratory for repelling "communists," since President Camargo had supported Kennedy's ill-fated Bay of Pigs invasion of Cuba. For the Alliance to work it required sticks—counterinsurgency operations—to supplement the carrots of liberal reforms. In February 1962, Kennedy dispatched General Yarborough and a special warfare team to Colombia from the newly established Special Warfare School at Fort Bragg, North Carolina to assess the feasibility for organizing Indigenous irregulars to conduct both offensive "guerrilla" and counterguerrilla actions to eliminate "communists."[364]

Yarborough's recommendations included instituting improved "intelligence" and population control through a government-run "intensive civilian registration program" that would collect fingerprints and photographs. Interrogation teams would question rural villagers believed to be "knowledgeable of guerrilla activities." The interrogation was to be "exhaustive," and to include sodium pentothal and polygraph testing to "elicit every shred of information."[365]

A month after Yarlborough's arrival in Colombia, U.S. Special Warfare Military Training Teams (MTTs) showed up to help Colombia create its own long-term counterinsurgency forces. Michael McClintock, an experienced human rights observer, called this plan "a virtual blueprint for the Colombian Army death squads" that are still active today.[366] The first MTT assignment sent five twelve-man Special Forces teams to train four Colombian counter-guerrilla brigades, including an administrative detachment and psychologi-cal warfare experts. This counterinsurgency model was formally adopted at the end of 1962 by the Colombian military in a comprehensive counterinsur-gency plan, called Plan Lazo.[367]

As the autonomous republics were being destroyed by these new national government forces with help from the U.S., people chose to take up arms rather than be mercilessly murdered or left to starve. By the mid-1960s, four major guerrilla groups were formed and employing their own force in order to create a more just society. Two of the groups remain active today: the Fuerzas Armadas Revolucionarias de Colombia, or Revolutionary Armed Forces of Colombia (FARC), and the Ejército de Liberación Nacional, or Army of National Liberation (ELN).[368]

It is astonishing how little U.S. policymakers appreciate, and how little the U.S. population at large knows about, the vast pain and misery caused by military policies instituted to ensure "stability" for investors such as Rockefeller, manufacturers such as Coca-Cola, and extractors such as Drummond Company and Occidental Petroleum. In attempting to repress the small, local people's republics, the U.S. government had drastically guar-anteed a bloody civil war that has raged for over two generations.

Plan Colombia

In 1992, three friends and I visited several South American countries to see first-hand the effects of U.S. intervention. We arrived in Colombia in March 1992 and promptly met with representatives of sixteen different human rights groups around the country to get an overview of recent Colombian political activity.

These human rights activists described a cycle of violence that was clear for all to see: (1) government policies benefit the rich at the expense of the poor with the collusion of the International Monetary Fund (IMF); (2) a nonviolent popular movement develops in response to the injustices; (3) the government declares a national security state (with aid from the U.S.) to stifle the popular movement (labeled "communist") enabled by domestic paramilitary death squads and U.S. Special Forces; and (4) armed peasant groups ("guerrillas") arise in response to the state's systematic violent repression.

According to the Agustín Codazzi Geographic Institute in Bogotá, the richest 3 percent of the landed elite own 71.3 percent of Colombia's arable land. Two-thirds of the population lives in poverty, with 40 percent of the people living in abject poverty. By 1992, there were reportedly more than 140 paramilitary groups roaming the country, most funded by the drug mafia.[369]

Because external corporations had a monopoly on legal exports such as bananas (Chiquita/Del Monte), cut flowers (Dole), coffee (Kraft), minerals (Drummond Company), and oil (Occidental), peasants were forced to rely on coca and opium poppies to bring in cash. These exports fed cocaine and heroin addiction in the United States, while funding both the paramilitary death squads and left-wing insurgencies. The United States reacted by staging a "war on drugs" to eradicate these crops, instead of addressing the demand here in the United States and the lack of other opportunities for cash in Colombia. The policy has been a colossal failure, resulting only in the repression of small farmers in Colombia, enriching Medellín cartels and other large organized crime operatives while aggravating drug addiction and increasing prison populations in the U.S.

We were briefed that, in the summer of 1989, the U.S. State Department had approved sending military equipment to the Colombian military for what was described as "antinarcotics" operations. In its justification, the State Department said Colombia had a "democratic form of government" that upheld human rights, conveniently ignoring a recent internal Colombian Commission report that documented *thousands* of politically motivated murders committed with almost total impunity within only a few months. Most victims were peasants and grassroots organizers, union leaders and teachers, leftist politicians and human rights workers.

During Colombia's 1988 electoral campaigns, nineteen of eighty-seven mayoral candidates of the lone independent political party, the Patriotic Union, were assassinated, along with more than a hundred other candidates from the party. From 1988 to the time of our arrival in March 1992, 9,500 Colombians had been assassinated for political reasons with another 830 disappeared. Between 1988 and 1990, Colombia witnessed 313 documented massacres targeting peasant groups. This sordid record was described in Colombian-born theologian Javier Giraldo's 1996 book, *Colombia: The Genocidal Democracy*.

By the 2000s, the social and economic pathologies of the early 1990s were institutionalized in what is called Plan Colombia, through which billions of dollars of U.S. aid have been given to Colombia, ostensibly to eliminate coca growing and the guerrillas. Colombia's previous president, Andrés

Pastrana, had originally proposed Plan Colombia as a comprehensive social and economic revitalization strategy to end armed conflict, serious class divisions, and economic inequality. U.S. President Clinton preempted that idea, instead investing in a massive antidrug and antiguerrilla military aid project while ignoring Colombia's severe underlying social inequities. Thus, more than 80 percent of the six billion dollars has gone to counterinsurgency training and purchase of U.S.-manufactured combat helicopters and fixed-wing herbicide-spraying planes. Essentially, nearly half the aid has gone directly to private U.S. military contractors such as Lockheed Martin, Dyncorp, Textron, and United Technologies, all of which have profited handsomely from these guaranteed deals.

Another big chunk of this military aid ended up in the hands of the paramilitaries. CIA reports have acknowledged active collaboration between the military and paramilitary forces in Colombia.[370] As of summer 2007, the vast network of military, political and business leaders supporting and working closely with the paramilitary included fourteen current and seven former members of Colombia's national Congress, the head of the nation's secret police, several mayors, former department governors, former generals, the current vice president and the current minister of defense. A leading ex-paramilitary commander admitted that "paramilitarism was state policy" and that the paramilitary had murdered "countless civilians in massacres" from the mid-1990s until the early 2000s, including many union members who were targeted for their "ideological posture," not for their alleged ties to guerrillas.[371]

Despite these obvious connections, successive U.S. administrations have expanded military aid to Colombia to foster a war in "the entire national territory" against our real adversary, the guerrillas. A U.S. congressional delegation to Colombia in May 1997 led by Rep. Dennis Hastert (R-IL), then-chair of the House Subcommittee on National Security, secretly encouraged Colombian military officials to ignore funding conditions related to human rights compliance. Thus, our Congress became complicit in terror by supporting the human rights atrocities carried out by Colombia's military and paramilitary forces.[372]

More than ten thousand soldiers from Colombia have been sent to Fort Benning, Georgia, to be trained at the U.S. Army's School of the Americas (now called the Western Hemisphere Institute for Security Cooperation). This is more than from any other Latin American country. In 2000, the U.S. State Department and Human Rights Watch each documented the involvement of a number of Colombian SOA graduates in kidnapping, murder, massacres and the establishment of paramilitary groups.[373] Furthermore, it has been determined from looking at training manuals that Colombian officers studying at the SOA have been encouraged to target those workers who participate in "union organizing or recruiting," or who distribute "propaganda in favor of the interests of the workers," or who "sympathize with demonstrations or strikes."[374] This is another insidious way the U.S. promotes terror in Colombia and elsewhere. It literally trains and encourages soldiers to kill organizing efforts by peasant-workers to ensure cheap labor costs for multinational corporations.

Under Plan Colombia, the average daily number of politically motivated murders is approaching twenty per *day*, and it is estimated that over the past nineteen years nearly forty thousand civilian lives have been taken. Poor farmers' crops and health are damaged by regular aerial spraying of fumigants while the amount of coca grown has continued to increase. Plan Colombia's emphasis on hard military and police tactics rather than social and economic restructuring has simply inflamed Colombia's political and class divisions, thus dramatically escalating violence on all sides. Because most of the multinational corporations operate in Colombia's mining and energy regions, it is no surprise that the majority of U.S. military aid goes simply to bulk up the military and paramilitary forces already engaged to protect these corporations' investments. Most of the worst human rights violations and massacres have occurred in this same region. The correlation is direct and undeniable.[375]

Coca-Cola

When we were in Colombia, we asked the human rights workers to suggest an area to visit where we might witness the effects of the policy of terror. They suggested the Santander Department (one of thirty-three in Colombia) in the middle Magdalena River valley region nearly two hundred miles north of Bogotá in north central Colombia where we might experience military and paramilitary operations. This area had been subjected to intense scorched earth campaigns by the paramilitary and military. They agreed to facilitate interviews with victims.

Soon, we were flying from Bogotá to Barrancabermeja (Barranca), a large oil-refining city in the coal- and oil-rich middle Magdalena River region. One week earlier, the refugee center for war victims in the Campesino Hostel at Barranca had been forcefully entered by paramilitaries who terrified its occupants for three hours. In October 1991, on two separate occasions, the paramilitary massed outside the hostel and massacred a number of people in the street. Ten weeks before our arrival, there had been ninety-six murders in the city with only three arrests. From 1987–1991, there had been 1,267 murders in Barranca of which only 35 were ever investigated. Six weeks before our arrival, the city's human rights director had been murdered. This was a region where people lived in constant terror as murderous thugs operated with total impunity.

Colombia is considered by many to be the world's most dangerous country for trade unionists. Between January 1991 and December 2006, Amnesty International reported 2,245 trade unionists murdered, with 3,400 other serious threats, and 138 forced disappearances.[376] We met with representatives of the seventy-two-year-old Union of Oil Workers of Colombia who the Colombian government had accused of working closely with the guerrillas. Forty oil workers had been murdered in the three previous years, while fifty workers in the Barrancabermeja refinery had received death threats and had temporarily gone into hiding. The president of their union had left the country after several assassination attempts. Union members told us they had reports of Israeli security specialists working hand-in-hand with the U.S. in advising and training the Colombian military and its associated paramilitary. This U.S.-Israel alliance to maintain national security states using paramilitary and death squads has been common throughout Latin America.

When we met with the oil unionists in Barrancabermeja, they described the sixty-year history of Coca-Cola in Colombia. They proceeded to tell us a story typical of the role of U.S. corporations in Colombia and other "Third World" countries.

Coca-Cola established its first bottling operations in Latin America in 1906, and established its first factory in the 1930s. The official company history points to the "increasing interaction between the people of Latin America and the United States," but the company also no doubt wanted to secure a foothold in the countries that supplied it with the coca leaf necessary to create its product.[377] While Coca-Cola no longer contains cocaine (benzoylmethylecgonine), the secret formula is still said to contain extract of coca leaf, now supplied mainly from Peru.

Coca-Cola has long enjoyed a cozy relationship with governments in the region. The company coyly suggests they form these alliances "to give back to the community," but they also function to protect the company's interest in obtaining cheap resources (especially sugar and water), not to mention labor. In 1986, workers at Colombia's Coca-Cola bottling plants pushed back, forming the Colombian Labor Federation in part to ensure better wages for workers. Union membership makes a big difference for workers. In 2002, for example, experienced unionized workers earned nearly $400 a month, while nonunion laborers at Coke plants earned only $130 a month.[378]

The paramilitary forces in Colombia were very antiunion and did not hesitate to target union members for assassination. The Colombian Labor Federation had already recorded nearly six hundred assassinations of its union members nationwide in its first few years of existence. One of the first Colombia Coca-Cola union members was murdered during a strike. The perpetrator was never apprehended. Since then, at least nine Coca-Cola union workers have been murdered, with hundreds threatened. Four of them were assassinated between 1994 and 1996 at the Carepa bottling plant in northwestern Colombia operating under the name Bebidad y Alimento, owned by Richard Kirby of Key Biscayne, Florida.

In the most clear-cut incident, armed men on motorcycles rode up to the plant on the morning of December 1996 and shot the plant's gatekeeper, the union's secretary general, as he opened the door. The paramilitary terrorists returned later that night and firebombed the union's offices. Within a few days, the paramilitaries returned, forcing the workers into the company cafeteria where they were given a choice between signing letters of resignation from the union or being shot.[379] Many union members understandably resigned while others quit their jobs and fled to other cities. Some were still in hiding twelve years later.

A 2001 lawsuit brought by Colombian unions against Coca-Cola alleged, among other complaints, that the Carepa plant manager was known for his friendship with the paramilitaries and had "boasted publicly that he would use paramilitaries to sweep away the union." The manager had even allowed paramilitary forces to camp out at the Carepa plant for months at a time.[380] The lawsuit was thrown out of court and the labor unionists at that plant never received reparations.

Coca-Cola did nothing to reprimand its antiunion manager or provide security for its workers. Instead, in response to pleas by union officials to Coca-Cola headquarters in Atlanta for protection, the company repeatedly denied any relationship between its bottlers and paramilitaries. A 2007 PR piece posted on its website, "The Facts about the Coca-Cola Company in Colombia," reported that third parties have "found no violations and uncovered no allegations with respect to human rights abuses at any of the plants" relating to its "bottling partners' current workplace practices, including wages and hours, facility security, freedom of association, collective bargaining, health and safety." Another statement boasts that in its seventy years of operation in Colombia, Coca-Cola ensures "the safety of workers" and respects union membership. In a 2006 press release, it claimed that for seventy years it has "supported programs that aid children, promote education, and bring relief to victims of the country's ongoing conflict." Whose children, I wonder?

Despite Coke's mendacious rhetoric, in 2007 human rights workers witnessed *at least* six serious death threats against union members, all reported to the bottling company and its in-country plant partners. These included a September 25 threat against three union officials in Bucaramanga who received a message at their union office that warned, "Get out of the department. . . . If you don't, we will . . . give your families your bodies in a mass grave for Christmas. . . . You will be cut up into pieces." The paramilitary group *Aguilas Negras* (Black Eagles) claimed credit for five other threats to union members. Two days later, the son of one of the three union leaders was kidnapped and ordered to tell his father "that we won't stop until you're cut up into pieces" before throwing him out of a vehicle in an industrial area of Bucaramanga.[381]

It is no wonder that the number of unionized workers at Coca-Cola plants in Colombia dropped by more than two-thirds from 1,300 members in 1993 to only 450 as of 2001.[382] In 2007, Coke reported that of its two thousand Colombian employees, 31 percent, or over six hundred, were union members. Even if this is accurate, it is still seven hundred members less than before the four assassinations took place in 1994–1996 at the Carepa plant.[383]

Coca-Cola has become the focus of reform activists, but it is not the only company deeply implicated in supporting paramilitary violence against unionists and peasants. It is well documented that many U.S. corporations pay "protection money" to Colombian paramilitary forces. Their services are seen as indispensable for companies extracting resources from a country where 40 percent of the people live in absolute poverty.

One notable example is Cincinnati-based Chiquita Brands (formerly United Fruit) which owns huge banana plantations in Colombia. In 2007, officials from Chiquita discussed with Michael Chertoff, then-assistant U.S. attorney general, their payments to the AUC paramilitary forces, seeking to ascertain whether these payments violated U.S. antiterrorism laws. At the same time, they made clear to Chertoff that Chiquita would pull out of Colombia if it could not continue to pay the right-wing paramilitary forces to protect its banana plantations and ensure the "safety" of its employees. Chertoff never responded, perhaps hoping that inaction would make the matter disappear.[384]

These corporate bribes have devastating consequences. It was after Chiquita payments began to flow to the AUC in 1997—ultimately in more than a hundred separate payments totaling $1.7 million—that the paramilitary group carried out some of its most shocking massacres. In July thirty civilians were murdered in Mapiripán, a coca region.[385] Between May and September of 1999, there were fifteen massacres by paramilitary in the northern portions of Santander near Bucaramanga, in which nearly 150 civilians were killed.[386]

Companies in Colombia suspected of collaborating with paramilitary terrorists include: Drummond Company from Birmingham, Alabama; Coca-Cola at its six in-country bottling plants; Florida-based Del Monte with its associated third-party banana growers; and California-based Dole Food which owns large cut-flower plantations. Ex-paramilitary commanders claimed that payoffs have been "routine," "pervasive," and "long-standing" from these and numerous other multinational companies.[387]

Networks protecting corporate exploitation are, of course, not new. But more recently, the secrets of how their power is maintained are being exposed as never before. Having once been a teamster driving a Coca-Cola delivery truck in the U.S., I found the Colombia Coke case especially interesting. It shows how seemingly innocuous corporations function in ways that literally kill thousands of innocent people, with complete detachment from the structurally unjust historical context in which they operate. Of course, the erasure of historical memory is a prerequisite for corporate profit-making endeavors. In essence, the original theft of land and elimination of its inhabitants based on an ideology of colonialism is the product of an arrogance built on racism and classism. The original crime has never been addressed by a conscious commitment to justice. That would require a social revolution. Oligarchic elites ensure their continued power over generation after generation, by whatever means necessary. Rarely is anyone in the chain of structural class-control necessarily intentionally plotting evil. Evil deeds often are executed unconsciously by "good people" just doing their job, as Hannah Arendt wrote in her book, *Eichmann in Jerusalem: A Report on the Banality of Evil* (1963). The problem is deeply structural and cannot be rectified by trivial reforms.

The story of Coca-Cola in Colombia illustrates how deceitful rhetoric about maintaining social "stability" is used to maximize corporate profits, even as it obscures and denies the reality of violent injustices on the society. This is how "exceptionalism" is glorified.

Witnessing "Democracy" at Work

After meeting with the labor unionists, we met with the leaders of CREDHOS (Regional Corporation for the Defense of Human Rights) in Barranca. The Magdalena River area is a beautiful region rich in resources where many drugs are grown. The alliance between paramilitary forces, landowners, drug growers, and the Colombian military permeates local politics.

We experienced the perverted power of that alliance when we traveled to one of the poor barrios of northeastern Barrancabermeja and met with ten families who had been raided the night before by the army. Five men were forcibly taken out of their houses in their underwear and disappeared because they were accused of being guerrillas. One resident of the barrio, Soloman, described how soldiers had stormed into his small home, poking their guns at his children in an effort to terrify them into telling the soldiers where the "guerrillas" were. We saw one mother and her children standing in their now doorless, ransacked home with debris everywhere, holding hands as they sobbed and sobbed. Her husband, the father of the children, was now disappeared. They had no idea if they would ever see him again.

These experiences were repeated all over the country. In San Vicente, we saw houses that had been bombed. In La Salina, we were supposed to be met by local villagers; instead, we were met by dozens of armed Colombian soldiers who surrounded our car, pointed their guns at us, and detained us for four hours. When we were finally released, we drove back toward San Vicente. We watched paramilitary units moving in the distance before we were stopped en route by masked ELN guerrillas, who claimed to be protecting us from the army. We talked with them for several hours and they, too, eventually let us move forward.

Even though we were prepared for this sort of thing, these events were still nerve-racking. We were protected to a great extent by virtue of our U.S. citizenship, and the fact that we were accompanied by a group of five journalists and a human rights ombudsman. I could only imagine what it would be like to be an impoverished villager living in this war zone with no protection at all.

We finally came upon a small village on the western side of Taguales where we had planned to interview torture victims. Among the campesinos were a father and two sons, one of whom was named Favio. Originally refugees from the reign of terror in El Salvador that left their mother murdered, the families had settled on a small farm (finca) in San Vicente. Because of persecution from paramilitary forces that constantly demanded to know "who the guerrillas are," and the military that required regular reporting to a security post, the father, another son, and Favio moved again, this time to Barrancabermeja.

Another son, Filemón, however, remained on the farm that he loved. One day when Favio and his other brother were visiting Filemón to help cut plantains for the market, the paramilitary forces showed up wanting to know about "guerrillas." They grabbed Filemón, tied his hands behind his back, and put a cord around his neck. They counted to thirty and, then, with a gun pressed against Favio's forehead, ordered him to tell them who the guerrillas were in the area and in Barranca. If Favio didn't give them this information, they said, they would kill him and Filemón. Then, suddenly, the paramilitary let Favio and his other brother go, while they continued to detain Filemón.

They said, "Go home and tomorrow you can come back for your brother." The next day, when Favio returned to Filemón's *finca*, he found the body of his brother lying fifty yards from the house. His head had been cut off and his torso showed signs of severe torture. There were stab wounds on his neck, shoulders and back, and on his head. A neighbor woman reported seeing the paramilitary "playing soccer with his head, laughing."

The Military-Corporate Complex

In just one afternoon, we witnessed the brutality of the Colombian military, the paramilitary, and the guerrillas, all within a few kilometers of one another. Every human rights group, every union person, every teacher, every researcher, every campesino with whom we talked told us of the tight relationship between the military and the paramilitary. We saw with our own eyes how the military and paramilitary worked in concert to control daily life through a reign of terror. We also witnessed how guerrilla groups formed in opposition to the paramilitary became the targets of violence, but also sometimes fought back using violent methods themselves, thus creating even more terror for the population. Violence begot violence, in a cruel calculus the paramilitary used to their advantage.

This was not counterinsurgency run amok. As I saw in Viet Nam, in Nicaragua, and again here in Colombia, counterinsurgency is an intentional *terror* operation designed to instill fear in people to exact their total obedience to authority structures bent on pillage for profit. Counterinsurgency terror tactics work well to preserve a system that requires wage slavery and views democracy as a risk, not an asset.

After I returned to the U.S. from South America, an article written by our translator in Colombia, Leslie Wirpsa, was published in the May 1992 issue of the *Progressive*. In her essay, titled "Leave the Region or Die," Wirpsa described the repression in Colombia's Middle Magdalena region where we had been. She reported testimony collected by the human rights group Justicia y Paz: "Army officials accompanied by paramilitary soldiers told the peasants to fight guerrillas by joining 'self-defense groups' [read paramilitary], or 'leave the region or die.'"

I left the region because I was only a visitor. Thousands of Colombians have left the region, and other regions, only to seek safety in yet another region, often in hiding. There are reportedly three million internally displaced Colombians, more than anywhere else at the time except Sudan.[388] Others have no choice but to live out their lives in constant fear from military, paramilitary, and guerrilla activities, or slowly starve to death from absolute poverty.

In the end, this structurally maintained separation between the minority Haves and the majority Have-Nots diminishes all of us. It is not sustainable ecologically, materially or morally. We in the U.S. feel the effects of the Colombian drug wars on our inner cities. One day, the corporations that allow and often enable terrorism in countries like Colombia will be pushed out of those countries. We will no longer be able to buy one-dollar Cokes or ninety-nine-cent-a-pound bananas. Maybe when that day comes, we will finally realize that we do not even desire cheap goods at the cost of others' lives. Maybe we will finally realize that we all share a common humanity.

They are us. We are them. Favio is me. I am Favio. Filemón is you. You are Filemón.

CHAPTER 26

Assimilation or Elimination

As I traveled through Latin America in the late 1980s and early 1990s, I saw the United States protecting its prosperity by proxy, funding the Contra counterrevolutionaries in Nicaragua, the military governments of El Salvador, Honduras, Guatemala, and Panama, and the military and paramilitaries of Colombia. I also had traveled to the Middle East, North and South Korea, and Ireland.

It is one thing to talk about a pattern of conquest: it is another thing to experience it. In country after country, I saw examples of dismal poverty and repression, all contributing to the creation of the comfortable lifestyle I enjoyed in the United States. In country after country, I saw inspiring examples of groups of poor people practicing local self-reliance while attempting to resist the forces of globalization. Each of these groups was faced with the same dilemma: assimilate to the economic model being imposed in order to feed the American Way Of Life, or be eliminated. Very few groups were able to create a third way and get away with it.

The danger to local resistance groups became especially apparent as the 1980s wore on, when the United States was shaking off the "Viet Nam Syndrome." After being humiliated by the fall of Saigon in 1975, the U.S. military was much less eager to wage overt war in the "Third World." The fear of humiliation did not, however, keep the United States from invading the tiny island of Grenada in 1983 or from invading Panama in 1989, both virtually defenseless. By 1990, having successfully parachuted into tiny countries with little resistance, the United States was ready to resume its global military endeavors with a full-scale invasion of Iraq.

For me, nothing about these years was easy. Traveling was difficult with prostheses. I was emotionally devastated with the effective crushing of the Nicaragua Revolution. Holley and I agreed to go our separate ways in 1990. Our lives had become stressful as we were pulled one way, then another, for attention. It was difficult to find the kind of quiet time I needed. My mother died in 1988, my father in 1989.

As I visited various countries, I experienced a sense of shame about our cultural wasteland back home. I felt like a pariah as never before. Most people I met in the United States were apathetic about what was happening elsewhere. Most did not bother to look at the systemic repression that made their own lives possible, nor at people's courageous and inspiring resistance to it. I knew no foreign language. I felt I had no skills to help people.

Panama after the Invasion

During 1989 I read a number of news stories that strongly suggested President Bush planned to militarily overthrow Panamanian strongman Manuel Noriega using the pretext of illegal drug operations. In mid-November I was attending the funeral of my father in Jamestown, New York, when I read a short November 16 AP story in the local paper: "The CIA has launched a $3

PANAMA

President George H.W. Bush's military invasion of Panama on December 20, 1989—the most significant invasion of another country by U.S. troops since Viet Nam—simply continued traditional U.S. imperial policy, hoping it had finally overcome the "Viet Nam Syndrome."

In November 1903, Theodore Roosevelt, our twenty-eighth president, secretly conspired with Wall Street investors, banker J.P. Morgan, and prestigious lawyer William Cromwell, to acquire the Isthmus portion of Colombia, i.e., the state of Panama, to build the long sought canal. Roosevelt ordered the U.S. military to prevent Colombian forces from quelling an Isthmus "rebellion," then quickly recognized "Panama" as a sovereign state. Twelve days later, the Hays Treaty was agreed to with "Panama," by which the U.S. was granted all it desired for the construction, maintenance, and protection of the canal. It is not certain that any "Panamanian" or Colombian signed the Hays Treaty (or the Isthmian Canal Convention).[389]

In Roosevelt's January 4, 1904, message to Congress, he responded to criticisms that he violated Colombia's sovereignty declaring that the U.S. had a "moral" duty to overcome the former's "selfish" interests and delays in granting U.S. canal rights in the Isthmus of Panama. He cited considerations of "treaty rights and obligations," of U.S. "national interests and safety," of the needs of "collective civilization," and even of the "interests of its [Colombia's] inhabitants."

This facilitated U.S. global expansionism. Prior to becoming president, as secretary of the Navy, Roosevelt had eagerly promoted the Spanish-American War, which led to U.S. control over Cuba, including its Guantánamo port, over the Philippine Archipelago, which served as coaling stations for early U.S. military force projections in Asia, and over Hawaii. The Panama Canal was necessary to facilitate shortened, expanded trade to these markets, marking the beginning of the globalization of the American Way Of Life through the advancement of million operation, with the approval of congressional oversight committees, to overthrow Panamanian Gen. Manuel Noriega. . . . The covert operation has 'no restrictions.'" Well, shit! It just keeps on and on. I suffer from multiple wars as much as others suffer from multiple tours.

Within two weeks I joined more than 120 other U.S. Americans to attend a conference in Panama City in efforts to deter a momentum building toward a U.S. invasion. As it turned out this was just three weeks before the invasion.

Since becoming a global power, the United States had kept the narrow isthmus that is now the nation of Panama under its control. President Theodore Roosevelt's unilateral intervention into the internal affairs of sov-

our messianic mission of bringing the linked goals of prosperity (markets) and Christianity ("civilization") to the "undeveloped" world.

It is instructive to read Roosevelt's words marking the beginning of the new "American Century" to understand better the racism and arrogance behind this U.S. takeover of Panama:

> The experience of over half a century has shown Colombia to be utterly incapable of keeping order on the Isthmus. Only the active interference of the United States has enabled her to preserve so much as a semblance of sovereignty. Had it not been for the exercise by the United States of the police power in her interest, her connection with the Isthmus would have been severed long ago.
>
> Every effort has been made by the government of the United States to persuade Colombia to follow a course which was essentially not only to our interests and to the interests of the world, but to the interests of Colombia itself. These efforts have failed; and Colombia by her persistence in replacing the advances that have been made, has forced us, for the sake of our own honor, and of the interests and well-being, not merely of our own people, but of the people of the Isthmus of Panama and the people of the civilized countries of the world, to take decisive steps to bring to an end a condition of affairs which has become intolerable. The New Republic of Panama immediately offered to negotiate a treaty with us. This treaty I herewith submit.[390]

In March 1911, two years after he left the presidency and three years before the completion of the canal, Roosevelt addressed the University of California where he unblushingly proclaimed he "took the canal zone and let Congress debate, and while the debate goes on the canal does also." In his memoirs he bragged, "I took Panama without consulting the cabinet."[391]

ereign Colombia in 1903, was deliberately orchestrated to wrest Panama from Colombia and then to construct and protect the interoceanic canal. President George H.W. Bush's military invasion of Panama on December 20, 1989—the most significant invasion of another country by U.S. troops since Viet Nam— simply continued this imperial policy.

About 1 a.m., Wednesday, December 20, 1989, without warning, the U.S. dropped twelve thousand troops, bombs and firepower into Panama, striking Panama City, Colón, and a number of Panamanian Defense Forces (PDF) installations simultaneously. The newly revealed Stealth bomber dropped two two-thousand-pound bombs on the Rio Hato Military School, believed to be the first combat mission for the Stealth. Two thousand additional troops were dispatched making a total U.S. invading force of fourteen thousand complementing thirteen thousand military personnel present prior to the invasion.

I followed the unfolding story, noting how the U.S. media performed a masterful job of being the unofficial propaganda organ for the U.S. government and its policies. While the non-U.S. media used the terms "invasion," "occupation," "imperialist act," and "lawless," the U.S. news media used phrases like "surgical strike," "restoring democracy," and "lawful."

In reality, Bush sold the invasion to Congress and the American public as the only possible way to bring the drug-running General Manuel Noriega, Panama's dictatorial strongman leader, to justice. While Noriega was undoubtedly mixed up in a drug cartel, the U.S. wanted him out because he was a CIA agent gone bad, a former U.S. "asset" who now appeared to balk at simply handing Panamanian policy over to U.S. control through his puppet government. Since Noriega could not be convinced to be totally compliant, Bush determined the easiest solution was to directly install a U.S. puppet government. The message sent out to U.S. citizens through the media was that this invasion was a "just cause" designed to end drug trafficking in the region. When our military forces invaded this tiny sovereign nation in violation of every legal principle and moral standard, killing, injuring and detaining thousands of Panamanian citizens, large numbers of U.S. citizens and upper- and middle-class Panamanians celebrated by wearing "just cause" t-shirts.

In 1991, I joined fifteen U.S. citizens returning to Panama for the second anniversary of the U.S. invasion. What were the real casualty numbers? What was the behavior of the U.S. troops? What areas were destroyed? What had the U.S. media not told us? We hoped to get answers to these and other questions.

Arriving in December 1991, we stayed in a house run by Daughters of Charity of St. Vincent de Paul and St. Louise de Marillac, an organization founded in 1617 in Paris to help the poor, of which Panama has plenty. One report indicated that 55 percent of Panama's 2.4 million people at the time were in extreme poverty.

The Daughters of Charity House was located in the poor Panama City neighborhood of El Chorillo, adjacent to the Panama Canal, and, unfortunately for them, close to the Panamanian Defense Forces headquarters heavily bombed by the U.S. This neighborhood of mostly wooden tenement houses was virtually destroyed. Looking out their front door, I saw acres and acres of rubble where eighteen thousand people had once lived in seven blocks of tenements and high rises. Fourteen thousand people remained homeless.

In separate meetings with officials of the U.S. Southern Command (Lt. Col. McMahon), the Minister of Panama's Presidency (Julio Harris), and the U.S. Embassy (Peter DeShazo), we were consistently told the number of U.S. dead from the invasion stood at twenty-three people. The "official" estimate of *Panamanian* deaths ranged from "over 500" (U.S. Southern Command), to "656" (Panama's "official" human rights group), to "up to 800" (U.S. Embassy). However, an official from the Panamanian Housing Ministry who asked to remain anonymous out of fear told us that he believed that the first day of bombings alone had killed three thousand, primarily in the El Chorillo barrio. Panama's minister of presidency said, "We really do not know how many died in the invasion." But some estimates by human rights workers placed the death toll as high as five thousand. We visited three mass grave sites containing many dozens of skeletal remains. Witnesses confirmed that the U.S. had directed backhoes to dig trenches, then dumped truckloads of bodies into them.

We received several briefings on the rapid privatization of Panamanian society since the U.S. invasion. Panamanian airlines, water, electricity, ports and phone services were being privatized, while public welfare programs were being reduced. Condominiums and shopping malls for the wealthy were being constructed seemingly everywhere. Crime and drug use were reported to have dramatically increased, and we were warned not to venture anywhere near the El Chorillo barrio. When we told them we were staying on the edge of the barrio, they urged us to move to another location. Perhaps they were right. One evening eight members of our group were mugged as we walked through the rubble near our Daughters of Charity lodging to a meeting of homeless refugee groups discussing new housing plans. I was tackled by a young thug and we both fell hard to the ground. I suffered minor injuries while the tackler was knocked nearly unconscious. Another delegation member grabbed my walking stick and wielded it in such a way that the five other muggers fled.

The U.S. invasion had dramatically decreased the quality of life for the poorest Panamanians. Nor did they have any say in the new "democracy" the

U.S. forcefully put in place. The new puppet government was termed "completely docile," as it acted in deference to policies dictated by global corporations. It was described by many as being controlled on a day-to-day basis by the U.S. ambassador and the U.S. Southern Command. This was not Panama for the people, but Panama for the banks, corporations, and drug traffickers. In its second post–Viet Nam military operation (Grenada was first in 1983), the United States had succeeded, once again, in protecting its way of life while thwarting people's movements.

Iraq: Facing Conquest Firsthand

Of all the interventions undertaken by the United States during the late 1980s and early 1990s, none was as violent and full of double standards as the first Gulf War. In Central America, the United States had been able, for the most part, to work through proxies, using covert and overt military aid to overthrow unyielding governments and support our puppets. In Iraq, however, as in Panama, the United States faced a former ally "gone bad."

In August 1990, President George H.W. Bush declared that Iraq's August 1990 "naked aggression" against the Sheikdom of Kuwait was unacceptable. There had been numerous instances of "naked aggression" committed by one country against another in the Middle East, as well as elsewhere, that the U.S. never protested. The United States had supported Iraq's invasion of Iran under Saddam Hussein in 1980, including the use of poison gas against both the Iranians and the Kurds. The United States had no trouble with Israel's "naked aggression" against Lebanon in 1982 nor against the Palestinians, including the illegal occupation of their lands, the bulldozing of their homes, and the random killings of their people. Historically, the United States has shown itself more than willing to support "naked aggression" when the aggressor supports U.S. policy objectives and the American Way Of Life. Saddam Hussein's mistake was to attack Kuwait, a major supplier of U.S. oil and client of the U.S. defense industry.

I visited Iraq with a veterans' delegation in 1991, following the conclusion of Operation Desert Storm, the short hot war waged by George H.W. Bush against Iraq. We knew that we might not be welcomed by the people of Iraq. We imagined being stoned, perhaps charged with some kind of trumped-up crime, or possibly even killed by people in a rage. But we wanted to make a serious effort to go there and say we were sorry for what our government had done, that the attack was inflicted in our names but without our consent.

We left Jordan on September 29. After a 590-mile trip by van through the Syrian desert, we arrived at the Iraq border town of Trabiel at 3 a.m. on September 30. Traveling on Iraq superhighway 10 through the large western

Governorate of al-Anbar, we observed the remains of burned-out buses, cars, and trucks along the road. As we drove through the cities of Rutba, Ramadi, Habbaniya, and Fallujah, we witnessed the bombed and completely destroyed infant formula factory between Fallujah and Baghdad.

On the morning of October 1 in the lobby of our Baghdad hotel, while reading that day's edition of Iraq's only English-language newspaper, the *Baghdad Observer*, I was startled to see a front-page story about a bloody coup the day before that ousted President Jean-Bertrand Aristide from Haiti. In June, exactly 104 days earlier, I had been part of a five-person veterans' delegation to Haiti where the liberation theology priest Aristide's recent popular election had finally broken the decades-long cycle of terror in that country. Wherever we went in Haiti, throngs of people celebrated a freedom and hope they had never before experienced. During our meeting with Aristide, he reminded us that the U.S. had seriously attempted to thwart his election (including efforts of Jimmy Carter who, as a U.S.-sanctioned election observer, asked Aristide to drop out of the election). Despite these efforts, Aristide said, Haiti was not an enemy of the U.S. He urged us to do what we could to convince our country's leaders to respect Haiti's sovereignty.

Here we were in Iraq, assessing the damage of forty-three days of U.S bombing (one United Nations report concluded that the U.S. had bombed the country back into the Stone Age), and now we were learning of another likely U.S.-prompted intervention: the overthrow of a revolutionary government halfway around the world. I felt sick. Wherever one goes, one walks in the shadow of U.S. imperialism.

Later that day, we visited the destroyed Amiriya bomb shelter. One of twenty-two underground shelters in Baghdad, it was constructed with five to ten feet of reinforced concrete. The U.S. government claimed it was a Saddam military command bunker. In fact, the shelter was full of women and children from the middle-class neighborhood of Amiriya when it was hit by the first "smart" cruise missile at 4:30 a.m. on February 13, 1991, the second one striking seven minutes later. The local school was damaged, most of the neighborhood houses suffered broken windows and cracked walls and ceilings, and the shelter itself was destroyed. The estimates of people murdered ranged from 400 to 1,600.

When walking the neighborhood around the shelter, we saw many men and older boys sitting on their front porches, angry and depressed, dressed in black as if in petrified shock and mourning seven and a half months after the murders of the wives, mothers, sisters, daughters, and very young sons. We talked with a man from the neighborhood named Asam who had lost his wife and two daughters in the shelter. Asam told us that the men and boys had remained outside to make room for more women and children in the shelter. Almost every household in that neighborhood lost at least three family members, some as many as nine. At least ninety-seven infants were murdered in the blast.

As we walked and drove around Baghdad and beyond, we observed people struggling to walk, and realized that many were amputees. When we visited a large food market in Baghdad, a vendor described the forty-three consecutive days of bombing as the ultimate in terror. For about ten or twelve days, he said, Baghdad was bombed every three to five minutes, at least ten hours a day, from about 8 p.m. to 6 a.m. The March 1991 United Nations report of the impact of the war on Iraq, prepared by Under-Secretary-General Martti Ahtisaari, listed 2,500 homes destroyed in Baghdad alone.

The nation's electrical power grid and sewage system were both destroyed. Blocked pipes forced sewage onto the streets and into buildings and homes, while one million cubic meters of raw, untreated sewage were being discharged into the Tigris River every day. I later learned that the U.S. government *intentionally* used bombing, then sanctions, to degrade the country's water supply.[392] UNICEF reported in 2007 that the rate of children dying of water-borne illness continued to threaten the health of millions of Iraqi children as shortage of potable water hit the youngest hardest.[393] My government knew the health costs to civilian Iraqis, especially children, and went ahead with its criminal intent to cause large amounts of pain and suffering.

Visiting doctors at the Saddam Central Teaching Hospital, we learned about their new phenomena of malnourished mothers, and shortages of infant formula, supplemental milk, medicine, and clean water. Thousands of Iraqi children under two years of age were suffering and dying in epidemic proportions from malnourishment and gastroenteritis caused primarily by the economic sanctions imposed in August 1990 by the U.S.-driven United Nations. The death rate for children following the imposition of the sanctions both before and after the bombing of January–February 1991 was initially four times greater than what it had been in mid-1990. We witnessed dozens of mothers and children in this heart-wrenching situation, some in hospitals, some in their homes, and some along the streets.[394]

From Baghdad, we headed south on Highways 8 and 9, driving 350 miles to Basra, then another thirty-seven miles south to the Persian Gulf port city of Umm Qasr, the terminal point of the famous Baghdad Railway, or Orient Express. From Baghdad to Basra we traveled through more than a dozen Shiite cities, including Karbala, Najaf, Diwaniya, and Nasiriya, all of which suffered extensive damage from both bombings and voluminous small arms fire, some of which occurred during the failed insurrection that followed the

U.S. war. Open sewage could be seen flowing on the streets. Most bridges had been destroyed as had virtually all electric facilities and factories.

We interviewed employees who had worked at a destroyed electric power plant in Najbiya that required thousands of unavailable spare parts to become operational again. When the plant was bombed at noon on January 17, much of the employee housing located two blocks away was bombed as well. We learned that thirteen houses were totally destroyed with one bomb, killing forty-one people inside. We saw a lot of dirt and the dusty remains of a neighborhood. Learning we were from the United States, young kids pointed to the dirt and dust and, with focused anger, yelled, "Bush here," "Bush here," "Bush here!"

Next we visited the Basra Teaching Hospital and received a briefing from its director, Dr. Walid W.H. al-Rawi. The hospital was bombed at 7:30 a.m. on January 26. The huge bomb crater was very visible in the ground only a few feet outside the intensive care unit. Three patients in the unit were instantly killed. Pieces of bomb fragments the size of basketballs were rocketed through the outer walls of the intensive care unit. All windows in the entire hospital were broken, most ceilings collapsed, water pipes broken, and the oxygen supply disrupted.

While exploring the areas near the Kuwait border we heard stories of people being paid to collect and redeem the thousands of unexploded land mines buried in the sand, left over from the Iraq-Iran war as well as the recent U.S. ground invasion. We discovered a Norwegian-operated United Nations desert tent hospital on the border with Kuwait. Conversing with a Norwegian surgeon, we learned that during the three weeks prior to our visit the hospital had received over a hundred victims, from three to nine Iraqi civilian casualties per day, each suffering from one to three limb amputations caused by the explosion of antipersonnel mines.

We interviewed the most recent land-mine victims, three young Iraqi males, each with one or two fresh amputations. They told us they were being paid 25 to 35 Iraqi dinars (U.S. $3.10–4.40) for each land mine they turned in. The economic conditions in Iraq were so desperate that finding, safely removing, then redeeming these mines was about the only available income for the people of the desert. It was a chilling thought that each of their limbs could be valued at the price of a hamburger in the U.S.

Their legs and mine: this was the price of the American Way Of Life. Our bodies had stood in the way of the train of prosperity and progress, so our limbs were cut off. Here was the clear evidence, so often hidden from U.S. citizens by the media, of the brutally violent means by which we maintain our prosperity.

Israel/Palestine

Two years earlier, in April of 1989, I visited the Middle East on a trip to Israel/
Palestine sponsored by the Middle East Children's Alliance. We flew into
Tel Aviv to witness the First Intifada (Arabic for "shaking off" or "waking
up") of the 1.7 million Palestinians living in the West Bank and Gaza Strip
against Israel's illegal, forty-year brutal military occupation. It was depressing
to observe an attitude and policy that seemed to ensure ethnic cleansing. It
seemed to me that Zionists were now acting like the Nazi monsters who had
once tried to eliminate the Jewish people.

That First Intifada started in December 1987; by April 1989 it was clear
the uprising was going badly for the Palestinians. Approximately twenty-five
Palestinians were being killed for every Israeli killed. All Palestinian elementary and high schools had been closed since December 1987. Some twenty
thousand Palestinians had been incarcerated in Israeli prisons, including a
brand new facility in the West Bank city of Nablus reserved for children ten
to fifteen years of age, most of whom were imprisoned with virtually no due
process. Vast numbers of Palestinians lived in twenty-eight total camps surrounded by multiple chain-link and razor-wire fences, with the Israeli military posted at the entrances and around the perimeters.

One of the camps I visited was Jabaliya, north of Gaza City. The largest
of all the Palestinian camps, Jabaliya at that time held nearly sixty thousand
residents in two square kilometers (.85 square miles). As we walked through
a large open area on our way to visit a health clinic, we suddenly found ourselves in the middle of a confrontation between several hundred youth carrying the banned red, green, white, and black Palestinian flag at their head and
Israeli Defense Forces (IDF) riding shotgun on several armored personnel
carriers. A blue United Nations vehicle sped toward the scene in an attempt
to ward off any further trouble. However, tempers were flaring, the encounter became more intense, and the angry youth began hurling stones at the
equally angry Israeli soldiers. I moved quickly toward a low rock wall and
vaulted over it for protection. As the stones kept flying, the soldiers began
shooting. A teenage boy was shot dead, becoming one of the five hundred
Palestinian victims killed during the Intifada up to that time. We joined his
family in mourning the next day in their Jabaliya home.

Later on that trip, we spent a few hours in the Makassed Hospital in
Jerusalem, the only Palestinian hospital in the country. We visited forty
patients, all but a couple of them between the ages of eleven and nineteen.
Most had been shot in the back, ostensibly as they ran away from soldiers.
Nine had been shot in the head, several with rubber bullets—the bullets were
permanently embedded deep inside their brains, clearly visible on x-rays. All

had been paralyzed. These survivors would have to live with no rehab or resources available to them or their families for the rest of their lives. While we were there, a seventeen-year-old arrived in an ambulance. He had been shot in the back at the base of the neck and died a few hours later.

Two years later, in 1991, I helped organize a veterans' delegation and returned to Israel/Palestine. I revisited Makassed, where I was distressed to find more Palestinian youth paralyzed by Israeli bullets. I also returned to Jabaliya, in the Gaza Strip, where the residents still lived under siege. One evening, while enjoying a delicious Arab dinner with a Palestinian family, we noticed a key hanging in a prominent place on the wall. Someone asked about it and it was explained that the key was from the family's furnished house less than ten miles away—the house this family had fled from in 1948 during the Israeli military blitz that created a state for the Jewish people. Despite the requirements of international law, there has been no right of return for the Palestinian people.

As we were bedding down on a steaming hot night in a workroom not normally used for sleep, one of our veterans, Mark Birnbaum, a Jew, asked if the one visible wall vent could be opened for some fresh air. Our host family politely asked us to keep the vent closed, because on the other side of the wall was an alley regularly patrolled by Israeli soldiers throughout the night. If soldiers heard any noises such as snoring, sneezing, or voices speaking a language other than Arabic, they would become suspicious. Entertaining unwelcome visitors was a violation of the law under occupation. Suspected violations could bring a loud knock on the door, followed by a forced entry. Soldiers would search the premises, and there would be a good chance that the men of the house would be taken away indefinitely for imprisonment and torture. After hearing this shocking explanation, Mark sadly remarked that he now knew what it must have been like to be trapped in the Warsaw ghetto during World War II.

In nearby Rafah, I witnessed Palestinian women yelling and gesturing to other family members in Egypt, *permanently* cut off from each other by a strip of no man's land fifty to seventy-five yards wide preserved by high cyclone fences. The fences had been quickly erected in 1981 as a result of the 1978 U.S.-sponsored Camp David Accords which changed the actual boundary between Egypt and Gaza. Palestinian families suddenly found themselves divided. Since they do not possess passports, they are prohibited from travel to another "country," even if it is only fifty to seventy-five yards away, separated by barbed wire and armed Israeli patrols. Many of the same women, we were told, had been present everyday at the "Flat of Shouts" for the ten years since the fence was built. We discovered a similar "Flat of Shouts" in the Israeli-occupied Golan Heights along its "new" boundary with Syria. The Syrian orchardists, stuck with living under occupation, were prohibited from drilling for water for drinking or irrigation, so instead had constructed large rainwater collection tanks. However, we saw large gauges mounted on the side of each tank. These were required, we were told, by the Israeli government, which placed a heavy tax on rainwater collection.

We also went to the West Bank. At Nablus, I visited with Bassam Shaka, the Palestinian ex-mayor of Nablus. Sitting in a wheelchair with two leg stumps hanging over the seat, he greeted us with a big smile. Like me, Shaka had lost both legs due to his political activities, and we greeted each other with an extended heartfelt embrace. His legs had been blown up in an assassination attempt when a bomb exploded on July 2, 1980, as he entered his car outside the very home in which we sat. He had been the most prominent Palestinian politician in the occupied territories during the 1970s and '80s. The known Israeli perpetrators of the bombing that took his legs were never apprehended. Thus, his situation is very much like mine: we each knew who tried to kill us, who took our legs in the process, but the perpetrators were never prosecuted.

From Nablus, we drove to the city of Nazareth, where Jesus reportedly grew up. There we visited the remains of a Palestinian house that had been dynamited only two weeks earlier just because one member of the family was suspected of organizers against the illegal Israeli occupiers.

When Mark, our videographer, and I went to Ramallah, we happened to witness several Israeli Defense Force soldiers beating up two young Palestinian boys on a side street. We thought we were protected from view by several thick bushes, but one of the soldiers spotted a reflection off Mark's camera lens and rushed over to see what it was. We were apprehended and taken to the Ramallah jail where Mark refused to hand over any of his tape. The law of Israeli occupation prohibits taking photos or filming of any of its soldiers. We waited in a makeshift cell for a couple of hours while the officials sent for an English-speaking Israeli intelligence officer. Once the officer arrived, he again asked for the footage. Mark again refused, identifying himself as a Jewish U.S. citizen and a Viet Nam veteran to boot. The angry Israeli captain was incredulous, but clearly realized that an international incident could result from forcibly taking footage from a Jewish U.S. journalist. After a couple more hours we were released to our fellow delegation members who were waiting outside the prison gate. We walked away to spend another day studying life under the occupation.

The worst part of that trip, for me, happened during our visit to East Jerusalem. While sitting in a Palestinian cafe, I noticed three Israeli soldiers stopping two young boys who were walking on a plaza across the narrow street, about fifty feet from where I was sitting. The soldiers began questioning the boys, a typical scene. But then the scene turned ugly. Two of the soldiers grabbed one of the boys and began shoving what appeared to be a small tree branch down his throat. The boy was drooling and gagging, bent over double. I felt sick as I watched this and I asked the Palestinian cafe owner what on earth they were doing. The cafe owner told me this was one of the methods the soldiers use to humiliate "Arabs," to keep them in their place. It was a measure of how arrogant the Israeli soldiers could be in their role of maintaining the occupation, knowing they could do almost anything without fear of punishment.

It was clear that the Israelis applied a policy of systematic terror to enforce occupation, an unfortunately typical practice when one group controls another. It was not uncommon to witness or hear testimony about on-the-spot beatings of Palestinians from rifle butts and police clubs. We also heard stories of the Israeli forces extracting "confessions" through torture. I believed them, after what I had seen.

I heard these stories during many evenings spent talking with Palestinians. I remember one night particularly well. It was the night before we left to go back home. We were at the Dheisheh Camp near Bethlehem, and the youth there were fascinated by my two stumps, which I had taken out of the prosthetics and let dangle over the back of a chair. Almost everyone I met had been wounded at one time or another or were currently nursing wounds, so they could easily relate to my now "deformed" body. We conversed about life in the United States and Palestine, politics, revolution, and the history of struggle. An eighteen-year-old boy, wanted by the soldiers, risked capture to meet me, maneuvering through alleys with his thirteen-year-old sister serving as a lookout. The youth wanted to know about my meetings with Daniel Ortega, whether I thought fascism was making a comeback, and if I had read Jack London's *The Iron Heel* (1908), which describes how a fascist state can quickly arise out of capitalism, a warning penned four decades before Orwell's *Nineteen Eighty-Four* (1949). We got almost no sleep that night, but I was animated by the spirit of these Palestinian youth.

There were also, I should add, some hopeful signs on the Israeli side. During our trip we had traveled to Mount Carmel to visit with dozens of Israeli peaceniks who were expressing solidarity with the Israeli Army refuseniks imprisoned in nearby Athlit prison, members of Yesh G'vul ("there is a limit"). Yesh G'vul is a group of Israeli soldiers who refuse military service as a matter of principle in the Palestinian occupied territories of the West Bank and Gaza Strip. Still, many of the Israeli people seemed, at best, resigned to the attacks by their government on the Palestinian people, or, at worst, wholly supportive.

I was appalled that a so-called democracy would be engaged in an occupation this diabolical, and even more so that the United States was—and is—substantially subsidizing this occupation, egregiously violating numerous international laws and human rights standards. The human rights abuses were as severe as anything I had witnessed in El Salvador and, though I had not been to South Africa, it was and remains just as tyrannical a regime as apartheid. Some estimates indicate the amount of U.S. aid given to Israel is so staggering that the average Israeli citizen annually receives more U.S. federal aid than the United States gives its own average citizen.

Nicaragua in Trouble

Throughout my travels, I continued to pay close attention to Nicaragua. In January 1988, Phil Roettinger joined Dan Ellsberg, Ed Asner, myself, and others in an eleven-day water fast against Contra aid on the east steps of the Capitol, the same location as our 1986 veterans fast. I returned to Nicaragua many times during 1988 and 1989 for meetings with NGOs and to mark the progress of the revolution.

New elections were scheduled for Nicaragua in February 1990, having been moved up from November 1990, a good faith effort of the Sandinistas to comply with the Tela Accords signed on August 7, 1989, by the six Central American presidents in the Honduran port of the same name. At a time when U.S. belligerence seemed never-ending, it was refreshing to observe the Sandinistas working hard to create peace and end the war of terror being waged against them.

According to the Tela Accords, the Contras were required to demobilize no later than December 5, 1989. However, despite making many promises, the Contras continued to escalate their attacks right up until election day on February 25, 1990, with the support of overt and covert U.S. funding. Indeed, during his Senate confirmation hearings in January 1989, soon-to-be U.S. Secretary of State James Baker testified that covert actions in Nicaragua "would not be inappropriate" including "covert support for a political party or candidate to influence the outcome of another's elections."[395] In early November, the New York Times reported four ways the U.S. was violating Tela: making sure the Contras remained as a fighting force in Nicaragua; handing out up to $200,000 cash every month to Contras inside Nicaragua; being aware of the Contras' continued human rights violations and not reporting them; and urging the Contras to commit egregious attacks hoping they would provoke President Ortega to do something "intemperate."[396]

In addition to funding the Contras during this period, the United States poured almost $50 million into the election campaign against the Sandinistas—this in a country with only 3.5 million people. That would be the equivalent of *another* country spending $3.5 billion on a U.S. election campaign. The Sandinistas were being opposed by UNO (United Nicaragua Opposition), an alliance of fourteen smaller parties, led by U.S.-selected Violeta Chamorro, an opposition completely directed and financed by the United States, including millions of CIA funds spent between 1984 and 1989. In addition, the National Endowment for Democracy (NED), in effect a CIA-like agency designed to influence elections and political "happenings" in other countries, spent anywhere from $12–18 million between 1984 and 1990 in support of UNO and an opposition newspaper. All these expenditures, plus others, are well documented.[397]

When Charlie Liteky, Jack Ryan, Bob Spitzer, and I traveled through Nicaragua in December 1989 after the mandated December 5 deadline for completion of Contra demobilization, we witnessed first-hand the continuation of Contra terrorist activities. We saw the immediate aftermath of destruction of a cooperative including the murders of several of its members, and the ambush of a public transport that killed or wounded over twenty civilians. Bands of Contras continued to roam in many areas, which actually prevented our intended travel due to increased danger, and U.S. planes continued to make regular reconnaissance flights over the country, providing the Contras with detailed intelligence on specific positions of Nicaraguan army units and campesinos targeted as local Sandinista leaders.[398]

While in the Department of Nueva Segovia near the Honduran border, we decided to investigate the October 29, 1988, ambush site of the El Carmen state coffee farm truck, which had been traveling to San Juan del Rio Coco, a few miles west of the city of Quilali. Dora Lopéz, six months pregnant, cradling her ten-month-old son Marlon while holding the hand of her five-year-old son Erick, was among the twenty-two passengers. After rounding a curve the truck was ambushed by about a dozen Contras with rocket propelled grenades and automatic weapons blazing, and subsequently crashed into a roadside ditch, now marked by a cross with flowers. Over 120 bullet holes were found in the truck body. Apparently at least one rocket-propelled grenade hit the truck as well. According to an area resident whose cousin was murdered in the ambush, a total of eighteen people were killed immediately, or soon died of their injuries. The four survivors included Dora Lopéz and her son, Erick Cano Lopéz. Dora's baby son Marlon died a few days later from shrapnel wounds to his young skull.

This attack had occurred despite the Sapoa Accords signed in March 1988 calling for a cease-fire agreement. This was one of many Contra ambushes that had continued all over the country following those accords, several on this very road. This particular site was on a well-traveled Contra infiltration trail from Honduras through eastern Nueva Segovia that intersected with this road. We found what looked like a large foxhole a few meters off the road. Contras regularly used trip wire mines funded by the U.S., M-79 grenade launchers firing 40 mm grenade shells, and automatic weapons. The site was south of an area along the Honduran border where twelve to fifteen Contra camps were concentrated, housing several thousand members of Contra terrorist bands and their families.

When Holley and I visited Dora for the very first time in the Managua hospital three days after the ambush, the doctors sheepishly asked Holley, who spoke Spanish, if she would inform Dora of the tragic news that her leg was about to be amputated, that her fetus had perished, and that her ten-month-old Marlon had just died. Holley and I were fresh from visiting Erick and Marlon at a nearby children's hospital when we learned of Marlon's death. Holley tightly held one of Dora's hands as she conveyed these three terrible pieces of news. Dora screamed in grief and I wept with her.

Holley and I later arranged for Dora and Erick to fly to San Francisco to be treated at Shriners Hospital for several rounds of surgery. Erick had been struck by a bullet through his right cheek and needed reconstructive facial surgery including an operation to save his tear ducts. Another bullet destroyed his right shoulder's growth center, which meant he would have a permanently withered right arm. Dora lost her left leg at the hip due to a gangrene infection from several bullet wounds. She lost her left eye to shrapnel, and her six-month-old fetus from bullet wound poisoning.

When Dora and Erick came to San Francisco for their respective surgeries, they lived with Holley and me. As serendipity would have it, one day when Erick and I were home alone playing checkers, the doorbell rang. I was in my wheelchair, so I rolled to the front door with Erick at my side. It was Mr. Kaminsky, the IRS agent who was in charge of my tax refuser case. I told Kaminsky that it was a perfect time for him to be visiting because I wanted him to meet Erick who had been seriously injured as a direct result of the U.S. taxpayer money the Reagan administration had used to buy automatic weapons and bullets for the Contras. I asked Erick, whose English had become conversational, to describe the ambush. He told Kaminsky that after the truck crashed into the ditch "everybody was hit by bullets and blood was everywhere, people screaming." Then he explained that he and his mother and baby brother, who were standing in the truck next to the tailgate, had been knocked out of the truck to the ground after the bullets hit them, and "his mother crawled with him and his baby brother further down the ditch and played dead" as the Contras looked for survivors. I reminded Kaminsky that Dora and Erick were two of only four survivors of the twenty-two people in the truck and told him, as I had before, that I could not sign any agreement to make any payments to the U.S. government whose policy was murdering and impoverishing people all over the world. Kaminsky showed no emotional response to Erick's revelations. He only said, as he finally turned and walked away, "I'll see you in court."

Empire Triumphant

In an editorial piece published in the *Boston Globe* on March 4, 1990, Noam Chomsky summarized the situation facing the campesinos quite well:

> Suppose that some power of unimaginable strength were to threaten to reduce the United States to the level of Ethiopia unless we voted for its candidates, demonstrating that the threat was real. Suppose that we refused, and the threat was then carried out, the country brought to its knees, the economy wrecked and millions killed. Suppose, finally, that the threat was repeated, loud and clear, at the time of the next scheduled elections. Under such conditions, only a hypocrite would speak of a free election. Furthermore, it is likely that close to 100% of the population would succumb. Apart from the last sentence, I have just described U.S.-Nicaraguan relations for the last decade.

In addition to pouring money into funding political opposition to the Sandinistas, the Bush administration told the Nicaraguan people that if they didn't vote for Chamorro, the embargo begun by Reagan would continue and banks would not lend the country money.

U.S. citizens are conditioned to think of institutions like the IMF and the World Bank as benevolent dispensers of wealth to impoverished nations. However, these U.S.-controlled institutions use money as a hammer to beat other nations into submission. The United States, through its own banks, typically loans countries huge amounts of money to pay for "infrastructure" the country either does not need or that will only benefit wealthy private corporations by subsidizing export crops and products. The loan is contingent upon allowing those corporations to exploit the country's resources ("the free market").

By 1987, the Nicaraguan economy had collapsed, with inflation having risen over 1,000 percent and food shortages common.[399] Workers were making only about $10/month, and the country was surviving only due to Soviet aid. The Nicaraguan currency was almost worthless in international markets.

The cost of fighting the Contras made it impossible for the Sandinistas to correct their economy. In 1987, war accounted for 18.2 percent of Nicaragua's Gross Domestic Product (GDP).[400] Moreover, the Contras targeted health centers, agricultural cooperatives and schools, the infrastructure that the Sandinistas had spent their scarce money to create. By the end of 1985, even though the Sandinistas had prioritized health care, 10 percent of the population lost access to that care because of Contra bombing and terror attacks.

Elections finally took place in Nicaragua on February 25, 1990. Violeta Chamorro, the candidate of UNO, handily won 55 percent of the vote with Daniel Ortega's receiving only 41 percent. That vote in effect ended the revolution, though remnants of *Sandinismo* remained deep within Nicaragua society.

When we heard the devastating news of the Sandinista election defeat on the morning of February 26, Holley, the nine other members of our election delegation, and I were sitting at a long outdoor table in Puerto Cabezas on the Atlantic Coast. We had been serving as official election observers in several small Miskito villages, including Krukira and Taupi, a half-hour drive from Puerto Cabezas, as well as Puerto Cabezas itself. I will say that the mechanical process of the election, at least the part that I observed, was fair. Without electricity, using only the light of candles, poll officials hand-counted ballots until one in the morning under the watchful eyes of numerous observers from each political party as well as internationalistas like myself. Looking back, however, I feel that the election cannot be called fair given the context of the active terror war being waged against the campesinos throughout Nicaragua. I carry some guilt that I helped to legitimize an election that took place in that atmosphere.

At the time, though, I was caught up in the excitement of the revolution and didn't understand the extent to which the people had been exhausted by ten years of war. I hadn't expected the Sandinistas to lose and it came as a real shock. As we had driven over 220 miles on the long road from Matagalpa to Puerto Cabezas in a large cattle truck to our observer location, *every* bridge had been blown up or otherwise destroyed by the Contras. From the cab of our truck I watched our experienced driver ford fifty-seven streams and rivers, knowing precisely where to steer the wheels as we crossed each bridgeless waterway. It was understandable that the people had simply voted to end the terror. The day after the election, a Sandinista Air Force helicopter flew our eleven-member delegation the 240 air miles back to Managua.

I've never regretted my support of the Sandinista revolution. Life is a process, and one makes decisions and takes steps based on what one feels is right at the moment. I believe the Sandinistas embodied a radical spiritual change experienced in the hearts and minds of the Nicaraguan people, and in people elsewhere. Even though that spirit has been repressed by capitalism, I think it invariably lives on in people's hearts and dreams.

I had a difficult time immediately after the election. I was mourning the end of the revolution. As Holley and I were flying home from Nicaragua in early March, I wondered whether I would ever return. The man sitting behind us was the Sandinista representative to Europe for the banana trade. He tapped me on the shoulder and asked, "Isn't it a pity that the United States wouldn't let our flower bloom?" to which I just burst out in tears.

Addendum

After losing elections in 1996 and 2001, Daniel Ortega won the presidential campaign in 2006 with 38 percent of the vote, thereby reclaiming the executive power he had so desperately sought since losing in 1990. However, by that time he was no longer a revolutionary. He agreed to controversial constitutional changes with Arnoldo Alemán, a former corrupt conservative president who had worked with Somoza before the revolution. At the time of the 2006 election, Alemán was serving a prison sentence for criminal misconduct while in office. Ortega's pact with Alemán included a change in the country's election procedures making it possible for a candidate to win in the first round with only 35 percent of the vote, while assuring a shorter prison sentence for Alemán.

Ortega also made deals with various political adversaries that included members of the old land-owning Somoza families and the Contras. He shocked many of his liberation theology supporters when he embraced the reactionary, hierarchical Catholic Church that had supported the Contras. He then supported the repeal of a century-old law permitting therapeutic abortion, joining El Salvador and Chile as the only Latin American countries with such a cruel, reactionary law prohibiting all abortions. And Ortega disappointed many with his support of the Central American Free Trade Agreement (CAFTA) and his embrace of the free market with its associated tax breaks for corporations and privatization of public utilities. These compromises have made Ortega a ghost of his former courageous, visionary self.

PART VII

Steady State

CHAPTER 27

Cuba—A Special Case

Afterthe fall of the Sandinista government in 1990, I became much more interested in the success of the Cuban Revolution. Cuba, as a country, presents us with a painfully instructive example of the paradigm of U.S. imperialism, what U.S. historian William Appleman Williams describes as the "tragedy of American diplomacy." Empire intervenes, then exploits, and finally imposes counterrevolution against the people's response to their exploitation.[401] The difference in Cuba is that the people, under the leadership of Fidel Castro, succeeded in establishing a revolutionary government explicitly in opposition to the American Way Of Life.

We don't hear much about Cuba's success in the United States, because it flies in the face of the American Way Of Life, but after the collapse of the Soviet Union, Cuba discovered a third way, enabling it to continue its revolutionary experiment. Out of necessity, Cuba created a kind of bioregional island sufficiency within a vertical structure, different from either the no-limits, oppressive capitalism of the United States, or the repressive bureaucratic industrial state-run economy, often referred to as socialism, of its former partner Russia. It is an informative model that begs careful examination.

The successes of the Cuban Revolution have been astonishing. After nearly a century of slave-like existence in the service of corporations from the north, Castro offered the Cuban people agrarian reform that would redistribute large tracts of land to the poor; new roads, schools and hospitals; homes at affordable rates; affordable phone and electric service for everyone; national health care; and education for all. In the first ten years of the revolution, the number of elementary schools skyrocketed from about six hundred to nearly fifteen thousand. The number of high school students went from nearly 64,000 to 186,000, and the number of teachers from 22,000 to 69,000.[402]

Today, in Cuba, every person has enough food to eat, even if sometimes it is skimpy, a house to live in, and clothes to wear. Literacy is at 96 percent and the education system is considered the best in Latin America. Excellent health care is free and available to all, even to those who come to Cuba simply to take advantage of their health care system. No wonder Cuba has become an international example of the power of a people's revolution.

I wanted to learn how Cuba had succeeded. I started by looking backward since I now knew that to understand a country's present I had to start with its past. I read a lot of Cuban history, particularly as it related to the Bay of Pigs and U.S. involvement. In the 1980s, while I was working to oppose U.S. policy of terrorist aggression against sovereign Nicaragua, I had often met people who had participated in the Venceremos Brigade, which had been sending people to Cuba since 1969 to harvest sugar and show solidarity with the Cuban Revolution. Phil Roettinger had gone to Cuba, and as ex-CIA, knew a lot about what was happening there. Over time, I met other ex-CIA agents who were familiar with U.S. attempts to overthrow Cuba, including Ralph McGhee and Phil Agee.

Finally, forty-two years after my interest in Cuba was aroused by my hatred for the 1959 revolution while a senior in high school, I traveled to Cuba with my brother Dwight, ex-FBI agent Jack Ryan, and several others. We arrived in June 1991, during Cuba's "Special Period," its most difficult economic time since the revolution of 1959.

By 1991, the USSR had collapsed, and had to withdraw practically all of its considerable support from Cuba, including subsidized oil imports and shipments of food and medical supplies. Meanwhile, the U.S. embargo, imposed since 1961, was being strengthened even more by new U.S. laws punishing third-party countries that chose to trade with the island. Cuba suddenly lost more than half of its oil. Imports of grains for human consumption were reduced by more than 50 percent, and foodstuffs were reduced by as much as 80 percent. Farmers had little fuel for tractors, and little or no fertilizers and pesticides. Soon Cubans caloric and protein intake dropped 30 percent, causing the average adult Cuban to lose thirty pounds.[403] It appeared the country might starve to death.

Despite this extreme hardship, Cuba offered me the most encouragement of all the places to which I traveled during 1991 and 1992. You could feel the Cuban people's gritty determination to survive and absolute refusal to "cry uncle." The majority of Cubans did not want to revert to the quasi-feudal society that had existed before the revolution. The majority recognized the myth that is the American Way Of Life, and refused to buy into a fundamentally unfair system in which prosperity is acquired by violence against others and guided by selfishness. Instead, they hunkered down, prepared to survive through sacrifice and frugality.

Also, throughout this difficult period, Cuba generously continued to support people's revolutions elsewhere. At the "July 26 Camp" we visited outside of Havana, Cuban doctors enthusiastically provided free care and rehabilitation to more than 300 injured Salvadoran guerrillas, 160 of whom were amputees. I, of course, immediately related to their situation and their long road of rehabilitation. One of the young soldiers, a male teenager with arms amputated at each elbow, was painting a beautiful picture by holding a paint brush between the ends of his elbows. Painted on the wall outside of the camp's cultural center was a mural of FMLN Comandante Dimas Rodríguez—the same Dimas who had given me an FMLN guerrilla daypack—who remained an inspiration to Salvadoran revolutionaries after he was killed in the November 1989 offensive in San Salvador.

We also visited the incredible "Chernobyl Village" where a thousand Soviet children up to the age of sixteen were being treated for radiation-related sickness, including cancers, caused by the April 1986 Chernobyl nuclear reactor disaster in Ukraine. Many of the children were accompanied by their mothers. By that time, six thousand Soviet children had been treated there, and thousands more since—all free of charge. The Cubans were experiencing terrible hardships, but their commitment to provide medical care for all in need was unwavering, an example of the universal medical care that has been one of the many success stories of the Cuban Revolution. During the early years of the revolution, Cuba had only one doctor for every 2,000 people; as of 2007, it had one doctor for every 155 citizens! In 2008, tiny Cuba with a population of 11 million had more than 38,000 physicians and health care professionals serving in seventy-five countries around the world, far more than are made available by the World Health Organization (WHO).[404]

Cuba also provides free training to future doctors from around the world, including those from the United States, at its medical schools on the condition that upon graduation they will serve the poor for a period of time.

Day care shares almost equal importance with health care. Universal day care for all families was maintained even throughout the Special Period. In 1991, we visited the International Year of Women Daycare Center near Havana where full-time staff work with more than a hundred deaf and hearing-impaired children. All families in Cuba, then and now, have access to staffed day care.

Despite continuing initiatives like universal health care and day care, however, Castro and his government advisers quickly realized that Cuba could not continue as it had during its Soviet period. With Soviet support—and oil—withdrawn, they would have to rethink the Cuban economy. It was time for the development of a "third way"—a way of living based neither on capitalism nor a high-tech, petroleum-based, state-run economy, often referred to as socialism. It was time to embark upon a national social program of self-sustainability and economic autonomy.

Cuba's Third Way

Though it clouded Cuba's short-term economical forecast, the Soviet collapse proved to have a silver lining over time. It forced the Cuban people and their government to understand the importance of self-sufficiency. The earth ultimately won't survive unless all of us live within our means and limit our own footprints, only consuming what we ourselves can grow locally or make or trade regionally. In the United States, we've been able to avoid living that way by stealing the lands and resources of others, and by plundering the earth's finite ecosystem.

When faced with the loss of Soviet oil, Cuba's first decision was to replace oil-consuming cars, whenever possible, with more sustainable transportation. The answer was bicycles. The week we were there in 1991, Cuba received a large shipment of thousands of bicycles. Now Cuba has built its own bicycle factories, and bicycles have become a major mode of transportation.[405]

Similarly, Castro's government observed that fuel-guzzling tractors and farm equipment could be replaced with teams of oxen, which had been used traditionally by Cuban farmers. According to the Cuba Organic Support Group in the United Kingdom, up to three hundred thousand teams of oxen were employed on the island in 2000, with numbers still rising.[406] In 2009, President Raúl Castro reiterated Cuba's commitment to use oxen to increase food sufficiency while conserving energy.[407] "Old-fashioned" technology was coupled to a serious investment in "green" technology. Cuba has plans to be completely solar by 2020, is now producing its own solar panels, and is beginning by solarizing schools throughout rural areas[408] By 2006, nearly 2,400 rural primary schools had been electrified with photovoltaic panels.[409] Through both old and new measures, Cuba has managed, in just over fifteen years, to reduce its energy consumption by 50 percent!

Cuba is the first country to successfully address peak oil. How has it done so? By contraction, localization, and conservation. Contraction was forced upon Cuba when, between the collapse of the Soviet Union and the continued embargo by the United States, the island nation lost the majority of its trading partners. Without access to many foreign goods, Cuba had to redefine its needs. For example, instead of using foreign-produced herbicides and petroleum-derived fertilizers, Cuba transitioned to organic and natural food growing systems. Farmers learned how to use biological pest controls, reinstituted traditional methods of plant rotation and intercropping, and emphasized composting. The oxen not only replaced petroleum tractors, but provide a natural source of nitrogen-rich fertilizer.

Cuba also survived its economic crisis by localizing production as much as possible. By decentralizing farming and setting up produce markets in local neighborhoods, the country saved on the tremendous amount of petroleum needed to move food from farmer to market. Community gardens were planted in every usable space within the cities utilizing raised beds. By 1995 there were thirty thousand community organic gardens in Havana alone, with more than a million across the country.[410]

Cuba conserves energy by asking its people to rely upon each other. For example, if folks need to get somewhere, they line up in designated spots, and vehicles going in that direction are required to pick up passengers. This policy has been in place since the Special Period of the early 1990s. The sense of community has been strengthened by Cubans' reliance on each other for transportation and other needs.

Cuba is often looked to by other poor nations as a model for political change, but what Cuba really offers is a model for lifestyle change. The first country to face a serious peak oil crisis, the *WWF Living Planet Report 2006* reveals that Cuba is the only country in the world approaching sustainability by achieving both a Human Development Index (HDI) higher than .80 (Cuba's is .82) and an Ecological Footprint (EF) of energy consumed per year of less than 1.8 hectares/person (Cuba's is 1.5)![411]

Think of that for a moment. No other country has both a Human Development Index of more than .80 (a U.N. formula for "high human development" based on life expectancy, literacy, and educational attainment) *and* an Ecological Footprint lower than 1.8 global hectares per person per year, the average biocapacity *available* per person on the planet. Though the United States enjoys an HDI of .94, the average person in the United States possesses a consumption index of 9.6 hectares per year, more than five times a sustainable rate. The world average is 2.23 hectares consumed per person per year, already 25 percent over the earth's capacity.

In my efforts to determine my own footprint after a period of several years of no flying in airplanes, buying more and more local food, cycling instead of driving for local travel, generating substantial solar electricity, I am still over the 1.8 target. Simplification is a process of extricating one's self from layers and layers of habits and unexamined assumptions. Consciousness enables us to be more engaged in taking personal responsibility for the consequences of every choice.

Return to Cuba

Nine years after my first visit, my partner Becky and I decided to return to Cuba. For me, it was extraordinarily revealing to see how Cuba had survived the Special Period of 1990–1994. We went to every province in Cuba except far eastern Guantánamo, and talked freely with people on the street as well as with some government officials. What struck me most, in our first days in Havana, was to see people talking to each other in parks, all day long. They talk about everything from baseball to politics. There was a real open, community feeling on the streets.

Life there can be difficult. At the time of our visit a painful dual economy was evident: a tourist economy in U.S. dollars and a local economy in Cuban pesos. Many people still don't have the variety and amount of food, or all the material goods they would like. The U.S. embargo continues to make it difficult for Cuba to acquire many of its needs through trade or loans.

The U.S. government also continues to agitate for the overthrow of the Cuban government. These intentions are openly, shamelessly expressed, and have been accompanied for nearly fifty years by countless instances of sabotage initiated or sanctioned by the United States. As a result, Cuba has necessarily been required to take very seriously the creation of a well-developed security infrastructure to counter the threat from its large, dangerous neighbor.

The continued threats from the United States have severely impeded Cuba from developing political autonomy for its people. Cuba has signs of local political autonomy: for example, issues directly affecting people locally are discussed in neighborhood groups called Committees for the Defense of the Revolution. The outcome of these meetings is then passed up to the 601-member National Assembly of People's Power, whose members are directly elected by secret ballot every five years. Yet ultimate power in Cuba rests in the hands of the country's leader, Fidel (and now Raúl) Castro, and a small cadre of state officials.

Politicians in the United States love to contrast our "open" political system with Cuba's dictatorship. From my perspective, we have a one-party system here (albeit with two right wings) whose job it is to preserve our version of a vertical authority structure—monopoly capitalism dependent upon expansion. Without doubt, the national government of Cuba suppresses criticism and dissent. But the history of suppression of *effective* dissent in the United States and the de facto censorship of factual history is so complete that we cannot presume to judge other nations' behaviors. Political philosopher Sheldon Wolin describes the United States as an inverted totalitarian state, a "democracy incorporated" where corporations dominate the entire political process while its majority apathetic citizenry seem deluded in their democratic exceptionalism.[412]

Essayist John Ralston Saul similarly describes the U.S. as dominated by corporatism, a foundation for fascism.[413]

For over four decades, the United States has worked covertly and overtly to plant antigovernment forces within Cuba. In the 1960s and 1970s the U.S. orchestrated hundreds of bombings of parts of Cuba and has hatched hundreds of plots to assassinate Castro. The security threat to Cuba is extraordinarily real. Who knows what would happen if the United States would just leave Cuba alone? Perhaps if the U.S. threat were to disappear, the national government might relax repression that up until now has been so important for preserving Cuba's national security.

When visiting in 1991 we saw many signs of Cuba's communal spirit. This was a difficult economic period for the country, so many government officials took ministerial breaks to work in agricultural positions to increase food production. We visited a farm where officials from the foreign ministry were taking their turns living and working for two weeks. It makes a community of each, for each, truly seem possible.

Capacity for Change

Seeing Cuba in 1991 and again in 2000 convinced me that we do have the capacity to change how we live, individually and collectively, if we can only recover the fundamental autonomy that is part of our evolutionary human condition. We are genetically capable and designed to do whatever is necessary to survive. It is important to recognize that these cooperative, empathic, archetypal human characteristics reside deeply within us.

Human beings can effect change through principled action. As a twenty-one-year-old student, Fidel Castro could see that the repression and class divisions in his country weren't right and he responded. During apartheid, Steve Biko refused to give the South African police any names of fellow ANC revolutionaries, and was murdered by them for his noncooperation. Bobby Sands and his comrades fasted to death in an Irish prison for the right and dignity of correctly being identified as political prisoners rather than common criminals.

Living is about dignity, not longevity. Embracing this simple truth makes it easier to choose a new, more vibrant life for ourselves and the planet.

Castro's journey from wealthy son to revolutionary, then to a leader in the sustainability movement, reminds me of Peter Kropotkin's (1842–1921) journey. Kropotkin renounced his privileged position with the Russian Czar's Military Corp to study biology, geography, and anthropology in the vast unknown regions of Siberia. The outcome of that study was his masterful long view of human evolution, *Mutual Aid: A Factor of Evolution* (1902). This work ultimately prepared a scientific foundation for anarchism by demonstrating that mutual aid—voluntary cooperation—is a much stronger tendency in human evolution than aggression and domination. His words bear repeating. He begins his treatise by stating:

> [I]t is not love and not even sympathy upon which Society is based in mankind. It is the conscience—be it only at the stage of an instinct—of human solidarity. It is the unconscious recognition of the force that is borrowed by each man from the practice of mutual aid; of the close dependency of every one's happiness upon the happiness of all; and of the sense of justice, or equity, which brings the individual to consider the rights of every other individual as equal to his own.[414]

Kropotkin concludes his book by declaring that "in the ethical progress of man, mutual support—not mutual struggle—has had the leading part."[415] Here is evidence that we are all intimately related, even at the molecular level, imbedded deeply in our ancient mind-body mechanisms. To realize this truth and act upon it enables us to discover the strength and wisdom to liberate ourselves from complicity with our nation's deep ideological and imperial insanity.

Castro, I think, understood this basic theme, even if his own ego sometimes demonstrated arrogance. He and the Cuban revolutionaries were never interested in empire—it is the United States, not Cuba, that wants to control the world. Castro was interested in empowering poor people to overthrow a feudal system, and to create a human system in which people would have enough to eat, a place to live, health care and an education. A human social system is sustainable when a community recognizes that it must live within the limits of the carrying capacity of the bioregion in which it is located, and consumes only what can be grown or made within its bioregion or easily traded with neighboring bioregions. Everyone genuinely knows and cares about each other, because everyone's well-being is dependent upon the well-being of all.

A STORY OF EMPIRE

Cuba was one of the lands subjected to the original Hemispheric Euro-American holocaust of 1492, when Christopher Columbus invaded the island. Within fifty years, Cuba's one hundred thousand Indigenous Tainos had been virtually eliminated by fire, slaughter and disease, a genocide paralleling the massive elimination of humans in nearby Haiti.[416]

Over the next several centuries, Cuba was repopulated by the Spanish. However, in the very first years of the new U.S. republic, its political and commercial "leaders" were expressing their desire for a Caribbean outpost. Benjamin Franklin linked U.S. prosperity to expansion, especially southward toward Florida and what was then called the West Indies.[417] Thomas Jefferson wrote in

1786 that "our confederacy must be viewed as the nest from which all America, North and South, is to be peopled."[418] And John Quincy Adams stressed that since Cuba was "almost in sight of our shores" it should become U.S. territory.[419]

In 1808 President Jefferson sent a military officer to Cuba to ask the Spanish to cede Cuba to the United States. In 1809 Jefferson wrote his successor, James Madison, that the acquisition of Cuba would enable "control over the Gulf of Mexico and the countries and isthmus bordering it." In 1823, Jefferson reminded President Monroe, that "Cuba's addition to our confederacy is exactly what is wanting to round out our power."[420] Secretary of State John Quincy Adams in 1823 wrote to the U.S. minister to Spain describing the likelihood of U.S. "annexation of Cuba." Henry Clay, the secretary of state in 1824 under new president John Quincy Adams, wrote the U.S. minister to Spain emphasizing Cuba's "connection with the prosperity of the United States."[421]

In 1854, President Franklin Pierce, in the confidential Ostend Manifesto, declared Cuba indispensable for the security of slavery, recommending that the U.S. make every effort to purchase Cuba from Spain, and if the latter refused, "then by every law human and divine, we shall be justified in wresting it."[422] In 1858 President James Buchanan agreed, saying of Cuba, "Whilst the possession of the island would be of vast importance to the United States, its value to Spain is comparatively unimportant."[423]

While U.S. politicians contemplated acquiring Cuba from Spain, U.S. investors were already profiting from Cuba's sugar and other harvests. U.S. trade with Cuba became larger than trade with all the rest of Latin America. The Spanish provincial government ran the country practically as a fiefdom,[424] allowing Cuba's sugar industry to become a virtual foreign enterprise—with foreign capital, foreign machinery, and often with foreign workers.[425]

Cubans resisted. The second Cuban war for independence from Spain, 1895–1898 (the first occurred 1868–1878) destroyed much of this feudal infrastructure. The Cuban people sought independence but, just as the sixty-thousand-strong Cuban revolutionary forces were on the verge of defeating the two hundred thousand Spanish occupying troops, the U.S. declared war on Spain and invaded Cuba in efforts to preserve its $50 million investment.[426] Cubans mistakenly believed the U.S. had come to assist its liberation.

After coveting Cuba for more than a century, the United States finally controlled it. Cuban rebels were furious when the U.S. flag was hoisted in Havana on January 1, 1899. Free of Spanish rule thanks mostly to their own valiant, exhausting efforts, they had been betrayed by the United States. The Platt Amendment (to the 1902 U.S. Army Appropriations Act) forced upon Cubans the option of either being a de facto "protectorate" owned by U.S. corporations, or being annexed altogether.

Under these rules, the U.S. would possess the right to intervene at any time to ensure "stability," which the U.S. military governor General Leonard Wood described as a condition of "business confidence" encouraging private investment.[427] The Platt Amendment also allowed the United States to establish a permanent Naval base at Guantánamo. Newly independent small farmers and planters were stuck. In desperate need of capital to rebuild their destroyed farms and mills, they knew that the only available capital was in U.S. investors' hands. In 1901, Military Governor Wood issued an order that allowed U.S. creditors to collect their debts from the now land-rich but cash-poor small Cuban farmers. The farmers had little option but to sell their lands to foreign investors at huge discounts. This opened the door for a major land grab by U.S. companies and others, a new breed of opportunist carpetbaggers. United Fruit Company (UFC), whose plantations in Central America would soon constitute the equivalent of a farm one-half mile wide and more than seven hundred miles long from Guatemala to Colombia,[428] was able to purchase two hundred thousand acres of land in Oriente Province for a mere $1 an acre.[429]

A 1914 history of the United Fruit Company, *Conquest of the Tropics*, makes absolutely clear the link between "prosperity" and empire, concluding that "Cuba raised nothing but revolutions, anarchy, and chaos until the United States was compelled, against its will, to interfere for the purpose of eradicating an international nuisance. . . . These tropics are productive . . . in proportion as American initiative, American capital, and American enterprise."[430] The Platt Amendment guaranteed that North American businesses could invest with confidence.

As a result, Cuba, as with other Latin American countries, became a virtual U.S. fiefdom. The needs of its inhabitants' were subjugated to the needs of U.S. investors whose "life and property" were guaranteed by the U.S.[431] Cuban hopes reemerged in 1933 when a popular general strike under the slogan, "Down With Yankee Imperialism," forced out dictator Gerardo Machado, the manager of the U.S.-owned power and light company. At the time, the United States controlled 70 percent of the Cuban economy. President Franklin Roosevelt sent twenty-nine warships to gain the upper hand. The U.S. refused to recognize the young rebel junta which quickly enabled an obscure Army sergeant, Fulgencio Batista from eastern Cuba, to seize power. The hated Platt Amendment was abrogated in 1934, but it was replaced by a treaty that granted only limited Cuban sovereignty that ensured increased sugar profits for U.S. businesses while retaining possession of Guantánamo.[432] The Batista era had begun.

CRIMES AGAINST THE PEOPLE
Iron-fisted Batista abolished the Cuban Constitution and suspended all political liberties. He enforced an ever-widening gap between the multitudes of poor and

the few rich and encouraged organized crime to enrich himself and his cronies. As many as twenty thousand discontented Cubans were murdered by Batista's security forces in the late 1950s alone.[433] The U.S. government never interceded.

By 1958, a half million Cubans out of a total population of 6 million were unemployed, and nearly 85 percent lived in shacks without electricity, water, or sewer. Only a small number of children attended school. The vast majority of adults were unemployed most of the year, working only during the short sugar cane harvesting season. Health care was only for the wealthy.

Meanwhile, Batista himself was taking $1.28 million a month as a partner with Meyer Lansky's casino gambling.[434] The Mafia controlled drug trafficking through Cuba, all the legendary casinos, and more than three hundred brothels, seven hundred bars, and fifteen thousand prostitutes, as thousands of U.S. Americans, the bulk of the clientele, flocked to the island orgy playground. The level of control exercised by the U.S. Mafia in cooperation with Batista created many interesting political connections. This helps explain the participation of U.S. organized crime with the U.S. government and its CIA in illegal counterrevolutionary activities against the 1959 revolution.

Wealthy U.S. citizens and corporations successfully invested nearly a billion dollars. They controlled 80 percent of Cuban utilities, 25 percent of Cuban banks, 50 percent of Cuban railways, 40 percent of Cuban sugar, 90 percent of Cuban mines, 90 percent of Cuban cattle ranches, and nearly 100 percent of Cuban oil refineries.[435] The U.S. happily furnished Batista's army and police with all their tanks, planes, bombs, and ammunition.

Cuban wealth interfaced with U.S. politics at home. United Fruit provides an example. The Eisenhower administration was full of people who profited from UFC operations. Secretary of State John Foster Dulles had been the long-time principal lawyer for UFC and a large stockholder. John's brother, Allen, director of the CIA, had been a lawyer for UFC, a stockholder and ex-board member. Henry Cabot Lodge Jr., U.S. ambassador to the United Nations, was an ex–board member. John Moors Cabot, assistant secretary of state for inter-American affairs, was a large stockholder; his brother Thomas Dudley Cabot, director of international security affairs in the State Department, was a former UFC president. Robert Cutler, Eisenhower's National Security adviser, was former board chair. Walter Bedell Smith, former CIA director under President Truman and under-secretary of state under Eisenhower, upon retirement in 1955 became a UFC board member.[436] It is worth noting John Foster Dulles's honesty when he reportedly declared that "the United States doesn't have friends, it only has interests."[437]

CHAPTER 28

Horizontalism

Different revolutionary movements in Latin America have experimented with a variety of egalitarian models. This includes creating social models based on horizontalism where power is shared laterally among the people. Examining each offers ideas of how we in the United States might rethink our own vertically structured, undemocratic society.

Haves and Have Nots

In early February 1992, I joined with three friends to form the Community for the Practice of Nonviolence (CPNV). CPNV members Scott Rutherford, Elizabeth Hallett, Karen Fogliatti, and I met with several activists from South America who had been touring the United States as they shared the gruesome facts of life on the ground south of the Rio Grande. The pattern of systematic impoverishment in Latin America was being dramatically worsened by imposition of severe adjustments to countries' economic structures by the International Monetary Fund, the World Bank, and other global financial institutions. These "structural adjustments" were introduced to cover the enormous debts that a small coterie of wealthy oligarchs had racked up while running their countries into the ground. The old formula was at work here: privatize the profit, socialize the debt.

The United States was, of course, instrumental in this restructuring, which also adversely affected our citizens at home. In the early 1980s, President Reagan initiated a destructive domestic version of structural adjustments, granting massive tax breaks for the rich while systematically scaling back the social safety net for most everyone else. He created a huge budget deficit by pouring staggering amounts of money into the military-industrial complex, in effect guaranteeing a massive public subsidy for a small network of plutocrats. These Reaganomic "adjustments" produced a dramatic increase in social decay at home.

In the United States, the term "welfare" is generally used to refer to government programs for the poor and lower middle class. However, the fact is that the majority of welfare in our country goes to the rich to become ever richer.

The shift of ever more resources from the commons to the plutocracy, from the poor and middle classes to the wealthy, has rapidly moved the

United States toward our own version of a "Third World" nation, headed toward neofeudalism.

Many of the homeless were mentally ill, wandering around with no safe haven after being systematically discharged from mental facilities that were being shut down as funding for social services was drastically cut. A large percentage were psychically traumatized war veterans without adequate VA assistance (the cost of war coming home to every community). And as discussed earlier, in a country that boasts that its way of life is the best on earth, the number of African American males who were incarcerated dramatically rose, while money for public housing programs was substantially cut; the era of free public universities ended; and the 1980s saw an alarming increase in numbers of people lacking any health care, or with only inadequate health care at best.

A summary of current statistics reveal that life in the United States is worse, twenty-five years later. The National Alliance to End Homelessness reports that 744,313 people are homeless in the United States, including almost 100,000 homeless families.[438] More than 100,000 Iraq and Afghanistan war veterans have sought help for mental illness since 2001.[439] One in ten Black males aged twenty-five to twenty-nine was imprisoned in 2007.[440] Average college tuition in 2006 was $30,000 for four years,[441] while the average yearly wage for nonsupervisory workers—miners, factory workers, salesclerks, teachers, etc.—was $30,798.[442] In 2007, more than 15 percent of the U.S. population (45.7 million out of 301 million) was without *any* health insurance.[443]

But because the United States is—materially— more prosperous than most other countries in the world, the fact that wealth is being absconded upward is rhetorically concealed. Those policies are far more transparent in smaller, poorer countries where wealth is not only concentrated in the hands of a few within the country, but actually being transferred out of the country into the hands of U.S. "interests" (i.e. multinational corporations).

Seeing the problems these structural injustices were producing in the United States, CPNV wanted to document what our South American activist friends were telling us was happening in their part of the world. We wanted to ask people about their attitudes as well as their physical, material circumstances. We especially wanted to know what resistance looked like there, so we could share ideas when we returned home.

In February 1992, Karen Fogliatti, Scott Rutherford, and I traveled to South America with videographer Mark Birnbaum. The North American Free Trade Agreement (NAFTA) was in its final preparatory stages, and we wanted to measure the deleterious changes sure to come after that agreement became law on January 1, 1994. Starting in Ecuador, we traveled to Colombia,

Brazil, and Argentina. Then I returned to the United States, while my friends continued on to Peru and Chile.

The travel exhausted me, both physically and emotionally. I realized that the poverty I saw when I visited the people of these countries (rather than their tourist attractions) was the result of centuries of repression and disloca- tion. I saw virtual feudal systems still intact outside the cities, and extensive slums inside them. Several times, I broke down thinking about how all this land had been taken from Indigenous people since the 1600s, their cultures decimated in attempts to eradicate them for profits. Miraculously, the people of these lands endure and their continued existence, though often compro- mised, offers us indispensable examples about how to live lightly on the earth.

Brazil

We spent more than five weeks in Brazil where we were met by a fifth friend, CPNV member Elizabeth Hallett. She grew up as a child of missionary parents in Brazil and spoke fluent Portuguese.

Brazil was first occupied in 1500 by the Portuguese at a time when as many as eight million Indigenous people lived in thousands of communities in the vast forested river system larger than the land area of the continental United States.

Brazil's rightist president at the time of our visit, Fernando Collor, was rapidly making structural adjustments under the neoliberal economic religion of privatization. Just as would later happen in the U.S. during the banking crisis of 2008, the government was paying the debts of the wealthy (in this case, wealthy planters) while cutting health care, housing, and social programs. Brazil had enjoyed a government committed to agrarian reform in the early 1960s under President Joao Goulart, a supporter of the Cuban Revolution, who was overthrown by the U.S. in 1964. This led to a modern line of dictatorial rulers who, in turn, opened the country to a rush by U.S. and Western corporations to exploit its vast resources.

We traveled for thirty-seven days, mostly by airplane, to a number of locations across the vast country, visiting thirty-four cities and towns from the interior of the country, and the western rubber-producing region in the State of Acre, to the cities along the Atlantic coast such as Belem in the north to Puerto Alegre in the south. We visited the cities of Rio de Janeiro and São Paulo as well. From the air, the Amazon River system was awesome to behold, though it was depressing to see the thousands of acres of logged rain- forest. On the ground, we witnessed land invasions by the landless, millions of poor living in hundreds of *favelas* (shantytowns), and thousands of home- less children wandering the streets. We strove to uncover who was suffering as a result Collor's neoliberal policies, and what they were doing, if anything, to fight back.

Brazil seemed ripe for a popular movement. When ruthless power exercises its repressive and systematic injustices, the consequential misery caused to the people and their land, invariably leads to rebellions. Unfortunately, those rebellions are all too often savagely repulsed. The fear of political defeat experienced by political rulers, the loss of their comfortable, privileged lifestyle, the threat to their insatiable corporate profits, so threatens them that they work desperately to silence the people's cries for justice.

It seems that unless we as a species mobilize against the perpetual oligarchic control of basic resources, ultimately we will be doomed to extinction. As we traveled through Brazil, we gathered evidence of this destructive paradigm and, more optimistically, for signs of its collapse.

A Devastated Land

When you fly into Brazil, one of the first things you notice from the air is the impact of clearcutting. Vast swathes of forest have been cut down, leaving gaping holes in the natural canopy.

We began our Brazilian trip with a flight from Bogotá, Colombia, to Manaus in the center of the Amazon region, where we visited large tracts of land clearcut from virgin forests. The change in temperature was dramatic as we walked from the suffocating heat of the clearcut areas into the cool shaded air of the forest. We traveled by boat up the Amazon and two of its tributaries for nine hours, and saw more clearcuts along the banks. Forests were being converted into "hamburger" ranches for red-meat eaters. Grasslands were being converted to soybean plantations for cattle feed, biofuels, and vegetarians. Genetically modified (GMO) soy is now Brazil's largest export crop.

Wide paths of clearcut forests became rutted roads enabling miners of gold, iron ore and bauxite, and oil drillers, to travel deep into the rainforest. Iron was turned into steel at factories built deep in the rainforest, powered by charcoal created from more cut trees. With nearly eighty hydroelectric dams already completed by Electronorte, Brazil's state dam company, thousands of square miles were being flooded, dislocating thousands, mostly Indigenous people. In the 1990s, Brazil planned nearly three hundred additional hydroelectric plants.[444]

One group that was trying to fight back against this ecological damage being done to the Brazilian rainforest was the rubber tappers' union. Before the rubber market collapsed in the early 1930s, Brazil's rubber trees had been owned by what were called rubber barons, with the tappers working like slaves, always in debt to the owners. Rubber seedlings were then exported to Malaysia and other parts of Asia where investors developed large rubber plantations. Some of these plantations even existed in Viet Nam (owned by Michelin tire company) when I was there in the late 1960s.

The market collapsed, but the rubber trees remained, and thousands of small-farm tappers eked out a subsistence living by selling nuts as well as small amounts of rubber. When the state decided to develop the land for cattle ranches in the 1970s, more than one hundred thousand tappers were forced out. Many of their houses were burned to drive them out, and armed ranchers shot at the stragglers. In response, the Rural Workers Union was formed in 1975, followed by the National Council of Rubber Tappers in 1985.

Despite this mass expulsion of tappers, fifty thousand, or 10 percent of the state's population, remained in the forests, committed to preserving sustainable rubber harvests and their way of life, even as threats from ranchers seeking expanded "hamburger" grazing lands continued. In the Acre region, as the tappers became more organized to preserve the trees, and their way of life, a man named Chico Mendes popularized nonviolent tactics such as group sit-downs with people locking arms surrounding the trees targeted for clear cuts. Mendes also advocated prolonged fasts while protesters sat by the trees day and night until the chainsaws were turned over.

The ranchers feared this tenacious effort, and decided that the only way to stop the rubber tapper movement was to eliminate their union leadership. On July 21, 1980, Wilson Pinheiro, president of the Rural Workers Union of Brasiléia, and a colleague of Chico's, was murdered. In the next twelve years, a total of 172 union leaders were murdered in the Acre region. Fifteen of these were leaders with the rubber tappers' union. Mendes himself was assassinated at his home in Xapuri on December 22, 1988, when he was only forty-four years old. He had experienced death threats for more than ten years and survived eight earlier attempts on his life. This reign of terror has not stopped.[445]

When we visited the rubber tappers' union office in Acre, we saw posted there a quote from Chico Mendes: "At first I thought I was fighting to save rubber trees, then I thought I was fighting to save the Amazon rainforest. Now I realize I am fighting for humanity." This man of the forest grasped the complex interconnection of everything.

A Devastated People

As we traveled through Brazil, meeting with popular organizations, research institutes, and community and union leaders, we saw and heard about the deleterious effects of "globalization" on the people of Brazil. One percent of the people owned 44 percent of the land. In fact, the 20 largest landowners in Brazil controlled 37 million acres and the 245 largest landowners controlled 125 million acres. Added to that, 75 million acres were controlled by multinational corporations. Brazil is a massive country with over 1.2 billion acres of potentially arable land, but in 1983, only 121 million acres of land were being farmed.[446] Essentially all the farmed land was owned by a small group of wealthy landowners and corporations.

The inequality was extreme. Over 23 million workers lived in dire poverty in rural areas and 4.5 million *families* had no land whatsoever. Since the U.S.-led coup in 1964, more than 30 million people had migrated to the cities. Once there, however, they could not find work—we were told that 10 million urban Brazilians were unemployed. Only 32 percent of Brazilians were adequately fed. More than 25 percent could not read or write.

Police and paramilitary violence was out of control, both in the cities and in the rural areas, with over two thousand community activists murdered since the 1960s, including union leaders. The killing of street children was an epidemic, with five thousand murdered in the three years before our arrival. We were told that formal slavery still existed in Brazil, with thousands of forced laborers working on farms. Seven million children were estimated to be homeless, more than half of them living on the streets of the big cities, many persecuted by police and a paramilitary financed by business owners who just wanted them eliminated.

Forced out of their homes by dams, clearcutting, and the takeover of their lands for export agriculture, the Indigenous and rural people of Brazil found refuge in vast slums. In Belem, the mouth of the Amazon, we witnessed an invasion community of ten thousand people that had been built on a swamp. It was the worst slum imaginable, and there were many others like it. The people had little choice but to become squatters on any land available.

When we visited Porto Alegre, near Brazil's southern coast, we were asked by our guides from the Movement of Landless Rural Workers (MST) and the Pastoral Land Commission (CPT), if we wanted to accompany them to witness a recent expulsion and reoccupation. After a four-and-a-half-hour drive, we arrived at an encampment near Não-Me-Toque, 160 miles northwest of Porto Alegre and almost 120 miles from Brazil's western border with Argentina.

Early the next morning, we visited the "Night Secret Camp" comprised of 1,200 people, including 270 who were children aged ten and under. They had begun to occupy the vacant land about a month earlier. Though the land was on the list of Agrarian Reform properties available for settlement, the legal process for receiving permission was cumbersome, and the state considered these people illegal occupiers. So just eight days before our visit, they had been evicted by a force of eighty federal and state police with a hundred other officers as backup.

With no place to go, these 1,200 people simply set up their plastic sheets as temporary tents in another open field across the road. Though MST and CPT were helping with food, the people were already adept at eating native weeds and roots. Since they had no place to go, these people told us, they were determined to stay put until jailed, killed, or until Agrarian Reform granted the legal papers enabling them to cross the road from where they had been evicted.

In Recife we met with then-eighty-three-year-old retired Archbishop Dom Hélder Câmara, an early liberation theologian noted for his famous statement, "When I give food to the poor, they call me a saint. When I ask why the poor have no food, they call me a communist." He reminded us that the fundamental issue since the time of Columbus continues to be lust for land and the gold under it, and that only Indigenous people understand the earth's sacredness.

After two weeks we arrived in the incredibly sprawling metropolis of São Paulo, one of the largest cities in the world, at the time home to 15 million inhabitants. In one view, we could see the concentration of generations of enforced impoverishment. There were over 1,500 favelas throughout the sprawling city, housing nearly 1.75 million of São Paulo's most impoverished residents. Many are on hillsides between gated enclaves. The juxtaposition of sickening opulence next to sickening impoverishment has to be seen to be believed. Three million other city residents lived in one-room shacks adjacent to the favelas.

It was depressing to see such a huge number of impoverished people—especially the swarms of street children. We saw them again and again in all the big cities, especially in São Paulo and Rio de Janeiro. Despite these harsh realities, we were also inspired during our time in Brazil by the incredible examples of resistance exhibited by the landless in rural areas and the tenacious organizing being done by the poor in urban slums. Starting in Manaus, we met with representatives of the active CPT that advocated for the poor in land conflicts throughout the country, the national Commission for Defense of Human Rights, and the Indigenous Missionary Council. We learned the most about the landless movement in São Paulo, in our meeting with the MST, a well-organized group advocating for 50 percent of the arable land in private hands to be returned to individual family farmers.

For much of our time in São Paulo, our host was activist priest Ticao who coordinated popular education programs developed by Paulo Freire, the famous Brazilian educator. Ticao rarely slept in the same location twice for security reasons, since his literacy campaign for favela residents—a campaign that often brought with it radical self-awareness—was considered dangerous to the status quo. As the poor came to understand the structural forces that perpetuated their impoverishment, generation after generation, they began to feel empowered to participate with others in struggles toward liberation. Tragically, popular organizing in the favelas, in turn, was stimulating an increase in terror against the people carried out by paramilitary forces.

Paulo Freire

Paulo Freire discovered how to use political literacy to unlock the colonization of the minds of the impoverished after generations of being enslaved. Freire's revolutionary educational methodology was considered so dangerous that the leaders of the 1964 coup ordered him out of the country, and he was kept out for sixteen years. Finally, by 1980, the repression had lessened and Freire returned to Brazil. During all these years, whether at home or abroad, he continued teaching his anticolonial pedagogical method. Freire found that when people are keen to understand the causes of their own misery, they are motivated quickly to become literate and critical thinkers. Perhaps a similar process had been provoked in my own psyche when I looked into Mai Ly's eyes. I had to know why this woman had lost her life; suddenly I had new eyes that could see what before I could not.

We met Paulo Freire on April 2 and enjoyed a very inspired discussion. At the time, Freire was seventy-one years old. Balding and sporting a full grey beard, he peered at us through thick eyeglasses. Physically a very small man, his passion for radicalization of the mind and consciousness was enormous.

Freire shared with us his conviction that *every* human being is capable of looking critically at his or her world situation and joining with others to creatively engage the power structures. He believed that with self-radicalization—which he described as seeing with new eyes—came hope and a willingness to take new risks, enabling a person to pursue radical justice through nonviolent struggle. Freire identified three principles of nonviolent, revolutionary education: to possess sufficient passion to seek justice for all; to possess convictions without imposing them; and to dream the world one seeks in order to create its reality.

He firmly believed that dreaming, which is part of human nature, is indispensable for achieving a society based on justice and mutual fairness. When asked about the prospects for a popular movement to overcome centuries of repression, he responded that his own dream is that the poor will prevail, that "in spite of the misery, in spite of the poverty, in spite of the imposition of silence on them, in spite of the lack of seriousness in the politicians and their lack of shame, in spite of the pain, in spite of the lack of hope, in spite of all, the Brazilian people have fought and . . . are creating possibilities for the country." Paulo believed that the potential of dreams must not be forgotten, that a new reality would emerge as a result.

I had read his book *Pedagogy of the Oppressed* in the late 1970s, and it struck me then that his principles for increasing radical self-awareness were as relevant to "First World" people as they were for impoverished peasants in the "Third World."[447] He stressed that a "culture of silence" is conditioned by social, economic and political domination and that that conditioning contributes to lethargy and ignorance.

Freire understood well the psychology of dominators. In *Pedagogy* he states:

> For the oppressors, what is worthwhile is to have more—always more—even at the cost of the oppressed having less or having nothing . . . The oppressors do not perceive their monopoly on *having more* as a privilege which dehumanizes others and themselves. They cannot see that, in the egoistic pursuit of *having* as a possessing class, they suffocate in their own possessions and no longer *are*; they merely *have*. For them *having more* is an inalienable right, a right they acquired through their own "effort," with their "courage to take risks" [emphasis in original].[448]

In reading—and later listening—to Freire, I have come to believe that the people of the United States suffer from this "culture of silence" he describes. Our worship of materialism has only produced lethargy and ignorance among most of us, while others suffer as a result.

It is said that Freire had great influence on people like Steve Biko and the Black Consciousness Movement in South Africa because his pedagogy emphasizes self-awareness, personal dignity, and possession of a dream for justice. When people passionately pursue their dreams, they are no longer the *objects* of domination, but participants in their own liberation; they become important *subjects*.

Freire's ideas seem to connect with at least two provocative revolutionary psychiatrists, Frantz Fanon, who grew up in Martinique Island in the Caribbean when it was a French colony, and Erich Fromm, the Jewish-German-American psychoanalyst. Fanon's classic work, *The Wretched of the Earth*, explores the psychopathology of colonized peoples, both individual and collective, and the process of their liberation and decolonization.[449]

Fromm, a giant in the field of political psychology, described in his profound essay *Escape from Freedom* the choices people make to healthfully embrace freedom, or to turn to escape mechanisms such as authoritarianism, destructiveness, and automaton conformity to avoid it.[450] The fear of uncertainty associated with freedom, he assessed, is often experienced as an unbearable burden which, in turn, creates deep psychological conflicts that manifest in behaviors such as sadism (by dominators), and obedience to authority (by the dominated). He advocated that people seek liberation by choosing to engage in solidarity with all people and nature—a form of libertarian socialism—while rejecting both Western capitalism and state socialism/communism as systems so dehumanizing and bureaucratic that universal alienation results.

The Columbus Enterprise continues in the Americas—five hundred years of plunder and the repression necessary to enforce it. The values, patterns, structures, and habits created to enrich a few at the expense of the many have only become more entrenched. Though the state at different times rhetorically talks of change and reform, it continues to move resources of the public commons into the pockets of the private rich—private power and profit, public decay and debt. The poor and their organizations valiantly continue to cry out, "Enough! Enough!" as they practice local organizing and sustainable living. Meanwhile, for those who have not freed their minds, the direct connection between wealth and privilege on one hand, and impoverishment and misery on the other, are ignored and denied. What a pity.

Ecuador

The impact of neoliberalism was, if anything, even more evident in Ecuador, a country of about 11 million people. My conversations with ex-CIA agent Phil Agee had alerted me to the heavy hand of U.S. intervention in Ecuador. Phil had been a covert operative there between 1960 and 1964. The election in September 1960 of José María Velasco Ibarra, a moderate, should not have upset the United States—after all, the immensely popular Velasco had already served three terms in office and would serve again in the late 1960s. But in 1960, Velasco made the mistake of insisting on maintaining diplomatic relations with Cuba in defiance of U.S. instructions, setting in motion a concerted effort to undermine the Velasco government.[451] He was forcibly replaced by his vice president, Carlos Julio Arosemena Monroy, in November 1961, but Arosemena turned out to be more leftist. The U.S. finally succeeded in putting in its own figurehead after a military coup took over the country in July 11, 1963.

Arriving in Ecuador three decades after this example of U.S. meddling in the affairs of this historically underdeveloped country, we sought to determine whether such intervention had improved the lives of the people. We spent a total of nineteen days, traveling from Machala, a lowlands city of two hundred thousand on the southwestern Pacific coast, to Otavalo, a city of twenty-five thousand residents three hundred miles further north in Imbabura Province in the highlands near the border with Colombia.

What interested us most was the continuing resistance of the country's Indigenous peoples to the commodification of their culture. From Otavalo we traveled to a small community of some 370 homes in Pijal where the residents were involved in the aftermath of the country's Indigenous uprising in 1990. They were striving to acquire and secure land, using what they described as their "Indigenous theology," stressing that "land is not a commodity" but the identity, mother, and culture of the Indigenous. They could not relate to the idea of land as private property.

Ecuador's Indigenous resistance was essentially nonviolent—they used no guns or arms, only rocks and sticks, in personal self-defense. They told us that during a tense moment during a face-off with the Ecuadoran army, five hundred women and children directly confronted the army by sitting firmly on the roads linked arm in arm. They said the soldiers had not wiped them out because they refused to fire directly at the women and children, while the men were elsewhere.

One of the most interesting conversations we had about the 1990 uprising took place in the small community of Ludo. There, members of the Indigenous movement described their vision of decentralized socialism—or communitarianism as some called it—which sought to preserve their culture, language, values, and natural medicine. They talked about creating a local parliament and land reform that would redistribute resources, equalizing the haves and the have-nots. They sketched a picture of a communal way of life I would encounter again and again among Indigenous communities, reaching its clearest expression in Chiapas, Mexico.

After meeting with Indigenous leaders in Riobamba, we accompanied representatives of Indigenous Agrarian Reform to witness a land dispute in Pulingui at the foot of the 20,500-foot-high, snow-covered Mt. Chimbarozo. We traveled by bus caravan packed with members of six different communities representing hundreds of Indigenous families. Suddenly, around a bend in the road, we encountered a number of Indigenous people wielding spears as we were stopped by a roadblock of fallen trees. We learned that they represented some twenty Indigenous communities, converted from Catholicism to evangelical Christianity, working for the mestizo landowners. Behind the felled trees, we could see two mestizo landowners accompanied by an evangelical preacher with a cross hanging from his neck.

The road was too narrow to turn around, so several people in our lead bus got out to negotiate with the blockers. The landowners and preacher remained behind the downed trees, along with a number of other Indigenous people with spears, their heads just visible above the branches. Words were exchanged, and then a fistfight broke out. For four hours the two groups alternately—and sometimes simultaneously—talked and fought. Finally, it was decided that we should back up our buses, one by one, for nearly a half mile until we could turn them around.

This event—which frankly was startling at the time—demonstrated quite literally how five hundred years of European conquest had pitted Indigenous people against Indigenous people in their quest for survival. Some were siding with the mestizo landowners to gain some semblance of security, while others were striving for genuine Indigenous identity. The Columbus Enterprise was being played out in front of our eyes, fist against fist, landowner against Indigenous, Indigenous against Indigenous, Western religion against traditional spiritual practices. Neoliberal globalization was making the original crime even worse.

Even so, I found inspiration in the Indigenous Agrarian Reform movement. There, at least, was a group of people who understood that the fundamental problem of the Columbus Enterprise was its verticality. It perpetuated a way of life dependent on domination by one group over another. They had a vision of a completely different way of life, in which each person would have an equal say and equal access to resources. If only these communities could be left in peace to pursue their vision!

Argentina

My last stop on our trip was Argentina. The four of us (now minus Mark Birnbaum) arrived in Buenos Aires on April 21 by way of Montevideo, Uruguay. The history of Argentina is like many of the other countries in the Hemisphere: European conquerors—in this case, the Spanish—arrived in the early 1500s and set about exterminating the Indigenous peoples and taking their land. By the early 1900s, the Spanish had succeeded in creating a landed oligarchy that joined with the Catholic Church to rule the country. In the early twentieth century, Argentina turned first to Prussia and Germany, then to the United States, for military support, developing a professional army that, during the 1970s and 1980s, was used by the United States to train counterrevolutionary forces such as the Contras in Nicaragua.

Argentina's politics have swung widely between left and right, from the soft socialism of Juan Perón (and his famous second wife, Evita) to the infamous reign of terror known as the "Dirty War" created by the March 1976 military coup, that lasted until 1983.[452] Over thirty thousand people were disappeared during this period. Though this coup was not instigated by the United States, the new Carter administration, known for talk about its commitment to human rights, enthusiastically maintained a "special relationship . . . with the Argentine Armed Forces."[453] Despite Carter's support of the regime, the U.S. Congress did impose limitations on military aid and some commercial transactions due to human rights violations. But monies to Argentina from the World Bank, International Monetary Fund, and the Inter-American Development Bank, along with private U.S. banks, *increased* during the dictatorship.[454]

Upon our arrival in Argentina, we learned there were 2,500 active Mothers of the Disappeared pressing fervently for more information about the earlier abductions of their loved ones. We met them at their office in Buenos Aires on a Thursday, then accompanied them to the Plaza de Mayo where they solemnly walked around the plaza holding white scarves to remind the government and the country of the scars caused by the military dictatorship. These mothers had gathered to walk on this plaza *every* week since the mid-1970s when the disappearances began. One of the mothers told us that their vigil had become a movement for "a radical transformation of their culture with a popular social system free of top-down authority."[455]

This was the context in which Adolfo Perez Esquivel left his university teaching position as a professor of architecture in 1974 to promote nonviolent liberation for the poor throughout Latin America. He founded SERPAJ (Service for Justice and Peace) as the vehicle for doing this, and we had met him when he was on a 1991 SERPAJ speaking tour in the U.S. He was an astute observer of the role political-economic structures have on the quality of human culture. Trained as a sculptor and architect, Esquivel had become a Christian pacifist sensitive to the conditions of the poor and the power structures that so selfishly preserved impoverishment. His work brought him the Nobel Peace Price in 1980.

When the military dictatorship came to power, Esquivel was imprisoned without trial for fourteen months and was consistently tortured during this time. He survived through deep meditation. He was released in 1978 on the condition that he report to the police regularly, with travel restrictions imposed. When the conditions were lifted in 1980 he started traveling to newly created SERPAJ offices throughout Latin America, some of whose representatives had hosted us on our South American trip.

We shared with him everything we had witnessed in Ecuador, Colombia, and Brazil. We wanted to hear his take on the history of repression, the history of resistance. He confirmed our belief that there was more dysfunction and disharmony than ever, and that the New World Order as described by U.S. President George H.W. Bush was simply the latest expression of a series of dominations that he called, as others had, "The Columbus Enterprise."

Esquivel described the problem of street children in Argentina, similar to what we had witnessed in Brazil. A recent census had counted two thousand street children in Buenos Aires alone, with another thousand children in prison. Forty percent of all Argentinian children lived in poverty. In a nation of 33 million people, half of whom lived in the metro Buenos Aires area, one-third lived in poverty, contrasted with 10 percent who were very comfortable. There were more than twenty squatter settlements in Buenos Aires housing 150,000 inhabitants. Thousands of others squatted in vacant buildings and run-down hotels.

Esquivel described the need for a "transformation of consciousness" that could move beyond resistance, to experimenting with alternative, local self-reliant communities. He stressed that to be sufficiently free to participate in radical change, risk-taking is essential. We were surprised to learn that he had been imprisoned in Ecuador, Uruguay, Chile, and Argentina for his organizing activities. Despite all that, however, Esquivel was enthusiastic about the emergence of hundreds of popular movements throughout Latin America that were primarily nonviolent in the spirit of Gandhian resistance, striving to move the consciousness of the "Enterprisers" toward humility and mutual respect.

In Ecuador, the Indigenous people were intent on creating a horizontal society. Some of the seeds of such a movement had been planted also in Argentina, and, a decade after our trip there, they began to sprout. After nearly twenty years of brutal IMF neoliberal policies being imposed on the people of Argentina, the country's economy collapsed in December 2001, and virtually everyone but the super rich were thrust into poverty. Massive capital flight, devaluation of currency, freezing of bank accounts, and bankruptcy of the government sent millions of people into the streets.

What emerged was amazing. With no formal leadership or hierarchical structures, without political parties, the people created a new, organic *horizontalidad* street democracy. Hundreds of neighborhood assemblies met every week to practice direct democracy, factories were occupied by workers who capably managed them without any owners or bosses. The same was true of bakeries, health clinics, child-care centers, etc.—all were self-organized within the respective neighborhoods. I believe this is another example of an archetypal human characteristic—autonomy—that thrives in *locally* organized society. Similar to Cuba's discovery of self-reliance out of necessity, Argentinians were forced to consciously break from dependence upon authority structures, whether in the form of ward bosses or elected representatives, and found they could be productive working in cooperation with their neighbors, without bosses. Vertical was out, horizontal was in.

Argentinians are now communicating directly with the MST in Brazil and the Zapatistas in Chiapas, Mexico, sharing information on land takeovers, herbal medicines, and various practices of autonomy in decentralized groups. More recently, various groups from all over Latin America and Europe have been meeting under the name, *Enero Autónomo* (Autonomous January) to share their vision and experiments with direct democracy.[456] This organic revolution is chronicled in the book *Horizontalism*, edited by researcher Marina Sitrin.[457] Sitrin emphasizes that horizontalism is not an ideology but a method of people relating to one another in direct democracy while discovering a new creative force that links with other social movements.

A Lot to Learn

We learned much from our trip to South America. We learned that neoliberal, "free-market," global supermarket economics are the *deus ex machina* of the new, post–Cold War unipolar "new world order." In a way, neoliberal economics was an advanced form of "low-intensity warfare" against the poor. The economic "structural adjustment" programs being forced onto entire nations of people through U.S.-controlled finance institutions such as the International Monetary Fund (IMF) and the World Bank were creating a staggering new debt to be paid by the poor for the benefit of the rich.

The callousness with which the institutions of the Global North and the ruling oligarchies in each nation were aggressively, relentlessly pursuing neoliberalism suggested to us a conscious attempt to eliminate marginalized people who, due to enforced unjust structures, were unable to participate, either as producers or consumers. These people were apparently perceived as increasingly expendable and the hope seemed to be, the sooner they die the better. The vast majority were pushed to the outer margins of human society to live in misery and fear until they met with premature death in favelas and squatter tent cities.

We discovered pockets of Indigenous prosperity and empowerment projects in both rural and urban areas, and here we found the best of the human condition. We were thrilled and inspired beyond expectations by people risking life for transformative ideas in the face of great odds. The struggle took many forms: nonviolent land occupations by the landless, especially in Brazil and Ecuador, who then farmed cooperatively and collectively; creation of community soup kitchens, health clinics, and community schools by millions of poor in the favelas, especially by women; and efforts toward autonomy and regional self-determination by the Indigenous.

As significant as anything else was the *process* of struggle engaged by those who, in Western terms, have nothing. These processes were highly democratic, cooperative, and daring. When people engage in this kind of process for a common goal of justice, it transforms their consciousness and their relationship with one another. They can be fierce advocates for change without imposing their ideas on anyone. Liberated zones are created—common spaces organized by the poor and preserved by them. Perhaps, those of us in the United States and the Western world in general, might feel a tug within us to participate in something similar, and I believe we would be transformed as well.

Maintaining a horizontal way of life in the face of global capital is not easy. In 2006, Argentine president Néstor Kirchner's refusal to comply with most of the IMF's ruthless demands contributed to a resurgence of his country's economy. However, Kirchner simultaneously repressed the new horizontal social movements and tried to co-opt the workers. According to activists, the government continues to support police brutality, to instill fear and criminalize protest.[458] Rulers in positions of authority have large egos that cripple their sensitivity to universalizing justice. The habit of government collaboration with private profit is a tough one to break. But the examples of the Indigenous people in Ecuador, the displaced in Brazil, and the workers in Argentina demonstrate that people are very capable of taking care of themselves.

The September 1992 Fast

Our sojourn through South America had overwhelmed us. We felt we had to find some way to show U.S. Americans the ravaging consequences of the Columbus Enterprise and "its capacity to stop at nothing," and to contrast it with the positive example of horizontalism.[459] We wanted once again to call attention to the egregious consequences of the American Way Of Life and demonstrate that there could be an alternative. Scott Rutherford, Elizabeth Hallett, Karen Fogliatti, and I decided to start a forty-two day water-only fast on September 1, 1992, and to end it on October 12, the five-hundredth anniversary of the invasion of the Columbus Enterprise. Popularly called "Columbus Day," we would call it "Indigenous People's Day."

Something is terribly wrong with celebrating an invasion that opened a continent to plunder, pillage, and proselytizing! Uruguayan historian Eduardo Galeano captures this upside-down nature of the modern world in his aptly named book *Upside Down: A Primer for the Looking-Glass World*: "'Developing countries' is the name that experts use to denigrate countries trampled by someone else's development."[460]

Soon twelve others joined in our fast on the east steps of the U.S. Capitol, including long-time pacifist Dave Dellinger, Marie Dennis of Pax Christi,

Quaker feminist Teresa Fitzgibbons, ex-stockbroker Vic Scutari who had been with me in Panama in 1989, ex-FBI agent Jack Ryan, and Ted Glick, long-time antiwar activist involved in third party politics.

We were acknowledging the dignity of the poor and their struggle of liberation, as well as our complicity as U.S. Americans in living a way of life dependent upon massive exploitation, and suffering of other people. The fast was an earnest effort to reflect on the consequences of each of our daily choices—whether they have a healthy or unhealthy affect.

The Luther Place Memorial Church offered space for sleeping. A support group ensured that fasters had sufficient water, provided transportation, and arranged for various speakers and community groups to meet with us during our public hours. We had regular visitors throughout the fast, including people from around the U.S., and from many Latin American countries. Miguel D'Escoto, former foreign minister for Nicaragua, joined us for a day. We also had a number of visitors from Europe, Middle East, Asia, and from New Zealand and Australia.

On October 12, the last day of the fast, we celebrated Indigenous People's Day by joining two thousand others at Washington's National Cathedral to hear Indigenous Alaskan Episcopal Bishop Steven Charleston summarize the Columbus legacy in four words—racism, oppression, exploitation, and destruction. Later that day we broke our fast with several hundred supporters, then enjoyed our first meal in forty-two days at the St. Aloysius Church in Washington. I wondered what was next.

CHAPTER 29

Arrowheads

By going to other countries, I had sought to learn more about the effects of the American Way Of Life on others around the world. I had succeeded in a quest for knowledge, and had learned more than I ever intended about U.S. interventions, and the devastation wrought by the capitalist pursuit of prosperity over everything else.

The question became: how to share this knowledge with the U.S. American people, how to convey that our drive for "prosperity" is destroying the lives of ordinary people around the globe, and ultimately will destroy us as well. I have done my best to educate my fellow citizens and continue with public demonstrations such as the fast in 1992. I also wrote up eyewitness accounts—some of which can be found on my website.[461]

Yet I failed, I think, to convey this understanding. Perhaps it was presumptuous of me, or arrogant, to think I could do so. I asked myself how many places do I need to go to witness what the American Way Of Life is doing to people? And how to communicate with people who have no frame of reference to understand what I am talking about?

After a while, even the best of my efforts felt like trying to empty the ocean with a teaspoon. The American Way Of Life is very powerful and enticing. Well-meaning people like myself are easily caught up in its seductive power.

I realized that my work had to include focus on myself—including changing my own consumption habits. My thoughts continually turned back to Cuba, and the way that island nation had to become self-sufficient after years of being isolated by the United States and more recently having lost their provider of critical resources, the collapsed Soviet Union. I began to appreciate ever more the importance of modeling a way of life on the principles of self-sustainability while sharing that with others in my local community.

The Gulf War: A New Massacre

These thoughts were forming during the long winter of 1991 and reinforced by my travels to South America in early 1992. At this time I was also feeling psychically devastated by the new war the United States decided to pursue against Iraq.

During the relentless January–February 1991 bombing of Iraq, I spent most of my time in seclusion in my boyhood home in rural New York State, contemplating the meaning of this darkness. I thought a lot about the Iraqi people, but the images in my mind were not restricted to those in Iraq and Kuwait. I also thought about the Palestinians, the Koreans, the people of East Timor, the Mozambiquans, the Blacks in South Africa, the Namibians, the Angolans, the Libyans, the Cubans, the Haitians, the Guatemalans, the Grenadans, the Panamanians, the Filipinos, the Mexicans, the Hondurans, the Chileans, the Peruvians, the Vietnamese, the Nicaraguans, the Salvadorans, the Indigenous Americans, the Blacks kidnapped from their cultures in Africa to build the "New World's" economy as slaves!

"I'm sorry you have all had to pay such a price for having run into the Columbus Enterprise and all its spinoff enterprises," I cried. "The haves have become so cruel, so bestial in their crimes against the have-nots, and nature herself. Oh, my god, forgive us, forgive me." My murmuring became a steady moan. "Oh, Great Spirit, help me feel my oneness with all of life, help me feel these people's suffering, let me see their visions for a just and fair world. Let my life express this oneness with them, including their suffering," I prayed out loud, over and over again. "We are not worth more, they are not worth less," I proclaimed almost endlessly through my anguished reflection.

It seemed like I had never experienced such anguish as I was feeling at that time, and about what seemed like the dehumanized automatons we U.S. citizens had become.

Floyd Redeye

What brought me back to the land of the living was a series of very personal, and very prophetic conversations with Floyd Redeye, a Seneca Indian. Our paths converged through a special connection.

My birthplace, Geneva, New York, had once been called Kanadesaga. It had been a major center of the Seneca Nation, one of the six nations of the powerful Iroquois Confederacy. Tragically, in early September 1779, General John Sullivan, with five thousand men of the Continental army, carried out General George Washington's orders: "The immediate objects are the total destruction and devastation of [the Indian] settlements. . . . [The Indian country] is not to be merely overrun, but destroyed." The Senecas were routed, many murdered, all their homes and crops destroyed, and the survivors driven to points further west. Most of the remaining Senecas today live in southwestern New York State, on two reservations in Cattaraugus County, not too far from Ashville, the small town my family moved to in 1951, from Geneva, the original home of the Seneca nation. In a way, my own life had followed the Seneca "trail of tears." But this only set up the geographical coincidence for our meeting. A more serendipitous force was at work.

Floyd Redeye was a Seneca whose family had been deeded land in southern New York State since the 1700s, as a result of historic treaties. Yet, that land was taken from him illegally in the early 1980s. The State of New York wanted to build a highway, and they asserted eminent domain. Under normal circumstances, they could not succeed—property that belongs to Indian Nations is considered sovereign and is not subject to eminent domain. The State of New York got around that technicality by pressuring the Seneca Tribal Council under direction from the Bureau of Indian Affairs to declare—without telling Floyd—that he, Floyd Redeye, was not an Indian, and that his land was private property rather than the property of an Indigenous Seneca.

As Floyd described the trickery and deceit used to rob him of his ancestral land, I had to work on calming my anger. Floyd had only learned of the ruling when he saw New York State highway equipment getting ready to gorge his sacred land. Outraged that no one had ever spoken to him about this matter, he and a handful of other Senecas proceeded to sit down in front of the road equipment, blocking its forward movement with their bodies. They repeated this action on several occasions, and thus managed to delay completion of the highway construction for more than a year.

On September 1, 1987, while Floyd was visiting his Seneca blood brother near Concord, California, he was shocked, along with millions of others, by the news that a U.S. Navy munitions train had viciously assaulted several people who had been peacefully blocking the shipment of lethal weapons from the Concord Naval Weapons Station. Many of these weapons were destined to be used against the people in Central America, many of them Indigenous, who were revolting against the unjust oligarchies in their native countries which were forcing virtually all the small farmers and working-class people into misery and starvation. One of the demonstrators assaulted at Concord, of course, was me.

A mutual acquaintance learned that Floyd wanted to meet me, and arranged our first meeting shortly after the U.S. had launched its genocidal bombing of Iraqi people and I had retreated to my boyhood home. We connected like brothers. We shared our experiences of blocking the White man's machinery, of challenging the onslaught of the American Way Of Life. We were both shocked and saddened over the U.S. bombing of the Cradle of Civilization in the Middle East. We were both seeking an end to the Columbus Enterprise, and a re-creation, a resurrection, of a more primordial, spiritually vibrant consciousness.

Floyd and I also shared a similar past. Like me, Floyd had given a lot to the White man's new world order. I served briefly in Viet Nam, but Floyd served thirty-one years in the U.S. Army, retiring as a master sergeant after having served in combat in three wars—World War II, Korea, and Southeast Asia. He and his wife raised three children, all now grown and working in professions. In 1991, at sixty-nine years of age, he hobbled around with arthritic knees, one of which was a plastic substitute. Floyd had a Veterans Administration disability from injuries suffered in combat in Korea.

After retiring from the military, Floyd returned to his family's aboriginal land on the Allegany Indian Reservation that included Salamanca, in southwestern New York. He was already upset about the federal Kinzua Dam and Reservoir project in the 1960s. The dam had flooded a third of the aboriginal land on the Allegany Reservation promised for eternity, first by President George Washington in the 1794 Pickering Treaty, and again by President John Adams in the 1797 Treaty at Big Tree. Floyd was striving to recover his Indigenous values and heritage, but when New York State insisted on routing Highway 17 through the reservation in the 1980s, he said, "Enough is enough."

When I met Floyd in 1991, he was in the middle of a new battle. The City of Salamanca, with about six thousand White residents, sits almost entirely within the Allegany Reservation. The land had been taken from the Senecas in 1892, under dubious circumstances, through an imposition of a ninety-nine-year lease. The Whites felt certain there would be no Senecas left in 1991 to reclaim the land. That lease expired on February 19, 1991. Floyd and a minority of other Senecas wanted the lease terminated at its expiration, and the land returned to the natives.

A series of tactics by the local Whites, New York State, and the U.S. Congress ended with the BIA-sanctioned Seneca Tribal Council giving in. For a cash settlement, they agreed to the equivalent of a new eighty year long lease, that has, at least temporarily, left Salamanca in the possession of the White residents. But the Senecas I know were determined not to let this blatant continuation of trickery and deceit stop their struggle to reclaim their aboriginal heritage. Incidentally, Floyd refused all the money offered by the state for his ancestral land. He said that by accepting the money he would only legitimize the theft of that land.

I had a number of meetings with Floyd, and sometimes with other Indigenous Senecas. In the most profound sense, they knew deeper than anyone else just how intrinsically corrupt the U.S. American way has been and how diabolical are its effects. It was comforting to share my anguish with kindred spirits.

Arrowheads Again

One day, Floyd drove me about thirty-plus miles down Highway 17 from my home to point out the stretch of road and the area along the Allegheny River that had been the Redeye land. I knew the spirit of this land. When I was a child, I used to bike from my home in Geneva to the nearby Seneca Burial Mound. There I would often uncover old arrowheads. Soon I had a treasure trove of arrowheads of various sizes that I kept safely hidden in my bedroom. I would hold them in my hand, feeling each one with my fingers, noting its texture, shape, weight, size, and sharpness. I loved the subtle color variations in the rock, from dark-grey to blue-black.

Though I wondered what life must have been like for the Indigenous people who once lived and hunted on the very ground I played on, as a child I never imagined that the Seneca story would open up the secrets of my own country's history, a much older history of plunder, always nobly rationalized by kings, dictators, and presidents demanding obedience to their authority. As a young boy living the American Way Of Life, I did not understand that the arrowheads were not only a symbol but direct evidence of the Columbus Enterprise. I did not then know that the Seneca culture was comparatively much more sustainable for people and for the earth than the greed-based way of life. I did not imagine that I was holding in my hand a symbol of everything I would have to work so hard to learn over the next fifty years.

As Floyd and I walked on the sacred land of his ancestors, he said to me, "The U.S. government could have avoided bombing Iraq. It was a conscious choice. It was easy to bomb. I know this way of thinking." I replied, "And the people, they're cheering, just as the German people cheered the exploits of Hitler and the German Army." Floyd and I were not cheering.

He looked at me as we stood on his sacred land, now lost to the White man's "progress." The U.S. flag was flying everywhere at that time. I don't remember when I've seen so many U.S. flags flying as during that bombing campaign. He said, "The flag, we call it 'Old Gory.' The red is our blood, violently spilled out of our bodies. The white, our bones, scattered around, buried, then dug up for highways and developments." As we were driving on Highway 17, the "Southern Tier Expressway," there were moments I couldn't tell whether I was in Viet Nam, Nicaragua, Iraq, or at the end of the Seneca Trail of Tears.

Walking the Walk

I believe that only a radical awakening, an unprecedented and comprehensive change in the way we relate to everyone and everything else, can save us from extinction.

Historian Lewis Mumford has argued that we may be nearing the end of a long epoch of several thousand years of living in what we call "civilization." After centuries of forcefully taking power from individuals in small groups and centralizing it in an ever smaller class of elite people, we ended up with societies gone mad, nation states convinced that its own continued power is the sole purpose of existence.[462] Since 1500, people of the West have been deluded into believing that their "superiority" justified the plundering of "inferiors." Systematic, massive theft and murder have been rationalized under noble sounding rhetoric to ensure extraordinary wealth to a handful of European-based societies while simultaneously bringing "democracy" and "salvation" to the non-European "savages" of the world. The United States emerged from this "colonizer's model of the world."[463]

The belief that we in the United States are better than others is called "American exceptionalism." We want material prosperity; our version of prosperity requires expansion; expansion requires that people move out of our way or be killed, if they do not agree to be assimilated. The people then generally become addicted to this prosperity, and thus addicted to the habit of intervening in other countries to maintain our way of life. We've militarily intervened over 550 times in other countries in just over two hundred years of national existence, carried out thousands of intimidating military port calls, and conducted many thousands of lawless and criminally covert interventions, while bombing twenty-eight countries since World War II.[464]

Those of us living in the United States are so comfortable, we have a hard time understanding the negative impact our way of life has had—and continues to have—on people around the world. For example, the average American consumes thirty-two times more resources than the average Kenyan.[465] Thirty-two times! Following World War II, the U.S. developed its Cold War "forward strategy as far east as possible" and had troops positioned in more than seventy countries.[466] At the conclusion of the Korean War the U.S. developed hundreds of new Air Force, Navy, and ground bases around the world, with as many as 950 overseas military installations.[467] At the height of the Cold War the U.S. nuclear infrastructure possessed nearly 1,600 military facilities in forty countries, and more than 4,100 facilities in our fifty states.[468]

Even today, after the fall of the Soviet Union, the U.S. military has nearly 255,000 personnel stationed in 153 countries around the globe, with at least 725 identifiable bases in thirty-eight countries.[469] U.S. military personnel, including Special Forces, train foreign troops in 180 countries.[470] The U.S. military presence around the world is not altruistic. They make sure we control the political circumstances in other countries and the events that impact our way of life, and ensure that hundreds of mineral resources (not just oil since the

1970s), continue to flow our way. Our dependency on these resources has grown increasingly significant since the early 1900s. [471]

After all, why does the United States care about a little island like Cuba, or a relatively poor country like Nicaragua? The seemingly thoughtless American Way Of Life demands compliant populations elsewhere and obedient citizens at home, as "prosperity" gobbles up supplies of raw materials and goods manufactured elsewhere with cheap labor. Our dependency on imports is obscene, and it is across the board. For example, the following dollar amounts were spent on imported products in 2007 alone.[472]

Foreign foods, feeds, and beverages: $8,975,000,000

Industrial supplies and materials: $326,459,000,000

Automotive vehicles, parts, and engines: $149,499,000,000

We are several times more dependent on foreign manufactured consumer durable and nondurable goods than on OPEC (Organization of Petroleum Export Countries), as we no longer manufacture our own clothes, shoes, or household appliances, creating a trade deficit in consumer manufactured goods of billion of dollars, and an overall cumulative trade deficit now in the trillions.

Consumption habits that outstrip domestic supply of resources is a classic definition of empire, one that John Locke described long ago—a way of life that justifies taking wealth and freedom from others to enrich oneself. The land the United States stole by force from the Native Americans was verdant, with more than enough resources to feed, clothe, and house everyone in comfort, but in moderation consistent with the carrying capacity of nature. That egregious theft was committed over the bodies of millions of Indigenous residents, which to this day has not been honestly addressed. This enabled the European settlers to prosper in the manner of a robber who never gets caught—and is deluded into thinking he or she can continue stealing without consequence. Our avarice won't allow us to leave other people's resources alone. This enabling and defining experience of our culture has spoiled our modern people, and we have never been held accountable for our murderous, thieving behavior. I believe this toxic impunity—an entrenched narcissism—will destroy us if nothing else does.

The U.S. government decided as early as 1890 to spurn the idea of a healthy subsistence economy, for an expanding, imperial global economy. Even with our massive theft we are not satisfied. Prosperity requires an ever-larger number of resources, and more is never enough, so expansion is endless.[473]

To repeat: the American Way Of Life, and the Western Way of Life in general, is unsustainable. It has radically harmed other societies and destroyed countless lives. It is now collapsing in on itself. In trying to protect and extend our interests against an increasing array of mythical enemies (including imagined weapons of mass destruction, while we possess the majority of them right here at home), we have borrowed against our future. We have funded hundreds of foreign wars while ignoring the needs of real people here at home. And we have undermined our own farmers and manufacturers in the quest to obtain ever-cheaper goods from abroad. Is this not an evolutionary moment of incredible opportunity to entertain a radical shift that can experience consequences of our actions, building a foundation for rediscovering our deeper, interconnected selves?

Global warming, whether from natural cycles, human activities burning fossil fuels, or a combination, is melting the glaciers and burning the plains, suggesting that in the near future we may all drown or starve. If we want to continue as a species, or to increase our chances to do so, we can *choose* to break our addiction before it breaks us.

For example the average U.S. American consumes over forty-two pounds of corn a year in the form of sugary sweeteners like high-fructose corn syrup! It could more wisely be used to feed an average person for thirty-seven days.[474] The U.S. exports corn to other countries as feed for meat, which we then import back. During the 1980s the U.S. was a net exporter of corn to Nicaragua, corn that fed beef cattle, not campesinos, before the beef was exported to the U.S.

I had seen the effects of these kinds of policies with my own eyes. I had seen people begging for food while fields were planted with sugar cane for the U.S. market. I had seen campesinos killed for wanting to grow—and eat—their own corn. Once I experienced the realities of impoverishment as a direct consequence of accumulation of wealth, I was able to see through the mythology of the "exceptional" American Way Of Life. I cannot even look at a Coke machine without feeling a twinge of nausea. How do we begin to feel our very direct, spiritual and visceral connection to the hunger experienced this very moment by millions, even billions of people in the world. We are really all part of *one* interconnected weave.

Overwhelmed

I started thinking I needed to walk more and talk less.

Faced with the enormity of confronting the American Way Of Life in my own life, part of me wanted to drop out completely. In hindsight, I also was increasingly battling post-traumatic stress related to my Viet Nam experiences, compounded by lingering trauma from the train assault. As soon as I recovered physically from being hit, I immediately began traveling, without taking the time to adequately process the psychic content of that traumatic experience. I also had avoided certain emotional dimensions of my Viet Nam experience, partly by convincing myself that, since I had not been a grunt, I would not have to contend with postwar trauma like other Viet Nam veterans.

By 1993, however, I was overwhelmed by stress and depression, faced with an enormous amount of grief—over the earlier defeat of the Sandinistas, my parting from Holley, the death of my parents, numerous premature deaths and suicides of Viet Nam veteran acquaintances, the deaths of dozens of friends and acquaintances in El Salvador and Nicaragua, the intrusive memories of the murders of hundreds of Vietnamese villagers after bombings, and the terrible impoverishment I had witnessed around the globe. I felt I was on the verge of a total meltdown and, on the advice of a friend, checked myself into a Quaker psychiatric hospital in Philadelphia.

Checking into that hospital was one of the best things I could have done for myself. I stayed a whole month, and eagerly attended several prescribed group sessions every day. My regular treating psychologist was a Viet Nam veteran and also happened to be an amputee. The director of the hospital at the time, Dr. Delaplane, served as my overseeing psychiatrist. It was during a session in his office that I was able to confess, for the first time, the way I had tortured my dog Lucky, the assault I made on my father when I was fourteen, and the deep grief I felt from witnessing the murder of so many Vietnamese villagers. My month-long stay ensured adequate time to think about and process deeper questions about how to walk on this path I was stumbling along.

By the time I left the hospital, I was thinking more seriously about living in a local community and practicing what the Buddhists call "right livelihood." I wanted to be with people who were purposefully living lives of simplicity. I had seen how difficult it was to put a roadblock in front of the American Way Of Life—when I tried that, I got run over—literally. I needed to step back and critically reflect on my actions. By pursuing a life of simplicity, a life not driven by the fetish of prosperity, I hoped to learn a different way of being in the world.

My friends and mentors, Wally and Juanita Nelson, had succeeded in creating that kind of simple life for themselves on a homestead surrounded by friendly neighbors in western Massachusetts. I hoped that I might be part of a larger community to practice a similar kind of balance with the earth that many of our ancestors lived.

Limits

I set out to find a right-living community where I could settle. Most of the self-sustaining communities that have been founded in the United States are either religious communities, like the Amish, or based in a drug counter-culture. Being an anomaly among most of my peers, I never have been attracted to mind-altering substances, finding that life itself is mind-altering enough. And I am not interested in living in a religious community.

In 1994, I found a place that I thought might work. A small group of people had founded a land trust in west-central Massachusetts and were looking for new members. After designing an all-natural straw-bale house and getting approval from the local building inspector, I assembled a wonderful three-man crew. We spent three summers building my house on that land trust property. Each spring, I drove from California to Massachusetts to work on the house; each fall, I drove back to the San Francisco and Monterey Bay Areas to spend time with the community of peace veterans there. The house was finally finished in 1998. It was everything I had dreamed of: a solar-powered, energy-efficient house with walls made of straw bales, built with timber sustainably harvested from the immediate property surrounding the house and custom sawed on site, plus some recycled materials. There was enough land for a garden to grow vegetables in cooperation with like-minded neighbors.

But the dream ended almost immediately upon completion of the house. Through the three years I had spent building it, I had not been willing to face my own limitations. The first autumn I spent in the house, an early snowstorm made me into a prisoner. I could not go outside without fear of falling down in the ice and snow with my prosthetic legs. I would have to continue driving to San Francisco every winter, and only live in my chosen community the rest of the year.

The permanent, disabling injuries resulting from the train assault have understandably had a huge impact on my life. During the first few years I successfully projected an image, to myself as well as to others, that my new physical limitations would not hold me back. And by all outward appearances, it had not slowed me down at all. But I tired of traveling, especially when considering the huge carbon footprint it requires.

Another effect has been a huge growth in consciousness about what it means to be disabled and the struggles of disabled people. The Americans with Disabilities Act (1990) placed this country in the forefront for helping disabled folks—institutionalizing access to facilities and public spaces through wheelchair ramps, audible crosswalk signals, and properly equipped bathrooms. Despite this progress, there is much education still needed. "Able-bodied" people typically reveal insensitivity to needs of "disabled" folks unless they are forced to, or unless they have a friend or family member who has brought a specific need to their consciousness. Because I am ambulatory and usually make walking look "easy," people don't realize how difficult it is for me to climb stairs. Any stump sore leaves me in a wheelchair. I regularly need to educate the people about my special needs, by asking questions such as, "Is this venue ramp accessible? How many stairs? Is there a secure handrail? Accessible bathroom?" It is crucial for community organizers and educators who strive for inclusivity to develop consciousness about what "open to the public" means for people with physical limitations.

I had chosen to live in west-central Massachusetts because I had enjoyed living there in the early-to-mid-1980s. I had a number of friends there and the area had plenty of forests surrounding small villages. The last thing I wanted to do was to continue to *burn* fossil fuels for travel, and that's what I'd be doing if I continued commuting between East and West coasts. Keeping the Massachusetts house would have meant betraying the very ideals that had led me to the community in the first place. Leaving was another of those difficult choices I had to make. I felt my only responsible choice was to return to the West Coast where the climate enabled me to walk safely year around. I sold the house to other members of the land trust.

Though I occasionally mourn the loss of that house, the experience of building it—and of realizing I could not live there—was all part of my journey. Living in this new way of life is not easy. It's much easier to drive a three-thousand-pound car ten blocks to the nearest supermarket to purchase twenty pounds of groceries than to bike twenty blocks to the nearest natural foods grocery. It's cheaper to buy clothes made overseas by underpaid workers than to save up money to buy locally made clothes from artisans using locally produced materials (or to learn to make your own). It would have given me a lot of pleasure to keep the Massachusetts house and become a "snowbird," leaving each winter and returning in the spring. Yet choosing what is easier, cheaper, and more gratifying in the short run—choices enabled by our conditioning that there are no limits—is precisely what is destroying this planet. The temptation to go this route was threatening to pull me off my path.

Our current way is out of balance with the earth. Even more problematic than reaching peak resources is the insatiable *consumption* by too many people, especially in the U.S. That includes me, of course. This pattern speeds up depletion of our finite resources. It seems suicidal to me to continue behavior that is contributing to the demise of the ecosystem, which means the demise of us since we are part of that ecosystem.

We are very capable, as individuals in concert with others in our local communities, of transforming our consciousness leading to radical changes in our social behavioral patterns. Embracing changes toward lives of simplicity—a life based on relationships rather than on accumulation of things—promises liberation and feelings of relief.

One of the twentieth century's greatest physicists, David Bohm, has remarked that what relativity and quantum theory have in common is their understanding of the undivided wholeness of everything and every particle in the universe. This knowledge requires breaking our cognitive thought structure, which historically is based on a mechanistic order commonly expressed through what Bohm calls the Cartesian grid. As he says, it is not easy to change this because our notions of order are so pervasive, they affect not only our thought processes, but our sense of ourselves, our feelings, our intuitions, our physical movement, and our relations with others and society, in fact with everything. Our problems originate in our *thought*, and as our thinking structures are rooted in mechanistic reduction and separation rather than the undivided whole, it is *thought* that is the problem.[475] This is an astounding conclusion in our age of "reason."

We forgot long ago that our brains are connected to our physical bodies and the earth as part of one undivided whole. Locked as we are in the Cartesian grid, we can easily become deluded and dangerously arrogant as we conform to the edicts of authority figures and ideologies that lead us to think and act stupidly, preempting our development as critical thinking, cooperative and empathic human beings functioning in the undivided whole of the universe. I have discovered, from experience, that the only way I can share what I have learned, while continuing to learn from others, is through practicing consciousness as it unfolds each day. While building my Massachusetts house I discovered a number of people who were willingly, consciously *contracting* their consumption. It becomes increasingly clear that our long-term security requires living simply in the present such that a future is possible for life itself. I am learning that slow and small are beautiful.

A life defined by sustainability is a life more or less permanently able to perpetuate itself, generation after generation. Perhaps if we choose to recover our senses, we will recognize the basic requirements for survival, with dignity, tapping into our deepest evolutionary mechanisms.

In Cuba, I had seen sacrifice creating new thinking and practices. Then I heard that the Zapatistas in Chiapas, Mexico, were committed to preserving their local noncash economy and cultural autonomy. In 1995, I traveled to Chiapas to study the lives of the Zapatistas.

CHAPTER 30

Zapatistas! An Archetype

The Zapatistas emerged on January 1, 1994, in an uprising in Chiapas, southern Mexico, to coincide with enactment on that day of the North American Free Trade Agreement (NAFTA). When they started organizing in the jungles in the early 1980s influenced by liberation theology, they represented the poorest of the poor. At the same time, the U.S. was pressuring Mexico to adopt draconian structural adjustment policies increasing impoverishment. In 1992, Mexican President Salinas repealed Article 27 of the Mexican Constitution that had emerged from its 1917 Revolution, a provision that guaranteed secure communal farmlands for all Mexicans, prohibiting privatization. This repeal was a precondition for acceptance into NAFTA with Canada and the U.S. as it opened Mexico's lands to the free market. The Zapatistas knew that NAFTA meant more impoverishment, more death.

I was attracted to the Zapatistas because they represented a culture of Indigenous Mayas who, repressed for generations, still possessed the clarity, courage and energy to organize for their own dignity and justice, two of the most basic of human characteristics.

I first traveled to Chiapas for an initial introduction to the Zapatistas in February 1995, but returned at the end of that year and stayed for several months to discover more about these people and their lives.

One event that resonates with me today happened in late March 1996, when I joined a number of other observers at talks between the Zapatista people and the Mexican government. The talks were focused on the implementation of the San Andrés Accords, signed in February 1996, that were intended to guarantee various rights of autonomy for the Indigenous peoples of Mexico. The Zapatistas actually wanted virtually nothing from the government except to be left alone, and truly respected. I was not all that surprised when the talks failed—Mexican President Ernesto Zedillo decided not to honor the accords, mainly because he had no intention of leaving the Zapatistas alone. They sit on too many valuable natural resources like natural gas, timber, and hydropower.

The negotiations were held in a well-kept, white-painted community building surrounded by three rings of security observers to ensure respect for the discussions going on inside. The inner ring was comprised of Red

Cross representatives standing about twenty-five feet apart, each holding a rope in a big circle. The middle ring was similar, made of poor but very proud campesinos—men, women and children—standing six feet apart from one another, each holding onto a rope. The outer ring was comprised of helmeted Mexican soldiers, every other one alternating facing inward or outward, standing at parade rest ten feet apart, wearing brand new uniforms, new shiny boots, carrying night-sticks but no firearms. The officers wore black gloves, the regular soldiers white.

Each ring had regular replacement shifts every four hours. One evening a light rain was falling. The soldiers wore new green ponchos over neatly pressed uniforms. The Red Cross representatives sported new raincoats over nice clothing. The campesinos, short and of slight build, had plastic sheets wrapped around themselves. Some wore sombreros, others had no hats; many were barefoot, a few had old footwear held together by tape. The circles revealed class differences so dramatically—but they also demonstrated the power of a people's movement. I will never forget the excitement evident on the faces and in the body language of the campesinos standing in that ring, as they protected the representatives inside the white building who were negotiating for *their* autonomy. Their dignity brought tears. I loved the fact that they were determined to never again work for "the Man," even if they had to die in that struggle.

Chiapas

The Mexican peso collapsed in December 1994 jeopardizing NAFTA. Emergence of the "threatening" Zapatistas was considered a cause. A leaked January 13, 1995, Chase Bank memo declared that successful international investment depended upon "elimination" of the Zapatistas. President Clinton rallied $50 billion despite opposition from Congress to bail out Mexico's economy. With this kind of pressure, I sensed the U.S. was prepared to militarily involve itself to ensure elimination or neutralization of the Zapatistas to salvage NAFTA.[476]

Thus, in February 1995 I joined eleven other U.S. Americans to observe whether there might be evidence of U.S. military influence in Chiapas. On February 9, 1995, while traveling south on curvy, mountainous Chiapas Highway 173, the group I was riding with encountered a long, heavily supplied Mexican military convoy. Carrying hundreds of newly uniformed, armed soldiers in troop trucks, armored personnel carriers and jeeps, among other equipment, I sensed most everything was U.S. supplied except the Mexican soldiers themselves.

The convoy was moving north toward Simojovel, thirty miles northwest of San Cristobal, the highland village we had just left. Later I learned that what we had seen was the beginning of a major military offensive that ravaged many communities, and whose goal was the capture of Zapatista leaders.

I had witnessed this sort of counterinsurgency so many times before—in Nicaragua, in El Salvador, in Colombia, in Israel/Palestine—all over the globe. But on this trip my purpose was not only to observe U.S. intervention in other people's lives. I also sought to learn from the Indigenous people of Chiapas a new way of life.

What I found was a movement that exhilarated me. Here was an uprising based on a philosophy of horizontal, direct democracy; local self-sufficiency; and regional autonomy. The Zapatistas understood that a local, steady-state economy was best achieved through horizontal relationships. They also understood the dangers that monopoly capitalism—a system based on vertical economic structures—posed for people's souls and for the land to which they were inextricably connected. These people wanted to preserve their cultural heritage and their sovereignty. They wanted to be free of outside imperial control. They were willing to sacrifice everything to preserve their integrity. They did not want to be wage slaves. They did not want to join the global capitalist economy.

I returned to Mexico in December 1995 to study Spanish and to learn more about the lives of these people, and gain a fuller understanding of how the Mexican government was treating its poorest citizens. Driving 4,400 miles round trip by car with my wonderful Spanish-speaking friend Joanne, we traveled through eighteen of Mexico's thirty-one states. Once in Chiapas we visited more than thirty Indigenous communities, most but not all of them Zapatista, and I twice flew over the conflict region in a small Cessna plane, observing the scarred jungle, the numerous military outposts scattered throughout the region, and noting many military convoys traveling on the numerous dirt and paved roads. We made extended visits to four communities, and were fortunate to meet and talk with many citizens of Chiapas—small farmers, business people, anthropologists, church and human rights workers, and various people I met on the streets of San Cristóbal, the cultural capital of Chiapas.

The accumulated impact of the many painful stories people told me was crushing. My heart ached as it had in war-ravaged Viet Nam, Nicaragua, and El Salvador. The government troops I had seen—all over Chiapas during the February 1995 offensive—were operating as a terrorist force. The army's strategy in the 1995 offensive was simple and cruel. Soldiers would enter a Zapatista community and drive the people into the mountains with just the clothes on their backs. Soldiers would burn buildings, destroy crops, damage precious water supplies, then leave. Costs to the government for this kind of war are relatively low. Few soldiers are endangered, and nothing makes the newspapers. But the targeted small vibrant communities of human beings are devastated.

The connections between the Mexican Army and their closely associated paramilitary terror groups were effective. General Mario Renán Castillo, the commander of the Seventh Military Region in Chiapas at the time, was a career officer trained at the counterinsurgency (COIN) warfare school at Fort Bragg, North Carolina.[477]

Castillo was in charge of the February 1995 offensive. I later learned from Bishop Ruiz's human rights office in San Cristóbal, Chiapas, Castillo was recruiting, training and arming as many as twelve paramilitary groups. The paramilitaries' systematic campaign of terror and repression relieved Castillo's military forces of having to publicly undertake the shameful, despicable task of terrorizing the Indigenous communities.

Castillo's friendship with the paramilitary forces is illustrated by the fact that he proudly displayed posters promoting the *Paz y Justicia* (Peace and Justice) paramilitary group at his office in Tuxtla Gutierrez, the state capitol of Chiapas—I know this because I read them while sitting in his office waiting room in April 1997.[478] And, further, Castillo was present as an "honorary witness" when Chiapas Governor Ruiz Ferro formally turned over 4,600,000 pesos (nearly $600,000 U.S.) to *Paz y Justicia* at a public ceremony in 1997.[479] A few days before Castillo stepped down from the Seventh Military Region, *Paz y Justicia* gave him a going away party at which he was honored with the words, "We will never forget you, sir, for all that you have done for us.[480]

The paramilitary groups committed acts of terror in cities as well as in small towns, against civilians as well as against political targets. In February 1995, while in San Cristóbal, I witnessed the aftermath of an attack on a human rights office there—equipment destroyed, supplies and documents, many shredded, strewn around on the floor. The staff was filled with terror, so afraid to go home that they slept in our hotel rooms that night. The human rights workers shared with us their anxiety about reports that U.S. military personnel had been spotted in Chiapas. Unlike most U.S. Americans, Mexicans are quite aware of the long history of eleven U.S. military interventions into their country dating to the 1830s. And with some bitterness, they remember that the Mexican-American War had been concocted by U.S. President Polk to acquire additional slave territory that stole nearly half of Mexican lands to become parts or all of ten U.S. states. We discussed this history most of the night.

The Massacre at Acteal

The most widely publicized of these terrorist acts was committed on December 22, 1997, when paramilitary units massacred forty-five Tzotzil

Indigenous Mayas while they were worshiping in their makeshift church in Acteal, Chiapas. Acteal, twenty miles north of San Cristóbal, was a community of refugees camped on a steep slope along the side of a major road. The refugees were largely members of the *Sociedad Civil las Abejas* (Civil Society of the Bees) who had already recently fled paramilitary terror in a nearby village. The Bees were sympathetic with the Zapatistas, but their total commitment to nonviolence prevented them from any formal relationship with the Zapatista Army, called the EZLN (Ejército Zapatista de Liberación Nacional, or Zapatista National Liberation Army).

The massacre at Acteal was not a mistake or an unforeseen consequence of the war on the Zapatistas. It was a predictable outcome of President Zedillo's (and the Clinton administration's) policy of encircling Indigenous communities with military forces while *pretending* to initiate a peace process. It was an outcome of the Zedillo and Clinton administrations' willingness to look the other way while allowing unaccountable paramilitary units to commit acts of terror with virtual total impunity.

In fact, Acteal was the largest single instance of the murder and rape of the people of Chiapas that had been ongoing since the mid-1990s. It has been estimated that in the two-and-a-half years leading up to the Acteal massacre, a minimum of 1,500 Indigenous people were murdered, and that at least sixty Zapatista communities suffered severe arson, thefts, and harassment, mostly committed by the paramilitary with the backing of the Army.[481]

This style of warfare was sickeningly familiar to me. It is another U.S. export and it is called "low-intensity" counterinsurgency or COIN warfare. It has been taught at the U.S. Army's School of the Americas in Fort Benning, Georgia and at the Special Warfare School at Fort Bragg for years. After the Chiapas insurgency in 1994, Mexico quickly accelerated training of military officers in the United States, paid for by the U.S. government. That deal was sealed on October 23, 1995, when U.S. Secretary of Defense William Perry visited Mexico's military high command under the guise of fighting the drug war.[482] What really mattered to Perry, however, as reported in Mexican (but not U.S.) papers, was that Mexico and the United States would sign a new security agreement that would complement the political and commercial cooperation already embodied in NAFTA. Perry was quoted as saying, "When it comes to stability and security, our destinies are inextricably linked."[483]

Perry's trip was a success. The major agreement he signed authorized transfer of an additional $50 million worth of military equipment to Mexico, including seventy-three Huey helicopters to the Mexican Air Force. In addition, thirty Huey helicopters were to be given to the Mexican Attorney

General's Office, technically for the drug war, but the State Department indicated that these helicopters need not be used exclusively in the war on drugs.[484] The 1996 military aid package also included four C-26 reconnaissance planes, five hundred additional armored personnel carriers and much more, along with funding to train at least fifty-five Mexican soldiers a year at SOA.[485] By 1998, according to School of the Americas Watch, Mexico "became the largest SOA client, accounting for one-third of all soldiers trained there." At least eighteen SOA graduates, top military officials, have been identified as having committed human rights abuses and murders in Chiapas, as well as in other Indigenous rebellions in Guerrero, and Oaxaca.[486]

Large amounts of military aid continue flowing from the United States to Mexico. In 2007 Mexico received nearly $46 million in U.S. military and police aid.[487] Many of these funds are technically dedicated to counter-narcotics programs, but evidence suggests that they are in fact going into counterinsurgency training and operations. As the Center for International Policy points out, most of this military aid actually flows to Mexico through the Defense Department, which is "notoriously resistant to 'burdensome' reporting requirements" and thus provides an easy funnel to "off-the-books" programs. The United States expects a return. They expect the Zapatista revolution to be neutralized.

Resistance

The Zapatistas have refused to capitulate. People in Nicaragua, too, declared they would not surrender. They had a famous slogan, "¡No Pasaran!" ("They will not pass!") But after ten years of relentless, U.S.-funded and directed terrorism, the people of Nicaragua did capitulate. Understandable, yes. That the United States would shamelessly terrorize an entire country into submitting to its own reenslavement is diabolical, beyond comprehension. It could happen to the Zapatistas, too—but I think the Zapatistas would choose to die rather than submit. Martin Luther King Jr. said, "Until you are willing to overcome the fear of death, you are not free." I think that is true.

They are up against a sizable military threat. As of early 2008, Mexico had fifty-six permanent military bases in Chiapas, with nearly two-dozen smaller installations. The paramilitary groups remain active, as well. The thousands of acres of land retaken by the Zapatistas in 1994 are threatened to be stolen once again by land barons with the force of the state's army. In my travels to Chiapas I heard people voice fears that Mexico had napalm and cluster bombs in its weapon's inventory, though I don't know if these have been used.

And the threat is not only military. Journalist John Ross, in his book *Zapatistas! Making Another World Possible*, summarizes some of the lethal effects of the first ten years of NAFTA on the people of Chiapas: *millions* of farmers already forced off their lands; all Mexican banks controlled by foreigners, mostly from the United States; all railroads sold to Union Pacific; all mines and airlines in private hands; five million acres of tropical forest already destroyed for private development with eucalyptus junk trees being grown for paper pulp in southern Mexico by companies such as International Paper; most homegrown industries shut down due to inability to compete with U.S. corporations; the "Maquiladora Miracle" already losing out to China in a race to the bottom; six hundred Wal-Mart megastores putting hundreds of homegrown retailers out of business; real wages down 20 percent with disparity between Haves and Have-Nots growing dramatically; *thousands* of new fast-food chain restaurants such as McDonald's and Burger King; importation of genetically modified corn threatening to contaminate the ancient Maya corn staple, among many destructive developments.[488]

Dangerous risks are often faced by humans wishing to preserve their dignity, no matter the cost. For example, the Korean people mounted a strong resistance to U.S. occupation forces from 1945 to 1951. After all, unbeknownst to most U.S. Americans, it was the U.S. enforced division and occupation following Japan's surrender in World War II that became the deep cause of the Korean War. I have seen photos taken by U.S. military intelligence officers in 1949–1951, of Koreans being tied to stakes and shot for being "Communists." These men actively resisted U.S. occupation and in the photos they appear quite stoic. They lived their lives with political integrity; they accepted their deaths with dignity. U.S. officers reported that they sang as they were shot. Without integrity, habits of obedience tend to make us robots to authority.

The idea that dignity trumps longevity, that a life without autonomous freedom is not worth living, is a very difficult concept for many U.S. citizens to understand, so spoiled are we with our material comforts. But as the reader knows by now, in my search for deeper human dimensions to guide my own journey, I have discovered that clarity of purpose and quality of life are critically important to a life well lived. Knowing about the struggles faced by people in Korea, Nicaragua, Chiapas, and elsewhere affirms that purpose and meaning are more important than longevity.

The essence of the Zapatista struggle is a desire for autonomy. Some analysts see this as a new type of revolution—a revolution that resists vertical political systems while distinctly rejecting the goal of taking state power. John Holloway, a social science professor in Mexico, has written a treatise, *Change the World Without Taking Power*, in which he explains this new political search for direct democracy and local self-sufficiency—for autonomy.[489] As he writes, the Zapatistas share a common history and a common plight.

Their life revolves around their village and the seasons of corn, or maize. What matters most is their ability to make their own decisions, to have a voice in their common life. They *are* corn, which has grown unmolested by "development" for millennia from the sacred microbial ecosystem in the soil under their feet. The Maya have listened to that wisdom and rediscovered their dignity, even as their corn and its sacred DNA is threatened today with contamination from U.S.-imported GMO varieties under NAFTA rules so that companies such as Monsanto can rake in obscene profits.

Representative vs. Direct Democracy

What the United States calls democracy is actually a vertical model of remote governance by oligarchs—economic barons and their political representatives. The result is that citizens in the United States have little control over what the U.S. government does.

In Chiapas, the Zapatistas believe in direct democracy. No one is elected to represent others. Instead, everyone in the *room* discusses every issue that is raised, and a resolution occurs only when there emerges a clear consensus. In this horizontal model of governance, every single person's say matters. No one can claim to represent another's point of view. Known as direct or radical democracy, it comprises *everyone in the room.*

The villages work together by informing each other of the decisions they have made. They communicate with each other through runners, or men on horseback, so that everyone knows what others are thinking. Now they also use photovoltaic solar-powered Internet connections. They remain in daily contact with very little or no dependence upon petroleum.

Of course, sometimes it is necessary for villages to send representatives to meet with each other, since it would be impossible—and dangerous—for these people of the corn to all leave their villages and land in order to meet with each other. More recently they have organized their more than 1,300 communities in eastern Chiapas into twenty-nine autonomous municipalities, which in turn work with five regional "good government councils" (*caracoles*). However, the representatives, or "coordinators" as they are sometimes called, generally serve only one year. There are no professional representatives, no politicians. Very few villagers actually want to serve as coordinators because it means they will have less time for tending to food growing and harvesting. However, those who serve do so out of a sense of responsibility for the whole community, and the community in turn helps provide for their family.

When the coordinators of the different villages get together, they don't act like our Congress or legislatures. The real political unit of the Zapatistas is the village, so if even one village is opposed to a plan, it cannot move forward without more discussion. Sometimes this form of consensus-building takes many months before clarity is reached on an issue. This is direct participatory governance from below rather than authoritative rule demanding obedience from above.

The Zapatistas have their own military, the EZLN, which ironically does have a vertical, hierarchical organization. The EZLN is directed by *comandantes*, both men and women who lead willing combatants, because military decisions cannot always wait for long group discussions. However, support for the EZLN is a decision undertaken by each village on its own. If a particular village does not want to be affiliated with the EZLN, they are not pressured to do so. Their autonomy is recognized.

Zapatistas who volunteer to serve in the EZLN must agree to avoid alcohol and drugs, and to limit the number of children they have if they are in a relationship. The commitment is to the revolution, and a permanent new liberation for the Indigenous people.

The EZLN also differs from most military forces in its embrace of militant nonviolent resistance among the Zapatista communities in civil society. While the EZLN has modest weapons and will use military force, its members prefer to put their bodies on the line in confrontation with military forces. I was in a Zapatista village when a Mexican Army convoy of armored personnel carriers, troop trucks, and jeeps arrived. Presumably they hoped the residents would be terrified enough to flee to the nearby mountains, freeing up the area for mestizos to farm and develop export crops. The men of the village quickly hid, while the women and children stood across the entire road, blocking the army's way. The idea was that the army would be more likely to shoot men, than to shoot at women and children. It was pretty gutsy.

As is often the case, the heavily armed soldiers in this army unit were primarily Indigenous. The captain and several troops disembarked from their vehicles and ordered the women to get off the road. The Zapatista women with their children firmly stood their ground, berating the soldiers and the officer, saying, "You are Indians. We are Indians. Why are you hassling and troubling us?" After a standoff of perhaps fifteen or twenty minutes, the officer ordered his troops to turn their vehicles around and return in the direction from which they had come. That is nonviolent resistance.

Local Self-Sufficiency

The Zapatista resistance is fueled by an overwhelming desire to nurture people's humanity while building their local, steady-state economy. These Indigenous villagers understand what capitalism can do to one's body, thought patterns and culture. They have a very advanced critique of neoliberalism and globalization that it would behoove all "First World" people to study.

In early April 1996, Joanne and I attended the four-day "First Continental Encounter for Humanity and Against Neoliberalism" at La Realidad, the jungle headquarters for the Zapatistas.[490] With five hundred other Mexicans, Latin Americans, and North Americans, including movie actor Edward Olmos and members of the American Indian Movement, we listened to astute critiques of neoliberal economics and descriptions of the deleterious effects of these policies on culture and peoples. We participated in a number of workshops discussing both how people have personally experienced market-driven societies and to envision alternatives for promoting autonomy and what some call a rhizomatic society. Like my Nicaraguan mother, the Maya know that dignity trumps longevity, but they also know that dignity is not private. Regaining our humanity is one part of a shift in which the inner world is integrated with the outer, based on mutual aid and respect, as Peter Kropotkin so eloquently describes in his book *Mutual Aid* (1902). Evolutionary biology teaches us that in fact we are wired as social beings.

The Zapatistas know that access to land is an indispensable necessity for their autonomy and that when a few people, that is an oligarchy, control most of the land area, impoverishment is ensured for the vast majority of the people. Part of a new "antisystem movement," they are directly communicating with other horizontal organizations such as the MST (landless movement) in Brazil and the emerging movement in Argentina where workers and neighborhood residents take responsibility for managing and operating factories, schools and health clinics, sharing experiences on land takeovers, herbal medicines, and various practices of autonomy in decentralized groups.

One choice communities are making is to take themselves off the grid. I saw how successful an off-grid economy could be in Cuba, where the people were forced out of necessity to learn self-sufficiency. In Chiapas, the people recognized for themselves the value of self-sufficiency. They have chosen to live off the grid. To preserve their autonomy, they have chosen to not make utility or tax payments to the government, knowing that their limited telephone and electrical service would be cut off as a result. They increasingly use herbal medicine. For transportation, they use horses and bicycles, with very few cars, and use the rural bus system. They are dependent on few external inputs, though they are now interacting with many outside support organizations in order to create local education, health, and justice systems, and to promote limited fair-trade coffee.

In several of the poorest Maya communities where people live on back roads that are barely passable, I was shocked to discover that the one vehicle that visited every week was the Coca-Cola truck. Being a former Coca-Cola truck driver, I was stunned by the size of the trucks in Mexico. Some tandem trucks have as many as ten bays, twelve cases high, meaning that one truck could deliver as many as thirty-four thousand bottles of nutritionless sugar water. I sadly watched a young malnourished mother nursing her baby with a bottle full of Coca-Cola. She had no breast milk and no corporate baby formula.

I later found out that Coca-Cola is one of several corporations seeking to tap into plentiful surface and aquifer water supplies in Chiapas, now up for grabs under NAFTA. That the water is being bottled and sold as sugar water is but another example of how natural resources under neoliberal global economics are purchased by predators then sold back to the people whose resource it was in the first place.

One of the villages we visited was San José del Rio, a relatively new community of forty families of Tojolabal Maya origin, situated in the beautiful Dolores River valley. They had settled in this uninhabited valley a few years earlier, leaving an oppressive life under a patron only a two-hour walk west. The community already had established a small store, a church without a priest, a school through the fourth grade, a Mexican Red Cross office, and a two-cell jail.

Joanne worked in the school and in the school's community organic garden while I maintained a vigil along the single road that passed in front of the Campamentos Civiles por la Paz (Civil Peace Camps) house created by the Bishop of San Cristóbal. In the eleven days I acted as an international observer, I witnessed sixty-three military vehicles moving slowly in eleven convoys carrying various supplies and more than 350 heavily armed soldiers; seven military helicopters flying low over the village residences; and two fixed-wing military aircraft passing overhead. The children in the village knew by the sound of vehicles in the distance, long before they were visible, when the military was getting close. "Military, military, military coming!" These events always changed the tenor and activities of the villagers, who quickly moved out of sight from the road, while for me it was time to be standing right next to the road with notepad and pencil, binoculars around my neck, waiting to record data as the military slowly moved through the village. Often, the soldier riding on top of an armored personnel carrier positioned a video camera directly at me as other soldiers made their firearms menacingly visible.[491]

While serving in this role as international observer, I slept in a hammock like the villagers, and enjoyed community meals with residents. In this village, the adults, men and women, gathered every afternoon for a meeting. They discussed how to approach their planting and harvesting, secure better health care, maintain security from military and paramilitary, expand their school, and so forth. Each village is responsible for itself and has authority for itself. Though they do not accept the authority of the state of Mexico, they are proud to be *Mexicans*. They fly the state flag of Mexico along with their own.

Every day, people are very busy. Many of the community members work on the land, hoeing and planting maize, beans, and chilies. When they walk the roads to their fields they have to watch for military, paramilitary, and bandits on the road, and they know that at any time the force of the military could "eliminate" their emerging liberated community.

The women collect and sometimes chop firewood, and do traditional chores like going to the river to wash clothes with babies and children strapped to their backs. In the village there are local teachers working to ensure that the children become both linguistically and politically literate. People of all different ages paint murals—you see them everywhere. This communal artistic expression reminded me of revolutionary Nicaragua.

Three men from the community take turns being the village *migra* (their local migration "officials"). They are the watchful eyes examining every vehicle and pedestrian traveling through their village, day and night. They search for alcohol and drugs and, if found, the alcohol is dumped on the ground, drugs are destroyed. These substances are considered threats to the clear hearts and minds needed to conduct a revolution against great odds. In a translated conversation, I joked with Zapatista Comandante Tacho at a middle-of-the-night meeting deep in the jungle that if the United States wanted to fight the drug war in Chiapas they should hire the Zapatistas. He laughed, but then proceeded to explain how serious their revolution was. "We will never return to a position of obeying a system requiring our enslavement, and, yes, I and most Zapatistas would rather die than comply."

Even without alcohol and drugs, the residents know how to celebrate. Two marimbas and a male crew of marimba players had become popular throughout the region. In the eleven days we were in San José del Rio, they produced five fiestas of lively music and dance. There was a makeshift soccer field where kids played everyday, and one basketball hoop and backboard. We enjoyed lots of wonderful discussions with community members.

These villagers grow a number of vegetables and fruits, and have plenty of chickens and the occasional cow, but their sustenance and their spiritual life revolves around maize. It is maize that keeps these People of the Corn rooted to their land and to their communities. They used to sell excess corn to local markets, which gave them some currency or trading capacity. Now they can't do that, because the United States is importing so much cheap corn. Except for coffee, the Zapatistas don't export or import much of anything at all, and the trading they do is mainly within eastern Chiapas.

I don't want to suggest that the Zapatistas live a utopian life. They are materially very poor. Some barely have shoes. However, despite their impoverishment, caused by centuries of Eurocentric enslavement, they are determined and enthusiastic about their new freedom—freedom achieved through their own education, sacrifice, and a keen understanding of the structural injustices that have oppressed them and their ancestors since Columbus.

What the U.S. government and many of its citizens can't understand is that attaining material prosperity is not a life goal for all people. The Zapatistas don't want to be part of the market economy and they are willing to live with the consequences, which may include a certain amount of material deprivation. They understand that we as a species are not designed to be cogs in a wheel. We are meant to be autonomous beings in small, cooperative communities, in turn communicating with residents living in hundreds of other similar villages.

A Different Way of Life

The deep human experiences of Indigenous people provide them with a profound understanding of the pathology of the Columbus Enterprise, and an even more profound self-awareness of their innate capacity to reorganize in local, self-sufficient, durable communities. This is true of all *Homo sapiens*. We were all autonomous Indigenous human beings once. We don't need to be tethered to a global economy that promulgates wars in the name of peace, or poverty in the name of prosperity. We can choose a different way of life.

Autonomy does not mean anonymity. On the contrary. When we express our deepest selves, we discover our connection to one another, fostering empathy, equity, and cooperation in community interdependence.

The Hebrew prophets, Jesus, Buddha, the Confucianists—they all understood that the force within us is the same force that links all of us. We are the product of a long journey of matter that has spirit and soul embodied in it. We can't eliminate that. We can condition ourselves to be obedient to ideologies, but at some point our original sacred soul seeks expression. It is naturally part of who we are. The Zapatistas are an expression of that basic autonomous spirit.

We in the United States are socially atrophied. Our focus tends to be on making money, and many of us have very little time left over to actually participate in the life of our community. One of the pathologies of the modern age is that we become spectators rather than participants in our own lives. Yet, that passiveness, that nonparticipation, is a choice—one that is killing our world. We destroy the earth by our inaction, or by thoughtless consumption with no concern for consequences.

Why do we live and act in a way that is so against our nature? We have become unhealthy as we endanger others around the world. Our purchase of material goods may make us feel good temporarily—a kind of high—but they don't make us feel really good, through our whole body. Psychiatrist Peter C. Whybrow, in his studies of addictive patterns in people, examined brain dopamine reward systems. He discovered that shopping provides a "rush" similar to that produced by addictive drugs. He attributes our U.S. American addiction pathologies to desperate attempts to relieve epidemic stress and anxiety, what he describes as the American "paradox of prosperity."[492]

What meaning does life have if it is lived without humanity? The average U.S. consumer life is conditioned by economics and a market-driven ideology that has nothing to do with humanity. We still build shelters for our bodies, we still have sacrificial rituals—but they have grown way out of proportion: we call them mansions and war.

I don't want my life defined by a bunch of White men (or anyone acting like them) who ask others to kill and possibly be killed to protect *their* money interests. Was the purpose of thousands of years of evolution merely to send young people like me to Viet Nam and other countries to kill people on the orders of another man (or woman)? I don't think so. But to be true to myself, I have had to learn the art of constructive disobedience. Obedience has been our paradigm for so long, that apparently we need an epistemological break to shatter our passive obedience to vertical authority. We are capable of developing a deeper consciousness that mindfully disobeys top-down authority while seeking wholeness in community.

The ability to live as cooperative beings in small cultural units is already embedded within us as part of our evolutionary genetic history. We simply need to access it in our bodies. For centuries it has been blocked by the familiar, and therefore comfortable, conception of the world dominated by the dualism of Cartesian thinking—the terribly misguided idea that our feelings (our bodies) can be separated from our thoughts (minds) or that we as a species are somehow set apart from and superior to the rest of the natural world.

We create ourselves. We are shaped by tradition, but we also create tradition. We can change whatever is necessary to survive. Thus, we humans make ourselves.[493] Mumford echoes this: "What the human mind has created, it can also destroy."[494] And, therefore, create anew.

Conclusion

In Country: USA

How was it so easy for me to follow an order to travel nine thousand miles to another land, another people, another culture—and participate in a grand effort to destroy them?

As a young man, I believed in the American Way Of Life. Just obey! Don't question our formula for success, or our way of life. Obedience of the masses enables power to preserve its control. But after tragedy, trauma and struggle, I began discovering a different Brian.

I started a new path having no idea where I was going. I still don't know. I told my family that I was done with the notion of church and state, of religion and government as I had been taught. I began crafting a new value system that is still unfolding. Writing this memoir is part of my unfolding journey.

Even now, more than forty years after Viet Nam, I am reminded of that war's moral pain. In 2003, our 823rd intelligence officer, Captain Paul, tracked me down with this message: "I'd get reports like 24 VC KIA and two pistols captured. Never made sense until I started talking to people like you. You came to Tan Son Nhut and I showed you one of the after action reports of a hundred VC killed. You confirmed my suspicions that we weren't killing VC." Shortly after receiving this message Captain Paul died of an Agent Orange related illness. He was one of five officers in the 823rd whom I considered friends. I decided to track down the other four, three of whom were section commanders like myself. One of them, a psychologist, had died of an Agent Orange related illness a few years earlier. Another, a police officer, had committed suicide after murdering his wife. The third, an opera singer, hasn't been heard from since 1984 and no one seems to know what happened to him. The fourth, my immediate superior in Viet Nam, Captain Joel, died of an Agent Orange illness in 1979. And so it goes, on and on, the price of war.

When I was born on the fourth of July in 1941, I was born into the American Way Of Life. Embedded deeply within me, and each of us, however, are our species' characteristics of cooperation and mutual respect, developed in small groups that prevailed until the advent of hierarchical "civilization" and its required obedience some six thousand years ago. I now realize that it is the American Way Of Life that is truly AWOL. As with all empires, it has taken a criminal departure from our deepest humanity. If my journey has a direction, it is to rediscover the psychological, spiritual wholeness that the Western way of life discourages and discards.

Drunk on the American Way Of Life

During the 1960s and 1970s, we were often told that Viet Nam was a "different kind of war." Bullshit! We began fighting against Indigenous peoples in the 1600s and have never let up. In our nation's history, we have overtly intervened in other countries at least 550 times, and since World War II, covertly thousands of times, while bombing twenty-eight countries. What was unique about our war in Viet Nam was that the United States did not win in the traditional military sense, even though it destroyed much of Viet Nam's ecosystem, infrastructure, village life, and murdered approximately 15 percent of its 1965 population.[495] This would be the equivalent of 46 million U.S. Americans murdered based on our country's 2009 population of 307 million.

These interventions are driven by our narcissistic addiction to material prosperity. Our culture of prosperity demands that we constantly find new resources, new sources of cheap labor, and new markets, at the expense of our espoused ideals of "freedom" and "democracy." Our desire for material goods far outweighs our commitment to these ideals, even treats them with contempt. Consequently, most of the pain, suffering, and plunder are outsourced to other lands, cultures, future generations, while the earth's health is compromised beyond repair.

Virtually all of us in the United States are drunks. We are drunk on stuff. Even though we know that we are devouring our planet, we can't stop consuming. Our addiction to technology has only accelerated our consumption. Like a drunk, our pain at hurting the earth, our sadness at being cut off from communal life by our electronic gadgets, our anger at the frenetic pace of daily life, only sends us back to the bottle. Studies show that when we feel sad, angry, or depressed, we go shopping.[496] Thus the addict's cycle begins again.

Of course, we don't realize we are addicts. We tell ourselves we are living the good life, that we are better off than any other society on earth. But this culture of comfort and convenience is also a culture of inequality and destruction. The problem with prosperity is that we never have enough. With computer technology we have become ever more addicted.

As computer chips grow smaller, they must be fabricated from very specialized metals, such as hafnium oxide. The United States currently mines hafnium, but our domestic mines are being quickly depleted. So we are now importing the mineral at a rate of four to five metric tons a year.[497] Many of these mines are located in Africa. Who owns the mines? How much are workers being paid? At what cost to their environment and their lives are we enjoying the convenience of our electronic gadgets?

We answer these questions by looking at the Congo, a country that has been raped for 125 years by European powers for resources such as ivory, rubber, and diamonds. The Congo possesses a vast wealth of minerals—such as cobalt, coltan, niobium, and germanium—required to create the innards of virtually every pager, cell phone, computer, VCR, CD player, TV, and fiber optic cable. Our ability to control the world depends upon these rare metals. Should we be surprised, then, that U.S. and other Western corporations and even the U.S. government have been found to be encouraging civil wars in the Congo, in order to extract resources using cheap labor while displacing ancient cultures from their land base? As many as 10 million moms, dads, and children in the Congo have been murdered since 1996, abetted by the corporate grab for these extraordinarily profitable resources.[498]

Compounding the cost of extraction are the extraordinary environmental costs of manufacturing microchips, far exceeding their small size. A *single* two-gram chip requires at least 3.7 pounds of fossil fuels and chemical inputs plus 8.5 gallons of water. The amount of energy needed to reach temperatures at the outer limits of technology to "fix" or "bake" every layer of "information" on a computer chip means its energy requirements *per weight* are hundreds of times greater than those of manufacturing an automobile.[499]

And the manufacture of an average desktop computer (like the one I am using) uses more than ten times its weight in fossil fuels and chemicals according to the United Nations University study which has called for a worldwide halt to the "growth of high-tech trash."[500]

A culture of inequality that is drunk on stuff and continues to depend on mining metals in distant countries will have to constantly be prepared to fight those countries to keep supply lines open. With the American Way Of Life, where more is never enough, resources have to be squeezed out of the hides of other people and a finite earth.

A Society in Crisis—The Long View

It's not easy to admit the fact that our everyday comforts are built on the oppression and conquest of other peoples and the destruction of the earth. It's frightening to face serious challenges to our thought structure; it's frightening to begin taking on a new consciousness. It's frightening to ask—honestly—questions such as: Why does nothing make sense according to the way I was raised? Was it ever the way I was taught? Why was I raised to believe in freedom and democracy if those are not values our country truly holds dear? The only way I could come close to understanding was to see the long view.

The longest view starts about 15 billion years ago when the primordial universe flowed into being. Our sun is but one of 300 billion stars in our Milky Way, and there are billions of galaxies in the cosmos, quite staggering to the human mind. Our earth and other planets were formed about 4.5 billion years ago, and the first pre-cell bacteria emerged about 4 billion years ago. At 2 billion years the first true nucleus cells with genetic material emerged, and over time multicellular eukaryotes (you-KARR-ee-ohts) evolved into animals, plants, and fungi. Though we humans tend to fear bacteria and don't much think about eukaryotic cells, our bodies contain trillions of each. Without them we could not exist. In a most authentic way, each of us started out as a microscopic organism.

Our closest living relatives in the animal kingdom are the seven-million-year-old chimpanzees, bonobos, and gorillas. About four to five million years ago the first bipedal hominid emerged. The first humans, *Homo habilis*, evolved about 2.6 million years ago, then the hunter *Homo erectus* at 1.5 million years. Some two hundred thousand years ago archaic humans evolved, and fifty to seventy thousand years ago modern *Homo sapiens* began migrating out of our species' birthplace in the central lakes region of Africa.[501] Every human being alive today shares a very recent (in geological terms) common ancestor from a male Y chromosome Adam and a female mitochondrial Eve that emerged out of Africa.

Scientific evidence shows that after the decline of the last major Ice Age about twelve thousand years ago, humans began to shift from hunting and gathering to settled communities. Through the domestication of plants and animals, a secure surplus of food enabled human numbers to surge. This agricultural revolution included the first Neolithic villages able to sustain populations of more than a thousand people and is considered one of the most radical social transformations in human evolutionary history. It was during this period that irrigation was developed, and pottery, weaving, architecture, and the wheel were invented.

Another huge change occurred around 5,500 years ago, or 3500 BCE, when these relatively small Neolithic villages began mutating into larger urban "civilizations." Domestication of plants and animals was followed by the domestication of people—creating slavery, class divisions, and imperial societies whose expansion was driven by the acquisition of more materials and enabled by slave labor. Over time, civilization, which we have been taught to think of as so beneficial for the human condition, has proven severely traumatic for our species, not to mention for other species and the earth's ecosystem. As modern members of our species (excluding the lucky Indigenous societies that somehow escaped assimilation), we have been stuck in this model of large vertical power complexes requiring massive obedience now for three hundred generations.

With "civilization," a new organizational idea emerged—what cultural historian Lewis Mumford calls a "megamachine" comprised totally of human parts to perform tasks on a colossal scale never before imagined.[502] In Mumford's analysis, civilization saw the creation of a bureaucracy directed by a power complex of an authority figure (a king) with scribes and speedy messengers, which organized labor machines (masses of workers) to construct pyramids, irrigation systems, and huge grain storage systems among other structures, all enforced by a military. Its features were centralization of power, separation of people into classes and lifetime division of labor, slavery and forced labor, arbitrary inequality of wealth and privilege, and military power and war.[503] Mumford makes clear his bias that autonomy in small groups is a human archetype that has become repressed in deference to obedience to technology and bureaucracy. The creation of human urban civilization has brought about patterns of systematic violence and warfare previously unknown,[504] what Andrew Schmookler calls the "original sin" of civilization,[505] and Mumford, "collective paranoia and tribal delusions of grandeur."[506] Joseph Conrad, in his 1899 novel *Heart of Darkness*, captured this ugly side of humans, depicting how "civilization" covers over the harsh realities of the cruel exploitation upon which it is built.[507]

"Surplus," a sanitized word for the accumulation of wealth, bred another new problem, institutionalized greed. Initially this was manifested in king-directed city-states and early empires. Eminent social scientist Riane Eisler argues that patriarchy (Eisler prefers the term "andocracy") gradually replaced goddess cultures with a warring male dominator model destroying a cooperative, partnership one.[508] Reportedly, 14,600 wars have occurred during the 5,600 years of written history.[509]

"Civilization" has required massive civil obedience to enable the vertical authority structures to prevail. Autonomous freedoms that people once enjoyed in precivilization tribal groups now defer to belief in authority structures and their controlling ideologies, which have been described as oppressive "domination hierarchies" where private property and male subjugation of women prevail, by force if necessary.[510]

The emergence of vertical authority structures, the rule of kings and nobles, ripped people from historical patterns of living in small tribal groups. Along with forced stratification, the separation of people from their intimate connections with the earth produced deep insecurity, fear, and trauma to the psyche. Ecopsychologists suggest that such fragmentation led to an ecological *un*conscious.[511] This trauma is exacerbated by the acceptance of vertical authority structures that require us to bury unpleasant feelings of unworthiness and invalidity that are associated with class. These feelings can quickly turn to shame, a dreaded emotion that remains buried so deeply in our psyche that we normally do not recognize it.

A major consequence of civilization, then, is that each of us likely nurses deep psychic trauma in the form of insecurity and shame. These feelings are usually so unbearable that to create viable personas we must develop defense mechanisms to mask them. Carl Jung described how we often play a trick on ourselves by projecting our dark inner shadows onto others. Arrogance rather than humility, ignorance rather than awareness, and violence against "others" rather than mutual respect, became major mechanisms to relieve the anxiety created by these insecurities.[512] Denial serves as a convenient, unconscious defense mechanism that covers over or obscures painful reality. Because our official life as a nation is enabled and built on collective denial of extremely painful realities—the dispossession of others—fantasy politics in the U.S. has become a way of life in our country.[513]

Individual psychic defenses are reflected in the development of civilization itself, as successive generations of shame-based upbringing and shame-based ethics have led civilized cultures to systemic patterns of violence, a "poisonous pedagogy"[514] and a "pathology of violence."[515] Ancestral desire for collective mutuality has been turned into collective blood-lust against our "enemies."[516] Societies based on materialism have hampered the development of deeper human relationships based on mutual respect and caring.[517]

The American Way

These words sound harsh but there are many examples in our nation's history and contemporary society. Many U.S. Americans do not realize that our political and economic interests brutally and systematically eliminated those people who fought Fascism during World War II. The Cold War Red Scare was, in fact, a smokescreen used by those with private wealth to insure expansion of profits at the expense of meeting basic social needs of people here and abroad.

During the 1960s, Martin Luther King Jr. expressed a powerful vision of a world built on mutual respect, a time when democracy was threatening to break out in our society as youth, women, Indigenous people, and African Americans began to empower themselves in opposition to the repressive status quo. Tragically, King was assassinated on the eve of his call for a massive Poor People's Campaign intended to force a restructuring of U.S. American society by redirecting massive funds from Viet Nam to serve the needs of the people at home.

Beginning in the 1970s, we witnessed a concerted repression of participatory democracy from which we still suffer. As William Appleman Williams has suggested, our country's original and sustaining ethos operates on the principle of advancing prosperity for a small number of elite, mostly White males, through endless expansion at virtually any cost. Any perceived impediment to that push to prosperity must be assimilated or eliminated, whether the language and tactics are masked (the tendency of Democrats) or unmasked (the tendency of Republicans).

Put another way, political power in the United States is concentrated at the top in a vertical authority structure as much as it was in any historical kingdom. Tyranny is inherent in the concentration of political, social, and economic power, whether achieved through elections, force of arms, or inheritance. The method of rule is essentially the same—achieving massive consent for hierarchies and bureaucracies, either through fear or propaganda/ myth.[518] It is ironic, then, that it is we the people who keep this tyranny in place. So, what happens when the people choose to cease being compliant even to the risk of death, seeking dignity?

What marks the United States as unique is our successful post–World War II effort to exert control throughout the entire world. And to repeat once again a most important reality for us to grasp: Though the U.S. represents only 4.6 percent of the world's population, its citizens consume at least 25 percent of the world's various resources. We have taken from others by force much of what we have, in the fashion of our European ancestors, through centuries of systematic blatant theft and gruesome murder expressed in at least three genocides that we must not forget, committed with virtual total impunity: (1) the murder of millions of Indigenous peoples so that we could steal their land; (2) the capture and ultimate murder of millions of African Americans (and others) so that we could steal their labor; and (3) the murder of millions of impoverished people throughout the "Third World" so that we could steal their resources. We outsourced all the consequential pain, suffering, and destruction to others, including future generations, and to the habitability of the earth itself. Since everything is part of a connected weave, this painful plunder will inevitably return to its sender like a toxic boomerang with extreme vengeance—"blowback." By choosing to not address this historic pattern of forcefully stealing from others with impunity, we ensure its pathological continuation.

You and I are the engine that keeps this system going. In the end, each of us needs to understand how our complicity fuels it. Our power lies in discovering how to create a completely different type of social system. It is worth noting that Riane Eisler makes a distinction between civilization's inhibiting domination hierarchies and a second type, actualization hierarchies of biological systems (e.g., molecules, cells, and organs of the body), which progress toward more evolved levels of functioning.[519] The former are applied with force, usually driven by fear and greed, subverting the natural flow of individual and collective energy. The latter are trust- and empathy-based in partnership systems, maximizing each organism's natural potential and evolution.

Facing our individual and collective complicity is difficult, but becomes an evolutionary/revolutionary leap as we relearn the moral truth that no one deserves a bigger share of the earth's wealth than anyone else. Then we have the opportunity to experience the deep feeling of mutual love and respect that is humanity's birthright. Learning how, once again, to experience ourselves as part of a greater, awesome undivided whole—that is the real revolution.[520]

The Real Revolution

I believe that deep within each of us is a soul and an ecological consciousness that totally grasps that all life is part of one evolving universe. To the degree we continue to put energy and faith in the political structure we grew up with—an oligarchy as it turns out—and participate in the monopoly capitalist market economy, to that degree we inhibit the space available in our lives for the Tao, or the Great Spirit, or our own soul, for a truly imaginary energy.

Former *New York Times* war reporter and author Chris Hedges characterizes U.S. democracy as an illusion—a useful fiction that serves to keep most people believing in and supporting a system that in fact protects imperial projects. A healthy society lies in rediscovering that genuine democracy, or biocracy (people *with* nature), only happens in small groups where all persons know one another practicing ancient values of empathy, mutual respect, and cooperation.

I do not like to think about what may happen if we are unable to take a leap of consciousness. We are not, after all, in control of the earth. A number of credible observers are warning us about tipping points signaling catastrophic changes to our ecosystem. Others describe the impending collapse of every centralized system,[521] and other sobering wake-up calls.[522]

Evolutionary biologist Jared Diamond has studied a number of societies to determine the factors that led to their collapse.[523] He identifies five contributing factors: environmental damage, climate change, hostile neighbors, change in friendly trade partners, and a society's responses to its problems. How we respond to environmental problems is totally within human control.[524] With humor, he makes his point:

> What did the Easter Islander who cut down the last palm tree say while he was doing it? Like modern loggers, did he shout "Jobs, not trees!"? Or:

"Technology will solve our problems, never fear, we'll find a substitute for wood"? Or: "We don't have proof that there aren't palms somewhere else on Easter, we need more research, your proposed ban on logging is premature and driven by fear-mongering"?[525]

There is nothing built into the life formula that says we are indispensable. Extinction is well within the realm of possibility. The late evolutionary theorist Stephen Jay Gould helped develop the theory of "punctuated equilibria" which states that evolution of any species, including ours, is most likely characterized by periods of geologically rapid change followed by long periods of stasis, with most change happening at the point when a new species is formed.[526] Gould suggests that evolution is not progressive, and that the present is a product of many contingencies over time, with no directional trend, no linear path. Human history has wandered across a landscape of possibility governed primarily by happenstance. That we are the only hominid in existence, he concludes, is historically atypical.[527] We are not immune from such a pruning.

The most dire prediction comes from James Lovelock, the independent scientist who proposed the Gaia hypothesis that the earth is a self-regulating "super living organism."[528] He believes that global warming has passed the point of no return and that by the end of the twenty-first century billions will have died with only scattered breeding pairs of humans remaining in mild Arctic regions.[529] Other scientists' predictions are not as dire, but none dare to totally refute the prestigious scientist's predictions. Increasingly, there are informed suggestions that due to interrupted supplies of petroleum upon which agribusiness is totally dependent, food famines will result in as many as five billion deaths in the next forty years.[530] Petroleum-dependent food production artificially enabled an exponential explosion of human numbers from 1.6 billion in 1900 to 7 billion today, a totally unsustainable number on a finite earth.

Petroleum, mining metals, and electricity are so inextricably codependent that very soon electricity shortages caused by interrupted supplies of petroleum will play havoc with all the systems we are dependent upon for virtually every aspect of our lives. I still remember the question an Amish blacksmith used to ask me: "What are you moderns going to do when the electrons stop?" I laughed then. Now, it seems prophetic. Beginning around 1900, the expanding use of the private automobile and the national electrical grid, both fueled by the flow of seemingly endless supplies of petroleum, have a century later devoured a majority of our basic earth resources while egregiously polluting our air, water, and soil. The 1890s, the era in which both sets of my grandparents were married, was possibly the last window of opportunity for collectively designing a sustainable society.

Growing awareness leads naturally to right livelihood. As Indigenous activist and environmentalist Winona LaDuke says, "Get some place, stay there, live in a way that is peaceful to that place. Dig in." What excites me is that we have the capacity to stop what we are doing, just stop. The alternative to genocide and ecocide is living humanly and wholly in local, steady-state, relatively small, food- and simple-tool-sufficient communities. By contracting, relocalizing, and conserving, we might discover what social critic Barbara Ehrenreich calls the joy of the rallying together, the community dance. These ideas echo the insights of Kropotkin published more than a century ago.[531]

We need to learn the art of becoming *uncivilized*. I can imagine some intermediate step where soon, out of necessity, members of our species revive what might be described as a form of bioregionalism, or federations of thousands of local communities that resemble Neolithic-type models. To thrive as human beings, it would be instructive to synthesize the wisdom of tribes, villages, and cultures based on a partnership model. Such social organization is the only known sustainable model found in human evolutionary history, a paradigm well worth revisiting.[532]

I was first exposed to the elements of local, steady-state societies when growing up near the Amish, then later observing rural village life in Viet Nam and campesino communities in Central America. These people generally had very little in terms of material wealth, yet were able to sustain a relatively stable, warm, and rich culture with the "little" they had.

But to develop an awakened consciousness also requires engagement in *internal* work, beyond changing lifestyle and consumer habits. I am examining with great difficulty the more shadowy, emotional dimensions of my psyche. I learned to accept and love my father without particularly liking him. Learning to be emotionally honest, not just with those who are close to me, but people in general, has meant learning an entirely new skill—taking responsibility for my own feelings. I have been in counseling for many years, and participated in safe, guided weekend sessions with other men expressing painful family memories, adult misbehaviors, resentments, grief and emotional hurts. Nonviolent communication teaches awareness by careful identification of one's feelings as they relate to real, specific needs. This takes substantial practice with others. It is part of the revolutionary process.

Less and Local—Small, Slow, Simple

As I finish this book, I'm experimenting with reducing my energy dependence, including dramatically cutting back on private auto travel and totally eliminating air travel. My partner Becky and I are working with others in our city's "Transition" movement to prepare for a dramatic energy descent by taking steps toward relocalization and the creation of a non-carbon-based local economy. Transition Town Initiatives are now being explored in nearly three hundred communities worldwide. Some of the essential elements of this movement are: developing resilience by building community within local neighborhoods, protecting diversity in various local sufficiency efforts, reskilling to fulfill basic human needs, increasing neighborhood emergency preparedness, promoting local banks and credit unions, and creating local currency. Instructive examples that provide inspiration include Cuba's transition toward creative self-sufficiency and its exemplary emergency preparedness following the devastating loss of its oil supply and the decades-long sanctions imposed by the United States. The Mondragón Cooperative in Spain, the Zapatista autonomous municipalities in Chiapas, Mexico, and the neighborhood assemblies in Argentina after their currency collapsed in 2001 are also excellent examples.

Personally, it's been easiest to contract our energy usage, although it requires an up-front financial investment. My partner and I very consciously reduce our electrical consumption by frugal use of lighting and appliances. We heat our house with wood and with an efficient electric heat pump. We replaced our gas appliances with very efficient electric ones. We fully insulated our house while installing a solar preheated water system and photovoltaic solar panels that are already producing a good percentage of the electricity we use. The remainder is generated from all-renewable sources purchased from our local utility company (no coal, no oil, no natural gas, no nuclear). This option is not available to everyone, and even renewables are not sustainable, except in local and limited applications, because of the vast energy inputs required and extensive pollution caused by mining, manufacturing, and distribution of the infrastructure.

My discovery of arm-powered handcycling opened a new world—an enjoyable way to stay fit while practicing a personal political policy of local transportation without use of fossil fuels. The sign on the back of my trike says: "Cycling: A quiet statement against oil wars."

For the past thirteen years I have traveled over fifty thousand miles on a three-wheeled handcycle. For fun I have participated with other handcyclists in five marathons, including Boston and New York. I average about a hundred miles a week between local errands and food shopping, meetings, and recreation.

We have a small 1984 Chevy pickup truck converted to all-electric that we use sparingly for local trips. Becky also drives an old car fueled primarily by recycled, second-use, local "waste" grease converted to biodiesel. While sustainable for a limited number of local drivers, biodiesel is not something that can be universalized because the growth of monocultural biofuel crops is supplanting food crops. It is a cruel irony that 2 billion people are starving or nearly starving, while big ag turns from producing food for people to producing fuel for the world's 800 million motorists.

We also save conserve by using various water-saving devices, including a low-water-use washing machine. We often take sponge baths instead of showers. We recycle greywater and a hundred percent of rainwater from our roof diverts into garden beds, swales, and collection tanks for irrigation. Our waterless composting toilet separately collects urine which, when diluted, provides valuable nutrients for our permaculture gardens. This practice of eliminating flush toilets saves five thousand gallons of water a year, keeping our valuable composted "wastes" on site rather than flowing to a central sewer.

Much of the food we choose to eat is local, and that does take a very conscious decision as to where to live, and how to live. We are fortunate to have a generous yard converted into a permaculture edible landscape featuring many fruit and nut trees and berry bushes as well as raised beds for vegetable growing. Permaculture (a contraction of the words permanent and culture) is a human ecological design system mimicking nature. We grow as much of our own vegetables as possible and buy what we cannot grow from sources within a hundred-mile radius—the "hundred-mile diet"—whenever possible. We buy produce in season at our local co-op and grocery stores, farmer's markets, or through community-supported agriculture (CSA), and try to avoid consuming fruits and vegetables flown in from faraway places. Still, some of the foods we most take for granted—salt, pepper, sugar, flour, and spices—are very hard if not impossible to come by locally produced. However, we increasingly are able to use local honey in place of sugar, grind flour in our kitchen from organic grains grown regionally, and use ground kelp from the nearby ocean in lieu of salt.

It takes an ongoing effort to cut down on the number of nonfood items we consume. So much of our culture tells us to buy, buy, buy. Becky and I practice conservation by using recycled materials, radically reducing purchase of consumable items, and trying to avoid excess packaging, especially plastic. We strive not to purchase consumer items manufactured elsewhere, an increasingly difficult challenge leading us to question just what we really need. We try to practice conscious consumerism instead of compulsive shopping, and buy recycled goods whenever possible. We sometimes choose to pay more than an item's value to have it repaired rather than send it to the landfill.

We still use computers, knowing that their manufacture is based on exploitation of resources, including the murder of people who get in the way of those resources. I am aware there are health issues for the workers assembling the very piece of technology with which I am composing the manuscript for this memoir. I struggle with this knowledge—and that's part of my journey. There may come a day soon when I stop using computers entirely for this reason. We extend the life of our personal computers for longer than was previously considered possible, resisting the heavy pressure from the industry to continually upgrade. Nonetheless, I am wrestling with an emerging question that I am unwittingly part of a process of great waste and destruction.

William McDonough and Michael Braungart wrote a book called *Cradle to Cradle*, espousing the principle that there is no need for waste, and advocating the development of products that require zero net energy from beginning, to end, to beginning for everything.[533] Nature knows no waste, and such a concept is purely a figment of the modern human mind. McDonough and Braungart argue that the environmentalist's refrain, "reduce, reuse, recycle" still perpetuates the one-way, cradle-to-grave manufacturing model that is now at least two hundred years old. They haven't completely figured it out yet either, but know we have to develop a way of life that understands all the inputs and the consequences of every consumer item. It means redesigning everything such that all ingredients are based on simple, natural resources so all their parts can be reused or go back into the soil. And, we know more clearly now, that unless technology is quite simple it is not sustainable.

Smaller and slower is a more engaging, more conscious way to live. This was first validated in my personal life when I read Schumacher's *Small Is Beautiful* in 1974.[534] But let me be clear: as noble as radical downsizing of personal lives is, and important that it spreads as a social movement, it is equally important to actively support for collapse of industrial civilization and eliminate our roles that continue to legitimize it.

Last Words

The destruction left by the incredible wars between nations, causing 100 to 200 million deaths as a result in the twentieth century alone, is now dwarfed in significance by the plunder of natural earth systems and Indigenous human cultures by industrial civilization. If our species is to survive, we must leave behind the rhetoric of entitlement and begin facing the reality of consequences. We need to look beyond "civilization."

From an evolutionary perspective this is an unprecedented opportunity for an explosion of consciousness, an awakening begging to happen. Disobedience to, and withdrawal of support from vertical power becomes natural as we rediscover locally sufficient horizontal communities throughout habitable regions, roughly following the pattern of our evolutionary social origins. A horizontal revolution will require us to make (what we perceive to be) extraordinary sacrifices as we give up our individual, selfish desires in order to preserve our collective life on this planet. However, the life-affirming nature of the revolution will bring many rewards.

We miss many of the meaningful relationships of life because we are distracted by frenetic activity facilitated by speed and technology. Practicing stillness for a few minutes each day helps nourish our imaginary beings. For the human species to survive, we can learn that the issues are deep within our tissues—in our cells—and that we are all interconnected—molecularly as well as in our social humanity.

As much as we are the problem, the destroyers of our home, we are also the solution, the antidote. Paul Hawken, in *Blessed Unrest*, identifies more than a million examples around the world of people reclaiming power in local communities, extricating themselves from dependency upon external inputs from corporations.[535] No longer spectators, they have become participants in creating viable local communities.

An old, wise maxim says "what resists supports," an understanding from physics that resistance to materials makes for strong construction. Applying this principle to the traditional struggle of people against entrenched power suggests that, instead of fighting vertical power, and therefore legitimizing and strengthening it, a better way may be to ignore that version of "power" and move the struggle to spaces where self-rule can take root,[536] i.e., creating people power in the interstices of the oligarchic structure. Gandhi deeply understood this concept. In the Indian independence struggle, he advocated the twin prescription of noncooperation with imperial authority and the construction of a model of self-reliance in every community.

When I handcycled with others from Eugene, Oregon, to Seattle in 2006 to attend the Veterans For Peace convention, I did so as an example of transportation policy as well as for recreation. Every rotation of my handcycle's twenty-inch wheel carried me six feet. Nearly 270,000 revolutions later I had traveled over three hundred miles, one revolution after another, modeling an alternative transportation pattern. We don't have to wait for the capital-R Revolution. Small acts, millions of them, are essential. Each turn of the bicycle wheel is a revolution.

The revolution is in us. We cannot depend on the state, on authority figures, on technology, or some other outside force to humanize our world. It is up to each of us to reawaken our ancient consciousness in cooperation with others in our local community. You and I *are* the world. We cannot depend on governments to protect the environment. But we do need each other! You and I *are* the environment. Less and local. Contraction, relocalization, conservation. What we consciously choose to do becomes the revolution, one moment, one choice at a time, honoring our evolutionary, social wiring.

The more we obstruct continuation of industrial civilization, and withdraw our cooperation and support, and the more we reconstruct *locally sufficient economies*, the better chance our species, and millions of other life forms, have for a dignified survival.

NOTES

CHAPTER 1

1 Florence Baldrich, my Sunday school teacher from 1946 to 1950 at the Geneva, New York, First Baptist Church, was thus quoted in the *Finger Lakes Times* (Geneva, NY) a week after I was struck by the munitions train at Concord Naval Weapon Station (Concord, CA) on September 1, 1987.

2 IBM had developed a sophisticated punch card and sorting system—precursor to the computer—that was first used to tabulate voluminous data managing the New Deal's social programs. But what made IBM the wealthiest corporation was its business association with Nazi Germany, beginning when Hitler first came to power in 1933. IBM's president, Tom Watson, an acquaintance of my uncle, was a fan of Hitler who awarded Watson in 1937 the Führer's Merit Cross of the German Eagle with Stars. IBM established a special lucrative alliance with the Nazis to create a data system for tracking and cataloging the location, movement, and status of every Jew and Gypsy from points of apprehension to camps and extermination in gas chambers. In effect, IBM had automated the "Final Solution." This taught me another lesson that when following profits to their origins, one generally discovers grievous theft, exploitation, or genocide. See: Edwin Black, *IBM and the Holocaust: The Strategic Alliance Between Nazi Germany and America's Most Powerful Corporation* (New York: Crown Publishers, 2001).

3 Bertrand M. Wainger, Edith Brooks Oagley, *Exploring New York State* (New York: Harcourt, Brace and Company, 1946), 20, 39, 50, 88, 89.

4 See: T.W. Adorno, et al., *The Authoritarian Personality* (New York: Harper & Row, 1950); Alice Miller, *For Your Own Good: Hidden Cruelty in Child-Rearing and the Roots of Violence* (New York: Farrar, Straus, & Giroux, 1983); and Michael A. Milburn and Sheree D. Conrad, *The Politics of Denial* (Cambridge, MA: The MIT Press, 1996). These are excellent sources for understanding a relationship between authoritarian personality, parental upbringings, and development of political attitudes as adults and consequent policies.

CHAPTER 2

5 William Appleman Williams, *Empire as a Way of Life* (New York: Oxford University Press, 1980), 198–99.

6 Richard J. Walton, *Cold War and Counter-Revolution: The Foreign Policy of John F. Kennedy* (Baltimore: Penguin Books, Inc., 1973), 55.

7 Ibid., 169–70; John S. Bowman, ed., *The Vietnam War: An Almanac* (New York: World Almanac Publications, 1985), 50–51.

8 Fidel Castro and José Ramón Fernández, *Playa Girón* (New York: Pathfinder, 2001), 222–23.

9 Jesús Arboleya, *The Cuban Counterrevolution* (Athens, Ohio: Ohio University Center for International Studies, 2000), 120–21.

10 James Bamford, *Body of Secrets: Anatomy of the Ultra-Secret National Security Agency from the Cold War through the Dawn of a New Century* (New York: Doubleday, 2001), 82–91.

11 Cecil B. Currey and Edward Lansdale, *The Unquiet American* (Washington: Brassey's, 1998), 139–55; Marvin E. Gettleman, Jane Franklin, Marilyn B. Young, and H. Bruce Franklin, eds., *Vietnam and America: A Documented History*, rev. ed. (New York: Grove Press, 1995), 81–92.

CHAPTER 3

12   Theodore H. White, *The Making of a President 1964* (New York: Atheneum, 1965), 106.

13   Gettleman et.al, *Vietnam and America*, 241–48.

14   Frances Fitzgerald, *Fire in the Lake: The Vietnamese and the Americans in Vietnam* (Boston: Little, Brown and Co., 1972), 264.

15   Gettleman et al., *Vietnam and America*, 240; Bowman, ed., *The Vietnam War*.

16   Gettleman et al., *Vietnam and America*, 241.

17   Harold Evans, *The American Century* (New York: Alfred Knopf, 1998), 147.

18   At a campaign speech in Boston, October 30, 1940, FDR swore: "I have said this before, but I shall say it again and again: Your boys are not going to be sent into any foreign wars." See Charles A. Beard, *President Roosevelt and the Coming of the War, 1941: A Study in Appearances and Realities* (New Haven: Yale University Press, 1948), 3–4.

19   John T. Robinson, *Honest to God* (Philadelphia: The Westminster Press, 1963). He proclaimed that "The first thing we must be ready to let go is our image of God himself." Bonhoeffer, a German Lutheran pastor, was arrested after joining the resistance to Hitler, then executed only a month prior to Germany's surrender in 1945. In the United States, he is best known for *Letters and Papers from Prison* (1953). Bonhoeffer advocated a "situational ethics" and religionless Christianity. German-born Paul Tillich, a Christian existentialist philosopher, became one of the most influential theologians of the twentieth century.

20   Alfred W. McCoy, *The Politics of Heroin: CIA Complicity in the Global Drug Trade* (Brooklyn: Lawrence Hill Books, 1991), 31–38 and R. Harris Smith, *OSS: The Secret History of America's First Central Intelligence Agency* (Berkeley: University of California Press, 1972), 85–87.

21   I used Harvey Cox's *God's Revolution and Man's Responsibility* (Valley Forge, PA: The Judson Press, 1965) as a text in the Oxon Hill, MD, Methodist Church Sunday school class. Cox, an ordained Baptist minister, was and remains an eminent theologian at Harvard Divinity School. In *God's Revolution* Cox declared that "as Christians we have no special entrée to what is happening in the world" (25) and that "Change is the way the God of justice shatters an unjust order and opens up the way of God's will for justice" (34). He argued that God has given us an assignment to love the world, which means "to take upon our shoulders the responsibility for its reconstruction and renewal" (36). My obsession at that time with the evils of Communism created an arrogant perspective on personal "responsibility" clearly not shared by Cox. Cox is popularly known for his 1965 essay "The Secular City," which postulates that the church is not an institution, but a people of action in the forefront of change in society.

22   Associated Press, "Geneva Church Conference Criticizes U.S. Viet Bombing," *Washington Star*, July 26, 1966. The World Conference on Church and Society, representing more than two hundred religious denominations from eighty countries, were meeting with four hundred delegates in Geneva, Switzerland. They overwhelmingly declared: "The massive and growing American military presence in Viet Nam and the long-continued bombing of villages in the south and of targets a few miles from cities in the North cannot be justified." Ironically, Harvey Cox was one of the signers of the declaration that, nonetheless, did not deter our sending a letter condemning that church body for its criticism of U.S. Viet Nam policy. We thought the delegates were "unrealistic" and concluded that "fighting may be necessary to attain constructive future goals."

CHAPTER 4

23   Asher Price, "New LBJ White House Tapes Released," *Austin American-Statesman*, November 18, 2006.

24   William F. Pepper, *An Act of State: The Execution of Martin Luther King* (London: Verso, 2003), 205. Pepper cites the Report of the Subcommittee on Constitutional Rights, Senate Committee on the Judiciary, *Military Surveillance of Civilian Politics*, 93rd Cong., 1st sess., 1973, 21. The U.S. Army's domestic surveillance program of the late 1960s was first exposed by a young Army captain, Christopher Pyle. Pyle, a lawyer, was teaching constitutional law at the U.S. Army Intelligence School at Fort Holabird, near Baltimore, Maryland, when he learned that the Army had dispatched 1,500 plainclothes military personnel to spy on antiwar and civil rights activists all across the United States. He brought this practice to public light in his article "CONUS Intelligence: The Army Watches Civilian Politics," *Washington Monthly* (January 1970), 4–16. His follow-up article, "CONUS Revisited: The Army Covers Up," *Washington Monthly* (July 1970), 49–58, intensified the public reaction such that Senator Sam Ervin, then the chair of the Senate Judiciary Subcommittee on Constitutional Rights, launched two series of hearings, and published two committee reports on the subject of military surveillance of civilians: "Federal Data Banks, Computers and the Bill of Rights," Hearings, 92nd Cong., 1st sess., 1971; "Military Surveillance," Hearings, 93rd Cong., 2d sess., 1974; "Army Surveillance of Civilians: A Documentary Analysis," Staff Report, 92nd Cong., 1st sess., 1972; and "Military Surveillance of Civilian Politics," Subcommittee Report, 93rd Cong., 1st sess., 1973. Pyle, who has taught politics at Mt. Holyoke College in South Hadley, Massachusetts, since 1976, was an important witness at the 1971 hearings. For a thorough examination of the covert spying by U.S. Intelligence operations over its own citizens, see Senate Select Committee to Study Governmental Operations with Respect to Intelligence Activities, *Supplementary Detailed Staff reports On Intelligence Activities and the Rights of Americans*, Book 3, Final Report, 94th Cong., 2d sess., April 23, 1976 (Washington, DC, GPO). The Select Committee was chaired by Senator Frank Church (D-ID), and it became popularly known as the Church Committee, producing fourteen reports in all.

25   Jonathan Neale, *The American War: Vietnam 1960–1975* (London, Chicago, and Sydney: Bookmarks, 2001), 92.

26   Stanley Karnow, *Vietnam: A History* (New York: Penguin Books, 1984), 514.

27   "Viet Cong" (VC) was a derogatory term meaning "Vietnamese Communist," shortened from Viet Nam Cong San. The Vietnamese described those same forces as the People's Liberation Armed Forces (PLAF). Similarly, what we termed the North Vietnamese Army (NVA), the Vietnamese called the People's Army of Viet Nam (PAVM). Apparently, the United States is not fond of using the word "people" in describing mass movements. And, of course, there was no authentic division of Viet Nam into a North and a South. That there was even terminology of two countries was simply a result of the temporary dividing line created by the July 1954 Geneva agreements ending the French-Indochina War that was to have been extinguished upon results of the mandated July 1956 unifying elections which never happened due to deliberate U.S. obstruction.

28   James F. Dunnigan and Albert A. Nofi, *Dirty Little Secrets of the Vietnam War* (New York: St. Martin's Griffin, 1999), 108–9.

29   Ecologist David Abram discusses how the body can be motivated "by a wisdom older than my thinking mind," in "The Ecology of Magic," *Ecopsychology: Restoring the Earth, Healing the Mind*, Theodore Roszak, Mary E. Gomes, and Allen D. Kanner, eds. (San

Francisco: Sierra Club Books, 1995), 301–15, esp. 313. Ecologist Paul Shepard describes the "secret person undamaged in each of us" in "Nature and Madness," *Ecopsychology*, Roszak, Gomes, and Kanner, eds. 21–40, esp. 39. Professor of philosophy and consciousness Christian de Quincey discusses the soul and wisdom in all matter in his provocative work, *Radical Nature: Rediscovering the Soul of Matter* (Montpelier, VT: Invisible Cities Press, 2002).

30   The Air Force defines the control roster as an "observation period for individuals whose duty performance is substandard or who fail to meet or maintain Air Force standards of conduct, bearing, and integrity." [See http://pdg.af.edu/Web%20Site/CHAPTERS/Chapter%2007/TEXT/7.12.html]

CHAPTER 5

31   Taylor Owen and Ben Kierman, "Bombs Over Cambodia: New Light on U.S. Air War," *Japan Focus*, May 12, 2007, http://www.japanfocus.org/-Taylor-Owen/2420.

32   McCoy, *Politics of Heroin*, 193–261, especially the discussion of Binh Thuy, 199, 233, 234.

33   My combat security and ranger training at Fort Campbell, Kentucky, included instructions in the rules of engagement that incorporated the Nuremberg Principles. The seven Nuremberg Principles are set forth in the London Agreement and Charter, an Executive Agreement signed on August 8, 1945, by the four major victorious allies in World War II, the U.S., U.S.S.R., United Kingdom, and France. The Agreement and Charter provided that the *major* war criminals whose offenses had no particular geographical location would be tried by an International Military Tribunal (IMT) at Nuremberg, Germany, for three major crimes—those against Peace, against Humanity, and against the Laws of War. U.S. Supreme Court Justice Robert Jackson, loaned to be one of the four prosecutors at Nuremberg, upon signing the London Agreement on behalf of the United States, stated: "For the first time, 4 of the most powerful nations have agreed not only upon the principle of liability for war crimes of persecution, but also upon the *principle of individual responsibility for the crime of attacking international peace*" [emphasis added].

Nineteen additional nations signed the London Agreement and Charter. The IMT at Nuremberg tried twenty-four major German Nazi offenders, from November 14, 1945, to October 1, 1946. From October 1946 to April 1949, the U.S. conducted a series of twelve subsequent trials, each centered on an *occupation group*, in which 836,000 former Nazis were tried, 503,360 of whom were convicted.

At the very first session of the U.N. General Assembly on December 11, 1946, the Nuremberg Principles, first identified at the London Agreement, were unanimously adopted. In June 1950, the U.N. General Assembly instructed the International Law Commission, a U.N. body of expert international lawyers, to reformulate the Nuremberg Principles and that was so done.

Among the most important of the seven Principles of International Law Recognized in the Charter of the Nuremberg Tribunal and in the Judgment of the Tribunal, which were adopted by the International Law Commission of the U.N. in 1950, are:

Principle 1: "Any person who commits an act which constitutes a crime under international law is responsible therefore and liable to punishment."

Principle IV: "The fact that a person acted pursuant to order of his government or of a superior does not relieve him from responsibility under international law, provided a moral choice was in fact possible to him."

Principle VI: "The crimes hereinafter set out are punishable as crimes under international law:

(a). *Crimes against peace:* (i) Planning, preparation, initiation or waging of war of aggression or a war in violation of international treaties, agreements or assurances; (ii) Participation in a common plan or conspiracy for the accomplishment of any of the acts mentioned under (i).

(b). *War Crimes:* Violations of the laws or customs of war which include, but are not limited to, murder, ill-treatment or deportation to slave-labour or for any other purpose of civilian population of or in occupied territory, murder or ill-treatment of prisoners of war or persons on the seas, killing of hostages, plunder of public or private property, wanton destruction of cities, towns, or villages, or devastation not justified by military necessity.

(c). *Crimes against humanity:* Murder, extermination, enslavement, deportation and other inhuman acts done against any civilian population, or persecutions on political, racial or religious grounds, when such acts are done or such persecutions are carried on in execution of or in connection with any crime against peace or any war crime."

The "Law of Land Warfare" found in the U.S. Army Field manual (FM 27-10, July 18, 1956), incorporates the Nuremberg Principles, which define and make criminal war crimes, crimes against humanity, and crimes against peace, e.g., planning or waging a war of aggression. These Principles apply to "any person," whether a member of the U.S. armed forces or a civilian.

The Declaration of the Judgment of the International Military Tribunal at Nuremberg concluded:

"To initiate a war of aggression is the *supreme international crime,* differing only from other war crimes in that it contains within itself the accumulated evil of the whole" [emphasis added].

Extracts of the Nuremberg Charter and Judgment can be found in B. Ferencz, *Defining International Aggression: The Search for World Peace* Vol. 1 (Dobbs Ferry, NY: Oceana Publications, 1975), Documents 18–20.

34   Neil Sheehan, *A Bright Shining Lie* (New York: Random House, 1988), 732.

35   There was a history from as early as 1962 of disaffected South Vietnamese pilots, mostly flying U.S.-supplied A-1 Skyraiders, defecting to nearby Cambodia. See Albert Grandolini, Tom Cooper, and Truong, "Cambodia, 1954–1999, pt. 1," Air Combat Information Group (AGIC), http://www.acig.org/artman/publish/article_410.shtml; and Cambodia: Aviation Royale Khmere/Cambodia Air Force, http://www.aeroflight. co.uk/waf/aa-eastasia/cambodia/cam-afi-aircraft.htm. On February 26, 1962, two disgruntled VNAF pilots flying A-I Skyraiders in broad daylight strafed and bombed the presidential palace in Saigon. One was shot down, but the other escaped to Cambodia. See John Morrocco, ed., *The Vietnam Experience: Thunder from Above, Air War, 1941–1968* (Boston: Boston Publishing Company, 1984), 14.

36   Douglas Valentine, *The Phoenix Program* (New York: William Morrow, 1990; Lincoln, NE: iUniverse.com, 2000), 215–16.

CHAPTER 6

37   Regarding Viet Nam: On April 4, 1995, the Vietnamese Government reported official figures of their citizens killed during the war—5.1 million. This was reported by Agence France-Presse (French Press Agency), April 4, 1995; and by BBC, "Vietnam War: History," http://news.bbc.co.uk/2/shared/spl/hi/asia_pac/05/vietnam_war/html/introduction.stm. The total 5.1 million Vietnamese dead was the equivalent of a staggering 14 to 15 percent of their 1965 population. In comparison, using today's popu-

lation numbers, the equivalent percentage of U.S. citizens would be about 43 million. Regarding Cambodia (Kampuchea) and Laos: Edward Herman and Noam Chomsky reported in *Manufacturing Consent* (1988; New York: Pantheon, 2002, 263) that six hundred thousand Cambodians, or 8 percent of its population of 7 million, were killed in U.S. bombings from 1969–April 1975, citing *Kampuchea in the Seventies: Report of a Finnish Inquiry Commission* (1982). This number of dead roughly coincides with that cited by U.S. government sources (CIA) of six to seven hundred thousand. Herman and Chomsky cite the August 24, 1975, *New York Times* conclusion that 350,000 Laotian citizens, more than 10 percent of the population, had been killed in Laos from bombings during the war. (*Manufacturing Consent*, 260). Thus, over 6 million Southeast Asians were murdered due to the planning, preparing, and waging of aggressive war by the U.S., the supreme international crime against peace, crimes against humanity, and systematic war crimes, especially from incessant bombings, as defined by the Nuremberg Tribunal (see n. 33 above).

38   David Hunt, "Villagers At War: The National Liberation Front in My Tho Province, 1965–1967," *Radical America* 8, nos. 1–2 (January–April 1974), 3–20.

39   Gettleman, *Vietnam and America*, 464.

40   Raphael Littauer and Norman Uphoff, eds., *The Air War in Indochina*, rev. ed. (Boston: Beacon Press, 1972), Statistical Summary 5b, 276.

41   Sheehan, *A Bright Shining Lie*, 112–14.

42   *The Uncounted Enemy: A Vietnam Deception*, CBS documentary, aired January 23, 1982. Regarding pressure placed on military officers to achieve high body counts, see David H. Hackworth, *About Face* (New York: Simon and Schuster, 1989), 677; in general, see Christian G. Appy, *Working-Class War* (Chapel Hill: University of North Carolina Press, 1993), esp. 156, 228–29, 231.

43   "The Road from Laos to Nicaragua," *The Economist*, March 7, 1987, as quoted in Noam Chomsky, *The Culture of Terrorism* (Boston: South End Press, 1988), 82, 106n20; John K. Singlaub, *Hazardous Duty: An American Soldier in the Twentieth Century* (New York: Summit Books, 1991), 474; Roger Warner, *Shooting at the Moon: The Story of America's Clandestine War in Laos* (South Royalton, VT: Steerforth Press, 1996), 192–98.

44   Warner *Shooting at the Moon*, 201.

45   Philip Jones Griffiths, *Vietnam, Inc.* (New York: Collier Books, 1971; repr., London: Phaidon Press Ltd., 2001), 120–23; "Slaughter Goes On," *The New Republic*, February 24, 1968.

46   James S. Hirsch, *Riot and Remembrance: The Tulsa Race War and its Legacy* (Boston: Houghton Mifflin Co., 2002), 6, 93–94, 106, 259–60, 285; Adrian Brune, "Tulsa's Shame," *The Nation*, March 18, 2002; Carla Blank, "Historical Amnesia: Worst U.S. Massacre?" *CounterPunch*, May 2, 2007, http://www.counterpunch.org/blank05022007.html.

CHAPTER 7

47   Gloria Emerson, *Winners and Losers: Battles, Retreats, Gains, Losses and Ruins from the Vietnam War* (1972; New York: Harcourt Brace Jovanovich, 1976), 343–46; Valentine, *Phoenix Program*, 348–49.

48   Fitzgerald, *Fire in the Lake*, 366–67.

49   James M. Carter, "The Merchants of Blood: War Profiteering from Vietnam to Iraq," *http://www.counterpunch.org/carter12112003.html*, December 11, 2003.

50   Noam Chomsky and Edward S. Herman, *The Washington Connection and Third World Fascism: The Political Economy of Human Rights*, vol. 1 (Boston: South End Press, 1979),

321; Harry G. Summers Jr., *Historical Atlas of the Vietnam War* (New York: Houghton Mifflin Co., 1995), 154.

51   "Memories of a Massacre," CBS's *60 Minutes II,* May 1, 2001; Gregory Vistica, "What Happened in Thanh Phong," *New York Times,* Sunday, April 29, 2001; Gregory Vistica, *The Education of Lieutenant Kerrey* (New York: St. Martin's Press, 2003), 240. CBS's *60 Minutes II,* also known as *60 Minutes Wednesday,* was intended to replicate, but not replace, the investigative style of the original *60 Minutes.* It first aired in January 1999; its last airing was in September 2005, while the original *60 Minutes* continues weekly broadcasts.

52   Daniel Ellsberg, *Papers on the War* (New York: Simon and Schuster, 1972), 237.

53   Emerson, 154.

54   The HERBS tapes, a computerized record from MACV (Military Assistance Command, Viet Nam) log books of time, date, place and amount of Operation Ranch Hand aerial fixed-wing herbicide spraying in Viet Nam between 1965 and 1971, were tabulated and mapped in Clark Smith and Don Watkins, *The Vietnam Map Book: A Self Help Guide To Herbicide Exposure* (Berkeley, CA: Agent Orange Veteran's Advisory Committee, November 1981); Winter Soldier Archive, 2000 Center St., Box 1251, Berkeley, CA 94704.

55   "First Dioxin Disaster," *Parade,* February 5, 1984, 20.

56   The reputation of the ARVN was generally as bad or even worse than that of U.S. troops. Trained by the U.S., they were corrupt, often stealing villagers' goods and selling them on the black market, or trafficking in drugs. See Barbara Tuchman, *March of Folly* (New York: Knopf, 1984), 360. In cities such as Vinh Long in the Mekong Delta, it was reported that ARVN troops backed up military trucks to storefronts and stole large amounts of merchandise. See Don Luce and John Sommer, *Viet Nam: The Unheard Voices* (Ithaca, NY: Cornell University Press, 1969), 272. Worse, it was well established that the ARVN routinely, and casually brutalized Vietnamese villagers.

57   For examples of atrocities and policies of terror carried out by U.S. military, see Edward Doyle and Stephen Weis, eds., *The Vietnam Experience: A Collision of Cultures* (Boston: Boston Publishing Co., 1984), esp. Chapter 7, "An Environment of Atrocity," 148–69; subsection "A Continuum of Terror," 150–53; subsection "An Environment of Atrocity," 153–58; sidebar "Fear and terror," 154–55; sidebar "A Strategy of terror," 156–57; and subsection "A Contagion of Slaughter," 158–60. From page 153: "That U.S. soldiers would commit acts of casual terror against helpless civilians was a disturbing discovery for many Americans. That they would be responsible for the annihilation of whole villages was incomprehensible. The men who served in Vietnam were no different from those who remained at home. But they found themselves in a situation for which they had not been prepared, an environment of fear and uncertainty where restraint could mean death and the distinction between enemy and civilian could lose its reality, an environment of atrocity with its own logic of crime and punishment. 'I gave them a good boy,' despaired the mother of Paul Meadlo, one of those accused of participating in the My Lai massacre, 'and they made him a murderer.'"

58   John Prados, *Lost Crusader: The Secret Wars of CIA Director William Colby* (New York: Oxford, 2003), 186–88, 194–97, 220–38; Sheehan, *A Bright Shining Lie,* 731–33.

59   "Thieu's Political Prisoners of War," *Time,* December 25, 1972.

60   Luce and Sommer, *Viet Nam: The Unheard Voices,* 157.

61   Sheehan, *A Bright Shining Lie,* 733.

62   Chomsky and Herman, *Washington Connection,* 323–24.

63   Fitzgerald, *Fire in the Lake*, 418; and Ralph McGehee, *Deadly Deceits: My 25 Years in the CIA* (New York: Sheridan Square Publications, 1983), 155–57.

64   New York: The Dial Press, 1967.

65   Philadelphia: Lippincott, 1966; Harrisburg: Stackpole, 1966, 5th rev. ed.

66   Nancy Zaroulis and Gerald Sullivan, *Who Spoke Up? American Protest Against the War in Vietnam, 1963–1975* (New York: Holt, Rinehart and Winston, 1984), 1–5; Charles DeBenedetti, *An American Ordeal: The Antiwar Movement of the Vietnam Era* (Syracuse: Syracuse University Press, 1990), 107, 129–30, 186, 194, 280. The other quite normal U.S. Americans who immolated themselves: Alice Herz, 82, a retired professor, holocaust survivor, Quaker, Unitarian, and WILPF (Women's International League For Peace and Freedom) member, on a Detroit street corner, March 16, 1965, died March 26; Roger LaPorte, 21, a Catholic Worker, on the Dag Hammarskjold U.N. Plaza, November 9, 1965; Navy veteran J.D. Copping, on a street in Panorama City, California, August 19, 1967; Hiroko Hayashi, 36, a Buddhist, on a street in San Diego, October 12, 1967; Florence Beaumont, 55, a housewife and mother of two in a neighborhood in La Puente, California, October 15, 1967; Erik Thoen, 27, a Zen Buddhist, in a field in Sunnyside, California, December 4, 1967; Ronald Brazee, 16, a high school student, near his home in Auburn, New York, March 19, 1968; and George Winne Jr., 20, a student, at the University of California–San Diego, May 12, 1970.

67   Robert Topmiller PhD, assistant professor of history, Eastern Kentucky University, e-mail message to author, October 14, 2006. Topmiller, a Viet Nam veteran who served as a medical corpsman at the battle of Khe Sanh in 1968, is author of *The Lotus Unleashed: The Buddhist Peace Movement in South Vietnam, 1964–1966* (Lexington: University of Kentucky Press, 2002).

CHAPTER 8

68   Roger P. Fox, *Air Base Defense in the Republic of Vietnam, 1961–1973* (Washington, DC: Office of Air Force History, United States Air Force, 1979).

CHAPTER 9

69   Seymour Hersh filed the breaking story on November 12, 1969, with Dispatch News Service, and it was subsequently picked up the next day by a number of newspapers in the United States, in articles such as "Lieutenant Accused of Murdering 109 Civilians," *St. Louis Post-Dispatch*, November 13, 1969, 1A, 19A.

70   David Cortright, *Soldiers in Revolt: GI Resistance During the Vietnam War* (1975; Chicago: Haymarket Books, 2005), 35.

71   Joel Geier, "Vietnam: The Soldier's Revolt," *International Socialist Review* 9 (August-September 2000), www.isreview.org/issues/09/soldiers_revolt.shtml.

72   Steve Starr, "Set Free in Angola Prison," *Decision Magazine*, June 2006, reprinted in *Good News Magazine*, September-October 2006, online at http://www.billygraham.org/articlepage.asp?ArticleID=681.

73   "The Farm: Angola State Penitentiary," *Democracy Now!* March 16, 1999, http://www.democracynow.org/1999/3/16/the_farm_angola_state_penitentiary.

74   George McTurnin Kahin and John W. Lewis, *The United States in Vietnam* (New York: The Dial Press, 1967).

75   "Policy Planning Study 23: Review of Current Trends in U.S. Foreign Policy," February 24, 1948, *Foreign Relations of the United States*, vol. 1 (Washington, DC: GPO, 1948; declassified in 1975), 509–29.

76 James B. Davies et al., *The World Distribution of Household Wealth* (Helsinki: United Nations University, World Institute for Development Economics Research, December 5, 2006).

77 Jared Diamond, "What's Your Consumption Factor?" *New York Times,* January 2, 2008.

78 George Monbiot, "Our Quality of Life Peaked in 1974. It's All Downhill Now—We will pay the price for believing the world has infinite resources," *The Guardian/UK,* December 31, 2002. Monbiot's report concluded that the U.S. quality of life peaked six years earlier than the U.K.'s.

79 WWF, "The Footprint and Human Development," *Living Planet Report 2006.* The WWF originally stood for the World Wildlife Fund, but its legal name has changed to "World Wide Fund For Nature," and the organization now uses only "WWF" as its formal public name.

80 William Appleman Williams, *The Tragedy of American Diplomacy* (1959; New York: W.W. Norton & Company, 1972). Williams is my favorite U.S. American historian. Born in a small town in Iowa in 1921, he was a graduate of the U.S. Naval Academy where he studied engineering and served as a Naval officer in the Pacific during World War II where he incurred a war injury. The fact that he was from a small town and was a war veteran immediately endeared him to me, as did his analysis of the political and diplomatic history of the United States. He received his doctorate in history at the University of Wisconsin, where he later was a popular professor during the Viet Nam War years. *Tragedy* was his most influential work, first published in 1959. Other works of his that have influenced me include *The Contours of American History,* 1961; *The Roots of the Modern American Empire,* 1969; and *Empire as a Way of Life,* 1980. He died of cancer at sixty-eight years of age in 1980.

81 Noam Chomsky, *Turning the Tide: U.S. Intervention in Central America and the Struggle for Peace* (Cambridge, MA: South End Press, 1985), 43–84.

82 Williams, *Empire,* ix.

83 George Orwell, *1984* (1949; New York: Signet, 1950), 4.

84 Gore Vidal, *Imperial America: Reflections on the United States of Amnesia* (New York: Nation Books, 2004).

CHAPTER 10

85 As Appy assessed, "American policy did not . . . make atrocities by individual soldiers inevitable, but it certainly made it inevitable that American forces as a whole would kill many civilians," *Working-Class War,* 201.

86 Richard Stacewicz, *Winter Soldiers: An Oral History of the Vietnam Veterans Against the War* (New York: Twayne Publishers, 1997), 318; Senate Select Committee, *Intelligence Activities,* 534 (see n. 24 above for full citation); Robert J. Goldstein, *Political Repression in Modern America* (Cambridge, NY: Schenkman Publishing Co., Inc., 1978), 466.

87 Philip Caputo, *10,000 Days of Thunder: A History of the Vietnam War* (New York: Atheneum, 2005), 102; Richard Pyle and Horst Faas, *Lost Over Laos* (Cambridge, MA: Da Capo Press, 2003), 148n2.

88 Citizens Commission of Inquiry, *The Dellums Committee Hearings on War Crimes in Vietnam: An Inquiry into Command Responsibility in Southeast Asia* (New York: Vintage Books, 1972).

89 Ira Glasser, "The Constitution and the Courts," in *What Nixon Is Doing to Us,* eds. Alan Gartner, Colin Greer, and Frank Riesman, 162 (New York: Harper & Row, 1973), as quoted in Goldstein, 499.

90   From the time the Marines first landed at Da Nang in Viet Nam in early March 1965 to the Paris Peace Accord on January 27, 1973, the cumulative data now suggest that more than 6 million Southeast Asians were killed due to the U.S. aggression. In the nearly 95 months of that inclusive period, the average was approximately 2,080 Asians killed per day, or 86 per hour.

91   David Zeiger, "Farewell Dave Cline," *Sir! No Sir!*, http://www.sirnosir.com/dave_cline. html, September 18, 2007. A tribute to Cline after his September 14, 2007 death.

92   "Willson Called Not Eligible as Democrat," *Post-Journal* (Jamestown, NY), April 6, 1972; "Sheriff Candidate Held Ineligible," *Courier-Express* (Buffalo, NY), April 6, 1972.

93   Ellsberg, *Papers on the War,* 42–135.

94   Senate Select Committee, *Intelligence Activities,* 980 (see n. 24 above for full citation).

95   Curt Gentry, J. Edgar Hoover, *The Man and the Secrets* (New York: W.W. Norton & Company, 1991), 652–58; Loch K. Johnson, *America's Secret Power: The CIA in a Democratic Society* (New York: Oxford University Press, 1989), 140–46; Evans, *The American Century,* 573.

96   Senate Select Committee, *Intelligence Activities,* 740.

97   Pepper, *An Act of State,* 11; Senate Select Committee, *Intelligence Activities,* 81.

CHAPTER 11

98   Sources: Bureau of Justice, *Corrections Statistics,* by year; Federal Bureau of Prisons, *Quick Facts,* by various dates; Bureau of Justice Statistics, *Census of State and Federal Correctional Facilities,* by year; Bureau of Justice Statistics, *Census of Jails,* by year; Bureau of Justice Statistics, *Jails in Indian Country,* by year; U.S. Department of Justice, Office of Justice and Delinquency Prevention, *Juvenile Residential Facility Census,* by year; and Fox Butterfield, "Despite Drop in Crime, An Increase in Inmates," *New York Times,* November 8, 2004.

99   Public housing data: "At Last, A Slowdown," *Time,* January 15, 1973; "Sources of Misery: When the Government Left the Poor in the Cold," *San Francisco Chronicle,* December 13, 2006; Todd Depastino, *Citizen Hobo: How A Century of Homelessness Shaped America* (Chicago: University of Chicago Press, 2003), 255–56; Joint Center For Housing Studies, Harvard University, *The State of the Nation's Housing,* 2001.

100   Paul Street, "Color Bind: Prisons and the New American Racism," in *Prison Nation: The Warehousing of America's Poor,* eds. Tara Herival and Paul Wright, 31–40 (London: Routledge, 2003).

101   Randall Mikkelsen, "Prison System a Costly and Harmful Failure: Report," *Reuters,* November 19, 2007.

102   Solomon Moore, "Justice Dept. Numbers Show Prison Trends," *New York Times,* December 6, 2007.

103   Bruce Franklin, *Vietnam and Other American Fantasies* (Amherst, MA: University of Massachusetts Press, 2000), 126–27. Regarding Reagan, Franklin cites Deborah Davis, "Free Tuition Is Dead—And Who Killed It," *Village Voice,* December 8, 1975; regarding Ford, Franklin cites Ira Shor, *Culture Wars: School and Society in the Conservative Restoration, 1969–1984* (Chicago: University of Chicago Press, 1992), 7.

104   Fernando E. Gapasin and Michael D. Yates, "Labor Movements: Is There Hope?" *Monthly Review* 57, no. 2 (June 2005), www.monthlyreview.org/0605gapasinyates.htm.

105   Jeffrey Reiman, *The Rich Get Richer and the Poor Get Prison: Ideology, Class, and Criminal Justice,* 7th ed. (Boston: Pearson, Allyn and Bacon, 2007), 5.

106   Ibid., 1–156.

107   Thorstein Veblen, *The Theory of the Leisure Class* (1899; New York: Mentor, 1953). Veblen is my favorite U.S. homegrown sociologist. Being from a small town and possessing such a careful yet searing critique of the country of both his and my birth was impressive.

108   Ibid., 60–80.

CHAPTER 12

109   Lee Nichol, ed., *The Essential David Bohm* (London: Routledge, 2003), 306–10.

110   Ibid., 84.

111   Ashley Montagu and Floyd Matson, *The Dehumanization of Man* (New York: McGraw-Hill Book Co., 1983), 219–20.

112   Peter Kropotkin, *Mutual Aid: A Factor of Evolution* (1902; Montreal: Black Rose Books, 1989), xli–xlii. Citations are to the Black Rose edition.

113   Ibid., 300.

114   Respected Danish sociologist Svend Ranulf suggested seventy years ago that the level of bourgeois psychology, i.e., whether upper bourgeois, petty bourgeois, or proletariat, in the origins of a modern country substantially determined the character of each nation, conceivably more important than heredity characteristics. See Svend Ranulf, *Moral Indignation and Middle Class Psychology* (Copenhagen: Levin & Munksgaard, Ejnar Munksgaard, 1938), 55–59. He cites, among others, V.F. Calverton, *The Liberation of American Literature* (New York: Charles Scribner's Sons, 1932), 50, 52, 55, 167, 169, 170. Calverton, born in 1900 in Baltimore, MD, was editor of the radical *Modern Quarterly*, later *Modern Monthly*, and an intellectual critic of American culture. He argued that "the American colonists in the main were drawn from this lower middle-class element" (45). He concluded that "in America it was the petty bourgeoisie which shaped our cultural attitudes from the very beginning," and that "Nowhere else was the petty bourgeoisie able to secure or assume so important a role in the cultural process" (170). In the main, Ranulf also concluded that this was true.

115   Bernard Bailyn, *Voyagers to the West: A Passage in the Peopling of America on the Eve of the Revolution* (New York: Alfred A. Knopf, 1986), 92 (Table 4.1), 166–67, 168–69 (table 5.15).

116   Calverton, 167.

117   Alexis de Tocqueville is commonly credited with coining the concept of American exceptionalism in his *Democracy in America* (1835). A recent essay on American exceptionalism can be found in Kevin Phillips, "American Self-Perceptions of Being a Chosen People and Nation," *American Theocracy* (New York: Viking, 2006), 125–31. Also see Seymour Martin Lipset, *American Exceptionalism: A Two-Edged Sword* (New York: W.W. Norton & Company, 1996). For a helpful summary overview of the origins of American empire and its sense of superiority, see Williams, *Empire*, 3–76. A sense of superiority was intrinsic to the first Puritans who believed they were God's chosen people tasked with founding a "Bible Commonwealth" to be perceived "as a city upon a hill" attracting "the eyes of all people." See Page Smith, *A New Age Now Begins: A People's History of the American Revolution* (New York: McGraw-Hill Book Company, 1976), 19–20. For an instructive history of Manifest Destiny, see Albert K. Weinberg, *Manifest Destiny: A Study of Nationalist Expansion in American History* (1935; Chicago: Quadrangle Paperbacks, 1963).

118   Charles Beard, "The Constitution in Operation," *Economic Origins of Jeffersonian Democracy* (1915); New York: The Macmillan Company, 1949), 108–31. Beard is my

second favorite U.S. historian, ranking close with William Appleman Williams. Born in a small town in Indiana in 1874, he became an academic focusing on the economic motives behind the Founding Fathers, the Constitution, and the new republic. In 1917, Beard, a Quaker, resigned his teaching position at Columbia University in protest of the draconian 1917 Espionage Act, which perturbed him even more than his opposition to U.S. entrance into World War I. He was a prolific writer of books, monographs, and magazine articles, often with his historian wife Mary. I have been most influenced by his *An Economic Interpretation of the Constitution of the United States*, 1913; *Economic Origins of Jeffersonian Democracy*, 1915; and *President Roosevelt and the Coming of the War, 1941: A Study in Appearances and Realities*, 1948. Beard has written many other provocative works, but due to my slow reading capacity, I have not yet studied most of these. He died in 1948 at seventy-four years of age.

119 Williams, *Empire*, 51.

120 James Madison, "The Federalist No. 10," *The Federalist: A Commentary on the Constitution of the United States* (published originally in the New York Packet, November 23, 1787 (New York: The Modern Library, 1937), 61.

121 Ibid., "The Federalist # 14," November 30, 1787, 84.

122 The U.S. Operations Mission–Saigon, detailed census data of South Viet Nam, 1964, which I studied while stationed at Binh Thuy.

123 Kahin and Lewis, *United States in Vietnam*, 140–42.

124 McGehee, *Deadly Deceits*, 138, 156; and Kahin and Lewis, *United States in Vietnam*, 140–42. The consequences of such insensitivity resulted in poor intelligence and an inability to penetrate the Communist hierarchy, as discussed in Harold P. Ford, *CIA and Vietnam Policymakers: Three Episodes 1962–1968* (History Staff, CIA, Center for the Study of Intelligence, 1998), 129.

125 E.F. Schumacher, *Small Is Beautiful: Economics as if People Mattered* (New York: Perennial Library, 1973).

126 Karl Hess, *Dear America* (New York: William Morrow & Company, 1975).

127 Ben Bagdikian, *The Media Monopoly* (Boston: Beacon Press, 1983).

128 Leopold Kohr, *The Breakdown of Nations* (1957; New York: E.P. Dutton, 1978); Leopold Kohr, *The Overdeveloped Nations: The Diseconomies of Scale* (New York: Schocken Books, 1978).

129 Schumacher, "Social and Economic Problems Calling for the Development of Intermediate Technology," *Small Is Beautiful*, 181–201.

130 Kohr, *Breakdown of Nations*, 26, 33–35, 45, 48, 84n1, 106–8, 145–53. For further discussions complementing both Schumacher and Kohr, see Gustavo Esteva and Madhu Suri Prakash, *Grassroots Post-Modernism: Remaking the Soil of Cultures* (London: Zed Books, 1998), esp. "Global Thinking Is Impossible," 22–23; "The Wisdom of Thinking Small," 23–26; "Downsizing To Human Scale," 26–27; and "Escaping Parochialism," 27–28.

131 Schumacher, "Buddhist Economics," *Small Is Beautiful*, 56–66.

132 Ibid., 62 [emphasis added].

133 Ibid., 60–61 [emphasis added].

134 Jim Merkel, *Radical Simplicity: Small Footprints on a Finite Earth* (Gabriola Island, B.C., Canada: New Society, 2003), 62–63.

CHAPTER 13

135 Hannah Arendt, *Eichmann in Jerusalem: A Report on the Banality of Evil* (1963; New York: Penguin Books, 1994), 276.

136 Lisa M. Krieger, "Shocking Revelation: Santa Clara University Professor Mirrors Famous Torture Study," *San Jose Mercury News*, December 20, 2008.

137 Stanley Milgram, "The Perils of Obedience," *Harper's*, December 1973, 62–66, 75–77; Stanley Milgram, *Obedience to Authority: An Experimental View* (1974; New York: Perennial Classics, 2004), 6–8, 11.

138 Milgram, *Obedience to Authority*, 179.

139 In general, see Philip Zimbardo, *The Lucifer Effect: Understanding How Good People Turn Evil* (New York: Random House, 2007). Zimbardo distinguishes dispositional (personal) factors, from situational (social) and systemic (political) ones, concluding that the situational is far more powerful than the other two.

140 Dave Grossman, *On Killing: The Psychological Cost of Learning to Kill in War and Society* (Boston: Little, Brown, 1995).

141 Milgram, *Obedience to Authority*, 182.

142 Craig Haney, Curtis Banks, and Philip Zimbardo, Department of Psychology, Stanford University, California, "Interpersonal Dynamics in a Simulated Prison," *International Journal of Criminology and Penology* 1 (1973): 69–97; Philip Zimbardo, "Stanford Prison Experiment" Web site, http://www.prisonexp.org/.

CHAPTER 14

143 "Defining and enabling experience" is a term used by Richard Drinnon, *Facing West: The Metaphysics of Indian-Hating and Empire-Building* (Minneapolis: University of Minnesota Press, 1980), 461.

144 David C. Korten, *The Great Turning: From Empire to Earth Community* (San Francisco: Berrett-Koehler Publishers, 2006), 126–41.

145 Williams, *Empire*, 37.

146 Ibid., 59; Robert W. Tucker and David C. Hendrickson, "The Empire of Liberty: The Conflict Between Means and Ends," *Empire of Liberty: The Statecraft of Thomas Jefferson* (New York: Oxford University Press, 1990), 157–171, 313n168.

147 John J. Carter, *Covert Operations as a Tool of Presidential Foreign Policy in American History from 1800 to 1920: Foreign Policy in the Shadows* (Lewiston, NY: The Edwin Mellen Press, 2000), 16, 24.

148 William Appleman Williams, *The Contours of American History* (Cleveland: The World Publishing Company, 1961), 192.

149 Williams, *Empire*, 65.

150 William Appleman Williams et al., eds., *America in Vietnam: A Documented History* (Garden City, NY: Anchor Books/Doubleday, 1985), 11.

151 Greg Grandin, *Empire's Workshop* (New York: Metropolitan Books, 2006), 24; Max Boot, *The Savage Wars of Peace* (New York: Basic Books, 2002), 125; "Kipling, the 'White Man's Burden,' and U.S. Imperialism," *Monthly Review*, November 2003.

152 Ivan Musicant, *The Banana Wars: A History of United States Military Intervention in Latin America From the Spanish-American War to the Invasion of Panama* (New York: MacMillan Publishing Company, 1990).

153 S. Brian Willson, *United States Intervention into Western Hemisphere Countries* (self-published, October 1990). The following sources were examined: Tom Barry and Deb Preusch, *The Central American Fact Book* (New York: Grove Press, 1986); "Black Ops, 1963 to 1983," *Harper's* (April 1984); William Blum, *The CIA: A Forgotten History* (London: Zed Books Ltd., 1986); Center For National Security Studies, *30 Years of Covert Action* (Wash., DC, 1977); *Rand McNally Atlas of World History* (map # 85), 1983;

Holly Sklar, "Who's Who: Invading 'Our' Hemisphere 1831–," *Z Magazine*, (February 1990), 53–54; John Stockwell, "Destabilization and Deceit," *Nicaragua Perspective* 13 (Spring 1986): 14–21; *Third World Guide '86-'87* (New York: Grove Press, 1986), Appendix, 530–40; Foreign Affairs Division, Congressional Research Service, Library of Congress, *Instances of Use of United States Armed Forces Abroad, 1798–1945* (Washington, DC: GPO), 1975; Harvey Wasserman, *Harvey Wasserman's History of the United States* (New York: Four Walls Eight Windows, 1988), Map of Some American Interventions, 41; Howard Zinn, *A People's History of the United States* (New York: Harper Perennial, 1980).

154 Grandin, *Empire's Workshop*, 3.

155 Stuart Creighton Miller, *Benevolent Assimilation* (New Haven: Yale University Press, 1982), 213.

156 Ibid., 184, 213.

157 Ibid., 235.

158 Ibid., 251, citing *New York Times*, May 31, July 5, 1902; citing *San Francisco Call*, May 31, June 13, June 29, July 5, 1902.

159 Dana Priest, "U.S. Instructed Latins on Executions, Torture Manuals Used 1982–91, Pentagon Reveals," *Washington Post*, September 21, 1996.

160 Dana Priest, "Army's Project X Had Wider Audience," *Washington Post*, March 6, 1997; Robert Parry, *Lost History* (Arlington, VA: The Media Consortium, 1999), 9–10.

161 Associated Press, "CIA Allegedly Supplied Psychological War Book," *Boston Globe*, October 15, 1984; William M. LeoGrande, *Our Own Backyard: The United States in Central America, 1977–1992* (Chapel Hill: University of North Carolina Press, 2000), 363.

162 Richard Wilkinson, *The Impact of Inequality* (New York: The New Press, 2005), 306.

163 See, in general, Murray Bookchin, *The Spanish Anarchists: The Heroic Years, 1868–1936* (New York: Harper and Row, 1977).

CHAPTER 15

164 Michael Segal and Richard Gaines, "Strategic Forces: Kerry in the Clutch," *The Boston Phoenix*, September 25, 1984; "Vietnam Key to Kerry Focus on U.S. Foreign Policy," *Recorder* (Greenfield, MA), July 22, 1985. Reprinted from *Christian Science Monitor*.

165 Seymour M. Hersh, *My Lai 4: A Report on the Massacre and its Aftermath* (New York: Random House, 1970), 9.

166 Fox Butterfield, "Massachusetts Senate Race Narrows," *New York Times*, October 30, 1984.

167 Kenneth J. Cooper, "Veterans Divided on Kerry, Shamie," *Boston Globe*, October 15, 1984.

168 Louise Sweeney, "Vietnam Key to Kerry's Focus on U.S. Foreign Policy," *Recorder* (Greenfield, MA), July 22, 1985.

169 Senate Foreign Relations Subcommittee on Terrorism, Narcotics and International Operations, *Drugs, Law Enforcement and Foreign Policy*, 100th Cong., 2d Sess, December 1988, 41 (Washington, DC: GPO, 1989). This was popularly termed the Kerry Committee.

170 Susan F. Rasky, "Senate Approves Democrats' Plan to Assist Contras," *New York Times*, August 11, 1988; Associated Press, "Democratic Senators Near Accord on Contras," *Boston Globe*, August 3, 1988; "John Kerry's Senate Voting Record, 13 October 2004," http://voteview.com/kerry_voting_record.htm.

171 My reading list at the time included: Chomsky and Herman, *Political Economy of Human Rights*, vols. 1 and 2; Zinn, *A People's History of the United States*; Sidney Lens, *The Forging of the American Empire* (1971); Drinnon, *Facing West* (1980); Weinberg, *Manifest Destiny* (1935); Williams, *Empire as a Way of Life* (1980) and *The Contours of American History* (1961); ex-CIA officer John Stockwell, *In Search of Enemies* (1978); ex-CIA officer Philip Agee, *Inside the Company: CIA Diary* (1975); and ex-CIA operative Ralph McGehee, *Deadly Deceits* (1983), including a description of his role in Viet Nam.

172 Associated Press, "Envoy is said to Assert Nicaragua is 'Infected,'" *New York Times*, October 5, 1984.

173 Bob Woodward, *Veil: The Secret Wars of the CIA 1981–1987* (New York: Simon and Schuster, 1987), 281.

174 Robert Parry, *Lost History*, 61.

175 "President Calls Sandinista Foes 'Our Brothers,'" *New York Times*, February 17, 1985.

176 Lindsey Gruson, "Ortega Now Says End to Rebel Aid Can Save Truce," *New York Times*, October 29, 1989.

177 Philip Taubman, "2 Nicaraguans Dead Identified as U.S. Veterans," *New York Times*, September 5, 1984: "Two Americans killed when their helicopter was shot down in Nicaragua on Saturday were identified by associates today as Vietnam veterans and members of an anti-Communist group formed to assist the Nicaraguan insurgents"; The National Security Archive, *The Chronology: The Documented Day-by-Day Account of the Secret Military Assistance to Iran and the Contras* (New York: Warner Books, 1987), 63–64.

178 Lester H. Brune, *Chronological History of U.S. Foreign Relations*, 2nd ed., vol. 2, 1933–1988 (London: Routledge, 2002), 1015.

179 Knight-Ridder, *Miami Herald*, December 16, 1984, and Alexander Cockburn, "Beat the Devil" column, *The Nation*, February 9, 1985, as quoted in Chomsky, *Turning The Tide*, 129, 276n117.

180 Knight-Ridder, *Miami Herald*, December 16, 1984 as quoted in Robert Parry, *Lost History*, 270.

181 Bradley Graham, "Medals Granted after Acknowledgement of U.S. Role in El Salvador," *Washington Post*, May 6, 1996, 1A.

182 Envio team, "Nicaragua—Who is Going to Say Uncle? The Terms of the Conflict Become Clearer," Envio, March 1985, http://www.envio.org.ni/articulo/3392; later reported in "Contra Takeover May Be Necessary, Reagan Declares," *New York Times*, August 20, 1986.

183 "Key Congressmen Praise Embargo," *New York Times*, May 2, 1985.

184 Joel Brinkley, "Nicaragua and the U.S. Options: An Invasion Is Openly Discussed," *New York Times*, June 5, 1985.

185 Bill Keller, "U.S. Military is Termed Prepared for any Move against Nicaragua," *New York Times*, June 4, 1985.

186 Shirley Christian, "Reagan Aides See No Possibility of U.S. Accord with Sandinistas," *New York Times*, August 18, 1985.

187 Edgar Chamorro, affidavit given in Washington, DC, September 5, 1985, submitted to the International Court of Justice (World Court) Case Concerning Military and Paramilitary Activities In and Against Nicaragua, (NICARAGUA VS. UNITED STATES OF AMERICA). Copy of affidavit appears in Peter Rosset and John Vandermeer, eds., *Nicaragua: Unfinished Revolution* (New York: Grove Press, 1986), 237. Photocopy in author's possession.

188   See also Parry, *Lost History,* 74–75 and Holly Sklar, *Washington's War on Nicaragua* (Boston: South End Press, 1988), 224–25.

CHAPTER 16

189   Diana Melrose, *Nicaragua: The Threat of a Good Example?* (London: Oxfam America, 1985).

190   Elliott Abrams, editorial, "Keeping Pressure on the Sandinistas," *New York Times,* January 13, 1986.

191   William Clark, "Public Diplomacy (Central America)," July 1, 1983, published as Document 6 in *The Iran-Contra Scandal: The Declassified History,* eds. Peter Kornbluh and Malcolm Byrne, 21 (New York: The New Press, 1993).

192   "Virus" is a term often used by Noam Chomsky.

193   Richard N. Ostling, "Power, Glory—and Politics," *Time,* February 17, 1986.

194   Group Watch Profile, "Christian Broadcasting Network," interview with Honduran human rights official, Dr. Ramon Custodio, December 1985. Group Watch Profile was a project of the Interhemispheric Resource Center, now located at Political Research Associates in Somerville, MA (www.publiceye.org) that profiled right-wing private organizations and churches in the United States.

195   Tom Fiedler, "Robertson Pledges to Support Nicaragua Invasion," *San Jose Mercury News,* November 13, 1987.

196   Tom Barry, Deb Preusch, and Beth Sims, eds., *The New Right Humanitarians* (Albuquerque, NM: The Resource Center, 1986), 39; Thomas B. Edsall, "'Moral Majority' Name Changed to Boost Image," *Washington Post,* January 4, 1986.

197   Edgar Chamorro, letter, "Terror Is the Most Effective Weapon of Nicaragua's 'Contras,'" *New York Times,* January 9, 1986.

198   Sklar, *Washington's War on Nicaragua,* 245–46.

199   Alfonso Chardy, "N.S.C. Supervised Office to Influence Opinion," *Miami Herald,* July 19, 1987: "'If you look at it as a whole, the Office of Public Diplomacy was carrying out a huge psychological operation of the kind the military conducts to influence a population in denied or enemy territory,' a senior U.S. official familiar with the effort said"; Robert Parry and Peter Kornbluh, "Reagan's Pro-Contra Propaganda Machine," *Washington Post,* September 4, 1988: "The campaign came to resemble the sort of covert political operation the C.I.A. runs against hostile forces overseas but is outlawed from conducting at home"; Alfonso Chardy, "Secrets Leaked to Harm Nicaragua, Sources Say," *Miami Herald,* October 13, 1986, reporting that a disinformation campaign named "Project Truth," designed to set the agenda for debate over Nicaragua, apparently was activated in a secret National Security Directive titled "Management of Public Diplomacy Relative to National Security," dated January 14, 1983. See, for example, Robert Parry, "Iran-Contra's 'Lost Chapter,'" *CommonDreams News Center,* June 30, 2008, http://www.commondreams.org/archive/2008/06/30/9992/.

200   George Creel, *Complete Report of the Chairman of the Committee on Public Information, 1917, 1918, 1919* (Washington, DC: GPO, 1920), 2–6.

201   Stuart Ewen, *PR! A Social History of Spin* (New York: Basic Books, 1996), 6, 34, 102–27, 147.

202   Woodward, *Veil,* 37, contempt for Carter; 105, ruthless and cutthroat; 119, tough and cold, knew right from wrong. During the 1980 presidential campaign, President Carter's briefing book was surreptitiously copied by hostile parties prior to a TV debate, ending up in the possession of Reagan's staff which enabled them to prep the candidate to

respond to what Carter was expected to say. James Baker, who subsequently became Reagan's chief of staff, admitted having seen Carter's briefing book, saying that he had gotten it from William Casey, Reagan's then campaign manager. Casey claimed not to remember any such book. See Ed Magnuson, "I Never Knew There Was Such a Thing," *Time*, July 11, 1983. One historian reported that a copy of Carter's briefing book was kept in Casey's safe. See John Prados, *President's Secret Wars: CIA and Pentagon Covert Operations From World War II Through the Persian Gulf* (Chicago: Ivan R. Dee, 1996), 371.

203   Alfonso Chardy, "North and the 'Secret Government': Martial Law Plan Among Work of Reagan Advisors," *San Jose Mercury News*, July 5, 1987; Dave Lindorff, "Oliver's Martial Plan," *Village Voice*, July 21, 1987.

204   Ross Gelbspan, *Break-ins, Death Threats and the FBI: The Covert War Against the Central America Movement* (Boston: South End Press, 1991), 184.

205   Harold Denny, "Wall Street Role Large in Nicaragua," *New York Times*, July 29, 1928; repr. in *Central America and the Caribbean: The New York Times*, eds. Graham Hovey and Genee Brown, 114–15 (New York: Arno Press, 1980).

206   "American Marines Land at Capital of Nicaragua Rebels," *New York Times*, December 25, 1926, repr. in Hovey and Brown, eds., *Central America and the Caribbean*, 108–9.

207   Calvin Coolidge Special Message to Congress, "American Intervention in Nicaragua" (extracts), 69th Cong., 2d sess., *Congressional Record* 1324–26 (January 10, 1927): H 633; Vincent Ferraro, "Calvin Coolidge, 'Intervention in Nicaragua,' 1927," http://www.mtholyoke.edu/acad/intrel/cc101.htm; "Coolidge Openly Accuses Mexico in Unexpected Message to Congress, Defending His Policy Nicaragua; Warns Against Meddling," *New York Times*, January 11, 1927.

208   Richard O'Connor, "Mr. Coolidge's Jungle War," *American Heritage* 19, no. 1 (December 1967): 36–39, 89–93.

209   Godfrey Hodgson, *The Colonel: The Life and Wars of Henry Stimson, 1867–1950* (New York: Knopf, 1990), 108.

210   Ibid., 108–9.

211   Richard V. Oulahan, "Kellogg Offers Evidence of Red Plots In Nicaragua and Aid from Calles," *New York Times*, January 13, 1927, repr. in Hovey and Brown, eds. *Central America and the Caribbean*, 110–11.

212   Hodgson, *Colonel*, 119.

213   "1,000 Additional Marines are Ordered to Nicaragua to Quell Sandino Revolt," *New York Times*, January 4, 1928, repr. in Hovey and Brown, eds., *Central America and the Caribbean*, 112–13.

214   Joseph H. Alexander, *The Battle History of the U.S. Marines* (New York: HarperPerennial, 1997), 56–58.

215   Colman McCarthy, "In Nicaragua, An Ex-Marine's Campaign of Conscience," *Washington Post*, Sunday, March 2, 1986.

216   Ibid.; See also: Michael Parenti, *The Sword and the Dollar: Imperialism, Revolution, and the Arms Race* (New York: St. Martins Press, 1989), 41.

217   Envio team, "Nicaragua: Who Is Going to Say Uncle? The Terms of the Conflict Become Clearer," *Envio*, March 1985, http://www.envio.org.ni/articulo/3392.

218   Leonel Rugama Rugama, from an Esteliano family, is one of Nicaragua's most famous revolutionary poets. He was killed in 1970 at age twenty fighting Somoza's National Guard near Estelí. His powerful poem, "The Earth is a Satellite of the Moon," is known throughout Latin America.

219 Adon Taft, "TV Evangelist Defends Aid to Nicaragua," *Miami Herald,* June 14, 1985; Sara Diamond, "Right Wing's Televangelists Manipulate U.S. on Contra Aid and Apartheid," *Sequoia,* September/October 1986.

220 James LeMoyne, "U.S. is Said to Aid Contras via Salvador," *New York Times,* February 13, 1986.

221 M.K. Gandhi, *Non-Violent Resistance* (New York: Schocken Books, 1961), 86.

222 Helen Michalowski and Robert Cooney, eds., *The Power of the People: Active Nonviolence in the United States* (Culver City, CA: Peace Press, 1977), 137.

223 Ibid.

224 Jim Ridgeway, "Veterans Revolt," *Village Voice,* November 8, 1983.

CHAPTER 17

225 United Press International, March 3, 1986, reporting remarks at a White House meeting for supporters of U.S. assistance for the Nicaraguan Democratic Resistance (Contras): "It'd be a major defeat in the quest for democracy in our hemisphere, and it would mean consolidation of a privileged sanctuary for terrorists and subversives just two days' driving time from Harlingen, Texas." See Ronald Reagan, "Remarks at a White House Meeting for Supporters of United States Assistance for the Nicaraguan Democratic Resistance," http://www3.niu.edu/~tdorafi/history468/apr1805.htm. This statement was considered so absurd it became famous, and ubiquitous, repeated thousands of times with no specific attribution. For example see *New York Times,* "Another Kind of Peace Dividend?" April 27, 1990, which begins, "Four years ago, President Reagan warned that the Sandinistas in Nicaragua were consolidating 'a privileged sanctuary for terrorists and subversives just two days' driving time from Harlingen, Texas.' Mr. Reagan's histrionic threat of invasion never materialized. Now, as Nicaragua's democratically elected President, Violeta Barrios de Chamorro, is taking office in Managua, Border Patrol stations near Harlingen and San Diego are reporting something like the opposite: fewer undocumented immigrants from Central America."

226 Philip Shenon, "U.S. Aide Terms Nicaragua 'Aggressor State' In Region," *New York Times,* March 29, 1986.

227 "If we don't stop the Reds in South Vietnam, tomorrow they will be in Hawaii, and next week they will be in San Francisco": Michael Kort, *The Colombia Guide to the Cold War* (New York: Columbia University Press, 1998), 56.

228 James McCartney, "The Threat Posed by Sandinistas is at Center of Debate," *Philadelphia Inquirer,* March 20, 1986.

229 Landon Lecture Series, Kansas State University, April 14, 1986.

230 Such disregard for the rule of law was, sadly, not unprecedented. During the Banana Wars at the start of the twentieth century, the United States destroyed the Central American Court of Justice, established at U.S. initiative, when it ruled against the U.S. in regard to its earlier interventions in Nicaragua in 1912 and 1916: Noam Chomsky, "U.S. Polity and Society: The Lessons of Nicaragua," in *Reagan Versus the Sandinistas: The Undeclared War on Nicaragua,* ed. Thomas W. Walker, (Boulder: Westview Press, 1987) 288.

231 Marvin Gettleman et al., eds., *Guatemala In Rebellion: Unfinished History* (New York: Grove Press, 1983), 53.

232 Mary McGrory, "Struggle Against Contra Support," *Times-Argus* (Barre-Montpelier, VT), August 15, 1986.

233 Bernard Weinraub, "Contra Takeover May Be Necessary, Reagan Declares," *New York Times*, August 20, 1986; Richard Halloran, "U.S. Gets Ready to Send G.I.'s to Train Contras," *New York Times*, August 21, 1986.

234 Will Lindner, "Willson: Fasting Vets Are Doing Well," *Times-Argus* (Barre-Montpelier, VT), September 24, 1986.

235 Jonathan Tilove, "Kerry Pleads for Veterans to End Fast, Four at Capitol 'Willing to Die,'" *Morning Union* (Springfield, MA), October 8, 1986.

236 Eduardo Paz-Martinez, "Rudman Likens Fasting Veterans to Terrorists," *Boston Globe*, October 11, 1986.

237 Stephen Engelberg, "U.S. Officials Said to Have Aided Private Suppliers of Contra Units," *New York Times*, October 11, 1986.

238 For example, Bella English, "Rally Against Contra Aid Draws 1,000," *Boston Globe*, September 29, 1986, reporting on a new Boston group, the "Veterans Vigil For Life."

239 Judy Keen, "Vets Cast Off Medals in Protest," *USA Today*, October 10, 1986.

240 James LeMoyne, "U.S. Officials Linked to Airlift of Contra Supplies," *New York Times*, October 14, 1986; Lydia Chavez, "The C.I.A. Role in Salvador: Air Base Described as the Key," *New York Times*, October 15, 1986.

241 See, for example, Joel Brinkley, "Four Veterans Ending Fast on Policy in Nicaragua," *New York Times*, October 17, 1986, which reported the end of the fast with a large photo of the fasters, quoting George Mizo: "'We have 500 documented solidarity activities.' . . . The fasters . . . now plan a new strategy. They hope to recruit hundreds of other veterans who will be willing to go with them to Central America, where they will try to intervene with Nicaraguan rebel offensives."

CHAPTER 18

242 John Greenwald, "World," *Time*, October 27, 1986.

243 Mark Johnson, "Willson Leads Protest," *Burlington Free Press*, October 26, 1986.

244 Jerome P. Curry, "Smuggling Probe Hits Peace Convoy," *The Sunday Express-News* (San Antonio, TX), August 14, 1988; Associated Press, "Nicaragua Peace Convoy Under Investigation," *Houston Chronicle*, August 15, 1988; Associated Press, "Smuggling To Guatemala Alleged: Was Peace Convoy a Cover?" *Houston Post*, August 15, 1988; Jerry Urban, "Veterans Planning New Move," *Houston Chronicle*, August 19, 1988. The latter article described federal intelligence reports held by the FBI, the Air Force Office of Special Investigations, and the U.S. Customs Service identifying five veterans, including myself, participating with the Veterans Peace Convoy crossing into Mexico carrying humanitarian supplies to Nicaragua while smuggling antiaircraft parts into Guatemala. Though I publicly supported the convoy, I was not one of its organizers, nor did I accompany it.

245 The Sandinista National Liberation Front (Frente Sandinista de Liberación Nacional), known as the FSLN, was formed in 1961 as an armed group aimed at organizing the poor and middle class to overthrow the government of the Somozas that had ruled with an iron fist since the United States put Anastasio Somoza García in power in the 1930s. The only serious opposition to the 1926–1933 U.S. military occupation of Nicaragua had been led by Augusto César Sandino who, with his ragtag army of peasants, held the five thousand Marines to a stalemate. Soon after the frustrated U.S. forces departed in 1933, the United States installed Anastasio Somoza García, son of a wealthy coffee planter who was educated in the United States, as head of the National Guard. In 1934 Somoza lured Sandino to the presidential palace and had him assassinated. By 1936 Somoza was the president

and his family held the reins until overthrown by the FSLN on July 19, 1979. Thus, the heroism of Sandino inspired the founding of the FSLN. See Liza Gross, *Handbook of Leftist Groups in Latin America and the Caribbean* (Boulder: Westview Press, 1995), 125–30.

246 Stephen Kinzer, "Managua Holds a Parade to Show its Resolve," *New York Times*, November 9, 1986; Tracy Wilkinson, "On Sandinista Anniversary, Ortega Warns U.S.," *Philadelphia Inquirer*, November 9, 1986.

247 National Security Archive, *The Chronology*, 325, 425.

248 Ibid., 325.

249 Roger Warner, *Shooting at the Moon: The Story of America's Clandestine War in Laos* (South Royalton, VT: Steerforth Press, 1996) 201.

250 Barry, *New Right Humanitarians*, 56.

251 White phosphorous has been used by the United States in a number of countries, including Viet Nam in the 1960s–1970s, and Iraq in the 2000s. It has also been used by Israel against the people in Gaza in 2008–2009. It burns at three thousand degrees, hotter than napalm, and once a person is hit by one of the many burning fragments it is almost impossible to extinguish as it burns down to the bone. Generally, people do not survive phosphorous wounds. Viet Nam veteran Dr. Charlie Clements, a former executive director of the Unitarian Universalist Service Committee, served as a physician in the war zones of El Salvador in the early 1980s and reported that white phosphorous was routinely fired against civilian targets by U.S. O-2 spotter planes piloted by Salvadorans, despite the Salvadoran army's claims that they were merely marking bombing targets with the white smoke created by the rockets. Dr. Matthew Meselson who taught genetics at Harvard University for many years, and became an expert on chemical and biological warfare, said the evidence of the nature of severe wounds from El Salvador strongly confirmed Clements's observations. See also Chris Hedges, "Salvador Charged with Dropping Incendiary Bombs," *Christian Science Monitor*, April 17, 1984.

252 Beginning in December 1985 and continuing into 1986, the San Francisco Pledge of Resistance filed a series of FOIA requests with the Department of Navy in Washington, D.C., seeking data on shipment of weapons from the Concord Naval Weapons Station to El Salvador. By summer 1986 the Pledge had received computer printouts and copies of contracts with El Salvador that listed identified weapons shipped on November 10, 1984, and June 10, 1985, from CNWS. Local newspapers took an interest upon the start of our vigil: "Concord Weapons Station Linked to El Salvador Arms Shipments," *San Francisco Examiner*, June 10, 1987; "All Sorts of Military Weapons Handled by Concord Station," *Oakland Tribune*, June 14, 1987.

253 Photocopy (in author's files) of lay missionary's June–July 1983 diary entry, reporting bombings in Chalatenango Department, El Salvador, describing discovery of an unexploded bomb with data printed on its casing revealing its origin from the Umatilla Arms Depot in Hermiston, Oregon, tracing its movement to Concord, California, then shipment to El Salvador's Air Force via the Pacific Coast port of Acajutla. Separately, Detroit Auxiliary Bishop Thomas Gumbleton told me of his 1990 visit to the village of Corral de Piedra in Chalatenango Department where he examined the results of the February 11 attack by two U.S. A-37 planes and three U.S. helicopter gunships, piloted by Salvadoran military, that murdered four children and one father as they huddled in a small house attempting to find safety from the terror from the air. The house was destroyed as well. Gumbleton had picked up several pieces of shrapnel found at the scene, remains of a rocket likely shipped from Concord, California. He described the gory details of the attack from his interviews with survivors still living in terror in the village. See his article

published in the *National Catholic Reporter,* March 23, 1990, "U.S.-Made Rockets ravage a Tiny Village in El Salvador." Gumbleton gave me one of the pieces of shrapnel found near the destroyed house, which I retain in my archives.

254 NARMIC/AFSC staff, *Invasion: A Guide to the U.S. Military Presence in Central America* (Philadelphia: NARMIC, 1985), 12–15.

255 Envio team, "Hasenfus: Nothing But the Facts," *Revista Envio* 65 (November 1986), http://www.envio.org.ni/articulo/3243.

256 Ibid.; National Security Archive, *Chronology,* 515.

257 United Pres International, "Protest Accuses Sandinistas of Raiding a Honduran Post," *New York Times,* December 7, 1986; "The White House Crisis: Pressure on Sandinistas; U.S. Copters Ferry Honduran Troops to Face Nicaragua," *New York Times,* December 8, 1986; James LeMoyne, "The White House Crisis: A Latin Skirmish; U.S. Copters Finish Honduran Mission; Clashes May Go On," *New York Times,* December 9, 1986.

258 Photocopies of the following are in author's files: U.S. Major C.A. McAnarney, U.S. Military Group El Salvador, letter to Thomas Posey, November 16, 1983, favorably responding to Posey's earlier letter offering support from Civilian Military Assistance mercenary group; General Gustavo Alvarez Martínez, chief of Honduran Armed Forces and director of Honduran death squad Battalion 316, letter to Posey, November 25, 1983, favorably responding to Posey's November 5 letter offering support from Civilian Military Assistance mercenary group. These copies were given to me by a source who insisted on remaining anonymous.

259 Ken Lawrence, "From Phoenix Associates to Civilian-Military Assistance," *Covert Action* 22 (Fall 1984): 18–19.

260 Michael Dobbs, "Papers Illustrate Negroponte's Contra Role: Newly Released Documents Show Intelligence Nominee Was Active in U.S. Effort," *Washington Post,* April 12, 2005.

261 Ambassador Negroponte cable to Secretary of State George Schultz, January 11, 1984, photocopy in author's files, given to me by a source who insisted on remaining anonymous.

262 C. Enrique Bermúdez, military director of the FDN Contras, letter to Posey, January 23, 1984, accepting Posey's offer of military support, photocopy in author's files, given to me by a source who insisted on remaining anonymous.

263 Taubman, "2 Nicaraguans Dead Identified as U.S. Veterans"; Lawrence, "From Phoenix Associates to Civilian-Military Assistance."

264 Russell Watson, Kim Willenson, and Ron Moreau, "The Friends of Tommy Posey," *Newsweek,* September 17, 1984, 55.

265 For more information regarding U.S. veterans support for Contras in Honduras-Nicaragua, and the El Salvadoran military against the FMLN guerrillas, see: Bryan Burrough and Dianna Solis, "Private Wars: U.S. Citizens Plunge Into Latins' Conflicts For Peace and Profit," *Wall Street Journal,* June 14, 1985; Brian Barger, "Fools Rush In: The Inside Story of Viet Vets in Central America," *VVA Veteran,* February 1985, 10–11; Freddy Cuevas, "Contras Seek Training From Vietnam Vets," *Sunday Rutland Herald and Sunday Times Argus,* July 6, 1986; Lawrence, "From Phoenix Associates to Civilian-Military Assistance."

266 Cuevas, "Contras Seek Training from Vietnam Vets."

267 Barger, "Fools Rush In," 10.

268 Lloyd Grove, "Rallying Round the Contra Cause: The Gathering of the Die-hard Anti-Sandinistas," *Washington Post,* September 8, 1987.

269 Stephen Kinzer, "2 Towns Bombed, Nicaraguans Say," *New York Times*, December 9, 1986; Stephen Kinzer, "Honduran Envoy Tells of Bombing of Nicaraguans," *New York Times*, December 11, 1986; Sklar, *Washington's War on Nicaragua*, 315–16.

270 Heron Marquez Estrata, "Nicaraguan May Let U.S. Vets Observe," *Santa Cruz Sentinel*, December 24, 1986; Kathy Salamon, U.S. Veterans to Set Up 'Nicaragua Patrol,'" *Register-Pajaronian* (Watsonville, CA), December 24, 1986.

271 "U.S. Troops to Start Exercise in Honduras," *New York Times*, February 12, 1987; Richard Halloran, "700 U.S. Paratroopers Fighting Mock Battles in Hills of Honduras," *New York Times*, February 19, 1987.

272 Julia Preston, "Contras Burn Clinic During Raid on Village," *Washington Post*, March 7, 1987.

273 Kennan, "Policy Planning Study 23," 23.

274 Read about Cabezas' experience as a guerrilla fighter in Omar Cabezas, *Fire from the Mountain* (New York: Crown Publishing, 1985).

275 "New U.S. Exercises Set for Honduras," *New York Times*, March 22, 1987.

276 See Associated Press, "Americans March Through War Zone, Former Franklin County Resident among Protesters in Nicaragua," *The Recorder* (Greenfield, MA), March 28, 1987; "San Rafael Man Sees Ambush Site," *Marin Independent Journal*, March 29, 1987; "Contra Raid Site 'Bloody,'" *Santa Cruz Sentinel*, March 29, 1987; "Protester Reports Contra Ambush," *Oakland Tribune*, March 29, 1987.

277 Stephen Engelberg, "Contras to Start New Radio Station; Move Is Called a Key Element in Plan to Improve Rebels' Support in Nicaragua," *New York Times*, November 5, 1986; "Powerful New Radio Station for Contras," *San Francisco Chronicle*, December 25, 1986."

278 Knight-Ridder-Tribune News Information Services, "CIA Dropping Contra Commandos onto Nicaragua," *Marin Independent Journal*, April 1, 1987.

279 In March 1988, after the September 1987 train assault, I was awarded the Leonel Rugama Rugama Heroic Youth Award by the July 19th Sandinista Youth, Managua, Nicaragua.

280 Personal conversations with David Linder; Judy Butler, "Nicaragua: On the Nicaragua Solidarity Trail," *Envio* 74 (August 1987), http://www.envio.org.ni/articulo/3207.

281 United Press International, "Contras Admit Killing American, Blame Sandinistas," *San Francisco Chronicle*, April 30, 1987.

282 Stephen Kinzer, "American Died in Rebel Ambush, Nicaragua Says," *New York Times*, April 30, 1987.

283 Gary Handschumacher, "Mourn Ben Linder, Not His Killer: Ronald Reagan's Death Squads," *CounterPunch*, June 16, 2004, http://www.counterpunch.org/lindner06162004.html.

284 Jules Lobel, *Success Without Victory: Lost Legal Battles and the Long Road to Justice in America* (New York: New York University Press, 2003), 228–29.

285 "Foreigners Aren't Safe, Contras Say, Rebels Urge Volunteers to Get out of Nicaragua," *Miami Herald*, May 4, 1987.

286 "The World: Marchers Honor Linder," *Los Angeles Times*, May 19, 1987: "Nicaraguan soldiers deactivated two land mines along the path of about 70 U.S. citizens as they marched to the site where an American engineer was killed in a northern war zone, the government newspaper Barricada said."

287 Judy Butler, "Nicaragua: Ben Linder's Dream: Electricity Comes to Bocay," *Envio* 156 (July 1994), http://www.envio.org.ni/articulo/3034.

288 Ibid.

CHAPTER 19

289 Jonathan Marshall, Peter Dale Scott, and Jane Hunter, *The Iran Contra Connection: Secret Teams and Covert Operations in the Reagan Era* (Boston: South End Press, 1987), 83–124; Andrew Cockburn and Leslie Cockburn, *Dangerous Liaison: The Inside Story of the U.S.-Israeli Covert Relationship* (New York: HarperCollins Publishers, 1991), 223–36; Sklar, *Washington's War on Nicaragua*, 224–25. Israel had been supplying arms and training to Somoza's repressive government since the 1950s, a favor being paid for Somoza's early support of Zionist forces in the late 1930s and 1940s. See Cockburn and Cockburn, *Dangerous Liaison,* 216, 242 and Jack Colhoun, "Israel in Central America: Arms to the Contras," *Covert Action Information Bulletin* 30 (Summer 1988): 46–48.

290 Stephen Engelberg, "Lehrman Takes to Road for Conservative Cause," *New York Times,* May 5, 1985.

291 Bryan Burrough and Dianna Solis, "Private Wars: U.S. Citizens Plunge into Latins' Conflicts for Peace and Profit," *Wall Street Journal,* June 14, 1985.

292 Barry, *New Right Humanitarians,* 24.

293 "Thunder to the Right," *Time,* December 29, 1986; Barry, *New Right Humanitarians,* 35–37.

294 William M. Arkin and Richard W. Fieldhouse, *Nuclear Battlefields: Global Links in the Arms Race* (Cambridge, MA: Ballinger Publishing Company, 1985), 176.

295 "Concord Protesters Claim Lawmen Used Unnecessary Force," *The Tribune* (Oakland, CA), June 19, 1987.

296 Franklin Zahn, *Deserter from Violence: Experiments with Gandhi's Truth* (New York: Philosophical Library, 1984), 259–60.

297 See, for example the following: Keith Pope, *A Year of Disobedience* (Boulder: Daniel Productions, 1979) about the blocking of nuclear trains at Rocky Flats, CO; United Press International, "Police Rout 300 in Troop Train Protest," *Los Angeles Times,* August 13, 1965: "Several demonstrators sat down on the tracks as the train approached. They were seized by plainclothesmen," accompanied by photos; Cooney and Michalowski, 230, 238; "Hands Across the Tracks That Stopped the Trains," *Life,* October 8, 1956; Photo with caption, "Attempting "a blockade of military supplies just like Nixons', demonstrators hold up a Southern Pacific freight near Davis, California for six hours, protesting the President's Vietnam escalation," *Life,* May 19, 1972; Ray Bonds, ed., *The Vietnam War: The Illustrated History of the Conflict* (New York: Crown Publishing, Inc., 1979), 118, photo showing Buddhist monk sitting in path of an ARVN tank; "21 Arrested in Jersey Trying to Block Loading of Munitions Ship," *New York Times,* April 24, 1972; Bob Levering, "People's Blockade," *WIN* 8, no. 3 (August 1972): 5–8; "Protestors Block Arsenal Rail Line," *Minneapolis Star,* August 28, 1972, B13; "Arsenal Demonstrators Hope to Keep Vietnam War 'Visible' to Local Public," *Minneapolis Tribune,* September 19, 1972; "Five Charged With Stopping Ammo Train," *Seattle Times,* August 27, 1972; Seabury Blair, Jr., "'People's Blockade' Again Stops Ammo Train," *Bremerton Sun* (Bremerton, WA), August 29, 1972; and "12 War protesters Jailed After Blocking Munitions Train," *Seattle Times,* September 13, 1972, A15.

298 We chose not to marry in compliance with California law because we believed strongly that the law of the state possessed no legitimate authority to sanctify our personal decision to begin a partnership.

299 Independent radio journalist Bill Fisher was present with his audio tape recorder on September 1, 1987, for our commencing "interfaith" circle about 10 a.m., at which time several of those gathered made opening remarks which Bill taped. My remarks were

among them. This was followed by a small press conference about 11 a.m. that more formally announced the beginning of our planned forty-day, water-only fast and blockade of munitions trains.

CHAPTER 20

300 Fisher's audiotape recording continued as we began our blocking action a little before noon when the first train of the day began to move from the bunker side of the base toward the docks on Suisun Bay in the nearby Sacramento River. He caught the sounds of the oncoming train, the clanging of the traffic warning bells, and all the pandemonium, shouting, and various remarks made by whomever was within recording distance of his microphone as the train accelerated through the block and continued for several hundred feet before stopping and being surrounded by armed Marines. Some of the comments on the recording are his own. Learning of the existence of the tape, my lawyers soon acquired it and had it transcribed for evidence.

CHAPTER 21

301 Karen Sheldon, Criminalist, Contra Costa County Criminalistics Laboratory Division, Report of Laboratory Examination, September 17, 1987, revealing FBI Laboratory examination of Bob Spitzer's videotape calculated train speed at 16 mph across the paved section of the road where Willson was struck, and that the tape was accurate and unaltered; Ronald Kessler, *The FBI* (New York: Pocket Books, 1993), 310–11, 562n316.

302 Navy investigation conducted by Navy Captain S.J. Pryzby for the Naval Sea Systems Command, completed October 2, 1987.

303 "Weapons Train that Maimed Pacifist was Under Navy Orders Not to Stop: Reports Revealing Order Not Shared with Congressional Investigators," *National Catholic Reporter,* January 29, 1988.

304 Bob Cialdini, *Influence: Science and Practice,* 4th ed. (Boston: Allyn and Bacon, 2001), Ch. 6, "Authority," Willson reference, 184. His text is used in college courses in media studies and psychology such as at Malaspina University-College in Nanaimo, B.C., Canada and at Appalachian State University in North Carolina.

CHAPTER 22

305 "Peoria-Area Peace Groups Bitter over FBI Agent's Firing," *Journal Star* (Peoria, IL), September 17, 1987.

306 Such as: *Christian Science Monitor,* October 3, 1986; *Village Voice,* October 7, 1986; *USA Today,* October 8, 10, 1986; *Miami Herald,* October 9, 1986; *Los Angeles Times,* October 10, 1986; *Boston Globe,* October 11, 12, 1986; *Philadelphia Inquirer,* October 13, 1986; *The New Yorker,* October 13, 1986.

307 FBI, Chicago Office, "Domestic Security/Terrorism Sabotage," Memorandum to the Director and *All* Offices of the FBI, October 31, 1986. This memorandum ordered the investigation of the Plowshares group and the Veterans Fast for Life group, both suspected of being part of "an organized conspiracy to use force/violence to *coerce* the United States Government into *modifying its direction"* [emphasis added]. Photocopy of FBI memo provided to author by Jack Ryan, the fired agent.

308 *Ryan v. United States Department of Justice,* 950 F.2d 358 (7th Circuit 1991).

309 Jay Peterzell, *Reagan's Secret Wars* (Washington, DC: Center for National Security Studies, 1984), 75.

310 Gelbspan, *Break-ins, Death Threats and the FBI*, 190; Ellen Ray and Bill Schaap, "Pentagon Moves On 'Terrorism,'" *Covert Action Information Bulletin* 22 (Fall 1984): 4–9; Brian Glick, *War at Home* (Boston: South End Press, 1989), 29–33; Ellen Ray and Bill Schaap, "Pentagon Moves on 'Terrorism,'" *Covert Action Information Bulletin* 22 (Fall 1984): 7.

311 Woodward, *Veil*, 361–62; Ellen Ray and William H. Schaap, eds., *Covert Action: The Roots of Terrorism* (Melbourne, Victoria, Australia: Ocean Press, 2003), 64–66, 76–77.

312 United Press International, "House OKs Spy Funding," *The Morning Union* (Springfield, MA), July 19, 1985.

313 Photocopy in author's files; available from National Security Council (NSC) List of Policy Documents for 1961–1992 Presidencies, and from Federation of American Scientists (FAS) Web site, http://www.fas.org/irp/offdocs/nsdd/nsdd-179.htm.

314 *Covert Action Information Bulletin* 33 (Winter 1990): 13; Federal Bureau of Investigation, *Terrorism in the United States* (1998, 1999) posted in Jeffrey Richelson and Michael L. Evans, eds., Volume I: Terrorism and U.S. Policy, National Security Archive Electronic Briefing Book no. 55, Document 6, September 21, 2001: http://www.gwu.edu/~nsarchiv/NSAEBB/NSAEBB55/fbiterrorism98.pdf

315 International Center for Development Policy (Washington, DC), "Bush, Iran-Contra, and Counterterrorism: A Chronology," Memorandum, November 4, 1987, citing articles in the *Washington Post*, February 17, 1987, February 20, 1987, and February 22, 1987.

316 Peter Dale Scott and Jonathan Marshall, *Cocaine Politics: Drugs, Armies, and the CIA in Central America* (Berkeley: University of California Press, 1991), 143, 148; Parry, *Lost History*, 112–13.

317 Alfonso Chardy, "North and the 'Secret Government'; Martial Law Plan Among Work of Reagan Advisors," *San Jose Mercury News*, July 5, 1987.

318 Gelbspan, *Break-ins*, 20–23. For a summary of break-ins and harassments, see House Subcommittee on Civil and Constitutional Rights, Committee of the Judiciary: Hearings before. *Break-Ins at Sanctuary Churches and Organizations Opposed to Administration Policy in Central America*, 100th Cong., 1st sess., February 19–20, 1987 (Washington, DC: GPO, 1987); Center for Constitutional Rights and the National Lawyers Guild, *Harassment Update: Chronological List of FBI and Other Harassment Incidents* (New York: Center For Constitutional Rights, January 1987) and *Harassment Update* (January 27, 1988), 1.

319 John Stockwell, *The Praetorian Guard: The U.S. Role in the New World Order* (Cambridge, MA: South End Press, 1991), 105–6.

320 U.S. General Accounting Office, *International Terrorism, FBI Investigates Domestic Activities to Identify Terrorists*, Report to the Chairman, Subcommittee on Civil and Constitutional Rights, Committee on the Judiciary, House of Representatives, Washington, DC, September 1990; Gelbspan, *Break-ins*, 50.

321 Gary M. Stern, *The FBI's Misguided Probe of CISPES* (Washington, DC: Center For National Security Studies, 1988), 2, as quoted in Greg Grandin, *Empire's Workshop: Latin America, The United States, and the Rise of the New Imperialism* (New York: Metropolitan Books, 2006), 138–39.

322 Ross Gelbspan, "More Probes Found of Latin Policy Foes; FBI Surveillance Called Pervasive," *Boston Globe*, June 18, 1988 as quoted in Grandin, *Empire's Workshop*, 138.

323 Chardy, "North and the Secret Government"; Gelbspan, *Break-ins*, 184.

324 Letter dated December 14, 1987 from Department of Justice to Congressman Edwards, copy in author's files.

325 While I was recuperating at John Muir Hospital under twenty-four-hour armed guard, Contra Costa County Sheriff's Department detective Ed Nunn interviewed me at bedside on September 18 with my lawyer, Tom Steel, present. One of the questions he asked was, "Were there any plans . . . to board the train?" I was flabbergasted and as yet had no clue about having been considered a "domestic terrorist suspect" by the FBI.

326 Rob Morse column, *San Francisco Examiner*, September 3, 1987: "What I was really saying in Wednesday's column . . . was that what happened out at Concord Tuesday looked an awful lot like attempted murder; Stephen Babb, "Attempted Murder," *The Guardian, Independent Radical Newsweekly* (San Francisco, CA), September 16, 1987; Paul Rauber, "Fast Train Coming," *East Bay Express* (Emeryville, CA), October 16, 1987; Stockwell, *The Praetorian Guard*, 105–6.

327 Peter Dale Scott and Jonathan Marshall, *Obstruction of Justice: The Reagan-Bush Coverup of the Contra Drug Connection*, pamphlet published for Christic Institute (Berkeley: University of California Press, 1990), 78–79.

328 Rob Morse's column, *San Francisco Examiner*, November 19, 1989.

329 Just as in 2008 Congress approved domestic warrantless surveillance of U.S. citizens, as reported by Eric Lichtblau, "Senate Approves Bill to Broaden Wiretap Powers," *New York Times*, July 10, 2008.

330 Brad Kessler, "Body on the Line," *The Nation*, October 3, 1987.

331 My views on nonviolence cannot be dogmatically applied, especially not to those suffering from impoverishment and repression due to the imposed structural injustices created and preserved by the imperial policies of the United States and its European teachers. If we do not offer people a concrete way of liberating themselves from these deprivations, or join with them in facing the risks they face everyday, we have no moral authority to judge their responses.

332 An example of this kind of government terrorism occurred in Israel on March 16, 2003, when Rachel Corrie, an Olympia, Washington, resident and student, was killed while serving as a participant in a peaceful protest against house demolitions in Occupied Palestine. She was standing with other members of the International Solidarity Movement in front of a Palestinian house to protect it from demolition when an approaching Israeli bulldozer ran over her once, then a second time, and crushed her to death.

CHAPTER 23

333 "Nicaragua-Sapoa: Will Peace Last?" *Revista Envio*, no. 82, April 1988. Notably, on March 16, 1988, President Reagan launched "Operation Golden Pheasant," sending paratroopers from Fort Bragg's 82nd Airborne and ground troops from Fort Ord's 7th Infantry Division to Honduras, threatening to invade Nicaragua. See "Operation Golden Pheasant," *Wikipedia*, http://en.wikipedia.org/wiki/Operation_Golden_Pheasant (accessed December 20, 2008).

334 Joel Brinkley, "News Analysis: Plan For Peace, or Arms?" *New York Times*, August 6, 1987.

335 Ibid; Anthony Lewis, "The Peace Scare," *New York Times*, November 19, 1987.

336 "Sandinistas Accuse Contras of New Attack; Ortega Delays His decision on Suspending Cease-Fire," *San Francisco Chronicle*, November 1, 1989.

CHAPTER 24

337 James R. Brockman, *Romero: A Life* (Maryknoll, NY: Orbis Books, 1989), 241–42, 274n37–40.

338 Michael McClintock, *The American Connection*, Volume I: *State Terror and Popular Resistance in El Salvador* (London: Zed Books, 1985) 18–23, 201–2, 210, 328; David Kirsh, "Death Squads in El Salvador: A Pattern of U.S. Complicity," *Covert Action Information Bulletin*, no. 34 (Summer 1990), 51–53.

339 Thomas Sheehan, "Friendly Fascism: Business As Usual in America's Backyard," in *Fascism's Return: Scandal, Revision, and Ideology Since 1980*, ed. Richard J. Golson, 270–71 (Lincoln, NE: University of Nebraska Press, 1998).

340 Raymond Bonner, *Weakness and Deceit: U.S. Policy and El Salvador*, (New York: Times Books, 1984), 178; House Foreign Affairs Subcommittee on Human Rights, *The Situation in El Salvador*, Hearings before, 98th Cong., 2d sess., January 26, February 6, 1984, 50.

341 Douglas Farah, "2 Salvadorans Detail Origins of a Death Squad," *Washington Post*, August 29, 1988, 26; McClintock, *The American Connection*, 218.

342 Marshall, *The Iran-Contra Connection*, 22.

343 House Foreign Affairs Subcommittee, *The Situation In El Salvador*, 48; Douglas Farah, "2 Salvadorans Detail Origin of a Death Squad," *Washington Post*, August 29, 1988.

344 William Blum, *Rogue State* (Monroe, Maine: Common Courage Press, 2000), 156, 54.

345 Van Gosse, "Shame & Salvador," *The Nation*, November 29, 1993.

346 McClintock, *The American Connection*, 306.

347 James Petras, "El Salvador: White Paper on the White Paper," *The Nation*, May 28, 1981.

348 Bonner, *Weakness and Deceit*, xvii.

349 Ibid., xviii.

350 Raymond Bonner, "U.S. Advisers Saw 'Torture Class,' Salvadoran Says," *New York Times*, A2, January 11, 1982. Bonner's source was twenty-one-year-old Carlos Antonio Gomez Montano who was interviewed in the January 1982 issue of *El Salvador Alert*. The transcription of that interview, "Salvadoran Deserter Discloses Green Beret Torture Role," was reprinted in *Covert Action Information Bulletin* 16 (March 1982): 17–18.

351 Torture reports in author's possession provided by Human Rights Commission of El Salvador (CDHES); Ron Ridenhour, "In prison, Salvador rights panel works on," *San Francisco Examiner*, November 14, 1986. Interestingly, Ridenhour was an ex-Army helicopter door gunner in Viet Nam who in March 1969 publicly wrote letters revealing what he had learned from other soldiers about the massacre at My Lai a year earlier that had been kept under wraps by senior officials.

352 "For a CIA Man, it's 1954 Again," *Los Angeles Times*, March 16, 1986.

353 "Lifting the 'C' from Covert Action," *Washington Post*, November 26, 1987.

354 See, for example, "214 Arrested During Protest over U.S. Policy on El Salvador," and accompanying AP photo with caption, "Brian Willson Joins Protest," *The Post Journal* (Jamestown, NY), October 18, 1988; "Protest At Pentagon," *Baltimore Sun*, October 18, 1988; "Pentagon Besieged in Protest on Salvador," *Los Angeles Times*, October 18, 1988; "Protest Knots Early Traffic at Pentagon," *The Washington Times*, October 18, 1988; "1,000 Protest Role Of U.S. in El Salvador, 215 Arrested in Blockade at Pentagon," *Washington Post*, October 18, 1988; "Pentagon Entrance Blockaded," *Argus* (Fremont, CA), October 18, 1988; among many stories.

355 Associated Press, "Salvadoran Marchers Call For Peace Talks," *San Francisco Chronicle*, November 16, 1988, reporting an estimated fifteen to twenty thousand marchers.

356 A.J. Bacevich, et al., *American Military Policy in Small Wars: The Case of El Salvador* (Washington, DC: Institute for Foreign Policy, 1988), 5.

357   Bradley Graham, "Medals Granted after Acknowledgement of U.S. Role in El Salvador," *Washington Post*, May 6, 1996, 1A

358   Frank Smyth's Web site, "No Passage," July 13, 2000, http://www.franksmyth.com/intellectualcapital-com/no-passage/. This essay is a detailed account of life in San Salvador during the November 1989 FMLN Offensive.

CHAPTER 25

359   Grandin, *Empire's Workshop*, 14, 16–17.

360   Gerard Colby and Charlotte Dennett, *Thy Will Be Done—The Conquest of the Amazon: Nelson Rockefeller and Evangelism in the Age of Oil* (New York: HarperCollins, 1995), 116.

361   Jenny Pearce, *Colombia: Inside the Labyrinth* (London: Latin American Bureau, 1990), 63.

362   Colby and Dennett, *Thy Will Be Done*, 349.

363   Dennis M. Rempe, "An American Trojan Horse? Eisenhower, Latin America, and the Development of U.S. Internal Security Policy 1954–1960," *Small Wars and Insurgencies* 10 (Spring 1999): 34–64.

364   Michael McClintock, *Instruments of Statecraft: U.S. Guerrilla Warfare, Counterinsurgency, and Counter-terrorism, 1940–1990* (New York: Pantheon Books, 1992), 222–23.

365   Ibid, 222.

366   Ibid., 223.

367   Ibid.

368   Gross, *Handbook of Leftist Groups in Latin America and the Caribbean*, 47–59.

369   New Internationalist, *The World Guide* (Oxford, U.K.: New Internationalist Publications, Ltd., 2001), 175.

370   Documents obtained by the National Security Archive presented in its *Electronic Briefing Book* no. 69, "War in Colombia: Guerrillas, Drugs and Human Rights in U.S.-Colombia Policy, 1988–2002," May 3, 2002.

371   Ibid.

372   Ibid.

373   School of the Americas Watch, "Colombia and the SOA," *School of the Americas Watch Update*, Winter 2001.

374   Karen Smith, "Coca-Cola and Latin American Death Squads," Council on Hemispheric Affairs, Washington, DC, July 20, 2002.

375   Francisco Ramirez Cuellar, *The Profits of Extermination: How U.S. Corporate Power Is Destroying Colombia* (Monroe, Maine: Common Courage Press, 2005).

376   Amnesty International, "Colombia: Killings, Arbitrary Detentions, and Death Threats—The Reality of Trade Unionism in Colombia," July 2007, 8, citing data from the National Labor School (Escuela Nacional Sindical) in Medellín, Antioquia, Colombia.

377   Coca-Cola Company, *The Centennial of Coca-Cola in Latin America, 1906–2006*, http://www.thecoca-colacompany.com/citizenship/pdf/Centennial_Coca-Cola_Latin_America_English.pdf.

378   David Bacon, "The Coca-Cola Killings: Is Plan Colombia Funding a Bloodbath of Union Activists," *The American Prospect*, January 28, 2002.

379   Michael Blanding, "The Case Against Coke," *The Nation*, May 1, 2006.

380   Smith, "Coca-Cola and Latin American Death Squads."

381   "Son of Coca-Cola Worker Kidnapped and Tortured," *Colombia Support Network News*, October 31, 2007, October 8 entry.

382 Jeremy Rayner, "The United States and the War on Trade Unions in Colombia," The John F. Henning Center for International Labor Relations, Berkeley, CA, http://www. irle.berkeley.edu/henningcenter/gateway/columbia.html.

383 The Coca Cola Company identifies two thousand employees in Colombia, of which 31 percent belong to unions. http://www.thecoca-colacompany.com/dynamic/press_center/2006/01/the-facts-the-coca-cola-company-and-colombia.html

384 Michael Evans, "'Para-politics' Goes Bananas," The Nation, April 4, 2007; Carol Leoning, "In Terrorism-Law Case, Chiquita Points to U.S.; Firm Says It Awaited Justice Dept Advice," Washington Post, August 2, 2007.

385 Evans, "'Para-politics' Goes Bananas"; Leoning, "In Terrorism-Law Case."

386 "Paramilitaries as Proxies: Declassified Evidence On the Colombian Army's Anti-Guerrilla 'Allies,'" National Security Archive Electronic Briefing Book no. 166, October 16, 2005.

387 Josh Meyer, "U.S. Bending Rules on Colombia Terror?" Los Angeles Times, July 22, 2007.

388 Dianna Harman, "Colombia's Displaced Trickle Home," Christian Science Monitor, June 20, 2006.

CHAPTER 26

389 Ovidio Diaz Espino, How Wall Street Created a Nation: J.P. Morgan, Teddy Roosevelt, and the Panama Canal (New York: Four Walls Eight Windows, 2001).

390 James D. Richardson, A Compilation of the Messages and Papers of the Presidents, 1789–1904, vol. 10 (Washington, DC: Bureau of National Literature and Art, 1904), 603–4, 606.

391 Ibid.

392 Thomas J. Nagy, "The Secret Behind the Sanctions: How the U.S. Intentionally Destroyed Iraq's Water Supply," The Progressive, September 2001. Defense Intelligence Agency (DIA) documents, "Disease Information: Effects of Bombing on Disease Occurrence in Baghdad" and "Iraq Water Treatment Vulnerabilities," both dated January 22, 1991, only six days after the bombing had begun, explain that, "Increased incidence of diseases will be attributable to degradation of normal preventive medicine, waste disposal, water purification/distribution, electricity, and decreased ability to control disease outbreaks. Any urban area in Iraq that has received infrastructure damage will have similar problems." A third document, "Disease Outbreaks in Iraq," dated February 21, 1991, boasts that, "Conditions are favorable for communicable disease outbreaks, particularly in major urban areas affected by coalition bombing." To directly access the DIA documents, Google "Iraq water treatment vulnerabilities."

393 UNESCO, "Safe Water Shortage Threatens Iraq's Children," March 22, 2007; Greg Barrett, "Running Dry: Sanctions Hit Iraq's Young the Hardest," Seattle Times, August 4, 2002.

394 In 1995, researchers for a Food and Agricultural Organization (UN/FAO) study wrote to The Lancet, the journal of the British Medical Society, that U.S.-enforced sanctions were responsible for the deaths of over five hundred thousand Iraqi children. A New York Times story declared "Iraq Sanctions Kill Children." On CBS's 60 Minutes, May 12, 1996, Lesley Stahl asked U.S. Secretary of State Madeleine Albright: "We have heard that a half million children have died. I mean, that's more children than died in Hiroshima. And, you know, is the price worth it?" Albright responded: "We think the price is worth it."

395 "Baker Would Weigh Covert Acts to Influence Foreign Elections," *Los Angeles Times* printed in the *San Francisco Chronicle,* January 19, 1989.

396 Robert Pear, "U.S. Has Resisted Central American Peace Agreement," *New York Times,* November 3, 1989.

397 S. Brian Willson, "How the U.S. Purchased the 1990 Nicaragua Elections," http://www. brianwillson.com/awolnicelection.html; William I. Robinson, *A Faustian Bargain: U.S. Intervention in the Nicaragua Elections and American Foreign Policy in the Post-Cold War Era* (Boulder: Westview Press, 1992).

398 S. Brian Willson, "U.S.-Waged 'Low Intensity' Warfare in Nicaragua, Excerpt from Report of Veterans Peace Action Team Pre-election Observation Delegation to Nicaragua, November 30 to December 14, 1989," December 30, 1989: http://www.brianwillson.com/awolnicaragua.html.

399 James LeMoyne, "In Nicaragua, Economy is Hobbling Sandinistas," *New York Times,* December 20, 1987.

400 Emma Curtis, "Child Health and the International Monetary Fund," *The Lancet* 352, no. 9140 (November 14, 1998): 1622–24, http://www.thelancet.com/journals/lancet/article/PIIS0140-6736(98)03248-6/fulltext.

CHAPTER 27

401 William Appleman Williams, *The Tragedy of American Diplomacy* (New York: W.W. Norton & Company, 1972).

402 Rius, *Cuba For Beginners* (New York: Pathfinder Press, 1986), 141.

403 Peter M. Rosset, "A Successful Case Study of Sustainable Agriculture," in *Hungry For Profit: The Agribusiness Threat to Farmers, Food and the Environment,* ed. Fred Magdoff, John Bellamy Foster, and Frederick H. Buttel, chap. 12, 203–13 (New York: Monthly Review Press, 2000); Megan Quinn, "The Power of Community: How Cuba Survived Peak Oil," *Permaculture Activist,* Spring 2006.

404 Steve Brouwer, "The Cuban Revolutionary Doctor: The Ultimate Weapon of Solidarity," *Monthly Review* 60, no. 8 (January 2009): 30–31, 37; Quinn, "The Power of Community"; Cliff DuRand, "Humanitarianism and Solidarity Cuban-Style: A Healthcare Model for the World," *Z Magazine,* November 1, 2007.

405 *Culture Change* 12 (1997); "Signs Of The Times—Encouragement Found in Unexpected Places," *In Context, A Quarterly Of Humane Sustainable Culture* 40 (Spring 1995).

406 Mike Weaver, "Gardening Brigades, Havana," Cuba Organic Support Group (UK), February–March 2000, http://www.cosg.org.uk/mike2000.php.

407 Associated Press, August 9, 2009, "In Cuba, the Ox is Mightier than the Tractor," August 9, 2009.

408 I attended a 2000 meeting in Santa Cruz, California, at which geophysicist Bruno Enriquez, cofounder and director of Cuba Solar, a division of Cuba Energy, discussed Cuba's present and future decentralized renewable energy plans, including solar, wind biomass, and energy efficiency.

409 Quinn, "The Power of Community."

410 "Signs Of The Times," *In Context.*

411 WWF, *Living Planet Report 2006:* http://wwf.panda.org/about_our_earth/all_publications/living_planet_report/living_planet_report_timeline/lp_2006.

412 Sheldon Wolin, *Democracy Incorporated: Managed Democracy and the Specter of Inverted Totalitarianism* (Princeton: Princeton University Press, 2008).

413 John Ralston Saul, *The Unconscious Civilization* (New York: The Free Press, 1997).

414 Peter Kropotkin, *Mutual Aid: A Factor of Evolution* (Montreal: Black Rose Books, 1989), xli–xlii, 300.

415 Ibid.

416 David Stanley, *Cuba* (Victoria, Australia: Lonely Planet Publications, 1997), 13; Kirkpatrick Sale, *The Conquest of Paradise: Christopher Columbus and the Columbian Legacy* (New York: Alfred A. Knopf, 1990), 161.

417 Williams, *Empire*, 337–38.

418 Sidney Lens, *The Forging of the American Empire: From the Revolution to Vietnam: A History of U.S. Imperialism* (1971; Chicago: Haymarket Books, 2003), 2.

419 Louis A. Perez, Jr., *The War of 1898* (Chapel Hill: University of North Carolina Press, 1998), 3.

420 Ibid., 5.

421 Jane Franklin, *Cuba and the United States: A Chronological History* (Melbourne, Australia: Ocean Press, 1997), 2–3; Rius, *Cuba For Beginners* (New York: Pathfinder Press, 1986), 33.

422 Richard B. Morris and Jeffrey B. Morris, eds., *Encyclopedia of American History*, Bicentennial Edition (1953; New York: Harper & Row, 1976), 259.

423 Richardson, *A Compilation of the Messages*, vol. 5, 511.

424 Stanley, *Cuba*, 18.

425 Peter Wollen and Joe Kerr, *Autopia: Cars and Culture* (London: Reaktion Books, 2002), 170.

426 Rius, *Cuba For Beginners*, 36–37.

427 Perez, *The War of 1898*, 32.

428 Willis J. Abbot, *Panama and the Canal* (New York: Syndicate Publishing Co., 1913), 291.

429 J.A. Sierra, "The Bitter Memory of Cuban Sugar," pt. 2, *History of Cuba* website: http://www.historyofcuba.com/history/havana/Sugar1b.htm (accessed November 30, 2008). Sierra relies on the academic scholarship of Cuban historian Louis A. Perez, Jr, especially his piece, "Insurrection, Intervention, and the Transformation of Land Tenure Systems in Cuba, 1895–1902," *Hispanic American Historical Review* 65, no. 2 (May 1985): 229–54.

430 Frederick Upham Adams, *Conquest of the Tropics: The Story of the Creative Enterprises Conducted by the United Fruit Company* (Garden City, NY: Doubleday, Page & Company, 1914), 36–37.

431 Ted Szulc, *Fidel: A Critical Portrait* (New York: Avon Books, 1987), 13.

432 Rius, *Cuba For Beginners*, 48–52; Franklin, *Cuba and the United States*, 12–13; Morris, *Encyclopedia*, 386.

433 Rius, *Cuba For Beginners*, 67.

434 David Halberstam, *The Fifties* (New York: Villard Books, 1993), 714.

435 Felix Greene, *The Enemy: What Every American Should Know about Imperialism* (New York: Random House, 1970), 139.

436 Stephen Kinzer, *Overthrow: America's Century of Regime Change From Hawaii to Iraq* (New York: Times Books/Henry Holt and Company, 2006), 129–30; Franklin, *Cuba and the United States*, 24; Tim Weiner, *Legacy of Ashes: The History of the CIA* (New York: Doubleday, 2007), 79–104.

437 Kitty Felde, "Oscar Arias: Harsh Words for the U.S. From a Voice for Peace and Prosperity," *Los Angeles Times*, February 20, 2000; Rius, *Cuba For Beginners*, 105.

CHAPTER 28

438 Homeless Research Institute of the National Alliance to End Homelessness, *Homelessness Counts*, January 2007, http://www.endhomelessness.org/content/article/detail/1440.

439 Gregg Zoroya, "Veteran Stress Cases Up Sharply," *USA Today*, October 18, 2007, http://www.usatoday.com/news/washington/2007-10-18-veterans-stress_N.htm.

440 The Sentencing Project, "Facts About Prisons and Prisoners," July 2008, http://www.sentencingproject.org/PublicationDetails.aspx?PublicationID=425.

441 Rob Kelley, "Average College Cost Breaks $30,000," *CNNMoney.com*, October 27, 2006, http://money.cnn.com/2006/10/24/pf/college/college_costs/index.htm.

442 Bureau of Labor Statistics, U.S. Dept. of Labor, "Economic News Release Table B-3, Average hourly and weekly earnings of production and nonsupervisory workers (1) on private nonfarm payrolls by industry sector and selected industry detail," September 5, 2008, http://www.bls.gov/webapps/legacy/cesbtab3.htm

443 Ian Urbina, "A Decline in Uninsured is Reported for 2007," *New York Times*, August 26, 2008. Note that this article lists only raw numbers—percent is from census figures showing U.S. population at 301 million as of July 2008.

444 Leinad Ayer de O. Santos and Lucia M.M. de Andrade, *Hydroelectric Dams on Brazil's Xingu River and Indigenous Peoples* (Cambridge, MA: Cultural Survival, 1990).

445 "Chico Mendes's Legacy," *New York Times*, December 26, 1998: "According to Brazil's Catholic Church, Mr. Mendes was one of 982 activists murdered in land disputes in the Amazon between 1964 and 1988, the vast majority by ranchers' hired guns"; Bradley Brooks, "Amazon Killings Go On Despite Chico Mendes' Legacy," http://www.commondreams.org/headline/2008/12/21-1: "More than 1,100 activists, small farmers, judges, priests and other rural workers have been killed over preserving land since Mendes' murder."

446 Frederick Ungeheuer, Charles P. Alexander, and Charles Thurston, "Rainy Days in Brazil," *Time*, July 25, 1983, http://www.time.com/time/magazine/article/0,9171,954015-4,00.html.

447 Paulo Freire, *Pedagogy of the Oppressed*, trans. Myra Bergman Ramos (New York: Seabury Press, 1973).

448 Ibid., 44–45.

449 Frantz Fanon, *The Wretched of the Earth*, trans. Constance Farrington (1961; New York: Grove Press, 1963).

450 Erich Fromm, *Escape from Freedom* (1941; New York: Henry Holt and Company, 1994).

451 Blum, *Killing Hope*, 153–56; Agee, *Inside the Company*, 133–204, describing day-by-day details.

452 Lernoux, *Cry of the People*, 332.

453 Chomsky and Herman, *Washington Connection*, 270.

454 Ibid., 270.

455 The group Women in Black, which does not consider itself a formal organization, was started in Jerusalem in 1988 by Israeli women distressed by Israeli violations of human rights against Palestinians during the First Intifada. It was reportedly inspired by the "Mothers of the Plaza de Mayo."

456 Marina Sitrin, *Voices of Popular Power in Argentina* (Oakland: AK Press, 2006).

457 Ibid., 16. Also see Roger Burbach, Orlando Nunez, and Boris Kagarlitsky, *Globalization and Its Discontents: The Rise of Postmodern Socialisms* (London: Pluto Press, 1997).

458 Marie Trigona, "Workers' Power in Argentina: Reinventing Working Culture," *Monthly Review* 59, no. 3 (July-August 2007): 110–19.

459 Hans Koning, *Columbus: His Enterprise* (1976; New York: Monthly Review Press, 1991), 116.

460 Eduardo Galeano, *Upside Down: A Primer for the Looking-Glass World* (New York: Picador, 2001), 37.

CHAPTER 29

461 http://www.brianwillson.com.

462 Lewis Mumford, *The Myth of the Machine: Technics and Human Development* (1966; New York: Harcourt, Brace & World, Inc., 1967), 186.

463 J.M. Blaut, *The Colonizer's Model of the World: Geographical Diffusionism and Eurocentric History* (New York: Guilford Press, 1993).

464 Congressional Research Service (CRS) Report for Congress, February 5, 2002, *Instances of Use of United States Armed Forces Abroad, 1798–2001;* B.M. Blechman and S.S. Kaplan, *Force Without War: U.S. Armed Forces as a Political Instrument* (Washington, DC: The Brookings Institution, 1978), Appendix B; J.M. Collins, *America's Small Wars: Lessons for the Future* (Washington: Brassey's (U.S.), Inc., 1991); Joseph Gerson and Bruce Birchard, eds., *The Sun Never Sets . . .: Confronting the Network of Foreign U.S. Military Bases* (Boston: South End Press, 1991), 3–14, 360–63; Williams, *Empire*, 122, citing S.S. Roberts, "An Indicator of Informal Empire: Patterns of U.S. Navy Cruising on Overseas Stations, 1869–1897," available at Center for Naval Analysis, Alexandria, Virginia; Grandin, 3; John Stockwell, *The Praetorian Guard: The U.S. Role in the New World Order* (Cambridge, MA: South End Press, 1991), 70; Prados, *President's Secret Wars: CIA and Pentagon Covert Operations from World War II through the Persian Gulf,* 336.

465 Jared Diamond, "What's Your Consumption Factor?" *New York Times,* January 2, 2008

466 George Stambuck, *American Military Forces Abroad* (Columbus, OH: Ohio University Press, 1963), 4.

467 Ibid., 4–5, 5n8.

468 Arkin and Fieldhouse, *Nuclear Battlefields,* 40–41, table: "The U.S. Nuclear Infrastructure," and 147, table: "The U.S. Nuclear Infrastructure Overseas," and 171–249, "Appendix A. United States Nuclear Weapons Infrastructure."

469 Chalmers Johnson, *The Sorrows of Empire: Militarism, Secrecy, and the End of the Republic* (New York: Metropolitan Books, 2004), 154–61, citing the "Base Structure Support" of the Department of Defense, and separately, "Worldwide Manpower Distribution by Geographical Area."

470 Lora Lumpe, "U.S. Foreign Military Training: Global Reach, Global Power, and Oversight Issues," *A Foreign Policy In Focus Special Report,* May 2002.

471 Albert Perry Brigham, "American Dependence on Foreign Products," *The Geographical Journal* 63, no. 5 (May 1924): 412–24; John M. Dunn, "American Dependence on Materials Imports the World-Wide Resource Base," *The Journal of Conflict Resolution* 4, no. 1 (March 1960): 106–22; Roger Prestwich, "America's Dependence on the World's Metal Resources: Shifts in Import Emphases, 1960–1970," *Transactions of the Institute of British Geographers* 64 (March 1975): 97–118.

472 Paul Craig Roberts, "American Economy: R.I.P.," *Information Clearing House,* September 10, 2007, citing data from two official U.S. government sites: Bureau of Economic Analysis: *U.S. International Transactions Accounts Data,* and Bureau of Labor Statistics:

Employees on nonfarm payrolls by industry sector and selected industry detail, http://www.informationclearinghouse.info/article18350.htm.

473 Peter C. Whybrow, *American Mania: When More Is Not Enough* (New York: W.W. Norton & Co., 2005).

474 Adam Voiland, "Health Reasons to Cut Back on Corn Consumption," *U.S. News and World Report,* December 17, 2007.

475 Lee Nichol, ed., *The Essential David Bohm* (London: Routledge, 2003), 83–84, 306.

CHAPTER 30

476 Ken Silverstein and Alexander Cockburn, "Major U.S. Bank Urges Zapatista Wipe-Out: 'A Litmus Test for Mexico's Stability,'" *CounterPunch,* February 1, 1995.

477 Darrin Wood (Nuevo Amanecer Pres-Europa), "Paramilitary Groups in Chiapas: Under the Doctrine from Ft. Bragg," *Masiosare* Sunday Supplement, *La Jornada,* January 11, 1998, quoted in Willson, *Slippery Slope,* 46.

478 I was present with four other U.S. military veterans seeking a meeting in Tuxtla with General Castillo on April 11, 1997, and while sitting in his waiting room we noted two prominently displayed posters on the wall supporting the *Paz y Justicia* paramilitary group. Though we had made an appointment in advance and driven three hours to get there, we were told after waiting for an hour that the General was not in his office.

479 "Ruiz Ferro and the Paramilitaries: Relations Exposed," *Masiosare* Sunday Supplement, *La Jornada,* December 21, 1997, quoted in Willson, *Slippery Slope,* 46, reporting formal agreement signed July 4, 1997 between then-Chiapas Governor Julio Cesar Ruiz Ferro and PRI Deputy, Samuel Sanchez Sanchez, founder and director of the paramilitary group, *Paz y Justicia,* in which the governor handed over 4,600,000 pesos (about $600,000 in U.S.) to Sanchez for various promises, including not to commit violence during and after the then impending July 6 Mexican elections. General Renán Castillo was present at the signing ceremony as an "honorary witness."

480 Wood, "Paramilitary Groups in Chiapas, quoted in Willson, *Slippery Slope,* 46.

481 Alejandro Nadal, "Terror in Chiapas," *The Bulletin of the Atomic Scientists,* March–April 1998, 21.

482 Anthony DePalma, "U.S. Defense Chief Meets Mexican to Discuss Military Distrust," *New York Times,* October 24, 1995: "Mr. Perry said the United States next year would double the Pentagon's $500,000 budget for training 55 Mexican military officers at American military schools."

483 *La Jornada,* October 25, 1995, quoted in Willson, *Slippery Slope,* 8.

484 *La Jornada,* May 17, 1996, quoted in Willson, *Slippery Slope,* 35.

485 *La Jornada,* September 20, 1996, quoted in Willson, *Slippery Slope,* 17; Jeffery St. Clair, "The 'Drug War' Against the Zapatistas," Interpress Service, January 14, 1997; "U.S. Offer Raises Sticky Questions," *San Francisco Chronicle,* December 10, 1996.

486 SOA Watch, "SOA/WHINSEC Background," http://www.soaw.org/about-the-soawhinsec/history; Stanley Meisler, "U. S. Bolsters Mexican Military, Report Says," *Los Angeles Times,* July 15, 1998, A4.

487 "Below the Radar," *Center For International Policy,* http://www.ciponline.org/facts/below_the_radar_eng.pdf.

488 John Ross, *Zapatistas: Making Another World Possible: Chronicles of Resistance 2000–2006* (New York: Nation Books, 2006).

489 John Holloway, *Change the World Without Taking Power,* New edition (London: Pluto Press, 2005).

490   The First Continental Encounter for Humanity and Against Neoliberalism was dupli-
cated in several locations worldwide, leading to the First Intercontinental Encounter for
Humanity and Against Neoliberalism, July 1996 in Oventic, Chiapas.

491   Observation functions were shared with citizens from Mexico, Italy, Germany, and the
Basque region in Spain. These witness efforts were coordinated by the human rights
center of the Diocese in San Cristóbal, with the intention of providing some protection
for Zapatista villages. There were twenty-five such peace camps located throughout the
Zapatista zone.

492   Whybrow, American Mania, 71, 85, 93–96, 186–87.

493   V. Gordon Childe, Man Makes Himself (1936; New York: New American Library, 1983),
xviii–xix, 179–80. Childe was an Australian archaeologist who, in this brilliant essay, syn-
thesizes archaeology with philosophy, history, and the social sciences, arguing that the
first significant break in humans' past was the shift from Old Stone Stage food-gatherers
to New Stone Age agriculturalists, what he called the Neolithic Revolution. The second
break was the emergence of urban dwellers from the New Stone Age agriculturalists,
what he called the Urban Revolution. The latter produced the new idea of civilization,
which led to plundering empires that were, in effect, tribute-collecting machines maintained by war for the benefit of the vertical monarchies. The vast majority of people,
however, suffered from severe degradation. But Childe insists that nothing that humans
create is fixed and immutable, that "Man makes himself," that choices for change are
always available.

494   Lewis Mumford, an intellectual giant, was a contemporary of Childe and echoed
a similar chord: "What the human mind has created, it can also destroy." See Lewis
Mumford, The Myth of the Machine: The Pentagon of Power (1964; New York: Harcourt
Brace Jovanovich, Inc., 1970), 421.

CONCLUSION

495   General Department of Statistics, National Institute of Labour Protection of Vietnam
reported nearly 35 million people as of 1965; On April 4, 1995, the Vietnamese
Government released official figures on numbers of their citizens killed during the
war—5.1 million, reported by Agence France Presse (French Press Agency), April
4, 1995; and BBC, "Vietnam War: History," http://news.bbc.co.uk/2/shared/spl/hi/
asia_pac/05/vietnam_war/html/introduction.stm. Thus, about 14.5 percent of the
Vietnamese population was killed during the U.S. war waged against them.

496   Whybrow, America Mania; Barbara Ehrenreich, Bait and Switch (New York:
Metropolitan Books, 2005).

497   Richard Martin, "Dwindling of Rare Metals Imperils Innovations," Information
Week, May 29, 2007, http://www.informationweek.com/story/showArticle.
jhtml?articleID=199703110.498 Keith Harmon Snow and David Barouski, "Behind the
Numbers: Untold Suffering in the Congo," ZNet, March 1, 2006, http://www.zmag.org/
content/showarticle.cfm?ItemID=9832.

499   Environmental Literacy Council, "Computer Chip Life Cycle," updated April 3, 2008,
http://enviroliteracy.org/article.php/1275.php, read online March 22, 2010; "The
Three-and-a-Half-Pound Microchip: Environmental Implications of the IT Revolution,"
November 5, 2002, Beverly Hassell, American Chemical Society, http://www.eureka-
lert.org/pub_releases/2002-11/acs-ttp110502.php, read online March 22, 2010.

500 UN News Service, "Computer Manufacturing Soaks up Fossil Fuels, UN University Study Says," http://www.un.org/apps/news/printnewsAr.asp?nid=10007, read online March 22, 2010.

501 Brian Swimme and Thomas Berry, *The Universe Story* (New York: HarperSanFrancisco/ HarperCollins, 1992), 273–74; Paul Rincon, "DNA Project To Trace Human Steps," BBC News, April 13, 2005.

502 I learned about the "megamachine" when exposed to the ideas of cultural historian Lewis Mumford, who started critiquing civilization in the early 1920s. Among his works are two complementary books: *The Myth of the Machine: The Pentagon of Power* (1964; New York: Harcourt Brace Jovanovich, Inc., 1970) and *The Myth of the Machine: Technics and Human Development* (New York: Harcourt, Brace & World, Inc., 1967). Mumford, born in 1895 in urban Flushing, New York, was a brilliant observer of the traumatic effects to humans and the earth of so-called civilization, and his thinking on the long view remains extremely illuminating.

503 Mumford, *Myth of the Machine: Technics and Human Development,* 186.

504 Ashley Montagu, *The Nature of Human Aggression* (Oxford: Oxford University Press, 1976), 43–53, 59–60; Ashley Montagu, ed., *Learning Non-Aggression: The Experience of Non-Literate Societies* (Oxford: Oxford University Press, 1978); Jean Guilaine and Jean Zammit, *The Origin of War: Violence in Prehistory,* trans. Melanie Hersey (2001; Malden, MA: Blackwell Publishing, 2005).

505 Andrew B. Schmookler, *Out of Weakness: Healing the Wounds That Drive Us to War* (New York: Bantam Books, 1988), 303.

506 Mumford, *Myth of the Machine: Technics and Human Development,* 204.

507 *Heart of Darkness,* written by Polish-born English novelist Joseph Conrad (1857–1924), was originally published in 1899 as a three-part series in *Blackwood's* Magazine (U.K.). It is considered one of the most-read works of the last hundred years, largely an autobiographical description of Conrad's six-month journey in 1890 into the "Congo Free State," at the time being plundered by Belgium. In fact the story could apply to almost anyplace in the world where European nations, later the United States, plundered peoples for profits and material privileges without acknowledging the terrible, ugly consequences. Francis Ford Coppola's 1979 movie *Apocalypse Now* translates the "Heart of Darkness" to Viet Nam and Cambodia. Adam Hochschild's *King Leopold's Ghost* (New York: A Mariner Book, 1999) describes the diabolical exploitation of the Congo Free State by King Leopold II of Belgian between 1885 and 1908. Estimates of murdered Congolese in this period run as high as 13 million. Please don't read this as if this is something that the United States or other European nations would not do, or have not done. Indeed the U.S. and Europe are founded on these practices, all under the cover of "civilization."

508 Riane Eisler, *The Chalice and the Blade* (San Francisco: Harper & Row, 1987).

509 James Hillman, *A Terrible Love of War* (New York: The Penguin Press, 2004), 17.

510 Etienne de la Boetie, *The Politics of Obedience: The Discourse of Voluntary Servitude,* trans. Harry Kurz (ca. 1553; Montreal: Black Rose Books, 1997), 46, 58–60; Eisler, *The Chalice and the Blade,* 45–58, 104–6.

511 Roszak, Gomes, and Kanner, eds , *Ecopsychology.* Ecopsychology concludes that there can be no personal healing without healing the earth, and that rediscovering our sacred relationship with it, i.e., our intimate earthiness, is indispensable for personal and global healing and mutual respect.

512 Michael A. Milburn and Sheree D. Conrad, *The Politics of Denial* (Cambridge, MA: The MIT Press, 1996), 1–29.

513 Ibid., 3.

514 Alice Miller, *For Your Own Good: Hidden Cruelty in Child-Rearing and the Roots of Violence* (New York: Farrar, Straus, & Giroux, 1983), 3–91.

515 James Gilligan, *Violence: Reflections on a National Epidemic* (New York: Vintage Books, 1997), 1–85.

516 Barbara Ehrenreich, *Blood Rites* (New York: Metropolitan Books, 1997).

517 Kropotkin, *Mutual Aid*.

518 De La Boetie, *The Politics of Obedience*, 58–59.

519 Eisler, *The Chalice & the Blade*, 105–6, 205n5.

520 David C. Korten, *The Great Turning: From Empire to Earth Community* (San Francisco: Berrett-Koehler Publishers, 2006). Three of Korten's earlier works: *When Corporations Rule the World* (San Francisco: Berrett Koehler Publishers, 1995); *The Post-Corporate World* (Berrett Koehler, 1999); and *Globalizing Civil Society: Reclaiming Our Right to Power* (New York: Seven Stories Press, 1998). Korten is a former Harvard Business School professor and cofounder of *Yes!* Magazine.

521 Jared Diamond, *Collapse: How Societies Choose to Fail or Succeed* (New York: Viking, 2005).

522 Ibid., 486–96.

523 Ibid., 114.

524 Richard Heinberg, *The Party's Over: Oil, War and the Fate of Industrial Societies* (Gabriola Island, BC, Canada: New Society Publishers, 2003).

525 Ed Ayres, *God's Last Offer: Negotiating for a Sustainable Future* (New York: Four Walls Eight Windows, 1999) and Chellis Glendinning, *My Name Is Chellis Glendinning and I'm in Recovery from Western Civilization* (Boston: Shambhala, 1994).

526 Richard York, "Homo Floresiensis and Human Equality, Enduring Lessons from Stephen Jay Gould," *Monthly Review* 56, no. 10 (March 2005): 15.

527 Ibid., 14–19.

528 James Lovelock, *The Ages of Gaia: A Biography of the Living Earth* (New York: W. W. Norton & Company, 1995).

529 James Lovelock, *The Revenge of Gaia: Earth's Climate Crisis and the Fate of Humanity* (New York: Basic Books, 2007), xiv.

530 Peter Goodchild, "The Century of Famine," *Culture Change*, March 2, 2010.531 Barbara Ehrenreich, *Dancing in the Streets: A History of Collective Joy* (New York: Metropolitan Books, 2007); Kropotkin, *Mutual Aid*, xli–xlii, 300. Kropotkin's masterful study reveals the indispensable role human solidarity plays in human evolution—"the close dependency of every one's happiness upon the happiness of all" and our "oneness with each human being," validating sages such as Martin Luther King Jr., who wisely observed that "an injustice anywhere is a threat to justice everywhere."

532 Daniel Quinn, *Beyond Civilization: Humanity's Next Great Adventure* (New York: Three Rivers Press, 1999), 91.

533 William McDonough and Michael Braungart, *Cradle to Cradle: Remaking the Way We Make Things* (New York: North Point Press, 2002).

534 Schumacher, *Small Is Beautiful* .

535 Paul Hawken, *Blessed Unrest* (New York: Viking, 2007).

536 Gustavo Esteva and Madhu Suri Prakash, *Grassroots Post-Modernism: Remaking the Soil of Cultures* (London: Zed Books, 1998); Mumford, *Myth of the Machine: The Pentagon of Power*, 421.

RECOMMENDED READING LIST

Adorno, T.W., E. Frenkel-Brunswik, D.J. Levinson, and R.N. Sanford. *The Authoritarian Personality*. New York: Harper & Row, 1950.

Agee, Phil. *Inside the Company: CIA Diary*. 1975; New York: Bantam Books, 1986.

Allen, James, et al. *Without Sanctuary: Lynching Photography in America*. Santa Fe: Twin Palms, 2000.

Andreas, Joel. *Addicted to War: Why the U.S. Can't Kick Militarism*, 3rd ed. Culver City, California: Frank Dorrel/Oakland: AK Press, 2004

Appy, Christian G. *Working-Class War*. Chapel Hill: University of North Carolina Press, 1993.

Arboleya, Jesús. *The Cuban Counterrevolution*. Athens, Ohio: Ohio University Center For International Studies, 2000.

Arendt, Hannah. *Eichmann in Jerusalem: A Report on the Banality of Evil*. 1963; New York: Penguin Books, 1994.

Armstrong, Karen. *A Short History of Myth*. Edinburgh, Scotland: Canongate, 2005.

Baker, Russ. *Family of Secrets*. New York: Bloomsbury Press, 2008.

Bamford, James. *Body of Secrets: Anatomy of the Ultra-Secret National Security Agency from the Cold War through the Dawn of a New Century*. New York: Doubleday, 2001.

Berry, Thomas. *The Dream of the Earth*. San Francisco: Sierra Club Books, 1988.

Berry, Wendell. *The Unsettling of America: Culture & Agriculture*. San Francisco: Sierra Club Books, 1977.

Beard, Charles A. *An Economic Interpretation of the Constitution of the United States,* New York, Macmillan, 1913.

Black, Edwin. *IBM and the Holocaust: The Strategic Alliance Between Nazi Germany and America's Most Powerful Corporation*. New York: Crown Publishers, 2001.

Blaut, J.M. *The Colonizer's Model of the World: Geographical Diffusionism and Eurocentric History*. New York: Guilford Press, 1993.

Blum, William. *Killing Hope*. Monroe, Maine: Common Courage Press, 1995.

Bonner, Raymond. *Weakness and Deceit: U.S. Policy and El Salvador*. New York: Times Books, 1984.

Bookchin, Murray. *The Spanish Anarchists: The Heroic Years, 1868–1936*. New York: Harper and Row, 1977.

Brune, Adrian. "Tulsa's Shame," *The Nation*, March 18, 2002.

Butler, Smedley D. *War Is A Racket*. Los Angeles: Feral House, 2003, orig. 1935.

Carey, Alex. *Taking the Risk out of Democracy: Corporate Propaganda Versus Freedom and Liberty*. Urbana: University of Illinois Press, 1997.

Carson, Rachel. *Silent Spring*. New York: Fawcett Crest, 1962.

Carter, John J. *Covert Operations as a Tool of Presidential Foreign Policy in American History from 1800 to 1920: Foreign Policy in the Shadows*. Lewiston, NY: The Edwin Mellen Press, 2000.

Catton, William R., Jr. *Overshoot: The Ecological Basis of Revolutionary Change*. Urbana: University of Illinois Press, 1982.

Childe, V. Gordon. *Man Makes Himself*. London: Watts & Co, 1936; New York: New American Library, 1983.

Chomsky, Noam. *The Culture of Terrorism*. Boston: South End Press, 1988.

———. *Turning the Tide: U.S. Intervention in Central America and the Struggle for Peace*. Cambridge, MA: South End Press, 1985.

Chossudovsky, Michel. *The Globalization of Poverty*. Pelang, Malaysia: Third World Network, 1997.

Churchill, Ward. *A Little Matter of Genocide: Holocaust and Denial in the Americas 1492 to the Present*. San Francisco: City Lights, 1997.

Cockburn, Andrew, and Leslie Cockburn. *Dangerous Liaison: The Inside Story of the U.S.-Israeli Covert Relationship*. New York: HarperCollins Publishers, 1991.

Colby, Gerard, and Charlotte Dennett. *Thy Will Be Done—The Conquest of the Amazon: Nelson Rockefeller and Evangelism in the Age of Oil*. New York: HarperCollins, 1995.

Congressional Research Service. CRS Report for Congress, February 2, 2009, *Instances of Use of United States Armed Forces Abroad, 1798–2008*. http://www.crs.gov.

Conrad, Joseph. *Heart of Darkness*. Mineola, New York: Dover Publications, 1990. (First published in a three-part series in *Blackwood's* magazine, 1899.)

Cortright, David. *Soldiers in Revolt: GI Resistance During the Vietnam War*. Chicago: Haymarket Books, 2005, orig., 1975.

Creel, George. *Complete Report of the Chairman of the Committee on Public Information, 1917, 1918, 1919*. Washington, DC: GPO, 1920.

DeBenedetti, Charles. *An American Ordeal: The Antiwar Movement of the Vietnam Era*. Syracuse: Syracuse University Press, 1990.

De La Boetie. *The Politics of Obedience: The Discourse of Voluntary Servitude*, trans. Harry Kurz. ca. 1553. Montreal: Black Rose Books, 1997.

De Quincey, Christian. *Radical Nature: Rediscovering the Soul of Matter*. Montpelier, VT: Invisible Cities Press, 2002.

Dellinger, David. *From Yale to Jail: The Life Story of a Moral Dissenter*. New York: Pantheon, 1993.

De Waal, Frans. *The Age of Empathy: Nature's Lessons For A Kinder Society*. New York: Harmony Books, 2009.

Diamond, Jared. *Collapse: How Societies Choose to Fail or Succeed*. New York: Viking, 2005.

Douglass, James W. *JFK and the Unspeakable: Why He Died and Why It Matters*. Maryknoll, New York: Orbis, 2008.

Drinnon, Richard. *Facing West: The Metaphysics of Indian-Hating and Empire-Building*. Minneapolis: University of Minnesota Press, 1980.

DuRand, Cliff. "Humanitarianism and Solidarity Cuban-Style: A Healthcare Model for the World," *Z Magazine*, November 2007.

Ehrenreich, Barbara. *Blood Rites*. New York: Metropolitan Books, 1997.

———. *Dancing in the Streets: A History of Collective Joy*. New York: Metropolitan Books, 2007.

Eisler, Riane. *The Chalice and the Blade*. San Francisco: Harper & Row, 1987.

Emerson, Gloria. *Winners and Losers: Battles, Retreats, Gains, Losses, and Ruins from the Vietnam War*. 1972; New York: Harcourt Brace Jovanovich, 1976.

Escalante, Fabian. *The Cuba Project: CIA Covert Operations 1959–62*. Melbourne, Australia: Ocean Press, 2004.

Espino, Ovidio Diaz. *How Wall Street Created A Nation: J.P. Morgan, Teddy Roosevelt, and the Panama Canal*. New York: Four Walls Eight Windows, 2001.

Ewen, Stuart. *PR! A Social History of Spin*. New York: Basic Books, 1996.

Fanon, Frantz. *The Wretched of the Earth*, trans. Constance Farrington. 1961; New York: Grove Press, 1963.

Fitzgerald, Frances. *Fire in the Lake: The Vietnamese and the Americans in Vietnam*. Boston: Little, Brown and Co., 1972.

Fleming, D.F. *The Cold War and Its Origins 1917–1960,* Vols. I–II. Garden City, New York: Doubleday & Company, Inc., 1961.

Fogelsong, David S. *America's Secret War Against Bolshevism: U.S. Intervention in the Russian Civil War, 1917–1920.* Chapel Hill: University of North Carolina Press, 1995.

Foucault, Michel. *Madness and Civilization.* New York: Vintage, 1973.

Frankl, Viktor E. *Man's Search for Meaning.* New York: Touchstone, 1984, orig. 1959.

Franklin, Bruce. *Vietnam and Other American Fantasies.* Amherst: University of Massachusetts Press, 2000.

Franklin, Jane. *Cuba and the United States: A Chronological History.* Melbourne, Australia: Ocean Press, 1997.

Freire, Paulo. *Pedagogy of the Oppressed,* trans. Myra Bergman Ramos. New York: Seabury Press, 1973.

Fresia, Jerry. *Toward an American Revolution: Exposing the Constitution & Other Illusions.* Boston: South End Press, 1988.

Fromm, Erich. *Escape from Freedom.* 1941; New York: Owl Books, Henry Holt and Company, 1994.

Galeano, Eduardo. *Open Veins of Latin America: Five Centuries of the Pillage of a Continent.* New York: Monthly Review Press, 1973.

Gelbspan, Ross. *Break-ins, Death Threats and the FBI: The Covert War Against the Central America Movement.* Boston: South End Press, 1991.

Gentry, Curt. *J. Edgar Hoover: The Man and the Secrets.* New York: W.W. Norton & Company, 1991.

Gerson, Joseph, and Bruce. Birchard, eds. *The Sun Never Sets.* Boston: South End Press, 1991.

Gettleman, Marvin E., Jane Franklin, Marilyn B Young, and H. Bruce Franklin, eds. *Vietnam and America: A Documented History,* rev. ed. New York: Grove Press, 1995.

Gilligan, James. *Violence: Reflections on a National Epidemic.* New York: Vintage Books, 1997.

Glendinning, Chellis. *My Name Is Chellis and I'm in Recovery from Western Civilization.* Boston: Shambhala, 1994.

Goldstein, Robert J. *Political Repression in Modern America.* Cambridge, NY: Schenkman Publishing Co., Inc., 1978.

Goleman, Daniel. *Emotional Intelligence: Why It Can matter More Than IQ.* New York: Bantam Books, 1997.

Goodman, Paul. *Growing Up Absurd: Problems of Youth in the Organized System.* New York: Random House, 1960.

Grandin, Greg. *Empire's Workshop: Latin America, the United States, and the Rise of the New Imperialism.* New York: Metropolitan Books, 2006.

Greco, Thomas H. Jr. *The End of Money and the Future of Civilization.* White River Junction, Vermont: Chelsea Green, 2009.

Green, James. *Death in the Haymarket: A Story of Chicago, the First Labor Movement and the Bombing that Divided Gilded Age America.* New York: Pantheon, 2006.

Greene, Felix. *The Enemy: What Every American Should Know about Imperialism.* New York: Random House, 1970.

Griffiths, Philip Jones. *Vietnam, Inc.* New York: Collier Books, 1971; repr., London: Phaidon Press Ltd., 2001.

Grossman, Dave. *On Killing: The Psychological Cost of Learning to Kill in War and Society.* Boston: Little and Brown, 1995.

Harman, Chris. *A People's History of the World.* London: Verso, 2008.

Hawken, Paul. *Blessed Unrest: How the Largest Movement in the World Came Into Being.* New York: Viking, 2007.

Hedges, Chris. *War Is a Force that Gives Us Meaning.* New York: Public Affairs, 2002.

Heinberg, Richard. *The Party's Over: Oil, War and the Fate of Industrial Societies.* Gabriola Island, BC, Canada: New Society Publishers, 2003.

———. *Peak Everything: Waking Up to the Century of Declines.* Gabriola Island, BC, Canada: New Society Publishers, 2007.

Herival, Tara, and Paul Wright, eds. *Prison Nation: The Warehousing of America's Poor.* London: Routledge, 2003.

Herman, Edward S. *The Real Terror Network: Terrorism in Fact and Propaganda.* Boston: South End Press, 1984.

Herman, Edward, and Noam Chomsky. *Manufacturing Consent: The Political Economy of the Mass Media.* 1988; New York: Pantheon, 2002.

Higham, Charles. *Trading With the Enemy: The Nazi-American Money Plot 1933–1949.* New York: Barnes & Noble, 1983.

Hillman, James. *A Terrible Love of War.* New York: The Penguin Press, 2004.

Hirsch, James S. *Riot and Remembrance: The Tulsa Race War and Its Legacy.* Boston: Houghton Mifflin Co., 2002.

Hochschild, Adam. *King Leopold's Ghost.* New York: A Mariner Book, 1999.

Holloway, John. *Change the World Without Taking Power,* New edition. London: Pluto Press, 2005.

Illich, Ivan. *Tools for Conviviality.* New York: Harper & Row, 1973.

———. *Toward a History of Needs.* Berkeley: Heyday Books, 1977.

Jensen, Derrick. *Endgame, Volume I: The Problem of Civilization; Endgame, Volume II: Resistance.* New York: Seven Stories Press, 2006.

Johnson, Chalmers. *The Sorrows of Empire: Militarism, Secrecy, and the End of the Republic.* New York: Metropolitan Books, 2004.

Josephson, Mathew. *The Robber Barons: The Great American Capitalists 1861–1901.* New York: Harcourt, Brace and Company, 1934.

Kahin, George McTurnan, and John W. Lewis. *The United States in Vietnam.* New York: The Dial Press, 1967.

Kinzer, Stephen. *Overthrow: America's Century of Regime Change From Hawaii to Iraq.* New York: Times Books/Henry Holt and Company, 2006.

Klein, Naomi. *The Shock Doctrine: The Rise of Disaster Capitalism.* New York: Metropolitan Books, 2008.

Kohr, Leopold. *The Overdeveloped Nations: The Diseconomies of Scale.* New York: Schocken Books, 1978.

Koning, Hans. *Columbus: His Enterprise.* 1976; New York: Monthly Review Press, 1991.

Korten, David C. *The Great Turning: From Empire to Earth Community.* San Francisco: Berrett-Koehler Publishers, 2006.

Kropotkin, Peter. *Mutual Aid: A Factor of Evolution.* Montreal: Black Rose Books, 1989, orig. 1902.

Kunstler, James Howard. *The Long Emergency: Surviving the Converging Catastrophes of the Twenty-First Century.* New York: Atlantic Monthly Press, 2005.

———. *World Made by Hand.* New York: Grove Press, 2008.

LaFeber, Walter. *The New Empire: An Interpretation of American Expansion 1860–1898.* Ithaca: Cornell University Press, 1963; repr., 1987.

Lens, Sidney. *The Forging of the American Empire: From the Revolution to Vietnam: A History of U.S. Imperialism.* 1971; Chicago: Haymarket Books, 2003.

LeoGrande, William M. *Our Own Backyard: The United States in Central America, 1977–1992.* Chapel Hill: University of North Carolina Press, 2000.

Lifton, Robert Jay, and Greg Mitchell. *Hiroshima in America: Fifty Years of Denial.* New York: Putnam and Sons, 1995.

Lovelock, James. *The Revenge of Gaia: Earth's Climate Crisis and the Fate of Humanity.* New York: Basic Books, 2007.

Lumpe, Lora. "U.S. Foreign Military Training: Global Reach, Global Power, and Oversight Issues," *A Foreign Policy In Focus Special Report,* May 2002.

Lynd, Staughton. *Intellectual Origins of American Radicalism.* New York: Cambridge University Press, 2009, orig. New York: Vintage Books, 1969.

Mander, Jerry, and Edward Goldsmith, eds. *The Case Against the Global Economy and For A Turn Toward the Local.* San Francisco: Sierra Club Books, 1996.

Marshall, Jonathan, Peter Dale Scott, and Jane Hunter. *The Iran Contra Connection: Secret Teams and Covert Operations in the Reagan Era.* Boston: South End Press, 1987.

Marshall, Peter. *Demanding the Impossible: A History of Anarchism.* Oakland: PM Press, 2010.

McClintock, Michael. *Instruments of Statecraft: U.S. Guerrilla Warfare, Counterinsurgency, and Counter-terrorism, 1940–1990.* New York: Pantheon Books, 1992.

McCoy, Alfred W. *The Politics of Heroin: CIA Complicity in the Global Drug Trade.* Brooklyn, NY: Lawrence Hill Books, 1991.

McDonough, William, and Michael Braungart. *Cradle to Cradle: Remaking the Way We Make Things.* New York: North Point Press, 2002.

McGehee, Ralph W. *Deadly Deceits: My 25 Years in the CIA.* New York: Sheridan Square Publications, Inc., 1983.

Meadows, Donella, et al. *Limits to Growth: The 30-Year Update.* White River Junction, Vermont: Chelsea Green, 2004.

Merkel, Jim. *Radical Simplicity: Small Footprints on a Finite Earth.* Gabriola Island, B.C., Canada: New Society, 2003.

Michalowski, Helen, and Robert Cooney, eds. *The Power of the People: Active Nonviolence in the United States.* Culver City, CA: Peace Press, 1977.

Milburn, Michael A., and Sheree D. Conrad. *The Politics of Denial.* Cambridge, MA: The MIT Press, 1996.

Milgram, Stanley. *Obedience to Authority: An Experimental View.* 1974; New York: Perennial Classics, 2004.

Miller, Alice. *For Your own Good: Hidden Cruelty in Child-Rearing and the Roots of Violence.* New York: Farrar, Straus, & Giroux, 1983.

Miller, Stuart Creighton. *Benevolent Assimilation: The American Conquest of the Philippines, 1899–1903.* New Haven: Yale University Press, 1982.

Monbiot, George. "Our Quality of Life Peaked in 1974: It's All Downhill Now: We Will Pay the Price for Believing the World Has Infinite Resources," *The Guardian/UK,* December 31, 2002.

Montagu, Ashley, ed. *Learning Non-Aggression: The Experience of Non-Literate Societies.* Oxford: Oxford University Press, 1978.

Montagu, Ashley, and Floyd Matson. *The Dehumanization of Man.* New York: McGraw-Hill Book Co., 1983.

Mumford, Lewis, *The Myth of the Machine: Technics and Human Development.* 1966; New York: Harcourt, Brace & World, Inc., 1967.

———. *The Myth of the Machine: The Pentagon of Power.* 1964; New York: Harcourt Brace Jovanovich, Inc., 1970.

Nearing, Scott. *Civilization and Beyond: Learning From History.* Harborside, Maine: Social Science Institute, 1975.

Nichol, Lee, ed. *The Essential David Bohm.* London: Routledge, 2003.

Nicosia, Gerald. *Home to War: A History of the Vietnam Veterans' Movement.* New York: Crown, 2001.

Orwell, George. *Nineteen Eighty-Four.* New York: Signet, 1950.

Papworth, John. *Small Is Beautiful: The Future as if People Really Mattered.* Westport, Connecticut: Praeger, 1995.

Patti, Archimedes L.A. *Why Viet Nam?* Berkeley, California: University of California Press, 1980.

Pepper, William F. *An Act of State: The Execution of Martin Luther King.* London: Verso, 2003.

Polanyi, Karl. *The Great Transformation: The Political and Economic Origins of Our Time.* Boston: Beacon Press, 1944.

Postman, Neil. *Amusing Ourselves to Death. Public Discourse in the Age of Show Business.* New York: Penguin, 1985.

Prada, Pedro. *Island Under Siege: The U.S. Blockade of Cuba.* Melbourne, Victoria, Australia: Ocean Press, 1995.

Quinn, Daniel. *Beyond Civilization: Humanity's Next Great Adventure.* New York: Three Rivers Press, 1999).

Quinn, Megan. "The Power of Community: How Cuba Survived Peak Oil," *Permaculture Activist,* Spring 2006.

Raphael, Ray. *Founding Myths: Stories that Hide Our Patriotic Past.* New York: The New Press, 2004.

Reiman, Jeffrey. *The Rich Get Richer and the Poor Get Prison: Ideology, Class, and Criminal Justice,* 7th ed. Boston: Pearson, Allyn and Bacon, 2007.

Robinson, William I. *A Faustian Bargain: U.S. Intervention in the Nicaragua Elections and American Foreign Policy in the Post-Cold War Era.* Boulder: Westview Press, 1992.

Ross, John. *Zapatistas: Making Another World Possible: Chronicles of Resistance 2000–2006.* New York: Nation Books, 2006.

Roszak, Theodore, Mary E. Gomes, and Allen D. Kanner, eds. *Ecopsychology: Restoring the Earth, Healing the Mind.* San Francisco: Sierra Club Books, 1995.

Sale, Kirkpatrick. *The Conquest of Paradise: Christopher Columbus and the Columbian Legacy.* New York: Alfred A. Knopf, 1990.

———. *Dwellers In the Land: The Bioregional Vision.* San Francisco: Sierra Club Books, 1985.

Saul, John Ralston. *The Unconscious Civilization.* New York: Penguin, 1997.

Schmookler, Andrew B. *Out of Weakness: Healing the Wounds That Drive Us to War.* New York: Bantam Books, 1988.

Schumacher, E.F. *Small Is Beautiful: Economics as if People Mattered.* New York: Perennial Library, 1973.

Scott, Peter Dale, and Jonathan Marshall. *Cocaine Politics: Drugs, Armies, and the CIA in Central America.* Berkeley: University of California Press, 1991.

Sheldrake, Rupert. *The Presence of the Past: Morphic Resonance and the Habits of Nature.* New York: Vintage, 1989.

Simpson, Christopher. *Blowback: The First Full Account of America's Recruitment of Nazis and Its Disastrous Effect on Our Domestic and Foreign Policy.* New York: Weidenfeld & Nicolson, 1988.

Sitrin, Marina, ed. *Horizontalism: Voices of Popular Power in Argentina.* Oakland: AK Press, 2006.

Sklar, Holly. *Washington's War on Nicaragua.* Boston: South End Press, 1988.

Soloman, Norman. *War Made Easy: How Presidents and Pundits Keep Spinning Us to Death.* Hoboken, New Jersey: John Wiley and Sons, 2005.

Stacewicz, Richard. *Winter Soldiers: An Oral History of the Vietnam Veterans Against the War.* New York: Twayne Publishers, 1997.

Stannard, David E. *American Holocaust: The Conquest of the New World.* New York: Oxford University Press, 1992.

Stinnett, Robert B. *Day of Deceit: The Truth about FDR and Pearl Harbor.* New York: The Free Press, 2000.

Stockwell, John. *In Search of Enemies: A CIA Story.* New York: Norton, 1978.

Stone, Christopher D. *Should Trees Have Standing?* Dobbs Ferry, New York: Oceana Publications, 1996.

"South Viet Nam: Thieu's Political Prisoners of War." *Time,* December 25, 1972, 18.

Swimme, Brian, and Thomas Berry. *The Universe Story: From the Primordial Flaring Forth to the Ecozoic Era.* San Francisco: HarperSanFrancisco, 1994.

Tanaka, Yuki, and Marilyn B. Young, eds. *Bombing Civilians: A Twentieth-Century History.* New York: The New Press, 2009.

Thornton, Russell. *American Indian Holocaust and Survival: A Population History Since 1492.* Norman: University of Oklahoma Press, 1987.

Tick, Edward. *War and the Soul. Healing Our Nation's Veterans from Post-Traumatic Stress Disorder.* Wheaton, Illinois: Quest Books, 2005.

Tolstoy, Leo. *The Kingdom of God Is Within You.* Lincoln: University of Nebraska Press, 1984, Orig, 1894.

Tuchman, Barbara. *The March of Folly: From Troy to Vietnam.* New York: Knopf, 1984.

U.S. Congress. Senate. Committee on the Judiciary. Subcommittee on Constitutional Rights. *Military Surveillance of Civilian Politics.* 93rd Cong., 1st sess., 1973.

U.S. Congress. Senate. Final Report of the Select Committee To Study Governmental Operations With Respect to Intelligence Activities [aka Church Committee Report]. Book III: *Supplementary Detailed Staff Reports on Intelligence Activities and the Rights of Americans.* 94th Cong., 2d sess., April 23, 1976.

Veblen, Thorstein. *The Theory of the Leisure Class.* 1899; New York: Mentor, 1953.

Vidal, Gore. *Imperial America: Reflections on the United States of Amnesia.* New York: Nation Books, 2004.

Vistica, Gregory. "What Happened in Thanh Phong," *New York Times,* Sunday, April 29, 2001.

Walker, Thomas W., ed. *Reagan Versus the Sandinistas: The Undeclared War on Nicaragua.* Boulder: Westview Press, 1987.

Weinberg, Albert K. *Manifest Destiny: A Study of Nationalist Expansion in American History.* 1935; Chicago: Quadrangle Paperbacks, 1963.

Weisman, Alan. *The World Without Us.* New York: St. Martin's Press, 2007.

Welsh, Anne Morrison. *Held in the Light: Norman Morrison's Sacrifice for Peace and His Family's Journey of Healing.* Maryknoll, New York: Orbis, 2008.

Whybrow, Peter C. *American Mania: When More is Not Enough.* New York: W.W. Norton & Co., 2005.

Wilcox, Fred A. *Waiting For an Army to Die: The Tragedy of Agent Orange.* Cabin John, Maryland: Seven Locks Press, 1989

Wilkinson, Richard, *The Impact of Inequality.* New York: The New Press, 2005.

Williams, William Appleman. *Empire as a Way of Life*. Oxford: Oxford University Press, 1980.

————. *The Tragedy of American Diplomacy*. 1959; New York: W.W. Norton & Company, 1972.

Willson, S. Brian. *The Slippery Slope: U.S. Military Moves into Mexico*. Self-published zine, 1998. http://www.brianwillson.com/the-slippery-slope-u-s-military-moves-into-mexico/

Woodward, Bob. *Veil: The Secret Wars of the CIA 1981–1987*. New York: Simon and Schuster, 1987.

WWF. "The Footprint and Human Development." *Living Planet Report, 2006*.

York, Richard. "Homo Floresiensis and Human Equality, Enduring Lessons from Stephen Jay Gould," *Monthly Review* 56, no. 10 (March 2005): 15.

Zaroulis, Nancy, and Gerald Sullivan. *Who Spoke Up? American Protest Against the War in Vietnam, 1963–1975*. New York: Holt, Rinehart and Winston, 1984.

Zimbardo, Philip. *The Lucifer Effect: Understanding How Good People Turn Evil*. New York: Random House, 2007.

Zinn, Howard. *A People's History of the United States*. New York: Harper Perennial, 1980.

Acknowledgments

The people who most inspired me to write this memoir are the "shirtless and barefoot" women, children, and men who have risen up, and continue to do so, against repressive power regimes around the world, including "the greatest purveyor of violence," my own government, which inflicts and preserves violence virtually everywhere. The Vietnamese, Nicaraguans, Salvadorans, Haitians, Mexicans, Colombians, Brazilians, Palestinians, and many others around the world have in different ways and times stimulated in my own soul, mind, and body, an irreversible knowledge of our awesome interconnectedness with one another.

Friends who have helped me write and fine tune my story during countless hours of reading, correcting, rewriting, and engaging me in provocative conversation, include Bob Goss, Nicole Bowmer, Frank Dorrel, Karen Fogliatti, and George Hill. Becky Luening, with whom I share the more intimate aspects of my life, has been a constant reader offering innumerable helpful suggestions, and with the patience to tolerate my ups and downs. Pedro Kropotkin, our Welsh Corgi dog, provided many hours of comic relief and support.

Holley Rauen rescued and revived me from near death on the tracks at Concord Naval Weapons Station with immediate assistance from Gerry Condon, Duncan Murphy, Dave Hartsough, and Steve Brooks providing emergency medical attention before the delayed ambulance arrived. Norman B. Livermore III, orthopedic surgeon, Cavett M. Rogers, Jr., brain surgeon, and Nourollah Ghorbani, plastic and reconstructive surgeon, spent nine hours salvaging my mangled body in the emergency room at John Muir Hospital's trauma unit, Walnut Creek, California.

Upon release from the hospital, I was immediately blessed with the services of physical therapist Tom Koren who came to my home numerous times to teach me to walk once again on my new "stilts." Tom referred me to premier prosthetist Wayne Koniuk who quickly fitted me with my first of many pairs of artificial legs, which have enabled me to walk comfortably now for nearly twenty-four years. My most worrisome problem was the severe "phantom pain" in my now-missing feet and ankles, which was so severe that I actually contemplated suicide. Doctors indicated the phantom pain might be only partially relieved with long use of morphine. Thankfully, another angel, acupuncturist Brian La Forgia, arrived on the scene. An expert in advanced pulse diagnosis, Brian was able to completely eliminate the pain in just two treatments. It is thanks to these empathic health providers that I am still breathing, walking, and handcycling.

Fellow Viet Nam veteran and photographer Mike Hastie spent countless hours pouring over and helping select from among hundreds of photos those best to complement my story.

Roxanne Dunbar-Ortiz encouraged me for years to write this memoir and directed me to developmental editor Jo Ellen Green Kaiser who greatly assisted in organizing voluminous material into the basic story. I am greatly appreciative of PM Press for agreeing to publish my memoir when it seemed no other publisher would. PM copy editor Romy Ruukel spent countless hours poring over the drafts to shape the story into its final read.

And, of course, there are hundreds of fellow travelers I have encountered along my path, through conversation, reading books and essays, and serendipitous meetings, who have affected my life in numerous significant ways.

INDEX

"Passim" (literally "scattered") indicates intermittent
discussion of a topic over a cluster of pages.

ABOUT PM PRESS

PM Press was founded at the end of 2007 by a small
collection of folks with decades of publishing, media, and
organizing experience. PM Press co-conspirators have
published and distributed hundreds of books, pamphlets,
CDs, and DVDs. Members of PM have founded enduring book
fairs, spearheaded victorious tenant organizing campaigns, and worked closely with
bookstores, academic conferences, and even rock bands to deliver political and
challenging ideas to all walks of life. We're old enough to know what we're doing
and young enough to know what's at stake.

We seek to create radical and stimulating fiction and non-fiction books, pamphlets,
t-shirts, visual and audio materials to entertain, educate and inspire you. We
aim to distribute these through every available channel with every available
technology — whether that means you are seeing anarchist classics at our bookfair
stalls; reading our latest vegan cookbook at the café; downloading geeky fiction
e-books; or digging new music and timely videos from our website.

PM Press is always on the lookout for talented and skilled volunteers, artists,
activists and writers to work with. If you have a great idea for a project or can
contribute in some way, please get in touch.

PM Press
PO Box 23912
Oakland, CA 94623
www.pmpress.org

FRIENDS OF PM PRESS

These are indisputably momentous times — the financial system is melting down globally and the Empire is stumbling. Now more than ever there is a vital need for radical ideas.

In the three years since its founding — and on a mere shoestring — PM Press has risen to the formidable challenge of publishing and distributing knowledge and entertainment for the struggles ahead. With over 100 releases to date, we have published an impressive and stimulating array of literature, art, music, politics, and culture. Using every available medium, we've succeeded in connecting those hungry for ideas and information to those putting them into practice.

Friends of PM allows you to directly help impact, amplify, and revitalize the discourse and actions of radical writers, filmmakers, and artists. It provides us with a stable foundation from which we can build upon our early successes and provides a much-needed subsidy for the materials that can't necessarily pay their own way. You can help make that happen — and receive every new title automatically delivered to your door once a month — by joining as a Friend of PM Press. And, we'll throw in a free T-shirt when you sign up.

Here are your options:

- **$25 a month** Get all books and pamphlets plus 50% discount on all webstore purchases

- **$25 a month** Get all CDs and DVDs plus 50% discount on all webstore purchases

- **$40 a month** Get all PM Press releases plus 50% discount on all webstore purchases

- **$100 a month Superstar** — Everything plus PM merchandise, free downloads, and 50% discount on all webstore purchases

For those who can't afford $25 or more a month, we're introducing Sustainer Rates at $15, $10 and $5. Sustainers get a free PM Press T-shirt and a 50% discount on all purchases from our website.

Your Visa or Mastercard will be billed once a month, until you tell us to stop. Or until our efforts succeed in bringing the revolution around. Or the financial meltdown of Capital makes plastic redundant. Whichever comes first.

About Face: Military Resisters Turn Against War

Edited by Buff Whitman-Bradley, Sarah Lazare, and Cynthia Whitman-Bradley

ISBN: 978-1-60486-440-3
$20.00   272 pages

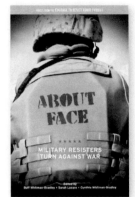

How does a young person who volunteers to serve in the U.S. military become a war-resister who risks ostracism, humiliation, and prison rather than fight? Although it is not well publicized, the long tradition of refusing to fight in unjust wars continues today within the American military.

In this book, resisters describe in their own words the process they went through, from raw recruits to brave refusers. They speak about the brutality and appalling violence of war; the constant dehumanizing of the enemy—and of our own soldiers—that begins in Basic Training; the demands that they ignore their own consciences and simply follow orders. They describe how their ideas about the justification for the current wars changed and how they came to oppose the policies and practices of the U.S. empire, and even war itself. Some of the refusers in this book served one or more tours of duty in Iraq and Afghanistan, and returned with serious problems resulting from Post-Traumatic Stress Disorder. Others heard such disturbing stories of violence from returning vets that they vowed not to go themselves. Still others were mistreated in one way or another and decided they'd had enough. Every one of them had the courage to say a resounding "NO!" The stories in this book provide an intimate, honest look at the personal transformation of each of these young people and at the same time constitute a powerful argument against militarization and endless war.

"About Face *gives us important insights into the consciences of women and men who volunteer for the military but find they cannot obey orders to fight in illegal wars. These are brave and loyal Americans who are willing to challenge the U.S. government and perhaps go to jail rather than betray their inner voices that say NO to these wars!"*
—Ann Wright, retired U.S. Army colonel and diplomat who resigned in protest at the invasion of Iraq, author of DISSENT: Voices of Conscience

"About Face *pulls down the veil of what honorable service in today's U.S. military really means. When new soldiers swear to support and defend the U.S. Constitution by following lawful orders, what are they to do when they are given unlawful orders?* About Face *provides raw examples of precisely what soldiers are doing who take their oath seriously."*
— Dahr Jamail, author of The Will to Resist: Soldiers Who Refuse to Fight in Iraq and Afghanistan

From Here To There: The Staughton Lynd Reader

Edited with an Introduction
by Andrej Grubačić

ISBN: 978-1-60486-215-7
$22.00   320 pages

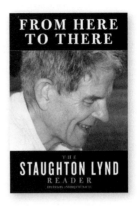

From Here To There collects unpublished talks and hard-to-find essays from legendary activist historian Staughton Lynd.

The first section of the Reader collects reminiscences and analyses of the 1960s. A second section offers a vision of how historians might immerse themselves in popular movements while maintaining their obligation to tell the truth. In the last section Lynd explores what nonviolence, resistance to empire as a way of life, and working class self-activity might mean in the 21st century. Together, they provide a sweeping overview of the life, and work—to date—of Staughton Lynd.

Both a definitive introduction and further exploration, it is bound to educate, enlighten, and inspire those new to his work and those who have been following it for decades. In a wide-ranging Introduction, anarchist scholar Andrej Grubačić considers how Lynd's persistent concerns relate to traditional anarchism.

"I met Staughton and Alice Lynd nearly fifty years ago in Atlanta. Staughton's reflective and restless life has never ceased in its exploring. This book is his great gift to the next generations."
— Tom Hayden

"Staughton Lynd's work is essential reading for anyone dedicated to implementing social justice. The essays collected in this book provide unique wisdom and insights into United States history and possibilities for change, summed up in two tenets: Leading from below and Solidarity."
— Roxanne Dunbar-Ortiz

"This remarkable collection demonstrates the compassion and intelligence of one of America's greatest public intellectuals. To his explorations of everything from Freedom Schools to the Battle of Seattle, Staughton Lynd brings lyricism, rigour, a historian's eye for irony, and an unshakable commitment to social transformation. In this time of economic crisis, when the air is filled with ideas of 'hope' and 'change,' Lynd guides us to understanding what, very concretely, those words might mean and how we might get there. These essays are as vital and relevant now as the day they were written, and a source of inspiration for activists young and old."
— Raj Patel

On the Ground: An Illustrated Anecdotal History of the Sixties Underground Press in the U.S.

Edited by Sean Stewart
with an Introduction by Paul Buhle

ISBN: 978-1-60486-455
$24.95   208 pages

In four short years (1965-1969), the underground press grew from five small newspapers in as many cities in the U.S. to over 500 newspapers—with millions of readers—all over the world. Completely circumventing (and subverting) establishment media by utilizing their own news service and freely sharing content amongst each other, the underground press, at its height, became the unifying institution for the counterculture of the 1960s.

Frustrated with the lack of any mainstream media criticism of the Vietnam War, empowered by the victories of the Civil Rights era, emboldened by the anti-colonial movements in the third world and with heads full of acid, a generation set out to change the world. The underground press was there documenting, participating in, and providing the resources that would guarantee the growth of this emergent youth culture. Combining bold visuals, innovative layouts, and eschewing any pretense toward objectivity, the newspapers were wildly diverse and wonderfully vibrant.

Neither meant to be an official nor comprehensive history, *On the Ground* focuses on the anecdotal detail that brings the history alive. Comprised of stories told by the people involved with the production and distribution of the newspapers—John Sinclair, Art Kunkin, Paul Krassner, Emory Douglas, John Wilcock, Bill Ayers, Spain Rodriguez, Trina Robbins, Al Goldstein, Harvey Wasserman and more—and featuring over 50 full-color scans taken from a broad range of newspapers, the book provides a true window into the spirit of the times, giving the reader a feeling for the energy on the ground.

"On the Ground *serves as a valuable contribution to countercultural history."*
— Paul Krassner, author of *Confessions of a Raving, Unconfined Nut: Misadventures in the Counterculture*

"One should not underestimate the significant value of this book. It gives you real insights into the underground press and its vast diversity of publications, which translated into a taste of real people's power."
— Emory Douglas, former Black Panther Party graphic artist and Minister of Culture

Resistance Against Empire

Interviewer/Editor: Derrick Jensen

ISBN: 978-1-60486-046-7
$20.00   280 pages

A scathing indictment of U. S. domestic and foreign policy, this collection of interviews gathers incendiary insights from 10 of today's most experienced and knowledgeable activists. Whether it's Ramsey Clark describing the long history of military invasion, Alfred McCoy detailing the relationship between CIA activities and the increase in the global heroin trade, Stephen Schwartz reporting the obscene costs of nuclear armaments, or Katherine Albrecht tracing the horrors of the modern surveillance state, this investigation of global governance is sure to inform, engage, and incite readers.

Full list of Interviewees:

Stephen Schwartz	Katherine Albrecht
Robert McChesney	J.W. Smith
Juliet Schor	Alfred McCoy
Christian Parenti	Kevin Bales
Ramsey Clark	Anuradha Mittal

"Derrick Jensen is a rare and original voice of sanity in a chaotic world. He has wisdom and wit, grace and style, and is a wonderful guide to a good life beautifully lived."
— Howard Zinn, author of A People's History of the United States

"Derrick Jensen is a man driven to stare without flinching at the baleful design of our culture... His analysis of our culture's predilection for hatred and destruction will rattle your bones."
— Daniel Quinn, author of Ishmael

Capital a⌐ ⌐F D⌐⌐
Conversa⌐ io⌐ ⌐ith f.⌐dic⌐
Thinkers in a Time of Tumult

Sasha Lilley

ISBN: 978-1-60486-334-5
$20.00 320 pages

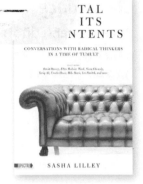

Capitalism is stumbling, empire is faltering, and the
planet is thawing. Yet many people are still grasping
to understand these multiple crises and to find a way
forward to a just future. Into the breach come the essential insights of *Capital
and Its Discontents*, which cut through the gristle to get to the heart of the matter
about the nature of capitalism and imperialism, capitalism's vulnerabilities at this
conjuncture—and what can we do to hasten its demise. Through a series of incisive
conversations with some of the most eminent thinkers and political economists
on the Left—including David Harvey, Ellen Meiksins Wood, Mike Davis, Leo
Panitch, Tariq Ali, and Noam Chomsky—*Capital and Its Discontents* illuminates the
dynamic contradictions undergirding capitalism and the potential for its dethroning.
At a moment when capitalism as a system is more reviled than ever, here is an
indispensable toolbox of ideas for action by some of the most brilliant thinkers of
our times.

*"These conversations illuminate the current world situation in ways that are very useful
for those hoping to orient themselves and find a way forward to effective individual and
collective action. Highly recommended."*
—Kim Stanley Robinson, *New York Times* bestselling author of the *Mars Trilogy* and
The Years of Rice and Salt

*"In this fine set of interviews, an A-list of radical political economists demonstrate why
their skills are indispensable to understanding today's multiple economic and ecological
crises."*
—Raj Patel, author of *Stuffed and Starved* and *The Value of Nothing*

"This is an extremel⌐ ⌐ and best
study yet published⌐ ⌐ ⌐sha Lilley
sets each interview⌐ ⌐ ⌐ut ideas and
philosophies."
—Andrej Grubači⌐ ⌐blies and
Zapatistas